International
Handbook of
Bilingualism
and
Bilingual
Education

INTERNATIONAL HANDBOOK OF BILINGUALISM AND BILINGUAL EDUCATION

EDITED BY

Christina Bratt Paulston

GREENWOOD PRESS

NEW YORK • WESTPORT, CONNECTICUT • LONDON

Library of Congress Cataloging-in-Publication Data

International handbook of bilingualism and bilingual
  education.

  Bibliography: p.
  Includes index.
  1. Bilingualism.   2. Education, Bilingual.
I. Paulston, Christina Bratt, 1932-
P115.I58   1988   404'.2   87–263
ISBN 0–313–24484–7 (lib. bdg. : alk. paper)

British Library Cataloguing in Publication Data is available.

Library of Congress Catalog Card Number: 87–263
ISBN: 0–313–24484–7

First published in 1988

Greenwood Press, Inc.
88 Post Road West, Westport, Connecticut 06881

Printed in the United States of America

The paper used in this book complies with the
Permanent Paper Standard issued by the National
Information Standards Organization (Z39.48–1984).

10 9 8 7 6 5 4 3 2 1

CONTENTS

Contents

PREFACE

The International Handbook of Bilingualism and Bilingual Education consists of twenty-seven chapters. The first chapter, ''Bilingualism and Bilingual Education: An Introduction,'' presents a theoretical framework of the contextual situations of language maintenance and shift in which we find bilingualism and bilingual education. The second chapter, ''Languages of the World,'' presents the basic facts about languages and language families in the world and where they are located. The chapter spells out the range of possibilities of languages in contact.

The other twenty-five chapters are case studies of bilingualism/multilingualism within nation-states, the norm around the world in spite of the nineteenth century's European model of one nation—one language. (In today's Europe, only two countries—Iceland and Portugal—are monolingual.) Because some of the chapters contain fairly technical vocabulary from linguistics and the social sciences, a glossary has been included. The book closes with some suggestions for further reading.

The case study chapters are arranged in alphabetical order and were selected to represent specific situations from all corners of the world. In Europe, Belgium is a trilingual country with considerable tension (and legislation) accompanying the language contact situation. In contrast, Switzerland, with its four official languages, presents a much more peaceful situation. In the United Kingdom, to the north and west, we find the Celtic languages slowly dying out, while the urban centers of England face the uneasy educational problems of a second (and third) generation of immigrants. Socialist Sweden has an easier time with her educational policies for immigrant children. And in post-Franco Spain we find a reemergence of minority languages, with Catalan in a strong position of language maintenance beyond what one might have expected.

In the Americas, we have a chapter on the American Indian situation in Canada (similar to that in the United States and so not duplicated) which is basically one of assimilation and language death or language maintenance through physical isolation. Owing primarily to Canadian legislation vis-à-vis language, we find parents resorting to a very unusual educational experiment, now established as routine, the French-English immersion programs. The chapter on the United States reveals, *inter alia*, the different course of educational programs for children of colonized groups compared with those of the European immigrants, who have completely assimilated.

In Latin America, the chapters on Mexico, Bolivia, and Peru present another form of colonization from the North American, that of colonization by men without women, and the subsequent course of mother-tongue diversity, which is basically one of slow shift motivated by economic necessity. In contrast, Paraguay presents a picture of maintenance of Guarani with Spanish bilingualism, rooted in the functional distribution of the languages. Finally, in the Caribbean, Jamaica is our one case study of a creole continuum and its educational problems.

The Arabic-speaking countries have their own characteristics. The chapter on the linguistic situation in Arabic-speaking nations is the only chapter that describes in detail the linguistic features of a bilingual situation. Stable Arabic diglossia is a very poorly understood phenomenon and is frequently given to misunderstanding and misinformation. The chapter on Morocco provides a case study of Arabic diglossia and Berber bilingualism.

China, India, and Soviet Central Asia are examples of enormous, multilingual nations with considerable language problems, which have been submitted to conscious efforts of language planning. Only China can claim to have been successful in its planning programs. Singapore, a nation-city, is another success story with four official languages but, unusually, without any strife among linguistic-ethnic groups.

The extremely multilingual sub-Sahara Africa provides four case studies. The three nations of East Africa—Kenya, Tanzania, and Uganda—and Nigeria in western Africa all have retained the ex-colonial English as a national language. Only Tanzania has been successful in implementing a native African tongue, Kiswahili, as a national language in common usage. Zaire (with Morocco), our example of a Francophone African state, shows a similar pattern to that of the other African countries. The chapter on the Republic of South Africa shows how the educational policies and language borders of ethnic minority groups are used to shore up the tragic policy of apartheid in an officially bilingual country.

No collection of case studies on bilingualism would be complete without a chapter on Israel. The successful revival of Hebrew is a unique occurrence in the world. There have been many attempts at language revivals, Irish, for example, but they have invariably failed. The historical account of the revival of Hebrew and the sociocultural conditions under which it took place make the case of Israel uniquely interesting, and the chapter primarily addresses itself to the problem of explaining the success of Hebrew.

Each chapter stands alone and can be read simply for the information it contains. If the chapters are considered together, however, trends and generalizations of societal bilingualism emerge, and this handbook with its case studies lends itself very well to theory testing.

Christina Bratt Paulston

Christina Bratt Paulston

BILINGUALISM AND BILINGUAL
EDUCATION: AN INTRODUCTION

Ethnic groups in contact within one state create certain characteristic problems, one of which is sociostructural. As R. A. Schermerhorn states, "The probability is overwhelming that when two groups with different cultural histories establish contacts that are regular rather than occasional or intermittent, one of the two groups will typically assume dominance over the other" (1970:68). Elsewhere he observes that the nature of this dominance is the major factor in ethnic relations (1964). The dominance of apartheid in South Africa is extreme, but to a lesser extent we see similar relations in Latin America. The Swedish laissez-faire policy for immigrants represents the other extreme of tolerant acceptance in educational policies. Typically, the ethnic minority groups are structurally subordinate with concomitant economic disadvantage. Catalonia in Spain is very much an exception. Occasionally, language becomes coupled to religion, and the chapters on Israel and the Arab-speaking nations show us the power of such a combination. Many bilingual nations recognize only the language of the dominant ethnic group as the official language, but other nations recognize more than one national language. (The situation of the United States which does not legally have an official, national language is unusual.) Official bilingualism may be peaceful as in Singapore and Switzerland, or it may be accompanied by occasional strife as in Belgium and Canada. The key to understanding such relations is often economic. In fact, the central question in understanding ethnic relations concerns the social conditions that hinder or foster the integration of ethnic groups into their environing societies (Schermerhorn, 1970:14).

Another characteristic problem of ethnic groups in contact concerns language and language planning, especially in educational policies. In her study of language policy in Mexico (1972), S. B. Heath makes clear that language decisions are based primarily on political and economic grounds and reflect the value of those in political power. Linguistic issues per se are of minor concern. Since the matters discussed are overtly those of language, there frequently is confusion about the salient issues discussed in language planning, whether they are matters of political, economic, religious, sociocultural, or linguistic concerns, or even moral concerns. The chapters in this book document the range of educational policies for minority social groups and emphasize the legitimate and important scholarly study which the topic merits.

Language choice is one of the major language problems, whether it be choice of national language (as in Israel), choice of national alphabet (as in Somalia), or choice of medium of instruction (as in Sweden). In Israel, social conditions and religious attitudes toward Hebrew and the Promised Land made possible the rebirth of Hebrew and its implementation as a national language. "As to the success of the Hebrew revival, it was probably due largely to the prevalence of the required conditions" (Nahir, 1984:302); that is, Israel serves as an example of social forces facilitating national language planning. In contrast, during the Velasco government Peru officialized Quechua as a national language (Mannheim, 1984) with resounding failure of implementation. In Peru, as in much of Latin America, race is defined primarily by cultural attributes: wear a long braid and many *faldas* (wide Indian-type skirts) and speak Quechua and you are an Indian; cut your hair, wear European-style clothing and speak Spanish, and you become, if not white, at least mestizo (Patch, 1967). To embrace Quechua would be to declare oneself Indian with all the accompanying socioeconomic stigmatization, and such planning held no hope of successful implementation. Peru serves as an example of language planning which goes counter to existing sociocultural forces.

The problem, of course, is to be able to identify relevant social forces and predict their outcomes. For example, contrary to expectation, choice of medium of instruction in the schools, especially for minority groups, has very little predictive power in the final language choice of the ethnic group. The difficulty is that we have a very poor grasp of what the relevant social forces are and of what the corresponding educational, social, and cultural outcomes will be. Three points need to be made here. The major point to understand about language as group behavior is that language is almost never the causal factor that makes things happen; rather, language mirrors social conditions and human relationships. It is quite true that denying blacks access to schooling as was common in the U.S. South in the last century made them unfit for anything but menial jobs, but black illiteracy was not the cause of black/white relations and exploitation. Rather, it was the result of it, much as is the situation in South Africa today.

The corollary to this simple, yet hard to grasp, point is that bilingual education (mother-tongue education, home language education, that is, education in both the national language and the ethnic group's own language) is in itself not a causal factor. Schools and schooling can facilitate existing social trends, but they cannot successfully counter social, economic, and political forces. English-medium schools were the major language learning facility for the children of the European immigrants to the United States, but the same schools have not been successful in teaching English to Navajo children on the reservations and they have had their fair share of failure in Chicano education. One key question that remains is, Under what social conditions does the medium of instruction make a difference for school children in achieving success?

The third point relates to the possible linguistic outcomes of the prolonged contact of ethnic groups within one nation, the typical background situation that necessitates special educational policies for minority groups. There are not many possibilities: the three main ones are language maintenance, bilingualism, or language shift. (Another possibility is the creation of pidgins and creoles as we see in Zaire with Lingala.)

The major point to be made here is that, in order to understand bilingualism and bilingual education, one must consider whether the general situation is one of language maintenance or language shift. Provided both opportunity and incentive are present, the norm for ethnic groups in prolonged contact within one nation is for the subordinate group to shift to the language of the dominant group, either over several hundred years as happened with Gaelic in Great Britain or over a span of three generations as has been the case of the European immigrants to Australia and the United States in an extraordinarily rapid shift. Precisely the language shift and attempts to stop it have caused much of the trouble in Quebec (from French to English) and in Belgium (from Flemish to French).

LANGUAGE MAINTENANCE AND LANGUAGE SHIFT

To the study of language maintenance and shift, we need to add two other related topics: language spread (Cooper, 1982) and language death (Dorian, 1981; Dressler and Wodak-Leodolter, 1977). R. L. Cooper defines language spread as ''an increase, over time, in the proportion of a communication network that adopts a given language or language variety for a given communicative function'' (1982:6). Most language spread probably takes place as lingua francas, as LWCs (languages of wider communication), and English is a good example (Fishman, Cooper, and Conrad, 1977). On the whole, such spread is neutral in attitudes.

But languages also spread for purposes of within-nation communication, and when they do so, not as an additional language like English in Nigeria but as a new mother tongue, then language spread becomes a case of language shift. When such language spread through shift takes place within groups that do not possess another territorial base, we have a case of language death. Languages do become extinct. The many dead Amerindian languages are mute witnesses to the spread of English (Bauman, 1980), as is also the case of the Celtic languages. Language shift, especially if it involves language death, tends to be an emotional topic. Social scientists who are not basically interested in language and culture per se will simply have to accept the idea that it is often futile to insist on a reasoned view in matters of language shift where it concerns the opinions and attitudes of the speakers of the shifting groups. Linguists and anthropologists frequently belong to this category.

Still, we can make some generalizations about language shift and maintenance which seem to hold in all cases. One of the primary factors in accounting for the subsequent course of mother-tongue diversity, to use S. Lieberson's phrase, lies in the origin of the contact situation (Lieberson, Dalto, and Johnston, 1975; Schermerhorn, 1970). Voluntary migration, especially of individuals and families, results in the most rapid shift, whereas annexation and colonialization—whereupon entire groups are brought into a nation with their social institutions of marriage and kinship, religions,and other belief and value systems still more or less intact—tend to result in much slower language shift, if at all.

The mechanism of language shift is bilingualism, often but not necessarily combined with exogamy, where parent(s) speak(s) the original language with the grandparents and the new language with the children. The case of bilingualism holds in all cases of group shifts, although the rate of shift may vary with several bilingual generations rather than just one.

Laymen and social scientists alike often treat language shift as an incontrovertible indicator of cultural assimilation, and it is often the painful thought of foresaking the culture and values of the forefathers that is at the root of the strife over language shift. Assimilation is a much more complex issue than language shift, but a few points need to be considered. First, we need to make a careful distinction, in Schermerhorn's terms (1970), between social and cultural institutions. Economic incorporation of an ethnic group with access to the goods and services of a nation (which is the common goal of minority groups and the most common reason for voluntary migration) is different from cultural assimilation and the giving up of values and beliefs. It is primarily to the perception of forced assimilation that the issue of the medium of instruction in the national language becomes tied. Many Chicanos, for example, bemoan the loss of Chicano culture with the loss of Spanish. But there is not necessarily an isomorphic relationship between language and culture; Spanish is the carrier of many other cultures besides Chicano, and as is less commonly accepted, language maintenance is not necessary for cultural and ethnic maintenance, as indeed D. E. Lopez (1976) documents for the Chicanos in Los Angeles. In other words, groups can maintain their own ethnic culture even after language shift takes place, as we see in groups like the English gypsies and many Amerindian tribes.

Although most ethnic minority groups within a nation do shift language, they will vary in their degree of ethnic maintenance and in their rate of shift. Groups also vary in group adhesion, and there is wide intragroup variation in members' attitudes toward language maintenance and cultural assimilation.

Where shift does not take place, it is for three major reasons:

1. Self-imposed boundary maintenance (Barth, 1969), always for reasons other than language, most frequently religion, for example, the Amish and the

orthodox Jewish Hassidim. The Hassidim are perfectly aware of the role of English, but their choice is group cohesion for religious purposes.

Many (Lubovitch) families elect to send their children to the Yiddish speaking school [no English curriculum]. In so doing, they increase the possibility of upward mobility within the ethnic group and decrease the probability that these children will gain the secular and technical skills necessary for employment in the economy of the larger society. All Lobovitchers are aware of the potential usefulness of secular skills and an English curriculum, but few . . . families elect the bilingual school for their children (Levy, 1975:40).

Such extreme measures of language maintenance are very unusual and are never undertaken over time only for the sake of language itself.

2. Externally imposed boundaries, usually in the form of denied access to goods and services, especially jobs. The black community of the past in the United States is an example. Geographic isolation (which is theoretically un-interesting but nevertheless effective) is also a form of external boundary that contributes to language maintenance, as Gaelic in the Hebrides or Quechua in the Andes.

3. A diglossic-like situation in which the two languages exist in a situation of functional distribution where each language has its specified purpose and domain and the one language is inappropriate in the other situation, as with Guarani and Spanish in Paraguay or with Modern Standard Arabic and their mother tongues in Morocco.

We see then that the major linguistic consequence of ethnic groups in prolonged contact within one nation is language shift of the subordinate groups to the language of the dominant group. The major dependent variable is the rate of shift. But this shift only takes place if the group has the opportunity and incentive to learn the national language. There are probably many kinds of incentives (the data base here is very inadequate), but the two major ones are (1) economic advantage, primarily in the form of source of income, and (2) social prestige. In L. Brudner's terms (1972), jobs determine language-learning strategies, which is to say wherever there are jobs available that demand knowledge of a certain language, people will learn it. Without rewards, language learning is not salient. Sometimes language shift is held to be problematic (Quebec), sometimes it is encouraged as national policy (France), sometimes it is resisted by the ethnic groups (Catalan), and sometimes it is encouraged (European immigrants to Aus-tralia and the United States), but one must invariably look to the social conditions to understand the attitudes and values that accompany language shift.

Another less common result of languages in contact is language maintenance, frequently with bilingualism, and it is always for reasons other than appreciation of the language per se. The third consequence is prolonged group bilingualism. This Introduction is not the place for a thorough discussion of the linguistic nature of bilingualism (Albert and Obler, 1978; Grosjean, 1982; Hornby, 1977; Lambert, 1972), but it should be mentioned that full-fledged, balanced bilingualism is the exception rather than the rule. Bilingualism spans a range from passive, imperfect knowledge of dead sacred languages (Sanskrit, Classical Arabic, Classical Hebrew, Suryoyo, etc.) to the linguistic competence necessary for simultaneous interpretation, (but even so U.N. interpreters only translate into one language, not back and forth). Degree of proficiency has little to do with language attitudes, and the sacred languages particularly assert a vast influence on attempts to orderly language planning (e.g., choice of national language in India). When we talk about bilingualism and bilingual education as an educational policy, we should therefore be careful to consider the degree and functional possibilities of the linguistic competence of the group discussed. I have observed ''mother-tongue'' education for Assyrian children in Sweden who could not even count to ten in their mother tongue but were fluent in the national language. In the same country, I have seen classes for Turkish primary students who knew very little Swedish. The highly varied nature of bilingualism forces us to face the problem of whether equity in education will allow the same educational policies for all ethnic groups. Indeed, the U.S. Supreme Court has suggested that equal treatment does not constitute equal opportunity in the matter of education of ethnic minority children compared to mainstream children. One can easily take that argument a step further and consider that the various ethnic groups may merit differential treatment.

When immigrant groups see that learning the national language well and fluently is in the best interest of their children (and social institutions like the schools and the church are available to help them do so), very few problems are associated with the educational policies for minority groups. Within the single city-state of Singapore with its four official languages and three major religions, there is no sign of ethnic strife or educational problems. Many Singaporeans favor the ex-colonial English as a medium of instruction. The simple explanation is to be found in Singapore's very strong and expanding economy. There is enough of the good of this life to go around for everybody, and competition takes place on the basis of individual qualities, not ethnic lines.

But when these same immigrant groups encounter stigmatization, economic exploitation, and systematic unemployment rather than socioeconomic opportunity, they are likely to use the original mother tongue as a strategy for mobilization. Language boundary maintenance reinforced with religion is an even stronger tool. The Turks in Europe have frequently followed this latter process. It is not that mainstream members and those from assimilated former ethnic groups like the Poles and Slovaks in Pittsburgh don't face difficulties in a declining economy; it is rather that they don't feel a we-they injustice and antagonism and (through language shift) they have lost language as a mobilization strategy. In Pittsburgh, the City Council recently decided to merge the Police Force and the Fire Fighter units. Both groups perceive this new policy as being against their best interests and are violently opposed to it. As both groups share the same ethnic mix, language and ethnicity are not available resources. Instead, both groups have mobilized along the lines of their labor unions. Had ethnicity been an available resource, they would very likely have mobilized along ethnic lines, to judge from D. Elazar and M. Friedman's (1976) case study of teachers in Philadelphia who did just that and who were able to successfully defend their jobs in that fashion.

Almost twenty years ago, Nathan Glazer asked: "Just why America produced *without* laws that which other countries, desiring a culturally unified population, were not able to produce *with* laws—is not an easy question" (1966:360). There is a fable by Aesop which holds the answer to that question and which best illustrates the points raised here. The sun and the wind see a man with a cloak (read language) walking along the road. They decide to enter a contest to see who can first cause him to shed his coat. The wind tears at him for hours, but the man only wraps himself more tightly in his cloak. The sun takes over and spreads her benevolence over the man, who, after a short time, divests himself of his cloak. Moral: In hard times, people will cling to their language and ethnic group; in times of plenty, they pay little attention to resources like ethnic languages.

Ethnicity and Nationalism

The preceding discussion has dealt exclusively with the course of language and the linguistic consequences of ethnic minority groups in prolonged contact within one nation. But groups can find another focus of social mobilization than ethnicity. In the rest of this Introduction, it is argued that there are four distinct types of social mobilization, which under certain specified social conditions result in different linguistic consequences: ethnicity, ethnic movements, ethnic nationalism, and geographic nationalism.[1]

Past scholarship on language and ethnic groups often used the term *nationality* synonymously with *ethnic group* (Deutsch, 1953). There is merit in reconsidering the phenomena of ethnic groups in contact, and instead of entwining the concepts of ethnicity and nationalism, we would have a better understanding of language maintenance and shift if we were to differentiate the two. Four types of social mobilization come close to forming a continuum rather than four distinct types: (1) Ethnicity, which closely corresponds to the old notion of ethnicity; (2) ethnic movement, which is based on the concept of the new ethnicity (Bennett, 1975); (3) ethnic nationalism; and (4) geographic nationalism which corresponds to H. Kohn's closed and open nationalism (1968) as well as to J. A. Fishman's nationalism and nationism (1968).

Ethnicity

An "ethnic group" is a reference group invoked by people who share a common historical style (which may be only assumed), based on overt features and values, and who, through the process of interaction with others, identify themselves as sharing that style. "Ethnic identity" is the sum total of the group members' feelings about those values, symbols, and common histories that identify them as a distinct group. "Ethnicity" is simply ethnic-based action (Royce, 1982:18).

Ethnicity tends to stress roots and a shared biological past and the common ancestors (factual or fictional). The basis of personal identity is cultural (including religion), and ethnicity is a matter of self-ascription. Cultural values and beliefs, which are held in common, are unconsciously learned behavior, and ethnicity is just taken for granted. The members tend to feel comfortable with past and future, and no opposition or violence is involved.

Ethnicity involves little power struggle and not much purpose, and so the common course is assimilation and concomitant language shift. For example, the Walloons were brought to Sweden in the 1600s to develop the iron industry and have completely assimilated into Swedish culture (Douhan, 1982). Ethnicity will not maintain a language in a multilingual setting, if the dominant group allows assimilation, and incentive and opportunity of access to the second language (L_2) are present. Some general social conditions that influence access to the L_2 are:

1. Participation in social institutions, primarily universal schooling, exogamy, and required military service, and often religious institutions.
2. Access to the mass media, especially television.
3. Access to roads and transportation versus physical isolation, like islands and mountains.
4. Travel, including trade, commerce, war, and evangelism.
5. Some occupations.
6. Demographic factors, like size of groups, vast in-migration, continued migration, back-migration, and urbanization.

A discussion of these social conditions would take us too far afield, and so only a few comments are made here.

Exogamy, that is, marrying outside the ethnic group or other social unit, obviously necessitates language shift for one partner, at least within the family. This shift typically is in the direction of the language of the socioeconomically favored group (Gal, 1979). Exogamy, showing definite trends of direction, is the most positive indicator of incipient shift, and an important mechanism for language shift and assimilation.

This list has been collected from a reading of case studies where these conditions are often treated observationally and anecdotally. No doubt some additions can be made.

Ethnic Movement

The major difference between ethnicity and ethnic movement develops when ethnicity as an unconscious source of identity turns into a conscious strategy, usually in competition for scarce resources. An ethnic movement is ethnicity that has turned militant, consisting of ethnic discontents who perceive the world as against them, an adversity drawn along ethnic boundaries. Although ethnicity stresses the content of the culture, ethnic movements will be concerned with boundary maintenance, in Barth's terms, with "us" against "them." It is very much a conscious, cognitive ethnicity in a power struggle with the dominant group for social and economic advantage, a struggle that frequently leads to violence and social upheaval. Many ethnic movements have charismatic leaders (probably always born a member of the ethnic group) like Stephen Biko in South Africa and Martin Luther King, but they need not have an intellectual elite or a significant middle class.

Movements need rallying points, and language is a good obvious symbol if it is available. (It may not be. The Irish Republican Army, for example, uses English.) So is religion. Original mother tongues and sacred languages are powerful symbols and may serve to support people in their struggle for what they perceive as a better life (that life may be after death, as in Jihad, Holy War). But note that language as a symbol need not be the ethnic group's mother tongue. Both Stephen Biko and Martin Luther King used English and partially for the same reason—the diversity of African languages. The symbol in Biko's case was the choice of language, English rather than Afrikaans; in King's case, the symbol lay with the characteristic style of Black English rhetoric, many of whose features originated with the West African languages.

When an ethnic movement draws on religion as a resource for its identity base as strategy in social competition, when cognitive ethnicity is joined with religious fervor, the likely consequence is one of language maintenance, probably of a sacred language (only). Sacred languages tend with great diligence to be kept unchanged. The result is that sacred languages are seldom spoken and exist only in written forms. Groups that maintain a sacred language, the Assyrians, for instance, will typically shift their everyday language to that of the surrounding community. Hence, we find all Assyrians maintaining Suryoyo (a form of Aramaic) but speaking Arabic, Turkish, Swedish, or American English. Maintaining two extra languages seems too cumbersome.

There are exceptions. Pre-Israeli Jews maintained both Hebrew and Yiddish, but as a result of externally imposed boundary maintenance and the environing community's refusal to let them assimilate. When allowed to assimilate, Yiddish disappeared. That explains why Yiddish was maintained in Slavic East Europe but not in Germany, that is, as a factor of degree of social enclosure (Schermerhorn, 1970). The dropout rate is likely to be high for such religious groups if the host community allows assimilation, as it is for the Amish and as J. W. Bennett cites for the New York Hassidim. Ethnic movements by themselves probably cannot maintain a language but will affect the rate of shift so that the shift is much slower and spans many more generations.

Nationalism

There seems to be as many definitions of nationalism as there are scholars of nationalism, basically because, in Boyd C. Shafer's words (1972), nationalism has many faces. Shafer concludes that it is impossible to fit nationalism into a short definition (1972:5). But H. Kohn points out that, while all instances of nationalism will vary according to past history and culture, as well as the present social structure and geographical location, all forms of nationalism still share certain traits (1968:64). R. W. Cottam's insistence that nationalism not be dealt with as a thing reified but rather as a manifestation of nationalistic behavior is very useful here. He identifies some of the shared traits in his definition of a nationalist "as an individual who sees himself as a member of a political community, a nation, that is entitled to independent statehood, and is willing to grant that community a primary and terminal loyalty'' (Cottam, 1964:3). Group cohesion to the end, a goal orientation of self-determination, a perceived threat of opposing forces, and above all access to or hope of territory are characteristics of all national movements. Both A. P. Royce's and Cottam's definitions stress that ethnicity and nationalism are sets or syndromes of behavior, perceptions, and attitudes of a group of people. Given certain social conditions, they will behave in certain predictable fashions, including language behavior which is our present interest.

Ethnic and geographic nationalism share all of these features. The goal is independence, their own political status, and social institutions on their own territory. The most common ideal is the nation-state, but there are others. Catalunya, Quebec, and Flemish Belgium are content to remain part of a larger state as long as they can safeguard their own social and cultural institutions, of which language becomes a very prominent symbol.

The improvement of one's own lot in life or at least of one's children's status is probably a common goal of all national movements. The motivation, as in ethnic movements, is one of perceived self-interest, a self-chosen state. Very often nationalism takes place as a protest against oppression, against a common enemy, whether it be against a (dominant) group within the same state or against another state. Euskadi, the Basque nation within Spain, is an example of the first type, and it introduces another problem of interpretation, the unanimity of degree of intensity of a national movement. The Basques range from terrorists and separatists to assimilists with language shift more common than admitted. There is typically a great emphasis on loyalty and group cohesion, which are consciously taught behaviors, taught through social institutions like school, church, and army, with typical symbols being the flag, the national anthem, and, above all, the language. To admit to language shift is to be disloyal, and this very deep-seated feeling of disloyalty is an additional problem in eliciting valid survey data in this type of research (Thompson, 1974).

The goals of national movements, besides general independence, tend to be quite definite and specific. These goals are often legitimatized by or based on historical past events or conditions. During the Finnish school strike in Stockholm during February of 1984, when Finnish parents kept their children out of school in support of their demand for Finnish-medium schooling in kindergarten through university-level courses, the reason given was that Finland was bilingual in Swedish-Finnish and that Sweden should reciprocate. It is a demand legitimized on the national law of the ethnic immigrant group and its past history. It is much more characteristic of nationalism than of ethnic movements which tend to base their claims on a rationale of equity with others within the nation-state.

A national movement must have a well-developed middle class in which condition it differs from ethnic movements. Victor Alba's (1975) anecdote of the Catalan workers who considered issues of language immaterial is representative. "We don't care if we are exploited in Castilian or Catalan," was their rejoinder, and they aligned themselves with the workers' unions and the Socialist party rather than mobilize themselves along national lines. Without a stake in property, nationalism is not perceived to further one's self-interest.

When ethnic discontents turn separatist, we get ethnic nationalism. A. P. Royce considers the situation of the Basques. The ETA, the Basque national organization, is led by members of the middle class. The lower class perceived no advantage in a Basque movement, and the concerns and economic interests of the elite are primarily state/national and international. The regional economic interests are in control of the middle class, who feel they carry an unfair share of Spain's economic burden and are given no adequate compensation. "The important point in this case is that the impetus for ethnic nationalism came from the sector whose privileges and power depended on the economic well-being of the Basque provinces. Basque nationalism was the obvious way to maintain their position" (Royce, 1982:104).

The crucial difference between ethnic movement and ethnic nationalism is access to territory; without land one cannot talk about Basque nationalism. It is also access to territory that gives viability to a separatist movement.

Ethnic nationalism and geographic nationalism share a great many features, as the previous discussion makes obvious. The difference between them is the same as that which Hans Kohn outlines for "open" and "closed" nationalism (1968:66). In ethnic or closed nationalism, the ethnic group is isomorphic with the nation-state. The emphasis is on the nation's autochthonous character, on the common origin and ancestral roots. In ethnic nationalism, language can attain an importance that is far out of proportion of its communicative function. The typical claim is that the deep thoughts and the soul of the nation can only be adequately expressed in the common mother tongue. Hitler's Germany, with its emphasis on racial exclusiveness and rootedness in the ancestral soil, was the most extreme form of ethnic nationalism. (It is an interesting observation that the leaders of national movements need not be original members of that nation; Hitler, Stalin, and de Gaulle—and Napoleon before them—did not have their original roots in the state of which they became national leaders.)

Kohn calls "open" nationalism a more modern form; it is territorially based (hence geographic nationalism) and features a political society, constituting a nation of fellow citizens regardless of ethnic descent. The so-called great immigration countries of Canada, Australia, and the United States are good examples. As Kohn observes, they rejected the notion of a nation based on a common past, a common religion or a common culture. Instead, "[They] owe their nationhood to the affirmation of the modern trends of emancipation, assimilation, mobility, and individualism" (1968:66).

In ethnic nationalism, language is a prime symbol of the nation, but that is not necessarily so with geographic nationalism. Actually, the United States does not even legally have a national language. Canada has two national languages, but English and French are not thought of as national symbols of Canada. Rather, the maintenance of a common language was undertaken primarily for pragmatic LWC (language of wider communication) purposes. At the same time, although one cannot change one's genes, one can learn a new language, and in a nation that does not care about genes but uses language to define its membership, as does Catalunya, learning the new language obviously held both practical and symbolic significance: knowing the national language became the hallmark of membership and in-group status. The combination of voluntary migration, the social incentives of in-group membership, and easy access to the new language has tended to result in very rapid bilingualism, often with consequent shift to the national language.

CONCLUSION

The uncertainty of language planning in education will be reduced if we consider the social context of language problems, especially the social, cultural, and economic forces that contribute to language maintenance and shift. The most elegant educational policies for minority groups are doomed to failure if they go counter to prevailing social forces, especially the economic situation. Language planning efforts are most likely to be successful when they are supported by economic advantage or similar social incentives for the minority groups.

At the same time, we need to acknowledge and respect the fact that there are other points of view on language maintenance and shift than the strictly pragmatic aspects argued here. Religious groups take language maintenance seriously without any immediately obvious incentives, and so do a few ethnic groups. Actual tolerance of religious disparity varies from nation to nation, but the principle of religious freedom is well recognized in most countries. Simply, it is one of respect for the right of a group to self-determination, to hold the values and beliefs as its chooses. Similarly, we should hold the truth self-evident that an ethnic group has a right to its own language if it so chooses. The point made in

this chapter, that ethnic groups very rarely opt for continued language maintenance if the social conditions favor a shift to the national language, is no coun-
terargument to the ethical principle that minority groups have a right to cultural
self-determination.

NOTE

1. Parts of this chapter are based on "Linguistic Consequences of Ethnicity and Nationalism in Multilingual Settings," a paper presented at the Organization for Economic
Cooperation and Development (OECD), Paris, 1985.

BIBLIOGRAPHY

Alba, Victor. 1975. *Catalonia: A Profile*. New York: Praeger Publishers.
Albert, M., and L. Obler. 1978. *The Bilingual Brain*. New York: Academic Press.
Barth, F. 1969. *Ethnic Groups and Boundaries*. Boston: Little, Brown and Co.
Bauman, J. J. 1980. *A Guide to Issues in Indian Language Retention*. Washington, D.C.:
Center for Applied Linguistics.
Bennett, J. W. 1975. "A Guide to the Collection." In *The New Ethnicity: Perspectives
from Ethnology*, ed. J. W. Bennett. St. Paul: West Publishing Co.
Brudner, L. 1972. "The Maintenance of Bilingualism in Southern Austria." *Ethnology*
11, 1: 39–54.
Cooper, R. L., ed. 1982. "A Framework for the Study of Language Spread." *Language
Spread: Studies in Diffusion and Social Change*. Arlington, Va.: Center for Ap-
plied Linguistics, and Bloomington: Indiana University Press.
Cottam, R. W. 1964. *Nationalism in Iran*. Pittsburgh: University of Pittsburgh Press.
Crewe, W., ed. 1977. *The English Language in Singapore*. Singapore: Eastern Uni-
versities Press.
Deutsch, K. W. 1953. *Nationalism and Social Communication: An Inquiry into the
Foundations of Nationality*. Cambridge, Mass.: MIT Press.
Dorian, N. 1981. *Language Death: The Life Cycle of a Scottish Gaelic Dialect*. Phila-
delphia: University of Pennsylvania Press.
Douhan, B. 1982. "The Walloons in Sweden." *American-Swedish Genealogical Review*
2:1–17.
Dressler, W., and R. Wodak-Leodolter, eds. 1977. "Language Death." *International
Journal of the Sociology of Language*, No. 12 (Special Issue).
Elazar, D., and M. Friedman. 1976. *Moving Up: Ethnic Succession in America*. New
York: Institute on Pluralism and Group Identity of the American Jewish
Committee.
Fishman, J. A. 1968. "Nationality-Nationalism and Nation-Nationism." In *Language
Problems in Developing Nations*, eds. J. A. Fishman, C. A. Ferguson, and J.
Das Gupta. New York: John Wiley.
————. 1977. "Language Maintenance." *Harvard Encyclopedia of American Ethnic
Groups*. Cambridge, Mass.: Harvard University Press.
Fishman, J. A., R. Cooper, and A. Conrad, eds. 1977. *The Spread of English*. Rowley,
Mass.: Newbury House.

Gal, S. 1979. *Language Shift: Social Determinants of Linguistic Change in Bilingual Austria.* New York: Academic Press.

Glazer, N. 1966. "The Process and Problems of Language Maintenance: An Integrative Review." In *Language Loyalty in the United States*, ed. J. Fishman. The Hague: Mouton.

Grosjean, F. 1982. *Life with Two Languages: An Introduction to Bilingualism.* Cambridge, Mass.: Harvard University Press.

Heath, S. B. 1972. *Telling Tongues: Language Policy in Mexico—Colony to Nation.* New York: Teachers College Press.

Hornby, P. 1977. *Bilingualism: Psychological, Social, and Educational Implications.* New York: Academic Press.

Kohn, H. 1968. "Nationalism." *International Encyclopedia of the Social Sciences* 11: 63–70.

Lambert, W. E. 1972. *Language, Psychology, and Culture.* Stanford, Calif.: Stanford University Press.

Levy, S. B. 1975. "Shifting Patterns of Ethnic Identification Among the Hassidim." In *The New Ethnicity: Perspectives from Ethnology*, ed. J. W. Bennett. St. Paul: West Publishing Co.

Lieberson, S., G. Dalto, and M. E. Johnston. 1975. "The Course of Mother Tongue Diversity in Nations." *American Journal of Sociology* 81, 1: 34–61.

Lopez, D. E. 1976. "The Social Consequences of Chicano Home/School Bilingualism." *Social Problems* 24, 2: 234–46.

MacDougall, J. A., and C. S. Foon. 1976. "English Language Competence and Occupational Mobility in Singapore." *Pacific Affairs* 49, 2: 294–312.

Mannheim, B. 1984. "Una nación acorrolada: Southern Peruvian Quechua Language Planning and Politics in Historical Perspective." *Language in Society* 13: 291–309.

Nahir, M. 1984. "Language Planning Goals: A Classification." *Language Problems and Language Planning* 8, 3: 294–327.

Painter, M. 1983. "Aymara and Spanish in Southern Peru: The Relationship of Language to Economic Class and Social Identity." In *Bilingualism*, ed. A. Miracle. Athens: University of Georgia Press.

Patch, R. W. 1967. "La Parada, Lima's Market. Serrano and Criollo, the Confusion of Race with Class," *AVFSR*, West Coast South America Series, 14, 2 (February): 3–9.

Paulston, C. B. 1975. "Ethnic Relations and Bilingual Education: Accounting for Contradictory Data." In *Proceedings of the First Inter-American Conference on Bilingual Education*, ed. R. Troike and N. Modiano. Arlington, Va.: Center for Applied Linguistics.

———. 1977. "Language and Ethnic Boundaries." In *Papers from the First Nordic Conference on Bilingualism*, ed. T. Skutnabb-Kangas. Helsinki: Helsingfors Universitet.

Rosier, P., and W. Holm. 1980. *The Rock Point Experience: A Longitudinal Study of a Navajo School Program.* Washington, D.C.: Center for Applied Linguistics.

Royce, A. P. 1982. *Ethnic Identity: Strategies of Diversity.* Bloomington: Indiana University Press.

Schermerhorn, R. A. 1964. "Towards a General Theory of Minority Groups." *Phylon* 25: 238–46.

————. 1970. *Comparative Ethnic Relations*. New York: Random House.

Shabad, G., and R. Gunther. 1982. "Language, Nationalism, and Political Conflict in Spain." *Comparative Politics* 14, 4: 443–77.

Shafer, Boyd C. 1972. *Faces of Nationalism*. New York: Harcourt Brace Jovanovich.

————. 1976. *Nationalism: Its Nature and Interpreters*. Washington, D.C.: American Historical Association.

Snyder, L. L. 1976. *Varieties of Nationalism: A Comparative Study*. Hinsdale, Ill.: Dryden Press.

Spolsky, B., ed. 1972. *The Language Education of Minority Children*. Rowley, Mass.: Newbury House.

Thompson, R. M. 1974. "Mexican American Language Loyalty and the Validity of the 1970 Census." *International Journal of the Sociology of Language* 2: 6–18.

Tosi, A. 1984. *Immigration and Bilingual Education: A Case Study of Movement of Population, Language Change and Education Within the EEC*. Oxford: Pergamon Press.

UNESCO. 1984. "Mother Tongue and Educational Attainment." *Prospects* 14:1.

Veltman, C. 1983. *Language Shift in the United States*. The Hague: Mouton.

Verdoodt, A. 1972. "The Differential Impact of Immigrant French Speakers on Indigenous German Speakers: A Case Study in the Light of Two Theories." In *Advances in the Sociology of Language*, ed. J. A. Fishman. Part II. The Hague: Mouton.

Weinstein, B. 1983. *The Civic Tongue: Political Consequences of Language Choices*. New York: Longmans.

2

Sarah Grey Thomason

LANGUAGES OF THE WORLD

The ideal starting point for a discussion of languages of the world would be the first human language. From there we could trace the diversification process that ultimately produced the several thousand languages now spoken. Unfortunately, this orderly historical path is not open to us: hominid remains several million years old have been found in Africa, but languages are not fossilized with the bones. Linguistic ''fossils'' appear only with the invention of writing about six thousand years ago. Historical linguistic methodology permits the partial reconstruction of prehistoric languages, but the time depth achieved by those methods is still only about ten thousand years at most. We cannot even be certain that language evolved only once in human history. It is possible that early human populations separately developed language, though in that case we might expect greater organizational differences among widely separated languages, and more difficulty in learning a distant culture's language. At any rate, the direct linguistic evidence dates from a period when there were at least as many languages spoken as there are today.

Given the continuing spread of the languages of politically and economically dominant groups at the expense of the languages of less powerful cultures, it is safe to assume that the number of human languages is rapidly decreasing. Such a decrease can be traced directly in the histories of countries like the United States and Australia, where many languages spoken at the time of first contact with Europeans have vanished. New languages may still be emerging in some parts of the world, but certainly not at a rate that matches the dismaying rate of language disappearance.

For this reason, today's guess at the total number of languages must differ from tomorrow's. Other factors, too, make any such estimate tentative. In particular, some regions of the world probably still harbor a few languages undiscovered by outsiders; and two different language names may in fact designate merely separate dialects (or even the same dialect!) of a single language. It is therefore not surprising that linguists' guesses at the number of the world's languages vary widely, roughly from three thousand to six thousand. The first figure is surely too low. There are about a thousand languages in Africa alone and another thousand in the New Guinea area (including New Guinea itself and neighboring islands). Over one thousand American Indian languages are probably still spoken in the Americas. Europe has only about fifty living languages, but Australia may still have about two hundred. Hundreds of languages are spoken in mainland Asia, and several hundred more on the islands of the Pacific and neighboring seas.

Sometime in the last few million years, the first human language (or the first few) evolved and then, over time, diversified into thousands of different languages. The processes of diversification that produce two or more daughter languages from a single parent language are well understood, because they can be more or less directly traced in real time. This is possible for those few groups in which an ancient language preserved in written records has split into several daughters. The best documented case is that of Latin, which gave rise to the modern Romance languages after Roman power spread over Western Europe and parts of Eastern Europe. Chinese has a much greater time depth than the Romance group, since written Chinese dates from the Shang dynasty (1766–1123? B.C.); but since Chinese writing itself has changed relatively little over the centuries, the processes of change into the various modern Chinese "dialects"—actually separate languages, judged on a criterion of mutual intelligibility—are not represented in the writing system. Greek has an attested history intermediate between that of Latin and Chinese, but in this case virtually no diversification has taken place: of the several Ancient Greek dialects, only Attic survives (except perhaps for a minor relic of a Doric dialect in the Peloponnese), and Greek is still just one language. Other languages are documented from a very early date but have left no living descendants. Sumerian has pride of place in this category: it is the earliest documented human language, with written records from as early as the fourth millennium B.C. But Sumerian died out long before the turn of our era, and, indeed, is not known to be related to any other language. Other ancient Mesopotamian languages, notably Akkadian (with its dialects Assyrian and Babylonian), dating from the third millennium B.C., and Hittite, the language of an empire that flourished from 1700 to 1200 B.C., are related to groups with living representatives, but not in a direct line of descent with any modern languages. The same is true of the North African language Egyptian: it is attested from 3200 B.C. and is distantly related to modern Semitic and other Afro-Asiatic languages, but Egyptian itself (in its modern form Coptic) had died by the end of the seventeenth century A.D.

From the direct evidence provided by the Romance group and languages that have diversified into several modern dialects, and the indirect evidence provided by groups whose time depth can be tentatively determined through

extralinguistic means, we can make at least a rough guess at the time required for a single language to split into two or more daughter languages.
We start with a premise whose empirical foundation is solid: all living languages are constantly changing. If a speech community divides into two
groups that have no further contact with each other (for instance, if one
group moves far away from the original homeland), the two versions of the
original community's language will diverge, because language change is not
deterministic—that is, it is impossible to make specific, detailed predictions
about the exact changes that a given linguistic system will undergo. After
five hundred to a thousand years, the two groups will be speaking separate,
mutually unintelligible languages. The process of language split may be hastened if the speech of one (or more than one) group is heavily influenced by
some foreign language, and it may be slowed in the unlikely event that neither group is influenced by any foreign language contact.

Given enough time and appropriate geographical spread and isolation, the
daughter languages produced by language split may split again and again, until
an elaborate branching family tree has sprung from the single original language.
Most family trees that linguists construct have an unattested starting point, called
a proto-language, whose existence is inferred from the evidence of certain kinds
of similarities in the attested daughter languages. Family trees are thus hypotheses, and the extent to which interrelationships within language families can
be absolutely determined continues to be a much-debated issue. The greater the
time depth in a proposed language family, the less detailed our historical hypotheses are. The methods for establishing branching family relationships, like
the methods for reconstructing unattested stages in the history of a language
family, break down at about ten thousand years. If all human languages arose
from a single parent language, our current methods would never permit us to
prove the point, because the time depths required to produce all the attested
human languages are clearly far greater than ten thousand years. This means,
among other things, that we can never prove two languages to be *un*related; we
can only note the absence of evidence that they are related. Linguists often talk
about unrelated languages, to be sure, but such statements always carry the
implicit hedge "as far as we know."

Numbers of language families are even trickier to estimate than numbers of
individual languages, because in most areas scholars disagree about the family groupings they consider adequately demonstrated. To give just one example, some linguists have claimed just six large language families among
American Indian languages north of Mexico, while others—almost everyone
nowadays—are much more cautious about accepting family (or genetic)
groupings, estimating about thirty-five to forty families. Probably there are at
least a hundred language families in the world. A few of the most diverse
families, notably Austronesian in the Pacific and Niger-Kordofanian in Africa, contain five hundred to a thousand languages each; Indo-European, with
over a hundred languages, is still among the most diverse families. Most lan-

guage families have only a few member languages, and scattered about the world are a number of language isolates, or one-language "families." Examples of isolates are Burushaski in India, Basque in Europe, and Kutenai in northwestern North America, as well as the extinct language Sumerian. Further research may well consolidate some sets of language families into single larger families; Kutenai, for instance, is believed by some linguists to be related to the Algonquian family of Canada and the northern United States. But there will no doubt still be many separate language families even after all the methodologically feasible consolidating has been done.

Surveys of the world's languages according to family groupings can be found in a number of sources. Linguistics textbooks often include a chapter on the subject, for example, Henry A. Gleason (1961) and Victoria Fromkin and Robert Rodman (1978). More ambitious lists and classifications are rarer. The first authoritative modern linguistic work that aimed at completeness was that by Antoine Meillet and Marcel Cohen (1952, but originally published earlier), which includes twenty-one maps, discussions of classifications, lists of languages, structural sketches, and brief analyzed texts for one or more important languages in most groups. More recently, the journal *Anthropological Linguistics* (1964–66) published a series of issues by C. F. and F. M. Voegelin surveying all the world's languages, with classifications and lists, and, occasionally, a bit of structural information. Merritt Ruhlen (1975) differs in scope from both of the earlier sources, since the bulk of the volume is taken up with some seven hundred representative phoneme inventories. But it also includes family trees and descriptions of most of the world's language families, so it is useful as a reference work. These three publications also differ in quality. Meillet and Cohen is consistently of very good quality, but many of its classifications are now seriously out of date. The other two vary in quality from family to family, and the reader is seldom warned that some family groupings are highly controversial (or even generally rejected nowadays). All these sources must therefore be used with caution. Readers interested in classifications for particular areas should consult the more specialized surveys that are available for many families and many regions of the world; some of these are listed in the reference to this chapter. A good source for general information is the *Encyclopedia Britannica*, whose most recent edition has a number of good articles on major families and some minor ones as well. The various volumes of the *Current Trends in Linguistics* series, edited by Thomas A. Sebeok, have more comprehensive surveys of most families. Here I will discuss the world's most firmly established language families, concentrating on those with the most member languages and the most speakers. This survey will then serve as background for a discussion of the world's languages in political terms, that is, a look at the national and international status of particular languages. The geographically designated section headings below are not meant to imply exclusivity: language families can, and frequently do, spill over continental boundaries.

LANGUAGE FAMILIES CENTERED IN EUROPE AND NORTHERN ASIA

Even before the Age of Exploration, the Indo-European family had one of the greatest geographical ranges in the world. At the time of the earliest historical records, as the family name suggests, Indo-European (IE) languages spread from India to northwestern Europe. The easternmost IE language, Tocharian, has long been extinct and is known only from documents discovered in Chinese Turkestan (western Sinkiang). Of the ten IE branches, seven are attested before 500 A.D.: Anatolian, an entirely extinct branch whose major representative was Hittite (Asia Minor); Greek, attested in the ancient Mycenean form from ca. 1400 B.C.; Indo-Iranian, with Indic attested in Sanskrit hymns from about 800 B.C. (and even earlier Indic words in a document from 1300 B.C.), and Iranian in the religious writings of Zarathustra (who is believed to have been born in 637 B.C.), written in the ancient language Avestan; Italic, including Latin, with inscriptions beginning about 600 B.C.; Germanic, with the oldest extensive texts in the now extinct language Gothic from about 350 A.D. and runic inscriptions in Early Norse from the third century A.D.; Celtic, with inscriptions in the continental language Gaulish, which became extinct in about 500 A.D., and in Old Irish from the fourth or fifth century A.D.; and Armenian (the USSR and elsewhere), a one-language branch first attested in the fifth century A.D.

Besides these seven early-attested IE branches, there are three more recently documented ones. Of these, only Balto-Slavic diversified into a number of modern languages, the two living Baltic languages Lithuanian and Latvian and the several Slavic languages. The other two branches contain just one language each: Albanian and Tocharian. The earlier attested IE branches, except for Anatolian, have left one or more modern descendants. In the Indo-Iranian branch, there are over twenty living Indic languages (mainly in India and Pakistan) and about thirty Iranian ones (Iran, Afghanistan, the USSR); and there are close to twenty languages, for example, Kashmiri, in Dardic (northern Indian subcontinent), the third sub-branch of Indo-Iranian. The Germanic, Celtic, and Italic branches have several languages each (the last comprises the modern Romance languages). Most of the Indian subcontinent and almost all of Europe are now IE territory—as well as almost the entire Western Hemisphere, thanks to European colonizers.

Two language isolates have been important in European history. These are Basque, which is spoken in the Pyrenees Mountains of Spain and France, and the extinct language Etruscan, which was spoken in what is now Italy. Aside from these two languages, only one other family besides IE occupies a significant portion of Europe: the Uralic family, whose most prominent members are Finnish, Hungarian, and Estonian. Most of the twenty-eight or so Uralic languages are spoken in both the European and the Asian parts of the Soviet Union, and the family name is derived from its proposed original homeland—the Ural Mountains. The family is divided into three main branches, Finno-Permic (e.g., Finnish, Estonian, and Lappish), Ugric (e.g., Hungarian), and Samoyed, a small group located in north central subarctic Siberia.

Between Europe and Asia, in the Caucasus Mountains of the USSR and neighboring parts of Iran and Turkey, are a number of languages to which the umbrella term *Caucasian* is given. In spite of their geographical proximity, these languages seem to be divided into two quite distinct genetic groups: the more diverse (over thirty languages) North Caucasian family and the South Caucasian, or Kartvelian, family (four languages). The most important language in either family is the South Caucasian language Georgian, which has been a literary language since the fifth century A.D.

The Altaic family, whose name comes from the Altai Mountains of Central Asia, stretches from the borders of Europe across Northern Asia to the Pacific Ocean. Its major representatives are found at the extremes of its range: the Turkic language (Ottoman) Turkish is the westernmost language of the family nowadays (though the country of Bulgaria is named after a Turkic people—no longer there—who once penetrated into Europe); and in the east, many (perhaps most) specialists now classify both Korean and Japanese as branches of Altaic. Most of the other twenty or more languages of the Turkic branch are spoken in the Soviet Union, but a few spill over into Afghanistan, Iran, Mongolia, and China (Sinkiang). The other two branches of the family, both in Northern Asia, are Mongol (nine languages) and Tungus (seventeen languages). Tungus is the least important Altaic branch now, but one of its members, Manchu, was the language of the rulers of China from 1644 to 1911. Wider relationships have been proposed for Altaic, especially with Uralic, but none of these is considered well established by most historical linguists.

In the far north of the Soviet Union, particularly in northeastern Siberia, are a few languages that do not fit into any of the families discussed so far. Siberian Eskimo belongs to the circumpolar Eskimo-Aleut family. It is closely related to the Eskimo languages of Alaska, Canada, and Greenland, and more distantly related to Aleut, which is spoken on the island chain between the USSR and Alaska. Then there is a set of eight languages often called Paleosiberian—a strictly geographical designation indicating that their speakers were in Siberia before others (Uralic, Altaic, and then Russian speakers) arrived in the area. Several of these belong to the same family, Luoravetlan (or Chukotian); these include, in particular, Chukchi, which was a language of political and economic importance in the region before the Russians came in numbers. The remaining Paleosiberian languages are not known to be related to each other or to any other languages, though hypotheses about possible genetic groupings are often put forward. Among the most interesting hypotheses are those that link one or more Paleosiberian languages, especially the Luoravetlan, with Indian languages of North America or with Eskimo-Aleut. Some of the research along these lines looks promising, but the time depth is great, and none of the cases is generally considered as proven—at least not yet.

LANGUAGE FAMILIES CENTERED IN AFRICA

In Western Asia and Northern Africa, the most important language family is Afro-Asiatic, whose five firmly established branches are Semitic, Egyptian, Berber, Chadic, and Cushitic. Only the Semitic branch is spoken in Asia as well as Africa. Five members of this branch have particular historical importance. Hebrew and Aramaic are the languages in which the Old Testament of the Bible is written, and Aramaic was the native language of Jesus. Arabic was the language of Muhammad and of the Qur'an; starting in the seventh century A.D., it was spread with Islam from Arabia over most of North Africa and large parts of Asia. Akkadian, now extinct, was the earliest written Semitic language and the major lingua franca of the Near East until it was displaced by Aramaic toward the turn of our era. Finally, Phoenician, with its offshoot Punic, was the language of the great Mediterranean sea power based in Carthage (modern Tunisia) in North Africa. It was probably the Phoenicians from whom the Greeks learned to write, perhaps as early as the ninth century B.C. Phoenician, like Akkadian, is long dead.

Besides Semitic, Afro-Asiatic has four or five other branches. Egyptian forms a one-language branch, now extinct. The several languages of the Berber branch, for example, Tuareg and Shilha, are spoken by isolated groups in northwestern Africa; they were once widespread throughout this region, but in recent centuries they have steadily lost ground to Arabic. Chadic languages are still little known. There are probably over one-hundred languages in this branch, clustered in the vicinity of Lake Chad and spoken mainly in Nigeria, Chad, Cameroon, and the Central African Republic. The best known Chadic language by far is Hausa, which is a lingua franca of great importance in large parts of West Africa and is the official language of Nigeria's northern provinces. The Cushitic branch is subdivided by some specialists into Cushitic proper and an independent sixth Afro-Asiatic branch, Omotic. Cushitic languages are spoken on the African side of the Red Sea, in Somalia, Ethiopia, Jibouti, the Sudan, Kenya, and Tanzania; the most important languages in this branch are Somali (Somalia and elsewhere) and Galla or Oromo (Ethiopia).

The vast majority of the territory in sub-Saharan Africa is occupied by the Niger-Kordofanian family, which contains nearly nine hundred languages. Although many details of the genetic groupings remain tentative, Joseph H. Greenberg's 1966 classification of Niger-Kordofanian into Kordofanian and six branches of Niger-Congo is widely accepted. All but one of these seven branches have relatively modest numbers of languages. Kordofanian, with about thirty-one languages (e.g, Koalib and Tegali), is spoken in the Kordofan region of the Sudan, south of Khartoum. Four of the six Niger-Congo branches are West

African. The twenty-three or so West Atlantic languages are spoken primarily in Senegal, Guinea, and Sierra Leone; the most important language in this branch, in terms of numbers of speakers, is Fula (Senegal and several other countries). The Mande branch is about the same size and is nearby in West Africa. Its twenty-six languages are spoken in Sierra Leone, Liberia, Ivory Coast, Mali, and other countries. They include the important language known variously as Malinke, Mandinka, Bambara, and Dyula, which was the language of the great thirteenth-century Mali empire (Bird and Shopen, 1979: 59) and is now spoken in several countries. The Gur branch is larger, with about fifty languages (e.g, Dagomba and Bariba) spoken in Ghana, Upper Volta, Benin, Ivory Coast, and elsewhere. The Kwa branch has about fifty languages and includes several of the most important languages of West Africa. Probably the best known of these are Yoruba and Igbo in Nigeria and Akan (Twi-Fante) in Ghana, each with several millions of speakers. The fifth Niger-Congo branch, Adamawa-Eastern, contains about eighty languages (e.g., Ngbandi and Gbeya) spoken in Central Africa, from eastern Nigeria to the western Sudan.

The remaining branch of Niger-Congo is the huge Benue-Congo group, which consists of nearly six hundred Bantu languages and about eighty non-Bantu languages. Non-Bantu languages belonging to this branch are spoken as far north and west as Nigeria (e.g., Tiv and Efik); Bantu languages spread from Cameroon in the northwest and Kenya in the northeast all the way south to southern South Africa. The great East African lingua franca Swahili is a Bantu language; so are kiKuyu (Kenya), Zulu (South Africa), and ki-Kongo (the Congo and Zaire).

Beside Afro-Asiatic and Niger-Kordofanian, the remaining two language families of Africa—Nilo-Saharan and Khoisan—are relatively insignificant, both in numbers of languages and in numbers of speakers. Most of the eighty or so Nilo-Saharan languages are spoken in Central and East Central Africa, but two of the most important members of this family, Songhai and Kanuri, are spoken farther west (Niger, Nigeria). The largest branch of the family, Chari-Nile, with about sixty languages, includes several important languages of the Sudan, for example Dinka and Nubian, and also Maasai in Tanzania.

Finally, there are about twenty languages in the Khoisan family, whose name derives from the Hottentot's self-name (Khoi) combined with their name for the Bushmen (San). Most of these languages, including Hottentot itself—now known as Khoikhoi—and the Bushman (San) languages, are spoken in South Africa; the other two members of the family, Sandawe and Hatsa, are spoken farther north in Tanzania. The Khoisan languages are apparently remnants of earlier populations whose languages were largely abandoned for Bantu as the Bantu speakers increased their territory: evidence of influence of Khoisan on Bantu is found in the presence of the most famous Khoisan structural feature—the click phonemes—in several southern Bantu languages, notably Zulu and Xhosa.

LANGUAGE FAMILIES OF SOUTHERN AND EASTERN
ASIA AND OCEANIA

Immediately to the east of Africa (if we ignore Madagascar for the moment) are Arabia, which is solidly Semitic-speaking, and then Iran, which is linguistically dominated by Indo-European languages of the Iranian sub-branch, especially Persian (Farsi). Neighboring Pakistan is mostly divided between the IE sub-branches Indic (e.g., Urdu) and Iranian (e.g., Balochi), but in India Indic languages compete for territory with languages of two other families, Dravidian and Austro-Asiatic.

Like the Indic speakers, but much earlier, the linguistic ancestors of the modern Dravidians entered the Indian subcontinent from the northwest. Southern India is now solidly Dravidian-speaking, while Indic languages dominate in the north. Only one Dravidian language is spoken entirely outside India—Brahui, in Pakistan. There are about thirty Dravidian languages in all, but as of the 1961 census 96 percent of all Dravidian speakers spoke one of the four literary languages: Tamil, Telugu, Kannada, and Malayalam. Various proposals have been made about genetic links between Dravidian and other language families, for example, Uralic and Altaic. The best developed hypothesis connects Dravidian with the extinct language Elamite, an ancient language of western Asia (modern western Iran) attested as early as the third millennium B.C.

The Austro-Asiatic family is represented in central and eastern India by the sixteen or so languages of the Munda branch (e.g., Santali and Mundari), but Munda speakers are thought to have entered India from the east; most of the other Austro-Asiatic languages, perhaps over a hundred of them, are spoken in mainland Southeast Asia, the proposed original homeland of the family. Proposed subgroupings within Austro-Asiatic vary so widely that no consensus seems clear (compare, for instance, the divergent classifications of Pinnow, 1963, Benedict [as cited by Matisoff, 1973], and Ruhlen, 1975:89). Munda, at least, is well established as a branch of the family. So is the large Mon-Khmer branch, which includes Khmer (Cambodian) of Kampuchea and may also include the Viet-Muong group (e.g., Vietnamese). The interrelationships of many of the other languages, for example, Nicobarese, the language of the Nicobar Islands in the Bay of Bengal, are less well understood. In any case, most Austro-Asiatic languages are clustered in Vietnam, Kampuchea, and Laos, but others are scattered through Thailand, Burma, Malaysia, and China, as well as India.

The enormous Austronesian family (sometimes also known as Malayo-Polynesian) also has a firm toehold in mainland Southeast Asia, though the vast majority of the three hundred to five hundred languages in the family are spoken on almost all the islands in the Pacific, from Hawaii all the way west to Madagascar—thus giving this family the largest geographic range of any language family in the world, before Europeans colonized the Americas. On the mainland, Austronesian languages are spoken in Malaysia (notably Malay) and southern

Vietnam. The great majority of Austronesian speakers speak languages of the Indonesian (or Western) branch, which includes Malay; Indonesian and other languages of Indonesia, for instance, those on Sumatra, Borneo, and Sumatra; Malagasy on Madagascar; the languages of the Philippines, for example, Tagalog, Visayan, and Ilocano; and some of the non-Chinese languages of Taiwan. (At least one Austronesian language of Taiwan, Atayal, may belong to a third branch of the family, independent from both Indonesian and Oceanic.) The second large branch of Austronesian, Oceanic (or Eastern), contains over half of the languages of the family but has far fewer speakers than Indonesian languages. The Oceanic branch is generally further subdivided into three groups of languages named after geographically contiguous groups of islands: Micronesia (e.g., the Marianas, Marshalls, Carolines, and Gilberts); Melanesia (e.g., New Guinea, New Britain, New Ireland, the Solomons, Vanuatu or New Hebrides), New Caledonia, and Fiji; and Polynesia (e.g., Hawaii, Samoa, the Marquesas, the Society and Cook Islands, Tonga, Easter Island, and New Zealand). There is considerable controversy over the validity of these groupings as genetic linguistic sub-branches, but the broad outlines of the classification are probably reasonably accurate. Not all the languages spoken in each area belong to the area's sub-branch, but for the most part the geography and the linguistic classification match rather well.

The Micronesian sub-branch is the smallest; its languages include Marshallese and Trukese (or Truk). Melanesian is by far the largest branch, with well over two hundred languages. A large percentage of these are spoken on New Guinea, for example, Motu and Buang, though Austronesian languages are in the minority there. The Polynesian branch contains a number of languages whose names are familiar to outsiders because the islands are famous: examples are Hawaiian, Tahitian, Samoan, and Tongan. Maori, spoken on New Zealand, is also Polynesian.

Not all the languages of Oceania are Austronesian, however. As mentioned above, most New Guinea languages—perhaps six hundred of them—are non-Austronesian. In general, Austronesian languages are spoken in the coastal areas, while non-Austronesian (NAN or Papuan) New Guinean languages are spoken in the interior of the island. The genetic affiliations of the NAN languages are much disputed, partly because very few of the languages have been studied extensively. (A few of the better known languages are Enga, Usurufa, and Wahgi.) Some scholars divide these languages into five separate families, the largest of which is the Trans-New Guinea group, with over three hundred languages. In this classificatory schema, besides these five families, a rather large number of languages remain unclassified. At the other extreme is Joseph H. Greenberg's (1971) Indo-Pacific hypothesis, according to which all the NAN languages of New Guinea are genetically related to each other and to some other languages as well—namely, the indigenous languages of Tasmania, which have been extinct since about 1900; some languages spoken on the Andaman Islands; and others spoken on several islands closer to New Guinea. Even some of the conservative groupings are considered highly tentative by various scholars, so it is not surprising that many or most linguists are unwilling to accept the Indo-Pacific hypothesis until and unless much more evidence can be adduced to support it.

One point on which specialists do agree is that there is no evidence that either the NAN New Guinea languages or the Tasmanian languages are related to the languages of Australia and the western Torres Strait Islands. Moreover, there is quite general agreement that, within Australia and the western Torres Strait Islands, all the languages are genetically related. Estimates of the total number of languages spoken in this area before Europeans arrived range from 150 to 650 (Yallop, 1982:27), but S. A. Wurm (1972) and Colin Yallop (1982) agree on an estimate of around 250; of these, perhaps fifty have become extinct since European colonization began in the late eighteenth century. Of the roughly two hundred extant languages, most have only a few speakers each, and only five have over a thousand speakers: the Western Desert Language (3,000–4,000), Warlpiri (ca. 2,500), Mabuyag (2,000+), Aranda (1,500+), and Tiwi (ca. 1,400) (Yallop, 1982:44). Australian languages have been tentatively subdivided into twenty-seven branches. One of these, Pama-Nyungan, occupies the vast majority of the continent's territory and contains by far the largest number of languages (ca. 175), including the Western Desert Language, Warlpiri, Mabuyag (spoken on the Torres Strait Islands), and Aranda. The remaining twenty-six branches are clustered together in north central Australia.

To return to mainland Asia, from which the ramifications of Austronesian led us into Oceania, we find two major remaining genetic groups. The larger is Sino-Tibetan; this is the second largest language family in the world in terms of speaker numbers, after Indo-European. At least, this is the standard claim, but it may no longer be accurate: the total number of Chinese speakers has recently been estimated at 900 million (Li and Thompson, 1979:295), and if this is correct, the family's speakers may now outnumber Indo-European speakers, even with the huge figures for English (as a first language), Hindi-Urdu, Spanish, and other widely spoken IE languages. Sino-Tibetan is also one of the most diverse of all families, though Chinese is far and away the largest, in territory as in speakers.

Classification in this family, as in so many others, is highly controversial, but Chinese itself is generally considered to form its own branch, Sinitic. Chinese is divided into several traditional dialects bound together by their ancient national unity and by their common writing system, which has the longest continuous history of any writing in the world (from the Shang dynasty, which began in 1766 B.C., until today). Although no single criterion offers a foolproof way of distinguishing dialects of one language from separate languages, the linguistic criterion of mutual intelligibility is most often appealed to, and it gives rather reliable results except when cultural factors interfere. With Chinese, history and shared culture (including the writing system) dictate status as a single language; but applying the criterion of mutual intelligibility would yield at least five separate Chinese languages. The largest by far is Mandarin, the native language of over half of the Chinese people and of most of the territory of China. The other four languages are spoken in eastern and southeastern coastal China and on nearby islands: Wu, including the dialect of Shanghai; Min, including the dialect of Chaozhou on the mainland and most dialects spoken on Taiwan; Yue or Cantonese, on the South China coast, including the dialect of Hong Kong; and Hakka in southeastern China and Taiwan.

Tibetan and Lolo-Burmese have traditionally been classified into a single branch of Sino-Tibetan, called Tibeto-Burman, but some specialists now split these into two or more branches. The Tibetan branch proper consists of only two or three languages, with many dialects. Tibetan itself has a long tradition as a literary language, with Classical Tibetan texts dating from the seventh century A.D. and written in a script derived from north Indian writing. In the Lolo-Burmese branch, Burmese is the major language and the only one with national and literary status (it is attested from the twelfth century A.D.). It is closely related to languages of the Lolo group (China, Burma, Thailand, Laos, Vietnam), for example, Lahu and Lisu.

Over two hundred Sino-Tibetan languages are spoken in the eastern Himalayan region, especially Assam in eastern India and down into Burma. These are sometimes grouped into the one Tibeto-Burman branch and sometimes split into several branches independent of Tibetan and Lolo-Burmese. Few of the languages are well studied, so it is not surprising that their detailed interrelationships remain obscure. Among the eastern Himalayan languages are two completely different groups called Naga, one comprising several languages of Burma and the other spoken in Sikkim, Nepal, Bhutan, and elsewhere. The important Bodo group, including Bodo proper and Garo, is centered in Assam and is closely related to the second group of Naga languages (i.e., those outside Burma) and to Kachin (Jinghpaw) in Burma. Other groups are Chin and Kuki in Burma, closely related to the Naga languages of Burma, and the Gyarung-Mishmi group in the Himalayas (especially Nepal, Assam, and Tibet).

Karen, which consists of several languages spoken primarily in the Irrawaddy delta of southern Burma, apparently belongs either in a separate Sino-Tibetan branch or in a branch with Tibetan and Lolo-Burmese as opposed to Sinitic. Finally, the few Miao-Yao languages are spoken in southern China (especially Guizhou and Hunan) and nearby northern Vietnam, Laos, and Thailand. The genetic affiliation of these languages is still controversial, but they are now sometimes classified as an independent branch of Sino-Tibetan.

One other important genetic group remains in Asia. This is the Tai-Kadai group (sometimes called Kam-Tai), comprising thirty to fifty languages, and its wider genetic affiliations are so much disputed that I will give it here as an independent family. It was long classified as a sub-branch of Sino-Tibetan, but a counterproposal to group it with Austronesian has gained ground in recent decades. Both proposals have been challenged on methodological grounds. Probably most scholars now reject the Sino-Tibetan connection; nevertheless, the Austronesian link is by no means generally accepted. The best known Tai-Kadai languages are in the Tai branch, notably Thai (or Siamese) in Thailand and Lao in Laos. Although a number of the other languages are spoken in Thailand, Laos, Vietnam, Kampuchea, and even Assam (India), probably most Tai-Kadai languages, including all four members of the Kadai branch, are spoken in China (Yunnan, Guizhou, Hunan, Guangxi, and Hainan Island).

A few southern Asian languages have not been classified into any of the genetic groups mentioned above. Some of these, for example, Burushaski and Khasi in India and Ainu in Japan, are genetic isolates, with no relationships established to any other languages. Others, such as the small (ca. twelve languages) Palaung-Wa family of Southeast Asia (Burma, Thailand, Laos, Vietnam, and China), have not been grouped with any of the several large families in their region.

LANGUAGE FAMILIES OF NORTH AMERICA NORTH OF MEXICO

The native languages of the Americas have evolved from the one or more languages spoken by hunters who crossed to North America on a land bridge over the Bering Strait, from Siberia to Alaska. The dates of their crossings are still disputed; land bridges emerged there several times during the last ice age. Archaeological evidence from as early as 10,000 B.C. is abundant, and early humans reached Tierra del Fuego by about 8,000 B.C. (Driver, 1969:3–4). But recent archaeological findings support a much earlier estimated date of man's arrival in the New World—at least as early as ca. 20,000 B.C. (Adovasio and Carlisle, 1984), and quite possibly thousands of years earlier.

As mentioned above, views on the classification of American Indian languages have varied from extremely broad to extremely conservative narrow groupings. The latter type is currently in fashion. As Mary Haas observed not long ago, today "there is a greater willingness to leave some things unassigned and to admit our inability to tie up all loose ends" (1976:32)—or, at least, to admit that we have not yet gathered sufficient evidence to justify many of the groupings that were popular until recently. In the discussion below, languages are referred to as being where they were at the time of the first European contact, rather than where they were, or are, during the reservation period. For the southeastern United States in particular, entire Indian communities were forced to move westward to Indian Territory (Oklahoma) as the number of white settlers increased.

In North America, most of the six huge genetic groups proposed by Edward Sapir (1921) have been split and split again. Only one remains intact: Eskimo-Aleut, which was discussed above.

Another of Sapir's groups has been separated from one, or perhaps two, of its putative members. This is Na-Dene, consisting of Athabaskan-Eyak, a well-established grouping; Tlingit (Alaska, British Columbia), whose relationship to Athabaskan-Eyak is considered shaky by many (or most) specialists; and Haida

(British Columbia, Alaska), whose genetic connection with the other two is no longer viewed even as promising, much less as established. Tlingit, Haida, and Eyak (Alaska) are single languages, but Athabaskan consists of about thirty languages spoken in three widely separated areas: Alaska and Canada (e.g., Kutchin and Chipewyan); connected coastal areas of Oregon and California (e.g., Hupa); and the Apachean languages, spoken primarily in Arizona and New Mexico—notably Apache itself and Navajo (Arizona), whose approximately 120,000 speakers make it the most widely spoken Indian language north of Mexico.

None of Sapir's other proposed groupings of North American Indian languages has remained intact. A recent conservative classification into sixty-two genetic units that are well supported by the available evidence is presented by Lyle Campbell and Marianne Mithun (1979b), and the discussion below follows their analysis. No one argues, however, that the classificatory work in this area is complete: future research will almost surely permit us to reduce the total number of families.

Among the sixty-two families are twenty-eight isolates, for instance, Haida, Kutenai, Tsimshian, Cayuse, Natches, Zuni, Yuchi, and Tunica. All twenty-eight have, of course, been claimed to be related to other languages (for example, Haida to Na-Dene, Kutenai (Montana, British Columbia) to Algonquian, Zuni (New Mexico) to "Penutian," and Yuchi (Tennessee, Kentucky, and elsewhere) to Siouan. But none of the groupings is currently accepted by all specialists, and for at least some of the isolates new groupings are being proposed (e.g., Yuchi with Tunica).

There are also, of course, well-established families, though very few have more than twenty languages. In the Northwest, immediately to the south of northern Athabaskan territory, the largest family is Salishan, with about twenty-three languages in Washington, Idaho, Montana, Oregon, and southern British Columbia. Among the Salishan languages are Bella Coola, Tillamook, Shuswap, and Kalispel. The Pacific Northwest coast of the United States and Canada is an area of great linguistic diversity, so the coastal Salishan languages in particular have many non-Salishan neighbors. Among these are the six languages of the Wakashan family, notably Kwakiutl (or Kwak'wala), on northern Vancouver Island and the neighboring British Columbia coast, and Nootka, on the west coast of Vancouver Island. Just south of Wakashan territory, in the Olympic Peninsula of Washington, are (or were) the two languages of the Chimakuan family: Quileute (with about ten remaining speakers) and Chemakum (extinct since about fifty years ago).

Twenty or more languages spoken to the north and to the south of Salishan and Wakashan were once classified into a group which Sapir called Penutian. This classification has now fallen apart completely, but current research will probably provide solid evidence of relationships among some (sub)groups that were included in "Penutian" (Silverstein, 1979). Among the genetic groups already solidly established are Chinookan, consisting of two or more languages along the Columbia River, Sahaptian, with two or three languages farther up the Columbia (e.g., Nez Perce), Kalapuya-Takelma in Oregon, and California Penutian, with about five languages (e.g., Yokuts). An important isolate originally placed in Penutian is Tsimshian, with several dialects—or, perhaps, several separate languages—on the British Columbia coast. A proposed genetic link of "Penutian" languages of North America and Mayan and other Mesoamerican groups has not been widely accepted by specialists in any of the groups. Little systematic evidence has ever been presented in support of that ambitious hypothesis (or in support of an alternative hypothesis connecting Mayan with Hokan).

Much of California and small areas in Arizona, Texas, Mexico, and even Central America are, or were, occupied by the numerous languages of the controversial Hokan group. William H. Jacobsen (1979) mentions thirteen branches of the family; eleven of these are located at least partly in California, and six of the eleven are now entirely extinct. Lyle Campbell and Marianne Mithun (1979b) list twenty genetic units, but they do not classify them further into a single established Hokan family. Many of the thirteen to twenty units of the proposed Hokan family contain only one language, but others have several languages each, for instance, Pomoan, with seven languages. As with "Penutian," many specialists now prefer to abandon the Hokan hypothesis entirely, start anew with more modest genetic hypotheses, and see whether those will in turn provide evidence for wider groupings. Examples of "Hokan" languages, in any case, are Shasta and Karok (northern California), Washo (east of the Sierras), Tequistlatec (Oaxaca, Mexico), and Jicaque (Honduras).

Among the neighbors of these languages is the important Uto-Aztecan family, with about thirty languages in California, Nevada, Arizona, New Mexico, Texas, and Mexico. Subgrouping within this family is still a matter of some dispute, but the family itself is well established as a genetic unit. Several Uto-Aztecan languages are now extinct, and others are moribund. But the family includes a number of languages whose names are likely to be familiar to outsiders, for instance, Shoshone, Southern Paiute, Comanche, Luiseno, Hopi, Pima, Yaqui, Huichol, and Nahuatl (or Aztec). The last was the language of one of the great pre-Conquest Mesoamerican civilizations, and is still spoken, in various dialects, by well over a million people in Mexico. Classical Nahuatl is well attested in numerous texts dating mainly from the sixteenth century. Before the Spanish Conquest, the Aztecs used a symbolic system that has been called "rebus writing," but this was used only to name people and places and was essentially pictorial, rather than a true writing system (Terrence Kaufman, personal communication, 1984). This leaves the Mayans (see below) as the only New World people who developed a genuine writing system before contact with Europeans.

The small Kiowa-Tanoan group, consisting of a few languages spoken in Oklahoma, Mexico, and elsewhere, has often been linked with Uto-Aztecan, but this grouping is not universally accepted.

In the central and eastern United States, and extending north into Canada, are (or were) languages of three families that may turn out to be distantly related to each other: Siouan, Caddoan, and Iroquoian. The eleven Siouan languages once occupied most of the Great Plains region and a few areas in the southeastern United States. The four southeastern languages are Catawba (North and South Carolina), which is distantly related to the rest of Siouan, and the extinct languages Ofo, Biloxi, and Tutelo. Siouan languages of the Great Plains have names familiar to outsiders, mostly because they have been used as American place names: Dakota, with its dialects Assiniboin, Dakhota (or Yankton), and Lakota (or Teton, or Oglala); Mandan; Winnebago; Cinwere, including Iowa and the extinct dialect Missouri; Dhegiha, whose dialects include Omaha, Osage, and the extinct Kansa; Hidatsa; and Crow.

The four or five Caddoan languages are (or were) also Great Plains languages, spoken in small areas from South Dakota to the Gulf states: Pawnee (Nebraska), with its offshoot Arikara; Wichita (Kansas, Oklahoma) and the nearby Kitsai; and Caddo (Louisiana, Arkansas, east Texas).

Iroquoian languages were once spoken around and to the northeast of the eastern Great Lakes, and in a separated area in southern Appalachia. There is evidence for the existence of perhaps fifteen Iroquoian languages, but most of these, for example, Huron-Wyandot, Erie, and Susquehanna (or Andaste), have long been extinct. Cherokee, the only member of the southern branch of Iroquoian, has the largest number of speakers today, about eleven thousand (North Carolina, Oklahoma) (Mithun, 1979). The famous Cherokee Sequoya invented a syllabic writing system for the language early in the nineteenth century, not long before most of his people were force-marched from Appalachia to Oklahoma. Of the northern Iroquoian languages, the most famous are those of the Five Nations: Seneca, Cayuga, Onondaga, Oneida, and Mohawk.

When Europeans first arrived on the Atlantic coast of North America, the northern Iroquois were almost surrounded by (and in conflict with) speakers of languages belonging to the Algonquian family. This family is one of the largest in North America, in terms of number of languages, number of speakers, and amount of territory. The twenty-six or so known Algonquian languages once occupied most of the Atlantic seaboard from North Carolina to Newfoundland (but not Newfoundland Island), and extended across Canada and the northern United States into the Great Plains. In the West, speakers of the Algonquian languages Cree (Saskatchewan and eastward), Blackfoot (Montana), and Cheyenne (Wyoming, South Dakota) are neighbors of Salishan, Athabaskan, and Siouan speakers. The most widely spoken Algonquian languages today are Cree and Ojibwa (Minnesota, North Dakota, and elsewhere), but so many Eastern and Midwestern place names derive from the names of Algonquian tribes that the language names are familiar: Delaware, Passamaquoddy, Connecticut (extinct), Narragansett (extinct), Menomini, Illinois-Peoria-Miami, Ottawa (the same language as Ojibway), and Fox (Wisconsin) are examples. Other familiar names (for other reasons) are Shawnee (Tennessee), Kickapoo (Michigan, Illinois, and elsewhere), Potawatomi (Michigan), and the extinct languages Mahican

(New York and elsewhere) and Powhatan (Virginia). Most of the wider genetic groupings that have been proposed for Algonquian have generally been abandoned (at least temporarily), but one proposal is now universally regarded as firmly established: Algonquian has been shown to be distantly related to two languages of the northern California coast, Wiyot and Yurok. The entire family is variously called Algonquian-Ritwan or Algic.

Only one other major family is primarily a U.S. group. This is Muskogean, whose six member languages originally occupied most of the southeastern corner of the country. Most Muskogean speakers were forced to move west of the Mississippi River to Indian Territory in 1836–40, but Seminole (a dialect of Creek) is still spoken in Florida as well as in Oklahoma, and Choctaw is spoken in Mississippi and Louisiana as well as Oklahoma. Other Muskogean languages are Chickasaw (actually a dialect of Choctaw), Alabama-Koasati, Hitchiti, Mitasuki, and the extinct language Apalachee.

LANGUAGE FAMILIES OF MESOAMERICA

South of the U.S. border is the rather well-defined linguistic area called Mesoamerica, which includes Mexico and Central America. The languages of several families are spoken in this area and share a number of linguistic traits. Two of the most important families in Mexico, Uto-Aztecan and Mayan, are represented more extensively outside Mexico, in the United States and Central America, respectively. A third important family, Otomanguean (twenty-five to thirty-five languages, or perhaps more), is located entirely in Mexico, except for the extinct language Mangue, which was spoken in Central America (coastal Nicaragua, Costa Rica, El Salvador, and Honduras). One branch of the family, including Otomi and Pame, is found north of Mexico City. The remaining Otomanguean languages are spoken in Chiapas (just one extinct language, Chiapanec), Puebla (central Mexico), Guerrero (Pacific Coast), and Oaxaca (southern Mexico). Among them are Mixtec, Mazatec, Zapotec, Chatino, and Amuzgo.

Two small language families are also found in Mexico. These are Totonacan (Hidalgo, North Puebla, and Veracruz), with just two members, Totonac and Tepehua; and Mixe-Zoquean (southern Mexico), with about eight member languages, notably Mixe and Zoque and their offshoots. Both of these groups may be related to Mayan (and thus to each other), but the classification is by no means universally accepted by specialists in Mesoamerican languages.

The thirty or so languages of the Mayan family are spoken in Mexico, Guatemala, Belize, and Honduras. Their territory is continuous (including the entire Yucatan Peninsula) except for Huastec, which is located on and near the Gulf Coast in Northern Veracruz and San Luis Potosi, Mexico. Two parts of the Mayan area are of particular historical importance: many inscriptions and documents from the great Mayan civilization have been found in Yucatan, where Yucatec or Maya proper is now spoken, and (to a lesser extent) in the Peten region of Guatemala, where the Island of Itza in Lake Peten was the last independent lowland Mayan kingdom (finally conquered by the Spanish in 1697). After a long period of doubt and controversy, it is now universally acknowledged that these records represent the only firmly established pre-conquest writing system in the New World. (Mayan writing is the only well-understood writing system in the world, other than Sumerian, that is definitely known to be an independent development: all of the world's other writing systems apparently derive, by imitation or by adaptation, from Sumerian.) The Mayan system is a syllabary—with each symbol representing a whole syllable—rather than an alphabet, and it has many logographs (word symbols) as well. It may be as old as ca. 100 A.D. (but its precursors go back to at least 300 B.C.). Many of the symbols have already been deciphered, though much work remains to be done. Probably both Cholan and Yucatecan are represented in these writings—that is, the ancestors of the modern languages Chol, Chorti, and Chontal, and Yucatec (Maya), Lacandon, Mopan, and Itza, respectively (Terrence Kaufman, personal communication, 1984). The modern Mayan language with the most speakers is Quiche (Guatemala); others with several thousand speakers each are Yucatec (Mexico), Mam (Guatemala), Kekchi (Guatemala, Belize), and Cakchiquel (Guatemala). Other important languages in the family are Tzotzil, Tzeltal, Tojolabal, Chuj, and Pocomchi.

Mesoamerica also contains a number of isolates and small families, such as Huave (Oaxaca, Mexico), Tarascan (Michoacan, Mexico), Xincan (with four languages, in Guatemala), and Misumalpan, a small family (including Miskito) in Honduras and Nicaragua.

LANGUAGE FAMILIES OF SOUTH AMERICA

The hundreds of Indian languages that are spoken in South America constitute one of the least studied groups of languages in the world, though a considerable number of investigations are in progress. Tentative genetic classifications of the whole area range from three (Greenberg's hypothesis, reflected in Ruhlen, 1975) to thirty-seven families, plus a hundred isolates (Meillet and Cohen, 1952). Not even the latter classificatory schema is firmly established by comparative evidence, so the broad three-unit schema is so far quite unsubstantiated. The genetic picture in South America is so very murky that no attempt will be made here to survey all the families in this area, as has been done for all the other regions of the world (except New Guinea). Instead, this section will mention only a few representative families that appear to be well established.

Of these families, the most prominent is the proposed Quechumaran family in Bolivia, Peru, and Ecuador. This family contains three branches, Quechua (consisting of three to four languages) and Aymara and (probably) Jaqaru (Peru) together in the other. Even with so few languages, the family is of considerable importance: not only was Quechua the language of the Inca Empire, but Quechua and Aymara are the most widely spoken of all American Indian languages:

Aymara (southern Peru, Bolivia) has well over a million speakers, and the various forms of Quechua (Peru, Ecuador, Bolivia) have ten million.

The next most important family is Tupi-Guarani. Guarani (Paraguay, southwestern Brazil) is the first or second language of most of the people of Paraguay, non-Indians as well as Indians—the only American Indian language spoken by such a high proportion of the population of a country. (Most Paraguayans also speak Spanish, the country's official language.) The numerous languages (about fifty) of the Tupi branch are spoken in Brazil, especially on the coast and in the central interior south of the Amazon River.

Sizable portions of northern South America, especially Colombia and Venezuela, are occupied by the fifty or so languages of the Cariban family. This group is noteworthy for having given its name to the Caribbean Sea; a few Carib speakers still live in the Lesser Antilles, but most of the languages are spoken only on the mainland, for example, Mapoyo in Venezuela and Bacairi in Brazil.

The hundred or so Arawakan languages are neighbors of the Cariban languages in the north, and they extend south through Brazil and Bolivia to the Paraguay-Argentina border. They, too, were once widely spoken in the Caribbean. Among the mainland Arawakan languages are Guajiro (the Guajira Peninsula in Colombia and Venezuela), Campa and Piro (Peru), Baure (Bolivia), and Terena (Brazil).

Languages of the Chibchan family (at least twenty-five in all) are spoken in Central America (Honduras, Nicaragua, Costa Rica, and Panama) as well as in South America (Colombia, Ecuador, and elsewhere). Among them are Cuna and Guaymi (Panama) and Cayapa (Ecuador).

The Panoan languages, for example, Cashibo and Shipibo (or Chama) in Peru, may be related to the Tacanan languages of Bolivia. Farther to the south are the Araucanian (Mapuche) dialects of Chile and Argentina. Still farther to the south—in fact, the southernmost language in the world—is (or was) Yamana, an isolate, at the extreme south of Tierra del Fuego.

The brevity of this sketch of South American Indian languages underscores the lack of consensus on, and often even preliminary guesses at, the genetic groupings on the continent. Given the startling number of "extinct" notations in language lists from South America, much crucial information has already been lost, and many or most of the remaining languages are rapidly disappearing. It may well be, therefore, that the interrelationships among these languages can never be established as firmly as genetic groups in other parts of the world.

PIDGIN AND CREOLE LANGUAGES

The foregoing continent-by-continent survey of the world's languages in terms of genetic categories leaves one significant group of languages unmentioned. This group comprises all the contact languages called pidgins and creoles— languages that did not arise by gradual change from an ancestor language, but rather by a relatively sudden process in a multilingual (or, rarely, a bilingual) setting where no common shared language was available for intergroup communication. In many contact situations, of course, one group simply learns the other (or another) group's language. But sometimes, especially when more than two languages are present, this does not occur, and a new language—a pidgin or a creole—develops. Two kinds of contact situations in particular have led to the emergence of pidgins and creoles: trade situations, when foreign traders visit a multilingual area, and plantation situations, when linguistically diverse groups of laborers are brought in (as slaves or otherwise). Contact languages that arise through trade are likely to be pidgins—that is, languages with no native speakers and, at least at first, limited vocabulary and morphosyntactic resources. By definition, pidgins are spoken only as second (or third) languages. Contact languages that arise on plantations may develop rapidly into creoles; that is, they may be spoken almost immediately by children as their first language (and thus actually developed partly by children learning the new language). The difference is that indigenous peoples who trade with occasional foreign visitors, or who occasionally travel to trade centers, may maintain their own native languages for intragroup communication; but plantation workers from any one language background may be too few to maintain their native language even as a home language.

Pidgin and creole languages are found all over the world, but almost all of the best known languages reflect the history of European trade and colonization: trade pidgins and creoles cluster on the coasts of Africa, Asia, several islands in the Pacific, and eastern North and South America, while plantation creoles are found in the Caribbean, coastal northern Australia, and several Pacific islands, including Hawaii. The most famous early pidgin was the lingua franca, whose vocabulary derived primarily from a Romance language; it probably arose in the Near East at the time of the Crusades, which began in 1095. But the earliest evidence of any pidgin is a pidginized form of Arabic recorded briefly in an Arab traveler's account from about 1050 A.D. Later, Arab trade and colonization activities led to firmly established Arabic-vocabulary pidgin/creole languages, for instance, Juba Arabic in the southern Sudan.

The Caribbean creoles, such as Jamaican Creole (English vocabulary) and Haitian Creole (French vocabulary), are the most studied of all pidgin/creole languages. Several West African pidgins and creoles are also well known, among them Cape Verde Creole (Portuguese vocabulary), Ivory Coast Pidgin French, and Cameroon Pidgin English. Afrikaans (South Africa) is variously regarded as an offshoot of Dutch or as a Dutch-vocabulary creole; its status is probably best described as semi-creole. Farther east are Mauritian Creole (French vocabulary; on the island of Mauritius), Sri Lanka Creole Portuguese, China Coast Pidgin English, and Tay Boi, a French-vocabulary pidgin of Vietnam that is now extinct, or nearly so. In the Pacific, the most important pidgin/creole language is Tok Pisin (or Neomelanesian), a hundred-year-old New Guinea pidgin that is now creolizing, that is, acquiring native speakers. At least three languages that arose as plantation creoles are still spoken in the United States: Gullah

(English vocabulary) in South Carolina, Louisiana Creole French, and Hawaiian Creole English.

It is by no means the case, however, that all pidgins and creoles have vocabularies derived mainly from the languages of foreign traders (European or Arab). At least some trade languages with non-European lexicons arose as a result of European trade activities and colonization, but others apparently arose without even a European catalyst, for use among non-European peoples before (as well as after) first contact with Europeans. Unfortunately, since in most cases the languages were not recorded until Europeans discovered them, it is often difficult to tell whether or not such a language predates European contact.

Africa has a large number of pidgins and creoles with non-European (and non-Arabic) vocabularies. Examples are some varieties of the Bantu language Swahili, the major lingua franca of East Africa, which has been pidginized and creolized in many parts of its territory; Sango (Central African Republic and elsewhere), which is based lexically on Ngbandi, a Niger-Congo language of the Adamawa-Eastern branch; and Fanagalo (used in the South African mines), whose vocabulary is derived mainly from Zulu, a Bantu language. A number of lesser known languages are spoken in Asia, among them Naga Pidgin (Assam; vocabulary from the Indic language Assamese) and Bazaar Malay, a pidginized form of the Austronesian language Malay (Malaysia and Indonesia). In New Guinea, besides Tok Pisin, there is a pidgin called Hiri Motu (or Police Motu), which is based lexically on the Melanesian (Austronesian) language Motu.

In the New World, several pidgins with Native American lexicons have been recorded. The most prominent North American pidgin is the Chinook Jargon of the Pacific Northwest, with a polyglot vocabulary derived from Chinook (Chinookan), Nootka (Wakashan), Salishan, and (latterly) English and French. Chinook Jargon is known from as early as 1840 (perhaps earlier), was in use among Indians for intertribal communication, and served as the major medium of communication between whites and Indians in the Northwest throughout the second half of the nineteenth century. The Delaware-vocabulary Traders' Jargon in the northeastern United States gave way to American Indian Pidgin English (and then to English itself) by the end of the seventeenth century, and Mobilian Jargon (Gulf Coast and Mississippi River Valley), with Choctaw (Muskogean) vocabulary, has recently become extinct. Pidgin Eskimo is also extinct. In South America, the Lingua Geral of Brazil, with Tupi vocabulary, was the major lingua franca in the Portuguese colony until it was gradually replaced by Portuguese in the eighteenth century, but was still used as late as 1900 in Manaus (Brazil, on the Amazon).

Estimates of the total number of pidgins and creoles vary. A recent comprehensive list (Hancock, 1977) contains 127 entries, which gives some notion of the size of the group.

Pidgins and creoles have often been called "mixed languages" because one result of their origin in multilingual contact is that their grammatical structures are not derived from one single language (though their vocabularies usually do come from one main source language). The notion of mixed languages is a controversial one, but more and more scholars are beginning to recognize the usefulness of such a category in historical studies of language. This acceptance has been encouraged by the discovery of a second type of mixed language—one in which the basic vocabulary comes primarily from one language, but one or more entire grammatical subsystems come from another language. So far only a few languages of this type have been adequately described. The major examples are Ma'a (also called Mbugu), a Tanzanian language with much inherited Cushitic basic vocabulary but with elaborate inflectional structures borrowed from Bantu; Michif (North Dakota), a language whose verb lexicon, morphology, and syntax are derived from the Algonquian language Cree, but whose noun lexicon, morphology, and (mostly) syntax have been borrowed from French; and Mednyj Aleut, spoken on Mednyj (or Copper) Island in the Bering Sea, whose inflectional verb morphology has been borrowed from Russian.

OFFICIALLY RECOGNIZED NATIONAL AND INTERNATIONAL LANGUAGES

Reading through a survey of the languages of the world tends to have a numbing effect: so many language families, so many more separate languages, and such a large proportion of both with names few readers have ever encountered before. If we narrow our focus to languages with official status or national importance, the picture is considerably simplified—primarily as a result of the expansionist histories of a few European and other cultures, most notably the English, the French, the Spanish, and the Arabs. Even in countries where these groups' languages dominate, indigenous languages often enjoy prestige too. Nevertheless, the international political dominance of a small number of languages is striking in view of the great diversity of languages in many parts of the world.

The discussion below is based primarily (though not entirely) on information from four sources: the 1984 edition of the *Europa Yearbook*, the 1981 National Geographic atlas, and two 1971 "Language Files" lists compiled by the Center for Applied Linguistics. Readers should keep in mind that the status of a language may change suddenly, so that even recently published information may be out of date. In particular, former European colonies in Africa, southern Asia, and Oceania are likely to replace (or supplement) a European official language with an indigenous one.

English has no serious competition as the world's most prominent international language. A total of forty-six of the world's nations, and fifteen nonindependent possessions, have English as an official national language, and in two others English has semi-official status. Of the forty-six, twenty-eight countries have only the one official language; in the other eighteen nations, English shares official status with at least one other language. Moreover, English is an official language in at least one country on every continent (except, of course, Antarctica, which has no permanent human population).

English is official in only three European countries, none of them on the continent itself: the United Kingdom; Ireland, where it shares official status with Irish (or Gaelic), though the great majority of the people speak only English; and Malta (official status shared with Maltese, an offshoot of Arabic). It is not official anywhere in northern or western Asia, but sixteen African nations use English officially: Botswana, Cameroon (with French), the Gambia, Ghana, Lesotho (with seSotho), Liberia, Malawi (with chiChewa), Mauritius (with French), Nigeria, Sierra Leone, South Africa (with Afrikaans), Swaziland (with siSwati), Tanzania (with Swahili), Uganda, Zambia, and Zimbabwe. In addition, Namibia has both English and Afrikaans as official languages, and English is semi-official in Ethiopia, where Amharic is the official language.

In southern Asia, English has official status in three countries: India (with Hindi), Sikkim, and Singapore (with Malay, Chinese, and Tamil). English is semi-official in Sri Lanka (where Sinhalese is official) and is the official language of the British dependency of Hong Kong.

In Oceania, English is the official language of Australia and New Zealand, of a number of dependent islands, and of the following island nations: Kiribati, Papua New Guinea (with Tok Pisin and Hiri Motu), the Solomon Islands, Tonga, Tuvalu, Vanuatu (formerly the New Hebrides; with French and Bislama), and Western Samoa (with Samoan).

English is, of course, also prominent in the New World. It is official in the United States, though only *de facto*, and in Canada (with French), Belize in Central America, Guyana on the South American mainland, and in the Caribbean island nations of Antigua and Barbuda, Bahamas, Barbados, Dominica, Grenada, Jamaica, St. Kitts and Nevis, St. Lucia, St. Vincent and the Grenadines, and Trinidad and Tobago. It is also official in British and U.S. dependencies in the Caribbean, for example, Puerto Rico (with Spanish).

Besides the countries in which English has official or semi-official national status, it is widely spoken in a number of other countries as well, among them Panama and Egypt.

French ranks second among the world's official national languages, with thirty-one countries. Five of these are in Europe: France itself, Belgium (with Dutch and German), Luxembourg (with German and Letzeburgesch), Monaco, and Switzerland (with German, Italian, and Romansch). It is semi-official in Andorra, where Catalan is the official language. Most of the other countries in which French is an official language are in Africa—twenty-two in all: Benin, Burundi (with kiRundi), Cameroon (with English), Central African Republic, Chad, Comoros (with Arabic), Congo, Djibouti (with Arabic), Gabon, Guinea, Ivory Coast, Madagascar (with Malagasy), Mali, Mauritania (with Arabic), Mauritius (with English), Niger, Reunion, Ruanda (with kinyaRuanda [also called kiRundi]), Senegal, Togo, Upper Volta, and Zaire. In addition, French has semi-official status in Algeria, Morocco, and Tunisia. Elsewhere, French is official only in

Canada (with English), Haiti, and Vanuatu (with English and Bislama) and in a number of French dependencies, such as French Guiana in South America.

Arabic has recently moved past Spanish into third place among international languages as measured by national language status, with twenty-three countries (versus twenty for Spanish). Arabic has official status in twelve Asian countries and ten African ones, as well as on the Mediterranean island of Malta. The Asian countries are Bahrain, Iraq, Jordan, Kuwait, Lebanon, Oman, Qatar, Saudi Arabia, Syria, the United Arab Emirates, and the two Yemens; in Africa there are Algeria, Comoros (with French), Djibouti (with French), Egypt, Libya, Mauritania (with French), Morocco, Somalia (with Somali), the Sudan, and Tunisia. It is semi-official in Israel and is widely spoken in the non-Arab Muslim world, for example, Chad and Niger.

Spanish is the sole official language of Spain and of sixteen Latin American nations: Costa Rica, Cuba, the Dominican Republic, El Salvador, Guatemala, Honduras, Mexico, Nicaragua, Panama, Argentina, Chile, Colombia, Ecuador, Paraguay, Uruguay, and Venezuela. It has the same status in Equatorial Guinea in Africa and shares official status in Bolivia (with Quechua and Aymara), Peru (with Quechua), and Puerto Rico (with English). It is widely spoken elsewhere as well, notably in the mainland United States on both coasts.

Portuguese is the only official language in Portugal, Brazil, and five African countries: Angola, Cape Verde, Guinea-Bissau, Mozambique, and Sao Tome and Principe; it is also official in a remaining Asian Portuguese possession, Macau. German has official status in seven European countries: Austria, Belgium, East Germany, West Germany, Luxembourg (with French and Letzeburgesch), Liechtenstein, and Switzerland (with three other languages). Of the remaining IE languages of Europe, only Dutch has national language status on another continent, in Suriname in South America as well as in the Netherlands and Belgium (with French and German). Italian, finally, is an official language in Italy, San Marino, Switzerland (with other languages), and the Vatican (with Latin).

Twenty-two other European languages have official national status, most of them in one European nation. Two of these, Finnish (Finland; with Swedish) and Hungarian (Hungary), are Uralic; the others are all Indo-European. Four are Germanic languages: Danish (Denmark; also official in Greenland), Swedish (Sweden and, with Finnish, Finland), Icelandic (Iceland), and Norwegian (Norway). Four belong to the Italic branch, Latin (Vatican City) and three Romance languages: Romanian (Romania), Catalan (Andorra), and Romansch (Switzerland, with other languages). Eight Slavic languages are official in five countries: Bulgarian (Bulgaria), Czech and Slovak (Czechoslovakia), Polish (Poland), Russian (USSR), and Serbo-Croatian, Slovenian, and Macedonian (Yugoslavia). The remaining official IE languages of Europe are Albanian (Albania), Greek (Greece and, with Turkish, Cyprus), and Irish or Gaelic (Ireland, with English). Besides these national languages, a number of other European languages are at least semi-official in parts of European countries, notably those with their own

Soviet Socialist Republics in the linguistically diverse USSR: Lithuanian (Baltic; Lithuania), Latvian (Baltic: Latvia), Armenian (Armenia), the Moldavian variety of Romanian (Moldavia), Ukrainian (Slavic; the Ukraine), Belorussian (Slavic; Belorussia), and the non-IE language Estonian (Uralic; Estonia). Another IE language, Tadzhik (a variety of the Iranian language Persian), also has its own Soviet Socialist Republic within the Soviet Union.

Four Altaic languages have national language status in six countries: Turkish in Turkey and (with Greek) in Cyprus, Mongolian (specifically, Khalkha Mongol) in Mongolia, Japanese in Japan, and Korean in both North and South Korea. Five other Altaic languages are official languages in their own Soviet Socialist Republics in the USSR. All of these belong to the Turkic branch of the family: Uzbek, Kazakh, Azerbaijan, Kirghiz, and Turkoman. A number of other Altaic languages, and languages of other families too, have official status in Autonomous Soviet Socialist Republics (e.g., the Mongol Altaic language Buryat and the Uralic language Mordvin); one other Soviet language, the Caucasian language Georgian, is the official language of its own SSR.

Besides Arabic, two other Semitic languages are official national languages: Hebrew in Israel and Amharic in Ethiopia. Non-Semitic Afro-Asiatic languages are widely spoken in a number of African countries, though usually without official status. Prominent among these are the Cushitic language Somali, one of the official languages of Somalia, and the Chadic language Hausa, a major West African lingua franca spoken by some 14 million people in Nigeria, Niger, Togo, Ghana, Benin, and other countries.

Five Bantu (Niger-Congo) languages have official status in sub-Saharan African countries. Swahili is now the official language of Kenya. In other countries, Bantu languages share official status with a European language: seSotho in Lesotho, chiChewa in Malawi, siSwati (probably the same language as Zulu) in Swaziland, and Swahili in Tanzania—all sharing official status with English; and kinyaRuanda (or kiRundi) in Ruanda, with French. In addition, Swahili is semi-official in Comoros, where Arabic and French are official.

South of the Soviet Union and in the Indian subcontinent, eight Indo-Iranian IE languages are official national languages. Only two of these, Farsi (a Persian dialect) in Iran and Pushtu and Dari (another Persian dialect) in Afghanistan, are Iranian; the rest are Indic: Urdu (basically the same language as Hindi; Pakistan), Hindi (India; with English), Bengali (Bangladesh), Nepali (Nepal), Sinhalese (Sri Lanka), and Divehi (the Maldives). In India, the various states have their own official state languages. Most of these are Indic, for instance, Assamese and Gujarati, but the four southern states have official Dravidian languages (Tamil, Malayalam, Telugu, and Kannada). Several languages of India, especially Hindi-Urdu and Tamil, are also spoken by large emigrant groups outside Asia, for example, Guyana in South America (where East Indians constitute half of the country's population), Mauritius in the Indian Ocean, South Africa, and Fiji in the Pacific. Tamil even has official status in one Southeast Asian country, Singapore (with Malay, Chinese, and English).

In Southeast Asia, the Austro-Asiatic languages Khmer (Cambodian) and Vietnamese are the official national languages of Kampuchea and Vietnam, respectively. Vietnamese is widely spoken by emigrant groups as well, notably in the United States. Laos and Thailand have as their national languages the Tai (of Tai-Kadai) languages Lao and Thai, respectively. Countries with official Austronesian languages are located both on the Asian mainland and on islands off the coast of Asia and elsewhere: Malay (Malaysia and, with other languages, Singapore), Indonesian (Indonesia), Tagalog or Pilipino (Philippines), and Malagasy (Madagascar; with French), Fijian (Fiji), Samoan (Western Samoa; with English), I-Kiribati (or Gilbertese; Kiribati), Nauruan (Nauru), and Tuvaluan (Tuvalu).

Sino-Tibetan languages, for all of their diversity and vast numbers of speakers, have official national status in only four countries: Chinese in China, Taiwan, and (with three other languages) Singapore; and Burmese in Burma. Chinese is semi-official in the British colony of Hong Kong and in the Portuguese possession Macau. In addition, large emigrant Chinese populations, speaking various "dialects" of Chinese, are found in many countries, especially the United States, Indonesia, and Mauritius.

Only two American Indian languages have official national language status: in Bolivia, Quechua and Aymara share this status with Spanish, and in Peru the official languages are Spanish and Quechua. Guarani (Paraguay) should be mentioned here too, since it is the only Indian language spoken by the majority of the people in its country. Greenlandic Eskimo, though not (strictly speaking) an American Indian language, is also relevant here, as it has official status (with Danish) in Greenland.

Several pidgins and creoles have at least semi-official status. Afrikaans, which may be a semi-creole, is one of South Africa's two official languages. Sango is the national language of the Central African Republic (though French is the country's official language). The forms of Swahili that are official in Kenya and semi-official in Comoros may be creolized (though most people classify most versions of Swahili as ordinary Bantu). The French-based Creole has recently replaced French and English as the official language of the Seychelles. The English-vocabulary pidgin Bislama is the constitutionally established national language of Vanuatu (formerly the New Hebrides) and shares official status with French and English. In Papua New Guinea, the English-vocabulary pidgin Tok Pisin has recently gained official status, and a second New Guinea pidgin, Hiri Motu, has the same status; English is the country's third official language. In a number of Caribbean countries, notably Haiti, the official language is a European one, but most of the people speak the local creole natively.

CONCLUSIONS

Both of the surveys in this chapter—languages of the world according to genetic groupings, and languages of the world according to political status—

could be expanded greatly. Only a tiny fraction of the world's individual languages were mentioned in the first survey, and in the second many languages of considerable national and even international importance were omitted. One obvious desideratum would be a list of the languages that have the most speakers; this gap is filled by "Language Files" (1971a), which has speaker figures for about three hundred major languages. (Fromkin and Rodman, 1978:347–50, provide a less systematically chosen list with speaker figures.)

To a linguist, a language with only a few remaining speakers might be the most fascinating of all the world's languages. To a native speaker of such a language, the dying language might symbolize the loss of an entire culture. One lesson history teaches us is that the languages most likely to survive (and to leave descendants) are those that have official national status and/or millions of speakers. Powerful nations spread their languages at the expense of other languages; and when empires fail, as did those of the Sumerians and the Hittites, their languages are likely to die as well. The histories of languages are a direct reflection of the histories of their speakers, so the study of linguistic diversity ultimately leads us to the study of the whole of human history.

BIBLIOGRAPHY

Note: Starred entries provide useful surveys of the languages of particular families or regions.

Adovasio, J. M., and R. C. Carlisle. 1984. "An Indian Hunter's Camp for 20,000 Years." *Scientific American* 250, 5:130–36.

*Benedict, Paul K. (Contributing editor: James A. Matisoff.) 1972. *Sino-Tibetan: A Conspectus*. Cambridge: Cambridge University Press.

*———. 1973. *Austro-Thai*. New Haven, Conn.: Human Relations Area Files Press.

Bird, Charles, and Timothy Shopen. 1979. Maninka. In Timothy Shopen, ed., *Languages and Their Speakers* (Cambridge, Mass.: Winthrop), 59–111.

*Campbell, Lyle, and Marianne Mithun, eds. 1979a. *The Languages of Native America: Historical and Comparative Assessment*. Austin: University of Texas Press.

*Campbell, Lyle, and Marianne Mithun. 1979b. "Introduction." In *The Languages of Native America*, ed. L. Campbell and M. Mithun.

*Capell, Arthur. 1969. *A Survey of New Guinea Languages*. Sydney: Sydney University Press.

*Catford, J. C. 1977. "Mountain of Tongues: The Languages of the Caucasus." *Annual Review of Anthropology* 6:283–314.

*Collinder, Bjorn. 1965. *An Introduction to the Uralic Languages*. Berkeley: University of California Press.

*Comrie, Bernard. 1981. *The Languages of the Soviet Union*. Cambridge: Cambridge University Press.

Driver, Harold E. 1969. *Indians of North America*. 2d ed. Chicago: University of Chicago Press.

Fromkin, Victoria, and Robert Rodman. 1978. *An Introduction to Language*. 2d ed. New York: Holt, Rinehart and Winston.

Gleason, Henry A., Jr. 1961. *An Introduction to Descriptive Linguistics*. 2d ed. New York: Holt, Rinehart and Winston.

*Greenberg, Joseph H. 1966. *The Languages of Africa*. Bloomington: University of Indiana Press and The Hague: Mouton.

———. 1971. "The Indo-Pacific Hypothesis." In *Current Trends in Linguistics*, ed. Thomas A. Sebeok. Vol. 8: *Linguistics in Oceania*. The Hague: Mouton.

Haas, Mary R. 1976. "American Indian Linguistic Prehistory." In *Native Languages of the Americas*, ed. T. A. Sebeok. New York: Plenum Press, Vol. 1:23–58.

*Hancock, Ian F. 1971. "A Map and List of Pidgin and Creole Languages." In *Pidginization and Creolization of Languages*, ed. D. Hymes. Cambridge: Cambridge University Press, pp. 509–23. [This list includes eighty languages.]

*———. 1977. "Repertory of Pidgin and Creole Languages." In *Pidgin and Creole Linguistics*, ed. A. Valdman. Bloomington: University of Indiana Press, pp. 362–91. [This list includes 127 languages, so it is more complete than the preceding item; but it is harder to use, because the numbered items are not discussed in order, but rather according to vocabulary language.]

*Holm, John. Forthcoming. *A Survey of Pidgin and Creole Languages*. Cambridge: Cambridge University Press.

*Jacobsen, William H., Jr. 1979. "Hokan Inter-branch Comparison." In *The Languages of Native America*, ed. L. Campbell and M. Mithun, pp. 545–91.

*Landar, Herbert. 1976. "South and Central American Indian Languages." In *Native Languages of the Americas*, ed. T. A. Sebeok. New York: Plenum Press, Vol. 2:401–527.

Language Files: List of languages with numbers of native speakers. 1971a. Washington, D.C.: Center for Applied Linguistics.

Language Files: List of political units with languages spoken in each. 1971b. Washington, D.C.: Center for Applied Linguistics.

Li, Charles N., and Sandra A. Thompson. 1979. "Chinese: Dialect Variations and Language Reform." In *Languages and Their Status*, ed. T. Shopen. Cambridge, Mass.: Winthrop, pp. 294–335.

*Loukotka, Cestmir. 1968. *Classification of South American Indian Languages*. Los Angeles: UCLA Latin American Center.

Matisoff, James A. 1973. "Tonogenesis in Southeast Asia." In *Consonant Types and Tones*, ed. L. M. Hyman. (S C Occasional Papers in Linguistics, no. 1), pp. 73–95.

Meillet, Antoine, and Marcel Cohen. 1952. *Les langues du monde*. 2 vols. Paris: Champion.

*Mithun, Marianne. 1979. "Iroquoian." In *The Languages of Native America*, ed. L. Campbell and M. Mithun, pp. 132–212.

National Geographic Atlas of the World (1981; updated by later supplements). Washington, D.C.: National Geographic Society.

*Pinnow, Heinz-Jurgen. 1963. "The Position of the Munda Languages Within the Austroasiatic Family." In *Linguistic Comparison in Southeast Asia and the Pacific*, ed. H. L. Shorto. London: School of Oriental and African Studies, pp. 140–52.

*Poppe, Nicholas. 1965. *Introduction to Atlaic Linguistics*. Wiesbaden: Otto Harrassowitz.

Ruhlen, Merritt. 1975. *A Guide to the Languages of the World*. Stanford, Calif.: Language Universals Project.

Sapir, Edward. 1921. "A Bird's-eye View of American Languages North of Mexico." *Science* 54:408.

Sebeok, Thomas A., ed. 1963–. *Current Trends in Linguistics.* A multivolume series. The Hague: Mouton.

*———. 1976. *Native Languages of the Americas.* 2 vols. New York: Plenum Press.

*Silverstein, Michael. 1979. "Penutian." In *The Languages of Native America*, ed. L. Campbell and M. Mithun, pp. 650–91.

Voegelin, C. F., and F. M. Voegelin. 1964–66. "Languages of the World." *Anthropological Linguistics*, Vols. 6–8.

———. 1973. *Index of the World's Languages.* Washington, D.C.: U.S. Department of Health, Education, and Welfare.

*Wurm, S. A. 1972. *Languages of Australia and Tasmania.* The Hague: Mouton.

*———, ed. 1977. *New Guinea Area Languages and Language Study.* 3 vols. (Pacific Linguistics, C38-C40.) Canberra: Australian National University.

*Yallop, Colin. 1982. *Australian Aboriginal Languages.* London: Andre Deutsch.

*Zvelebil, Kamil. 1970. *Comparative Dravidian Phonology.* The Hague: Mouton.

3

Alaa Elgibali

THE LANGUAGE SITUATION IN ARABIC-SPEAKING NATIONS

The etymology of the word "Arab" is obscure. Some scholars, however, believe that it is derived from the Semitic root *cabar* meaning "pass" or "cross," which implies nomadism. The name was originally used to refer to the nomadic tribes (the Bedouins) that inhabited the northern parts of the Arabian Peninsula, with the corollary "raider." The first documentation of the word "Arab" in history exists in an Assyrian inscription of 853 B.C., commemorating the defeat of a rebellious tribal chief called Gindibu the Arab (see Carmichael, 1967). From the very earliest times on, Arabic-speaking town- and village-dwellers (al-Hadar) were clustered around commercial centers located along the trade routes and in the fertile lands in the peripheries of the Arabian Peninsula. Nonetheless, the term "Arab" was commonly used by non-Arabic speakers, especially orientalists or Arabists, to refer to "a native or inhabitant of Arabia, or a member of the Arabic division of the Semitic peoples" (Webster's Dictionary, 2d edition, 1979). Currently, however, the term "Arab" is used indiscriminately to refer to all Arabic-speaking people regardless of their diverse ethnic roots, national, or religious affiliations. This is partially due to the frequent reference in the mass media to the "Arab-Israeli conflict," following the creation of Israel in 1948, without differentiating between the different ethnic groups that exist in each Arabic-speaking (or Arab) state.

The extension of the word "Arab" to include all Arabic-speaking people is a convenient, though ambiguous, simplification. This is the case because, although the overwhelming Muslim majority of the inhabitants of the modern Arabic-speaking nations assume the identity "Arab" as a national identity disguising their diverse ethnic roots, some minority groups prefer to ascribe to themselves other primary national identities. These minority groups either completely dissociate themselves from the identity "Arab," which has too often been erroneously equated with "Muslim," or assume it as a secondary identity. Christian Lebanese, for example, privately resent being called Arabs, although publicly they refer to themselves as such. Ethnically, the Copts in Egypt see themselves as Copts (or the descendants of the ancient Egyptians) and nationally as Egyptians. The Copts accept the identity "Arab" as a global national identity only in the presence of a common cause unifying the entire region of Arabic-speaking people, for example, the beginnings of pan-Arab nationalism in the 1880s or the threat of Zionism in this century. The ambiguity of the term "Arab" is also a result of the superficial paradox between the fact that Islam considers distinctions based on national, ethnic, or racial grounds as totally unimportant, while, on the other hand, one effect of the spread of Islam was to create racially mixed and religiously heterogeneous communities whose people were keenly aware of their differences. These communities were created by the Arab migrants (from Arabia) throughout East, Central, North Africa, Greater Syria, Iraq, and other parts of Asia.

INTRODUCTION

Although the language situation in Arabic-speaking nations may not at first glance appear particularly complex, a closer look will reveal an intricate array of languages, dialects, and intradialectal variation. The complexity is not that of a multiplicity of languages all contending for a share in national life. Rather, the region is characterized by the persistent interplay of two themes running through several hundred years of history. These two themes are bidialectalism (diglossia) within Arabic and the bilingualism of contact situations that have often but not always resulted in a shift to Arabic. This chapter discusses these two themes separately and includes historical and linguistic data pertinent to each. The reader should remember, however, that this is an unnatural dissection and that bidialectalism and bilingualism are not completely separated either chronologically or geographically. On the contrary, they represent two basic components of a single picture: that of the language situation in the Arabic-speaking nations.

LANGUAGE SITUATION BEFORE AND AFTER ISLAM

Bidialectalism

The existence of divergent Arabic dialects can be traced back to pre-Islamic periods, that is, before the seventh century A.D.[1] In the Arabian Sahara several tribes coexisted, enjoying different degrees of prestige and power and speaking different dialects of Arabic. M. Eid (1981), through anecdotal evidence, shows that such different dialects existed, and indicates that the domain of divergence included lexicon, morphology, syntax, and semantics. Immediately after the inception of Islam, that is, during the period when missionaries and written communications were being dispatched to spread the new religion, several scholars took upon themselves the task of recording the Hadith (speech) of the prophet Muhammad. One such scholar was Ibn Al-'athir, who recorded the following anecdote:

Having heard the prophet speak to a delegation from Bani Nahd, Ali Bin Abi Talib said to Muhammad, "We are the sons of one father; we hear you talk to Arab delegates and yet we do not understand most of what you say." The prophet answered, "God educated me well!"

In another Hadith Muhammad says, "I was ordered to talk to people in such a way that they can understand." Commenting on a letter which Muhammad sent to the tribe of Hemyar, Eid mentions that in a forty-two word paragraph fifteen words were exclusive to the local dialect of Hemyar. In addition, he notes a replacement of the voiced pharyngeal fricative within the imperative form of the triradical verb *?acta* ("give"). Perhaps the best proof for the divergence of the dialects immediately before Islam is the fact that there are still seven different acceptable pronunciations for reciting the Qur'an. These *al-qiraa'aat al-sabc* ("the seven readings") reflect the seven most prestigious or influential dialects at the time of the documentation of the Qur'an.

At all times then there was an awareness of and an aspiration to acquire a prestigious superposed standard variety. Before Islam, the selection of one tribal dialect rather than another as the standard linguistic norm was determined by intricate interactions of socioeconomic, cultural, tribal, and/or literary considerations. The tribes in Arabia never shifted to any of the assumed standards and always maintained their own dialects as a mother tongue and as a symbol of tribal honor and pride (see Abou-Seida, 1972). However, with the inception of Islam in 640 A.D. and the documentation of the Qur'an, the rivalry among the various dialects for the position of the superposed standard came to an abrupt end. In the early days of Islam, the linguistic model of the Qur'an immediately assumed supremacy over all regional dialects, so much so that even non-Muslims viewed it as the linguistic model to emulate. Pretending to be a prophet himself, one of the most ardent enemies of the new religion, Musailama al-Kadhab, declared that the ocular proof to the authenticity of his prophethood lay in the linguistic sophistication of his "religious" texts which he compared to that of the Qur'an. The fact that Arabs have traditionally been language-oriented is best demonstrated by the existence of *Souq Ookadh* ("Okadh market") which was held annually during the *Hajj* ("pilgrimage") season. *Souq Ookadh* served as the stage for political and cultural activities and trade. The most prominent cultural activity was the literary contests among poets. Poets competed, and the winning poems (*al-Mucalaqat*) were permanently displayed on the walls of *al-kacba*, the most sacred place for the Arabs.

Bilingualism

Before Islam (i.e., before 640 A.D.), the northern parts of the Arabian Peninsula, known as "Badiyat al-Shaam," served both as a large buffer zone of desert-like land separating the Persian and Roman empires and as a target of expansion for both empires. Badiyat al-Shaam represented a triangle situated in the middle between the fertile lands of Iraq to the north, the Sinai Desert, the Dead Sea, the fertile lands of the Jordan Valley, Palestine, and Greater Syria (the Fertile Crescent) to the west, and the Dajla and Furat rivers to the east. It served as a battlefield in the series of indecisive, intermittent wars (330–648 A.D.) between the Persian and Roman empires (Byzantium) to dominate the Fertile Crescent and gain access to the major trade routes passing through Badiyat al-Shaam. Some of the inhabitants of Arabia and Badiyat al-Shaam allied themselves with the Romans, and others with the Persians. These military alliances also opened the door for some cultural contacts that resulted in the creation of a bilingual elite. The bilinguals acted as military mediators and trade middlemen between the Arabs on one hand and the Persians or the Romans on the other. The linguistic influence of the bilingual elite on Arabic was minimal, however, and its domain was confined mainly to lexemes particular to the Roman or Persian cultures, with no equivalent in the culture of the Bedouins or al-Hadar. Moreover, because both the Persians and the Romans, at the time, were the superpowers in the area, they looked in disdain at the Arabic culture and, therefore, were not influenced by the Arabs or their language.

The seventh and eighth centuries A.D. witnessed the era of great Muslim expansion which reached inside the borders of India and China in Asia, Sudan, Egypt, and all the way west through Morocco in Africa, and Spain and parts of France in Europe. Linguistically, Arabic, which by then was well established as *the* language of Islam and the new Islamic state, faced several challenges during that period: the languages of the former colonists (mainly Hellenic Greek, Persian, and Vulgar Latin) which were used as the languages of administration and government, competition from the local languages (for example, Coptic in Egypt and Berber in Morocco), and the challenge of adapting to the new and widely diverse local cultures in the opened territories.

The consolidation of Arabic as the official language of government replacing the languages of the former colonists was not a major problem because these languages had always remained just that: the languages of government. In Egypt, for example, Hellenic Greek did not infiltrate or replace Coptic, even though it had been the official language of government for three centuries (333–30 B.C.). Latin left only few linguistic traces on the local languages in northwest Africa, despite the Roman control of the area for five decades (see Abdul-Rahman, 1971:61). The peoples of the opened countries simply did not care if one colonial language replaced another.

Not surprisingly, the immediate reaction of the local peoples was to adhere to their own languages in the face of the new language of administration. Of extreme importance to understanding the language situation at that time is the distinction between *Arabization* (i.e., the Arabs attempting to make non-Arabs become Arab-like) and *Arabophilia* (i.e., non-Arabs wanting to become like Arabs). The term *Arabization*, though commonly used, is a misconception since the expanding Arabs only wanted to spread Islam and nothing more. Arabization was never a declared policy of the Islamic state. The literature is full of anecdotal references to the effect that the Arab immigrants respected the local customs and cultural norms. The effects of the so-called Arabization movement on the language situation in that period led to a slow shift to Arabic in the absence of coercive policy, forcing the subjects of the Islamic state to shift to Arabic. It was the Arabophile who, adopting Islam as a faith, accepted the premise that Arabic, the language of the Qur'an, was the appropriate language for every Muslim to learn and speak. It was the Arabophile who, in the beginning of the Muslim administration, learned Arabic and acted as a translator between the local people and the Arabs. Other translators were Arabs who were commissioned by the state to learn the languages of the new territories. Together, the Arabophile and the Arab translators represented the first generation of bilinguals, in Arabic and some other language, in these territories.

The emergence of larger bilingual communities was heralded by the mass migration movements of Arabic tribes that came to settle in the new territories for religious and economic reasons, and the more intense cultural and social contacts and intermarriages between them and the local people. The nature and size of the migration movement resulted in extending the domain of Arabic to other local cultural, judicial, military, and literary aspects of daily life. With the increase in the number of locals becoming Muslims, and the upset in the numerical balance of the population created by the migration of Arab Muslims from Arabia, Arabic began to take over as the common language as well as the language of wider communication. Although the rate of shift to Arabic varied from one place to another for different reasons, the typical pattern was for the local people, at least in urban centers, to shift to Arabic over three generations. Abdul-Rahman (1971:67) reports that as early as 710 A.D. ten thousand Berbers were conscripts in the army invading Spain, and the language of the army was Arabic. The local languages, however, did not disappear; instead, they were usually maintained as religious languages, like Coptic in Egypt, or as a home language, like Nubi in upper Egypt or Berber in the African sub-Sahara.

CURRENT LANGUAGE SITUATION

Diglossia Versus Continuum

The codification of Classical Arabic by the grammarians, who were motivated primarily by their desire to preserve the linguistic model of the Qur'an and its purity, led to the maintenance of a "fossilized" language form that became, for every Muslim, the object of reverence which one might aspire to master. However, the attempts of Arabic speakers to attain or master this strictly codified, revered model remained, except for a dedicated few, mainly fruitless. Meanwhile, the real language of Arabic speakers, as represented in their dialects, followed the natural path of language growth and change. The result was the widening of the gap between the local dialects and the superposed variety that existed in the traditional, that is, pre-Islamic, model of bidialectalism. The more the dialects changed and adapted themselves to new cultures and technological advances—while Classical Arabic remained artificially stabilized—the greater the differences became between them and the classical form. The following sections outline the relationships between the classical form and the dialects, as the first step toward an understanding of the current language situation in Arabic-speaking nations.

Two descriptions of the current language situation in the Arabic-speaking nations exist. In his classic article on the subject, Charles A. Ferguson (1959) characterizes the language situation in Arabic-speaking nations as one of diglossia.[2] He defines this term as:

A relatively stable language situation in which in addition to the primary dialects of the language (which may include a standard or regional standards), there is a very divergent, highly codified (often grammatically more complex) superposed variety the vehicle of a large and respected body of written literature either of an earlier period or in another speech community which is learned largely by formal education and used for most written and formal spoken purposes but not used by any sector of the community for ordinary conversation (232).

Ferguson thus recognizes only two levels of Arabic: H, a superposed variety with no regional variants, and L, a collective term for the regional dialects. According to Ferguson, each level has its own linguistic properties and codified set of functions. Ferguson acknowledges only slight overlapping between the two levels and, therefore, predicts that in one speech episode only L or H will be used with minimal overlapping. Overlapping, Ferguson states, refers to the switching from L to H, or vice versa, but not to what we may term *fusion of features* in the same utterance. Each utterance, therefore, is clearly either H or L but not a mixture of both.

Expanding on the work of Ferguson, El-Said Badawi (1973) characterizes the language situation in Egypt as one of a continuum. He maintains that within each regional speech area in Egypt five linguistic levels coexist, each with its own distinctive phonological, morphological, and syntactic properties.[3]

Badawi claims that the different levels of Arabic found in Egypt are not segregated entities as Ferguson suggests. Rather, they are all interrelated. The five levels which Badawi characterizes for Arabic in Egypt (and by extension in the Arabic-speaking nations) are the following:

1. *fuSHa al-turaθ* (i.e., Classical Arabic, corresponding to Ferguson's H).

2. *fuSHa al-caSr* (i.e., Modern Standard Arabic, the modern literary language, written only—has no immediate correspondence in Ferguson's analysis).

3. *cammiyyat al-muθaqqafin* (i.e., High Standard Colloquial, the everyday spoken language of educated people in dealing with serious matters—corresponding to Ferguson's regional standard which is part of L).

4. *cammiyyat al-mutanawwirin* (Middle Standard Colloquial, the everyday language of educated people when speaking informally—part of Ferguson's L).

5. *cammiyyat al-ummiyyin* (Low Colloquial, everyday language of the illiterate—part of Ferguson's L).

Badawi, like Ferguson, discusses the discourse rules that govern the use of the proposed levels in relation to the social and educational background of the speaker and the addressee, and to the discourse content. Thus, both authors explain the sociolinguistic bases of the speaker's choice and his motivations for moving occasionally from one linguistic level to another within the same speech episode. A university professor lecturing in the humanities, for example, will explain a specific point in level 3 (educated spoken), but will occasionally move up the linguistic continuum to level 2 (Modern Standard Arabic) to summarize or give titles of topics. The same professor will then move down again to level 3 when he steps out of the lecture hall and chats informally with a student or a colleague; when he goes home and sits at the dinner table, he will still move further down to level 4 (Middle Standard Colloquial) when he talks to his wife and children. The code-switching of this professor will not stand out as unique because it conforms to the expected linguistic behavior in these situations. On the other hand, another university professor lecturing in the sciences will code-switch between levels 3, in formal situations, and 4, in informal situations, but will not reach level 2. The range available for each of the two professors for code-switching differs because those who study or teach arts and humanities are generally expected to possess, and perhaps do, a higher level of linguistic sophistication in Arabic than those who work in the sciences and whose jargon contains many specialized terms from English, French, and, to a lesser degree, German.

The general pattern of code-switching exhibited by these two professors is essentially the same in form as one would observe in a similar situation in, say, the United States. One fundamental difference, however, has to do with the mechanism by which code-switching is carried out in each case of style variation. In the Arabic case, the professor will code-switch by changing the ratio of *cammiyyiat* features to *fuSHa* features, or vice versa, in the same utterance. It is indeed difficult, if not impossible, to define whether any one utterance is clearly H or L. This process of fusing features from different linguistic levels in the same utterance makes the phenomenon of code-switching in the Arabic case more complex to perform and, consequently, harder to describe than in the case of American English or any non-"diglossic" language situation. This process of code-switching and style variation takes place at the phonological, morphological, and syntactic levels.

Classes of true bilinguals emerged in all the Arabic-speaking nations as a result of long-term and close contact with one or more European languages. Thus, we find bilinguals in Arabic on the one hand, and English (Egypt, Sudan, Jordan, Iraq, and Palestine), French (Northwest Africa, Lebanon, and Syria) or Italian as was the case in Libya and parts of Somalilands. The size of bilingual sections in these societies varied considerably and depended mainly on length of time of the contact situation, and the nature of the contact, cultural versus military. Bilingualism in Arabic and English in Egypt, and French in Lebanon, for example, was confined primarily to the upper classes, who associated themselves with the "developed" Westerners, and parts of the middle classes who correctly viewed mastering the languages of the rulers as a necessary step to achieve upward mobility. In Northwest Africa, French thoroughly infiltrated many domains of daily public life, the government, and education. This was so much the case that, given the French attitude that Algeria should be permanently annexed to France, Arabic was becoming the second language to many residents.

DIGLOSSIA AND BILINGUALISM

Since 1959 when Ferguson highlighted the term *diglossia*, attempts have been made to extend its scope and to redefine its basic set of implications. Several scholars advocate the use of a single theoretical model to handle all code variation, whether monolingual or bilingual. J. Macnamara notes that "in the decade following the publication of Ferguson's article the term diglossia was extended to refer to all situations in which a standard variety is used for the purposes of more formal communication, and a relatively 'uncultivated' variety is used for more intimate communication" (1967:3).

Macnamara attributes the source of the generalization of the domain of Ferguson's term to the attempts of Joshua Fishman (1964) and John Gumperz to provide a single theoretical framework to describe the societal norms that control the use of linguistic varieties in bi- or multilingual speech communities. John Gumperz (1961, 1962, 1964, 1966) extends the domain of the term to refer to all multilingual or multidialectal societies that manipulate the different registers or codes according to rules of discourse. The views expressed by Gumperz, Macnamara, and Fishman only help to trivialize the term *diglossia*, especially when the Arabic case is concerned. The model they propose is so general that it is certain not to grasp the special characteristics initially outlined by Ferguson and later detailed by Badawi. Moreover, the existence of Classical Arabic, with its intimate association with Islam, makes the Arabic language situation unique. It is the awareness of the uniqueness of the Arabic case that perhaps makes both Ferguson and Badawi meet on common ground.

The extension or redefinition of the term by the proponents of one theoretical model for code variation has been rejected by several scholars for different reasons. André Martinet rejects the attempts to treat diglossia as a type of bilingualism.

Talking about a specific diglossic language situation, Anghelescu (1974:89) argues that diglossia is a term that is so intimate to the Arabic language situation that application to other supposedly similar situations is an "unjustified extrapolation." Few will agree with Anghelescu about limiting the scope of the term to just one specific language situation, since the purpose of studying any phenomenon is to arrive at some generalization, or theory, to help us understand and make predictions about similar situations.

Indeed, it can be further argued that diglossia is not a form of bilingualism, because the term *diglossia* refers to how the speakers view what they speak. In bilingualism, the two linguistic forms are acknowledged as separate entities by the members of the community; in diglossia, they are viewed as constituting only one language by the same members. This argument deals with an essential aspect of the term as Ferguson originally defined it in 1959, that is, with the psychological reality of the linguistic varieties involved. Arabic speakers, for example, will use their colloquial variety (L) to argue strongly against any characterization of their speech as colloquial. Unfortunately, the proponents of a unified model ignore this essential aspect of the phenomenon (see Anghelescu, 1974).

Nadia Anghelescu warns against attempts to mix diglossia with bilingualism on the grounds that any such attempts will lead to the trivialization and/or "the dissolution of the term"; the incorporation of the term into that of stylistic functional variation will disguise its unique psychological and linguistic traits. This is the case because "diglossia implies sufficiently similar languages for the speakers to feel that it is the same language, yet remote enough, so that the acquisition of the literary language implies long-term efforts and can never be fully achieved" (1974:83).

The desires of the proponents of one theory of all types of code variation constitute a legitimate cause. However, the frameworks proposed by these proponents of one model have ignored the unique characteristics of the term in Ferguson's sense, and have so far only led to the dissolution of the term—as Anghelescu warned. We have not gained any new insights into the interaction of sociological and psychological phenomena. Instead, we have lost a term that was capable, in Ferguson's sense, of helping us understand, interrelate, and make predictions about the behavior of a particular type of language situation and the psychological attitudes of its speakers.

LANGUAGE POLICIES

Dialect Variation

Interest in studying the dialects began in the early days of Islam as a result of the codification of Classical Arabic. Not surprisingly, the grammarians viewed the dialects as bastardized or debased forms of Arabic and studied them in order to "purify" them of any regional features. Of great importance to the grammarians was that the Muslims should recite the Qur'anic verses "correctly." The model of "correctness," however, was not limited to the speech patterns of one dialect. Instead, a set comprising seven dialects was widely recognized as acceptable models for recitation. The differences among the members of this set never went beyond the phonetic level. I. Anis (1975) claims that the rise and consolidation of Islam during the seventh century A.D. created even more awareness of the importance of linguistic correctness and "purity." This increasing importance stemmed from the Muslim's belief that Muhammad was only a messenger whose main task was to deliver the Qur'an, which was composed by God Himself. The Qur'an was documented in the dialect of Quraish, the tribe to which Muhammad belonged. By the middle of the seventh century A.D., to the Muslims Arabic meant the language of God. Any colloquial tribal dialect other than that of Quraish was viewed even by its native speakers as a bastardized variety whose most natural domain of usage was in the home and for intragroup activities.

When Islam began to spread widely as a faith and as a way of life, the grammarians began to have a different problem: the non-Arab Muslims had to learn the language of the new religion. The grammarians started to face yet another problem, that is, *laHn* ("diversity from the linguistic model of the Qur'an"). In addition, the self-appointed guardians of the language faced the influx of borrowing of vocabulary items from the languages in contact with Arabic in the domains of culture and know-how. These two problems initiated the thereafter extremely influential work of Arab grammarians and authors of dictionaries whose work was intended mainly to preserve the "purity" of the language among the Arabs and to facilitate teaching it to nonnative speakers who were increasingly adopting Islam as a faith.

The question of linguistic diversity and mutual intelligibility among the speakers of the numerous geographical modern Arabic dialects began to be seriously entertained by the turn of this century. Some arabists (see Said, 1980) contributed the major share in directing the attention of Arab nationalists and educators to the importance of addressing the question of dialect variation. Since then, Arab politicians and thinkers have adopted stances ranging from one extreme to the other. A group of pan-Arab nationalists (for example, Abdul-Rahman, 1971) advocates the gradual elimination of the local dialects in favor of a unified standard linguistic variety, which they equate with Classical Arabic. Sharing the goals of this group, which is mainly motivated by the desire to preserve the language of the Qur'an and to achieve the long-desired Pan-Arabism from Iraq to Morocco (see Anis, 1970), the influential Al-Azhar University offered financial and moral support to their common cause.

The second group (for example, Vilhelm Spitta, 1880) takes the other extreme and demands the elimination of the artificially superposed classical in favor of the local dialects which, they believe (perhaps rightly), are full-fledged languages. This group claims that the artificial maintenance of the "fossilized" Classical Arabic is responsible for the "retardation" of the Arabs today (see Shoubi, 1951; Spitta, 1880). Two problems are associated with this movement: first, it was started by Westerners which, in light of the fact that its claims threatened the eventual death of the language of the Qur'an, made its proponents suspect; and, second, its demand meant the elimination of what is perceived as a powerful unifying factor essential to achieving the goals of the pan-Arab movement.

The third group, led mainly by the three language academies in Damascus (Syria), Cairo (Egypt), and Rabat (Morocco) and the Arab League, takes a middle position by (1) acknowledging the importance of maintaining Classical Arabic as a unifying force in the Arab world, and (2) having the common sense and linguistic sophistication to admit that dialects are not bastardized forms of the classical. This third group takes credit for most of the serious research done in the area of pan-Arab education (see Abou Seida, 1972), which aims at coordinating the various educational curricula in the Arab world today.

The official language policies that support the spread and consolidation of Standard Arabic, often confused with the classical form, have in general been ineffective and noncomprehensive. For example, there is no coordination between all the various organizations controlling the linguistic level presented to the people as a model to follow. Textbooks and curricula are scrutinized only for their content but never for their linguistic form. Most college graduates complete their academic studies without ever having to consult an Arabic dictionary. In fact, Arabic dictionaries are no longer a required educational aid. Moreover, research pertinent to language planning is virtually nonexistent.

Bilingualism

The spread of the Arabic language was a major priority to Muhammad and his followers. The prophet was quoted as once saying, "seeking knowledge is the duty of every Muslim." To him, the appropriate language for seeking knowledge was Arabic. Thus, in the early days of Islam, messengers (educators) were routinely dispatched to spread literacy in Arabic. During the first two centuries of Muslim expansion in non-Arabic-speaking areas, conflicts arose as to whether the language of education, especially among non-Muslims, should be Arabic or the already established language of education which was usually the local language. The official policy of the Islamic state was to allow bilingual education— in Arabic for the Muslims and in the local language for the others. These conflicts were eventually and amicably resolved as the majority of the local populations gradually adopted Islam and shifted to Arabic.

Current government policies in Arabic-speaking nations vary considerably as to the role bilingual education should play in national life. Northwest African countries have adopted and seriously pursued an Arabization movement in all fields of education to offset the formerly pervasive practice of offering education in French. Egypt, on the other hand, allows bilingual education in the hard sciences and fields, relying on European languages for know-how, but not in the humanities. Pressed for the knowledge and know-how applied through the major European languages, most governments agree that, while bilingual education should be kept to a minimum, European languages should be offered as second or foreign languages.

The indigenous home languages that are scattered around the Arabic-speaking nations do not contend for a place in the educational system and continue to remain just that: home languages. Perhaps the explanation of this attitude is practicality and economy. Even if speakers of indigenous languages are granted bilingual education, the domain of their local languages will remain the home. In addition, it is Arabic that will allow them to join the mainstream of contenders for upward mobility. Moreover, these speakers are mostly Muslim and therefore look favorably at Arabic, the language of Islam. The only example of an indigenous group demanding the right to bilingual education and a national place for their languages is the southern Sudan where the pagan inhabitants are also seeking to have an independent state.

CONCLUSIONS

The above discussion cannot pretend to be complete. Only a few of the issues are detailed in a few countries over centuries of conflict and development. The points discussed, however, are intended to illustrate the importance of the twin themes of bidialectalism (diglossia) and bilingualism.

Three points need to be emphasized. First, a description of Arabic is incomplete without adopting Ferguson's notion of diglossia and incorporating Badawi's analysis of the continuum. Furthermore, the condition of diglossia can be understood only if one recalls the supreme authority of the Qur'an in all matters, especially language.

Second, we should keep in mind that bilingualism is not a novel condition in the Arabic-speaking nations. It is regarded as a fact of life. For hundreds of years, Arabic has been one of the languages involved; the ''other'' language has been different at different times and in different places. In addition, bilingualism has persisted for a considerable time and has resulted in shift only when cultural assimilation has occurred. Where large numbers of people chose to adopt Arabic, as in Egypt, and where large numbers of Arabic-speaking migrants settled on a permanent basis, the bilingual contact situation led to a general shift to Arabic. In cases of shift, the indigenous language may have been retained for religious purposes (Coptic) or as a home language (Berber). On the other hand, where bilingualism occurred only for the purpose of upward mobility into government and administration, as in the case of the Greek domination in Egypt, the bilingual situation was limited in the extent of its domain, the length of time it persisted, and the final outcome. That outcome was maintenance of the indigenous language. On the basis of this historical tendency, we might expect a similar outcome for modern bilingualism in colonial settings that involves the use of one of the European languages.

The third and final point of emphasis is that formal efforts at language planning, such as those of the academies, have only succeeded in preserving the high form of Arabic. There is general agreement that a unified pan-Arab standard should exist for all Arabic-speaking nations, but there is no agreement on what the standard should look like. Governments in the region have not provided comprehensive plans for the language in education, and the plans that exist have not been implemented as they were intended. It is perhaps ironic that a coherent policy for the teaching of second or foreign (European) languages does exist, while no such effective policy is available for Arabic. Such a lack is not surprising in light of the complexities of the language situation in Arabic-speaking nations.

NOTES

1. Classical Arabic is classified as a South Semitic language, a subgroup of Greenberg's (1955) Afroasiatic language family.

2. D. Sotiropoulos (1977) mentions that the term *diglossia* was first used by Karl Krumbacher (1902) in his book *Das problem der Modernen Griechischen Schriftsprache*, where he dealt with the origin and characteristics of diglossia with special reference to the Greek and Arabic language situations. Nonetheless, it is commonly held in the literature that the term was first coined by the French linguist W. Marçais in 1930. Marçais used the term to describe the situation in the Arab world as "la concurrence entre une langue savante écrite et une langue vulgaire parfois exclusivement parlée" (401).

3. To Badawi, a linguistic level is a set of linguistic properties that characterizes a group as separate from other groups. The line between one linguistic level and another is drawn based on the level of education.

BIBLIOGRAPHY

Abdel Malik, Zaki N. 1972. "The Influence of Diglossia on the Novels of Yunsif al-Sibaaci." *Journal of Arabic Literature* 3:132–41.
Abdul-Rahman, A. 1971. *Our Language and Life* (in Arabic). Cairo: Dar al-Ma'arif.
Abou-Seida, Abdelrahman, A. 1972. "Diglossia in Egyptian Arabic: Prolegomena to a Pan-Arabic Socio-Linguistic Study." *Dissertation Abstracts International* 33:739A–40A.
Altoma, Salih J. 1969–70. "The Problem of Diglossia in Arabic: A Comparative Study of Classical and Iraqi Arabic." Cambridge, Mass.: Harvard University Press.
Amin, Mostafa. 1956. *Al-Nahw Al-wadih*. Cairo: Dar al-Ma arif.
Anghelescu, Nadia. 1974. "Arabic Diglossia and Its Methodological Implications." In Angelescu, M. (sic) ed., *Romano-Arabica*. Bucharest: Romanian Association for Oriental Studies, pp. 81–92.
Anis, I. 1975. *Of the Secrets of Language* (in Arabic). Cairo: Anglo-Egyptian Bookstore.
Badawi, El-Said. 1973. *Mustawayat al-'arabiyya al-mucaSira fi miSr*. Cairo: Dar al-Macarif.
Blau, Joshua. 1977. *The Beginnings of the Arabic Diglossia: A Study of the Origins of Neoarabic*. Santa Barbara, Calif.: Afroasiatic Linguistics.

Dahdah, A. 1981. *A Dictionary of Arabic Grammar in Charts and Tables.* Libraire du Liban.

Daltas, P. 1980. "The Concept of Diglossia from a Variationist Point of View with Reference to Greek." *Archivum Linguisticum: A Review of Comparative Philology and General Linguistics* 11:65–88.

Eid, M. 1981. *The Linguistic Levels of Classical and Dialects: Poetry and Prose* (in Arabic). Cairo: Alam al-Kutub.

Elgibali, A. 1981. "Correlation Between Cultural Affinity and the Domain of Contact-Induced Language Change." Unpublished manuscript.

El-Hassan, S. A. 1977. "Educated Spoken Arabic in Egypt and the Levant: A Critical Review of Diglossia and Related Concepts." *Archivum Linguisticum: A Review of Comparative Philosophy and General Linguistics* 8:112–32.

Ferguson, Charles A. 1959. "Diglossia." *Word* 15:325–40.

Fishman, Joshua. 1964. "Language Maintenance and Language Shift as a Field of Inquiry." *Linguistics* 9:32–70.

———. 1967. "Bilingualism With and Without Diglossia; Diglossia With and Without Bilingualism." *Journal of Social Issues* 23, 2:29–38.

Gumperz, John. 1961. "Speech Variation and the Study of Indian Civilization." *American Anthropologist* 63:976–88.

———. 1962. "Types of Linguistic Communities." *Anthropological Linguistics* 1:28–40.

———. 1964. "Linguistics and Social Interaction in Two Communities." In *The Ethnography of Communication*, ed. J. Gumperz and D. Hymes. *American Anthropologist* 2:137–53.

———. 1966. "On the Ethnography of Linguistic Change." In *Sociolinguistics*, ed. Wm. Bright. The Hague: Mouton.

Hall, Robert A., Jr. 1978. "Bi-(Multi-)lingualism and Diglossia in Latin Romance." *Forum Linguisticum* 3:107–17.

Hymes, Dell. 1967. "Models of Interaction of Language and Social Setting." *Journal of Social Issues* 23, 2:8–28.

Kaye, Alan A. 1972. "Remarks on Diglossia in Arabic." *Linguistics: An Interdisciplinary Journal of the Language Sciences* 81:32–48.

Krumbacher, Karl. 1902. *Das Problem der Modernen Griechischen Schriftsprache.* Munich.

Krysin, Leonid P. 1979. "Command of Various Language Subsystems as a Diglossic Phenomenon." *International Journal of the Sociology of Language* 21:141–51.

Labov, W. 1964. "Phonological Correlates of Social Stratification." *American Anthropologist* 2:164–76.

———. 1967. *The Social Stratification of English in New York City.* Washington, D.C.: Center for Applied Linguistics.

Macnamara, J. 1967. "Bilingualism in the Modern World." *Journal of Social Issues* 23, 2:1–7.

Marçais, W. 1930. "La diglossie arabe." *L'enseignement public* 97:401–409.

Martinet, André. 1966. "Bilinguisme et Plurilinguisme." In Actes du seminaire de Linguistique des 14, 15 et 16 Avril 1965 on "Les Faits de contact linguistiques et les niveaux de langue." *Revue tunisienne de sciences sociales* 3, 8.

McKay, Jym M. 1973. "Syntactic Similarities in Arabic Diglossia." *Dissertation Abstracts International.*

Parasher, S. V. 1980. "Mother Tongue English Diglossia: A Case Study of Educated Indian Bilinguals' Language Use." *Anthropological Linguistics* 22:1511–62.

Said, Z. 1980. *History of Propagation of Colloquial in Egypt* (in Arabic). Cairo: Dar al-Ma'arif.

Schmidt, Richard W. 1975. "Sociostylistic Variation in Spoken Egyptian Arabic: A Re-examination of the Concept of Diglossia." *Dissertation Abstracts International*.

Shoubi, E. 1951. "The Influence of the Arabic Language on the Psychology of the Arabs." *Middle East Journal* 5:284–302.

Sotiropoulos, D. 1977. "Diglossia and the National Language Question in Modern Greece." *Linguistics: An Interdisciplinary Journal of the Language Sciences* 197:5–31.

Spitta, W. 1880. *Grammatik des arabischen Vulgardialekts von Aegypten*. Leipzig.

Zughoul, Muhammad Radji. 1980. "Diglossia in Arabic: Investigating Solutions." *Anthropological Linguistics* 22:201–17.

BILINGUALISM AND LINGUISTIC
SEPARATISM IN BELGIAN SCHOOLS

On April 23, 1968, two language inspectors, one representing the Dutch-language Ministry of Belgian Education, the other the French-language Ministry, interrogated four-year-old Luc in a classroom of the Brussels French-language nursery school in which he was enrolled (Dossier 5/68/CP). The child, intimidated by this unexpected attention, remained stolidly silent while the adults introduced subjects that might interest him: toys, food, dogs, "tour a tour en français et en flamand," according to the report of the French-language inspector. Luc's brief response, when it finally came, was first in Dutch; then, after prodding from the French-language inspector, he spoke a few words of French—a performance that elicited contradictory appraisals of his linguistic orientation in their reports.

The French-language inspector reported difficulty in determining the dominant language of this bilingual child who answered questions as easily in French as in Dutch. Nonetheless, he recommended that Luc be allowed to continue his education in Francophone schools because French was the language used by Luc's mother, a Francophone Fleming, at home and in her job as a librarian. The Dutch-language inspector, on the other hand, pointed out that Luc had shown only minimal proficiency in French, answering merely "oui" or "non" to questions in that language. "An answer such as that is always fifty percent correct but is in no case proof of language dominance, and even less proof of an existing mother tongue." ("Een dergelijk antwoord is steeds 50% juist, maar is geen geval een bewijs van taalbeheersing en nog minder een biwijs van de bestaande moderstaal.") In his judgment this was no basis for accepting French as the mother tongue of a child born in Flemish Brabant. In August 1968, the Commission which adjudicates such disputes between language inspectors ruled that Luc must transfer to a Netherlandish school.

The assignment of Luc to a school that would reinforce his legal linguistic identity instead of to the Francophone school favored by his mother is a stark example of the polarities underlying language planning in Belgium. In Luc's case, of course, no placement could have precluded his receiving a bilingual education, which was the intent of this planning, for, although not highly verbal in either Dutch or French, Luc was already functionally bilingual. The language of instruction of whatever school he attended would differ from one of the languages which he had already internalized. In Belgium, a fragile equilibrium exists between bilingualism and the moral imperative for preserving the mother tongue, between linguistic integration and linguistic segregation, between cosmopolitanism and ethnicity; and the schools, particularly the schools of the capital city Brussels, are at its focal point.

Since 1971, parents in Brussels (but not in other parts of Belgium) have had greater freedom to determine the language of their children's education than they had at the time of Luc's interrogation, but the paradoxes surrounding bilingual education in this multilingual country remain. Bilingualism is a national necessity, but it is widely viewed as at best a necessary evil (Bustamante, Van Overbeke, and Verdoodt, 1978:20). "Bilingualism in education must be condemned" ("Le bilinguisme dans l'enseignement doit être condamné," states the final Report of the Harmel Center (Centre de recherche #326, 1954:6). This research became the basis for one of the most rigid exercises in language planning in the world, the Belgian Language Law of 1963.

LANGUAGES AND LANGUAGE COMMUNITIES IN BELGIUM

Close to 9.9 million people inhabit the 30,519 square kilometers of this multilingual country (*Annuaire Statistique*, 1980) which shares political borders, not natural boundaries, with the Netherlands, Germany, France, and Luxembourg. They live, however, within rigidly defined linguistic zones: approximately 56 percent in Flanders, Dutch-language territory; 33 percent in Wallonia, French-language territory; 10 percent in the officially bilingual (French/Dutch) capital, Brussels, a predominantly Francophone island within Dutch-language territory; and there is also a small German-speaking community, less than 1 percent of the total population, in the eastern section of the Province of Liege in Wallonia. The Dutch, French, and German languages have official status, but in addition there are international business firms that use English as a lingua franca; polyglot delegates to the European Economic Community and NATO, whose headquarters are in Brussels; migrant workers, primarily from Italy, Morocco, Spain, Turkey, and Greece, nearly 9 percent of the total population (Bastenier and Dassetto, 1981), many with linguistic and cultural concerns of their own. Bilingualism has a wide range of referents in this crowded Babel. It is, however, the frequently acrimonious quarrel between the French- and Dutch-language communities that has shaped the institutions of modern Belgium.

Scholars still debate the origin of the so-called language line that divides a

Dutch language north from a French language south (Dhondt, 1947:261–68; Draye, 1942; Kurth, 1896–98; Olyff, 1940–44; Stengers, 1959; Valkhoff, 1944). They hypothesize, however, that the Franks, who invaded this northern outpost of the Roman Empire in the fifth century A.D., succeeded in establishing their own Teutonic tongue in the sparsely populated north but adopted the Latin vernacular of the more densely populated south. According to Godefroid Kurth (1896–98, 2:5), a period of transitional bilingualism preceded this language shift, but it was the "barbarians" who were bilingual, not the more advanced Romanized population.

In the south, French emerged as the dominant language, although some traces of Walloon, Picard, and Lorrain survived as regional dialects. In the north, an area that included the Netherlands until the sixteenth century, *Nederduitsch*, a dialect of low German sometimes called *Thiois*, *Dietsch*, or *Duitsch*, evolved into modern *Nederlands* (Dutch), the term used to designate the official language of northern Belgium. Until recently, the Belgian dialect of Dutch was called *vlaams* (Flemish). This is a somewhat confusing designation, for *vlaams* was originally a dialect of the medieval County of Flanders, just as Brabantine and Limburger were dialects of Brabant and Limburg. Even today, Belgians whose mother tongue is Netherlandic are called Flemings and their entire region Flanders, just as Francophones who live in the south are called Walloons and their region Wallonia.

For Belgo-French, the standards of Paris have prevailed for centuries, although a small group still speak Walloon and books and articles on "belgicismes" (Hanse, 1974) and on syntactical differences between Belgo-French and the French of France (Cohen, 1905) all testify to Francophone concern over in-group identity. The language of Flemings, on the other hand, has had a more complicated struggle. From the first meeting of the Netherlandish Language and Literary Congress (*Nederlandse Taal- en Letterkundige Congressen*) in Ghent in 1849, Flemish nationalists urged adoption of standard Dutch. But getting the devoutly Catholic Flemings to accept the pronunciation and orthography of the Protestant Netherlands, a nation which many Catholic Belgians regarded as the seat of religious heresy, was not at first easy. A plan put forward in 1870 suggested that German rather than Dutch be the written language, leaving Flemish a spoken vernacular (Pirenne, 1922–32, 7:279–80). Others such as members of the West Flanders Movement promoted their own dialects. The linguistic situation was so fluid in the early years of the twentieth century that Flemish students at the University of Louvain, then a French-language institution, gathered in cafes that catered to their own local dialect group, using French, however, for communication with Flemings who spoke a different dialect and for intellectual matters (Daumont, 1911, 1:69–720).

Standard Dutch is now the official language of the Flemish community and its schools, but these schools still face a big task. There are still members of an older generation who encountered Standard Dutch for the first time in school, still intellectuals who question whether imitation of Hollanders is the best way of stabilizing their mother tongue (Boelen, 1972:129; Leenen and Clayes, 1972:134), and others who have made such a zealous attempt to weed French words from their language that Belgian Dutch now contains fewer borrowings from French than the Dutch of the Netherlands (Pée, 1970:20–21). To compound the problem, many non-Belgian scholars have continued to call the language of northern Belgium *Flemish* (Meillet and Tesnière, 1928; Rundle, 1946; ILEA, 1982). Even Flemings have shown reluctance to change old customs. The Netherlandic Cultural Council did not replace the *Vlaams* in its title with *Nederlandse* until 1972. Younger Belgians, however, now hear Dutch from early childhood on the radio and TV, as well as in school; for them (and for their children) standard Dutch is fast becoming a mother tongue.

Linguistic standards are further complicated by the status of Brussels, the capital city and a bilingual zone within Flemish Brabant. Brussels is not the only Flemish city in which French has coexisted with Dutch, but it is the only city north of the language line where the two languages officially coexist today. A center of governmental and economic power long feared and envied by the other regions—"Helsche duivel die tot Brussel sijt" ("the infernal devil who sits in Brussels") goes a sixteenth-century Counter-Reformation saying (quoted in Ombiaux, 1920:138)—Brussels has had a French-Dutch bilingual tradition since the Burgundians established their court there in the fifteenth century. The seat of government for a succession of foreign rulers: Spaniards (1579–1713), Austrians (1713–92), French (1792–1815), Dutch (1815–30)—all but the latter of whom used French for most affairs of state, in 1830 Brussels became the capital of a newly independent nation that continued this Francophone tradition. By then, however, Brussels was no longer a Flemish village but was instead a cosmopolitan city whose dominant culture was French.

The languages of Brussels span a broad continuum which itself constitutes a language community (Baetens-Beardsmore, 1971). At either end are the standard forms of Dutch and French, and in between an amalgam of the two languages. Within this spectrum are dialects such as Brabant, the speech most often used as an example of *Vlaams* in words of fiction. Of even greater importance is *bruxellois*, a patois of Netherlandish syntax and French vocabulary which some linguists view as a discrete linguistic system. *Bruxellois* has no official status, just a vital day-to-day life. The problems faced by purists go beyond the complexities of *bruxellois*, however. In the everyday speech of the city, imperfect bilinguals—the group castigated by Jules Destree ([1912] 1968:16–17) when he informed the King that separatism was preferable to a 'fusion' between Flemings and Walloons—regularly substitute the words of one language for those of the other. This linguistic interference even extends to the speech of Francophones, where it is likely to be done for comic effect. But, as Hugo Baetens-Beardsmore has demonstrated (1971), Flemish has had a demonstrable influence on the syntax of Brussels French whether or not this influence is recognized by the speaker. Small wonder that intellectuals from both language communities have tended to focus on standards of linguistic correctness.

TWO PERSPECTIVES ON DUTCH-FRENCH LANGUAGE CONTACT

When Ludovico Guicciardini, the famous Italian traveler, visited the Low Countries in the sixteenth century, he found astonishing linguistic prowess among citizens of the cities of Flanders, a population who, in addition to Flemish, knew French "comme langue maternelle" (Guicciardini [1557] 1943:30). This image of a quintessentially universal and benevolent bilingualism, and of the peaceful relations that such a state implies, represents a major strand in Belgian history. Henri Pirenne, for example, described Belgium as a microcosm of Europe (1928:43), a country without natural frontiers where people speak two languages (1922–32, 1:xi). Pirenne *did* note that "la civilization flamande" has "largement bénéficié du bilinguisme," that Flemings had more need to learn French than Walloons from the earliest days of their coexistence (1922–28, 7:384). Even the emergence of the nineteenth-century Flemish Movement, which he described as "l'agitation sentimentale," not to be disassociated from "les misères du prolétariat" (1922–28, 7:271), did not alter his belief in the benevolence of bilingualism—for Flemings.

The world-view of linguists in the early years of the twentieth century reinforced these assumptions. Antoine Meillet, for example, theorized the existence of two kinds of languages (Meillet and Sauvageot, 1934): those capable of expressing the subtleties and values of an advanced civilization and those outside the mainstream. Since only in the most fortuitous circumstance is a mother tongue likely to be a "langue de civilisation," members of less prestigious language groups who aspire to become "hommes distingués" must learn the language of the advanced culture, and it is quite possible that they will come to prefer this language to their own. "Hommes distingués," therefore, may have one or more language shifts in a lifetime—a point illustrated for Belgium (Meillet and Tesnière, 1928:294, 355) by reference to the fact that one-sixth of the children born into Flemish homes replaced their mother tongue with French by the time they reached adulthood, proof positive of "la prépondérance du français comme langue du civilisation" and of Flemish as "une langue d'intérêt local." Not surprisingly, Flemings concerned about language maintenance feared bilingualism.

Historians of the Flemish Movement (Clough [1930] 1968; Elias, 1969; Geyl, 1952, 1955; Picard, 1942–49; Willemsen, 1958) have their own interpretation of the history of language contact in Belgium. As early as the sixteenth century, Flemings such as Jacob de Meyere complained that the French language was making such gains in Flemish territory that it would eventually push the Teutonic tongue back to the Rhine (quoted in Armstrong, 1965:407–408). In the late eighteenth century, a Flemish lawyer, J.B.C. Verlooy, published a treatise on the decline of the Netherlandish mother tongue in the Low Countries in which he singled out for special concern the corruption of that language in Brussels, a city in which Flemings sometimes purposely spoke their mother tongue badly in order to give the impression that they had had a French education (Verlooy [1788] 1938:25–26). Flemish nationalists and their sympathizers have echoed his complaint ever since.

In their view, the introduction of French into Flanders by the Count of Flanders, a vassal of the French Crown, was an act of linguistic imperialism that was perpetuated by international entrepreneurs who settled in Flemish cities in the sixteenth century (Wilmars, 1968). The adoption of French by certain Flemings thereafter was a necessity for survival, but a necessity that corrupted and impoverished the life and culture of the Flemish people. According to the Dutch historian, Pieter Geyl, the historiography of Francophone writers such as Henri Pirenne is a conscious distortion of history which emphasizes relations across the language line but ignores natural ties between the northern half of Belgium and the Netherlands (Geyl, 1952:44–45). Pirenne himself, a Walloon teaching history at the then French-language University of Ghent, was an imperialist occupying "an advanced post in the movement of penetration and conquest which French civilization, under the auspices of the centralized Belgian state, was carrying on in Flanders" (Geyl, 1955:190–91).

Here then are the polarities. A Francophone interpretation of Belgian history has centered Belgian identity on a tradition of benevolent bilingualism based on a linguistic hierarchy which assumes the superiority of French and even allows for language shift to this more civilized tongue. Flemish nationalists have rejected this view of their history, pointing instead to Francophone linguistic, economic, and political dominance as a form of imperialism that has debased and impoverished the Flemish people. By the early years of the twentieth century, neither they nor maverick Walloons like Jules Destrée could find a viable source of national or personal identity in bilingualism.

PATTERNS OF BILINGUALISM IN THE PAST

At the First International Conference on Bilingualism in Education, which took place in Luxembourg in 1928, J. E. Verheyen (1929) pointed out that a majority of Belgians were not bilingual at all, only 13 percent of the total population, disproportionately represented in Brussels, were bilingual at the time of this conference. In that city, 41 percent of all residents, and 84 percent of Flemish residents, were bilingual (*Annuaire Statistique*, 1938:xxii). Belgium was a bilingual country because more than one language group lived within it, not because all Belgians were bilingual. To understand the urgency behind the sweeping language reforms initiated four years later in 1932 is to understand that bilingualism was a Flemish, not a Walloon, "problem."

In Flanders, the most common pattern of bilingualism was shaped by Flemings who used French for public life and reserved Flemish for intragroup contact and the home. French was the language of government, business, universities, and secondary schools; Flemish, the majority language, belonged to the common people. "Wanneer men alleen Vlaams sprak, kon men slechts een handarbeider zijn'' (Wilmars, 1968:54). A unilingual Fleming could be only a worker. A bilingual Fleming, on the other hand, could hope to join the Francophone power elite. This bilingualism with diglossia existed for centuries in Flanders, but the bilingual Fleming paid a price—perpetuation of a class structure in which language was the status marker.

A different pattern of bilingualism developed in Brussels, a mecca for ambitious Flemings willing and eager to pay the price for social and economic advancement. "Naturellement, mon père et ma mère parlant français, en plus du flamand; considérant cela comme une promotion, voulurent me donner l'instruction dans cette langue sans laquelle, socialement, rien n'était possible,'' notes the son of a Fleming who migrated to Brussels (Francis, 1974:27–29), the first member of his family to make a living with the pen instead of on the farm. ("Naturally, my father and mother, speaking French more than Flemish, considering that a promotion, wanted to give me an education in that tongue without which socially nothing was possible.'') In Belgium, Brussels was the melting pot.

The intermixture of these bilingual patterns was until recently part of the warp and woof of Belgian life. In *La maison du canal*, for example, a novel by Georges Simenon (1932), the heroine Edmée, the daughter of a Fleming who had migrated to Brussels, is sent to live with Flemish relatives in a small village in Flanders after the death of her parents. Her uncle and his sons all know French, which they use in their business, reserving Flemish for home and neighborhood—clear evidence of their prosperity and upward social mobility. There are also unilinguals in this story: Edmée, who knows only French, and her female relatives, who know only Flemish. For Edmée unilingualism is evidence of her privileged upbringing in Brussels where her parents spoke French and she attended a French language school. For her aunt and female cousins, however, unilingualism is evidence of a limited education that did not go beyond primary grades, a diglossic pattern that sheds light on spheres of language usage (as well as on the role of women in rural Flanders in the twentieth century).

Einar Haugen (1972:310–11) makes a distinction between *complementary bilingualism*, habitual use of a second language for clearly defined functions; *replacive bilingualism*, substitution of a second language for one's mother tongue; and *supplementary bilingualism*, the use of a second language on an occasional basis outside of a normal routine. A central theme in the Belgian-language controversy is not the necessity for learning a second language, although there is considerable resistance to learning Dutch among some Walloons. The issue is the kind of bilingualism to support. Complementary bilingualism connotes a social framework in which French is the elite language. Replacive bilingualism means gradual extinction of a Flemish identity group. The goal of language planning in Belgium, therefore, is to educate for mother-tongue dominance and for supplementary bilingualism in schools radically different from those that existed in the past.

THE WAXING AND WANING OF BILINGUAL SCHOOLS

Belgium has had bilingual schools throughout recorded history (Swing, 1980:29–51). Latin schools date from the Middle Ages, and vernacular schools, where ambitious Flemings learned French, from the Renaissance (Counson, 1922; Guicciardini [1567] 1943:57; Serrure, 1859–60). But it was not until Napoleon attempted to make French the language of instruction in schools throughout his realm that language became the dominant political issue that it still is today. William of the Netherlands, the foreign ruler (1815–30) who followed Napoleon, also viewed education, political rule, and language as intertwined. However, his attempts to impose the Dutch language on the government of Belgium and on its schools were so unpopular that his policies hastened the advent of the so-called bourgeois revolution which ushered in the independence of Belgium. That the Francophone leaders who led this revolt in 1830 made as overt a use of French as a tool for domination as their predecessor had of Dutch suggests how well they had internalized the instrumental use of language.

Article 23 of the first Belgian Constitution guaranteed linguistic freedom in education. Before the Constitution was even completed, however, a provisional government had made a basic decision about the language of official documents. That language could only be French, for no standard existed for the many dialects of Flemish and German in use in certain localities (Vanderkerckove, 1969:7). One of the first actions of the new government, therefore, was curtailment of the special Dutch course instituted in the schools by William of the Netherlands. Hereinafter, schools would use the language best suited to the needs of their students (Juste, 1844:332); the language of greatest utility was French. A few elementary schools in rural areas of Flanders and working-class districts of Brussels continued to use Flemish as the language of instruction, but in most schools Flemings had no alternative to a French-language curriculum. French was even the medium of instruction for evening courses at the Industrial School in Ghent, a short-lived experiment that failed (Nérum, 1838:143–44, 154–56).

In Brussels a curious byproduct of this policy of bilingual education by submersion is revealed in the census of bilinguals from the years 1866 and 1880. (No earlier census figures for bilinguals are available.) Between 1866 and 1880, the percentage of bilinguals declined from 32 to 23, but this decline was not accompanied by an increase in the number of unilingual Francophones, the goal of the assimilationist educational policies. The percentage of unilingual Francophones increased by only 1 percent—from 17 percent to 18 percent—whereas the percentage of unilingual Flemings rose from 51 percent to 59 percent [Table 4.1]. It is possible that the migration of large numbers of semiliterate rural Flemings to Brussels during these years (Boon, 1969:419) may have skewed the outcome, but it is also clear that schools were not turning large numbers of Flemings into Francophones, even though it was public policy to do so. Schools were not even doing an adequate job teaching Flemings the rudiments of literacy. By the 1870s, educators such as Charles Buls and Alexis Sluys (Sluys, 1939:29),

Table 4.1
Unilingual French, Unilingual Femish, and Bilingual Population of Brussels, 1866 to 1880

Year	Unilingual French		Unilingual Flemish		Bilingual French and Flemish	
	Popula-tion	Percent-age	Popula-tion	Percent-age	Popula-tion	Percent-age
1866	64,164	17%	205,645	51%	111,338	32%
1880	105,346	18%	338,821	59%	130,164	23%

SOURCE: Annuaire Statistique de la Belgique 33 (1903). Bruxelles: J. B. Stevens, p. 83. Percentages are derived from the population in the French-Flemish language groups, not from the total population, which included a very small group who knew neither language.

concerned about the high illiteracy rate among students taught to read what they did not understand, were ready to experiment with a different curriculum design.

The dual medium schools which proliferated in Brussels and other cities north of the language line during the last quarter of the nineteenth century were a direct response to this concern, a reform widely hailed by educators and Flemish nationalists alike. The availability of parallel French and Dutch classes did not, however, herald the demise of a unilingual French-language curriculum for Flemings. Many communal and most Catholic schools never adopted a dual medium pattern, and even where an alternative was available, Flemish parents continued to enroll their children in French schools. Dual medium schools, moreover, offered at best transitional bilingual education. That those Flemish students who stayed in school joined the French-language mainstream by the third or fourth year (Verheyen, 1929) was to be expected in a society in which French was the language of secondary schools and higher education. True, some secondary schools in Flanders offered certain subjects in Dutch, but secondary schools in Brussels remained French.

Nevertheless, these dual medium schools established Belgium as a world center for bilingual education, attracting many foreign visitors, some of whom (Dawes, 1902) optimistically predicted increased bilingualism among both Flemings and Francophones as a result of this pattern of education. What was not recognized at first, however, but what soon became apparent was that dual medium schools did not educate for a *stable* bilingualism. Before World War I, the number of bilinguals in Brussels *did* increase, testimony perhaps to the efficacy of the dual medium curriculum in easing the transition to French (Table 4.2). Thereafter, however, the bilingual segment of the Brussels population began slowly to decline: from 50 percent in 1910 to 41 percent in 1930. This decline, moreover, was accompanied by a sharp rise in the number of unilingual Francophones: 18

Table 4.2
Unilingual French, Unilingual Flemish, and Bilingual Population of Brussels, 1880 to 1930

Year	Unilingual French		Unilingual Flemish		Bilingual French and Flemish	
	Popula-tion	Percent-age	Popula-tion	Percent-age	Popula-tion	Percent-age
1880	105,346	18%	338,821	59%	130,164	23%
1890	112,402	16%	326,114	47%	258,677	37%
1900	144,723	19%	340,653	44%	294,901	38%
1910	205,217	27%	173,450	23%	372,193	50%
1920	253,226	34%	124,194	17%	371,012	49%
1930	326,929	43%	118,501	16%	308,414	41%

SOURCE: Annuaire Statistique de la Belgique 33 (1903). Bruxelles: J. B. Stevens, p. 83. Annuaire Statistique de la Belgique et du Congo Belgique 44 (1914). Bruxelles: A. Lesigne. p. 89. Annuaire Statistique de la Belgique et du Congo Belge 58 (1935). Gand: Vanderpoorten. p. 32.

percent in 1880, 27 percent in 1910, 34 percent in 1920, 43 percent in 1930; and a decrease in the number of unilingual Flemings: 59 percent in 1880, 16 percent in 1930. Were bilingual Flemings rearing unilingual Francophone children? It is possible to account for this language shift from any other segment of the population. An increase in bilingualism (among Flemings) preceded a clearly articulated language shift.

Given this reality, it is not difficult to see why Flemish nationalists came to view Brussels as a city of unique temptations where a metamorphosis from bilingual Fleming to unilingual Francophone could take place in two or three generations, and the curriculum of the schools of Brussels as a one-way road to unilingualism. Flemish nationalists had many complaints about the schools their children attended: the stigma attached to assignment to a Flemish regime (Cneudt, 1918:30); the shortage of trained Flemish teachers (Segers, 1907:37); the reluctance of communal authorities to create Flemish classes (Toussaint, 1935:40). These schools not only transmitted a negative message about the Netherlandic language and culture; in accelerating a language shift, they alienated children from their parents, "denationalizing" them—to use a word that appeared over and over in the polemics of the language controversy (Wezemael, 1937).

Acceleration of the language shift in Brussels was a major reason for rejection of bilingualism in education in Belgium, but another issue was also germane: the perceived relationship between bilingualism and cognition. At the First International Conference on Bilingualism in Education in 1928, all three of the papers given by Belgians focused on the high rate of failure among Flemings. Ovid DeCroly advanced an argument whose time had not yet come: that failure in school among Flemings should be correlated with low socioeconomic background (DeCroly, 1929:53–61). His two colleagues, however, looked for a different explanation. Both J. E. Verheyen (1929:137–45) and Nicolas Toussaint (1929:146–56) had made empirical studies comparing bilinguals with unilinguals, and on the basis of their research concluded that Flemings had difficulty in school because bilingualism inhibited intellectual development. If this were true, and many Belgian educators of that era were convinced that it was, there were sound pedagogical as well as political reasons to reject the bilingual educational patterns that had existed in the past, whether in unilingual French schools attended by Flemings or in dual medium schools.

EDUCATION FOR SEPARATISM

That language had become the central issue in Belgian life by the mid-twentieth century reflects both the growing power of Flemish nationalists and the potency of the singular mystique they espoused, a mystique far from unique to Belgium (Gillouin, 1930), but nevertheless well nurtured there. "Language is the most important characteristic of a people" ("Het voornaamste kenmerk van een volk is zijne taal"), states a nineteenth-century Flemish nationalist slogan (Temmerman, 1898:5). "Culture is almost always language," concludes the Final Report of the Harmel Center (Centre de recherche #32, ca. 1950:1). But "language" in this context is not a "language of civilization." It is the mother tongue. That in Belgium mother tongue would become a legal concept only in Brussels while "territorial language" (*landstaal*) would become the legal basis for schools and other institutions in Flanders and Wallonia are further examples of the paradoxes underlying language planning in this complex Babel.

The Language Law of 1932, which set the linguistic pattern for the rest of the twentieth century, called for the use of the territorial language as a medium of instruction in Flanders and Wallonia, for the mother tongue or usual language in Brussels. Dual medium schools were to be phased out except in Flanders where transmutation classes would ease the transition from French to Dutch. Second-language study would be mandatory, but only in the modern language classroom, and not until after the fifth year of school when the mother tongue was firmly established. That French-language schools continued to exist in Flanders (European Court of Human Rights, 1967–68), that Flemish families continued to choose French over Dutch as a language of instruction in the nation's capital (Vansiliette, ca. 1950), that transmutation classes became a means for evading Dutch-language education (*Transmutatie Klassen*, 1956), that dual medium schools did not fully die in Brussels (Ministère de l'Instruction Publique, 1953)—all are testimony to the problems inherent in implementing such a blueprint. But that outlawing bilingualism in education began to have an impact we can have no doubt. Even before passage of the more stringent Language Law of 1963, there existed a generation of Flemings educated from primary school through university in their mother tongue.

Education in modern Belgium still reflects this basic design: the principle of linguistic territoriality in Flanders and Wallonia, where only the legal language—Dutch in the north, French in the south—may be the language of education; the principle of personality in bilingual Brussels, where mother tongue is the determinant. But this organization is now far more total than its archetype in the 1930s. The Language Law of 1932 had allowed minorities in Flanders or Wallonia to begin school in their mother tongue in transmutation classes. The Law of July 30, 1963, mandated total hegemony of the regional language, a situation that led a number of Francophone parents in Flanders to seek a redress of their grievances at the Court of Human Rights in Strasbourg (Court of Human Rights, 1966–67), a case they lost. The Law of July 15, 1932, had permitted Flemings and Francophones to coexist within the same school in Brussels, sometimes even within the same class where a teacher taught first in one language and then in the other. Indeed, a few of these "bilingual classes" existed as late as 1962 (*Bulletin Communal*, 1962:407). The Language Law of 1963 not only split such schools into separate linguistic regimes, separately administered, but it also empowered a linguistic inspectorate to determine whether the mother tongue coincided with the language of the school (Law of July 30, 1963, Article 17, 18. Arrêté November 30, 1966). By 1971, the right of parents to select the language of their children's education (*liberté du père de famille*) was partially restored in Brussels, but in the years between 1966 when the law was first rigidly implemented and 1971, the parents of bilingual children in Brussels were sorely tried.

Universities were not included in the 1963 legislation, but they have also come to reflect its design. The state university of Liege (French) and Ghent (Dutch since 1930) have complemented one another for half a century, and they are now balanced by the newer universities of Mons-Hainaut (French) and Antwerp (Dutch). A source of considerable contention was the scission of the private universities, the University of Louvain (Catholic) and the University of Brussels (free-thinking). In 1968, riots in Louvain led to the downfall of the government of Premier Vanden Boeynants and to a decision to move the entire French-language faculty of this ancient university from Flemish soil to Louvain-la-Neuve in Wallonia. Shortly thereafter, in 1969, the University of Brussels divided, becoming the *Vrije Universiteit te Brussel* and the *Université Libre de Bruxelles* (Dejean and Binnemans, 1971; "Le dédoublement," 1969).

Except for a few international schools, a few schools run by the military, and occasional after-school community classes for the children of migrants, all education in Belgium now takes place in separate schools in the language of the separate linguistic communities. This is a bilateral design, each community a mirror image of the other, but basic to it is the scission that makes the complementary images possible. Subterfuges such as the building of a wall between Dutch and French sections of a school in order to retain subsidies have long passed. Dutch-French dual language schools no longer exist, although there *are* dual medium (French-German) schools in the German-language area. Schools may not even employ a teacher who did not receive his or her diploma in the language of the linguistic community to which the school belongs unless the teacher has passed a special examination before a state board (Law of July 30, 1963, Articles 13, 14, 15). By 1969, there were two ministries of education, one for Dutch and the other for French schools. By 1971, two semi-autonomous Cultural Councils, one Dutch, one French, took over responsibility for ministering to the educational, social, and cultural needs of Flemings and Walloons. A similar counsel was also created for the German-language community and would begin to take charge of German-language education in 1983 (Brassine and Kreins, 1984). Education for separatism is now complete.

Nevertheless, the design is not without its internal inconsistencies. That the revised constitution of 1971 provides all Belgians, including citizens of the bilingual capital, with membership in one or the other of three semi-autonomous communities—one French, one Dutch, one German, each administered by its own Cultural Council—implies that language determines cultural identity (Article 3C). But that this constitution also recognizes four geographical regions as language zones—Dutch, French, German, plus bilingual Brussels—implies that except in Brussels language is a function of geography (Article 3B). In Brussels, the choice of an educational regime is now largely a matter of self-definition, virtually a free choice since 1971, provided that parents can prove their residence within the city (Law of July 26, 1971, Article 88). In the unilingual territories, on the other hand, assimilation of linguistic minorities continues to be the policy, and—except in certain villages on the now immovable language line—there exists no legal alternative to education in the regional language except for the child to enroll in a school in a different linguistic zone. This distinction between territorial and individual identity is particularly important for Francophones living in Flemish villages on the Brussels perimeter. Even those living in communes with limited French-language "facilities" (*communes à facilités*) eye the freedom now enjoyed by the French-language community in Brussels with envy.

There is a further paradox here. In Brussels, the study of French in schools in the Dutch regime and of Dutch in schools in the French regime may now begin as early as first grade (Law of July 27, 1971). In the unilingual territories, however, second-language study may not begin before the fifth year, and then, under certain circumstances, another modern language may be substituted. Nevertheless, members of both communities appear to have signaled recognition of *de jure* linguistic parity. A leading Francophone newspaper even published an editorial calling for improvement in the quality of Dutch classes in French schools because Francophone children must compete with bilingual Flemings for government jobs (*Le Soir*, July 19, 1979). Competition exists between the

French and Dutch regimes in Brussels for students and resources, but debate over the democratization of the linguistic hierarchy is over—at least on a policy level.

ISSUES IN THE 1980s

That achievement of *de jure* linguistic equality has not produced linguistic peace in Belgium should surprise few observers of this beleaguered society in which symphony orchestras, television and radio stations, libraries, athletic leagues, as well as schools, are all conducted in the official languages of the discrete linguistic communities to which they belong. And the tendency is toward more segmentation, more separatism. The German Language Community, for example, a community not recognized in Harmel Center research and given only consultative power in the revised Constitution, now has the power to develop and generate its own institutions (Brassine and Kreins, 1984), and increased power over its schools, originally under the exclusive province of the French Ministry of Education. What this new autonomy will mean for the sixty-five thousand German-speaking Belgians is not yet clear, although the fact that they live within clearly defined borders that do not contain an official bilingual area like Brussels could make a difference.

This centrifugal impulse is even more notable in the larger language communities. By 1973, Flanders had completed an agreement with the Netherlands (Govaert, 1982), which later extended to agreements between the Belgian Netherlandish Minister of Education and the Dutch Minister of Education and Culture, and which included provisions for a permanent commission to meet three times a year, alternately in Brussels and the Hague. That Flanders acting unilaterally could conclude an accord on scholastic, scientific, and artistic matters with an independent foreign power with whom it shares a common language is evidence indeed that ethnolinguistic identity, not bilingualism, has become the center of individual reference in modern Belgium.

Nevertheless, *de facto* bilingual areas still remain, and in them the problems attendant when competing languages are in contact. We have already noted the difficulties faced by Luc and his mother in Brussels when rigid application of language legislation was applied to them. With resolution of that particular issue, the center of conflict has now shifted away from Brussels to the periphery, particularly to the predominantly Francophone villages in Flemish territory which surround Brussels. Six of these villages (*communes à facilités*) have special provisions for linguistic "minorities," but application of these provisions has led to considerable tension (*Le Soir*, February 24, 1979). Francophones argue that *their* cultural community should control *all* French-language education. Flemings insist on controlling all schools within the boundaries of *their* geographical territory.

Equally contentious are areas such as the Comines and the Fourons, places of unrest since the freezing of the language line in 1962. In the Fourons (Hermans

Table 4.3
Proportion of Neerlandophone and Francophone Students in the Fourons, 1961 to 1982

	61-62	71-71	76-77	79-80	81-82
Dutch Sector	408(64%)	316(44%)	229(42%)	181(38%)	197(46%)
French Sector	231(36%)	395(56%)	316(58%)	293(62%)	230(53%)
Total	639	711	545	474	428

SOURCE: Commissariat d'arrondissment adjoint pour Fouron. In
Courrier Hebdomadaire du CRISP, 1019 (2 decembre 1983), p. 14.

and Verjans, 1983), for example, a region that is now part of the Province of Limburg but was formerly part of the Province of Liege, Flemings seek to suppress facilities for Francophones and have closed the French-language school. Enrollment in the Dutch-language schools has shown a minor increase recently (Table 4.3), but is still well below the 64 percent it represented in 1961, a matter of small comfort to certain radical Flemings. Weekend riots are commonplace in the area. Francophones, meanwhile, are a majority in a population in which Flemings do not go below 30 percent. The war is far from over.

Another language issue deserves mention. Like other Western European countries, Belgium has had difficulty coming to grips with the multicultural nature of the population that lives within its borders. There are nearly nine hundred thousand migrant workers in Belgium (Bastenier and Dassetto, 1981), close to half in the coal mine areas of Wallonia and the rest almost equally distributed between Brussels and Flanders. Most of these workers are "migrant" in name only. They have come to Belgium to stay. The challenge they pose to Belgian schools is considerable, a point that becomes all the more apparent when the high birth rate of this population is taken into account (9.5 births per 100 females in the immigrant population versus 7 in the Belgian female population), and its youth (49.8 percent are under twenty-five years of age, a figure that translates into 32 percent of the population of Brussels, 16.8 percent of Wallonia, and 5.3 percent of Flanders) (Bastenier and Dassetto, 1981).

Until recently, little attempt was made to provide for the special needs of these immigrant groups. Children attended schools which, because of the rigidity of Belgium's language laws, assumed that either Dutch or French was the language of the home, an impossible situation in a number of schools. In Brussels, there are ninety-five schools with more Moroccan students than Belgian; twenty-one schools where immigrant children comprise 90 percent of the population; twenty schools with over 80 percent; twenty-five schools with over 70 percent

Table 4.4
Choice of a Second Language in the Dutch and French Sector

==

	Dutch	French	English	German	None
French sector	57.9%		36.2%	3.3%	2.6%
Dutch sector		90.7%	9.3%		

SOURCE: Courrier Hebdomadaire du CRISP 1026-1027 (20 janvier 1984).

(Roosens, 1981). Some supplementary instruction in French or Dutch is available, but little instruction in the native languages of these students was even considered, aside from a few after-school classes run by the immigrant groups themselves or their embassies, until passage of the European Economic Directive of 1977 on the education of the children of migrant workers in their mother tongue. That extranational pressure both from the European Economic Community (Balsa, 1984) and from the Council of Europe (Conseil de l'Europe, 1983) for intensification of the few mother-tongue programs that now exist should collide with Belgium's language laws is an area for further research.

Challenge to Belgium's linguistic balance comes from another direction. The present language structure is predicated on the assumption that all Belgians will be educated for dominance in French or Dutch (dominance in German is a recent and untried phenomenon) *and* for supplementary competency in the second national language. Except in Brussels where study of the second national language is mandatory, provisions *do* exist for the substitution of a modern language other than Dutch or French under certain circumstances. Recently, a number of parents have begun to exercise this option. In Wallonia, 36.2 percent of students now choose English instead of Dutch as a second language (Baeten and Verdoodt, 1984), a large enough group to have a real impact on the bilateral design implicit in the language legislation. Even in Flanders among students who have traditionally sought out instruction in French, 9.3 percent are selecting English (Table 4.4). Secondary and university students now rank English as *the* most important modern language, although for Flemings it ties with French (Table 4.5). The spread of English concerns both Flemings, for whom another language of wider communication has begun to challenge hard-won gains, and Francophones, for whom the unthinkable has begun to happen: the possibility that English may replace French as the language of European institutions such as Benelux (Grève, 1980). The achievement of a linguistic balance is at best ephemeral.

CONCLUSIONS

Although it is dangerous to generalize about a subject as complex as the relationship between bilingualism and linguistic separatism in Belgium, four

Table 4.5
Importance of Modern Languages

	Secondary Students	University Students	Workers (Public Service)	Workers (Private Enterprise)
Francophones				
German	3	3	3	3
Dutch	2	2	1	2
English	1	1	2	1
Neerlandophones				
German	3	3	3	3
French	*1	2	1	1
English	*1	1	2	2

*Tie.

SOURCE: **Courrier Hebdomadaire du CRISP** 1026-1027 (20 janvier 1984), p.34.

lessons can be derived from this examination of the transformation of Belgian schools from their role as an agency for acculturation to a Francophone national ethos to their role as an agency for acculturation to linguistic ethnicity.

Lesson One: Dual medium schools do not necessarily lead to language maintenance.

In societies where languages are in competition, a dominant language group will not readily accept a pattern of education which diminishes its hegemony. For such a group, a dual medium curriculum serves a necessary function. Such a curriculum looks like a concession to the demands of the "disadvantaged," but it actually favors rapid transition to the dominant language. Recognition of this fact ushered in the age of linguistic separatism in Belgian schools.

Lesson Two: Democratization of a linguistic hierarchy is likely to bring demands for separate linguistic structures.

The emergence of separatist educational structures in Belgium was a byproduct of the emergence of Flemings as a social, economic, and political force to be reckoned with, but the social, economic, and political emergence of Flemings also coincided with their espousal of a mother-tongue mystique. Their insistence on a linguistic and ethnic identity equal in dignity to that of Francophones was a logical preamble to the emergence of separate school structures that would nurture this identity. We may grant that the existence of Flanders, a linguistic homeland in which Flemings were in the majority, provided a favorable reinforcement for separatists in the capital city. Nevertheless, in any situation in which languages are in competition the endangered group may decide to pull away from the mainstream, to garner its strengths, to defend its young from the blandishments of assimilation, and to prepare for an assertion of its right to a viable separate existence.

Lesson Three: Democratization of linguistic function brings change in the kind of bilingualism found in a society where languages are in contact.

In a society where languages serve differentiated functions, the language of the dominant group is likely to have greater value. It is, of course, possible to argue that acceptance of one language for public life, another for private, need not connote a value system that debases the mother tongue of the subordinate group, but the child who never hears his or her language in a classroom, who is forbidden to use a mother tongue on the playground, who must learn a second language to apply for a job or to fill out a legal form is not likely to consider the forbidden language a hidden treasure. Belief in the value of the mother tongue, on the other hand, carries with it a desire to use the heretofore despised language for public functions where it was previously not used. Witness the proud use of Dutch on the floor of the Belgian Parliament by Flemings perfectly able to make their speeches in French.

Lesson Four: Linguistic equilibrium is at best ephemeral in a society where languages are in contact.

Language planning in modern Belgium started with the outlawing of "bilingualism in education" and has led to a complete restructuring of what was once a unitary nation-state. That this centrifugal evolution has produced fragmentation at the price of only partial linguistic stability is a reality in a country where contact on the language line remains tense, where provisions for the education of immigrant children may be in conflict with national law, where the spread of a language such as English looms as a threat. It is the juxtaposition of this instability with Belgium's position as an international capital that surprises, but then so does the fact of the linguistic revolution that has already taken place.

BIBLIOGRAPHY

Annuaire Statistique de la Belgique 33. 1903. Brussels: J. B. Stevens.
Annuaire Statistique de la Belgique et du Congo Belge 44. 1914. Brussels: A. Lesigne.
———— 58. 1958. Gand: Vanderpoorten.
Annuaire Statistique de la Belgique 100. 1980. Brussels: Institut National de Statistique.
Armstrong, C. A. 1965. "The Language Question in the Low Countries: The Use of French and Dutch by the Dukes of Burgundy and Their Administration." In *Europe and the Late Middle Ages*, ed. E. R. Hales et al. Evanston, Ill.: Northwestern University, pp. 387–409.
Baeten, R., and A. Verdoodt. 1984. "Les besoins en langues modernes/étrangères en Belgique et leur enseignement." *Courrier Hebdomadaire du CRISP*, 1026–1027.
Baetens-Beardsmore, H. 1971. *Le français régional de Bruxelles*. Institut de Phonétique, Conférence et Travaux. Vol. 3. Brussels: Presses Universitaires de Bruxelles.

Balsa, C. M. 1984. "Les communautés étrangères en Belgique. Le statut et les fonctions de l'enseignment des langues et des cultures." *Revue de la Direction Générale de l'Organisation des Etudes* 19, 1 (January 1984): 11–24.

Bastenier, A., and F. Dassetto. 1981. "La deuxième génération d'immigrés en Belgique." *Courrier Hebdomadaire du CRISP*, 907–908 (January 23).

Boelen, S.S.H.M. (1972). "De nederlandse taal in Vlaanderen." In *Taal of Talltje*, ed. Guido Gaerts. Leuven: Acco.

Boon, H. 1969. *Enseignement primaire et alphabétisation dans l'agglomeration de Bruxelles de 1830 à 1879*. Louvain: Publications Universitaires de Louvain.

Brassine, J., and Y. Kreins. 1984. "La réforme de l'Etat et la communauté germanophone." *Courrier Hebdomadaire du CRISP*, 1028–1029 (February 10).

Bulletin communal, rapport annuel (1962). Archives de la ville de Bruxelles.

Bustamante, H., M. van Overbeke, and A. Verdoodt. 1978. Bilingual Education in Belgium." In *Case Studies in Bilingual Education*, eds. B. Spolsky and R. L. Cooper. Rowley, Mass.: Newbury House.

Centre de recherche pour la solution nationale des problèmes sociaux, politiques et juridiques en regions wallonnes et flamandes. 1948–54. 326 typewritten documents. (Harmel Center.)

Clough, S. B. (1930) 1968. *A History of the Flemish Movement. A Study in Nationalism*. New York: Octagon Books.

Cneudt, R. de. 1918. *De vervlaamsching van het lager onderwijs in groot Brussel*. Brussels: A Hessens.

Cohen, G. 1905. "Le parler belge." *Rapport présenté au Congrès pour l'extension et la culture de la langue française*. Liège (September 10–13). Reprinted in *Skandinavisk Månadsrevy* 9 (April 1906): 163–68.

Conseil de l'Europe. 1983. "Symposium sur la formation initiale et continué des enseignants de langues vivantes." (Conclusions et recommandations.) *Revue de la Direction Générale de l'Organisation des Etudes* 18, 10 (December): 5–12.

Counson, A. 1922. "Le français en Belgique et les écoles wallonnes à l'époque de la Renaissance." *Mélanges G. Lanson*. Paris: Hachette.

Daumont, F. 1911. *Le mouvement flamand*. 2 vols. Brussels: Societé Belge de Librairie.

Dawes, T. R. 1902. *Bilingual Teaching in Belgian Schools*. Cambridge: Cambridge University Press.

DeCroly, Ovid. 1929. "Réflexions et enquêtes à propos du bilinguisme." *Le bilinguisme et l'éducation*. Travaux de la conférence international tenue à Luxembourg du 2 au 5 avril 1928. Geneva: Bureau International d'Education, pp. 53–61.

"Le dédoublement linguistique de l'Université de Bruxelles." 1969. *Courrier Hebdomadaire du CRISP*, nos. 458, 463.

Dejean, C., and C-L. Binnemans. 1971. *Université belge: du pari au défi*. Brussels: Editions de l'Institut de Sociologie. Université libre de Bruxelles.

Destree, J. (1912) 1968. *La lettre au Roi sur la séparation de la Wallonie et de la Flandre*. Gembloux: Wallonie Libre.

Dhondt, J. 1947. "Essai sur l'origine de la frontière linguistique." In *L'Antiquité Classique* 16:261–86.

Dossier 5/68/CP. "Bestuur Gemeenschappelijke Diensten voor Nationale Opvoeding en Nederlandse Cultuur—Taalinspectie."

Draye, H. 1942. *De studie van de Vlaamsch-Waalsche taalgrenslijn in Belgie*. Brussels: Standaard-Boekhandel.

Elias, H. J. 1969. *Vijfentwintig jaar Vlaamse beweging, 1914–1939.* 4 vols. Antwerp: Der Nederlandsche Boekhandel.

European Court of Human Rights. 1967–68. *Case Relating to Certain Aspects of the Laws on the Use of Language in Belgium.* 2 vols. Strasbourg: Registry of the Court, Council of Europe.

Francis, J. 1974. *Lettre ouverte à trois millions cent quatre-vingt cent dix-huit Wallons.* Brussels: Musin.

Geyl, Pieter. 1952. *From Ranke to Toynbee: Five Lectures on Historians and Historiological Problems.* Smith College Studies in History, Vol. 39. Northampton, Mass.: Smith College.

————. 1955. *Debates with Historians.* London: B. T. Barsford.

Gillouin, R. 1930. *De l'Alsace à la Flandre: le mysticisme linguistique.* Paris: Editions Promethee.

Govaert, S. 1982. "La flandre et les pays-bas: rapports nouveaux." *Courrier Hebdomadaire du CRISP,* 960–961 (April 30).

Grève, M. de. 1980. "Le français au Benelux." *Le Soir* (March 8), p. 1.

Guicciardini, L. (1567) 1943. *Belgique 1567.* Eds. Paul Ciselet and Marie Delcourt. Brussels: Office de Publicité.

Hanse, J., A. Doppagne, and H. Bourgeois-Gielen. 1974. *Nouvelle chasse aux belgicismes.* Brussels: Charles Plisnier.

Haugen, H. 1972. *The Ecology of Language.* Stanford, Calif.: Stanford University Press.

Hermans, M., and P. Verjans. 1983. "Les origines de la querelle fouronnaise." *Courrier Hebdomadaire du CRISP,* 1019 (December 2).

ILEA (Inner London Education Authority). 1982. *1981 Language Census.* RS 811/82.

Juste, T. 1844. *Essai sur l'histoire de l'instruction publique en Belgique depuis les temps les plus reculés jusqu'à nos jours.* Brussels: Librairie Nationale.

Kurth, G. 1896–98. *La frontière linguistique en Belgique et dans le nord de la France.* 2 vols. Brussels: Société Belge de Librairie.

Leenen, J., and R. Clayes. 1972. "De nederlandse taal in Vlaanderen." In *Taal of Taaltje?,* ed. Guido Geerts. Leuven: Acco.

Meillet, A., and A. Sauvageot. 1934. "Le bilinguisme des hommes cultivés." *Conférence de l'Institut de Linguistique.* Paris.

Meillet, A., and L. Tesnière. 1928. *Les langues dans l'Europe nouvelle.* Paris: Payot.

Ministère de l'Instruction Publique. 1953. *Rapport Triennal 1948–1950.* Brussels: Ministère de l'Instruction Publique.

Nérum, C. J. van. 1838. *Essai sur l'instruction primaire et en particulier sur les écoles gratuites de Gand.* Gand: Annoot-Braeckman.

Olyff, F. 1940–44. *La question des langues en Belgique: Etude historique à la recherche d'une solution saine et définitive.* Hasselt: Les Editions du Moulin.

Ombiaux, M. des. 1920. *Psychologie d'une capitale, Bruxelles.* Brussels: Librairie Moderne.

Pée, Willem. 1970. "Het algemeen nederlands in Vlaanderen." In *Taal en Dialekt.* Amsterdam: N. V. Noord-Hollandsche Uitgevers Maatschappij.

Picard, L. 1942–59. *Geschiedenis van de vlaamsche en Groot-Nederlandsche beweging.* 2 vols. Antwerp: De Sikkel.

Pirenne, H. 1928. *La Belgique et la guerre mondiale.* New Haven, Conn.: Yale University Press.

————. 1922–32. *Histoire de Belgique.* 7 vols. Brussels: M. Lamertin.

Roosens, E. 1981. "The Multicultural Nature of Contemporary Belgian Society: The Immigrant Community." In *Conflict and Coexistence in Belgium: The Dynamics of a Divided Society*, ed. A. Lijphart. Berkeley: University of California, pp. 61–92.

Rundle, S. 1946. *Language as a Social and Political Factor in Europe*. London: Faber and Faber.

Segers, G. 1907. *Onze taal in het middelbaar onderwijs*. Ghent: A. Siffer.

Serrure, C. P. 1859–60. "Pieter Heyns en het schoolwezen te Antwerpen," *Vaderlandsch Museum* 3, pp. 293–404.

Simenon, G. 1932. *La maison du canal*. Paris: Fayard.

Sluys, A. 1939. *Mémoires d'un pédagogue*. Brussels: Editions de la Ligue de l'Enseignement.

Stengers, J. 1959. *La réformation de la fortière linguistique en Belgique ou de la légitimaté de l'hypothèse historique*. Brussels-Berchen: Latomus.

Swing, E. S. 1980. *Bilingualism and Linguistic Segregation in the Schools of Brussels*. Publication B 95. Quebec: International Center for Research on Bilingualism.

Temmerman, H. 1898. *De moedertaal eenig doelmatig voertuigt der gedachte in opvoeding en onderwijs*. Ghent: Siffer.

Toussaint, N. 1929. "Problèmes et expériences." *Le bilinguisme et l'éducation*. Travaux de la conférence international tenue à Luxembourg du 2 au 5 avril 1928. Geneva: Bureau International d'Education, pp. 146–56.

———. 1935. *Bilinguisme et éducation*. Brussels: M. Lamertin.

De transmutatie klassen. 1956. Brussels: August Vermeylen-Fonds.

Valkhoff, M. 1944. *L'expansion du néerlandais*. Trans. Jules Sepulchre. Brussels: Les Editions Lumiere.

Vanderkerckove, R. G. 1969. *L'admission progressive de la langue néerlandaise dans les textes officièle en Belgique*. Brussels: UGA.

Vansiliette, M. ca. 1950. "Note concernant la repartition des classes primaires et gardiennes de langue flamande dans l'agglomération bruxelloise." In *Centre de recherche*, no. 153.

Verheyen, J. E. 1929. "Le bilinguisme en Belgique." *Le bilingualisme et l'éducation*. Travaux de la conférence tenue à Luxembourg du 2 au 4 avril 1928. Geneva: Bureau International d'Education, pp. 137–45.

Verlooy, J.B.C. (1788) 1938. *Verhandeling op d'onacht der moederlyke tael in de Nederlanden*. Antwerp: De Sikkel.

Wezemael, J. van. 1937. *Bruxelles: Trait d'union ou pomme de discorde*. Brussels: Le Rouge et le Noir.

Willemsen, A. W. 1958. *Het Vlaams-Nationalisme, 1914–1940*. Groningen: J. B. Wolters.

Wilmars, D. 1968. *De psychologie van het franstalige in Vlaanderen: De achtergrond van de taalstrijd*. Antwerp: Standaard Uitgeverij.

5

Xavier Albó

BILINGUALISM IN BOLIVIA

Present-day Bolivia is a landlocked country in the heart of the Andean region of South America, with an area of 1,098,581 square kilometers but a population of only 6,257,721 (1984 estimate).

The country is divided into two distinct ecological zones—the Andean and the Amazonian. Approximately three-quarters of the population live in the Andean zone, which covers only slightly more than one-third of Bolivian territory and is divided in turn into two subzones—the Altiplano (lit. "high plain"), a large plateau 3,600 to 4,200 meters above sea level, with mountain ranges easily exceeding 6,000 meters (21 percent of the country); and the Valles Interandinos (intermontane valleys), a complex, rugged network of mountains and generally narrow valleys extending eastward toward the Amazon region, with heights typically over 2,000 meters but often varying between 4,000 and 1,000 meters in altitude. These valleys occupy 16 percent of the area of the country. Lastly, there are the vast Llanos Orientales (eastern plains, also referred to as the Oriente), with extensions to the north and southeast. The Llanos cover 63 percent of the country, although only one-fourth of the population lives there. Most of the plains area belongs to the Amazon system, but has a tropical or semitropical climate and ecology. The drier southeastern section belongs to the Chaco region, which is part of the La Plata Basin. Excluding the new center of development around Santa Cruz, the second largest city of Bolivia, population densities of less than one person per square kilometer are found in the Llanos; in the Andean zone, on the other hand, densities of ten to twenty inhabitants per square kilometer are frequent, but there are variations ranging from a maximum of a little over one hundred inhabitants per square kilometer in the central valleys of Cocha-

Translated from Spanish by Lee Puig-Antich.

bamba Department and around Lake Titicaca in the Altiplano to less than one inhabitant per square kilometer in the arid Altiplano Sur (southern plateau).

The human geography corresponds to this major ecological and demographic division. The Andean region of Altiplano and Valles is populated basically by people of Andean origin. Today people of Aymara language and origin predominate in the Altiplano and Puna (the area above the limit of vegetation, about 15,000 feet), with extensions into the Valles and Yungas (steep, semitropical valleys sometimes treated as a separate region) nearest La Paz, while present-day Quechua speakers predominate in the Valles, with extensions to the Altiplano Sur and the easternmost part of Oruro Department. The Llanos Orientales, on the other hand, are populated by people of selva (jungle) origin, together with the majority of those of Spanish origin. The latter also occupy some of the intermontane valleys in the Departments of Tarija, Santa Cruz, and the edge of Chuquisaca. The entirety is interspersed with the urban population, where a dominant tendency toward the Spanish language and culture generally coexists with, and exerts pressure on, a population of Quechua or Aymara origin (usually somewhat over 50 percent). Only three cities in Bolivia exceed three hundred thousand (1984 projection)—one in each ecological area—and together they contain only 24 percent of the population. Secondary cities have 8 percent of the population, and towns with over two thousand inhabitants, 10 percent. The remainder (59 percent) live in rural settings that are even smaller (data from the last census, taken in 1976).

HISTORICO-LINGUISTIC EVOLUTION

Since ancient times, the historical evolution of the Andean region has proceeded separately from that of the Llanos Orientales, although contact between the areas has intensified. In the pre-Inca era, the tropical region was inhabited by small autonomous groups of diverse linguistic origins. There is archaeological evidence that one of these groups developed an important agricultural civilization in the Moxos area (today Beni Department), with a population of perhaps two hundred thousand (Denevan, 1966). In the fifteenth and sixteenth centuries, several waves of Guarani arrived from the east and southeast. Fusing with the ancient Chane population, they gave rise to the new Chiriguano group in the foothills of the Andes and to minor groups further north (Saignes, 1974). Altogether there were more than forty ethnic groups, with little articulation among them, in the Oriente.

The Andean region had a denser, more homogeneous, and more articulated population, which inhabited elevated, protected areas. One of the oldest groups is probably the Uru, who lived off fish and waterfowl along the interior basin running lengthwise through the Altiplano (Wachtel, 1978). Between 600 and 1200 A.D., a civilization centered in Tihuanaco, near Lake Titicaca (the organization of which is still not well understood), flourished, and expanded throughout a large part of the area occupied by present-day Bolivia and Peru. The linguistic structure from this period is not known. There were undoubtedly many local languages, now lost, but whose existence is attested by toponyms. Puquina and Uru were probably the dominant languages, perhaps in Tihuanaco also. But at a relatively late date, *Jaqi Aru* (literally "human language") began to take over. Today known as Aymara, Jaqi Aru apparently arrived from the north and may be related to Huari culture (Torero, 1970). Little by little, control was established by agricultural populations organized in *ayllus*, which were based on real or fictitious patrilineal descent from a common ancestor. The Uru were reduced to a subordinate ethnosocial group within the *ayllu*. The *ayllus* were grouped in turn into about ten ethnic units or domains on the Bolivian side of Lake Titicaca in addition to others on the Peruvian side. These units were organized into larger confederations having a bipartite structure, the function of which remains unknown (Bouysse-Cassagner, 1978; Platt, in press).

Neither the *ayllu* nor the ethnic domain occupied contiguous territory but was scattered across various locations in order to gain access to a maximum number of ecological niches (Murra, 1975). Consequently, various ethnic groups were able to coexist in each location, resulting in a high degree of linguistic intermingling. In the fifteenth century, the Inca conquest took place from Cuzco (where the Incas had gone after Titicaca). The framework described above was left intact, but it was integrated into a higher level of state organization called Twantinsuyu, "the four united suyu." The Andean section from Cuzco southward was the Qullasuyu; the lower area, toward the selva, was called Antisuyu and was paired with the Qullasuyu. The Antisuyu was never penetrated deeply by the Inca. For their political and economic ends, the Inca enlarged the framework in which access to distant places could be gained. Thus, there were great relocations of populations, called *mitma*, together with their respective languages. In addition, for administrative purposes, there were officials of the Empire throughout the area who spoke *Runa Simi* (literally "human language"), today called Quechua or Quichua. The language was spoken in the region in which the Inca had originated and was later converted into a state language. The expansion of this language throughout present-day Bolivia is due primarily to the dual Inca administrative and relocation policies, and was carried out only in the century prior to the Spanish invasion.

The situation changed with the invasion of the Spaniards in the sixteenth century. Since the Andean people were an important source of labor for the mines (especially in Potosi) and the new *haciendas* and cities, they became bound to specific localities, even though the majority continued to live in communities directly descended from the old *ayllu*. The former multiplicity of ethnic identities began to be lost, with the result that everyone was reduced to the caste or ethnosociocultural group of "Indian" or "native." A stratified, intermediate group of mestizos or "cholos" also arose, with the Spaniards and their Creole descendants establishing themselves at the pinnacle of the social hierarchy. At the same time, this geographical and social hardening, together with the need to facilitate the missionary effort, led to greater linguistic consolidation. Initially, the ecclesiastical authorities planned sermons, catechisms, and other materials in three "general" languages (or lingua francas)—Quechua, Aymara, and Puquina. Puquina soon lost its importance because its speakers were assimilated to one of the other languages. Aymara was consolidated principally in the Altiplano, while Quechua was established in the Valles, where the old *ayllu* organization was weaker. It was also easier for people from other regions to migrate to the Valles, and as they settled on the *haciendas*, their former identity began to be lost.

Colonization in the Llanos Orientales had characteristics of its own. Arriving from Paraguay, the main Spanish contingent settled around Santa Cruz and maintained relatively weak relations with the rest of the Audiencia of Charcas (extending over present-day Bolivia), to which it belonged. Penetration into other parts of the Oriente was due above all to the missionaries. The *reducciones* (enforced settlements of converted Indians) of Moxos and Chiquitos, which were run by the Jesuits according to the model already flourishing in Paraguay and adjoining regions, became renowned throughout the north. In these *reducciones* there arose a new culture—a hybrid created from missionary and native elements—which melded the many previous groups (Parejas, 1976). The chief towns in the Oriente today owe their origin to these *reducciones*, as indicated by their religious names: Trinidad, San Ignacio, and so on. Even some varieties of the old languages centered about the missions still bear these names (Trinitario, Ignaciano). Some groups remained apart from the Spaniards, and, with one group, the Chiriguanos, there was a permanent conflict over borders. The missionaries never managed to fully establish themselves in Chiriguano territory, and the complete conquest (not without elements of genocide) was only achieved in 1892, well within the republican period. Since that time, the Chiriguano population has remained extremely low (one-tenth of the original), similar to the effects of the Spanish invasion in other regions (Calzavarini, 1980).

Since the formation of the Bolivian republic in 1825, the following developments have taken place. In the second half of the nineteenth century, it began to be possible to implement the "liberal" program (in Bolivia as well as in Peru and other countries). This involved transforming the old Andean *comunidad* (indigenous community with membership usually based on descent and having some communal features) into small plots of marketable land which were then exposed to the greed of unscrupulous new landowners. In a few decades the community lands were reduced from approximately 66 percent to 22 percent, and the majority of the *comunarios* swelled the ranks of the *hacienda* peons, who were subject to a kind of feudal labor system. This resulted in further stereotyping of Indians as a group (the "*indiada*"), and in continued discrimination. In the Oriente the great cattle ranches had been continuing their advance since the expulsion of the Jesuits at the end of the eighteenth century. Here also the native population—constantly declining—received discriminatory treatment. After the defeats of 1875 and 1892, the Guarani people suffered similar vicissitudes. Nevertheless, a few pockets of *comunidades* still remained in various areas of the Altiplano and Oriente.

The economy of Bolivia, like that of the Audiencia of Charcas, has been based primarily on the export of minerals—first silver and since the end of the nineteenth century, tin. As well as affecting the growth and decline of many towns, this activity has caused shifts in workers, capital, and commercial undertakings. About half of the cities and large towns in Bolivia owe their origin and present livelihood to some kind of mining activity. At the linguistic level, these processes, in addition to greater Hispanization, have contributed to the advance of Quechua in former Aymara areas of the Altiplano, principally around Oruro and Potosi. There is a clear correlation between the location of the mines, the advance of mine-related railroads, and the lines of penetration by Quechua.

The twentieth century, especially since the Revolution of 1952, has seen a restructuring of Bolivian territory and society. This, in turn, has had sociolinguistic consequences. After the defeat in the Chaco, in which a large portion of the uninhabited southeast was lost to Paraguay (recalling the loss of the coastal lands in 1879 and the northern rubber regions in 1900), there arose a new national consciousness which sought greater integration of all social strata in the country and better utilization of the lowlands. These issues culminated in the government established in 1952. The rural masses recovered their lands with the Agrarian Reform of 1953; they were integrated into political and labor activities and partially incorporated into the dominant economy; and finally, they drew nearer to the dominant culture through a new network of rural schools. These changes also accelerated migration to the cities, and on the linguistic level, greater access to Spanish, the official language. To encourage growth in the Llanos, new channels of communication, resettlement programs, and injections of capital were initiated. As a result, important new development has arisen around Santa Cruz, which in three decades has become the second largest city in the country, with more than four hundred thousand inhabitants (the largest is La Paz, with approximately 1 million). Although the "march to the Oriente" has not involved the numbers of people originally hoped for, about one hundred thousand rural families from the "colla" region (the Altiplano and in particular, the Valles) have been established in newly opened agricultural areas, thereby bringing about the advance of the Aymara and Quechua boundaries (through La Paz, and Cochabamba and Santa Cruz, respectively). However, in these areas, which are predominantly Spanish-speaking, the transplanted population rapidly becomes bilingual, especially in the succeeding generation.

THE SITUATION TODAY

The current outcome of these changes has the linguistic, socioeconomic, and geographic characteristics described below (Albó, 1980).

The Spanish Area

According to the last two censuses, 36 percent of the 1950 population of Bolivia claimed Spanish as their principal habitual language. Twenty-six years later, in 1976, 54 percent made this claim. That is, habitual speakers of Spanish increased at an annual rate of 3.69 percent. Since the rate of demographic growth in the country was 2.11 percent during this period, the annual rate of increase of habitual speakers was 1.58 percent higher than the rate of natural increase in the population. These figures must be interpreted cautiously, inasmuch as census questions pertaining to attitudes which concern prestige (such as speaking a dominant language or one that is discriminated against) elicit responses that tend to be exaggerated on the side of greater prestige, in this case Spanish. Nevertheless, the trend toward the expansion of Spanish is evident. At the same rate, almost the entire population would claim Spanish as their habitual language by the year 2015 (with exceptions mainly in rural parts of Chuquisaca and Potosi Departments).

Many of these people—about 45 percent in 1976—are bilingual. In that year, 68 percent of the population knew one of the indigenous languages, and at the same time, 77 percent claimed to know Spanish. Considering the prestige effect mentioned above, the first figure should probably be higher and the second, lower.

The trend toward Spanish needs no further elaboration, as it is the dominant and official language of the country. If the levels of Spanish are analyzed by age group, we find that this trend has been in existence in a systematic way for a long time but that it has accelerated since the 1952 Revolution, owing to a new rural economic structure, migrations to the city, and proliferation of schools in the countryside. According to present trends (which are probably exaggerated), by 1990 all children ten years of age will know at least rudimentary Spanish, and by the time they are grown—around the year 2040—it could be expected that the entire population, including rural dwellers, would know at least this much Spanish, except for the very old and those from remote areas.

Judging from these projections by age group, however, bilingualism will continue to be important. It will reach its peak around 1988. Afterwards it will gradually recede in favor of Spanish monolingualism, even in the rural sectors. In 2021, half of the rural ten year olds will probably still know an indigenous language in addition to Spanish; in 2074, only a third will know one of these languages; and by 2131, possibly all rural children will be Spanish monolinguals. It is foreseeable that fifty years later, in 2181, when these children are adults of sixty, the country will have reached a condition of Spanish monolingualism, with only marginal bilingual groups.

Projections based on data from the last century are of interest for determining future trends, but their value is probably relative. If the present linguistic policy persists, it is probable that as Spanish continues to expand, the rhythm of change will accelerate, thus shortening the intervals indicated above. But neither should we ignore the possibility that as Quechua and Aymara peasants gain greater access to formal education and to political and economic power, the opposite situation could arise—comparable to what took place with various European minorities or in the new African countries during the last two centuries. In this case, even if universal access to Spanish were not to decrease, bilingualism might increase, and the progression toward Spanish monolingualism would be slowed, although probably not stopped.

Hispanization, at least as a habitual language, is obviously stronger in the cities. It is almost impossible to survive there without knowing and using Spanish. This pressure is at its height in Santa Cruz, in the Llanos, where there is a long Spanish tradition. Until the 1950s Santa Cruz was relatively small and isolated. Almost everyone was a Spanish monolingual except for a few *patrones* (landowners) and their servants, who perhaps knew one of the eastern languages as well. But in 1954 a highway was opened which linked it to the rest of the country by way of Cochabamba. Shortly afterwards, two railroads connected Santa Cruz with Brazil and Argentina. The city and surrounding countryside were inundated with people and capital. As a consequence, the city has grown at an annual rhythm of 7.3 percent, so that by 1976, 40 percent of its population had originated elsewhere. Of those, approximately half came from rural areas of the department (already largely Spanish-speaking) and the other half from the Andean region, among whom are a substantial number of Quechua-speaking ex-peasants. However, as the latter are in the minority, they neither use their maternal language frequently nor teach it to their children born and raised in the new environment. As a result, only 13 percent of the present residents of Santa Cruz know one of the indigenous languages (mainly Quechua).

On the other hand, the pressure to use Spanish in the cities of the Andean, or "colla," region (La Paz, Oruro, Cochabamba, Potosi, Sucre, as well as smaller towns), although it exists, is less strong. In these cities a little more than half the population, including large groups living in the city for several generations, know Aymara (dominant in La Paz; a minority language in Oruro) or Quechua (in the remainder). There are few monolinguals in indigenous languages (usually the elderly or new arrivals) because of the environmental pressures already indicated. All in all, it is evident that Spanish largely prevails in the urban setting, especially in the public arena.

In addition, there is a section of the country which is fundamentally Spanish-speaking in both its urban and rural areas. It covers the greater part of the Oriente and extends along the southeast to a region of valleys going from Tarija to Valle Grande (Santa Cruz Department). In this area, a large majority knows and speaks Spanish. Exceptions include: (1) the northernmost part of the country (Pando Department) where 20 percent habitually speak Portuguese owing to Brazilian influence; (2) a regionwide minority—between 56,000 and 132,000 according to estimates (about 10 percent)—which knows or speaks one of the indigenous languages of the Oriente; and finally, (3) the "colonization" areas (population resettlements) of Santa Cruz, where the new settlers are usually of Quechua

(12.4 percent) or, to a lesser extent, Aymara (1.8 percent) origin. In the north the linguistic boundary is being pressured on the east by Portuguese; in the central area it is being pressured on the west by colonization. On the other hand, the southeastern boundary is slowly advancing toward the northwest. A pocket has been created there, where the people, although not bilingual, use a form of colloquial Spanish with Quechua suffixes (known locally as *Llapuni*). Speakers say, for example:

Vendrás*chu?*	Vendré*llapuni*
('Vendrás?	Claro que vendré!')
[Will you come?	Of course, I will!]

In the rest of the country, that is, most of the Andean region and its smaller urban centers, Spanish is definitely a minority language, although it maintains high prestige. It is somewhat stronger in the principal mining centers, even though one or another Andean language is regularly used in the home and in the mines (and also for religious rites). However, Spanish is usually used for meetings, including labor meetings, and other public activities. In other places the presence of Spanish is even weaker. It is dominant only in the artificial environment of the school, where its use is obligatory. Even in many nonpeasant towns, which attempt to maintain their distinctiveness and superiority both socially and culturally with respect to the surrounding rural communities, Spanish prevails only at the public level, whenever it becomes desirable to emphasize these differences.

Various geographic and social dialects can be distinguished within Bolivian Spanish. Geographically, the three most conspicuous dialects are Colla, spoken in the Andean regions, Camba, spoken in the Oriente, and Chapaco, spoken in the southeast, especially in Tarija Department. Colla has various characteristics in common with other highland regions of Latin America, for example, the use of a sibilated *r* [z], as well as a number of traits derived from the Andean substrata. Some of these traits are found at any social level, for example, postpositive *ps* (for "pues") ("well" or "therefore" in the standard meaning; other uses dialectally); and *habia* + *-Vdo* (pluperfect tense form) to denote lack of personal knowledge. Others, however, are indicative of a type of colloquial Spanish associated with the lower classes. For example, the sentence, "De la Maria su marido esta en ahi" [Maria's husband is over there] contains several traits borrowed from Quechua and Aymara. Camba has many characteristics typical of hot lowland areas of South America, such as suppression of final or intervocalic *s*. In addition, it incorporates many words from eastern languages, including some endings (e.g., the diminutive *-inga*). The principal characteristics of Chapaco are its intonation, in which long and short syllables are marked, and the survival of many archaic Spanish expressions which have been lost in other regions. These traits are more pronounced in rural areas and are therefore the basis of social dialects. One of these dialects, nearer the Quechua boundary, is the previously mentioned Llapuni.

First, Spanish predominates in the areas of official and professional activities, modern technology, written and printed materials, formal education, and certain mass media (the press and television, in particular), as well as in material imported from other countries. As far as official activities are concerned, the advantage of raising the other national languages to official status has been discussed on various occasions. However, such a step has never been proposed, let alone implemented. In practice, the great majority of activities on the official level are carried out in Spanish, except for those referred to below.

Second, the professions and modern technology have also been cornered by Spanish. The monopoly held by the dominant sector on access to higher education, written material, and technical and academic advances, together with the indisputable fact that Spanish is one of the international languages, contributes to the sole development of Spanish in modern technical and academic fields. The other national languages are unquestionably capable of development in these areas, as were Spanish and German when they supplanted Latin, or languages that have gained official status in the new ex-colonial countries. However, the present configuration of social forces does not favor such a development, with the result that the Spanish monopoly in these areas is assured.

Third, written and, particularly, printed materials are almost exclusively in Spanish. The same monopoly exists in the educational system owing to the explicit policy of nearly all governments since the colonial era. The inclusion of the native language in educational programs has occasionally been discussed, but either has not reached a practicable level or has been limited to small experiments in the early grades in selected rural areas. As a result of this policy, the population that knows how to write only knows how to write in Spanish. Even the possibility of reading in another language is nonexistent. The main exceptions are some of the religious, didactic, and expressive literature. One national weekly regularly includes a column in Aymara (or sometimes Quechua), and three popular monthlies include sections in Quechua.

Other functional areas in which the dominance of Spanish is out of proportion to its number of speakers include politics and other channels of social communication, business and commercial networks, and other public services. What is noteworthy here is not that Spanish dominates (which has always been true), but that it no longer holds absolute dominion. In the last few decades, probably as a side-effect of the social transformations engendered by the 1952 Revolution, the indigenous languages have created a place for themselves in these areas. The only place where Spanish controls almost all the activity is in television, the newest means of communication. But even there Andean languages are occasionally used for certain programs and commercials. On the other hand, native languages have frequently been used in Bolivian cinema, which, although small in output, has achieved worldwide recognition for excellence. Likewise, radio, which until the 1950s broadcast almost exclusively in Spanish, now devotes ample air-time to Quechua and Aymara, with some stations specializing in these languages (see below).

The Andean languages obviously predominate in rural areas and, hence, among people engaged in agriculture. Within the cities, however, the differences in Spanish dominance are related to occupation. Except for rural teachers, professionals have the highest incidence of Spanish monolingualism. Less obvious is the fact that the other most Hispanicized occupational group (at times even more so than the professionals) are the office workers. At the other extreme in the urban world are the two areas in which bilingualism predominates—small business and the various craft occupations—although distinctions need to be made along occupational lines. A machinist (more Hispanicized) is not comparable to an embroiderer (more Aymarized); nor is a shopkeeper in the center of town comparable to the operator of a market stall. The craft occupations constitute the greatest percentage of the economically active population and represent to a great extent the informal sector of the economy, where a large part of the urban lower and lower middle class is found. They are numerically of greater importance than salaried workers in a country as little industrialized and undercapitalized as Bolivia. However, merchants who are bilingual are more successful, as they are able to develop favorable relations with customers of all kinds. This advantage becomes a necessity when their business requires frequent dealings between town and country. Comparable to the situation of the merchants is that of the workers engaged in transportation. Many truckers are also businessmen and, as such, belong to the group of bilinguals. But among urban transport workers properly speaking (taxi drivers, bus drivers, etc.), the prestige of Spanish prevails, even though many are bilingual by virtue of their social origin. A similar situation arises with domestic workers, who dominate the urban female workforce. Almost all are of rural origin and are generally unmarried. Many learn Spanish only after arrival in the city, but once well established in their new role, they readily switch to Spanish. Their constant presence in homes where Spanish is almost the only language undoubtedly reinforces this attitude while simultaneously raising their status vis-à-vis other rural women. However, migrants to Bolivian cities do not experience the linguistic and cultural shock that occurs in large cities like Lima and Buenos Aires, where women arriving from the country are able to survive only by making a total break (including mode of dress) with their original culture.

The Quechua Area

The second most important language in Bolivia is Quechua, even though it was largely introduced into the region during the few decades of Inca domination of the Qullasuyu, and consolidated even later, during the colonial period. In 1950, it was the habitual language of 36.5 percent of Bolivians, thus occupying first place over Spanish by a narrow margin. By 1976, however, only 26 percent claimed to prefer its use in the home, although 38 percent of the population still knew the language. Because it is a language of oppressed groups and therefore has less social prestige, these percentages are probably somewhat too low. In the interval between the two censuses, the absolute number of habitual Quechua speakers rose at an annual rate of 9.7 percent, but when the rapid population growth is taken into account, the relative importance of Quechua throughout the country declined by 1.3 percent annually.

Although it has important variants which at times could be considered distinct languages, Quechua is also spoken in other countries, from Santiago del Estero in northern Argentina, along the entire Peruvian and Ecuadorian sierra, to southern Colombia, where it is known as Inga. Thus, Quechua is by far the most widespread of the Amerindian languages and the one with the greatest number of speakers.

Half of the Bolivians who habitually speak Quechua live in the Department of Cochabamba. Potosi Department has 28 percent; Chuquisaca, 13 percent; and the remainder are almost equally divided among northern La Paz, eastern Oruro, and the colonized areas of Santa Cruz Departments.

Dialectically, Bolivian Quechua belongs to Quechua II, within which it is a simplified variant of Cusco Quechua (Torero, 1965). Even more than Cusco Quechua, it shows clear influences from Aymara, not only in the series of glottal stops (*p'*, *t'*, etc.) but also in vocabulary. There is not much dialectal variety within Bolivia, and problems of mutual intelligibility never arise. The main difference occurs between the Quechua of northern La Paz, which is much closer to the Cusco variant, and the rest of Bolivian Quechua. A purer form has been maintained in Chuquisaca and Potosi, although in some areas in northern Potosi, a recent change due to Aymara has been noted, that is, the use of suffixes like -*t'a*- instead of the Quechua -*ri*-. The most highly evolved variants are those of Cochabamba, which spread out from there with migrating miners and merchants to parts of Oruro and the mining district. In this dialect, innovations such as -*chaq* and -*sqa*- (instead of -*chis* and -*sha*-) have been introduced, and in addition, the influence of Spanish is much stronger at every level. For this reason it is sometimes characterized as ''Quechuanol'' (Quechua-español). Innovations of this kind have generated various social dialects within Quechua, of which ''Patron'' variants or those of the nonrural social groups most closely resemble the Cochabamban. The influence of Spanish is also very strong in urban areas, particularly in grammatical constructions incorporating various Spanish elements. One of the urban variants, Quechua radio speech, while portraying these grammatical characteristics, attempts to form new words from Quechua roots but with semantic areas borrowed from Spanish (Albó, 1974).

Quechua coexists with Aymara in two regions—northern Potosi, including parts of Oruro, and northern La Paz. In several cantons more than half the population knows both languages, without counting those who have learned Spanish in school or through travel.

The Oruro-Potosi situation of bi- and trilingualism has resulted in marked linguistic stratification. Spanish is at the apex of the hierarchy but at the same time is the language of the "others," the domineering *q'ara*. In second place is Quechua, considered to be the language of merchants, miners, and business transactions; and finally, Aymara, the language of farmers, especially in areas containing *ayllus* (indigenous *comunidades*). The two languages are also intertwined on the ecological level—Aymara prevails in the highlands and Quechua in the valleys, where formerly there were many more *haciendas*. Because they travel more, the men learn Quechua more easily, even if they are of Aymara origin. Analogous situations, with a similar ecological intermingling, occur in northern La Paz, but the social stratification is reversed. After Spanish, which is hardly spoken there, the language of prestige and commerce is Aymara, which extends down from Lake Titicaca and the capital through the highland *punas*; the least prestigious language is the Quechua of the valleys. Trilingualism or Quechua-Aymara bilingualism is less frequent there, although a situation has been created in which Quechua and Aymara speakers manage to understand each other while speaking their own language. For reasons already mentioned, Aymara is retreating before the Quechua advance in the Oruro-Potosi area, while in northern La Paz the opposite is occurring.

From the functional standpoint, Quechua has been frequently used in political activity since the 1952 Revolution. The Agrarian Reform of the following year originated in the intense popular movements in the Cochabamba valleys, and since then the peasant labor movement, led for many years by that region, has been an important component in national politics, regardless of ideology. In 1945, a Bolivian president, Colonel Gualberto Villarroel, who was a native of a Cochabamba town, convened the First National Indigenous Congress where he addressed the gathering in Quechua. Twenty years later another military president, René Barrientos, who was from a neighboring town, became famous for his frequent trips through the countryside where, besides speaking in Quechua, he participated in many other cultural activities—food, dancing, the *compadrazgo* relationship (ritual kinship system), and so on. But the principal use of Quechua in the political sphere is in the demonstrations and organizations of the peasants themselves and, to a lesser extent, of the miners and urban lower classes. Quechua also has a significant place in the radio broadcasts of the area. It is the most frequently used language on various educational stations, which have developed such creative programs as serial dramatizations, song contests, and other expressions of popular culture. In the populated valleys of Cochabamba and the mining districts there are a considerable number of local stations with frequent programming in Quechua. This language is also heard over many stations in the city, especially in the morning. Even some of the largest stations in La Paz, in the heart of the Aymara zone, have some morning programs in Quechua.

The Aymara Area

Aymara is the third most frequently spoken language of Bolivia and the second most frequently spoken Amerindian language at the present time. In 1950, 25 percent of the population used it habitually as opposed to only 19 percent in 1976 (although 28 percent knew it). In absolute numbers, habitual speakers of Aymara increased at an annual rate of 1.14 percent between 1950 and 1976. Taking a population growth into account, this means that the proportion of total Aymara speakers relative to speakers of Spanish has decreased by 0.9 percent annually. However, since the annual rate of growth in the rural sections of the Altiplano is about 1 percent (because of infant mortality and migration), then in these areas Aymara is remaining stable and is probably penetrating urban areas through migration. The figures given for this language indicate a degree of language and cultural loyalty superior to that of Quechua, whose relative annual loss was 1.34 percent.

Geographically, Aymara is spoken from Lake Titicaca (including three hundred and fifty thousand speakers on the Peruvian side), along the entire Altiplano in the departments of La Paz and most of Oruro (except in the east where a wedge of Quechua has recently penetrated), to the northern part of the Salar de Uyuni (Uyuni Saltpan). In Potosi, Aymara is spoken in the Llica region, located north of the saltpan, and in the provinces comprising the region known as Norte de Potosi (northern Potosi), as far as Urmiri in the Province of Frias and another enclave further south. In these areas, Aymara enters into symbiosis with Quechua in the manner described in the preceding section. Outside the Altiplano, Aymara extends into the valleys throughout La Paz Department, where (as already mentioned) it is advancing on a Quechua enclave in the northernmost section. Nearer the central area, it is penetrating the warm regions of the Yungas and, recently, the new resettlement areas. Islands of Aymara persist in southern La Paz, eastern Oruro, and northern Potosi, as well as in highland areas of Cochabamba. However, in Cochabamba Aymara is receding before Quechua, which is advancing from the Valles.

As with Quechua, the dialectal differences in Aymara are not so great that they create problems of mutual intelligibility (Briggs, 1976). The main geographical distinction is between dialects around Oruro and Potosi, which could be considered peripheral and more conservative, and those of La Paz, which are more innovative and socially prestigious. La Paz, the most densely populated department, contains 83 percent of the habitual speakers of Aymara. Oruro has 11 percent; Potosi, 4.5 percent; and Cochabamba, 1.5 percent. The Puna varieties, located in Peru, resemble the peripheral southern dialects more than they do the innovative one of La Paz. The few thousand Aymaras on the Chilean side, opposite Oruro, speak another variety, which has been much more influenced by Spanish. On the other hand, the Spanish influence on the remaining Aymara dialects is much weaker than in Quechua. For example, it is not unusual to find the five Spanish vowels and the voiced stops b, d, g in the Quechuan phonological system (especially in Cochabamba), whereas the opposite has occurred in Aymara. Many bilinguals who speak Spanish fluently waiver in the use of these Spanish sounds. Differentiation has also developed among social dialects, principally in La Paz, which some authors have termed Patron, Missionary, and

Radio Aymara. All of these dialects are characterized by weakening of the deep structures of the language owing to loanwords from Spanish (Hardman, 1981).

The foregoing underscores the statistically verified fact that there is greater language and cultural loyalty in the case of Aymara. This phenomenon can be explained historically by the greater length of time in which Aymara, in contrast to Quechua, has been established on the Altiplano. It is also significant from the social standpoint that the Aymara Altiplano and the *ayllus* of northern Potosi have spearheaded many more movements for the restoration of Indian rights and that these have attached greater importance to the ethnocultural and historical components than similar movements occurring in Quechua areas. This was what happened in the great general uprising against the Spanish regime in 1780—the Katari brothers of northern Potosi and Tupaq Katari of La Paz promoted these features of the movement, whereas the Amaru [*sic*] on the Cusco Quechua side sought greater participation from the mestizos and creoles. In recent times, there is a clear contrast between the powerful new *Katarista* movement (see below) and the more populist and clientalistic character of the 1952 peasant movement in the Quechua valleys of Cochabamba. Nonetheless, throughout the southeast the Quechua language has been advancing at the expense of Aymara during the last two centuries, owing to the inferior occupational status of the Aymaras vis-à-vis the Quechua miners and tradespeople. At the same time northern Potosi, which was more centrally located and had greater agroeconomic importance in the colonial era (because of its proximity to the Potosi mine), is now separated from the principal communication routes, and many of its *ayllus*, having become isolated, have slipped into subsistence agriculture. Thus, while the Katari brothers spoke Aymara in Macha in 1780, their descendants now know only Quechua.

The functional uses of Aymara resemble those of Quechua, with the same contrasts and general distinctions made in connection with Spanish in the previous Quechua discussion. When it comes to politics, however, the language is more often used by the Aymaras themselves than by mestizo presidents. With the weakening after two decades of the program begun in the 1952 Revolution, a new movement arose, led by both Aymara peasants and migrants to La Paz. Significantly, this movement adopted the name *Katarista* in memory of the 1780 leader, Tupaq Katari. If the 1952 program came from a new and innovative government (undoubtedly spurred by the popular uprising in the Cochabamba *haciendas*), the point of departure for the Kataristas of the 1970s stems from the necessity of being taken into account and from lack of confidence in measures promulgated from above. This movement has been effective in leading the reorganization of the entire national peasant movement and in forming a new and independent syndicalism. As a symbolic gesture, some of its more "Indianist" branches even launched Aymara presidential candidates. In all sectors of the movement, the reclaiming of the cultural and linguistic heritage is considered to be very important, although the majority do not disassociate it from economic, social, and political change. This development is in line with other events not necessarily arising from the *Katarista* movement. For example, La Paz has witnessed the emergence of Aymara-led organizations—such as ILCA (Instituto de Lengua y Cultura Aymara—Institute for Aymara Language and Culture) and the university group, Memoria Comunitaria Aymara (Aymara Community Memory)—for the study of the Aymara language, culture, and history, some of which have branches in other regions. The Aymara presence on radio is also stronger than formerly. In La Paz, five out of twenty-one stations broadcast in Aymara for most of the day. Of these, only one is an educational station, and it is the only one that covers the entire rural sector. The others are small, privately owned commercial concerns, whose broadcasting power (and programming emphasis) allows them to reach only the Aymara audience of the city and its environs. This in itself is indicative of the weight that the Aymara language and culture carry in the capital city—a phenomenon further corroborated by the many Aymara celebrations in the city, including some of recent origin. What has been evolving might be termed the urban variant of Aymara culture, in which traditional Aymara elements and the new necessities and stimuli of the big city are achieving a synthesis that is highly fluid and open to innovation (Albó, Greaves, and Sandóval, 1983).

Other Languages and Cultural Groups

According to the last two censuses, the remainder of Bolivia's native groups have little demographic importance. In 1950, 2.9 percent were said to habitually speak other languages. By 1976, the percentage had dropped precipitously to 0.9 percent, implying an annual loss of about 1.9 percent in absolute terms and 4.4 percent in relative terms. Accordingly, the languages of these numerous minority groups would seem to be on the way to immediate extinction. But these census data must be interpreted in light of other data compiled by ethnologists specializing in the Bolivian Oriente.

The prospect of imminent extinction is much more evident in groups with fewer speakers. An ethnographic recount in 1974 showed a total of forty ethnic groups in the Oriente, but of these twenty-three had populations estimated at less than one thousand, including ten that had no more than one hundred and another eight for which information was unobtainable (Riester, 1976). The only small group that maintains a certain solidarity and has even shown signs of growth is the Chipaya, descendants of the ancient Uru and situated in the heart of the Oruro section of the Altiplano. It is interesting that this has occurred, even though the Chipaya are frequent travelers and are under heavy pressure from many sides to assimilate.

Among the other minority groups, the Chiriguano (numbering about twenty thousand) and the Guarayo (about eight thousand) branches of the Guarani are the most stable and have shown the most signs of cultural and linguistic revival (but not the Siriono or the probably extinct Guarasug'we branches). The latter group, which was fully "conquered" in Chiriguano territory at the end of the last century, immediately underwent heavy demographic and cultural disintegration. However, in recent decades it has been making a comeback in areas in which the original *comunidades* had managed to resist domination by the cattle-raising haciendas.

In some of the other relatively large groups, such as the Moxos and the Chiquitanos of the old colonial Jesuit *reducciones*, there are marked statistical discrepancies between the 1976 census and the estimates of the ethnologists specializing in the Oriente. Aside from the certainty of technical errors, the census probably indicates that in these groups language does not have as central a place as other cultural traits (e.g., ceremonies and dances) for the maintenance of identity. It must also be remembered that the present cultural identity of these groups is actually a relatively recent amalgam—the product of new fusions in the colonial environment of the *reduccion*.

Efforts to organize these native groups have recently taken place in the Oriente, but they have not yet reached the level of importance achieved by similar attempts in other South American countries. On the other hand, these efforts—more than elsewhere—have had some contacts with the chief organization representing the entire peasantry. This has perhaps been facilitated by the fact that the Aymara leadership of this organization fosters the understanding of the ethnic dimensions of the problems in the Oriente.

BILINGUAL AND INTERCULTURAL EDUCATION

Despite the pluricultural character of Bolivia, the usual practice in education has been to ignore the problem and to simply impose the language and culture of the dominant groups. There have occasionally been some initiatives and even decrees favoring the use and teaching of vernacular languages, but these have proved to be rhetorical gestures. Because of strong economic and ideological pressures, the status quo has continued in force. Thus, to this day the almost universal practice has been the teaching of, and insistence on, Spanish throughout the school system—from pre-primary to the university, in both the city and the country. In rural areas, even the use of a vernacular is punishable.

At various times, however, several counterattempts—a few of which were governmental but the majority private—have been made to develop educational programs that more closely reflect the sociolinguistic and cultural reality of the country. These refreshing innovations, which have occurred particularly in the field of nonformal adult education, will be the main focus of this section.

Education and Religion

Historically, the great precursor of education in the maternal language was the missionary effort. At the beginning of the colonial period, the first printed books were invariably collections of sermons and other religious texts, in addition to grammars and vocabularies for the training of new missionaries. In many respects, some of these works, such as the variously reprinted Aymara vocabulary of Bertonio (1612), have not lost their timeliness. As inventory of the principal Quechua and Aymara bibliography (Rivet, 1951–55) shows that in the first century forty religious works (twenty-five Quechua, fifteen Aymara) and twenty-five linguistic works (nineteen Quechua, six Aymara) were produced. Among them mention is also made of a "cartilla quechua-castellano" (Quechua-Spanish primer) with six thousand copies. Thus, a certain degree of importance was accorded the use of the vernacular; however, the emphasis of the period does not allow the same to be said for other cultural manifestations. Preaching was done in the maternal language, but in other areas "se extirpaba la idolatria" (idolatry was eradicated).

In the second colonial period, ethusiasm and production declined. Even in the great rebellion of 1780 the only recorded work was the drama, *Ollantay*, which was prepared by the priest, Antonio Valdes, and performed for the Kuraka rebel, Tupaq Amaru.

In the nineteenth and especially in the twentieth centuries, religious motives again stimulated an increase in output. Various Protestant groups have now taken the initiative, among which the Bible Societies and more recently, the Summer Institute of Linguistics are prominent. The majority of their materials are purely religious, although there are also some linguistic ones; in addition, a new concern for maternal-language literacy is developing. With the Summer Institute of Linguistics, in particular, production has expanded to include various regions and minority cultures of the Oriente (as well as the Chipaya). As elsewhere, the Institute has been subject to controversy because of its fundamentalist outlook and presumed connections to less devout North American interests, although it has never had serious difficulty in remaining in Bolivia. On the Catholic side, there was an occasional pioneer, for example, the Oruro priest, Carlos Felipe Beltran, who published numerous educational pamphlets in Quechua in the nineteenth century; but as a whole, activity was limited to reprinting or improving catechisms and collections of songs, and, occasionally, a linguistic work. The widespread use of native languages in rural pastoral work, as well as the production and use of more secular educational materials, has only been more fully undertaken in recent decades. For example, five editions of a Catholic religious songbook in Aymara, in which the majority of the compositions are by peasants, have been published. In the latest edition, which has 250 pages, one hundred and twenty thousand copies were printed.

The "Indigenist" Phase

The monopoly held in this field by religious institutions has been gradually disappearing. By the War of Independence (1810–25) the principal speeches of the patriots were translated into Aymara and Quechua; one of these translations is attributed to Juan Wallpa Rimachi, a well-known Quechua poet and partisan. Several decades later, in the middle of the culturally romantic, but politically liberal, era, a painful paradox occurred: on the one hand, the *comunarios* (members of the comunidades) suffered the pillaging of their lands; on the other, the production of poetry, popular song collections, stories, and ever pedagogical proposals in favor of the Indian began to flourish in Andean languages. The notable poet and writer, Franz Tamayo, illustrates this paradox. Although he vigorously defended the Indian in his classic *Pedagogia Nacional*, he is remembered by his former peons and their descendants as a despotic *patron*. It never ceases to be ironic that the theme of ''Indian education'' reappears periodically in the press whenever a new uprising occurs. At the beginning of the twentieth century, during the liberal era, new pedagogical currents came to Bolivia. Their main proponent—hired by the government—was the Belgian, George Rouma, who measured the craniums of Hacienda Indians in his spare time in order to verify the theories of Social Darwinism then in vogue (Demelas, 1981). In the midst of these contradictions, there arose the first rural schools, first in the mestizo towns and then, little by little, in some of the *comunidades* (Montoya, 1983).

Two efforts deserve explicit mention. The first, and better known, is that of Professor Elizardo Perez, who against all odds, succeeded in establishing the indigenous school at Huarisata, on the Aymara Altiplano, in 1931. Shortly after, he extended the experiment to other regions of the Altiplano, to Ucurena in Cochabamba Department and to Casarabe, among the Siriono of Beni Department. Elizardo Pérez (1962) acknowledged important cultural features: he located the schools outside of non-Indian towns, and he modeled his system, consisting of a nuclear school surrounded by a cluster of satellite schools, on the traditional *ayullu* organization. But he did not grasp the importance of education in the maternal language. His pedagogical goal and medium of instruction was Spanish (Huacani et al., 1978). The second effort, almost forgotten, is being rescued thanks to new research by historians from the group, Memoria Comunitaria Aymara. In the years from 1910 to 1930, there arose an important movement of *caciques*, traditional Aymara leaders, who fought simultaneously for the defense of their lands and for the establishment of schools in their communities. Some of these leaders and the itinerant teachers they hired suffered from persecution, and finally the effort was brought to a halt by the Chaco War of 1932. However, this was the precursor of mass participatory education.

Mass Education and Literacy

The next phase opened after the Chaco defeat (1935) with the rise of a new national political venture focusing on the integration of the ''Indian.'' The main controversy at that time was between those who thought that this primarily involved returning lands, and the more conservative element who thought that the Indian should first be subjected to the slow process of ''education.'' Both sides shared the conventional belief that this education had to be imparted in the dominant language and culture (Spanish) in order for full integration to occur, and both were assimilationist. Nevertheless, in the first decade the few attempts at rural education are of interest in that they represent a challenge to the elitist education and politics of the past. For example, in Ucurena, where the first peasant syndicate was formed immediately after the Chaco War with the support of the Huarisata school, the birth of the struggle for land and associated productive activities occurred simultaneously. When the landowners seized the lands again a few years later, the school not only taught the children but was also the training center for syndicalism for their parents. There, too, instruction was in Spanish, but social events (such as sociodramas) with a strong social content took place in Quechua (Dandler, 1984).

Mass rural education was initiated with the triumph of the MNR (Movimiento Nacionalista Revolucionario—Nationalist Revolutionary Movement) Revolution in 1952 and the promulgation of the 1953 Agrarian Reform Law. In twenty years, the number of small rural schools quintupled. The rate of illiteracy (minimally defined) declined from 68 percent in 1950 to 32 percent in 1976. Greater knowledge of Spanish has also resulted from this massive effort. However, with rapid expansion came a sharp decline in quality. The rural school and teacher— a state-salaried bureaucrat—were converted into the last link in the penetration of the system and status quo in the countryside. On the cultural level, this fostered the imitation of everything Hispanic and urban both directly, and—perhaps even more effectively—implicitly through the attitudes of the teachers, and thereby marked the attitudes and aspirations of the peasants with escapism and even conflict and trauma. Their identity, as shaped by personal and cultural experience, found itself at variance with what the school advocated. In order to "be something," it was necessary to abandon what they already were. Various adult literacy campaigns proposed in these decades suffered from the same misdirection (Subirats et al., 1978).

During the same period there were also various private efforts which stressed literacy—considered to be the gateway to every opportunity. Almost every initiative was connected to a religious institution, and in several cases, the maternal language did in fact constitute the point of departure. The two principal Protestant efforts were (and still are) ALFALIT and CALA. Each of these is based on the maternal language and has prepared materials for both children and adults which emphasize reading mechanics rather than content. In addition, CALA (Comision de Alfabetizacion y Literatura Aymara—Aymara Commission for Literacy and Literature), which is connected to the Summer Institute of Linguistics (SIL) has produced many readers, particularly biblical texts. SIL has also produced other literacy materials in various languages of the Oriente. Among Catholics, the main effort has followed a different route: the radio. A network of radio-schools for adults, called ERBOL, has come into being. At present there are four in the Aymara region, four in the Quechua region, and three in the Oriente, although those in the Oriente use mainly Spanish. At first, these stations were little more than amplifiers for a kind of school teaching in which the teachers in quasi-schoolrooms assisted the station from afar by following the lessons given by radio to the letter, all at the same time and at the same pace. These lessons were frequently given in both the maternal language and in Spanish; however, only a few stations provided written materials in the vernacular. Another recent Catholic endeavor for children has been the preparation of bilingual texts for the early primary years.

In the 1970s, innovation in the area of bilingual education also occurred within the official educational system. For some time an agency of the Ministry of Education has been responsible for adult literacy and education. With creative staffing this agency has carried out relevant activities, although that has not often happened. However, during the 1970s, the U.S. Agency for International Development promoted programs in bilingual education for Quechua children similar to programs put into effect in Ecuador and Peru. The government (which at the same time was turning down other local projects based on the maternal language) accepted this package because it involved several million dollars worth of aid. As a result, Rural Education Project I came into being in the Cochabamba valleys and highlands. Good instructional materials in Quechua (adapted from a similar project in Ayacucho, Peru) were produced, but the project suffered from the same problems as its couterparts in other countries—that is, because it originated in the unwieldy bureaucracy of the rural educational system and the agencies of the Ministry of Education, it did not succeed in interesting teachers in a methodology so different from the traditional perspective (Montoya, 1983).

Toward Mass Education

In the same period, a new program was being proposed which went beyond simple literacy to a participatory education much more responsive to the overall needs of adults. This time, too, the initiative was from the private sector, and only later did it become part of the government program.

The pioneers of the new outlook have probably been the numerous private institutions for rural advancement which have been proliferating in recent years. The majority have not dealt with literacy but have concentrated on more specific tasks, for example, agricultural production, health, the advancement of women, and organization. For each of these tasks, however, some type of educational program immediately becomes necessary. In these programs incorporation of the language and culture of the participants has proved to be indispensable for success. Permanent written materials have not always been required; when produced, they are often written in Spanish, as they are for adults literate in only that language. In contrast, audiovisual aids often use the native language. Several of these institutions have also felt the need to rely on the existing radio stations, where they almost always use the maternal language. Beyond these general characteristics, there is a wide-ranging and often creative variety in the ideological and methodological approaches.

The ERBOL radio network has also been evolving. At first, the programming format utilized the methods of Gilberto Freyre, with his stress on group discussion of topics reflecting the key interests of the participants. Later, formats more suitable to radio speech were adopted, for example, talk shows with audience participation. Of recent creation is a network of ''people's'' reporters who periodically form a chain on all the ERBOL stations to report on and discuss events in various rural areas as well as in lower class urban and mining sectors. Interesting multilateral exchanges are thus generated among various social, cultural and linguistic settings.

Since the establishment of a democratic government at the end of 1982, a new plan for the systematic education of adults, rather than children and adolescents, has been in preparation on the governmental level—the Servicio Nacional de Alfabetizacion y Educacion Popular (SENELEP) (National Service for Literacy and Mass Education), which is supported by UNESCO and other international institutions. Among other things, its formal proposal emphasizes the following: the necessity for the entire educational process to be controlled by the people concerned and their organizations, rather than by the rural teaching profession and other outsiders (who would be limited to aiding and advising); the Freyre notion of stress awareness of the problems of each group; the merely subordinate role of literacy, properly speaking, in relation to broader tasks also affecting the already literate; the need to use diverse channels, such as direct contact, contests, and mass communication media; and the intercultural and bilingual character of all education. Up to now the main activity has focused on the design and development of materials. Two readers, which also incorporate many indigenous social and cultural features, have already been prepared for Aymara and Quechua, respectively, as a result of various workshops and seminars in which peasants, teachers, and representatives of various previously mentioned institutions participated. An ancillary development, by no means negligible, has been the official adoption of a "single alphabet" for the two main Andean languages, containing the principal features of each. This resulted from discussions among some twenty institutions and specialists; however, in light of the emotional factors and existing practices connected with this subject, it is not certain that the much needed unification will be successful. Prior attempts in 1954 and 1968 met with failure.

The foregoing suggests an optimistic outcome with respect to the future. It is nevertheless necessary to conclude on a note of caution. The almost chronic economic and political difficulties of Bolivia hinder the continuity and completion of many projects, especially those that depend on governmental entities. Furthermore, most of the innovations of interest are concerned with adult education; little headway has been made in the problems raised by bilingualism and interculturalism for the education of children and youth. In 1984, the government decreed the obligatory teaching of Andean languages at the secondary level, but the indications to date suggest that this decree will not be enforced. Moreover, there are no signs of change in the current insistence on education which is solely *in* Spanish and *for* Spanish in the rural sector.

BIBLIOGRAPHY

Albó, Xavier. 1974. "Los mil rostros del quechua." Lima: Instituto de Estudios Peruanos. (Original thesis in English.) Cornell University, 1970.

————. 1980. *Lengua y sociedad en Bolivia, 1976.* La Paz: Instituto Nacional de Estadística.

————. 1981. *Idiomas, escuelas y radios en Bolivia.* 3d ed. La Paz: UNITAS-ACLO.

Albó, Xavier, Tomás Greaves, and Godofredo Sandóval. 1983. *Chukiyawu, la cara aymara de La Paz.* Vol. 3, *Cabalgando entre dos mundos.* La Paz: CIPCA.

Andean Linguistics Newsletter. Publicada sucesivamente en las universidades de Wisconsin, Illinois y New Mexico. Posteriormente llamada *Correo de Lungüística Andina.*

Bertonio, Ludovico. 1612. *Vocabulario de la lengua aymara.* Juli (Ultima edición, Cochabamba: CERES-MUSEF-IFEA, 1984.)

Bouysse-Cassagne, Therese. 1976. "Tributos y etnías en Charcas en la época del virrey Toledo." *Historia y Cultura* (La Paz) 2: 97–113.

————. 1978. "L'espace aymara: urco et uma." *Annales* (Paris) 33, 5: 1057–80.

————. 1980. "Les hommes d'en haut. Rapports sociaux et estructures spatiotemporelles chez les aymaras (VX-XVIᵉ siècles)." Ph.D. thesis, Paris, Ecole des hautes etudes en sciences sociales.

Briggs, Lucy T. 1976. "Dialectal Variation in the Aymara Language of Bolivia and Peru." Ph.D. thesis, Gainesville, University of Florida.

————. 1979. "A Critical Survey of the Literature on the Aymara Language." *Latin American Research Review* 14, 3: 87–106.

————. 1981. Missionary, patron, and radio Aymara. In *The Aymara Language in Its Social and Cultural Context*, ed. M. J. Hardman. Gainesville: University Presses of Florida.

Calzavarini, Lorenzo G. 1980. *Nación chiriguana, grandez y ocaso.* La Paz: Los Amigos del Libro.

Correo de Lingüística Andina. ed. Garland D. Bills. University of New Mexico, Albuquerque (Ver *Andean Linguistics Newsletter*).

Dandler, Jorge. 1969. "El sindicalismo campesino en Bolivia: Los cambios estructurales en Ucureña." México: Instituto Indigenista Interamericano. M.A. and Ph.D. thesis, University of Wisconsin, Madison, 1967, 1971; Nueva edición, Cochabamba: CERES, 1984.

Demelas, M. Danielle. 1981. "Darwinismo a la criolla: El darwinismo social en Bolivia." *Historia Boliviana* (Cochabamba) 1, 2: 55–82.

Denevan, William M. 1966. *The Aboriginal Cultural Geography of the Llanos de Mojos of Bolivia.* Berkeley: University of California. (Iberoamericana, no. 48. Vérsion castellano: La Paz: Juventud, 1980.)

Escobar, Alberto, ed. 1972. *El reto del multilingüísmo en el Perú.* Lima: Instituto de Estudios Peruanos.

Hardman, Martha J. 1978. "La familia lingüística andina Jaqi: Jaqaru, Kawki, Aymara." *Vicus Cuyadernos, Lingüística* (Amsterdam) 2: 5–28.

————. 1979. "Quecha y Aymara: Lenguas en contacto." *Antropología* (La Paz) 1.

————. In press. "Jaqi Aru: Lengua humana." In *Raíces de América: Mundo Aymara*, ed. X. Albó. UNESCO-Siglo XXI.

————, ed. 1981. *The Aymara Language in Its Social and Cultural Context.* Gainesville: University Presses of Florida.

Huacani, Carlos, J. Subirats, B. Ledesma, and J. E. Mamani. 1978. *Warisata "Escuela-Ayllu." El por qué de un fracaso.* La Paz: CEBIAE.

Huanca L., Tomás. 1984. "La desestructuración de los espacios socioeconómicos andinos en el Altiplano lacustre: Agresión colonial y resistencia comunitaria." Ph.D. thesis, La Paz, Universidad Mayor San Andrés.

Kloss, H., and G. D. McConnell, eds. 1979. *Linguistic Composition of the Nations of the World/Composition linguistique des nations du monde*. III. Central and South America/ L'Amérique Centrale et l'Amérique du Sud. Quebec: Les Presses de l'Université Laval, CIRB/ICRB.

Montoya, M. Victor. 1983. "La educación bilingüe en los proyectos integrados." In *Educación, etnías y descolonización en América Latina*, ed. N. Rodríguez, E. Masferrer, and R. Vargas. Una guía para la educación bilingüe intercultural. México: UNESCO and Instituto Indigenista Interamericano. Vol. 1, 57–82.

Moreno, Gabriel René. 1888. *Catálogo del archivo de Mojos y Chiquitos*. Santiago de Chile. 2d ed. Introduction and notes by Hernando Sanabria. La Paz: Juventud, 1974.

Murra, John V. 1975. *Formaciones económicas y políticas del mundo andino*. Lima: Instituto de Estudios Peruanos.

Parejas, Alcides. 1976. *Historia de Moxos y Chiquitos a fines del siglo XVIII*. La Paz: Instituto Boliviano de Cultura.

Pérez, Elizardo. 1962. *Warisata, la escuela ayllu*. La Paz: Burillo.

Platt, Tristan. In press. "El pensamiento político aymara." In *Raíces de América: Mundo Aymara*, ed. X. Albó. UNESCO-Siglo XX.

Plaza, Pedro. 1975. "Algunos aspectos de la discriminación lingüística y social." In *Anales* de la I Reunión de Antropología de los países del área andina. La Paz: Instituto Boliviano de Cultura.

———, ed. 1977. *Lingüística y Educación*. III *Congreso de Lenguas Nacionales*. La Paz: Instituto Boliviano de Cultura.

Riester, Jürgen. 1975. *Indians of Eastern Bolivia: Aspects of Their Present Situation*. Copenhagen: IWGIA Document 18. (Parcialmente reproducido en castellano en J. Riester, En busca de la loma santa. La Paz: Amigos del Libro, 1976.)

Rivet, Paul, and G. de Créqui-Monfort. 1951–55. *Bibliographie des langues aymará et kičua*. Paris: Musée de l'Homme. 4 vols.

Saignes, Thierry. 1974. "Une frontière fossile. La cordillere chiriguano au XVIII⁰ siècle." Thesis, Paris, Ecole Pratique des Hautes Etudes.

Sanabria, Hernando. 1965. *El habla popular de la provincia de Vallegrande*. Santa Cruz de la Sierra: Universidad Gabriel René Moreno.

SENALEP. 1984. *Plan Nacional de Alfabetización y Educación Popular, prof. Elizardo Pérez*. Propuesta Técnica. La Paz: Ministerio de Educación y Cultura.

Subirats, José. 1983. "Una experiencia de educación intercomunitaria rural." In *Educación, etnías y descolonización en América Latina*, ed. N. Rodríguez et al. Una guia para la educación bilingüe intercultural. México: UNESCO–Instituto Indigenista Interamericano.

Torero, Alfredo. 1965. "Los dialectos quechuas." *Anales científicos de la universidad agraria* 2, 4: 446–78.

———. 1970. "Lingüística e historia de la sociedad andina." *Anales científícos de la universidad agraria* 7, 3: 231–64.

———. 1974. *El quechua y la historia social andina*. Lima: Universidad Ricardo Palma.

Van den Berg, Hans. 1980. *Material bibliográfico para el estudio de los aymaras, callawayas, chipayas, urus*. Cochabamba: ISET. 3 vols.

Wachtel, Nathan. 1978. "Hommes d'eau: Le problème uru (XVIᵉ siecle)." *Annales* (Paris) 33, 5: 1127–59.

Yapita, Juan de Dios. 1977. "*Discriminación lingüística y conflicto social.*" La Paz: Museo Nacional de Etnografía y Folklore.

———. In press. "La afirmación cultural aymara." In *Raíces de América: Mundo Aymara*, ed. X. Albó. UNESCO-Siglo XXI.

6

THE CELTIC LANGUAGES IN THE BRITISH ISLES

At the present day, three Celtic languages survive as mother tongues within restricted populations in the British Isles. These are Welsh, Irish Gaelic, and Scottish Gaelic; they are spoken, respectively, in Wales, Northern Ireland and the Republic of Ireland, and the Highlands of Scotland. In none of these areas is the Celtic language numerically dominant, and only in the Republic of Ireland (Eire) does a Celtic language have significant, strongly funded government support.

The three surviving Celtic languages are remnants of a much larger linguistic group. Celtic is an independent branch of the Indo-European family of languages, and at one time (roughly 800 B.C. to 100 B.C. [Filip, 1981:34–46]) the Celts were the dominant population of Western and Central Europe. Their geographical distribution eventually extended into the Iberian Peninsula and central Italy, and at least as far east as Bohemia, Moravia, and Silesia, and even at one point Transylvania and Bulgaria (Filip, 1981:40). One Celtic population (the Galatians to whom Paul addressed the letter which appears as a book of the New Testament) established itself as far to the south and east as Asia Minor. The Celts also expanded into the British Isles, where all of the Celtic languages that remain today took form: even Breton, spoken in Brittany in France, was taken to its present Continental location by British Celts during the period of turmoil and conquest at the hands of Germanic tribes after the Romans abandoned their British colony in the early years of the fifth century A.D. (Chadwick, 1970:81). At their peak the Celts were powerful enough to pose a threat to Greece and Rome. They sacked Rome in ca. 390 B.C. and attacked Delphi in 279 B.C. (Corcoran in Chadwick, 1970:38). Their metal work was superb, which gave them excellent weaponry, and it was characterized as well by outstanding decoration and artistic design (Cunliffe, 1979:24–25). The Celts were in decline by roughly the end of the second century B.C., however, and decline has continued to be the fate of the Celtic peoples and their languages up to the present time. (For cartographic exposition of the expansion and contraction of Celtic populations in the ancient world, see McEvedy, 1967:28 ff.)

The Celtic language family in the British Isles is represented by two branches: Brythonic and Goidelic (sometimes known as P-Celtic and Q-Celtic, respectively, after a major linguistic feature distinguishing the two branches). The two branches are not mutually intelligible. Welsh is a Brythonic Celtic language; its only close living relative is Breton, but the separation in time and space has been such that Welsh and Breton are not mutually intelligible either. Cornish, extinct as a mother tongue since the end of the eighteenth century (Ellis, 1974:95–124), was Brythonic, and so were the Celtic dialects of southern Britain which died out under the successive impact of Roman and Anglo-Saxon invasions and occupation. Irish Gaelic is a Goidelic Celtic language; Scottish Gaelic is an offshoot from it and is therefore likewise Goidelic. Manx, which perished as a true mother tongue as recently as the 1970s, was also a historical development out of Irish Gaelic and so Goidelic as well.

In modern usage the two forms of Gaelic, Irish and Scottish, are usually distinguished by terming the one simply *Irish* and the other simply *Gaelic*. This practice will be adopted for the most part in this chapter, although where quotations or historical references use the term *Gaelic* indiscriminately it will be necessary to add the additional qualifying term. Where *Gaelic* is intended as a cover term for both living Goidelic speech forms, this will be stated or made clear from context. Where the two forms of Gaelic are deliberately compared or contrasted with each other, the identifying labels will routinely be attached.

No generally valid statement can be made about the mutual intelligibility of Irish Gaelic and Scottish Gaelic. The northernmost dialects of Irish Gaelic and the southernmost dialects of Scottish Gaelic are mutually intelligible, and residents of the southernmost islands in the Inner Hebrides sometimes chose to listen to Radio Eireann broadcasts instead of BBC broadcasts in Scottish Gaelic because they understand the Irish as easily or more easily (personal communication). The officially promoted form of Irish is rather of the central variety than the northern, and is consequently less readily understood by speakers of any variety of Scottish Gaelic. At the extremes of the Goidelic speech area, southern districts of Ireland and northern districts of the Scottish Highlands, intelligibility is either minimal or absent, usually the latter.

HISTORICAL BACKGROUND

The loss of autonomy among the Celtic populations in the British Isles was gradual and piecemeal. Since the history of retreat was different in each area, the history of marginalization was also different in each area. So different have been the developments and outcomes for Ireland, Scotland, and Wales, despite certain general similarities, that it seems preferable to deal with each separately.

Ireland

In a number of respects, Ireland represents the most extreme case among those under consideration. It was least affected by contacts with Roman civilization in the early period, and it was by far the most fortunate in the preservation of the materials from the flowering of its own early Celtic tradition, among them legal, poetic, artistic, and mythological materials. The strongest Highland Scottish challenge to English hegemony came very late, chronologically, and the Welsh threat was relatively early and easily disposed of. The Irish challenge was more serious and more persistent over time; for these reasons, the weight of English political and military force fell most heavily on Ireland for many centuries. All of these facts have a bearing on the modern-day position of the Irish language.

By simplifying on a grand scale, one might point to religion as the single most important factor in the more than four centuries of English struggle to secure control over Ireland. There were, of course, problems prior to Henry VIII's break with Rome in the early sixteenth century. Some of the native Irish princes, as well as some of the great Anglo-Irish families produced by the partial Norman conquest of Ireland in the twelfth and thirteenth centuries, had shown a disturbing tendency to flaunt their own autonomy and pay insufficient attention to the claims of the English Crown. In addition, Ireland's most powerful leaders had supported the losing Yorkist side in the Wars of the Roses, so that Ireland was regarded as hostile by the Tudor monarchs who arose from Lancastrian victory in that struggle.

Nonetheless, the unwillingness of Ireland to accept Protestantism and to abandon its allegiance to a Church adhered to by England's Continental Catholic enemies was a pivotal factor in the alienation of the two peoples and in the English determination to neutralize Ireland, whenever possible, as a potential ally of France and Spain. From this need for security against a hostile Catholic alliance on its left flank, so to speak, arose the determination of Elizabethan England to suppress the great Ulster earl Hugh O'Neill and his allies, and the scheme to "plant" Ulster with Protestants, since the Irish refused to turn Protestant themselves. From the English refusal to distinguish between the "Old English" Catholics (descendants of the Normans who had first extended English rule to Ireland) and native Irish Catholics, as measures were increasingly taken to handicap Catholics in political and economic life, arose alliances and rebellions among *all* Catholics in Ireland against English rule. Cromwell's invasion of Ireland represented a Protestant conquest of a Catholic enemy, and in its aftermath Ireland emerged with an English Protestant upper class and an impoverished Irish peasantry. Irish support of the Catholic succession of the exiled James II brought about invasion and defeat by the Protestant forces of William of Orange and ushered in the age of the Penal Laws (1691–1778), a period when Catholics were bitterly oppressed by an Irish Parliament now altogether Protestant. By the late eighteenth century, despite the fact that the Penal Laws had largely been repealed, the subjection of Ireland to oppressive rule by England and by an Irish Parliament controlled from England had resulted in the emergence of a widespread spirit of rebelliousness in Ireland. For the first time in several centuries, Catholic Irishmen and a good many Protestant Irishmen were united by a common opposition to the English.

From this point in Irish history onwards, religion played a less important role in the Irish "troubles" except in Ulster, where religious divisions coincided with cultural divisions between Irish of all backgrounds and the Lowland Scots whose ethnic patterns had prevailed since the time of the seventeenth-century Plantation. The potato-blight famine which devastated the Irish population in the mid-nineteenth century fell most fatally on the native Irish poor, but to some extent the lesser Protestant landowners were distressed as well.

In the years after the repeal of most of the Penal Laws in 1778, the sentiment favoring more autonomy for Ireland, or even independent existence as a separate country, gradually grew. The leaders of the various political movements arguing—and sometimes fighting—for these viewpoints included, very significantly, both Catholics and Protestants. Wolfe Tone, who spearheaded the United Irishmen and finally brought French troops to Ireland to aid their cause in 1798, was a Protestant. Thus, by an irony England's great fear of an alliance between Catholic Ireland and Catholic France was realized in this instance under the leadership of an Irish Protestant. Daniel O'Connell, the preeminent voice in Irish struggles for autonomy in the the first half of the nineteenth century, was a Catholic; but Isaac Butt, who took up the home-rule battle in the latter part of the same century, was a Protestant, as was Charles Stewart Parnell, who soon eclipsed Butt politically in the same cause. Michael Davitt, who joined Parnell in the leadership of the Irish National Land League, was an Irish Catholic raised in England (Moody and Martin, 1967:238–84).

All thirty-two counties in Ireland achieved dominion status by treaty in 1921, after two years of war, and the Irish Free State was created. But the six counties of Northern Ireland were granted the option of withdrawing from the Irish Free State and choosing union with the United Kingdom, which they promptly did. In the remaining counties, a civil war lasting two years was fought over the acceptability of the treaty signed in 1921 and the division of the island into two political units. The Free State and Northern Ireland continued as in the agreements of the 1920s, however, and the changeover from dominion status to republic status was achieved for the twenty-six counties only in 1937. The Republic of Ireland (Eire) is today the sole formerly Celtic territory in the British Isles to have achieved political independence.

Scotland

If Ireland came to be divided *socially* between Celts (largely the peasantry) and non-Celts (the Protestant upper class), Scotland came instead to be divided *geographically* between Celts (the Highlanders) and non-Celts (the Lowlanders).

The Gaelicization of Scotland began in the fifth century A.D. with the arrival of Irish conquerors and settlers (the Scots) in what is now Argyll. The indigenous Picts, whose ethnic identity is uncertain but probably not originally Celtic, yielded gradually before the Scots; by way of conquest, alliance, and missionary zeal on behalf of Christianity, the Scots became the dominant cultural and linguistic element. They never became the *only* cultural and linguistic element in the country which bears their ethnic name, however. Although Pictish died out, and the Brythonic Celtic kingdom once prominent in the southwest disappeared, Anglian influence grew in the southwest and spread westward, while Celtic Scottish influence and power grew to the north. By the seventh century, the lines of linguistic and cultural division which held for centuries after had already substantially emerged. The lowland areas had come under the domination of the Germanic Anglians and their language, on the whole; the higher, more mountainous parts of the country were the domain of the Celtic Scots and their language (Chadwick, 1970:89).

The cultural differences between the two areas were notable, quite apart from language. The Highlanders lived under the clan system, practicing transhumant pastoralism and cultivating a warrior ethos. The Lowlanders, in their more fertile and accessible regions, took readily to clustered settlement patterns and the regular practice of agriculture. Since the two ways of life came into conflict often enough wherever the different populations lived in any proximity, and the cattle raiding of the Highlanders among Lowland farmers was a notorious cause of friction, hostility between the populations was not long in developing.

Although religion never became the persistent and irresolvable divisive factor within Scotland that it was in Ireland's relations with England, it did nonetheless play a major role at a critical time. The Reformation gained acceptance in the Lowlands in the sixteenth century, but parts of the Highlands remained Catholic under clan chieftains who did not embrace the new beliefs. The support of a number of Highland clans for the Catholic Stuart claimants to the throne of Britain against the Hanoverian line ushered in with George I was essential to the two great failed risings in the Highlands, in 1715 and 1745. The latter, the famous but unsuccessful campaign of Prince Charles Edward Stuart ("Bonnie Prince Charlie"), led to brutal suppression of Highland culture (clan leadership, Highland dress, Highland weaponry, the traditional martial bagpipe music, and even the language) in the wake of the Hanoverian victory.

In the Highlands and in the Hebridean Islands off the west coast, a very Celtic culture based on such values as a warrior aristocracy and its patronage of poetry, music, and genealogy in the oral rather than written mode survived even longer than in Ireland. English conquest, colonization, and political domination had seriously disrupted the warrior aristocracy and the values it cultivated in Ireland by the time Cromwell's soldiers and officers became the Irish landholding class in the mid-seventeenth century. In the Celtic regions of Scotland, traditional Celtic lifeways, though often enough under severe pressure, were not subjected to relentless suppression until almost a century later, after the 1745 rising. In the end, however, the outcome of the conflict between Celtic and Anglo-Saxon cultures was much the same in both areas.

Politically, Scotland's long-term fate was quite different from Ireland's. Ireland was made a part of the United Kingdom by an act of union passed in 1800. By this late date, there had been several centuries of serious conflict between Ireland and England, and the struggle for home rule (and ultimately independence) began immediately. The act of union which united the Scottish and English parliaments came in 1707, but the union of the Crowns of Scotland and England had come as early as 1603, with the succession of James VI of Scotland and I of England upon the death of Queen Elizabeth I. It was a king already in power in Scotland who inherited the English Crown as well; this prevented the union of the Crowns from appearing in the light of an English imposition of power over Scotland. Although even the Lowland Scots were rather different from the English at this period in their patterns of living, the form of English which they spoke, and their overseas alliances, the gulf which divided them from the English was not nearly as unbridgeable as the gulf separating any Celtic group from any Anglo-Saxon group at this time. Scotland was a country sharply divided internally between two cultures, each with its own geographical base. There was no revulsion of feeling against the English among the masses of common people throughout all Scotland, as there was in Ireland. Thus, it is not surprising that Scotland remains within the United Kingdom today, whereas all of Ireland except the Protestant-planted north has disengaged itself from that political entity.

Wales

In the relations between Wales and England, one feature that was minimized in the relations of the other Celtic areas with England is always to the fore: proximity. Ireland had the expanse of the Irish Sea as a buffer, and the Highlanders were buffered at least to some extent by their distance from the seats of first Lowland Scots governance (Edinburgh) and then English governance (London); and, of course, the difficulties of the Highland terrain before modern road- and bridge-building made the word "remote" apply well, despite the relatively small distances involved.

The Welsh terrain presented difficulties, too, to be sure. But the Normans of the eleventh-century conquest period did succeed in penetrating in many parts of Wales, whereas Anglo-Norman power first reached even Lowland Scotland more by way of invitation (under the Canmore line of Scottish kings, heavily allied with England) than by any exercise of military power. English hegemony was extended over Wales as early as the late thirteenth century. It was challenged in the next two centuries, most notably by the Welsh prince Owen Glendower in the early fifteenth century, but never fully cast off.

Ironically, a development that originally roused great hopes of more autonomy for the Welsh proved fatal to those hopes in the event: the rise of the Tudor monarchy. The Tudors originated in northwest Wales, but Henry Tudor had a claim on the English throne through his mother's line. The Welsh supported him militarily in the Battle of Bosworth Field, which was decisive for the Lancastrian victory in the Wars of the Roses and brought Henry to the throne.

It was Henry VII's son, however, who dealt the death blow to Welsh hopes. Far from honoring his Welsh heritage and favoring the land of his forefathers, Henry VIII wished to reduce Wales to political order and eliminate cultural and linguistic differences between his domains. The Act of Union came in 1536, making Wales the first of the Celtic areas by more than half a century to come directly and fully under English rule.

This early political domination by England, together with the fact that Wales *did* follow Henry VIII into Protestantism, had the effect of sparing Wales the hostility and suspicion engendered by possible alliance with England's Catholic enemies on the Continent—and the vengeance incurred by entry into such an alliance on the losing side. Ordinary Welshmen were able to live their lives out with less obvious interference or direct threat to their traditional lifeways than their counterparts in Ireland or the Highlands.

The great wave of change that eventually broke over Wales was not the result of dramatic military defeats like Hugh O'Neill's at Kinsale or the Jacobite failures at the Boyne and Aughrim in Ireland and Culloden in Highland Scotland, but the result of economic development. Wales was rich in coal and iron, and with the rise of the steel industry and the extractive technology to supply its needs, Wales became a center of industrial activity. This ushered in a century of abnormal population growth: the population tripled in Wales during the nineteenth century (Lewis, 1978b:268). Two features of this surge in population had important consequences for the Welsh language. One was the disparity in density of population and in lifeways which emerged between districts that had no significant coal or iron deposits, remaining rural and pastoral in character, and districts that did. Those with such resources inevitably urbanized and equally inevitably became less Welsh in character. The second important feature was a contributing factor to this very disparity: a considerable part of the population bulge was the result of the in-migration of English labor. Denbighshire, and especially Flintshire in the northeast, were affected, but Glamorgan and Monmouthshire in the southeast much more so, since the South Wales coalfield was the preeminent producer.

Summary

No two of the Celtic-speaking areas of the British Isles show the same pattern of retreat under pressure from English political and cultural expansion. A once wholly Celtic or celticized Ireland retained a peasantry deeply conscious of its Celtic and Catholic identity, but largely through military defeats yielded its landownership and its prosperity to a non-Celtic gentry and aristocracy. Scotland, with a small but very early Anglian population in the most fertile districts, experienced growth of the territorial and cultural strength of that Germanic element in its midst and retreat of the Celtic element to inaccessible and relatively infertile fastnesses. Wales, with a general population as universally Celtic or celticized as that of early Ireland, suffered neither the kind of crushing defeat that might have eliminated native culture altogether nor the overly successful rivalry of a local non-Celtic element that might have sent the native Welsh into the mountains to stay. Rather, Wales became the industrial handmaiden of its all-too-close neighbor, and its Celts left their mountains and remote valleys voluntarily for the economic opportunity of the coalfields. There they mingled with, and were sometimes submerged by, large numbers of immigrant Englishmen attracted to the same opportunity.

Cornwall, it might be noted, combined the Irish resistance to the Reformation with the Welsh proximity to England. Though remote by reason of its peninsular configuration and its location at the southwestern extreme of the British land mass, it lacked the mountainous impregnability of many parts of Scotland and Wales and lay more open to English armies moving to quell risings in the fifteenth and sixteenth centuries. It is not a matter of chance, then, that Cornish was the first of the Celtic languages with a large native speaker population still in evidence as late as the sixteenth century to disappear completely before the advance of English.

THE PRESENT SITUATION

Although the historical situations that affected the Celtic languages of the British Isles adversely were different in each region, the outcome for the various languages was strikingly similar regardless of region. The English confronted the Celts as enemies almost from the first. Originally invited as allies of the southern British tribes against the Picts after Roman withdrawal in the fifth century, the Anglo-Saxons soon became conquerors rather than allies. Throughout the subsequent centuries, despite many temporary military alliances of convenience and no lack of strategic intermarriages among the leading families of both populations, the cultural traditions never fully merged. Rather, the Celtic populations retreated into districts remote enough or undesirable enough for them to hold. Where they were able to find such strongholds they preserved their own traditions and languages against ever-increasing pressure from the Anglo-Saxons. Where they were not able to retreat, as in Cornwall, assimilation to English customs, laws, and language was inevitable, although aspects of folk life remain Celtic nonetheless.

Anglo-Saxon attitudes toward the Celts and their languages were much as one would expect from a dominant group constantly confronted with the need to quell yet another restive and rebellious Celtic population within their realm. The subordinate group in this case was not only markedly different in language, law, literary tradition, and rules of succession to the kingship (see Dillon and Chadwick, 1967, chapters 5, 7 and 9, for example), but it cultivated a warrior ethos.

Thus, the Celtic peoples of Britain relished warfare, and their pacification did not come easily from an Anglo-Saxon point of view.

It did come naturally, on the other hand, for the Anglo-Saxons to regard these warlike Celts, with their exotic lifeways and their unintelligible languages, as savages, barbarians, and lesser beings. Scathing Anglo-Saxon opinion (including Lowland Scottish opinion of the Highlanders) has come down to us in all too generous measure.

Two major works, M. Hechter's *Internal Colonialism: The Celtic Fringe in British National Development, 1536–1966* (1975), and R. N. Lebow's *White Britain and Black Ireland: The Influence of Stereotypes on Colonial Policy* (1976), argue persuasively that such attitudes as these were critical to the establishment and maintenance of a thoroughly colonial British rule over the Celtic parts of the British Isles.

In the Irish case, we have seen that the long-term effect of cultural hostility and political subjugation was a successful independence movement. In the case of Scotland and Wales, the 1960s were a watershed, with Nationalist candidates winning parliamentary seats for the first time in both countries (Cunliffe, 1979:211; Brand, 1978:262). A proposal for "devolution" (a policy that would grant Scotland and Wales somewhat more control over their own internal affairs) was put to the vote in those countries in 1979. It failed, and ironically some of the strongest opposition came from segments of the respective Nationalist parties. Those segments felt that the proposal lacked sufficient provision for political and cultural autonomy to warrant support.

The publicity attending first the election of Welsh and Scottish Nationalist members of Parliament and subsequently the debate over devolution has created a climate in which demands for concession in both symbolic and substantive matters of support for ethnic identity are somewhat more likely to bring results.

One enduring if unlikely-seeming focus of cultural tension and Nationalist demands has been road signs. In both Wales and Scotland, regardless of the proportion of Celtic mother-tongue speakers to English mother-tongue speakers in any given district, road signs have traditionally been posted in English only. In protest of this policy, vandalism to road signs has gradually become a serious problem over the past several decades, as signs have been removed, painted over, or adorned with Nationalist slogans. But when authorities finally yielded to the pressures by posting a number of bilingual road signs, critics were quick to point out that English always appeared first, with the Celtic language beneath. Vandalism has resumed, though at a lower level, and local newspapers in Wales and Highland Scotland remain full of articles and letters-to-the-editor arguing the road sign issue.

In a more critical matter, the amount of radio and television programming provided in Celtic languages, the debate has been hotter and has included the Republic of Ireland, despite ostensible government support for Irish-language programming there. In Scotland the issues have been amount of air-time, with Gaelic speakers comparing the hours of programming provided immigrant languages like Punjabi and Urdu with the hours provided their own language; and the lack of a full-time Gaelic radio station based in the Outer Hebrides, the heartland of Gaelic today. In Wales, where a larger proportion of the population speaks Welsh either natively or as a second language, the pressure has been for an all-Welsh television channel as well as for increased programming of all types. In the Republic of Ireland there have been charges of tokenism and insufficient variety in programming, with Irish supporters pointing to the great disparity between number of hours of broadcasting in Irish and number of hours of broadcasting in English. Sometimes they also claim that serious coverage of major national and international news stories is still too likely to be in English and not in Irish.

Governmental response to pressures for more favorable treatment of the Celtic languages has differed considerably by region. Clearly, the Republic of Ireland represents the most favorable case.

The Irish Constitution of 1937 declares: "The Irish language as the national language is the first official language. The English language is recognized as . . . [a] second official language" (Macnamara, 1971:76). Naming Irish the "first official language" did not lead automatically to its general adoption, however, even by the government itself. Irish has been promoted vigorously, especially at a symbolic level. Up to the present it remains true that coinage bears no English, only Irish, and bank notes and postage bear a minimum of English; letterheads are bilingual, but the Irish is usually in larger type and stands first in each line, with the smaller English version printed interlinearly. Seamus O Ciosain, who notes these facts in a recent paper, reports also of the Dail, or Parliament: "In Parliament, formal prayers and motions are usually in Irish while statutes are published in completely bilingual versions and debates are almost entirely in English" (1983:13).

The Commission on the Restoration of the Irish Language was set up by the government to investigate progress; it made an extensive report in 1964. A government White Paper published a year later in response to the Commission's Final Report repeats at the outset the relative position of the two languages as established by the Constitution, but follows this immediately with a paragraph headed "The National Aim." In this next paragraph, a relatively modest goal is set forth, namely, "to restore the Irish language as a general medium of communication" (*The Restoration of the Irish Language*, 1965:4). Thus, Irish may be accorded favored status, but in practical terms that does not necessarily mean ousting English from dominance or even creating a bilingual nation in which all citizens are fully at home in both languages. Of the content and effect of the 1965 White Paper, Macnamara writes:

The white paper further goes on to recognize—perhaps for the first time in such a document—that the country is dependent and will continue to be dependent on a knowledge of English. Although the terms of both the Constitution and the white paper are so vague that they rule out a firm conclusion that the official policy had changed, many people felt that a significant change had been signalled (1971:83).

All such matters are relative, of course. If the government of the United Kingdom were to make statements of support for Welsh or Gaelic echoing those of the Irish government, supporters of those languages would feel that a major victory had been won. The disappointments of the Irish attempt at language revival have been great in proportion to the rhetoric of governmental support and to the grandiose visions of the Irish nationalists at the time of the founding of the Free State and in the decades leading up to that event.

The Irish government has expended enormous energy and large sums of money in the promotion of Irish, which again makes the limited results of those expenditures particularly disappointing. The thrust of governmental support of Irish has been twofold: to preserve the small residual population of native Irish speakers which still remains, and to make the rest of the country as fully conversant as possible with its Irish heritage, linguistic and cultural. It has seemed crucial to the survival of Irish that a true native-speaker population survive as a validating entity, a signal to the rest of the country that Irish can serve as a genuine language of daily life. A serious obstacle in the battle to maintain the native-speaker population has been the fragmented distribution of the Gaeltacht, the residual Irish-speaking area. Small, discontinuous districts on the seaboards of the western counties of Donegal, Mayo, Galway, and Kerry contain the bulk of the Irish-speaking population. They are cut off from each other by intervening areas in which English is the only native language. The districts to be officially recognized as part of the Gaeltacht were defined by the Gaeltacht Areas Order of 1956. Within the Gaeltacht many special benefits are provided by the government as an inducement to the Irish-speaking population to stay and to remain Irish in speech. Since there is relatively little arable land in precisely these districts, and there was historically a notable lack of commercial development of any kind, a good deal of government intervention was required if devastating out-migration was to be avoided. Intervention has taken a number of forms: an outright grant (originally 2 pounds, later 10 pounds) to the parents in a Gaeltacht family for every child certified as Irish-speaking by the school inspectors, and special house-building grants, along with official status as a suitable host family for summer language students, for such families; special grants for agricultural improvement; grants for the construction of village halls for community gatherings and entertainments; and introduction of government-sponsored manufactures such as tweed, toys, and knitwear (Fennell, 1981:33; *The Restoration of the Irish Language*, 1965:54–56).

A particularly severe and well-informed critic of the failure of policies aimed at preserving a genuine Gaeltacht would seem to be Desmond Fennell, who made a survey of the Gaeltacht in 1975 and 1976. He notes that the officially designated Gaeltacht areas of 1956 were known even at the time to include considerable territory that was English-speaking (Fennell, 1981:35). The 1971 census gave a Gaeltacht population of seventy-one thousand, but Fennell's own survey a few years later turned up only twenty-nine thousand people who lived in districts, or in "pockets," where Irish was the "normal language of daily intercourse." His findings on the transmission of Irish were decidedly dismal:

[I]n the course of the 1970's, in the principal Irish-speaking territories, the majority of parents have begun to rear their children in English. A family rearing its children in Irish is now, in most places, a matter for comment. Since this kind of situation has been the usual preamble to the disappearance of an Irish-speaking district, it is fair to say that the final dissolution of the Gaeltacht is now in sight (1981:36).

If we look closely at Irish government policy in the Gaeltacht toward one of the tension-generating issues discussed above in relation to Wales and Scotland, namely, road signs, some of the ambivalence that vitiates official efforts to promote Irish becomes evident. The White Paper of 1965, which formed the government's response to the Final Report of the Commission on the Restoration of the Irish Language in 1964, takes up the issue of road signs. The Commission had recommended *for the Gaeltacht* that place names for which the Irish and the English were very nearly the same be rendered only in Irish, and when the Irish and the English were quite different that both be given with the Irish version in larger lettering than the English (printed as Recommendation 61 in *The Restoration of the Irish Language*, 1965:42–44). The White Paper response to this Recommendation in the same publication reads:

78. As the main purpose of road signs is to facilitate traffic, clarity and uniformity are of paramount importance. The signs must be designed so as to be easily understood without confusion or hesitation by drivers of mechanically propelled vehicles; they are not primarily intended for residents of the immediate locality. Until the majority of drivers can easily read and understand Irish, signs in all areas must give prominence to the English version of place names where the English versions are commonly used. Where, however, the English version is a direct or almost direct rendering of the Irish, the Irish version only will in future be shown on additional or replacement signs (*The Restoration of the Irish Language*, 1965:44).

This response, closely considered, amounts to a blunt statement that English is the working language of Ireland and that the right of Gaeltacht residents to protection of their native language may be worth 10 pounds per year for each Irish-speaking school child but it is not worth inconvenience to nonlocal drivers. One might almost as well suggest that since the bulk of people entering Hoek van Holland are taking the ferry to Harwich and are not Dutch, and since the Dutch residents already know their way around, road signs in that part of the Netherlands should be in English, French, and German, but not in Dutch. In any normal sovereign state in Europe, road signs are printed in the local language (very occasionally with a foreign language gloss added), and road maps are made available with local language place names rendered into whatever other language might be useful: German for the Germans, French for the French, and so forth. It is not Ireland generally which is at issue here—exclusively Irish road signs in Dublin might well be of dubious value. Rather, it is the Gaeltacht, an area officially designated as Irish-speaking by the government itself. There seems to be a message conveyed to Gaeltacht residents by the road sign policy to the effect that they should be Irish-speaking when it suits government convenience— for example, when the government wishes to send civil servants on summer courses to improve their Irish by living temporarily in the Gaeltacht—but not when it might be an inconvenience to the rest of the population or to tourists. Thus, the road sign issue, which seems trivial at first blush, is perhaps not an inappropriate focus for the attention of linguistic minorities after all, at least within their own heartlands.

Where efforts to promote a knowledge of Irish outside the Gaeltacht are concerned, there have been individual successes of note in the form of people who have achieved native-like control of Irish without benefit of an Irish-speaking home. The most serious problems identified in the *overall* achievement are: (1) the fact that the successful learners of Irish have been middle class, with the working-class population relatively untouched by government efforts on behalf of Irish, both of these results connected with the crucial role of a good secondary education in acquired fluency; and (2) the fact that the successful learners of Irish are not geographically clustered in neighborhoods or districts but scattered throughout the population, so that the likelihood of successful home transmission to the next generation is greatly reduced by the isolation of the family units in which transmission efforts are being made (Greene, 1981:6). In a survey that tackled the question of conversational ability in Irish outside the Gaeltacht, apart from 1.9 percent who were actual native speakers, there appeared among the respondents 7.4 percent who had acquired a fair degree of fluency (Committee on Irish Language Attitudes Research, 1975:129). Extrapolating from this sample to the population as a whole, D. Greene estimates that there might then be 220,000 people in the Republic of Ireland who have learned Irish to the point of reasonable fluency (Greene, 1981:6). He calls this a "reasonably respectable linguistic group," capable, for example, of supporting a certain number of writers and journalists who chose to use Irish (p. 6). But given the obstacles to trans- mission of such acquired fluency, this is not so much ground that is won as ground that has been taken for the moment and will need to be perpetually retaken by succeeding generations through their own efforts.

In the early 1970s, a pair of writers produced a book devoted to the successful revival of threatened folk languages explicitly to remind the Celtic peoples that their plight was not unique and that the goal of language revival was obtainable. Comparing Irish with Faroese, they stated:

Today in modern literature the names and works of Richard B. Thomsen, William Heinesen and Jorgen-Frantz Jacobsen are world famous. Yet the language they write in, Faroese, was dead as a written language by the 15th century and . . . [its] restoration only started about the time of the foundation of the Gaelic League in the 19th century (Ellis and mac a'Ghobhainn, 1971:7).

If "world famous" is a bit strong for the authors named, the general point is well taken (cf. Greene, 1981, and Poulsen, 1981). There is bite, therefore, in the same authors' comment that only the Republic of Ireland, among countries with a Celtic-speaking population, has been in a position to make language restoration an official policy, and that among countries attempting language revival, Ireland has been "the only country to undertake such a policy and fail" (Ellis and mac a'Ghobhainn, 1971:8). The reasons for the failure are complex, of course, and since they are bound up in many respects with Ireland's bilingual education policies, discussion will be postponed until the next section.

Neither Wales nor Highland Scotland has enjoyed the political independence that would afford them the luxury of establishing their own policies on language use and language promotion.

In Wales, the great advance of recent years was the Welsh Language Act of 1967, which gave Welsh "equal validity" with English (Khleif, 1980:84). Remarkable as the existence of such an act is for a Celtic country that has suffered the usual suppression or discouragement of its original language under English rule, the practical consequences of the Act are limited. Provision was made for the use of Welsh in court by any party to the court case, but subsequent clarifications of that provision have sharply limited its application. Thus, while accused persons have the right to translation of all evidence into Welsh for their benefit, lay litigants do not. Control over the use of Welsh in a given case resides with the court in which that case is being heard and thus with the officials presiding in each case; no courts were designated for regular use of Welsh so that laypersons could be sure of the use of Welsh by taking their case to such courts. A shortage of interpreters competent to handle legal terminology and the sort of abstract issues likely to arise in a court case further reduces the usefulness of the provision (Khleif, 1980:84–90).

Government departments, technically also covered by the Welsh Language Act, responded in equally limited fashion, making some official forms available in Welsh but not others, or laying out only English versions ready to hand, thus reducing the number of people who would ask for Welsh forms and use them (Khleif, 1980:90–91).

The "equal validity" provision of the Welsh Language Act has perhaps become more useful as a potential wedge by which future concessions can be demanded and by reference to which actual inequities can be highlighted than it was as a genuine source of immediate improvement in the position of Welsh in Wales at the time of its promulgation.

In matters less technically legal, the Welsh have had some marked success, especially by comparison with the Highland Scots. On an experimental basis at least, they have gained the all-Welsh television channel which they lobbied for. At the university level, the Welsh have been more successful than either the

Irish or the Gaels in pressing their national university system to accommodate their special needs and interests:

[T]he influence of the native speakers of Welsh among the university population is far greater than their numerical status would allow us to expect. Some of the colleges have residential hostels which are reserved for Welsh-speaking undergraduates. Some departments of the University . . . teach some of the course in Welsh and they have appointed members of the respective faculties with this purpose in mind (Lewis, 1978a:271).

In Scotland, there are no countrywide provisions for Gaelic, symbolic or otherwise. Scotland's internal division between the Lowlands, where either Scots or its relative English has dominated for centuries, and the Highlands, traditionally Celtic but increasingly English in popular speech, creates an unfavorable environment. The inherent difference between Scotland on the one hand and Wales and Ireland on the other is apparent from the obvious symbolic role which the Celtic language has in an independent Ireland and would without doubt have in an independent Wales, and the uncertainty as to what role Gaelic would play in an independent Scotland. English speakers were originally an unwelcome intrusion in conquered Ireland and the product of an industrially motivated migration into Wales, although in both countries, of course, many natives—even a majority—adopted the language of the intruders. In Scotland, speakers of English have a very long indigenous history, and although Gaelic was probably the language of the greater part of the country in the early twelfth century, it seems most likely that "this coverage varied regionally in intensity of Gaelic speaking and that at no period within early and medieval Scotland was Gaelic everywhere understood and used as a spoken language for all purposes by all persons" (Withers, 1984:18). Consequently, it is difficult for Scots to rally around Gaelic throughout the country even emblematically, although the Scottish National Party (SNP) has made support for Gaelic a plank of its platform for some years. It is probably not accidental that the most Gaelic-speaking region in Scotland, the Western Isles, has been rather more consistent in voting for the SNP than other regions, a number of which have elected an SNP political candidate to Parliament at one time or another in recent years, but then elected a rival party candidate in the subsequent campaigns.

In 1981, the SNP Member of Parliament for the Western Isles introduced a bill that would have given Gaelic legal status, but it was "talked out" (prevented from coming to a vote) in the House of Commons. Within Scotland itself a few concessions have been gained: several very decorative bilingual air letter forms have been produced by the postal service in Scotland, and the Gaelic Books Council, with grants authorized by the Secretary of the State for Scotland beginning in 1968, has been enabled to support the publication of new writing in Gaelic, to reissue Gaelic classics that have gone out of print, and to translate into Gaelic some works originally published in other languages (*The Oban Times*, December 15, 1977). The publication of Gaelic materials has important implications not only for the ability of a number of outstanding modern Gaelic poets to see their works into print, but also for the survival of Gaelic drama groups (always in need of fresh material) and especially for bilingual education, as will become clear in the next section.

BILINGUAL EDUCATION AND THE FUTURE

As a preface to discussion of bilingual education efforts in the three Celtic areas, the situation with regard to dialect diversity and the standardization problems can be quickly dealt with. The scattered distribution of the surviving Gaeltacht areas in Ireland has at least the one advantage of allowing for the recognition of three basic dialect clusters: Donegal (Ulster) dialects in the northwest, Connacht dialects in the central part of the western seaboard, and Munster dialects in the southwest. There was a great need for standardization of the written forms, if Irish was to be promoted officially, and for modernization and simplification of spelling and script. Both tasks were undertaken by the translation office of the Irish Parliament. A reformed spelling was achieved in 1945 and adopted for government use in the same year; the old orthography was anachronistic and difficult for modern speakers to master, so that the reforms—especially with official support—met with wide acceptance. Standardization of the grammar was somewhat more problematic, since it was hard to accommodate the variety found among living dialects and to modify modern Irish without divorcing the current language from its history and its literary tradition. In 1953, the translation office produced a simplified and standardized grammar, specifying four principles that guided the effort; these were authenticity (in terms of similarity to forms or grammatical rules found in living Gaeltacht dialects), widest currency among living dialects (where competing variants existed), preservation of historical continuity, and preference for regularity and simplicity. The result coincided with no actual spoken dialects, but it had many advantages and was in any case intended above all for writers and publishers and for learners who needed to use Irish in civil service and in ceremonial duties. In general, forms were closer to Connacht Irish than to the more northerly or southerly dialects, and since Connacht was geographically intermediate and also claimed the largest number of native speakers, this was an acceptable tilt (O Cuiv, 1969a:32–33; Macnamara, 1971:73–74).

In reading Irish government publications dealing with the actual form which the Irish language is to take, it becomes clear that a tension is inherent in the two quite different goals of language policy. On the one hand, written Irish must be rendered as regular and learnable as possible, so that the general populace will not see the task of acquiring it as impossible; yet, on the other hand, the actual spoken dialects, which alone demonstrate the color and authenticity of the language, must be encouraged, so that Irish does not become a lifeless Esperanto-like abstraction. Thus, the White Paper of 1965 speaks first of adapting Irish to the needs of modern life, but then in the very next paragraph takes pains to state: "This policy of standardization does not of course detract from the respect in which the living speech of the Gaeltacht, with its local tones and variations, is rightly held" (*The Restoration of the Irish Language*, 1965:14). The tension produced by the dual aim of government policy probably *cannot* be resolved. Despite the homage paid to Gaeltacht dialects, speakers of those dialects are unlikely to feel that their speech is honored in a deeply meaningful or even economically reinforcing sense if the ceremonial Irish spoken and broadcast on state occasions, and even the Irish of government forms and notices, is noticeably different from their own everyday language. However, the use by Radio na Gaeltachta (the state-operated all-Irish radio network opened in 1972) of the three spoken dialects in equal measure has greatly helped listeners in each Gaeltacht district to become accustomed to the variations in the other areas.

In Wales, the chief dialect division is between the north and the south. Gwynnedd and Powys, in the northwest and northeast, respectively, and Dyfed and Gwent in the southwest and southeast, respectively, contain characteristic dialect clusters (Lockwood, 1972:68–69). Although dialect diversity is fairly pronounced in the regional spoken variants of Welsh, as is true in the other Celtic areas of the British Isles, Welsh is more fortunate than the others in having a well-established, widely used literary and spoken standard form and a population that is on the whole accustomed to it and able to make active use of it, despite the fact that it does not coincide with any actual spoken dialect. The chief reason for this seems to be the early and continuing success of the "circulating schools" in Wales, and their successors. Begun in the first half of the eighteenth century, the circulating schools used Welsh as the language of instruction; the teachers quickly taught the pupils (adults as well as children) in a given location to read Welsh and then moved on to start the process again in another district (Durkacz, 1983:83). The wide and early use of Welsh in education and the success of the effort are directly traceable to religious and political conditions in Wales as compared to Ireland and Highland Scotland:

Because the Irish and Gaelic languages were associated with Catholic religion the [early] protestant schools emphasized English in their curriculum even to the extent of sacrificing meaningful education to this end.

In Wales on the other hand, a nation in which the jacobite tradition was a thing of straw, the mother tongue was not tainted with Catholicism or rebellion. Its use as a vehicle of religious instruction had been pioneered by the Welsh Trust in the late 17th century: Welsh was never alienated from religious life and education as were the Gaelic and Irish languages (Durkacz, 1983:81).

There is some difference in the spoken value of written vowels in even the standard Welsh language as between north and south Wales. But there is no doubt that the Welsh are far more familiar with the normalized form of their language, and comfortable with it, than is true of their counterparts in the other Celtic areas.

In Gaelic Scotland, perhaps two chief problems are connected with the form of the language; these problems cause special difficulties. One is that Gaelic spelling has not enjoyed the modernization which Irish has undergone, and it is both cumbersome and ambiguous; it poses a formidable problem for children and learners without knowledge of language history, as well as for anyone who has learned English spelling first, since many identical letter-combinations have very different sound values in the two languages.

The second problem is that the region which by itself accounts for a very large proportion of the native Gaelic speakers alive today, the Isle of Lewis, also happens to be the home of the dialect found most difficult to understand by speakers of most other Gaelic dialects. By simple availability, speakers of Lewis Gaelic occupy many Highland pulpits, and they staff or appear on a relatively large number of Gaelic radio and TV broadcasts. Complaint about the difficulty of making out Lewis Gaelic is widespread in much of the rest of Gaelic-speaking Scotland. Other "aberrant" dialects, typically located on the Gaelic periphery, now have so few surviving speakers that they cause no one else any difficulty, although the remaining speakers in those districts may have special problems in understanding the Gaelic they hear from broadcast media or from other Gaels with whom they come in contact.

As in Ireland and Wales, the form of the language officially disseminated in schools, used in formal broadcasting, and generally adopted for purposes of written communication does not coincide with any actual spoken dialect. Ordinary speakers seem to identify very little with it, and in the absence of strong support for it on any national or even regional level, it may actually be alienating for a good many native speakers (Dorian, 1978:651; 1981:87–89).

As with all other matters of public policy involving language, Ireland was the first of the Celtic areas to embrace bilingual education. The Irish Free State was requiring at least an hour a day of instruction in or through Irish in all national schools with a teacher competent in Irish as early as 1922. In 1934, teaching as far as possible through the medium of Irish was made obligatory for all national school teachers (Macnamara, 1966:3–4). Although actual practice has varied a good deal over the years, basic belief in the importance of schooling in Irish has repeatedly resurfaced as part of the national ideology, both within officialdom and among the populace. The White Paper of 1966 stated:

The Government adheres to the view that no Irish child can be regarded as fully educated if he grows up without a knowledge of the Irish language and that the educational system will be seriously defective if it does not provide for the teaching of Irish to all children (White Paper on the Restoration of the Irish Language, 1966:36).

In the following decade, 68 percent of a population sample of 2,443 persons outside the Gaeltacht agreed with the statement that "All children should be required to learn Irish as a subject in school": 93 percent of a 542-person sample within the Gaeltacht agreed with the same statement (Committee on Irish Language Attitudes Research, 1975:26).

Given the strength of government commitment and the apparent support of the public not just for availability of Irish in the schools but even for Irish instruction as an obligatory part of a child's education, one might reasonably expect very positive results to have emerged over a fifty- to sixty-year period. Yet, as noted above, only 7.4 percent of the 2,443 respondents outside the Gaeltacht in the survey published in 1975 claimed to have achieved a fair degree of fluency in Irish if it was not already their home language. This does not seem an impressive return on decades of instructional effort and heavy expenditure.

There are doubtless many contributing factors to the relatively low level of success. Some are more obvious than others. At the time of the founding of the Irish Free State, there were about two hundred thousand people in the Gaeltacht (O Danachair, 1969:118). But these were the poorest, least fertile, least developed regions in Ireland, and there was a long history of massive emigration from these districts, especially to America, since families were large and local prospects nil. Precisely in the Gaeltacht, English was highly valued because it was the language immigrants would need to make their way in the world. Patrick Pearse, a great Irish nationalist spokesman of the early twentieth century, was exhorting an audience in a poor Gaeltacht district to cherish their native language when he was silenced after ten minutes by a shout from someone in the audience to the effect that their native language would not be much use to them where they were going to have to go (Wall, 1969:87). Yet it was the people of the Gaeltacht who were expected, in the government's plan, to be "the natural reservoir from which large numbers of learners can draw knowledge and inspiration" (O Cuiv, 1969b:129). D. Fennell, in his critique of government policies, points out that the people of the Gaeltacht were never fully recruited into the restoration effort at a policy-making or decision-making level. Finally, at the end of the 1960s and the beginning of the 1970s, Gaeltacht natives did organize politically and ask for a locally elected regional authority to administer their own affairs; they also asked that the language organizations promoting Irish move their headquarters from Dublin to the Gaeltacht, where they might become the focus of a more realistic popular movement. Neither objective was fully obtained (although a partly elected Gaeltacht authority was set up in 1979 and some decentralization to the Gaeltacht occurred). Fennell considers that failure actively to involve the population most critical to revival to have sounded the death knell of the government's restoration policies (Fennell, 1981:36–38). Even such a seemingly worthy and useful step as the government-subsidized introduction of industry in Gaeltacht districts has not been an unmixed blessing. Industrialization has required the recruitment of a certain number of monoglot English speakers, and where the ratio of English speakers to Irish speakers rises too high, as in the occasional more technologically sophisticated enterprise, the gain in employment is offset by a tendency among native Irish speakers to shift to English, on and ultimately off the job (O Cinneide et al., 1985).

In legislating instruction in Irish from 1922 on, the Irish government also came up against a serious limitation imposed by the nature of the Gaeltacht. These poor districts, the population of which was largely peasant, were the only areas where the true native speakers were to be found. Who was to staff the Irish classes in all the national schools? Although scholarships for university training were reserved for Gaeltacht youngsters, and, of course, some Gaeltacht natives had already made their way into the teaching profession by reason of exceptional ability, the supply of trained native speakers could not possibly meet the demand. The compensatory strategy adopted was to require the teachers under age forty-five who were already in the national schools to take summer courses, usually in the Gaeltacht, to achieve enough proficiency to teach Irish and even to teach other subjects through Irish. The summer boarding of teachers and civil servants learning Irish or improving their Irish became a sort of "cottage industry" in the Gaeltacht and continues even at present. There was also, it should be noted, a certain number of teachers in the primary schools at the founding of the Free State who, through nationalist zeal and pride in Irish heritage, had already taken the trouble to learn Irish and were immediately available as instructors (Macnamara, 1971:70; Fennell, 1981:33).

The obvious questions raised by this situation, however, are how proficient and capable the Irish learners became as teachers of or through Irish, and what sort of image of the Irish language they projected to their pupils when Irish was even for them an acquired language turned on at the classroom door but not used otherwise in their daily lives. Macnamara, who was a schoolboy in the middle 1930s, states that "the typical primary teacher when I was a boy was, naturally, middle-aged and had learned Irish for the most part in summer courses." Macnamara suspects that his Irish "probably revealed strong influence from English in phonology, syntax, and vocabulary" and also probably included some mixture of dialect features. Tellingly, the young Macnamara, rebuked by an adult for not talking Irish with his older sister, asked her later in private with honest surprise "Is Irish for talking?" (Macnamara, 1971:72–73). By an irony, this same author, so keenly aware of the likely shortcomings in the proficiency of his own teachers and the artificiality of their presentation of Irish, produced a study showing the negative effects of primary school teaching through Irish, in which study the pupils are meticulously grouped according to sex, sex composition of the school, size and location of the school, and number of years of instruction in Irish in the subject being assessed (arithmetic); but the teachers' proficiency in Irish was not assessed in any way. The attitudes of teachers, parents, and pupils toward Irish were not assessed either, an omission very weakly defended by the investigator (Macnamara, 1966, especially p. 74).

The weaknesses of the Irish national program of bilingual education are thrown into sharp relief by comparison with the development of bilingual education in Wales. In Ireland, bilingual education was decreed, and subsequently measures were hastily adopted to make compliance possible. There has always been an aura of the obligatory about Irish instruction, and even though 68 percent of the non-Gaeltacht sample surveyed in the 1970s may have stated that they favored requiring Irish as a school subject, 56 percent of that same sample responded to other items in a way that revealed their belief that most children resented having to learn Irish and 60 percent similarly revealed a belief that children learning certain subjects through the medium of Irish do less well at those subjects than children learning the same subjects via English (Committee on Irish Language Attitudes Research, 1975:30). Instruction in and through Irish has been imposed from on high, in Ireland, and there are various indications that the success of the instruction has been hampered by that fact.

In Wales, on the other hand, the first efforts at education in and through Welsh were made without official sanction by individuals who cared passionately enough about Welsh to sacrifice financial reward and good instructional facilities in order to create Welsh-language schools. The year 1939 saw the beginning of the first Welsh-medium primary school, purely by private initiative, in Aberystwyth. Though intended for native Welsh speakers, it was also opened to some children lacking fluency in Welsh, and it was in part the success of these children in achieving bilingual proficiency that helped to establish the credibility of the Aberystwyth school. The second Welsh-medium primary school was not founded until 1947, but after that the number of such schools grew relatively rapidly. The first Welsh-medium secondary school was opened in 1956 in Flintshire, an unlikely location near the eastern border with England. The number of secondary schools using Welsh as a medium of instruction has been slower to increase, but nonetheless has shown modest growth over the intervening years. Facilities in the Welsh-medium schools have been notoriously poor, but the enthusiasm of the teachers has been exceptionally high (Khleif, 1980:116–23). Apart from the Welsh-medium schools, other schools make available a ''Welsh stream'' whereby some students within those schools can elect to take certain subjects in Welsh which are also taught in English for monoglot pupils (Khleif, 1980:124).

Education in and through Welsh, begun privately and in voluntary fashion and subsequently espoused by the Welsh Education Office and allowed to expand more or less according to demand, has not produced students who achieve at a lower level than those taught only through English. Thus, in marked contrast to the negative findings of Macnamara's 1966 assessment of the results of primary schooling through Irish on the achievement of the pupils, the Welsh Office was able to state in 1977:

The learning of the two languages can enrich the total educational experience of the child. The evidence suggests that this can be done without adverse effects on general educational progress. The results achieved in public examinations by pupils from more Welsh areas do not compare unfavorably with those from other areas of Wales. The national survey of reading standards conducted by the National Foundation for Educational Research in 1970/1 showed no significant differences in standards in the reading of English between the children of England and the children of Wales. Tests of attainment in English language and mathematics and non-verbal reasoning have been administered in the course of several recent Schools Council projects to examine the consequences of the use of Welsh as a

medium of learning experiences for children from both Welsh-speaking and English-
speaking homes; here again no adverse effects on general attainment levels have appeared.
(Welsh Office, 1977:16).

According to statistics for the school year 1982/83, 18.8 percent of all Welsh
primary schools, catering to pupils from both bilingual or monolingual homes,
were using Welsh as either the sole or the main medium of instruction. An
additional 14.2 percent of Welsh primary schools used Welsh as the medium
for some of the teaching. At that time sixty-three primary schools and thirteen
secondary schools were officially designated as bilingual schools *outside* the
mainly Welsh-speaking areas of rural north Wales. These "designated bilingual
schools" had a pupil population of 19,345 (Welsh Office, 1983:43–44). The
success of graduates from the schools of this category in national exams has
been high, so that they have a reputation for academic quality and attract pupils
from homes where the parents are monolingual but have high aspirations for
their children (Khleif, 1980:195).

The percentage of the Welsh population which speaks Welsh has shown a
steady decline for at least ninety years, and this general trend continued in the
latest census figures (1981). But while the percentage did drop overall, the decline
between 1971 and 1981 was only 1.9 percent, whereas between 1961 and 1971
it was 5.2 percent, and in the preceding decade it was 2.9 percent. The rate of
decline has slowed somewhat, and two other facts that appear in the 1981 census
report point to the influence of Welsh-medium schools in producing that result.
Most suggestive is the marked difference among age groups. Speakers over
fifteen years of age declined in number, but the number of speakers between
three and fifteen rose. For the age groups three to four and five to nine, the rise
between the years 1971 and 1981 were great enough to make the 1981 figure
higher than the figure for 1961, two decades earlier. Furthermore, the dropoff
in Welsh-speaking between the two most recent censuses was roughly 3 to 4
percent in age groups over twenty-five, but only 1 percent in age group fifteen
to twenty-four. Thus, slowing or reversal of the decline in Welsh-speaking is
characteristic of people under twenty-five, while decline continues at a fairly
stiff rate among older people. Similarly, decline continues in the more rural parts
of Wales in a way reminiscent of the Gaeltacht in Ireland. Here Welsh is the
normal language of daily life for a significant part of the population, but the
living is poor and out-migration is a long-established pattern. In Gwent and
South Glamorgan, however—Gwent bordering on England and South Glamorgan
a highly industrialized area that includes Cardiff, the capital—there was a slight
rise in the number of Welsh speakers. In South Glamorgan, though not in Gwent,
the rise again makes the percentage of Welsh speakers higher in 1981 than it
was two decades earlier, in the 1961 census (Census 1981:50). South Glamorgan
in the school year 1982/83 had forty-eight primary schools in which Welsh was
the sole or main medium of instruction; Gwent in the same year had fifteen
(Welsh Office, 1983:44). Other counties had still more such schools but may

have had more pupils who already knew Welsh entering them, so that attendance at them made less long-term difference to the percentage of speakers in the county.

The difference in the outcome of bilingual education policies in Ireland and in Wales is instructive. In Ireland, the impetus came from the government and was made official and universal policy before the wherewithal to implement the policy realistically existed. In Wales, the impetus came from zealous individuals, and the government soon embraced what was proving to be a successful enterprise. Policy has never been uniform throughout Wales, and a variety of options remain available.

Ireland has concentrated its completely Irish-medium primary schools within the traditional Gaeltacht area; there were 157 such schools, or 85 percent of all such schools, in the Gaeltacht in 1973–74, but only twenty-eight, or 15 percent, outside (O Domhnallain, 1977:89). In contrast, Wales has produced a slightly broader distribution of its Welsh-speaking primary schools, with 18 percent outside of traditionally Welsh-speaking areas in 1982/83 (Welsh Office, 1983:43–44). Since the "Welsh-speaking areas" are of far greater extent than the tiny Gaeltacht districts of Ireland, it has been generally true that Welsh-medium schools are fairly widely scattered throughout Wales and that relatively urbanized populations have had access to them. Transportation to Welsh-medium schools as much as ten or fifteen miles away has been made available to pupils in linguistically mixed districts, for example, if they especially wished to attend such a school (Lewis, 1978b:270).

As compared with Ireland (and also with Highland Scotland), Wales has a major asset in the existence of a relatively large middle class. The very industrialization that threatened to swamp Welsh has in the end made it possible for the upwardly mobile Welsh-speaking sons and daughters of rural workers and of coal miners to find appropriate jobs within Wales and to form a substantial pressure group for Welsh and for bilingual education (Khleif, 1980:77–78). As early as 1967, it seemed to be the case that professional and middle-class parents were the strongest supporters of the Welsh-medium schools (Lewis, 1978a:269). Thus, Lewis can claim with justification that

The system of bilingual education is more advanced in Wales than in Ireland or in Scotland if we regard general acceptability by the total population as one criterion. . . . So far as surviving in a modernized world goes, Welsh is far stronger in the urban areas, and it is in these urban areas that the fate of the Celtic languages will be decided (Lewis, 1980:86).

In-depth bilingual education is a far more recent phenomenon in Scotland than in Ireland or Wales. The undertaking was made feasible only with the reorganization of regional political units in 1975, when the Western Isles Region came into being. This Outer Hebridean region contains the great majority of the country's Gaelic speakers (and an even greater predominance of the young Gaelic speakers). Before this consolidation, various of the Outer Hebridean Islands were the westernmost districts of two large, chiefly mainland shires (Inverness, and Ross and Cromarty), the bulk of whose population was solely English-speaking. Under previously existing circumstances, it had proven possible to introduce Gaelic as a school subject, but not much more than that. It was typically poorly taught, by teachers who themselves might be fluent in Gaelic but lacked decent texts, audiovisual aids, interesting reading matter for their pupils, and training in methods of bilingual education. Many Gaelic-speaking teachers hired to offer Gaelic were confronted by mixed classes of learners and native speakers, especially outside the Outer Hebrides. One teacher handled the problem by simply refusing to accept any pupils who were not already fluent from home, and another by using essentially rote methods for pupils of all backgrounds. In the first case, parents were indignant but powerless, and in the second, the pupils were bored or confused, depending on how much knowledge of Gaelic they had in advance.

Even on an Outer Hebridean island, in the period just before the start of the major bilingual education project in the Islands, a researcher who looked closely at educational methods and the results found little of a positive nature. The primary school population of Harris in the first year of Kenneth MacKinnon's study had 66.7 percent whose first language was Gaelic, although 81 percent of the pupils whose first language was English also had some ability in Gaelic (MacKinnon, 1977:77 and 87). There were serious problems for the teachers because of limited instructional materials, but some of the other handicaps were probably more damaging to the prestige and standing of Gaelic among the youngsters, regardless of the individual teacher's energy or enthusiasm. In the first two primary grades, even Gaelic-speaking teachers used mostly English, although some Gaelic might be included. Later on in the secondary school years, Gaelic was relegated to the teaching of less "important" subjects. Gaelic itself, religious history, and local studies within the Gaelic class were taught in Gaelic, but "serious" subjects such as science, history, math, and natural history were taught in English. Posted displays, insofar as they were in Gaelic at all, were likely to appear only in the Gaelic classroom itself. Moreover, while posted materials, notices, and illustrations in English were obtained from outside and were of professional quality, nearly all posted material in Gaelic was homemade locally by pupils or teachers and looked it by comparison with the English materials (MacKinnon, 1977:86, 100, 102–103). Comparing the results of his survey specifically of primary school children's language use with those of a similar survey made fifteen years earlier, MacKinnon found a dropoff in the use of Gaelic within families, among siblings, and on the school playground. The only improvements in the position of Gaelic among children at this age range were a greater tendency among English mother-tongue children to acquire usable Gaelic and an increased willingness among all primary school children to use both Gaelic and English with the teacher, though the use of Gaelic alone with the teacher had dropped to a smaller percentage than in the earlier study (MacKinnon, 1977:93).

The data for MacKinnon's Harris study were gathered in 1972–74. In the Outer Hebrides, the situation changed dramatically with the creation of the Western Isles region, just a year after the in-residence phase of MacKinnon's research ended. The Western Isles Council showed their consciousness of the region's uniquely Gaelic-speaking population level (approximately 81.6 percent bilingual inhabitants) by choosing to use the Gaelic version of their title, that is, Comhairle nan Eilean, and by making an early declaration of equal status for Gaelic and English in their region (Bilingual Primary Education in the Western Isles, 1979:6:1).

Funded initially by the Scottish Education Department and co-sponsored by that body and Comhairle nan Eilean, a Bilingual Education Project was begun in 1975. In its first three-year phase, the Project included twenty schools in five parts of the Outer Hebrides, from Lewis in the north to Barra in the south. All of the schools were in rural districts, and 92 percent of the Project school population had some knowledge of Gaelic (Bilingual Primary Education in the Western Isles, 1979, 1:1,1:7). By comparison with current reports on bilingual education in Ireland and Wales, where the efforts have been underway much longer, the first and second phase reports (1979 and 1981, respectively) of the Western Isles Bilingual Education Project have the charming spontaneity of working papers as well as a disarming candor about problems, obstacles, and unexpected hazards (a dizzying rise in media coverage was among the last of these, for example). The draft versions used in the preparation of this chapter were published subsequently by Acair, a bilingual publishing company in Lewis. The very existence of Acair is one of the many related developments sparked by the Bilingual Education Project. A critical problem throughout the early period of the Project was almost total lack of reading materials, teaching aids, curriculum units for the teacher, films of any kind for the classes, and so forth. After various attempts to provide materials on an informal, trial basis, the frustrations of a slow, trial-and-error approach to the production of classroom materials in a situation of colossal dearth and desperate need became evident: "The project had to become involved in Gaelic publishing," concluded the leadership (Bilingual Primary Education in the Western Isles, 1979,4:1–4:4). Ultimately, the effort to produce teaching and learning aids led not only to the publication of over twenty books, but also to preparation of a tape/slide program on seashore life and a series of TV video cassettes on the local environment, as well as considerable use of still and cine cameras by teachers and members of the Project team for more personal (if less professionally polished) use of the film medium in local classrooms (Bilingual Primary Education in the Western Isles, 1979:4:10–4:12). Monies for much, but not all, of the production of teaching materials have come not from the Project's own rather limited funding, but from separate grants to other bodies which then worked in conjunction with the Project.

Because of the freshness of the Project's written reports and likewise the impact of a bilingual education project in an area where the native language was excluded from serious educational use (or at some periods, from *any* educational use) for at least a century, some use will continue to be made of home-made cine films, despite certain difficulties, because of the power of the film medium:

On one occasion in Uist during an exhibition of project school work the project team, on an impulse, screened two or three short films which had just returned from processing for a room full of secondary school pupils and teachers. Everyone sat down and watched these silent unedited films, utterly absorbed. Twice. The novelty of seeing one's own people and one's own environment as the only content in a film rather than as a decorative background to romantic and/or travel films transfixed that audience (Bilingual Primary Education in the Western Isles, 1979:4:11).

Happily for the Project, the BBC had taken steps to begin to provide Gaelic radio programs for school children not long before the start of the Bilingual Education Project. The newly appointed Gaelic Schools Radio Producer cooperated fully with the Project from the outset, and two years later, when commercial television in Scotland undertook the first-ever Gaelic children's television programming, the Project's assistance was sought. Thus, the efforts of the teachers in their own classrooms, those of the three-member Project team who directed overall planning and evaluation in the twenty schools, and the activities of print and broadcast media were all coordinated to the benefit of the Project overall.

Teacher evaluations of the success of the Project ran quite sharply to the positive side when the teachers were formally interviewed under guaranteed anonymity by specialists not directly connected with the Bilingual Education Project at the end of the first (three-year) phase (Bilingual Primary Education in the Western Isles, 1979:5:1–5:23). Because of the apparent success of the first phase, the second three-year phase was immediately begun. The number of schools and teachers formally involved was expanded, but as the Project's own second-phase report notes, by this time a fair number of teachers in schools not targeted by the Project and even in districts outside the Western Isles Region, were to some extent making use of Project-related or -generated materials and techniques and were carrying out a similar sort of expanded teaching-through-Gaelic program on their own initiative or within other regional authorities' schemes (Bilingual Education Project, 1981:3:1; Bilingual Education in the Western Isles, 1979:8:1:). (An experimental bilingual primary education program on the Inner Hebridean Isle of Skye is the chief example of the regional authorities' programs.)

Instruction via Gaelic has been slow to blossom in secondary education in Scotland as compared with Ireland and Wales, but in 1983, again in the Western Isles, the first official project came into being. It involves the teaching of history, geography, and Celtic studies through Gaelic as well as English, and has been undertaken in two secondary schools in Lewis where the school population was large enough to permit parallel age-group classes, one for native speakers of Gaelic and one for all others. As in the primary-level project, there was strong focus on local environment and local conditions as a source of natural interest and rich material for study (Dunn, 1984:1 and 2).

FUTURE PROSPECTS

In all three Celtic populations in the British Isles, the key question in maintenance (even survival) or growth is that of prospects for transmission of the Celtic language to the rising generation. In Ireland, the most serious problems seem to be the still contracting native-speaker pool in the Gaeltacht and the discontinuous, dispersed distribution of those fluent speakers produced by the relatively long experiment in bilingual education in that country. The *Action Plan for Irish 1983–86* published by Bord na Gaeilge addresses the latter problem clearly for the first time (the former problem having been focused on for many years now). Proposals include the establishment of new city projects in certain districts of Dublin where fluent speakers (especially the relatively young) can be encouraged by such inducements as entertainment and recreational facilities to socialize and use their Irish, and expansion of an existing tendency for Irish speakers in the urban areas to cluster in the vicinity of all-Irish schools by provision of additional Irish services and facilities in those vicinities (Bord na Gaeilge, n.d.:15–16). There seems little doubt that at least symbolic support for the Irish language will continue strong in the Republic of Ireland, and that a schoolbook knowledge of Irish will continue to be common. Whether such things can be translated into the creation of a healthy language, or even second language, of daily life is a question much debated in Ireland itself. The Irish do have to their credit a good record in the publication of Irish-language materials for children and for adults and an especially good record in the publication in English of popular and scholarly materials focusing on the Celtic past and on the nature of Celtic culture and civilization. All the other Celtic areas are in their debt for this last, as are all people generally with an interest in Celtic, since such materials are not so readily available elsewhere. Irish government support is in part responsible for the abundance, but surely so also is Irish political independence, which has led to the desire to discover the nature of the society from which the ancestral culture sprang.

In Scotland, the creation of the Western Isles Region has proved to be a highly positive step for Gaelic, collecting as it does a great majority of Gaelic native speakers under a single regional authority. Geographical concentration in the Outer Hebrides is a major advantage for Gaelic. Although there are mainland and Inner Hebridean areas which still have relatively high numbers of Gaelic speakers, these are aging speakers and transmission to new generations has largely ceased. The 1981 census showed only 743 children ages three to four as native Gaelic speakers. Of these, 403, or 54 percent, were in the Western Isles; in Skye, one of the very few Inner Hebridean islands with a strong focus on Gaelic in recent decades, only thirty-nine children (5.2 percent of the total) were in that group (An Comunn Gaidhealach, 1984:n.p.). Countrywide, there were only 3,800 children under age ten reported as Gaelic speakers in the 1981 census; 1,968 of these were reported for the Western Isles Region (Census 1981, Scotland Gaelic Report, 1983:4, 9). This is a very small pool from which enough young parents can later be drawn to transmit the language successfully, especially given the continuing tradition of out-migration from the Gaelic areas. In Scotland, as in Ireland, the contraction of heartland areas in which Gaelic is the normal everyday language is recognized as a linguistic emergency. In both countries, concern has reached a new high and major efforts are underway—in bilingual education, in consolidation of language-promoting agencies, in the devising of job opportunities, and so forth—to slow or halt the trend. The crisis is at a rather advanced stage, and only time will tell how much can be expected from even concentrated efforts.

In Wales, the situation is somewhat more positive than in either Ireland or Scotland, though not so much so as to induce complacency. Rural districts are still showing decline in the number of native speakers, but the size of the native Welsh middle class (which has no real parallel in Irish Ireland or Gaelic Scotland) and the relatively long history of Welsh literacy among the populace are two factors that have facilitated movements promoting the Welsh language. The notable increase in the number and percentage of quite young Welsh speakers in the population over the past two decades testifies to good success for the bilingual education programs and seems to promise a reasonably good chance for the long-term survival of the Welsh language. In the case of Wales there is some reason to look forward to the 1991 census report. In Scotland and Ireland, too, that report may make prognostication easier; one can only hope that it will also make it more cheerful.

ACKNOWLEDGMENTS

I am much endebted to colleagues in the British Isles and in the United States for making necessary materials available or helping me to obtain them: Catrin Moseley in Aberystwyth, Hywel Moseley in London; Seamus O Ciosain (especially generously and copiously) in Dublin; Catherine Morrison in Stornoway and Catherine Dunn in Stornoway; Dr. Lois Kuter, Brother Charles Quinn, and Professor John M. Jones in Pennsylvania, New York, and New Jersey, respectively. Mr. and Mrs. William MacKinnon of Tobermory and Ms. Elizabeth MacRae of Inverness (formerly of Golspie) have for many years faithfully sent me weekly newspapers from the Western and Eastern Highlands, respectively, thereby enabling me to stay in closer touch with developments involving Scottish Gaelic. Seamus O Ciosain kindly reviewed the original draft of this chapter with reference to the Irish-language situation, and I owe a number of refinements and corrections to his careful scrutiny. Responsibility for the final formulations and any remaining errors or eccentricities of emphasis is, of course, my own.

BIBLIOGRAPHY

An Comunn Gaidhealach. 1984. "Cunntas sluaigh 1981: Gaidhlig." *Aithisq na Blianna* [Annual Report] 1983–84. (No publisher or place of publication stated.)

Bilingual Education Project. 1981. *Report of the Second Phase, September 1978-September 1981*. (Mimeo.)

Bilingual Primary Education in the Western Isles (1979). *Report of the First Phase of the Bilingual Education Project, 1975–78*. (Mimeo.)

Bord na Gaeilge. n.d. *Action Plan for Irish 1983–1986*. (No place of publication and no publisher are given.)

Brand, J. 1978. *The National Movement in Scotland*. London: Routledge and Kegan Paul.

Census 1981, Scotland Gaelic Report. 1983. Edinburgh: Her Majesty's Stationery Office.

Census 1981. 1983. *Welsh Language in Wales*. London: Her Majesty's Stationery Office.

Chadwick, N. 1970.*The Celts*. Harmondsworth: Penguin Books.

Committee on Irish Language Attitudes Research. 1975. *Report*. Dublin: Oifig Dhiolta Foilseachan Rialtais.

Corcoran, J.X.W.P. 1979. "The Origins of the Celts: The Archaeological Evidence." In *The Celts*, ed. N. Chadwick. Harmondsworth: Penguin Books, pp. 17–41.

Cunliffe, B. 1979. *The Celtic World*. Maidenhead: McGraw-Hill.

Dillon, M., and N. Chadwick. 1967. *The Celtic Realms*. London: Weidenfeld and Nicolson.

Dorian, N. C. 1978. "The Dying Dialect and the Role of the Schools: East Sutherland Gaelic and Pennsylvania Dutch." In *International Dimensions of Bilingual Education*, ed. J. E. Alatis. Washington, D.C.: Georgetown University Press, pp. 646–56.

———. 1981. *Language Death: The Life Cycle of a Scottish Gaelic Dialect*. Philadelphia: University of Pennsylvania Press.

Dunn, C. M. 1984. *Social Subjects: A Bilingual Approach*. (Mimeo.)

Durkacz, V. E. 1983. *The Decline of the Celtic Languages*. Edinburgh: John Donald Publishers.

Ellis, P. B. 1974. *The Cornish Language and Its Literature*. London: Routledge and Kegan Paul.

Ellis, P. B., and S. mac a'Ghobhainn. 1971. *The Problem of Language Revival*. Inverness: Club Leabhar.

Fennell, D. 1981. "Can a Shrinking Linguistic Minority Be Saved?" In *Minority 52 Languages Today*, ed. E. Haugen, J. D. McClure, and D. S. Thomson. Edinburgh: Edinburgh University Press, pp. 32–39.

Filip, J. 1981. "Early History and Evolution of the Celts: The Archaeological Evidence." In *The Celtic Consciousness*, ed. R. O'Driscoll. New York: George Braziller, pp. 33–50.

Greene, D. 1981. "The Atlantic Group: Neo-Celtic and Faroese." In *Minority Languages Today*, ed. E. Haugen, J. D. McClure, and D. S. Thomson. Edinburgh: Edinburgh University Press, pp. 1–9.

Hearnshaw, L. S. 1981. *Cyril Burt, Psychologist*. New York: Vintage Books.

Hechter, M. 1975. *Internal Colonialism: The Celtic Fringe in British National Development, 1536–1966*. Berkeley: University of California Press.

Jones, B. 1974. "The Roots of Welsh Inferiority." *Planet* 22:53–71.

Khleif, B. B. 1980. *Language, Ethnicity, and Education in Wales*. The Hague: Mouton.

Lebow, R. N. 1976. *White Britain and Black Ireland: The Influence of Stereotypes on Colonial Policy*. Philadelphia: Institute for the Study of Human Issues.

Lewis, E. G. 1978a. "Bilingualism in Education in Wales." In *Case Studies in Bilingual*

Education, ed. B. Spolsky and R. L. Cooper. Rowley, Mass.: Newbury House, pp. 249–90.

———. 1978b. "Migration and the Decline of the Welsh Language." In *Advances in the Study of Societal Multilingualism*, ed. J. A. Fishman. The Hague: Mouton, pp. 263–351.

———. 1980. *Bilingualism and Bilingual Education: A Comparative Study*. Albuquerque: University of New Mexico Press.

Loch, J. 1820. *An Account of the Improvements on the Estates of the Marquess of Stafford, in the Counties of Stafford and Salop, and on the Estate of Sutherland*. London: Longman, Hurst, Rees, Orme, and Brown.

Lockwood, W. B. 1972. *A Panorama of Indo-European Languages*. London: Hutchinson University Library.

MacKinnon, Kenneth. 1977. *Language, Education and Social Processes in a Gaelic Community*. London: Routledge and Kegan Paul.

Macnamara, J. 1966. *Bilingualism and Primary Education: A Study of Irish Experience*. Edinburgh: Edinburgh University Press.

———. 1971. "Successes and Failures in the Movement for the Restoration of Irish." In *Can Language Be Planned?* ed. J. Rubin and B. H. Jernudd. East-West Center: University Press of Hawaii; pp. 65–94.

McEvedy, C. 1967. *The Penguin Atlas of Ancient History*. Harmondsworth: Penguin Books.

Moody, T. W., and F. X. Martin, eds. 1967. *The Course of Irish History*. Cork: Mercier Press.

Murray, J. and C. Morrison. 1984. *Bilingual Primary Education in the Western Isles of Scotland*. Stornoway, Isle of Lewis: Acair.

The Oban Times, December 15, 1977.

O Cinneide, M. S., M. Keane, and M. Cawley. 1985. Ms. "Industrialisation and Linguistic Change Among Gaelic-Speaking Communities in the West of Ireland." *Language Problems and Language Planning*. Vol. 9:1,3–16.

O Ciosain, S. 1983. "Bilingualism in Public Administration: The Case of Ireland." *Revista de Llengua i Dret* 1:11–19.

O Cuiv, B. 1969a. "The Changing Form of the Irish Language." In *A View of the Irish Language*, ed. B. O Cuiv. Dublin: Stationery Office, pp. 22–34.

———. 1969b. "Irish in the Modern World." In *A View of the Irish Language*, ed. B. O Cuiv. Dublin: Stationery Office, pp. 122–32.

O Danachair, C. 1969. "The Gaeltacht." In *A View of the Irish Language*, ed. B. O Cuiv. Dublin: Stationery Office, pp. 112–21.

O Domhnallain, T. 1977. "Ireland: The Irish Language in Education." *Language Problems and Language Planning* 1:83–94.

Poulsen, J.H.W. 1981. "The Faroese Language Situation." In *Minority Languages Today*, ed. E. Haugen, J. D. McClure, and D. Thomson. Edinburgh: Edinburgh University Press, pp. 144–51.

Quinn, D. B. 1966. *The Elizabethans and the Irish*. Ithaca, N.Y.: Cornell University Press for the Folger Shakespeare Library.

The Restoration of the Irish Language. 1965. Dublin: Oifig an tSolathair.

Wall, M. 1969. "The Decline of the Irish Language." In *A View of the Irish Language*, ed. B. O Cuiv. Dublin: Stationery Office, pp. 81–90.

Welsh Office. 1977. *Educating Our Children: A Background Paper for the Conference in Wales, 22 March 1977*. Welsh Education Office.

———. 1983. *Statistics of Education in Wales*. Government Statistical Service.

White Paper on the Restoration of the Irish Language. 1965. Dublin: Oifig an tSolathair.

Withers, C.W.J. 1984. *Gaelic in Scotland 1698–1981: The Geographical History of a Language*. Edinburgh: John Donald Publishers.

7

Barbara Burnaby

LANGUAGE IN NATIVE EDUCATION IN CANADA

Since Canada has two official languages (English and French) and a host of minority languages, schooling in this country is provided with a formidable challenge if it is to meet the needs, expectations, and requirements affecting its students. This chapter examines the role of language in schooling for one group of Canadian students, those who are descendants of the aboriginal peoples of North America (Native peoples). Both historically and in the present, schooling for Native Canadian students has manifested a variety of approaches to recognizing the language backgrounds that Native children bring with them to school and to teaching them English and/or French. In order to provide a realistic picture of these many approaches, this chapter will report on school programs that attempt to take account of the specific language backgrounds of Native students.

DEMOGRAPHIC FACTORS

Native people in Canada make up approximately 2 percent (about 481,000 people) of the total population (Canada, Statistics Canada, 1982–84). Although the majority live on reserve of land set aside for their exclusive use, the Native population is spread fairly evenly over the whole country. In other words, reserves can be found in densely settled industrial areas, in farming areas, and in northern areas where there is little settlement by other people. Some reserves are situated within or next to major Canadian cities, whereas others are far from even small towns and can be reached only by plane or boat. Up to one-third of Native people do not live on reserves, and many of these now live in towns and cities (Canada Department of Indian Affairs and Northern Development [DIAND] , 1980:5, 12). Thus, all school administrative authorities across the country can expect to have some Native pupils. In most highly populated areas, they are likely to be only a small minority in any school, but in some isolated areas they form the entire school population.

LANGUAGE BACKGROUND

The ancestral languages of Canada's Native peoples are divided into eleven language families, that is, groups of languages that can be shown to have a common ancestor. Thus, a language from one family is as different from a language from another as English is from, say, Korean. Some families are represented by only one language (Haida, Kutenai, and Tlingit), while the others have a number of languages. The largest, Algonquian, has nine. A total of fifty-three Native languages are spoken in Canada today. A number of these, or their close relatives, are also spoken in the United States or in Greenland (Sturtevant, 1978). In Canada, each language family covers a particular area, although these areas often partially overlap. What this means in terms of schooling is that, although a large number of Native languages have to be taken into account, it is the general rule that any one school will have Native students from only one Native-language background.

English and, to some degree, French have strongly influenced the use of Native languages in Canada, particularly in recent decades. Many people whose mother tongue is a Native language now speak English or French as well or exclusively. Other Native people have English or French as their mother tongue, and almost all of these do not speak a Native language. Table 7.1 shows percentages regarding mother tongue, language most often spoken in the home, and ability to speak an official language calculated from the 1981 Census of Canada on the basis of the population who declared themselves to be ethnically Native. These figures indicate that English is so strong an influence in Native communities that it is becoming the mother tongue of the majority of Native people, and that it is becoming the home language of some Native people whose mother tongue is a Native language. There is no reciprocal trend for those whose mother tongue is an official language to speak a Native language at home. English is the home language of about as many Native children who have not been to school as those who are in school, although a greater number of children who are below school age do not speak any official language. In other words, it appears that schooling is not the most prominent factor in language shift to English. The total French-speaking population of Canada is about a quarter of the total population, yet Native people have not associated themselves linguistically with French very much except in certain regions of Quebec. From the figures it appears that French is losing ground among Native people. (See Burnaby and Beaujot, forthcoming, for further analysis of language data on the Native peoples from the 1981 census figures.)

To the extent that self-reported language data such as census figures can be relied on to accurately represent how people actually use language, these figures indicate a strong trend toward the use of English and, to a limited degree, French

Table 7.1
1981 Census in Canada: Ethnically Native Population (in Percentage)

	All Ages	Age 0-5	Age 6-14
Total By Age	491,460	50,385	115,935
Mother Tongue			
English	62.42	71.38	70.29
French	4.62	2.68	2.43
Native	28.69	23.58	25.03
Other	2.21	2.37	2.35
Home Language			
English	71.66	74.72	70.62
French	3.95	2.54	2.11
Native	22.18	20.87	20.51
Other	2.21	1.87	1.76
Official Language			
English	85.75	83.63	89.68
French	3.62	2.8	3.26
Both	4.96	1.17	2.71
Neither	5.68	12.41	4.35

Notes: 1. Columns may not add up to 100% because of rounding procedures
            used by the author and the Census officials.

        2. Figures, particularly under 'other', may be contaminated by,
            people incorrectly identifying themselves as Native people.

to the detriment of Native languages among Native people in Canada. Analysis of figures from the census (Burnaby, 1980, 1984; Burnaby and Beaujot, forthcoming; Canada, Statistics Canada, 1984) and M. K. Foster (1982) indicate that some Native languages are in danger of becoming extinct, while others still have a reasonably large number of speakers. Younger Native people seem to use official languages more than their elders. The degree of isolation of Native communities from the rest of the population has something to do with Native-language retention, but isolation alone does not account for the trend to the official languages entirely (Burnaby, 1980; Burnaby and Beaujot, forthcoming).

LEGAL AND ADMINISTRATIVE FACTORS

Soon after the confederation of Canada in 1867, the federal government began to generate and adapt a body of legislation regarding Native peoples, most of which falls under the Indian Act. It included and continues to include aspects of laws and treaties relating to Native people which were brought into being before confederation. The Indian Act has evolved continually since then, and treaties have been signed with Native groups as recently as the 1950s. The important aspect of the Indian Act for the present discussion is that the majority of Native people in Canada are individually recognized by law to be "Indians." This status is passed on patrilineally. People who are legally Indians are affected by laws and services that refer specially and often exclusively to them.

A number of people who are descended from the aboriginal inhabitants of Canada do not have Indian status. This group includes people known as nonstatus Indians, those whose ancestors did not get status for various reasons when status was first being established, or those who have since lost it through several legal processes. Many nonstatus Indians have the same aboriginal blood quantum as status Indians and live in accordance with the same cultural traditions. In addition, there are the Metis, a group of people descended from Native and European ancestors, who did not get status originally because they were seen to be culturally different from pure-blood Native people when Indian status was being established among Native people on the prairies. Finally, there are the Inuit (Eskimos) who generally live apart from other Native groups in the far north. Since 1939, the federal government has provided similar services to them as to status Indians, but their legal position is not established in legislation in the same way that Indian status is.

In Canada, the responsibility for education rests with the provinces (Canada's term for "states"), not with the federal government. Thus, the ten provinces and the two territories have their own education acts and administer their own school systems. The federal government transfers some monies to the provinces for certain educational activities it wants to promote, but the provinces administer that money themselves. It does not legislate funds to be administered by the federal government itself for special educational purposes (cf. the federal Johnson-O'Malley Act in the United States which supports certain aspects of education for Native American students directly from the federal coffers apart from state financial provision for the education of Indian students). Metis and nonstatus Indian students attend provincial and territorial schools, and any special needs or aspirations they might have are dealt with as far as the provincial government or local school system see fit. Inuit students are a special case since most of them live in isolated areas. Provisions for their education will be mentioned in more detail below.

The legislative anomaly in this situation is that the education of status Indian students is the direct responsibility of the federal government through the Department of Indian Affairs and Northern Development (DIAND). Originally, the federal government contracted out the work of Indian education, mainly to religious groups. At that time there was no policy governing the education of all status Indian students. In practice, that education often consisted of a combination of agricultural or industrial training with some academic teaching.

After World War II, DIAND took direct control of Indian education. It built and ran elementary schools on reserves. These schools began to follow the curriculum of the province in which they were located and hired provincially certified teachers. In areas in which status Indian children lived close to provincial schools, DIAND also began to make agreements with provincial governments or individual school boards to educate these children in provincial schools, their tuition being paid by the federal government. Virtually all status Indian high school students attend provincial schools.

In 1972, in response to a 1969 federal government policy statement that advocated the abolition of Indian status and special services to Indians (Canada, Standing Committee of the House of Commons on Indian Affairs, 1969), the national Native association of the day issued a statement called *Indian Control of Indian Education* (National Indian Brotherhood, 1972) which outlined the position that education for Indian children should continue to be financed by the federal government and that it should be under the control of Indian people. DIAND accepted this position as the basis for its educational policy in 1973, and since that time partial or total control of federal schools has been handed over to some local bands (the government of Native groups, usually reserve populations). The administrative and legal position of band-controlled schools is still somewhat vague since they are neither federally administered nor are they provincial schools. (See Tschanz, 1980; Burnaby, 1980; Howard, 1983, for further details of the historical development of Native education policy.)

In some areas of the country, this general administrative pattern for Native education is altered for historical or geographic reasons. In the northern parts of the prairie provinces—Manitoba, Saskatchewan, and Alberta—DIAND and the provincial governments have combined forces to provide education to the Native and non-Native inhabitants of these areas in which the population is scattered and communities are isolated. In northern Quebec, where the Quebec government made an agreement with the Native population to facilitate a huge hydroelectric power project, two Native administrative areas were set up, one for the Cree and the other for the Inuit (Canada, Statutes, 1977; Richardson, 1975). In each of these areas, the Native people control their own school board which operates as a regular provincial school board.

In the past, education in the Yukon and Northwest Territories was administered directly by the federal government, so there was no distinction between federal schooling for Native or non-Native people there. In the last decade, these two territories established governments much like those of the provinces, including departments of education. Since Native people form a relatively large percentage of the population in the territories in comparison with the percentages in the provinces, they have more chance at democratic control now that their governments are elected. Newfoundland and Labrador, a province that did not join Canadian confederation until 1948, treats its Native citizens as any others. Therefore, the educational needs of the Indian and Inuit inhabitants are addressed by the relevant provincial school boards, with supplementary funding provided by the federal government chaneled through the provincial government.

LANGUAGE IN EDUCATION PRACTICES

Role of Official Languages

The norm in Canada is that education will be through the medium of one of the official languages, English or French. This holds as true for education for Native people as for other citizens. There is no doubt that Native parents across the country today value the opportunity that schooling provides for their children to learn one or both of the official languages (National Indian Brotherhood, 1972). The ability to speak an official language is seen as essential for participation in the economic and larger administrative systems of the country. The degree to which the development of official language skills can be accomplished in concert with the development of Native-language skills as well is the subject of considerable debate.

Historically, educators of Native students have taken essentially two positions on the role of English and French as the medium of instruction vis-à-vis that of the Native languages. From the time of early contact between Europeans and the Native inhabitants until well into this century, there were Euro-Canadians who took the attitude that it was valuable to provide European-style education for Native people, but that if Native people were to be successful in learning what was being taught, it would be better that they be taught in their own languages. Most of these educators were missionaries, and the primary subject of their teaching was Christianity. Often they developed writing systems for the Native languages of their area, and they taught Native people to use them. The implication here is that the content is more important than the medium and that Native people may not need to learn an official language. It has sometimes also implied a respect for the power and integrity of Native languages and cultures.

This approach has waned, particularly in this century, as Native people have become more integrated into official language-speaking society and as the Christian religion has become less of a part of the regular education systems. In many schools for Native-speaking children, however, Christian religious education is still taught in the Native language, even though most other subjects are taught in an official language (Tschanz, 1980; Howard, 1983; Toohey, 1982; Burnaby, 1984).

The other approach to the language of Native education is that Native people must learn, and in some cases be forced to learn, English or French. From early times of contact with Europeans, Native people have shown an interest in European education and a facility for learning European languages in or out of formal schooling. Native views on learning European languages notwithstanding, in many cases Euro-Canadian institutions felt called upon to force training on Native people who did not readily present themselves to be educated (Tschanz, 1980). The most common means of accomplishing this task was to remove young children from their homes to a residential situation in which they could be surrounded with the English or French language and disciplined if they used their Native tongue. While this approach was used in isolated cases in Canada as early as the seventeenth century (Patterson, 1972:109–11), it became the norm from the late nineteenth century until the 1950s as the federal government attempted to implement universal compulsory education among Native people (Hawthorn, 1967; Indian Chiefs of Alberta, 1970).

This approach implies the exertion of the power of Euro-Canadian society and the attempt to force Native people to assimilate to its norms. Some Native people have assumed that formal education in the European style automatically meant learning English or French and that it was a valuable exercise for them, but others have been subjected to it unwillingly. Today, the fact that English or French is the medium of instruction for almost all schooling for Native children is acceptable to Native parents because they feel that the children must learn an official language (e.g., Tanner, 1982). The important point in this context is that strong feelings remain in Native communities about the roles that official languages have played in education and the status of Native languages in respect to them (e.g., National Indian Brotherhood, 1972; Ontario, Ministry of Education, 1975; Curriculum Development Team, 1979). A complicating factor is the changing administrative and economic roles of official languages in Native communities (Burnaby, 1985). The ways in which educational programs have been modified to make such schooling appropriate given the needs and expectations of the Native community will be discussed below.

Which Official Language?

In some parts of the country, there are disputes over which official language will be the main medium of instruction in Native education. For the most part, these disputes do not affect Native people, but in French-speaking Quebec recently accommodations have been made for Native people. In western and northern Quebec, Native people have traditionally had closer ties with English-speaking Ontario than with the Francophone majority population of Quebec. Those who spoke an official language almost all chose English. In the past decade, Quebec has created legislation and policies intended to make French the only official language of provincial affairs and business (Quebec, National Assembly, 1977). Since DIAND provided English-medium schooling and administered local affairs in English in the English-speaking Native communities, Quebec's initiatives posed few problems.

When the agreement was negotiated between Quebec and the Cree and Inuit to make way for the hydroelectric power project (Burnaby and Mackenzie in Burnaby, 1985; Richardson, 1975), the issue of official languages in the schools came up since these schools would now become regular provincial schools under Native school boards. Quebec recognized the traditional association with English of Native people in this area and for at least the time being waived its general ruling that French would normally be the medium of instruction (Quebec, National Assembly, 1976). But the power project and other economic factors have also brought these Native people into closer contact with Francophone Quebec employment and government. The result is that in the nineteen communities affected, each with from about six hundred to fifteen hundred inhabitants, there is an English-medium and a French-medium school. Parents seem to be inclined to send some of their children to one and some to the other, apparently to ensure that the family and the community will collectively be able to make use of whatever advantages there are to speaking each of the languages (Burnaby and Mackenzie in Burnaby, 1985).

One further point regarding the role of the official languages must be brought out here. It involves the learning of a second official language. Since the late 1960s, there has been an increased interest in the majority culture Anglophone sections of the country to ensure that children learn French in school because changes in legislation and policies at the federal level have meant that access to jobs in the federal civil service is increased for those who are bilingual in English and French. Most provincial schools now offer French as a compulsory subject and even as an optional medium of instruction to Anglophone children at the elementary and secondary level (Canada, Statutes, 1968–69; see also Genesee, Chapter 8 of this volume).

For Native education, the increasing profile of French in the provincial school systems is beginning to provide a conflict with Native efforts to establish and maintain the teaching of Native languages in the elementary schools in Native communities in which English is the official language used. Federal elementary schools generally do not offer French as a subject of instruction in Anglophone areas, although most provincial schools do. Provincial schools that teach Native children through tuition agreements with the federal government may substitute Native-language classes for French classes at federal expense. The main problems with this arrangement arise when the Native children enter high school and must compete with other children who have studied French through elementary school. In addition, some Native parents have voiced the feeling that if French will give non-Native children an economic advantage in later life, then they would like Native children to have the same advantage. The question of how many subjects can be squeezed into one school curriculum becomes contentious. The process of deciding on priorities between French and Native-language teaching is just beginning, but promises to be difficult for some time to come.

TEACHING THE OFFICIAL LANGUAGES

Native Mother-Tongue Speakers

Most mother-tongue speakers of Native languages who have learned to speak an official language in Canada did so by submersion in an official language dominant in school, in a hospital, in a work situation, or the like. Methods of teaching English or French as a second language (ESL/FSL) were virtually

unknown in schools for Native-speaking children until ten or fifteen years ago
and are still far from universally practiced today (Burnaby, Nichols, and Toohey,
1980; Burnaby and Elson, 1982; Toohey, 1982). Since the 1960s, the teaching
of ESL/FSL to non-English/French-speaking immigrants has developed greatly,
and, to some small extent, the progress made in the immigrant field has rubbed
off on education for Native-speaking people.

General figures are not available regarding the number of teachers trained in
second-language teaching methodology and employed in Native-speaking communities, but at least one regional study indicated that there were very few
(Burnaby, Nichols and Toohey, 1980). Supervisory staff in federal schools are
not likely to have had ESL/FSL training either, although the Northwest Territories, the combined jurisdiction provincial/federal school administrations in the
prairie provinces, the Quebec Native school boards, and some provincial systems
put considerable emphasis on this qualification for its supervisory personnel in
Native-speaking areas. Supervisors who are experienced in ESL/FSL are likely
to do their best to provide in-service training on this topic. There is often some
material for ESL/FSL teaching available in schools for Native-speaking children,
but teachers do not usually know how to use it, and they complain that the
methodologies are unsuitable for the learning styles of the Native children and
that the content is culturally inappropriate (Burnaby, Nichols and Toohey,1980;
Burnaby and Elson, 1982).

Compared with the teaching of ESL/FSL to immigrants, official language
training for Native-speaking students has some unique problems. First, there are
many more non-English/French-speaking immigrant children in Canadian
schools than there are Native-speaking children. The 1981 census showed that
there were 313,850 children below the age of fifteen whose mother tongue was
not English, French, or a Native language. There were 40,780 Native mother-
tongue children in the same age range. The fact that Native education is divided
among many educational jurisdictions (federal, ten provincial, two territorial,
and many separate band-controlled) does not make matters any easier. Teachers
who work with Native-speaking students belong to different unions according
to the educational system they work for. Hence, there has been little pressure
from the large professional organizations of teachers to force the various school
systems to improve conditions. The problems of Native-speaking children get
lost in the many concerns of large provincial systems, and federal schooling and
Native school boards dealing with Native-speaking children have a sense of
isolation and poverty of resources (Burnaby and Elson, 1982).

This isolation is a real factor since most Native-speaking children live in small
(less than one thousand population) communities scattered across Canada's vast
northern areas (Canada, DIAND, 1980:12), and valuable resources must be spent
just to transport materials and personnel. Regular visits by supervisors or access
to in-service training are very difficult under these conditions. Under the circumstances, it is not surprising that there is a high rate of teacher turnover in

schools attended by Native-speaking children. By comparison, the teaching of ESL/FSL to immigrant children is much less difficult since immigrants mostly migrate to the large cities and their children attend provincial schools.

There are more fundamental differences between Native-speaking and immigrant students, however. One involves the fact that children from Native-speaking communities are more likely to have different attitudes to learning the language of the majority society of the country from those of the children of immigrants (Mallon in Burnaby and Elson, 1982). Their parents did not deliberately choose to immerse themselves in this alien language and culture. They generally live in communities that are to a considerable degree isolated from the cultural and economic activities of the majority.

A second point is closely associated with the first. Native-speaking children are not surrounded with oral and written uses of the official languages in the way in which immigrant children in the cities are. Radio and television have reached most isolated communities in the past few years, but social, economic, and administrative interaction in Native-speaking communities is in the Native language. The school is generally the only place in which the official languages are normally heard. Immigrant children are often placed in classes not only with children who are mother-tongue speakers of English/French, but also with other immigrant children from language backgrounds other than their own. The schoolmates of Native-speaking children generally all speak the same Native language, perhaps with the exception of one or two official language-speaking children of teachers. Thus, while immigrant children are motivated by a wish to integrate and by the demands of survival in their new surroundings, Native-speaking children live in a world dominated by their own language and culture. Native-speaking children are not presented with the many opportunities to hear, read, and practice the official language that immigrant children are (Burnaby and MacKenzie in Burnaby, 1985).

Thus, teachers of Native-speaking children have considerable basis for saying that their needs in terms of ESL/FSL teaching are different from those of teachers of immigrant children. They have a right to complain that they teach under difficult conditions. They can also rightly complain that they have virtually no appropriate materials to work from. Native children whose school bus is a sleigh pulled by a snowmobile and whose ambulance is a small plane, for example, have major cultural problems, much less language problems, in understanding the world of elevators and cars depicted in materials for immigrants and majority society children. Publishing firms in Canada produce very little material directly for the Canadian market in the ESL field, although FSL for majority culture Canadian children is quite well supported. Governments produce some support materials for ESL, mostly with a focus on immigrants or teaching a second official language. The larger school systems serving Native students are producing their own second-language materials (e.g., the Quebec Native school boards and the government of the Northwest Territories, and federal and provincial educational agencies in Ontario), but on the whole teachers of Native-speaking children must

Table 7.2
Native School Achievement by Mother-Tongue Percentages

Mother Tongue	English and French	Ameridian	Inkutitut
Level of Education			
Less than Grade 5	6	26.5	46.6
Grades 5-8	23.3	34.4	26.3
Grades 9-10	24.1	16.2	9.9
Secondary Certificate	19.1	8	4.2
Post-Secondary	24.4	13.9	12.5
University Degree	2.4	1	.7

Note: Columns may not add up to 100% because of rounding procedures used by the author and Census officials.

make or adapt the majority of the materials needed for their language programs (Burnaby and Elson, 1982).

The result of all this, predictably, is that Native-speaking children as a group do not do as well in school as English-speaking Native children (Canada, DIAND, 1980:49). One study done comparing the use of English in various language functions between a group of children from a Native-speaking community and from a comparable English-speaking Native community showed that children from grade six in a Native-speaking community did not score as highly as the grade two children in a comparable English-speaking community (Toohey, 1982).

English Mother-Tongue Speakers

Native children whose mother tongue is English are also the object of concern among educators and parents. Although they generally do better in school than Native-speaking children, as a group they do not do as well as the majority of the population. Table 7.2 shows the levels of schooling achieved by ethnically Native people aged fifteen years or older and not attending school, broken down by mother tongue. The figures given are percentages of totals given in the 1981 census.

Table 7.3 shows the levels of education achievement, calculated as percentages, for the whole Canadian population of fifteen years of age or older. Unfortunately, the published census figures do not match the format as displayed in Table 7.2 for the Native peoples, but the differences in general trends are evident nonetheless.

Educators are concerned that, although most Native children speak English

Table 7.3
School Achievement, Total Population of Canadan Aged 15 Plus, Percentages of Total

Level of Education	
Less than Grade 9	20.0
High School without graduation	31.3
Secondary Certificate	13.9
Post-Secondary	27.6
University Degree	8.0

as their first language, they are still not experienced enough with English as the majority society uses it to operate up to their potential in the eyes of the school systems (Burnaby and Elson, 1982). Because "Indian English" has not been much studied in Canada (Shrofel, 1985), it is not possible to identify the role that dialect variants of English used by Native people might play in creating the gap between the school achievement of English-speaking Native children and that of the majority of Canadian school children. There has been a call for further study of the potential for the use of standard English as a second dialect method with Native children who come to school speaking English but who are not succeeding in school as well as children from other cultural groups in the country (Burnaby and Elson, 1982). However, K. Toohey (1985) contends that dialectal differences per se are not likely to be the critical factors affecting the school achievement of Native children.

Cultural factors such as the Native children's learning styles (Brooks, 1978; Bowd, 1977) and the lack of learning materials that relate to their home and community experiences may play a strong part. The role of literacy in many Native communities has also been considered as a possible source of the misfit between the school's expectations and the Native students' experience (Burnaby and MacKenzie in Burnaby, 1985; Burnaby, 1982; Philips, 1975). Of course, there has never been any comprehensive explanation of why children from the lower socioeconomic levels of most societies do not normally achieve up to the level of their more advantaged peers in school. An analysis of the 1971 and earlier census figures regarding occupational prestige among ethnic groups in Canada showed Native people to be ranked anomalously low. This finding prompted the researchers to suggest that "structural discrimination" might be indicated to account for Natives peoples' place at the bottom of the occupational ladder (Lanphier, Lam, Clodman and Somogyi, 1980:230–31).

THE NATIVE LANGUAGES

Native Language as a Subject of Instruction Programs

Since about 1970, Native languages have been taught as the subject of instruction in some schools for Native children not, as mentioned above, at the instigation of non-Native educators, but on the initiatives of Native people who were concerned that Native children were growing up unable to speak their ancestral language (Clarke and MacKenzie, 1980a). This movement has grown to the extent that about one-third of Native school children are now able to study their ancestral language as a subject of instruction in elementary schooling (Foster, 1982). Native children who come to school speaking a Native language are sometimes given oral language development and Native literacy training, but these programs do not necessarily have a high priority according to parents' views (Tanner, 1982). English/French-speaking Native children study Native languages as second languages, the latter type of program being the most prevalent since the majority of Native children do not speak a Native language as their mother tongue. The parents and grandparents of these children are vocally concerned that most of Canada's Native languages are at risk because of the preference for official language use within the Native populations (Burnaby, 1984). Few educational jurisdictions in Canada consistently provide Native-language programs in their area (Clarke and MacKenzie, 1980a).

The challenges facing Native-language teaching are legion. Most Native languages do not have a prestige dialect or a standardized orthography (Burnaby, 1985). This hinders attempts to create learning materials on anything more than a community-by-community basis, and even results in dissensions within communities about the way written materials are spelled (e.g., Mailhot, Drapeau in Burnaby, 1985). For example, Ojibwe (called Chippewa in the United States) is spoken by as many as thirty thousand people in Canada (Foster, 1982). It has many dialects (e.g., Saulteaux, Odawa, Algonquian), some of which are considered to be separate languages by their speakers. Two sets of characters are used to write Ojibwe—the roman alphabet and a set of syllabic characters. Traditionally, Ojibwe communities have used one or the other. There is no widely accepted standard for spelling in either system. Governments, Native organizations, teachers, and other individuals have produced learning materials, dictionaries, newspapers, and booklets in Ojibwe, but each item has only a relatively small readership. The roles played by community or personal loyalty to one orthographic tradition, mutual intelligibility of dialects and spelling conventions, and community sense of ownership of written material have not been studied to determine how widely the available Ojibwe materials will be comprehended and accepted by Ojibwe speakers.

The relatively new phenomenon of teaching literacy in the Native languages to children who are used to a standardized spelling system in the official language has created new challenges and controversies around Native literacy since these children expect words to be consistently spelled (Drapeau, Mailhot, MacKenzie in Burnaby, 1985). Most Native-language instructors prepare the majority of the materials they use in class themselves, often without the help of any other professional resources. The rest of the school staff is indifferent or feels helpless because of their lack of knowledge of the language and culture involved. The larger educational systems have produced curriculum guides for some of the major Native languages in the past decade, but these generally have not been effectively implemented in the appropriate schools. It is asking a good deal of trained teachers to go into class to teach a subject without any curriculum guides or appropriate learning materials. We are asking a good deal more of the Native-language instructors since they normally have little or no training and no informed supervision (Burnaby, Nichols and Toohey, 1980; Burnaby and Elson, 1982).

Apart from the questions regarding standardization of the Native orthographies and acceptance of dialect to be used in teaching materials as mentioned above, there are technical issues that make the production of materials for Native-language teaching difficult. Many orthographies for Native languages use a unique set of written characters (e.g.,Cree and Inuktitut) or at least use diacritics that cannot be reproduced on an ordinary English or French typewriter. Amplify this problem of producing materials by the number of languages (and writing systems used for each language in some cases) and it is apparent that the resources for producing and reproducing materials for instruction in each Native language are reduced to near zero. Editorial facilities and even proofreaders for materials do not exist as they do for standardized languages (Burnaby, Nichols, and Toohey, 1980; Mallon, Hebert and Lindley; Guerin and Sawyer in Burnaby, 1985).

The training of Native-language instructors is circumscribed by the fact that those who are the most proficient speakers are often those with the least formal education. In school systems that have strict rules about the qualifications of instructors—that is, most Canadian school systems—this problem has provoked a number of solutions. There are now several universities, for example, Lakehead University in Thunder Bay and the University of Victoria, which train Native-language instructors whose credentials suit at least one of the local school systems. The University of Quebec at Chicoutimi has also had a program to train Native technolinguists to do research on their Native languages and help in the training of Native-language instructors and the preparation of Native-language teaching materials. Projected high school Native-language programs remain un-implemented for the most part because regulations regarding the qualifications of instructors are stiffer at this level. A considerable number of Native-language instructors have received no training at all. Since the qualifications of Native-language instructors are not firmly regulated and since they have no overall body to represent them, they are paid at an uneven rate (Clarke and MacKenzie, 1980b; Moore, 1981; Burnaby and Elson, 1982).

It is nevertheless the case that Native languages are being widely taught as first and second languages in schools for Native children. This teaching seems to have various outcomes. If it is badly taught, it seems to discourage Native children from any interest in their ancestral language. For example, a study of parents' views of Cree-language programs in the Cree School Board showed that many parents were concerned that their already Cree-speaking children were being hindered rather than helped in their Native-language development by the Cree subject of instruction given in the schools. Poor quality of teacher training and materials development along with a lack of coordinated policy for the program were the main reasons given (Tanner, 1982). On the other hand, Native-language subject programs often serve to give Native children the feeling that their backgrounds are important and valued by the school. This writer has heard from a number of Native-language instructors across the country that the establishment of a Native-language program in the school has improved children's attitudes to schooling in general. The Native-language instructor often becomes the go-between for the children to express their fears and frustrations to the school authorities and to their teachers. This is particularly the case when the Native-language instructor is the only Native member of the staff of the school (Mildred Millea, Veronica Waboose, Ida McLeod, and others, personal communication).

Native Language as a Medium of Instruction Programs

The literature on the education of minority language groups increasingly indicates the value of mother-tongue medium education in the early grades as a means of integrating the minority child into the school system and of introducing initial literacy through the mother tongue (Cummins, 1981). In North American Native situations, this approach has proven effective in some cases (Modiano, 1973; Rosier and Holm, 1980). It must be kept in mind, however, that programs that fail are not likely to be reported on in the academic literature, or even studied. In Canada, this approach has not been widely accepted by educators, particularly in the Native context. Such a reaction can perhaps be justified by the lack of standardization of Native literacies, by the small size of the populations represented by each Native language and/or dialect group in relation to the expense of producing the necessary materials, by the positions taken on the subject by Native communities, and by the conservatism of educational authorities.

A case in point is the Cree School Board, one of the Native school boards in Quebec. In its inaugural stages, the Board commissioned a report, based mainly on the advice of academics, on the route it should take regarding language and medium of instruction in its schools. The resulting report strongly recommended the implementation of full bilingual and biliterate education, with the Cree language still being the medium of instruction for at least half the classes by the end of secondary school (Curriculum Development Team, 1979). Despite concerted efforts on behalf of the Board since that time to train teachers and develop materials, the Board has been unable to get Cree-medium education past the kindergarten level—the level at which it was used when DIAND administered the schools before the Board took over. A review of the policy was conducted in 1982, and it became clear that parents and education authority officials were divided over the question of whether more Cree-language instruction would either enhance the children's knowledge of Cree (particularly given in inadequacies of the Cree-language program) or give the children an advantage in acquiring literacy in the official languages (a somewhat counterintuitive notion to the Crees) (Tanner, 1982).

A few other school jurisdictions have taken steps to implement Native-medium education for Native-speaking children. The other Quebec Native school board, the Kativik School Board which serves eleven Inuit communities in Arctic Quebec, has had Inuktitut-medium education go to grade three since the creation of the school board in 1978. Like the Cree School Board and several other Native school authorities across the country, it has arranged to have local teachers trained mostly on site while they work under supervision in the classroom. Kativik has built a research program into this teacher training, and trainees work with researchers to gather data on the learning styles and language development patterns of Inuit children (Stairs in Burnaby, 1985). Although some of the Kativik communities have had moments of doubt about the effectiveness of the Native-medium program, it is still being used in all of the communities. The Northwest Territorial government also began Inuktitut-medium programs up to grade three in 1982 in all its Inuit communities in the Eastern Arctic.

Earlier in the 1970s, the Manitoba Department of Education ran a Cree medium of instruction program in some schools for Cree-speaking children. The program had 90 percent Cree instruction in junior kindergarten, sliding to 10 percent by the end of grade four (Kirkness, 1976). The project began in 1971 and was conducted in six schools until 1976. It continued in one school until 1982. Documentation on the project since 1976 does not appear to have been made, so it is not clear why the program was abandoned. Powerful leadership by Native educators was an important factor in the initiation of this project. The fact that some of the main leaders have since moved on to other positions may have had an effect on the later life of the program.

Schools for Native-speaking children quite commonly teach several subjects through the medium of the Native language. Religion, Native crafts, Native studies, and occasionally art or physical education are taught in the Native language on an ad hoc basis depending on the personnel available and the attitudes of the community. Kindergarten is often taught in the Native language, and bilingual teachers or classroom assistants in higher grades use the Native language as they feel it to be appropriate (Burnaby, 1980; Tanner, 1982).

As mentioned above, French is now being taught extensively to Anglophone children in Canada at the elementary school level. A very popular program is called French immersion in which Anglophone children are taught almost entirely through the medium of French either from the kindergarten level up or starting in a higher grade. This program has been a great success both in terms of its results (Swain and Lapkin, 1983) and of public enthusiasm for it. Several Native communities have taken a leaf from that book and have attempted Native-language immersion programs for English-speaking Native children. It is fairly common in English-speaking Native communities for the Native language to be taught in preschool programs. In the early 1970s, an Ojibwe immersion program that was to begin with an all Ojibwe medium of instruction in kindergarten and transfer mainly to English by grade five was initiated in West Bay, Ontario (Wasacase, n.d.). The program continued for several years, but when parents appeared to be hesitant about it and feared that their children would suffer academically, it was dropped. However, the community is now attempting to mount the program again. On the Caughnawaga reserve just outside of Montreal, a Mohawk immersion program has recently been put in place under the leadership of an energetic elementary school teacher, Sister Dorothy Lazore. This program is projected to cover kindergarten to grade three. Sister Dorothy has mobilized community resources to produce the necessary curriculum and materials, and she has taught a good deal of the program herself. Other Native-language immersion programs are in Maria, Quebec, and Chapel Island, Nova Scotia.

SUMMARY

The task of creating a rational policy for the provision of language training in schooling for Native children in Canada is complicated by the diversity of conditions for every factor involved. There are over fifty Native languages spoken in Canada subsumed under eleven language families. More than half of Canada's Native people now speak one of the two official languages (English and French) as their mother tongue. The majority, but not all, of Native people in the country are distinguished legally from other citizens and are entitled to services provided by the federal government specifically for them. Since education is one such service, a federal educational jurisdiction must be added to the list of provincial and territorial jurisdictions to be considered in the creation of Native educational policy. One further factor is the distribution of the Native population across the country—some communities in great isolation and others in close contact with non-Native groups in rural or urban areas.

Approaches to the role of Native languages in education have fluctuated throughout the history of formal education for Native students. In the period in which most Native students spoke a Native language as their mother tongue (up to about World War II), there were two rival approaches: (1) Native students were taught through the medium of their mother tongue in order to get the content across and were slowly introduced to English or French; and (2) the students' exposure to English or French was maximized from the beginning of schooling, and students were often prohibited from speaking their Native language either inside or outside of school. The second approach was the most common during the latter part of the period in question.

Since World War II, there has been a slow recognition of a variety of roles which the Native languages might play in Native schooling. A number of models have been proposed, and some of these have been implemented with varying degrees of success and staying power. The oldest, most persistent, and most universal of these is Native language as subject of instruction for Native or official language-speaking children. The use of Native languages as the medium of instruction in the early years of transition programs for Native-speaking children or of second-language immersion programs for English-speaking Native children has only emerged in the past decade or so. The earliest of these were discontinued, but others have been initiated which are still in operation. Also since World War II, there has been a slow growth in the use of English and French as a second-language teaching method in classes for Native-speaking children. In the past five years or so, interest has arisen in the use of methods for teaching standard English as a second dialect with some English mother-tongue Native children.

Program models available in schools for Native or official language-speaking Native students vary from community to community and from school to school. One important factor in the choice of program is community will. A second is the political will of the school authority. In some school jurisdictions, Native people have all or at least some of the decision-making power. However, such jurisdictions are not necessarily those with the greatest proportion of Native language in the school program. Other factors include geographically related conditions such as the amount of isolation of the community or the proportion of Native children to others in one school or school system. Finally, some factors are related to the human and material resources available to support innovative programs, such as facilities to print materials in Native languages which use special characters or programs to train and support Native-language teachers and other specialists.

If there is a "best" model for the integration of Native languages into schooling for Native students, or even one for Native-speaking and another for official language-speaking students, there is no consensus in Canada on it. Changing community climates and wider political opinions about the role of Native languages in Native society, along with changes in the part Native people play in decision-making about Native schooling, have resulted in a variety of innovations in language programs. The rich diversity of factors that might influence the choice and success of school programs has produced a range of models across the country. The only widely available measure of the general success of such programs is their longevity. Although we can have some confidence in the value of some of the longest lived and widely spread programs (such as the Native language as a subject of instruction programs), it is crucial that support and encouragement continue for newer experiments—for example, the Native-language immersion programs for official language-speaking Native students. Through these innovations new models can be developed and schooling for Native students can be adjusted to changing conditions.

BIBLIOGRAPHY

Bowd, Alan D. 1977. "Ten Years After the Hawthorn Report: Changing Psychological Implications for the Education of Canadian Native Peoples." *Canadian Psychology* 18, 2:332–45.

Brooks, I. R. 1978. "Teaching Native Children: Lessons from Cognitive Psychology." *Journal of Educational Thought* 12, 1:56–67.

Burnaby, Barbara J. 1980. *Languages and Their Roles in Educating Native Children.* Toronto: OISE Press.

———. 1982. *Language in Education Among Canadian Native Peoples.* Toronto: OISE Press.

———. 1984. *Aboriginal Languages in Ontario.* Toronto: Ontario Ministry of Education.

———. 1985. *Promoting Native Writing Systems in Canada.* Toronto: OISE Press.

Burnaby, B., and R. Beaujot. *The Use of Aboriginal Languages in Canada: An Analysis of 1981 Census Data.* Ottawa: Department of the Secretary of State and Supply and Services Canada.

Burnaby, B., and N. Elson. 1982. *Language Development in Native Education.* Toronto: TESL Canada.

Burnaby, B., J. Nichols, and K. Toohey. 1980. *Northern Native Languages Project: Final Report.* Toronto: Ontario Regional Office of the Department of Indian Affairs and Northern Development, Ontario Ministry of Education, Wawtay Communications Society, Northern Nishnawbe Education Council, and Ojibway-Cree Cultural Centre. (Mimeo.)

Canada. Department of Indian Affairs and Northern Development. 1980. *Indian Conditions: A Survey.* Ottawa: Department of Indian Affairs and Northern Development.

Canada. Standing Committee of the House of Commons on Indian Affairs. 1969. *Statement of the Government of Canada on Indian Policy.* First Session of the 28th Parliament. Ottawa: The Queen's Printer.

Canada. Statistics Canada. 1982–84. *Census of Canada 1981.* Ottawa: Statistics Canada.

Canada. Statistics Canada. 1984. *Canada's Native People.* Ottawa: Supply and Services Canada.

Canada. Statutes. 1968–69. *The Official Languages Act.* C. 54.

Canada. Statutes. 1977. *James Bay and Northern Quebec Native Claims Settlement Act.*

Clarke, S., and M. MacKenzie. 1980a. "Education in the Mother Tongue: Tokenism Versus Cultural Autonomy in Canadian Indian Schools." *Canadian Journal of Anthropology* 1, 2:205–17.

———. 1980b. "Indian Teacher Training Programs: An Overview and Evaluation." In *Papers of the Eleventh Algonquian Conference*, ed. Wm. Cowan. Ottawa: Carleton University.

Cummins, J. 1981. *Bilingualism and Minority-Language Children.* Toronto: OISE Press.

Curriculum Development Team. The Council of Commissioners. Cree School Board (1979). *Position Paper on Bilingual Education: Cree as a Language of Instruction.* Val D'Or, Quebec: Cree School Board. (Mimeo.)

Foster, M. K. 1982. "Canada's Indigenous Languages: Present and Future." *Language and Society* 7:7–16.

Hawthorn, H. B., ed. 1967. *A Survey of Contemporary Indians of Canada: Economic Political and Educational Needs and Policies*. Vol. 2. Ottawa: Indian Affairs Branch.

Howard, P. G. 1983. "History of the Use of Dene Languages in Education in the Northwest Territories." *Canadian Journal of Native Education* 10, 2:1–18.

Indian Chiefs of Alberta. 1970. *Citizens Plus*. Edmonton: Indian Association of Alberta.

Kirkness, V. 1976. *Manitoba Native Bilingual Program: A Handbook*. Ottawa: Department of Indian Affairs and Northern Development.

Lanphier, M. C., L. Lam, J. Clodman, and A. Somogyi. 1980. *Ethnicity and Occupational Ranking: Socio-Demographic and Regional Perspectives*. Toronto: York University, Ethnic Research Program.

Modiano, N. 1973. *Indian Education in the Chiapas Highlands*. New York: Holt, Rinehart and Winston.

Moore, A. J. 1981. *Native Teacher Education: A Survey of Native Indian and Inuit Teacher Education Projects in Canada*. Vancouver: Canadian Indian Teacher Education Projects (CITEP) Conference.

National Indian Brotherhood. 1972. *Indian Control of Indian Education*. Ottawa: National Indian Brotherhood.

Ontario. Ministry of Education. 1975. *People of Native Ancestry: A Resource Guide for the Primary and Junior Divisions*. Toronto: The Queen's Printer.

Patterson, E. P., II. 1972. *The Canadian Indian: A History Since 1500*. Don Mills, Ontario: Collier-Macmillan Canada Ltd.

Philips, S. 1975. "Literacy as a Mode of Communication on the Warm Springs Reservation." In UNESCO, *Foundations of Language Development: A Multidisciplinary Approach*. New York: Academic Press.

Quebec. National Assembly. 1976. *The James Bay and Northern Quebec Agreement*. Quebec: Editeur Officiel du Quebec.

Quebec. National Assembly. 1977. *Charter of the French Language* (Bill 101). Second Session of the 31st Legislature.

Richardson, B. 1975. *Strangers Devour the Land: The Cree Hunters of the James Bay Area Versus Premier Bourassa and the James Bay Development Corporation*. Montreal: Alfred Knopf.

Rosier, P., and W. Holm. 1980. *The Rock Point Experience: A Longitudinal Study of a Navajo School Program*. Washington, D.C.: Center for Applied Linguistics.

Shrofel, S. M. 1985. "Studying Native Indian English: Problems in Methodology." Paper presented at the joint conferences of the Canadian Ethnology Society (12th Annual), the American Ethnological Society, the Canadian Association for Medical Anthropology, and the Society for Applied Anthropology in Canada, Toronto, May 9–12, 1985.

Sturtevant, W. C., ed. 1978. *Handbook of North American Indians*. Washington, D.C.: Smithsonian Institution.

Swain, M., and S. Lapkin. 1983. *French Immersion: The Trial Balloon That Flew*. Toronto: OISE Press.

Tanner, A. 1982. *Establishing a Native Language Education Policy: A Study Based on the Views of Cree Parents in the James Bay Region of Quebec*. Val D'Or, Quebec: Cree School Board. (Mimeo.)

Toohey, K. 1982. "Northern Native Canadian Second Language Education: A Case Study of Fort Albany, Ontario." Ph.D. diss., University of Toronto.

————. 1985. "Educational Impact of Dialect in English Among Canadian Native Children." Paper presented at the joint conferences of the Canadian Ethnology Society (12th Annual), the American Ethnological Society, the Canadian Association for Medical Anthropology, and the Society for Applied Anthropology in Canada, Toronto, May 9–12, 1985.

Tschanz, L. 1980. *Native Languages and Government Policy: An Historical Examination.* London, Ontario: Centre for Research and Teaching of Canadian Native Languages, University of Western Ontario.

Wasacase, I. n.d. *Bilingual "Immersion" Native Language Ojibwe Pilot Project, West Bay, Ontario.* Ottawa: Department of Indian Affairs and Northern Development.

8

THE CANADIAN SECOND LANGUAGE
IMMERSION PROGRAM

Canada is a relatively young nation, founded in 1867, with a population of approximately 25 million citizens who inhabit a territory that is second in size only to the USSR. The country has a federal form of government consisting of ten provincial legislatures, two territorial legislatures, and one national parliament located in Ottawa. Political power is highly decentralized, with the provincial government holding considerable legislative and political power in certain jurisdictions, including, for example, education, health care, and municipal affairs, and the federal government holding powers in other jurisdictions.

There are three founding groups—Native peoples (including the Inuit or Eskimos and Indians), the French, and the English. These groups differ greatly with respect to their population size, geographical distribution, and social and economic power. It is not certain when the Native people arrived in North America, although it was probably during prehistoric times and possibly during the last Great Ice Age. The Inuit have traditionally inhabited the northern regions, and the Indians the more southern parts of the country. Since confederation in 1867, the Native peoples have comprised a small and diminishing percentage of the total Canadian population (see Table 8.1, and Chapter 7 by Barnaby, this volume). They have no separate, elected political representation; they vote in elections in the same way as other Canadian citizens. Matters of special relevance to them are dealt with by the Federal Department of Indian and Northern Affairs.

Canadians of British and French origin constitute by far the largest ethnic groups in Canada, with those of British origin being more numerous (40 percent) than those of French origin (27 percent). French and English Canadians are unequally distributed across the country. This is most notable in the case of French Canadians who reside mainly in Quebec, northern New Brunswick, the eastern border of Ontario, and southern Manitoba. English Canadians constitute

Table 8.1
Ethnic Origin of the Canadian Population, 1901 to 1971

Origin	1901	1921	1941	1961	1971
British	57.0%	55.4%	49.7%	43.8%	44.6%
French	30.7	27.9	30.3	30.4	28.7
Indian and Eskimo	2.4	1.3	1.1	1.2	1.3
German	5.8	3.4	4.0	5.8	6.1
Italian	0.2	0.8	1.0	2.5	3.4
Dutch	0.6	1.3	1.9	2.4	1.9
Polish	0.1	0.6	1.5	1.8	1.4
Scandinavian	0.6	1.9	2.1	2.1	1.8
Ukrainian	0.1	1.2	2.7	2.6	2.2
Other	2.5	6.2	5.7	7.4	8.6
TOTAL	100.0	100.0	100.0	100.0	100.0

[1]Source: Report of the Royal Commission on Bilingualism and Biculturalism, Book IV, p. 248.

a large percentage of the population in all regions of the country with the one exception of Quebec where they make up only 17 to 20 percent of the population. It is clear from Table 8.1 that even Canadians of British or French origin are slowly diminishing in numerical importance as a result of a rise in the number of non-English, non-French immigrants. It is estimated that there are some seventy-eight different cultural groups in Canada. They constitute approximately 33 percent of the total population.

The historical and social significance of French and English along with the growing importance and recognition of ethnic diversity in Canada are two of the most salient features of Canadian culture. Indeed, in contrast to the notion of a cultural "melting pot" in the United States, Canada has been characterized as an "ethnic mosaic." In recognition of these characteristics of Canadian society, the federal government has adopted official policies of bilingualism and multi-culturalism. According to the Official Languages Act, passed in 1969:

The English and French languages are the official languages of Canada for all purposes of the Parliament and Government of Canada, and possess and enjoy equality of status and equal rights and privileges as to their use in all the institutions of the Parliament and Government of Canada (section 2).

This means that Canadians have access to services provided by the federal Parliament or government in English or in French anywhere in Canada. The Act does not require that all Canadians be bilingual, but rather only that government employees dispensing federal government services are required to be bilingual. This type of bilingualism is referred to as institutional bilingualism.

The multiculturalism policy adopted in 1971 is designed:

to encourage and assist within the framework of Canada's official languages policy and in the spirit of existing human rights codes, the full realization of the multicultural nature of Canadian society through programs which promote the preservation and sharing of ethnocultural heritages and which facilitate mutual appreciation and understanding among all Canadians.

Part of the multiculturalism program is concerned with the maintenance and development of heritage languages, including languages other than French, English, or Native peoples' languages. This is a relatively recent aspect of multiculturalism, and to date relatively little has been accomplished (for reviews of this work see Cummins, 1983; and O'Bryan, Reitz, and Kuplowska, 1976).

The remainder of this chapter will focus on French-English bilingualism and particularly on bilingual education programs oriented toward teaching English-speaking children French.Reference will also be made to bilingual programs that teach nonofficial languages, such as Hebrew and Ukrainian, to English-speaking children. In general, then, the focus will be on bilingual education for majority English-language children. The reader is referred to Chapter 7 in this volume for a review of educational programs designed for Inuit and Indian children.

A BRIEF SOCIOLINGUISTIC HISTORY OF ENGLISH-FRENCH RELATIONS

Like many parts of the New World, Canada was settled and governed by different European nations during its early development. The first colonization of Canada was undertaken by the French beginning with Jacques Cartier's landing in Canada in 1534. French control gave way to British control in 1763 when the British defeated the French at the Battle of the Plains of Abraham near Quebec City (Cook, Saywell, and Ricker, 1977). French Canadian culture was deeply rooted in North America at the time of the British conquest. Thus, it resisted the assimilationist effects of British legislation and immigration policy which would have eroded the vitality of a less entrenched ethnolinguistic group.

The British North America Act of 1867 legally constituted the Canadian confederation, which at the time consisted of Ontario, Quebec, New Brunswick, and Nova Scotia. Analogous to the American Declaration of Independence, the

BNA Act, as it is usually referred to, affirmed Canada's linguistic duality only in Quebec, where the use of both the French and English languages was required in the Parliament and Courts of the province. It was not until 1969, with the passage of the Official Languages Act, as described earlier, that both languages were actually accorded status as official languages nationwide. According to Canadian bilingualism policy, federal government services throughout the country must be made available in both French and English. This policy does not apply to services provided by Canada's ten provincial governments or the two territorial governments in the Yukon and the Northwest Territories. At the provincial level, only one province, New Brunswick, also recognizes French and English as official languages. The remaining nine provinces are monolingual, with eight recognizing English and one, the Province of Quebec, recognizing French as the official language. Despite the lack of official status for both English and French in most of the provinces, certain provincial government services are now available in both languages in most provinces. There is an increasing move in this direction. The official language policies of the provincial governments tend to reflect their respective constituencies. Thus, the one officially bilingual province, New Brunswick, has a sizable percentage of both French-speaking and English-speaking residents; Quebec, which recognizes French as the only official language, is inhabited predominantly by French-speaking residents; and the remaining eight provinces, which all recognize English as the official provincial language, have predominantly English-speaking residents.

Notwithstanding regional differences in the prevalence of English and French, in general the English and French languages are important features of Canadian life. Consequently, competence in both English and French is an important means of communication in Canadian political, cultural, and economic affairs, and bilingual competence is often associated with tangible and/or intangible rewards. The reward value associated with English-French bilingualism is enhanced by the international status and utility of English and French, be it in diplomatic, economic, or cultural spheres. Notwithstanding the historical importance of the French and English cultures in the early development of Canada, the federal government recognizes neither as official cultures. As already noted, Canada has adopted an official policy of multiculturalism which recognizes the legitimacy and value of all cultures represented among its citizenry.

THE QUIET REVOLUTION

Despite its historical importance during the early colonization and subsequent development of Canada; despite its contemporary status as an official national language; despite its demographic significance as the native language of approximately 25 percent of the Canadian population; and despite even its international status as a major world language, French has until recently been the disadvantaged partner in Canadian confederation.[1] This has been true to a large extent even in the Province of Quebec where the vast majority of the population speak French as a native language (viz., some 80 percent in a total population of 6 million); indeed, many Quebecers speak only French. Evidence of the inferior status of French can be found in at least three areas: (1) legislation, (2) patterns of language use, and (3) language attitudes.

Legislation and the French Language

As has already been noted, French is recognized as an official language by only two of Canada's ten provinces (namely, Quebec and New Brunswick) and by neither territorial government. While the eight "English provinces" do not presently recognize French as an official provincial language, they do not forbid its use. The legislative picture was not always so tolerant. The use of French, particularly in public schools, has been forbidden by law in certain provinces at certain periods during the years since confederation. For example, in 1890 the government of the Province of Manitoba revoked an earlier law requiring the use of French in the provincial Parliament and permitting its use in public schools. Students caught using French in school by the authorities could be physically punished. The 1890 law has since been repealed, and political efforts are being made to restore French to its original status. According to the new Canadian Charter of Rights and Freedoms (1982), public education will be available in all provinces in both official languages, where numbers warrant.

Patterns of Language Use

Widespread daily use of French, except in communication with official federal government agencies, is limited to the provinces of Quebec and New Brunswick and to other specific regions with sizable French-speaking communities (e.g., the Ontario-Quebec border, Northern Alberta, and parts of Ontario). Even in these areas, however,English often predominates over French as the lingua franca. This is particularly true in public settings and in business and commerce. In an extensive study of the language of work in Quebec in 1972, J. D. Gendron notes that

In the province of Quebec itself, French remains basically a marginal language, since non-French-speaking persons have little need of it and many French-speaking people use English as much as and sometimes more than their mother tongue for important work. This applies even though Quebec's French-speaking people constitute a vast majority both in the labor force and in the overall population (p. 108).

This means that "in interrelationships in mixed conversation groups, English-speaking persons concede much less to French than do French-speaking persons to English" (p. 93). Thus, "the burden of bilingualism is unequally distributed between French- and English-speaking people, both as regards the degree of competence in the other language and the language demands on a worker during the course of his career" (p. 94).

Language Attitudes

Perhaps no other single piece of evidence attests to the disadvantaged or inferior status that the French language has had relative to the English language than the results of a study carried out by Lambert, Hodgson, Gardner, and Fillenbaum (1960). In what has become a classic study in the social psychology of language, Lambert and his colleagues asked groups of English and French Canadians in Montreal to listen to and give their impressions of people speaking either French or English. Unknown to the listeners, they were actually hearing the same perfectly bilingual individuals on separate occasions, sometimes speaking French and sometimes English. Analyses of the listener's reactions to the speakers indicated that they were much more favorable toward the English "guises" than toward the French "guises." In other words, the same speakers were perceived significantly differently when heard using each of their two languages—it is as if they were two different people. Furthermore, it was found that not only did English Canadians form more favorable impressions of the English guises than the French guises, evidence of in-group favoritism, but so did French Canadians. That is, even the French Canadian subjects perceived the speakers more favorably when they spoke in English than when they spoke in French, even though this meant denigrating members of their own ethnolinguistic group.

Subsequent research has substantiated these findings (d'Anglejan and Tucker, 1973) and further indicates that the tendency for French Canadians to denigrate members of their own group is not manifest by children before the age of twelve but emerges around adolescence (Anisfeld and Lambert, 1964) and thus appears to be a socially learned phenomenon (see Day, 1982, for a recent review of similar research). Lambert has interpreted these results to mean that language can act as an important symbol of ethnolinguistic group membership, and that members of ethnic minority groups may internalize the negative stereotypes of their group that members of the majority group often have.

Discontent over these linguistic and cultural inequities had been developing for some time, particularly in Quebec. Early attempts by the French-speaking community to arrive at a more equitable relationship with the English community through negotiation had been largely unsuccessful. Repeatedly faced with an apparent lack of responsiveness on the part of the English community to their concerns, French-speaking Quebecers began to make vocal and public demands for change. This culminated in the early 1960s with concerted political, social, and, in some cases, militant actions to bring about change. There were, for example, mass demonstrations against public institutions that would or could not communicate with French-speaking Quebecers in French. The social unrest manifested during this period has come to be called the Quiet Revolution.

During the last twenty years, some Quebec politicians have called for separation from the rest of Canada. A political party whose avowed intentions are to seek Quebec's separation from Canada was elected as the provincial government in 1976. One of the most important pieces of legislation which this government passed after taking office was a law declaring French the only official language of the province.This law then assures the linguistic rights of the majority French-speaking citizens of Quebec. Some analysts believe that a 1978 referendum by this same government seeking support for Quebec's separation from Canada failed because of the reassurance that this law gave the French population that their language would be respected and safeguarded.

THE ST. LAMBERT EXPERIMENT: A COMMUNITY EXPERIMENT IN SOCIAL CHANGE

At the same time that the French community in Quebec was expressing dissatisfaction with inequities in the language situation, some English-speaking Quebecers began to grow more concerned about English-French relations. More specifically there was an emerging awareness in the English community, precipitated by events of the Quiet Revolution, that French was becoming an important language of communication in most spheres of life in Quebec and, concomitantly, that English alone would no longer assure social and economic success in the province. The coexistence of French and English Canadians has been characterized by Canadian novelist Hugh MacLennan (1945) as *two solitudes*, an apt metaphor in this and many other communities inhabited by people of different linguistic and cultural backgrounds. Faced with the evolving importance of French as the main working language of Quebec and with an increasing dissatisfaction with the linguistic barriers that separated English and French Canadians, a concerned group of English-speaking parents in the small suburban community of St. Lambert, outside of Montreal, began to meet informally in the early l960s to discuss the situation (Lambert and Tucker, 1972).

They felt that their incompetence in French contributed to, and indeed was attributable in part to, the two solitudes that effectively prevented them from learning French informally from their French-speaking neighbors. They felt that their inability to communicate in French was also attributable to inadequate methods of second-language instruction in English schools. At that time, French was taught for relatively short periods each day (twenty to thirty minutes) by teachers who were usually native English-speakers with competence in French-as-a-second language that varied from excellent to poor.There was an emphasis on teaching vocabulary and grammar rules and on using pattern practice drills based on then popular audiolingual techniques. This approach was common to many second-language programs throughout North America which retain some of the same characteristics even to this day. Unlike second-language instruction in other parts of North America, however, second-language instruction in Quebec began in elementary school and continued systematically until the end of secondary school. This is still true, and it has become customary to varying degrees in the other Canadian provinces.

Despite twelve years of second-language instruction, however, students graduating from the public schools of Quebec were inadequately prepared to deal with the demands of using a second language in diverse real-life situations. As one of the group of twelve St. Lambert parents who spearheaded interest in alternative methods of second-language instruction pointed out:

Children were graduating from English Protestant schools in this province with little more knowledge of French than their parents had had, despite claims that the programs had been considerably improved over the years. Their knowledge was not perceptibly superior to that of graduates from the English provinces of Canada and was not sufficient to enable the students to communicate with their French-Canadian neighbors. The parents felt their children were being short-changed and should have the opportunity to become 'bilingual' within the school system, since it was so difficult to achieve this skill outside of school (Melikoff in Lambert and Tucker, 1972:220).

Most of the St. Lambert parents who participated in these discussions could attest to the failure of second-language instruction, using their own experiences as evidence.

In their search for better methods of second-language instruction for their children, the St. Lambert Bilingual School Study Group, as they came to call themselves, sought the assistance and advice of experts within their community. In particular, they consulted with Dr. Wallace E. Lambert of the Psychology Department, McGill University, who had conducted research on social psychological and cognitive aspects of bilingualism, and with Dr. Wilder Penfield of the Montreal Neurological Institute, McGill, who had conducted research on brain mechanisms underlying language functions. The involvement of these two scholars was indeed fortunate because not only did they give their overall support to the parents' project, but their professional advice shaped the new program in some important ways.

The efforts of the St. Lambert group finally succeeded, with the school district agreeing to set up an experimental kindergarten immersion class in September 1965, some two years after their first meetings. In her description of events leading up to 1965, Olga Melikoff notes that school officials did not accept the experimental class because of any conviction that it was a worthwhile educational experiment, but rather because public pressure on them was too great to ignore. She characterizes the official school district attitude as follows: ''You asked for it, if it doesn't work, it's not our fault''(p. 227). ''At no time would the Board undertake to accept the experiment for more than a year at a time'' (p. 233). Despite a lack of official support from the school authorities, parents were surprisingly enthusiastic—registration for the experimental kindergarten class ''opened one spring day at 1 p.m., and by 1:05 p.m. the quota of 26 children was reached'' (p. 226).

The process of community involvement that has just been described has been repeated many times since the first immersion class was opened in St. Lambert in 1965. The introduction of French immersion programs in most school districts elsewhere in Quebec and Canada has been instigated and promoted by local community groups, along with the assistance of individual school district officials and researchers. Official support has customarily been lukewarm at the outset. Parents have continued to play an important role in the evolution of immersion programs, as evidenced by the establishment of Canadian Parents for French, a voluntary, nonprofit association of English-speaking parents who seek to improve the quality of second-language instruction in public schools across Canada.

It was in the educational system, and in French immersion in particular, that the St. Lambert parents sought a response to important sociolinguistic changes that were taking place around them. Moreover, it was through educational innovation that they also sought to bring about social change within their own communities. Improved French-second-language learning was not intended to be the sole goal of immersion. Rather, it was intended to be an intermediate goal leading to improved relationships between English and French Quebecers and thus ultimately to a breaking down of the two solitudes that had become unacceptable.

ST. LAMBERT: AN EXPERIMENT IN BILINGUAL EDUCATION

The St. Lambert French immersion program that was inaugurated in September 1965 was designed to achieve the following primary goals:

1. To provide the participating children with functional competence in both written and spoken aspects of French.
2. To promote and maintain normal levels of English-language development.
3. To ensure achievement in academic subjects commensurate with the students' ability and grade level.
4. To instill in the students an understanding and appreciation of French Canadians, their language and culture, without detracting in any way from the students' identity with and appreciation for English Canadian culture. These goals are shared by most immersion programs across Canada in essentially the same form.

The program in St. Lambert was an *early total* immersion program. That is, all curriculum instruction, beginning in kindergarten (five years of age) and continuing through the primary grades, was taught through French, although it is common for the children themselves to use English with one another and the teacher during kindergarten. (See Figure 8.1 for a schematic summary of the early total immersion program.) At first, French was to be used as the only medium of instruction until the end of grade three; this was later altered so that only kindergarten and grade one were taught entirely in French. When English was introduced into the curriculum, it was used to teach English-language arts, for approximately one hour per day. Instruction through English was subsequently expanded in successive grades to include other subjects, such as math or science. By grade six, or the end of elementary school, 60 percent of the

Figure 8.1
Schematic Representation of an Early Total Immersion and a One-Year-Late Immersion Program

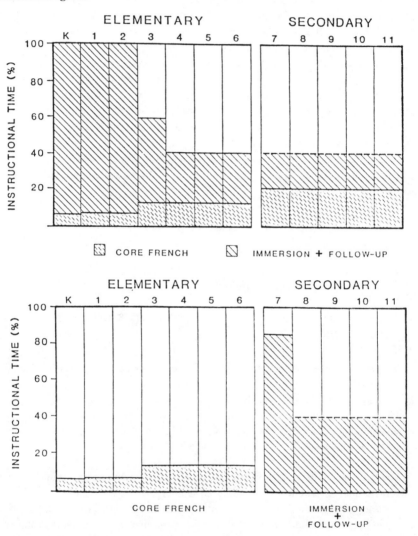

curriculum was taught in English and 40 percent in French. This was usually implemented by teaching through English during the morning and through French during the afternoon of each day and always with native speakers of English and French, respectively. This basic pattern is characteristic of many current early total immersion programs, although there are, of course, variations among programs. For example, early immersion programs offered elsewhere delay the introduction of English until grade three or even grade four or limit the amount of exposure to English once it is introduced (see Genesee, 1983, for a review). Some important variations will be discussed in a later section of this chapter. Follow-up to the early immersion years is often provided at the secondary school level by offering a number of selected courses in French. These may be either language arts or other subject courses such as geography or history. The particular courses and number of such courses that students take at this level are a matter of individual student choice.

The most distinctive feature of the St. Lambert immersion program was its use of the second language to teach regular academic subjects, such as mathematics, science, and social studies, in addition to language arts. This is one of the distinctive characteristics of all immersion programs. Immersion teachers teach regular school subjects using French much as they would if their pupils were native speakers of the language. The same subject matter is never taught in the same school year using both English and French. Formal instruction in the grammatical rules of French is presented in the French-language arts class, which constitutes a large part of the primary grades, as does English in the case of a regular English program. Clearly, however, the children are not native speakers, and so the teachers emphasize oral-aural communication skills during kindergarten and the first half of grade one. Reading, writing, and other literacy skills are introduced slowly and only when it is felt that the children have acquired the corresponding oral/aural language skills. The children are not required to use French with the teacher or with one another until the second half of grade one. In fact, the children commonly use English among themselves and with the teacher during this stage.

Generally, immersion programs are designed to create the same kinds of conditions that occur during first-language learning; namely, there is an emphasis on creating a desire by the student to learn the language in order to engage in meaningful and interesting communication (Macnamara, 1973; Terrell, 1981). Thus, language learning in immersion is incidental to learning about mathematics, the sciences, the community, and one another. This stands in sharp contrast to more traditional methods of second-language instruction where the emphasis is on the conscious learning of the elements and rules of language for their own sake. Moreover, the immersion program is designed to allow the student to apply his or her ''natural language learning'' or cognitive abilities as a means of learning the language. It is now generally accepted that first-language acquisition in children is a systematic process that reflects the child's active cognitive attempts to formulate linguistic rules that correspond to adult competence in the language. This process is called creative construction (Dulay and Burt, 1978; Slobin, 1973). According to this conceptualization, opportunities to communicate in the language are advantageous for learning, and ''errors'' are a normal and important part of the learning process. The immersion approach permits the learner to progress according to his or her own rate and style, again in much the same way that first-language learners do (Bloom, Hood, and Lightbown, 1974; Nelson, 1981).

Another distinctive pedagogical feature of the Canadian immersion program is the use of monolingual language models and "linguistic territories" within the school. The French teachers in the immersion programs present themselves to the students as monolingual French speakers, even though in most cases these teachers are very competent in English. The French teachers in kindergarten and grade one especially must know enough English to understand the students whose comments are initially all in English. Many of the students learn about their French teachers' bilinguality only in the later grades when they overhear them using English with an English teacher. The classrooms in which French and English instruction are presented are kept as distinct as possible. This means that the children usually change classrooms for the French and English parts of the school day once English is introduced into the curriculum. An explicit rule to use French in the French classroom and with the French teachers is established. These two strategies—the use of monolingual second-language teacher models and the establishment of French territories within the school—have been adopted and are observed very conscientiously in order to facilitate the students' second-language learning by encouraging, indeed requiring, their use of the second language. Otherwise, there would be a natural tendency for the students to use English, their stronger language.

THE SPREAD OF IMMERSION: THE PRESENT SITUATION

Since the St. Lambert experiment began, immersion has expanded dramatically. Immersion programs are now available in several different forms, in a variety of languages, and in all Canadian provinces and the territories. The number of students enrolled in immersion increased from approximately 17,763 in 1976 to 102,168 in 1982 (Stern, 1984). Participation in immersion programs is voluntary, and to date the majority of programs serve children from "middle-class" socioeconomic backgrounds. The alternative forms of immersion currently available differ primarily with respect to the grade level(s) during which the second language is used as a major medium of curriculum instruction. Differentiations are often made between (1) early, (2) delayed, and (3) late immersion. A secondary basis of differentiation is made according to the amount of instruction provided in the second language (viz., total versus partial) and/or the number of years during which the second language is used as a major medium of instruction. Excluded from this rough taxonomy are (1) second-language programs in which the second language is used for teaching language arts only and one nonlanguage subject and (2) programs in which the second language is never used to teach at least 50 percent of the curriculum during any school year. These latter types of programs would generally be regarded as *enriched* second-language programs.

Early Immersion

There are two main types of early immersion: total and partial. The *early total* immersion program has already been described in the section on the St. Lambert Experiment and is schematically represented in Figure 8.1. The *early partial* immersion program differs in that less than 100 percent of curriculum instruction during the primary grades (kindergarten, one, two, and three) is presented through the second language. The most common formula is 50 percent French—50 percent English. The amount of French instruction in early partial immersion programs tends to remain constant throughout the elementary grades, in contrast to total immersion programs in which the French component decreases. Another difference between these two types of immersion is the sequencing of literacy instruction. In total immersion programs, literacy training in the native language occurs after literacy training in the second language has begun. In partial immersion programs, literacy training tends to occur in both languages simultaneously from grade one on.

Among early total immersion alternatives, the main variation involves the grade level at which English instruction is introduced—it may be grade two, as in St. Lambert, grade three, or grade four. Another variation among early total immersion options is the amount of instruction presented through English once it is introduced into the curriculum. In some cases, English exposure increases quickly, for example, from 20 percent in grade three to 60 percent in grade five. In other cases, it increases very slowly (for example, remaining stable at 20 percent during grades three, four, and five).

Delayed Immersion

Immersion programs that postpone use of the second language as a major medium of instruction until the middle elementary grades (i.e., four or five) are classified here as delayed. These programs usually offer a core second-language course of twenty to forty-five minutes a day in the primary grades prior to the immersion component which may be of one or two years duration (see Cziko, Holobow, and Lambert, 1977, for an example). This may then be followed by partial immersion until the end of elementary school, during which language arts and other subject material are taught through the second language. In the delayed immersion, option training in first-language literacy precedes training in second-language literacy.

Late Immersion

Late immersion programs postpone intensive use of the second language until the end of elementary school or the beginning of secondary school (Figure 8.1). In *one-year* late immersion programs, all or most of the curriculum, except

English-language arts, is taught through the second language for one year (see, for example, Genesee, Polich, and Stanley, 1977). In *two-year* late immersion programs, this schedule is repeated for two consecutive years (see Genesee, 1981). Late immersion programs may be preceded by core second-language instruction throughout the elementary grades, or they may be preceded by special preparatory second-language courses one or two years immediately prior to immersion (see Swain, 1978). Most late immersion options—one-year/two-year and with/without prior core second-language instruction—are usually followed in the higher grades by advanced second-language arts courses and, in some cases, by selected nonlanguage courses, such as geography, that are taught through the second language.

Double Immersion

By far the most common alternative forms of immersion, as just described, involve the use of a single second language. Genesee and Lambert have investigated variations of immersion for majority English-speaking children in which two nonnative languages (French and Hebrew) are used as major media of curriculum instruction during the elementary grades (see Genesee and Lambert, 1983). French and Hebrew were selected as immersion languages in the programs in question because both have sociocultural significance for the participants but for different reasons. On the one hand, French, being one of the official languages of Canada, has social and economic relevance to these children and their families on a day-to-day basis. In this regard, the Hebrew-French double immersion programs are the same as the St. Lambert program and other French immersion programs for majority-language children in Canada. On the other hand, Hebrew is valued because of its religious and cultural significance and because of its increasing nonsectarian importance as a national language of Israel. In this respect, the Hebrew-French double immersion programs differ from French-only immersion in being heritage language or language revitalization programs. The underlying principles of both programs are nevertheless the same, and, in particular, their success is predicated on the participation of children who are members of the majority language group.

In one type of double immersion program studied by Genesee and Lambert, English-speaking children from Montreal received all their curriculum instruction during the primary grades in French and Hebrew. The French curriculum comprised language arts, mathematics, science, and social studies. The Hebrew curriculum comprised language arts, history, and religious and cultural studies. Native French- and Hebrew-speaking teachers were used to teach each curriculum. English was not introduced until grade three in the case of one school and grade four in the case of another. We have referred to this alternative as *early double immersion*. In contrast, in another double immersion program English along with French and Hebrew were used as media of instruction from kindergarten on. This program alternative has been referred to as *delayed double immersion* because the amount of exposure to French increased systematically from five hours per week in grade one to twelve hours per week in grades five and six. Instruction through English decreased somewhat from twelve hours per week in grade one to nine hours per week in grade six as a result. Exposure to Hebrew changed insignificantly.

These programs are described in some detail here because they represent effective and feasible models of multilingual/multicultural education of possible interest to ethnolinguistic groups who are interested in revitalizing heritage languages and at the same time wish to acquire competence in an additional second language of some local or national relevance. Examples other than Hebrew-French immersion for English children come to mind. For example, Ukrainian Canadians in western Canada might wish to have their children, who in most cases have become Anglicized, acquire competence in Ukrainian while also learning Canada's other official language, French.

RESEARCH FINDINGS

The extension of immersion programs to all the Canadian provinces and its evolution to include alternative forms is attributable in no small measure to the research component that has accompanied the development of immersion from the beginning. Several large-scale longitudinal evaluations have been set up in a number of Canadian centers to monitor the effectiveness of immersion programs in these locations. They include the Protestant School Board of Greater Montreal evaluations (Genesee, 1983), the Bilingual Education Project, OISE (Swain and Lapkin, 1982), the Ottawa Board of Education Project (Stern et al., 1976), and the British Columbia French Project (Shapson and Day, 1980), as well as the St. Lambert Experiment (Lambert and Tucker, 1972). The results of these evaluations provide a comprehensive and reliable indication of the linguistic and academic outcomes of immersion. The findings reviewed here pertain to students from middle socioeconomic backgrounds because they constitute the majority of participants (see Genesee, 1976b, for a discussion of the suitability of immersion for all children).

In brief, assessment of the English literacy skills (e.g., reading, spelling, writing) of early total immersion students has revealed that during the primary grades when no instruction in English is provided, they are usually behind their peers who have been in an all-English program. This is not surprising in view of the students' lack of training in English literacy. What is surprising is their ability to take English-language tests and complete them reasonably well despite a lack of such training. Quite likely, this is possible because the immersion students are able to transfer skills they have been taught in French to English, a language they already know well in its aural and oral forms. In other words, they do not have to learn to read and write in English from the beginning once they have acquired these skills in French. During the same grades, early total immersion students demonstrate no deficits in listening comprehension, aural decoding, or oral communication. A study by Genesee, Tucker, and Lambert (1975) found that in interpersonal communication early total immersion students were more sensitive to the communicative needs of their listeners than were nonimmersion students. The lag in English literacy that the immersion students experience during the primary grades is eliminated as soon as English-language instruction is introduced into the curriculum. Evaluation of different immersion variants has shown that this catch-up occurs at the end of one year of having received English-language arts instruction whether English is delayed until grades two, three, or four. This has also been found to be the case in double immersion programs (Genesee and Lambert, 1983). Furthermore, follow-up assessments in higher grades have revealed that there are no long-term advantages to introducing English instruction into the curriculum earlier (e.g., grade two) rather than later (e.g., grade four). Genesee and Lambert (1983) found that the use of English as a medium of instruction from kindergarten on in double immersion programs appears to inhibit second-language acquisition. Typically, early partial immersion programs, which use English 50 percent of the time and French 50 percent of the time, result in equivalent levels of English-language development as early total immersion programs. It has been found that students in delayed and late immersion programs also develop normal levels of English-language proficiency and experience no lags whatsoever.

The expansion of immersion programs shortly after their inauguration in 1965 raised concerns about the effectiveness of such an approach for children with low levels of academic or intellectual ability and for children who had relatively low levels of English-language development. In a series of studies, Genesee (1978) examined the English-language development of immersion students with low academic ability in comparison with that of similar students in all-English programs. Academic ability was assessed using IQ tests. He found that below-average students in immersion achieved the same levels of proficiency in English reading, spelling, vocabulary, and writing as below-average students in the English program. In other words, below-average students were not handicapped by the immersion experience as many had expected. M. Bruck (1982) has reported similar results for immersion children who were considered "language disabled" in English in comparison with similarly disabled children in the English stream.

Immersion students have been shown to achieve higher levels of proficiency in all aspects of French, including reading, writing, listening comprehension, and oral communication, than students receiving core French-language instruction. This is to be expected in view of the considerably greater exposure to French provided by immersion. Research by Genesee (1976a) has found that below-average students in early immersion programs cannot be distinguished from their above-average peers by native French-speaking evaluators who are asked to subjectively assess their oral production and listening comprehension skills. In contrast, above-average immersion students usually outperform below-average students on tests that assess literacy and academic achievement, for example, reading comprehension and mathematics. Comparisons of the French-language proficiency of immersion students with that of native French-speaking students has indicated that immersion students achieve very high levels of communicative ability but that their proficiency is not native-like even by the end of six or seven years.

The results of academic achievement testing have shown that immersion students achieve the same levels of academic proficiency in math and science, for example, as English control students who have been receiving all academic instruction in English.

Finally, investigations regarding some of the social psychological aspects of immersion indicate that the participating students develop the same identity with and positive attitudes toward the English Canadian culture and language as do students attending English-language programs (Genesee, 1984). The attitudes of immersion students toward French Canadians tend to be more positive than those of nonimmersion students during the early years of the program and then come to resemble those of their nonimmersion compatriots in later years. It is possible that lack of ongoing contact with French Canadians may account for this developmental shift. Immersion students generally indicate a willingness to use French when called upon to do so. Students in Montreal, for example, report using French in face-to-face encounters much more often than do nonimmersion students. At the same time, there is evidence that immersion students do not actively seek out contact with French Canadians or opportunities to use French. They also express reservations about using French at the expense of English. It seems quite likely that some of these feelings stem from conflicts between French and English Canadians in society at large. Notwithstanding such reservations and conflict, immersion students express positive attitudes toward learning French in the immersion programs. Many of their comments indicate that they are in favor of more French, especially during the followup years. In contrast, non-immersion students express relatively negative attitudes toward their French program and toward learning French in general.

Taken together, these findings indicate that immersion programs are suitable for children with diverse learning and language characteristics provided they are members of a majority language group, such as English Canadians. The suitability of immersion programs for children from minority language groups is an open question, subject to empirical investigation. In a review of research on the effectiveness of immersion programs for all children, Genesee (1976b) concluded that "the results from the existing research are generally inconclusive on the suitability of . . . immersion for minority group children" (p. 510). Only one study pertinent to this issue was available at that time. There has been no research progress since then. Proponents of second-language immersion programs for majority English-speaking children have generally doubted their applicability for children from minority language backgrounds who do not enjoy the same individual or social respect that English speakers in North America enjoy (Hernandez-Chavez, 1984). In Canada, English immersion programs for French-speaking Canadians have not been recommended because this form of education poses a wide-scale threat to French in North America. That is, too much English too soon could undermine the vitality of French. The important point here is that the implementation of specific forms of bilingual education must take into account the sociocultural context in which schooling takes place.

SUMMARY

Immersion programs were first instituted in the Province of Quebec, Canada, in the mid–1960s. They were developed in reaction to particular sociocultural events in the province at the time, and they were designed to respond to the needs and characteristics of a specific group of children. Since the original St. Lambert project, immersion has become a relatively widespread and common-place form of education in the Canadian public school system. The results of numerous longitudinal scientific evaluations have consistently indicated that ma-jority English-language children participating in these programs do not experience any long-term deficits in native-language development or academic achievement. At the same time, they achieve functional competence in the second language that is markedly better than that of students in core second-language programs. Although not truly native-like in all aspects, the second-language skills of im-mersion students are rated very highly even by native speakers of the language. Since immersion programs in Canada are optional, these results necessarily pertain to students who have chosen or whose parents have chosen on their behalf to attend the program instead of regular English schools.

The documented success of the Canadian immersion programs depends on a combination of pedagogical practices, as outlined earlier, as well as certain sociocultural conditions. The major sociocultural conditions include the follow-ing: (1) the participating children speak the language of the majority in North America, that is, English; (2) educational, teaching, and administrative personnel working in immersion programs value and support, directly or indirectly, the children's home language and culture; (3) the participating children and their parents similarly value their home language and culture and do not wish to forsake either; and (4) acquisition of the second language is regarded by all concerned as a positive addition to the child's repertoire of skills. Thus, the success of immersion is more than simply a question of when to use students' first and second languages for instructional purposes. It is equally dependent on an understanding of the sociocultural conditions in which the students are raised and educated.

Interest in immersion from both pedagogical and linguistic perspectives con-tinues as researchers continue to explore the suitability of immersion for all children. Genesee and Lambert, for example, are currently examining its effec-tiveness for black as well as white children from inner-city neighborhoods in U.S. school districts. Previous research has focused largely on middle-class, white children. An experimental early total immersion program in Mohawk, an

Amerindian language, is currently underway for Indian children who do not speak Mohawk but rather have learned English as a native language. A systematic evaluation of this project is planned by Genesee and Lambert as well. Researchers are beginning to address important issues concerning teaching approaches in immersion classes (Swain, 1984) and the relationship between intergroup relations in society at large and relations between English and French Canadian teachers in immersion schools (Cleghorn and Genesee, 1984). The findings from these studies will help to expand our already rich understanding of the immersion approach to bilingual education.

NOTE

1. Discussion of the social and political events that preceded the emergence of French immersion in 1965 focuses on issues pertaining to language and English-French relations. This coverage is necessarily simplified and is not intended to reflect a complete or unbiased interpretation of history.

BIBLIOGRAPHY

Anisfield, E., and W. E. Lambert. 1964. "Evaluational Reactions of Bilingual and Monolingual Children to Spoken Languages." *Journal of Abnormal and Social Psychology* 69:89–97.

Bloom, L. M., Hood, L. M., and P. Lightbown. 1974. "Imitation in Language Development: If, When, and Why." *Cognitive Psychology* 6:380–420.

Brown, R. C., Cazden, C. and U. Bellugi. 1970."The Child's Grammar from I to III." In *Psycholinguistics*, ed. R. Brown. New York: Free Press, pp. 100–54.

Bruck, M. 1981. "Language Impaired Children: Performance in an Additive Bilingual Education Program." *Applied Linguistics* 3:45–60.

Cleghorn, A., and F. Genesee. 1984. *Languages in Contact: An Ethnographic Study of Interaction in an Immersion School*. Montreal: Psychology Department, McGill University.

Cook, R., Saywell, J., and J. Ricker. 1977. *Canada: A Modern Study*. Toronto: Clarke, Irwin and Co.

Cummins, J., ed. 1983. *Heritage Language Education: Issues and Directions*. Ottawa: Ministry of Supply and Services.

Cziko, G. A., Holobow, N., and W. E. Lambert. 1977. *A Comparison of Three Elementary School Alternatives for Learning French: Children at Grades Four and Five*. Montreal: Department of Psychology, McGill University.

d'Anglejan, A., and G. R. Tucker. 1973. "Sociolinguistic Correlates of Speech Style in Quebec." In *Language Attitudes: Current Trends and Prospects*, ed. R. W. Shuy and R. W. Fasold. Washington, D.C.: Georgetown University Press, pp. 1–27.

Day, R. R. 1982. "Children's Attitudes Toward Language." In *Attitudes Toward Language Variation: Social and Applied Contexts*, ed. E. B. Ryan and H. Giles. London: Edward Arnold, pp. 116–31.

Dulay, H., and M. Burt. 1978. "Some Remarks on Creativity in Language Acquisition."

In *Second Language Acquisition Research: Issues and Implications*, ed. W. C. Ritchie. New York: Academic Press, pp. 65–89.

Gendron, J. D. 1972. *Commission of Inquiry on the Position of the French Language and on Language Rights in Quebec: Language at Work*. Quebec: L'editeur officiel du Quebec.

Genesee, F. 1976a. "The Role of Intelligence in Second Language Learning." *Language Learning* 26:267–80.

———. 1976b. "The Suitability of Immersion Programs for All Children." *Canadian Modern Language Review* 32:494–515.

———. 1978. "A Longitudinal Evaluation of an Early Immersion School Program." *Canadian Journal of Education* 3:31–50.

———. 1981. "A Comparison of Early and Late Second Language Learning." *Canadian Journal of Behavioral Sciences* 13:115–25.

———. 1983. "Bilingual Education of Majority Language Children: The Immersion Experiments in Review." *Applied Psycholinguistics* 4:1–46.

———. In press. "Beyond Bilingualism: Social Psychological Studies of French Immersion Programs in Canada." *Canadian Journal of Behavioral Science*.

Genesee, F., and W. E. Lambert. 1983. "Trilingual Education for Majority Language Children." *Child Development* 54:105–14.

Genesee, F., Polich, E., and M. H. Stanley. 1977. "An Experimental French Immersion Program at the Secondary School Level—1969 to 1974." *Canadian Modern Language Review* 33:318–32.

Genesee, F., Rogers, P., and N. Holobow. 1983. "The Social Psychology of Second Language Learning: Another Point of View." *Language Learning* 33:209–24.

Genesee, F., Tucker, G. R., and W. E. Lambert. 1975. "Communication Skills of Bilingual Children." *Child Development* 46:1010–14.

Hernandez-Chavez, E. 1984. "The Inadequacy of English Immersion Education as an Educational Approach for Language Minority Students in the United States." In *Studies on Immersion Education: A Collection for U.S. Educators*. Sacramento, Calif.: California State Department of Education, pp. 144–81.

Lambert, W. E., R. C. Hodgson, R. C. Gardner, and S. Fillenbaum. 1960. "Evaluational Reactions to Spoken Languages." *Journal of Abnormal and Social Psychology* 60:44–51.

Lambert, W., and R. Tucker. 1972. *Bilingual Education of Children: The St. Lambert Experiment*. Rowley, Mass.: Newbury House.

MacLennan, H. 1945. *Two Solitudes*. Montreal: Duell, Sloan, and Pearce.

Macnamara, J. 1973. "Nurseries, Streets, and Classrooms." *Modern Language Journal* 57:250–54.

Melikoff, O. 1972. "Appendix A: Parents as Change Agents in Education," in Lambert, W. and R. Tucker. 1972. *Bilingual Education of Children: The St. Lambert Experiment*. Rowley, Mass.: Newbury House.

Nelson, K. 1981. "Individual Differences in Language Development: Implications for Development and Language." *Developmental Psychology* 17:170–87.

O'Bryan, K. G., J. G. Reitz, and O. Kuplowska, eds. 1976. *Non-official Languages: A Study in Canadian Multiculturalism*. Ottawa: Ministry of Supply and Services, Canada.

Shapson, S. M., and E. Day. 1980. *Longitudinal Evaluation of the Early Entry Immersion*

Program in Coquitlam School District: Report to the End of Year 6. Burnaby, B.C.: Faculty of Education, Simon Fraser University.

Slobin, D. I. 1973. "Cognitive Prerequisites for the Development of Grammar." In *Studies in Child Language and Development*, ed. C. A. Ferguson and D. I. Slobin. New York: Holt, Rinehart and Winston, 175–280.

Stern, H. H. 1984. "The Immersion Phenomenon." *Language and Society.* Ottawa: Ministry of Supply and Services, pp. 4–7.

Swain, M. 1978. "French Immersion: Early, Late or Partial?" *Canadian Modern Language Review* 34:577–85.

———. 1984. *19th Report of the Activities of the Modern Language Centre.* Toronto: Ontario Institute for Studies in Education.

Swain, M., and S. Lapkin. 1982. *Evaluating Bilingual Education: A Canadian Case Study.* Clevedon, Avon, U.K.: Multilingual Matters.

Terrell, T. D. 1981. "The Natural Approach in Bilingual Education." In *Schooling and Language Minority Students: A Theoretical Framework.* Developed by the California State Department of Education, Office of Bilingual Bicultural Education. Los Angeles: California State University Evaluation, Dissemination, and Assessment Center, pp. 117–46.

9

James H.-Y. Tai

BILINGUALISM AND BILINGUAL
EDUCATION IN THE PEOPLE'S REPUBLIC
OF CHINA

According to the latest census conducted by the government of the People's
Republic of China in 1982, the country has a total population of 1,003,937,078,
of which 936,703,824 are ethnic Chinese, known as "Han" and 67,233,254
are members of fifty-five non-Chinese ethnic groups, referred to in China as
"national minorities." (The 1982 census data can be found in *Statistical Yearbook of China 1984*, compiled by State Statistical Bureau, the People's Republic
of China, and published by Economic Information Agency, Hong Kong.) In
terms of percentages, Han Chinese constitute 93.3 percent of the total population,
and the minorities, 6.7 percent. While Han Chinese live mainly in the densely
populated eastern plains and valleys, the minorities spread out along western
highlands and the northern and southwestern borders, their areas covering about
50 percent to 60 percent of the total national territory.

The work of identifying national minorities is not completely done yet. According to the 1982 census, there are still 879,201 persons whose ethnic identity
is not clear. There are also several languages whose relationship with other
languages is undecided. In identifying national minorities, criteria other than
linguistic and cultural factors are also taken into consideration. One criterion
has to do with historical background. The original Hui people came from Central
Asia during the Mongols' conquest in the thirteenth century and were comprised
of Arabs, Persians, and others who believed in Islam. In the course of history,
they lived among Han Chinese and were assimilated by them. On the other hand,
many Han Chinese have come to adopt Islam. Now "Hui" refers to Chinese
Moslems, who speak Chinese and differ from Han Chinese primarily in religion.
The Manchus have been completely assimilated to Han Chinese in both language
and custom, except for very few old persons living in some remote villages in
Heilongjiang, the northernmost province of China. The Manchus were recognized

for the undeniable historical evidence that they were originally a separate nationality. Another criterion employed in the identification work involves ethnic
self-identification of the ethnic group. Thus, the feelings of self-identity felt by
the Manchu people are used to reinforce the historical evidence (Lehmann,
1974:116–19).

Han Chinese speak a great variety of mutually unintelligible dialects, even
though they use one single written language and have adopted Standard Mandarin
as their common language. These dialects are usually grouped by Chinese linguists into eight major dialects (Egerod, 1967:95). They are similar in grammar,
and to a lesser extent in vocabulary, but very different in pronunciation. In terms
of intelligibility, they are perhaps as different from each other as Spanish, French,
and Italian within the family of Romance languages. Mandarin-speakers constitute the largest percentage, about 70 percent. They live north of the Yangtze
River and also south of the river in southwestern China. Although it is customary
to subgroup Mandarin dialects into Northern, Northwestern, and Southwestern
Mandarin, they are mutually intelligible. In the east, including the Shanghai
area, a large part of the population speaks Wu dialects. In the southeast, there
are Xiang dialects in Hunan, Gan dialects in Jiangxi, Min dialects in Fujian,
Yue dialects in Guangdong, and Hakka dialects in the junction area of Jiangxi,
Fujian, and Guangdong provinces. Within each of these dialect areas, many
dialects exist, some of which are mutually unintelligible, and many subdivisions
within each dialect can be made according to their degree of mutual intelligibility.
Dialectal differences are also exhibited in several of the national minorities (Ma
et al., 1981), though to a much lesser extent than Han Chinese. Yi has six very
different dialects. Tibetan, Mongolian, Miao, Dai, Nu, Hani, Dawoer, and
Ewenk each have three dialects. Qiang, Naxi, and Achang each can be divided
into two major dialectal groups. In the case of Miao, Nu, and Hani, the dialects
are unintelligible to each other. An extreme case can be found in Gelao, which
displays numerous mutually unintelligible dialects among some fifty thousand
individuals inhabiting a county-size area. Among the Yuku, with a population
of little more than ten thousand, three different languages are used by three
different groups—Chinese, Turkic Yuku, and Mongolian Yuku.

As far as written languages are concerned, Han Chinese share one single
written language, notwithstanding the great diversity of dialects. It is based on
the spoken Standard Mandarin and uses a system of ideographic symbols, known
as "Han characters" or "Chinese characters." Hui and Manchu also use the
system, having been assimilated by Han Chinese and speaking Chinese. It is
interesting to observe that while Hui, regardless of their Arabic and Persian
ancestry, probably had never developed their own writing systems, Manchu did
develop a system derived from the Mongolian alphabet at the end of the sixteenth
century. In addition to Hui and Manchu, several minorities also use Chinese
characters, even though they have not lost their spoken languages. Either they
never developed their own writing systems or they have been assimilated by
Han Chinese in this respect. They are Hezhe, Ewenk, Elunchun, Achang, Pumi,

Nu, Jing, Dongxiang, Tu, Tujia, Sala, Baoan, She, Benglong, Qiang, and Bai. Dawoer shifted from Manchurian orthography to Chinese characters after the fall of the Manchus' dynasty in 1911 (Ma et al., 1981).

Tibetan, Menba, and to a limited degree Luoba use Tibetan orthography, and the Mongolians and nomadic tribes among various minorities in the north and the northwest use Mongolian orthography. Korean orthography is used by the Koreans living in Manchuria as well as in Korea. Slavic orthography is used by the Russians. The Xibo group living in Xinjiang redesigned their Manchurian orthography in 1947. Kazakh, Khalkas, Uzbek, and Uighur, whose language is also used by Tajik, all have their own traditional orthography based on Arabic letters. Recently, they have also been provided with an orthography according to the Pinyin principles, the romanization principles for Standard Mandarin. Lahu and Jingpo each once used a Latin system designed by Western missionaries. Since they are outdated and have never been promoted, they have been updated according to the Pinyin principles (Ma et al., 1981).

Before the Communist Chinese came to power in 1949, only twenty-one minorities (including Hui and Manchu which had adopted Chinese spoken and written languages) had developed a written language. From 1955 to 1957, the Chinese government assisted the following minorities in developing their written languages in romanization based on the Pinyin principles: Zhuang, Miao, Dong, Hani, Buyi, Li, Lisu, Wa, and Naxi. Although Naxi has a traditional written language based on ideographic principles, its use is now limited to religion, folklore, and ballads. The government has also helped Dai systematize its various spelling systems into two sets to suit two major dialects. Yi has used a very complicated ideographic system since the thirteenth century, but the government helped Yi reform and simplify the system (Ma et al., 1981).

HISTORICAL BACKGROUND

Since the inception of Chinese civilization sometime before four millennia ago, China has been a stage for contacts, conflicts, coexistence, and assimilation for various races living in the eastern half of the Asian continent. Chinese civilization started around the middle reach of the Yellow River. Many Chinese historians tend to hold the view that the earliest dynasties, that is, Xia (ca. 2100–ca. 1600 B.C.), Shang (ca. 1600–ca. 1066 B.C.), and Zhou (ca. 1066–221 B.C.) actually represent three different races with some common customs and religious beliefs, even though the Chinese themselves since Confucius (551–479 B.C.) have perceived them as three different dynasties of one single race, that is, Chinese (Fitzgerald, 1961:1–33; Fairbank and Reischauer, 1960:32–52). All three groups lived around the middle reach of the Yellow River, competing with each other. Xia was conquered by Shang, which in turn was replaced by Zhou as the ruling group. They were surrounded by other races with names such as Yi in the east, Miao and Man in the south, Qiang and Rong in the west and Di in the north. These races have been regarded as non-Chinese in Chinese history.

The feudal states based on the vassal-fief relationship established in the beginning of the Zhou dynasty was finally replaced by independent warring kingdoms (403–221 B.C.). Many of these kingdoms were established by non-Chinese,
such as the powerful Qin in the west and Chu in the south, although they had
already adopted Chinese culture by that time. In 221 B.C., China was for the
first time unified by the Qin under a central government. Thus, from about 1600
B.C. to 221 B.C., people in the northern part of China proper underwent a long
period of migration and assimilation. As clearly expressed in Chinese classical
literature, by 221 B.C. people in northern China had come to view themselves
as belonging to one single race with a long cultural tradition.

The unification of China in 221 B.C. under one central government with an
elaborately designed and rigorously enforced uniform politico-economic system
throughout China resulted in a fundamentally important step for the self-identification of peoples in different regions with the Chinese civilization. The Qin
dynasty, primarily due to its extensive and rapid reform, was quickly replaced
by a more moderate Han dynasty in 206 B.C. During the Han dynasty (206 B.C.–
220 A.D.) China experienced a long period of prosperity and stability. Chinese
later began to use the word "Han" to distinguish themselves from other races.
It should be clear that from the very beginning the notion of Han Chinese has
been more of cultural content than of genetic composition. It was also during
this period that Chinese began frequent contacts with other races in what is
known as Xinjiang today and in Central Asia. These contacts introduced Chinese
inventions such as silk and paper to the West, and various kinds of fruits and
religions from Central Asia to China (Fitzgerald, 1961:174–201). It is possible
that Chinese words such as *putao* ("grape") and *pipa* ("loquat") are loan words
from Central Asia (Kratochvil, 1970:65).

Shortly following the end of the Han dynasty in 220 A.D., China suffered
more than three hundred years of disunification and wars. Many areas of northern
China were conquered by non-Chinese peoples at different times. According to
an official Chinese historical account, almost half of the inhabitants in northern
China were not Han Chinese. At the same time, a large number of Han Chinese
in northern China migrated to southern China. Thus, during the period 220–589
A.D., Han Chinese blended with other races in China proper, north and south
(Fitzgerald, 1961:249–64; Fairbank and Reischauer, 1960:131–33, 148–53).
While it is presumably true that the non-Han population was largely assimilated
into the Han population owing to the relatively higher culture of the latter, it
cannot be assumed that the impact of intermarriages among Han and non-Han
people had not reshaped Chinese culture and language.The extent of the cultural
reshaping during this period is yet to be examined in future research. One thing
for certain is that the genetic composition of Han-Chinese was once again altered
and enriched.

When China was unified again in the glorious Sui-Tang period (581–907 A.D.),
China was the most powerful and prosperous country in the world. Interactions
among different nationalities were accordingly enhanced to an extent hitherto

unseen. The emperors of the early Tang appointed leaders of various nationalities as governors in charge of administrative and military policies of their own states. More significantly, many nationalities including Greek, Jew, Persian, and Arab were living in China with their own religions (Fitzgerald, 1961:308–40; Fairbank and Reischauer, 1960:176–82). Another aspect of the internationalism of this period was reflected by the way in which neighboring peoples sought to imitate the Tang culture. The first unified Tibetan government, established in the seventh century, and the state of Nan-chao, founded by the Thai in Yunnan around 740, were both directly inspired by the Tang system of rule. Silla, the Korean empire in the seventh century, and the first Tungusic kingdom of Bohai in Manchuria and north Korea from 713 to 926 A.D., also closely copied Tang institutions (Fairbank and Reischauer, 1960:177). The Japanese in the seventh and eighth centuries adopted not only Tang institutions but also the Chinese writing system (Fairbank and Reischauer, 1960:473–75, 494–95). China was in a sense similar to the United States today in that it was a prosperous society open to different nationalities and religions and in that it was regarded as the paramount military power and as the obvious model for government and culture.

At the end of the Tang dynasty (618–907 A.D.), China was divided into many small kingdoms for about seventy years. Subsequently, northern China was ruled by a seminomadic Mongol people known as the Khitan and Tangut tribes of Tibetans (Fairbank and Reischauer, 1961:196–200) and then by Tungusic tribes known as the Jurched (Fairbank and Reischauer, 1961:208–11). Song, a Han Chinese dynasty, moved to the south in 1127 A.D. Again for more than one hundred and fifty years, northern China was ruled by non-Han peoples, and Han Chinese continued to move to the south. In 1279 A.D., Mongols conquered all of China and ruled it for nearly one hundred years, but later were overthrown by Han Chinese in 1368 A.D. However, the Manchus ruled China from 1644 A.D. until the 1911 revolution (Fairbank and Reischauer, 1960:243–393). The assimilation of Manchus into Han Chinese was due partly to their migration into China proper, and partly to the continuous migration of Han Chinese into Manchuria during the nineteenth and early twentieth centuries. In modern times, the Chinese Communist revolution from 1925 to 1949 involved many national minorities, especially during the period of the Long March from 1935 to 1941, in which Chinese Communists traveled mostly in the territory inhabited by national minorities. Recently during the Cultural Revolution (1966–76), hundreds of thousands of young and educated Han Chinese were persuaded or assigned to settle down in minority-dominated areas.

Han Chinese cannot be construed as a genetically homogeneous ethnic group. During its long course of evolution, this race has absorbed other racial stocks together with some selected features of their cultures. Likewise, Hui, Manchu, Mongol, Tibetan, Uighur, and other major national minorities are not homogeneous. Each of them, not unlike Han Chinese, has undergone a long history of formation, expansion, and transformation. The original ancestors of Hui were Arabs, Persians, and other peoples from Central Asia who believed in Islam and who were brought to China by Mongols to help them rule Han Chinese in the thirteenth century. In the next two centuries, they absorbed some Han Chinese, Mongols, Uighurs, and others, becoming an ethnic group identifiable with Islam. In the beginning of their formation, the Arabic and Persian languages were probably used along with the Chinese language. Later on, having spread over all of China and mingled with Han Chinese, these groups adopted Han Chinese surnames and eventually lost their languages (Ma et al., 1981:123–25).

The Manchus were a Tungusic people whose history can be traced back to about two thousand years ago. Throughout history, they had more frequent contacts with Han Chinese than other nationalities had. In the seventh century, they ruled a state subordinate to the Tang dynasty named Bohai and became acquainted with Chinese culture. In the twelfth century, they were called Jurched by the Chinese. They occupied Manchuria, part of Mongolia, and the northern part of China proper. In the thirteenth century, they were conquered by the Mongols and were under them until the Mongols were overthrown by Han Chinese in the late fourteenth century. In the Ming dynasty (1368–1644 A.D.), the Manchus were subordinate to Han Chinese. About the beginning of the seventeenth century, the Manchus were welded into a powerful organization under Nurhachi, who was conversant with the Chinese culture and political system. The name Qing was assumed at that time. Many Mongols and Han Chinese were incorporated into the Manchus' armies, and Koreans were also brought to acknowledge the Manchus' suzerainty. At the end of the sixteenth century, the Manchus developed their writing system from the Mongolian system, referred to as the "old Manchurian language." It was revised and improved in the early seventeenth century and was referred to as the "new Manchurian language" (Ma et al., 1981:27–28). In 1644 A.D., the Manchus marched on Peking and became the rulers of China, replacing the Ming dynasty. At the height of the Qing dynasty, it ruled over China proper, Manchuria, Mongolia, Xinjiang, and Tibet (Fairbank and Reischauer, 1960:354–63). During its more than two hundred and fifty years of rule, various nationalities increased their contacts significantly. In particular, a huge number of Han Chinese migrated into Manchuria. On the other hand, having successfully ruled China proper for such a long period, the Manchus eventually were assimilated into the Han Chinese culture, and lost their language as well (Guan, 1971).

The Mongols were related linguistically and possibly racially to the Turkish people and the Tungusic people who established a Khitan kingdom covering the present Mongolia and Manchuria toward the close of the ninth century and the beginning of the tenth century. Originally, "Mongol" was the name of a small tribe but later became the common name for many tribes living to the south and east of Lake Baikal, on the borders of what are now Outer Mongolia, Siberia, and Manchuria. In the twelfth century, under Genghis Khan's skillful and vigorous leadership, these tribes were welded into a formidable fighting force. Having brought together the peoples of Mongolia and the Uighurs in today's Xinjiang, Genghis Khan moved to the south and eliminated the Xi Xia kingdom, which had been established by a Tangut people speaking a Tibeto-Burmese language, and the Jin kingdom, which had been established by the Jurched. In 1260 A.D., Khubilai, a grandson of Genghis Khan, moved the capital to today's Beijing. In 1279 A.D., the Yuan dynasty was established in China. The Mongols were skillful at ruling different nationalities. Uighurs, Jurched, and other non-Han peoples were given high positions to rule the Han Chinese populace (Fairbank and Reischauer, 1960:243–76). They adapted the alphabetic Uighur script to form the Mongolian alphabet, which provided the base for the Manchurian alphabet. Young generations were put to school to study Confucian classics and other aspects of Han Chinese culture. Even after the collapse of the Yuan dynasty, the Mongols continued to keep close contacts with Han Chinese, Tibetan, Uighur, and Hui. Various kinds of literature from these nationalities with written traditions were translated into Mongolian. These translations not only enriched the Mongolian literature, but also contributed to the growth of vocabulary and standardization of this language. More importantly, many bilingual dictionaries and grammars were compiled and thus greatly facilitated communication between the Mongols and other nationalities (Ma et al., 1981:71–72).

The earliest Tibetans dwelled along the middle reach of the Brahmaputra River. In the sixteenth century, they established a kingdom called "Bod," a name the Tibetans have used to call themselves. They set up a legal system and designed the Tibetan alphabet, which consists of four vowels and thirty consonants (Ma et al., 1981:257–59). The Tibetans proved a formidable enemy even to the powerful early Tang dynasty. They were called "Turfan" by the Chinese. Twice (641 A.D. and 710 A.D.) a Chinese princess was given to the Tibetan rulers in marriage as part of the Chinese diplomatic policy to the Tibetans. The two princesses were known to have had much to do with introducing Chinese culture to the Tibetans. Many Tibetan students were also sent to study at Changan, the capital of China then (Ma et al., 1981:258–59). The Tibetans also overcame the Uighurs and the Turks in the Tarim Basin and other neighboring nationalities. In 763 A.D., they captured Changan (Fairbank and Reischauer, 1960:156, 157, 192). During the period from the tenth to the twelfth century, Buddhism, which was introduced into Tibet from northwest India in the eighth century, became fused with the native Tibetan cult known as Bon, which made much of magic and divination. The result was the development of Lamaism, which eventually penetrated into various cultural aspects of the Tibetans, and which in the thirteenth century spread rapidly into Mongolia and also China (Fairbank and Reischauer, 1960:277–78).

The history of the Uighurs can be traced back to the third century B.C. Their ancestors were nomadic people living south of the Baikal Lake and north of modern China. They could be related to the Tatars and the Turks (Ma et al., 1981:175). They had contacts with Han Chinese, when the Han dynasty sent two envoys to the West in 139 B.C. and 115 B.C., respectively (Fairbank and Reischauer, 1960:99). In the eighth century, they allied with the Tang dynasty against the Tibetans. In the middle of the ninth century, they blended with the

Tibetans, the Khitans, and the Mongols living in the Tarim Basin (Fairbank and Reischauer, 1960:155, 157, 191). In the twelfth century, they were converted to Islam. Based on the Sogdian alphabet, which had come indirectly from Syriac and thus ultimately from the ancient Phoenician alphabet, the Uighurs created the alphabetic Uighur script, which later provided the base for the Mongolian alphabet (Fairbank and Reischauer, 1960:264–65). As noted earlier, the Manchus had derived their alphabet from the Mongolian alphabet. The Uighurs, the Mongols, and the Manchus avoided the difficulties encountered by the Japanese and the Koreans in their adoption of the Chinese writing system. Throughout history, the Uighurs have been the most influential nationality in Chinese Turkestan, today's Xinjiang autonomous region of China.

Because of space constraints, we can only give a very brief historical account of the contacts among those nationalities that have exerted great influences on other nationalities in culture, language, and religion. For the present purposes, it suffices to make some general observations with regard to language maintenance and language shift of the above-mentioned nationalities from a historical perspective.

First, it must be recalled that Han Chinese have never been a pure race. They have absorbed blood from many different racial stocks, especially from the non-Chinese peoples from the north and the northwest. It is not difficult to notice that northern Chinese today look different from southern Chinese. For example, the northerners are in general taller and have lighter skin color than the southerners. The northerners also have sharper facial contours than the southerners. While the northern Chinese look more similar to the Mongols and the Koreans, the southern Chinese look more like the Vietnamese and the Thais. This seems to correlate with M. J. Hashimoto's (1976; forthcoming) observation that, whereas Mandarin Chinese shares some grammatical features with Altaic languages, southern Chinese dialects share features with Thai. In both physical and grammatical features, there exists a continuum, with the northernmost closest to Altaic and the southernmost to Thai.

Second, we have seen that both the Huis and the Manchus have lost their mother tongues. Despite the Islamic religion, the Huis have not been able to retain their languages, whether Arabic or Persian. This is perhaps in part because the Huis did not speak a common language to start with, and in part because they have thinly spread among other nationalities. The Manchus, having ruled China for more than two hundred and fifty years, have lost their language, customs, and indigenous shamanism (Fairbank and Reischauer, 1960:364). They are not unlike other non-Chinese peoples in history who ruled China, yet were in the long run assimilated into Chinese culture and language. The Mongols also ruled China for about one hundred years. Yet, they have maintained their language. At least four reasons account for the difference between the Manchus and the Mongols in language maintenance. First, the Manchus had long, close contacts with Han Chinese before they ruled China. This was not the case with the Mongols. Second, the Mongols did not rule China as long as the Manchus did. More importantly, unlike the Manchus, they did not establish a Chinese bureaucracy for administrative purposes. Third, while the Manchus were agricultural people like the Han Chinese, the Mongols were nomadic people who resisted agricultural living in China. Fourth, while Han Chinese continued to flock to Manchuria to settle down during the eighteenth and nineteenth centuries, few Han Chinese migrated to Mongolia for the pastoral living. As to the Tibetans and the Uighurs, they never ruled China. Geographically, they have been isolated, the Tibetans in the Tibet Plateau and the Uighurs in the Tarim Basin. Furthermore, they have their own religions and written languages. Similarly, the Koreans in Manchuria have been geographically isolated and have their own written language. In addition, they have lived in the border adjacent to Korea.

THE PRESENT SITUATION

For geographical, climatical, and historical reasons, the nationalities in China have not kept the same pace in social and economic developments. Throughout history, Han Chinese have been far more advanced than other nationalities in technology, production, and politico-economic organization as well as in the arts and literature. They have developed one of the most profound and influential cultures in the history of the world. History has witnessed that no nationalities can rule China successfully without adopting Chinese culture. Indeed, non-Chinese peoples have been given not only political but also economic incentives to adopt Chinese culture. In the course of history, the Huis and the Manchus and portions of other nationalities have been assimilated into Chinese culture. As a consequence, they have been able to enjoy the same living standard as Han Chinese. In contrast, the majority of Tibetan, Mongol, Kazakh, Khalkas, Tajik, and Yuku have remained as pastoral peoples. Dulong, Wa, and parts of Miao and Yao have engaged in relatively primitive agricultural production. On a still lower level, nationalities such as Hezhe, Elunchun, Owenk, Jing, and others have lived on fishing or hunting. Since the Communist Chinese came to power in 1949, the production, technology, and living standards for those minorities have been significantly improved. In some regions, they have caught up with those of Han Chinese.

Three types of socioeconomic structure could be found among the nationalities in China before the Communist revolution in 1949. The first type represents a traditional agricultural society with private ownership of land. Big and small landlords owned most of the land. The majority of peasants tilled the land as tenants. Often more than not, they were exploited and oppressed by the landlords. In conjunction with administrative officials, the landlords virtually ruled the society. Since only these two classes of people could afford education, they formed the gentry class for China (Meskill, 1973:123–24). This was typical of Han Chinese before the Communist revolution. To various degrees and in similar manner, more than thirty national minorities also displayed this type of social structure. They included Manchu, Hui, Zhuang, Uighur, Korean, Buyi, Tujia, and Dong. Most of these minorities have had close contacts with Han Chinese. In terms of language use, Manchu and Hui have shifted to Chinese, and a large number of the population among Zhuang, Buyi, Tujia, and Dong are able to use Chinese (Ma et al., 1981).

The second type of socioeconomic structure involved slavery. For the Tibetans, the masters were aristocrats, bureaucrats, and Lama clergymen of the highest ranks. They owned large tracts of land along with the slaves or slave families living on the land. The slaves were attached to the land and could not be freed. They were allowed to have only a small portion of land to cultivate for their own living (Ma et al., 1981:257–76). In the case of Dai, all of the land, rivers, and forests belonged to the highest tribal ruler, who kept a portion of land for himself and divided the rest among his subordinates. The slaves worked for the masters without any rewards, but were allowed to have a small portion of land to feed themselves (Ma et al., 1981:341–43). A slavery system also existed among some Mongol tribes living in the pastoral areas of Inner Mongolia. The slaves were forced to raise cattle for the aristocrats and high-ranking Islamic priests. Although the majority of Yi people had already advanced to the landlord-tenant system, a slavery system still existed for more than one million Yi before the Chinese Communists came to power. The whole population was ranked into four classes.Black Yi, which constituted only 7 percent of the population, were masters. The rest were three ranks of slaves, with the lowest rank subject to the cruelest form of slavery (Ma et al., 1981:299–300).

The third type of socioeconomic structure was the primitive commune system. Dulong, Nu, Lisu, Jingpo, Wa, Bulang, Elunchun, Qwenk, and Li on the Hainan Island could be construed as having this organization. To different degrees, they displayed the coexistence of community and private ownership with reference to both production and distribution (Ma et al., 1981:5).

Today, all three types have been replaced by the Chinese Communist system. Therefore, obvious differences in economic-social structure can no longer be found among the nationalities in China. The great economic disparities between Han Chinese and other minorities have also disappeared. At present, only small inequalities exist between urban and rural living, among different regions owing to geographical and climatical reasons, among different professions, and among different modes of production, for example, industrial, agricultural, and pastoral. While the Chinese Communists have striven hard to increase the production level of national minorities, it is perhaps generally true that they still lag behind Han Chinese in living standard as a result of various geographical and climatical limitations.

Before the Communist revolution, some national minorities lived under political systems different from the Han Chinese system, somewhat corresponding to their difference from Han Chinese in socioeconomic structure. For the Tibetans, the political system was inseparable from the Lama Buddhists' organization. In Inner Mongolia, while provinces and counties had been set up by the Nationalist Chinese government before 1949, the hereditary tribal aristocrats were still ruling many groups of Mongols. With the intricate slavery system, Yi people were governed by more than one hundred mutually independent families. These systems have been replaced by the Chinese Communist system. The minorities today are not so different from Han Chinese with regard to economic as well as sociopolitical structures. Not only minorities are more nearly equal to Han Chinese than before, but individuals in each nationality also enjoy more equality than before. Considering all the discrepancies that existed among all the nationalities and individuals, one cannot but be deeply impressed with the tremendous changes the Chinese Communists have brought.

Compared with social, economic, and political changes, relatively little change has occurred in different forms of religion in China. Before the Communist revolution, while a large number of Han Chinese were Buddhists and some were converted to Christianity, the vast majority of Han Chinese had assumed Confucian ethics and believed in ancestor worship with local deities. Despite its incompatibility with the Communist ideology, religion has been tolerated as long as it has not stood in the way of sociopolitical reforms. However, the Lama government was dissolved after the Tibetans' rebellion in 1959. During the Cultural Revolution (1966–76), religious groups were suppressed among Han Chinese more than among minorities. The custom of worshiping ancestors and deities, including Confucius himself, has faded significantly since 1949. However, it is difficult to assess to what extent Han Chinese have changed their beliefs, since Confucianism and ancestor worship embody deep philosophical beliefs rather than relying on ritual expression. Recently, Buddhism and Christianity have been revived among Han Chinese. Islam has remained as influential as before among Hui, Uighur, Kazakh, Khalkas, Tatar, Uzbek, Tajik, Dongxiang, Sala, and Baoan. Lamaism is still prevalent among Tibetans, Mongols, Tu, and Yuku people. A different form of Buddhism, Hinayana or the Lesser Vehicle, is widely followed among Dai, Bulang, Benglong, and some portion of the Wa population. Christianity is followed by Yi, a portion of Miao, and other smaller minorities in the southwest. Eastern Orthodox Christianity is followed by the Russians and some of the Ewenk people. Various primitive religions and the practice of shamanism still exist among Dulong, Nu, Wa, Jingpo, and Elunchun (Ma et al., 1981).

The Chinese Communists had developed a close relationship with many national minorities even before they came to power in 1949. During their long and hard struggle against the Chinese Nationalists, they often had to retreat to remote areas to live with and to seek support from national minorities. As early as 1931, the Communist party of China established a set of policies to encourage the development of language and culture among the national minorities (Lehmann, 1974:113). Shortly before the establishment of the People's Republic of China (PRC) in 1949, the Communist party, in consultation with representatives from various national minorities, formally announced its basic policies toward national minorities. These policies were later formalized in the 1954 Constitution of the PRC (Ma et al., 1981:13–14). They have remained intact in the latest revision of the Constitution, which stipulates that all nationalities in China be treated equally, that autonomous administrative districts be set up in areas with a concentration of national minorities, that all national minorities have the right to maintain their religions and customs and to use and develop their languages, and that the government assist national minorities to develop their economies and cultures.[1] Today, the PRC has five autonomous regions: Inner Mongolia for Mongols, Tibet for Tibetans, Guangxi for Zhuang, Ningxia for Hui, and Xinjiang for Uighur. They are equivalent to Han Chinese provinces. In addition, there are twenty-nine autonomous districts smaller than regions, seventy autonomous counties, and three autonomous tribes (Ma et al., 1981:16).

The Central Institute of Nationalities (Zhongyang Minzu Xueyuan) was established in June 1951 in Beijing in order to train cadres for national minorities. Nine local institutes of nationalities were subsequently established in the northwest, southwest, and south (Ma et al., 1981:17). Depending on the location, each local institute places emphasis on some particular minority languages and cultures. The Central Institute of Nationalities has a language department whose main function has been to train translators and interpreters for minority languages. While Han Chinese cadres learn minority languages, minority cadres learn Chinese (Lehmann, 1974:109–13). In recent years, the learning of minority languages on the part of Han Chinese cadres has been moved to local institutes so that minority languages can be more effectively learned. The Department of Languages at the Central Institute of Nationalities has thus concentrated on the teaching of Chinese to minority cadres.

The Chinese Academy of Social Sciences also has a department of minority languages. It focuses on research on minority languages and has maintained close ties with the Central Institute of Nationalities. In the early 1950s, it dispatched several teams of field workers to study minority languages and held extensive meetings and conferences. In 1956, the two organizations cooperated on an extensive research project that involved more than seven hundred linguists doing research on thirty-three minority languages in sixteen separate areas. After the research was completed, they went on to help several minorities design new alphabets or reform existing orthographies (Chang, 1967).

In the autonomous areas, the religions and customs of national minorities are taken into consideration for legal and administrative decisions, and their languages are used in administration, elections, publications, broadcasting, and law courts. In all of the five autonomous regions, and perhaps in many of the smaller autonomous units as well, the local national minority language is the medium of instruction in elementary and middle schools. The study of Chinese begins in middle school (Lehmann, 1974:114–15). Chinese is used as the medium of instruction in colleges and universities, when a professor cannot speak the local minority language or when the textbooks are available only in Chinese. The Central Broadcast Station in Beijing broadcasts in the major national minority languages. Local stations in the autonomous areas broadcast primarily in local minority languages. However, in areas with a large number of Han Chinese, the broadcasts are in Chinese as well as in local minority languages. For example, in Lhasa, the capital of Tibet, both Tibetan and Chinese are used in broadcasting. In Xinjiang, where about 40 percent of the population are now Han Chinese, broadcasts are in Chinese, Uighur, Kazakh, and Mongolian. The Nationalities Publishing House in Beijing publishes books in five minority languages: Mongolian, Uighur, Tibetan, Zhuang, and Korean. Local printing houses in major cities such as Lhasa, Urumchi, Kukuhoto, and other areas with a large number of Han Chinese in the autonomous regions also publish books, newspapers, and magazines in local minority languages and in Chinese (Lehmann, 1974:114).

The language policies of the Chinese Communists toward national minorities have sought to eliminate Han Chinese chauvinism and are in keeping with the egalitarianism of the Chinese Communists' ideology. Thus, standard Chinese is referred to as "Hanyu," the language of Han Chinese, rather than as "Guoyu," the national language, as by the Chinese Nationalists. Several cities in the autonomous areas have regained their original minority names. For example, Urumchi, the capital of Xinjiang, is now called Wulumuqi according to Uighur instead of Dihua, the name given by the Chinese Nationalists, which means "be assimilated" in Chinese. Similarly, Kukuhoto, the capital of Inner Mongolia, was called Guisui (meaning "be appeased") by the Nationalists and has been renamed Huhehaote. Chinese names for national minorities which are either derogatory or condescending have also been replaced (Tai, 1976).

Apart from the Chinese Communists' ideology, these language policies also serve political purposes. Never before has China been so tightly unified under one single effective socioeconomic system. The unification as well as the very security of China depends largely on the cooperation and support of many national minorities who live in the militarily crucial border areas adjacent to the Soviet Union, India, and Southeast Asia. It is imperative for national minorities to understand the political and economic policies of the Chinese Communist party. A great effort has been made to translate works on communism and government documents into minority languages to be published in local newspapers or to be broadcast by local stations. For national minorities to understand the party's policies is obviously more urgent than for them to understand the Chinese language. It is generally true that the Chinese Communists are more concerned with the socioeconomic development of national minorities than their acceptance of the Chinese culture and language. Besides, it is doubtful that they have ever had enough resources to conduct large-scale Chinese-language training programs among all of the national minorities.

A study of China's language policies on bilingualism cannot be sufficient without a brief discussion of the promotion of the so-called Putonghua ("common language") among Han Chinese, who speak many dialects. As the common language of the PRC, Putonghua was defined and endorsed at the standardization conference of October 1955. Its pronunciation is based on the general Beijing dialect, its grammar on northern dialects, and its vocabulary on modern colloquial literature (Lehmann, 1974:11). In essence, it is a continuation of Guanhua

("Mandarin" or "language of officials"), which served as a lingua franca in China for over five hundred years in the Ming and Qing dynasties, and Guoyu ("national language"), which was promoted during the Republican era (1911–49) on Mainland China and which has remained the standard language on Taiwan under the Chinese Nationalists. Although the three terms for the standard vernacular based on the Beijing dialect reflect three different attitudes toward a standard vernacular for this vast and populous country, the desirability of having a common speech that can be understood throughout the country has long been recognized. In dynastic times, it was simply a medium for official communication, and no attempt was made to popularize it among the people. During the Republic, while the popularization of the "national language" was set up as a goal, political chaos and wars precluded effective efforts.

In many senses, China was reunified by the Chinese Communists in 1949. The Communists' nationwide promotion of Putonghua began in 1955 with the Conference on the Standardization of the Modern Chinese Spoken Language. The State Council followed up in 1956 with a directive to popularize it throughout the country. It requested that all the schools of Han Chinese use Putonghua as the medium of instruction beginning in autumn 1956. It thus changed the hitherto common practice of using the local dialect as the medium. During the next two years, workshops were held to train primary, secondary, and normal school language teachers in the phonetics of Putonghua. In 1958, Zhou Enlai announced that the popularization of Putonghua was an important political and economic tool, the People's Congress approved the use of the Pinyin system as an invaluable tool for the spread of Putonghua, and Mao Zedong declared that all cadres must learn Putonghua (Lehmann, 1974:49). The campaign seemed to have gained considerable momentum before the Cultural Revolution started in 1966. During the Cultural Revolution, the campaign was neglected and interrupted. Yet, as hundreds of thousands of young students fervently traveled around the country to advocate the revolution and as thousands upon thousands of young and old educated citizens volunteered or were assigned to settle in rural areas, they contributed greatly to the spreading of Putonghua. The campaign was resumed after the Cultural Revolution, though without the initial vigor of the late 1950s.

The policy toward local dialects in China has been that they are useful and that cadres should learn to use the dialect of the area where they work (Lehmann, 1974:17, 50). Local television and radio stations broadcast in local dialects, in addition to Putonghua. Obviously, Chinese leaders have recognized that dialects cannot be eliminated by administrative order and they will not die out for a long time. To them, the popularization of Putonghua is motivated by national unity and need for communication, and not by any superiority over the dialects. In fact, many of the national leaders come from southern China and speak Putonghua with strong regional accents. On the other hand, it is not clear whether they have recognized the positive values of linguistic pluralism from an educational point of view. Perhaps they have accepted dialects on practical grounds rather than because of their appreciation of the educational philosophy behind bilingualism.

China treats Han Chinese dialects and minorities' languages differently in three respects. First, whereas Putonghua is required to be taught and used in elementary and secondary schools among the Han Chinese, it is to be taught only in response to the wishes of some national minorities. When Han Chinese have to work in minority areas, they are requested to learn the local languages. Second, while the Chinese government has helped many minorities romanize their languages according to the Pinyin principles employed for Putonghua, it has not allowed the romanization of local dialects of Han Chinese. Third, minority languages have been recognized on both ideological and practical grounds; local dialects are accepted only as a matter of practicality. Although the ultimate goal of the popularization of Putonghua involves the elimination of Han Chinese dialects, the ideology of the Chinese Communists prohibits the replacing of minority languages with Putonghua.

CONCLUSIONS

Constrained by the ideology of egalitarianism among different races, the Chinese Communists have attempted to maintain and to develop the cultures and languages of national minorities. On the other hand, on the grounds of national unity and the need for communication, they have made efforts to popularize Putonghua, a standardized Mandarin, throughout the entire country, especially among Han Chinese, Hui, Manchu, and some portions of the minority population which have adopted various Chinese dialects. The policy has been to proceed gradually through persuasion and encouragement, and not force (Seybolt and Chiang, 1979:25).

It is indeed difficult to assess in detail the achievement of the popularization of Putonghua in the past thirty years. However, several generalizations can be made. First, there are more minority people who have learned to speak Putonghua than Han Chinese who have learned to speak minority languages. This generalization also holds true for the bilingualism between Putonghua and Chinese dialects. Judging from China's policies toward bilingualism, it is not unreasonable to attribute the asymmetry to the very fact that a good command of Putonghua does provide more political and economical opportunities. Putonghua, as the common language for China, is analogous to English as an international language of politics and economics. Second, bilingualism between Putonghua and local minority languages or Chinese dialects is more common in urban areas than in rural areas, because the population in urban areas is in general more mixed than in rural areas and there is a higher concentration of government offices and schools in urban areas than in rural areas. Third, for both native speakers of minority languages and Chinese dialects, the more highly educated one is, the better one's command of Putonghua.

The following generalizations may be made with regard to the bilingualism between Putonghua and Chinese dialects only. First, the popularization of Putonghua has been more successful in the north than in the south. The primary reason is that northern dialects and the standardized Mandarin are mutually intelligible, whereas southern dialects and the standardized Mandarin are not. A secondary reason can perhaps be attributed to the geological and hence psychological distance between southern dialects and the standardized Mandarin. This may explain why the popularization of Putonghua has been more successful in Shanghai than in Guangzhou. Second, younger generations with more years of schooling in Putonghua have better command of Putonghua than their older counterparts. Thus, the generation under thirty is better than the generation of forty, which in turn is better than the generation of fifty years of age. The majority of the population above sixty years old in the south does not understand Putonghua at all. Third, there are many more people who can passively understand Putonghua than people who can actively speak the language. Especially in rural areas, youth tend to forget Putonghua after they leave school. This is particularly true in the south (Seybolt and Chiang, 1979:26–27, 382).

In recent years, the number of televisions in China has increased significantly to about thirty-eight per one hundred households. The nation has also made many efforts to expand education on all levels. In addition, a much improved transportation system has been implemented with less restricted traveling policies. It can be expected that the popularization of Putonghua will be enhanced accordingly. Nevertheless, without doubt very few minority languages and Chinese dialects will be replaced by Putonghua in the forseeable future. The future should see China as a more balanced bilingual nation, with Putonghua as a lingua franca throughout China.

NOTE

1. According to Zhang Jichuan and Zhang Liansheng, research fellows of the Institute of Nationality Studies of the Chinese Academy of Social Sciences. I have also benefited from discussions with them regarding bilingualism between Han Chinese and national minorities in China. I am solely responsible for any possible errors.

BIBLIOGRAPHY

Chang, K. 1967. "National Languages." In *Current Trends In Linguistics*, ed. T. A. Sebeok. Vol. 2. The Hague and Paris: Mouton, pp. 155–76.
DeFrancis, J. 1976. *Beginning Chinese*. New Haven and London: Yale University Press.
Egerod, S. 1967. "Dialectology." In *Current Trends In Linguistics*, ed. T. A. Sebeok. Vol. 2. The Hague and Paris: Mouton, pp. 91–129.
Fairbank, J. K., and E. O. Reischauer. 1960. *East Asia: The Great Tradition*. Boston: Houghton Mifflin Co.
Fitzgerald, C. P. 1961. *China: A Short Cultural History*. New York: Praeger Publishers.
Guan, D. G. 1971. "Manzu de ruguan yu hanhua" [The Manchu conquest of China and

their sinicization]. *Bulletin of the Institute of History and Philosophy, Academic Sinica, the Republic of China*, 43:445–88.

Hashimoto, M. J. 1976. "Language Diffusion on the Asian Continent: Problems of Typological Diversity in Sino-Tibetan." *Computational Analyses of Asian and African Languages*, 3:49–65.

————. Forthcoming. "The Altaicization of Northern Chinese." In *Nicholas C. Bodman Festschrift*, ed. W. J. McCoy and T. Light. Ithaca, N.Y.: Cornell University Press.

Kratochvil, P. 1970. *The Chinese Language Today*. London: Hutchinson University Library.

Lehmann, W. P. 1974. *Language and Linguistics in the People's Republic of China*. Austin and London: University of Texas Press.

Li, F. K. 1973. "Languages and Dialects of China." *Journal of Chinese Linguistics* 1:1–13.

Ma, Y., et al. 1981. *Zhongguo shaoshu minzu* [National minorities in China]. Beijing: People's Publisher.

Meskill, J. 1973. *An Introduction to Chinese Civilization*. Lexington, Mass.: D. C. Heath and Co.

Paulston, C. B. 1985. *Linguistics Consequences of Ethnicity and Nationalism in Multilingual Settings*. University of Pittsburgh.

Seybolt, P. J., and G. K. Chiang. 1979. *Language Reform in China*. New York: Sharpe, Inc.

Stern, H. H., et al. 1976. *Three Approaches to Teaching French*. Toronto: Ontario Ministry of Education.

Tai, J. 1976. *Lexical Changes in Modern Standard Chinese in the People's Republic of China Since 1949*. Washington, D.C.: U.S. Information Agency.

10

Carol Myers Scotton

PATTERNS OF BILINGUALISM IN EAST AFRICA (UGANDA, KENYA, AND TANZANIA)

LINGUISTIC GROUPINGS

Its large number of languages is one of the most distinctive features of sub-Saharan Africa. Since there is no generally accepted method for distinguishing between dialect and language, the precise number of African languages cannot be stated. Even by a conservative estimate, however, the number of distinct languages is well over eight hundred (Greenberg, 1971a:126). East Africa alone, the subject of this chapter, contains about 175 languages.[1] This three-nation area (Uganda, Kenya, and Tanzania) is especially diverse linguistically, with all four of the indigenous African-language families represented in Tanzania (the only African country with that distinction), three families in Kenya, and two in Uganda. As is the case elsewhere in Africa, most East African languages have small numbers of speakers, and their knowledge and use are largely synonymous with specific ethnic group membership. Only a handful of East African languages have more than a million speakers, and while the overwhelming majority of East Africans speak more than one language, the same second languages are not regularly learned by different speakers since neighboring languages differ. The outstanding exception to this statement is the learning of an ethnically neutral lingua franca. Swahili is widely spoken by all groups in all parts of East Africa—and beyond—as a lingua franca. English is also a lingua franca often known by the educated.

Relative to the diversity found elsewhere on the African continent, East Africa shows enough cultural and linguistic similarities to form a single, natural nation, had it not been for the fact that colonialism divided the area into three nations. Tanzania, Kenya, and Uganda contain basically the same indigenous ethnic groups with similar traditions, and they have adapted in similar ways to external influences: notably, all three are still very rural with few real towns and fewer cities; subsistence agriculture predominates; Christianity has many followers, but Islam is also an important influence on the coast.

The three nations of East Africa also group together linguistically as something of a transition zone between the Bantu-speaking area extending from Cameroon in the west to the tip of Southern Africa, the northeast in which Semitic and Cushitic languages dominate, and Central Africa just below the Sahara where Sudanic (Nilo-Saharan) languages are found. All three of these groups are present in East Africa. But, for example, to the south of Tanzania, in such nations as Mozambique and Malawi, the only indigenous languages are from the Bantu group.

Within the East African diversity, Bantu languages are prominent. This is no surprise since the Bantu group is the largest and most widespread in Africa as a whole; most scholars estimate that there are at least five hundred different Bantu languages. The Bantu group is less distinctive genetically than numerically; these languages simply constitute one small subgroup of the largest family in Africa, Niger-Kordofanian, showing closest affiliation (although distant) with coastal West African languages.

Relatively closely related Bantu languages are spoken by more than two-thirds of the East African population. Swahili, widely known as a second language and the official language of Tanzania, is also a Bantu language. Swahili is the national language of both Kenya and Uganda, but English is the official language there.

Language groups in general are larger in Kenya and Uganda than they are in Tanzania. Thus, there is an approximate total of thirty languages in Uganda (Ladefoged, Glick, and Criper, 1971:83) and twelve of these are Bantu. In Kenya, there are about fifteen Bantu languages out of an approximate total of thirty-four (Whiteley, 1974a:27). Estimates on the number of Tanzanian Bantu languages fluctuate, and no recent census includes data on mother tongue. It is generally agreed, however, that there are about one hundred and twenty different Bantu ones. Polomé (1980a:3–5) comments on the uncertainty as to the exact number.

In both Kenya and Uganda, Bantu languages represent about 66 percent of the population, but in Tanzania they constitute over 95 percent. In Uganda, a Bantu language, Luganda, has more native speakers than any other language, representing about 16 percent of the population. It is also something of a lingua franca there. In Kenya, Kikuyu has more native speakers than any other language, with more than 2 million speakers; other Bantu languages, Luyia (Luhya) and Kamba, each have well over 1 million native speakers. Although Sukuma in Tanzania is a Bantu language with over a million speakers, most other Bantu languages there have small numbers of speakers.

Recent studies of East African Bantu language classification include Guthrie (1967–71), Heine (1973), Henrici (1973), Möhlig (1980), Nurse and Philippson (1980), and Hinnebusch, Nurse, and Mould (1981).[2]

Although Bantu speakers predominate in Uganda and Kenya, more actual physical territory is covered by non-Bantu groups. The northern half of Uganda is non-Bantu, as are the northern half of Kenya and some large central regions. These non-Bantu groups are most prominently speakers of Nilotic languages, classified in three distantly related groups in the Sudanic family (Greenberg, 1963:85–148). Western Nilotic languages extend in a migration corridor from Sudan in the north to the northwestern corner of Tanzania in the south. Acholi and Lango are the major representatives in Uganda, and Luo is the only Western Nilotic language found in Kenya and Tanzania. Luo is a major language in Kenya, with over a million speakers. Its home territory is in the far west on the shores of Lake Victoria (including the city of Kisumu). But Luos, like many other ethnic groups in East Africa, are found far from their homes where they migrate for salaried positions. Luo extends across the border from the Kenya Luo home area into Tanzania, skipping over several Kenyan Bantu groups.

Eastern Nilotic is not a very populous group as a whole, but it includes Teso, one of the major languages of Uganda. Teso is spoken in central and eastern Uganda as well as in neighboring areas of Kenya. Karimonjong-Turkana is spoken in the northern border areas of Kenya and Uganda. The Maasai, a well-known pastoral group, also speak an Eastern Nilotic language. They are found in central areas shared by Kenya and Tanzania. Samburu (Sampur), spoken mainly in northcentral Kenya, is related to Maasai.

Southern Nilotic languages are found mainly in Kenya, although there are several minor ones in Tanzania. The Kalenjin group in Kenya consists of six related languages, with more than a million speakers in total. Kipsigis and Nandi are the largest. Speakers live in westcentral Kenya for the most part.

The Central Sudanic languages in northwestern Uganda are classified in the same family with Nilotic languages, but are very remotely related to them. Lugbara and Madi are the main representatives in Uganda, with their closest relatives across the border in Sudan.

Kenya's northeastern areas are largely Eastern Cushitic-speaking. Somali is the main language of the northeastern province, which borders on Somalia, where almost the entire population speaks dialects of Somali. Another Cushitic language is Oromo, a major language in Ethiopia, which is spoken in adjoining areas of Kenya as well.

Tanzania, in addition to having Bantu languages (Niger-Congo subfamily in the Niger-Kordofanian family) and Nilotic languages (Sudanic or Nilo-Saharan family), also has a pocket of Southern Cushitic speakers of Iraqw and several minor languages (Cushitic branch of Afro-Asiatic family), and two click languages, Sandawe and Hadza (Khoisan family).

For an overview on the genetic classification of non-Bantu languages in Kenya, see Heine (1980b and 1980c). For a discussion of the Nilotic languages of Tanzania, see Ehret (1980). Zaborski (1976) offers an overview on Cushitic languages.

As is the case elsewhere in the world, in a number of cases what are called separate languages in East Africa could be called dialects of the same language, if the criterion of mutual intelligibility were used. In some cases, the opposite is true; for example, not all the dialects of Chaga, a Bantu language of northern Tanzania, are mutually intelligible (Polomé, 1980a:3). In addition, there are several instances in East Africa of a standardized or "union version" being produced to stand for a number of related varieties. Thus, Luyia in western Kenya is really only a written version to represent eighteen closely related spoken varieties.[3]

There are also a number of Asians in East Africa, especially in Kenya but also in Tanzania. (General Idi Amin's policies in the 1970s meant an almost total exodus of the Asian population from Uganda.) Many Asians come from families who have been in East Africa for seventy years or more; two-thirds of the Asians in Kenya were born there (Neale, 1974:69). But citizens are a small minority, at least in Kenya, and further reductions in the Asian population are expected. The estimated Asian population in Kenya in the early 1970s was one hundred and seventy-four thousand (Bujra, 1974:263). According to the 1967 census, there were eighty-five thousand Asians in Tanzania (Polomé, 1980c:135). They speak about five different Indian languages, all of them Indo-Aryan. These include Kachi (a dialect of Sindhi), Konkani, Gujarati, Punjabi, and Urdu. Goans are often native speakers of English. Asians in business almost certainly speak Swahili as a second language; some know other African languages, and many speak English.

CHOOSING AN OFFICIAL LANGUAGE

Given the linguistic diversity outlined above, choosing an official language would not be easy for East African nations. As in most of Africa, in no country is one language numerically dominant. Choosing as official the language of one of several competing middle-sized groups is an unacceptable solution because of the clear advantages accruing to the native speakers of that language relative to those for persons who must learn it as a second language. Therefore, making an ethnically neutral language the official one has seemed the most feasible solution.

Tanzania was able to choose Swahili for this role because, although an indigenous language, Swahili was not associated with a numerically dominant or politically powerful group of native speakers. (Swahili had fewer than twelve thousand native speakers on the mainland, according to the 1957 census [Molnos, 1969:48]; in addition, of course, the total population of such offshore islands as Zanzibar and Pemba would be Swahili speakers.) Thus, the size of the group of those who gained by this move (mother-tongue speakers) was not large enough to threaten other groups. Furthermore, since Tanzania is a nation of many small language groups, no single group was large (or powerful) enough to dispute Swahili's claim as the most obvious indigenous candidate. Most important, however, were two interrelated factors: there was a tradition of at least a century of using Swahili as the main indigenous lingua franca across the entire country, and this tradition had "bleached" Swahili of much of its ethnicity, making it a neutral choice.

At the outset of the nineteenth century, Swahili was probably still largely a coastal language. "Swahili" is derived from the plural form *sawahil* of Arabic *sahil* ("coast") and originally referred to the language used in the coastal trade between the Arabs and local populations in precolonial times (Polomé, 1980b:79). Partly because of its history as a contact language, there has been much speculation about its origin. Many have assumed it is a creolized pidgin. In fact, there is strong evidence against this view. T. J. Hinnebusch (1976) presents detailed phonological comparisons to show that Swahili is closely related to other Kenyan coastal languages, such as Pokomo and Mijikenda, and that they show the regular sound correspondences constituting any linguistic subgroup. This places Swahili as one of the most northern of the Northeast Bantu group (Nurse and Philippson, 1980:46). Studies such as these and the fact that, in spite of its Arabic loan words, Swahili shows little Arabic structural influence point to the inevitable conclusion that Swahili is simply a coordinate member of the greater grouping of Bantu languages. True, it is different from its closest relatives in showing some structural divergences (loss of tone, for example), but this is because of its social history, not its origin. Present evidence indicates, therefore, that Swahili became differentiated from its cognate varieties and arose as a distinct language along the Kenya coast; then it spread mainly southwards along the coast and to the offshore islands, such as Zanzibar. It seems likely that Swahili was a coastal language before the tenth century (Whiteley, 1969:31; Hinnebusch, 1979:259). See Whiteley (1969) or Polomé (1980b) for more historical details.

Swahili native dialects today form a chain of mutually intelligible varieties that can be divided into three clusters. The Northern cluster is centered around Lamu Island on the northern Kenya coast (but also extends just across the Somali border). The Central dialects are mainly those spoken on the Island of Pemba and neighboring mainland Tanzanian areas. The Southern cluster includes Kiunguja, the dialect of Zanzibar town, which became the basis for Standard Swahili under colonial rule. A subgroup within the Southern cluster (but found geographically north of the rest of the cluster) includes Kimvita, the dialect of Mombasa.

Diverse circumstances created successive needs for a lingua franca in the East African interior, and Swahili fortuitously was on hand to meet these needs. First, the Arab traders who organized trading caravans to the interior from Zanzibar and coastal points needed a means of communicating with the indigenous peoples. There is no direct evidence regarding language use before the 1840s, but presumably these traders spoke Swahili as their own first language, or at least knew it, and it became the medium of trade. Second, the missionaries who arrived on the coastal scene in the mid- and late nineteenth century also needed a lingua franca. Since they set up initial operations where Swahili was a native language, since it was already in place as a lingua franca, and since it had a written literature (in Arabic script), it is not surprising that the missionaries considered Swahili worthy of their linguistic energies. Several grammars of Swahili were soon produced, the first in 1850. This, in turn, enhanced Swahili even more as a lingua franca. Third, the colonials also needed a lingua franca to govern. When the Germans arrived to colonize Tanganyika (now Tanzania, including Zanzibar as well as the mainland territory), they envisioned the area as a profitable colony and therefore wanted literate Africans, not expensive expatriates, filling at least minor civil service positions. They started with Swahili-speaking personnel from Zanzibar, founded schools that taught Swahili, and required the missionaries to produce Swahili-speaking graduates. In their administration of East Africa, the British (first in Uganda and Kenya and then also in Tanganyika after World War I) also wanted to use local resources in the civil service and therefore welcomed the idea of a lower level Swahili-speaking cadre. Under them, English did become the language of post-primary education and of higher administration, but they embraced Swahili as a general lingua franca. Many German and British civil servants, as well as settlers, also learned the language, although sometimes producing a somewhat pidginized version. Finally, especially in Tanganyika and to an extent in Kenya, when nationalists sought to unify the population in the push for independence after World War II, Swahili was the natural choice as the vehicle of mobilization. (See Whiteley, 1969, for a detailed history.)

The rise of Swahili as the main contact language in East Africa and neighboring areas is an excellent example of J. H. Greenberg's observation that the spread of a lingua franca takes on a life of its own. Having only a single lingua franca in an area becomes the dominant solution, not because anyone plans it that way, but because "once it becomes at all widespread, it has an advantage over other possible lingua francas so that its expansion continues" (1971b:201). Except in parts of Uganda, where Luganda remains a lagging but dogged competitor, Swahili has unquestioned status in all of East Africa as the expected medium of interethnic communication in an African language. Indeed, its domain includes large areas in neighboring countries on all sides as well. It is a significant lingua franca as far north as Juba in southern Sudan, and it may serve as a contact language as far south as northern Zambia. In eastern Zaire, it even has official status as a regional language used as a medium in the early primary grades.[4]

While programmed change making Swahili the official language and promoting its dominance has marked post-independence developments in Tanzania, gradual evolution and maintenance of the status quo have characterized this period in Kenya and Uganda. That is, little has been done systematically in Kenya and Uganda to change the arrangements that were in place at independence in the 1960s. Only in Tanzania could one use the term "language engineering." Thus, today English remains the official language of both Kenya and Uganda. In addition, a number of vernaculars have some official status, mainly as media in the lower school grades. There is also limited broadcasting in a long list of vernaculars on the state-owned radio systems. The only real change is that both nations have named Swahili the national language. This status entails no exact role, although Swahili enjoys many more public "national" uses in Kenya than in Uganda.

Only in Tanzania is Swahili paramount, where it was made both the official and national language in 1967, several years after independence. English is a compulsory subject in primary schools and remains the medium for most secondary schools and university subjects. Otherwise, Swahili is the only language with any official status, with policies to spread its use and thereby decrease the domain of other languages. There is a National Swahili Council to promote the language, and the university has both an Institute of Swahili Research and a Department of Swahili.

Tanzania believes that its choice of Swahili is necessary within its scheme of development. To promote socialism, Tanzania is trying to use Swahili as a leveling language. Since all public primary schooling is in Swahili, in theory all learn Swahili and enter the economic marketplace equally prepared (Scotton, 1978:729). In practice, however, English is still a qualification for better paying jobs; therefore, secondary school graduates, especially those attending one of several private primary schools, have a headstart. It is a fact, however, that all Swahili speakers have access to political office. Tanzania is also using Swahili to achieve national integration, promoting a sense of unity under a single transethnic symbol.

In contrast, in Uganda and Kenya English has been the solution to the problem of finding an ethnically neutral official language. English remains in place even though it still evokes images of the master-servant relationship characterizing colonial rule: those who do not know English complain they are relegated to the servant role, and even many who know it claim their nations will be colonies of the West as long as English is given high status. The most important problem concerns provisions to spread English, since socioeconomic opportunities typically are tied to knowing the official language in any nation. Adequate teachers or teaching materials in English are not equally available across the nation, and there are no arrangements to spread the language to the nonschool-age population. Thus, in both nations, the official language is still the language only of the elite, accessible only to those with special or higher education. In rural areas, perhaps only 20 percent or less know English, while in cities the proportion may rise to 40 percent. In such a situation, the result is that the official language does not promote a sense of national unity. Furthermore, it stratifies rather than integrates the population in a socioeconomic sense (Scotton, 1982b).

In such a situation, what about an official role for Swahili? Attitudes toward Swahili have always been volatile and complex in Kenya. Although it is the native language along Kenya's coast, Swahili first reached up-country Kenya via the caravan routes from Zanzibar through Tanganyika. (Fierce groups, such as the Maasai, deterred the idea of routes from Mombasa.) It was the Kiunguja dialect of Zanzibar that the colonials accepted as the basis for Standard Swahili in the late 1920s, not Mombasa's Kimvita dialect. (See Whiteley, 1969:79–95 for a full discussion of the rationale for this choice.) This was the Swahili learned up-country as it was spread via government notices, school texts, and other official channels.

Second, many up-country Kenyans associate Swahili with a Muslim coastal culture that is very different from their own indigenous or contemporary traditions or religious preferences. While today many of the advocates for a wider role for Swahili do come from up-country groups, primary supporters are typically coastal native speakers.[5] According to the 1969 census, there were no more than ten thousand native speakers of Swahili in Kenya. The much more numerous and politically powerful up-country Kenyans may see these supporters as espousing a variety of Swahili which they do not speak and an increasing role for a culture not their own. In addition, those in high position may see Swahili advocates as political competitors who would benefit from a change in Swahili's status, while they themselves have established and maintained their position through the medium of English.

Third, many up-country Kenyans see Swahili as a second-class language. This image is partly a result of colonial language policies. Provision for Swahili (but not English) in African education was seen as a means to ''keep Africans in their place.'' The fact that Swahili traditionally was learned informally (this also holds today) rather than necessarily through schooling means that knowledge of Swahili is not a symbol of education (Scotton, 1977).

Finally, even though Swahili is used for some interethnic communication by all socioeconomic levels, the fact that it is the main interethnic vehicle of the uneducated in low-status jobs has led to its primary association with such speakers.

At the same time, Swahili has unquestioned—and growing—preeminence as the language of urban life. Its role in politics is also important. This is related to its image as the language of the masses and to the fact that it is very widely known, attributes that English cannot claim. As M. H. Abdulaziz (1982:116) notes, ''A leader who cannot speak Swahili is unlikely to get support from members of their language groups. . . . The tremendous potential of this language as a rallying point for national aspirations and identity cannot be overemphasized in a situation with the potential of tribal conflicts.''

Largely because of ambivalence regarding Swahili's role, policies toward language in Parliament and in education have changed several times in Kenya. When it became independent in 1964, its Constitution specified ability to read English as a qualification for standing for election to Parliament. In 1974, however, then President Jomo Kenyatta announced that Swahili would be the sole language of parliamentary debate (although all laws would still be written in English). This decision was rescinded in 1978 when both English and Swahili were declared possible languages of parliamentary debate.

The vernaculars and Swahili have vied as media of instruction in Kenya's primary schools since early colonial times, with English also a contender from the 1960s. (English has always been the medium of post-primary school, but such facilities were very limited under colonial rule.) Africans themselves were at times suspicious of education offered to them in Swahili. They saw themselves as being educated only to become more useful to Europeans as their employers. In addition, some missionaries viewed education in Swahili with aversion since they believed a child should be taught first in his or her own language and that the vernacular was the necessary medium for inner religious conversion. Colonial administrators were of two minds: sometimes they saw Swahili as the efficient answer to the choice of a language for education, since preparing materials in even the main vernaculars was an unrealistic solution; other times they saw a child's first language as the most effective medium of instruction. (See Gorman, 1974a, for a detailed overview of language policy in Kenyan education.) Roughly speaking, the vernaculars were given priority in the primary schools until 1935, and then Swahili was in favor up to 1950. In the 1950s, there was another swing back to the vernaculars. Finally in the 1960s, English was becoming the popular choice as a medium right from primary one, but with Swahili gradually gaining favor again, but only as a subject.

Today, as noted above, official Kenyan policy sanctions the vernaculars once again as media, with both Swahili and English as subjects, but with only English taking over as a medium in primary four. The fact that Swahili was just made a compulsory subject on the primary school-leaving examination should mean its importance in the curriculum will grow. English is the medium for all higher education, although Swahili is an alternative subject to French in secondary schools and is emphasized in teacher training institutions. It is also a possible major subject at Kenya's two universities. There are about eighteen official school vernaculars, with Swahili one of them in coastal areas. A partial listing includes Kikuyu, Kamba, Meru, Embu, Pokomo, Taita, Mijikenda, Luyia, Luo, Kalenjin, Maasai, Samburu, Teso, and Somali.

The present policy to use vernaculars as a medium in the first three years of primary school is highly flexible (Sedlak, 1983). Headmasters and teachers seem to have a great deal of latitude in selecting a policy which they feel will produce the most effective education for their students. If a school serves a linguistically mixed population, the solution is most often Swahili as a medium. This is not only the case in urban areas, but also along ethnic group boundaries. But in Nairobi schools high up the socioeconomic ladder, for example, the sole medium will be English. This is also the case in some rural schools, with the vernacular possibly being used only for explanations. The reason is that educators feel the more English the students are exposed to, the better, since the primary school-leaving examination is in English.

Fairly complete sets of materials are available in most of the designated school vernaculars, with most work completed for the languages with the largest number of speakers. Still, these books are not always used. For example, it is possible that some of the better equipped schools will have a full range of English-language materials, while those in the vernacular will be found wanting. The reason is that the headmaster at each school has only a certain amount of money available each year and money tends to be spent more on English-language texts than on vernacular materials.

An experimental project to teach English via radio lessons (incorporated by the local teacher into a lesson plan) began in 1982 (under USAID auspices and part of a larger World Bank-financed program).

Even more than in Kenya, historical developments and linguistic groupings in Uganda mandated the choice of English as an official language. The association of education and high status with English, disapproval of Swahili as a foreign, non-Christian language of the uneducated, and strong ties to one's own vernacular are the threads which history provided as a basis for a Ugandan language policy. Since no indigenous language had a sufficient power base to be selected over others at independence in 1962, English became the sole official language of Uganda. Swahili had no status, and six vernaculars were designated as regional media in the schools, with English gradually taking over by primary four. While the 1970s under General Idi Amin included the designation of Swahili as the national language as well as many contacts with Swahili-speaking Tanzanians after the war resulting in Amin's overthrow, official policy has not changed. Practice favors English more and more rather than enhancing Swahili's status.

Swahili was also spread to Uganda in the way that it reached up-country Kenya, by traders in precolonial times from the Tanganyika coast. Colonial administrators also used it, but to a lesser degree than in Tanganyika or Kenya. While it was obviously useful as a needed lingua franca, Swahili was never well received by those in power in Uganda. Missionaries had much influence, and they generally favored using local vernaculars, or sometimes Luganda. In addition, it was feared that Swahili's spread might lead to a political union with Kenya and eventual domination by the Kenya colonists. (Uganda was a protectorate, not a colony.) The politically powerful Ganda felt that if any African language should be singled out for special status, it should be their own language, Luganda. Thus, as W. H. Whiteley comments,

In this land of Christians, Swahili was jeopardized from the outset by its association with Islam. . . . Whatever merits the language might have had from the administrative point of view, and these were frequently voiced between 1910 and 1920, it is clear that for the Church it was an alien tongue and for the Baganda a thinly veiled threat to their status (1969:69–70).

Yet whatever forces were marshalled against it, Swahili flourished in Uganda whether or not it had official status because it was useful. Especially in linguistically diverse eastern Uganda and in its cities of Jinja and Kampala, a lingua franca was clearly needed in multiethnic work environments. Swahili became heavily used (Scotton, 1972), as it still is today. The military was drawn from different ethnic groups, and Swahili was established as its official lingua franca (it was taught in schools for military children in the 1950s)—one reason why General Amin was predisposed towards Swahili. But military rule has been very unpopular in Uganda, and the association has left Swahili tarnished. A Ugandan academic commenting on its present status has said, "Admittedly many people understand Kiswahili but do not use it extensively unless, for example, they are confronted with security men at road blocks" (Walusimbi, 1984).

An indigenous alternative to either English or Swahili as an official language might have been Luganda, since it is the mother tongue of about 16 percent of Ugandans and a third of those surveyed nationally in 1968 claimed conversational ability in it (Ladefoged et al., 1971:25). But Luganda is colored by its association with Baganda "imperialism" before independence. Furthermore, speakers of other languages feel that elevating Luganda would put them at a disadvantage. A. Mazrui (1979:20) comments, "Luganda does pose problems comparable in kind, if not in magnitude, to the communal passions surrounding the issue of Hindi in India." Another observer today reports that many people have resorted to Luganda as a lingua franca, but no one suggests it as the main official language.

Just as Swahili serves as a force of political integration in Kenya today, English—if by default—must serve this function in Uganda. Although it is not well known in the nation even more than twenty years after independence, it is more or less *uniformly* less well known across the nation, giving no ethnic group special privilege. This, of course, has always been a factor in its appeal in both nations, in addition to its association with education and authority. While English retains its colonial image in Uganda as in Kenya, it was always a less highly colored image.

Since independence, English has been the dominant language in the schools at all levels, distinguishing Uganda from Kenya, where policy has changed several times and once again favors more use of vernaculars and Swahili, and from Tanzania, where English is only a medium in post-primary education. For many years, the same six vernaculars have been designated as official languages for the lower primary grades. They are Luganda, Runyoro/Rutooro, Runyankole/ Ruchiga, Lugbara, Lwo (Acholi), and Akarimonjong/Ateso. These are logical choices among the vernaculars, but the policy is still unworkable. Taking the country as a whole, about 40 percent of the population are not speakers of any of the official school vernaculars (Ladefoged et al., 1971:98). Many people also live outside the areas in which their own language is officially used in the schools. S. Heyneman's (1975) research in five rural and three urban areas showed that 47 percent of the classrooms contained four or more languages and only 20 percent of the schools had monolingual populations.

Given this situation and the fact that adequate materials were not available in all vernaculars even in the pre-Amin period and that the national financial crisis today does not permit increased production now, it is not surprising to learn that today English is increasingly becoming a medium in all schools from primary one onwards, with neither mother tongue nor Swahili considered as a medium (Walusimbi, 1984). Luganda is taught as a subject in some secondary schools, but Swahili is not, owing to lack of teachers. Both are possible major subjects at Uganda's single university, but Swahili has few students today. (In 1978, the

Ugandan Ministry of Education did propose an increased role for vernaculars and introducing Swahili as a primary school subject. But war broke out in 1979, and the present government is silent about the issue.)[6]

PATTERNS OF LANGUAGE USE

African attitudes in general toward bilingualism are far different from those of many in the Western world. When a middle-class person is bilingual, many Westerners see it as a definite advantage. Still, it is generally assumed that such bilinguals are "unusual" in some way, with a special upbringing or abilities. As E. Haugen points out, more Westerners probably associate bilingualism with the lower classes and then see it as a disadvantage. "For many people 'bilingual' is a euphemism for 'linguistically handicapped'. It is a nice way of referring to teaching them their mother tongue, which happens not to be the dominant language in the country they now inhabit" (1972:308). Thus, being bilingual is associated with being underprivileged.

Although East Africa is no different from the rest of the world in viewing some languages as symbols of power and socioeconomic prestige and others as not, East Africans definitely do not view knowing more than one language as unusual, nor do they necessarily see it as a status that is best if transitory. Speaking more than one language is the natural state of affairs all over East Africa. Bilingualism only becomes a problem when societal choices have to be made among languages for official purposes. Even at this level, societal monolingualism is not viewed as the ideal end product (although this may be less true in Tanzania).

Who becomes bilingual in East Africa? Bilingualism cuts across socioeconomic status and ethnic group memberships, and it may be for this reason that it carries no stigma. Rather, an "age syndrome" (Parkin, 1974a:163–64) or a "travel syndrome" (Kashoki, 1978:40–43) characterizes East African bilingualism. The syndrome is a composite of features favoring males over females as typical bilinguals. Other factors are education (the more education, the more bilingualism—although those at the top may know fewer languages, relying on the official language for their intergroup communications needs), age (under thirty-five, the more bilingual), travel (the more travel, the more intergroup contacts), and urban residence. These factors are obviously interrelated: males are more likely to receive higher education than females, and education typically involves travel, since many secondary schools are boarding schools. Studies by Whiteley (1974b), Heine (1980a), Scotton (1972; 1982a), Polomé (1980c), and Barton (1980) make this pattern clear.

In addition, certain attributes of a person's group affect degrees of bilingualism. Bilingualism is so prevalent in East Africa partly because of the large number of small ethnic groups, each with its own mother tongue. Small linguistic groupings all over the world produce good second-language learners: witness the Berbers in North Africa and the Danes or Flemish-speaking Belgians in

Europe. The reasons are obvious: when the numbers sharing one's mother tongue are small, chances are good that speakers will regularly have to deal with others not sharing that language. Communication will require bilingualism on someone's part, typically the small group member. Thus, Bernd Heine notes that "the highest numbers of Swahili speakers are found in Kenya's linguistic minorities" (1980a:64), results from a national survey. Scotton (1972:151–52) has found that some minority groups in Uganda's capital, Kampala, such as speakers of Ateso (an Eastern Nilotic language) know more Luganda and Swahili (Bantu languages) than speakers from some Bantu groups (for whom these languages should be easier to learn).

As a corollary, speakers from larger linguistic groupings are less bilingual. Heine notes that the larger the Kenyan ethnic group, the smaller the Swahili-speaking community tends to be. While his study showed that about 80 percent of some groups knew Swahili, only 49 percent of the Kikuyu, Kenya's largest group, claimed to know Swahili. Observers predict that research would show similar results for Tanzania's Sukuma and Haya, both large groups, whose members typically know less Swahili than small group members.

When a group is large, it can expect that interactions on home territory will be in the mother tongue. In reporting on Kenyan rural language-use patterns, Abdulaziz (1982:105) noted that in a Kikuyu village only seven miles from Nairobi on a main road, "At home, in spite of the proximity to Nairobi, the children know no other language before school. . . . And at the market place, since the buyers and sellers are almost wholly Kikuyu, the language used is Kikuyu." He notes that in other rural sites, more than one language often will be heard in markets.

Another reason speakers from the larger groups know fewer languages is that they can expect that others, if they learn another vernacular and not just a lingua franca, will learn their language. This is partly because of the patron-client relationship that often arises between members of large groups and small groups.[7]

Although there are no specific studies of its influence, another factor important in the learning of Swahili in particular is religion. Several studies in the Polomé and Hill (1980) volume make it clear that Swahili is more widely known in the eastern half of Tanzania where the majority of the population is Muslim.

One reason bilingualism is accepted as a way of life in East Africa may be that it is the vehicle of social compartmentalization which still characterizes daily interactions there. As J. A. Fishman (1980:5) points out, the allocation of different linguistic varieties to different uses depends on the maintenance of strict boundaries between societal functions. He goes on to say that modern life militates against such compartmentalization, listing a number of factors that diminish it. Most are associated with urbanism. Yet, urbanism in Africa is clearly associated with becoming bilingual and the need to compartmentalize. Possibly, the particular urban factors which Fishman discusses ("the increase in open network, in fluid role relationship, in superficial 'public familiarity' between strangers or semi-stranger, in non-status-stressing interactions . . . " [1980:5]) have yet to affect East Africa. Their coming influence, however, is apparent in the language-use patterns of the urban educated, who less and less deal with a single interaction in a single language. Much borrowing, but ultimately less bilingualism, would seem to be the end result of less compartmentalization.

PATTERNS OF BILINGUALISM

The most prevalent pattern of bilingualism in East Africa is speaking one's own mother tongue as well as Swahili. If a person is educated through secondary school, he or she may also speak English, but few persons are bilingual in English and not also in Swahili. This pattern is most likely to be the case in Tanzania. No national statistics exist, but such studies as Polomé (1980c) indicate that mother tongue-Swahili bilingualism exists everywhere, except possibly on the coast where uneducated persons may be monolingual in Swahili, or in remote rural pockets where the uneducated may be monolingual in a different tongue. This pattern is least likely in Uganda, where a 1968 study of a national sample showed only 35 percent claimed conversational ability in Swahili (Ladefoged et al., 1971:25). (But in eastern Uganda and in Kampala many people know Swahili. All but 3 percent in the sample of Kampala workers [N–223] studied by Scotton [1972] claimed to know some Swahili.) Bilingualism in Uganda may involve another vernacular or another lingua franca, Luganda. (In the 1971 Ladefoged et al. study, slightly more claimed conversational competence in Luganda than in Swahili.) Increasingly, educated Ugandans are making English their main contact language (Walusimbi, 1984), but in 1968 only 21 percent claimed conversational ability in it (Ladefoged et al., 1971:25).

Kenya represents the middle case regarding Swahili bilingualism, with possibly three-quarters of all Kenyans speaking at least minimal Swahili and almost all urban dwellers having real fluency. A national study in 1968–70 (Heine, 1980a:61) showed that 65 percent claimed to speak Swahili. Whiteley (1974b:59) reports on multilingualism in twenty rural samples. Well over 80 percent of half of the groups claimed competence in Swahili. Urban studies (Parkin, 1974a; Scotton, 1982a) report knowledge of Swahili by virtually every respondent.

These patterns suggest that if East Africans are bilingual, they most likely have learned a lingua franca, not simply the language of a neighboring group. Heine (1980a:61) reported that, while 42 percent of his Kenyan respondents spoke Swahili as their sole second language, only half of 1 percent spoke another vernacular if it was their only addition to the mother tongue. At the same time, however, one-third of his sample knew no second language.

Unfortunately, Whitely (1974b) reports no overall statistics for the Kenyan rural groups studied, but individual reports for each group show that either bilingualism or trilingualism involving only other vernaculars is low, while that involving Swahili and/or English is high. The most common trilingual pattern is mother tongue, Swahili, and English. C. M. Scotton (1982a:129), who studied three different samples from the Luyia ethnic group, also found such trilingualism most common.

Various urban studies show even more dramatically the dominance of lingua francas in the East African repertoire. While almost all the Kampala workers studied by Scotton (1972:56–58) knew some Swahili, 76 percent also knew some English. In addition, 46.6 percent of those who were not native speakers of Luganda reported knowing it as well. In Parkin's (1974a:148) study of a Nairobi housing estate (N–349), only one person claimed to know neither Swahili nor English; otherwise all the heads of household surveyed claimed to know Swahili and 42 percent also claimed to know English. Scotton (1982a) compared rural and urban patterns of language use among the Luyia ethnic group in Kenya. In both rural and urban sample (N–118), Swahili was the most widely known second language (92 percent overall). The high incidence of bilingualism found in the homogeneous rural sample is the result of labor migration patterns in East Africa: many men have worked at salaried jobs in multiethnic settings during their lives.[8]

In Tanzania, the crucial finding is not just that Swahili is almost inevitably the second language added, but that it is increasingly overwhelming mother tongues in terms of both frequency of use and situational allocation. A 1970 study of a Dar es Salaam suburb (N–221) showed that Swahili use predominated in almost all of the eighty-two individual situations for which respondents reported language use (Barton, 1980:197). In addition, Polomé (1980c:130) estimated that the usual pattern of difference in frequency of use in 1970 for people who use Swahili and their own vernacular was four to one. Specifically, Polomé reports on the usage of twenty-five Tanzanians, who were asked to keep language diaries. "For all of them Swahili was used more frequently than their own language in proportions that varied from a high of 15:1 to a low of 3:2" (Polomé, 1980c:109).

The trend toward eventual monolingualism in Swahili seems evident in a study of a sample of Haya (N–50) living in Dar es Salaam (Rubanza, 1971). While all could speak Haya, the inroads Swahili is making were shown by the fact that some learned Swahili, not Haya, as their main childhood language. Of those in semiskilled jobs, only 60 percent thought they could speak Haya better than Swahili; even fewer (42 percent) in white-collar jobs thought their Haya better. Even more revealing is the fact that 40 percent (four out of ten) of an additional sample of children aged seven to fifteen showed only weak ability to speak Haya and not one spoke it very well. Conversely, only 10 percent were weak in Swahili, and 30 percent spoke it very well (Rubanza, 1979:42). One secondary school student said, "I speak Kihaya in very limited circles. I usually speak Kiswahili. When one speaks Kihaya at school he is looked down upon and laughed at. Even at home I use Kiswahili more frequently even when I address my father" (Rubanza, 1979:45). Well-educated Haya maintain a bilingualism in English, which is used at times in the office, but Swahili is their main language, with Haya used only with friends or relatives. The only situation in which one can be sure Haya will be used is one in which traditional roles are stressed, such as burials. Language-use patterns in the Haya homeland in northwestern Tanzania are much different, to be sure, with more Haya used. Still, the trend is toward overall preference for Swahili.[9]

While Kenyans and Ugandans also use Swahili heavily as a lingua franca, the difference is that they also use their own mother tongues more than Tanzanians. In rural areas, the mother tongue is typically the only language used with parents and neighbors. Lingua francas may be used with outsiders, but anyone who does not speak the mother tongue with ethnic brethren is perceived as showing off and out of line. (I spent six weeks in a teacher's home in rural western Kenya in 1977 and never heard him speak English to his school-age children, even though he spoke it well and the children faced English-medium examinations determining their educational future.) Of course, school-age children themselves—especially teen-agers—may speak English or English/Swahili as an in-group language with peers.

In urban settings, the role of mother tongues is slightly different. Swahili, English, or English/Swahili becomes the main language any salaried worker uses (Parkin, 1974b:169; Scotton, 1982a:126). The higher the educational level, the more English used; see Scotton (1972:64) for Kampala and Parkin (1974a:152) for Nairobi. Yet, mother tongues are firmly in place in most nonwork settings. For example, M. H. Abdulaziz (1982:117) commented on the bars, lodges, and restaurants in Mombasa run by members of particular ethnic groups where many of the patrons are speakers of the same language as the proprietor. D. J. Parkin (1974a:149) reported that 94 percent of the Kikuyu workers in the largely Kikuyu area in Nairobi which he studied used their mother tongue most with neighbors. In the more multiethnic areas, more Swahili and even some English would be used. Yet most urban dwellers use their mother tongue everyday (Scotton, 1982a:26).

Mother-tongue maintenance, even in cities, may be related to the fact that an overt ethnic identity remains a necessary attribute for coping with daily life in both Uganda and Kenya. As Abdulaziz (1982:113) notes about urban Kenya, "There is . . . strong attachment to the mother tongue because one is continually labeled as belonging to such-and-such an ethnic group, a fact which has political and socioeconomic consequences for many." This was also the case in Kampala in 1970 (Scotton, 1972), and, from all reports, it remains true. Because of the military presence in recent years and negative attitudes toward it, more Ugandans than in 1970 may sanction use of mother tongues even in public situations, as a means of maintaining secrecy.

Still, in spite of the durability of mother tongues, both Swahili and English are moving into traditionally vernacular domains. A highly educated Kenyan reports that she finds Swahili use at the family level amazingly on the increase. "I can now name more than ten families in Nairobi where both mother and father belong to the same language group but they talk to their children in Swahili" (Angogo-Kanyoro, 1984). She also reports, "I have also met many young people of ages 25 and below who do not know any Kenyan vernacular language, but speak English first and then Swahili. These do not result from intermarriages, but just homes with affluent touches where mom and dad speak English only to the children.'' One reason English is spoken is to give children practice in the all-important medium of school-leaving examinations. Abdulaziz (1982) reports similar patterns, especially among the elite, but at least some use of mother tongue is usual.

In referring to language use in terms of this language or that, the above discussion has implied that speakers always maintain a single language for a single interaction. A good deal of code-switching characterizes many exchanges, especially between urban bilinguals. The social function of code-switching is to signal an attitude toward the relationship between participants, or to change that relationship. This is the argument of Scotton and Ury (1977) and Scotton (1982c); also see Parkin (1974c). Bilingual co-equals from the same ethnic group may code-switch to symbolize their mutual dual identities, with the overall pattern of use of two languages meeting this function. As noted above, such switching is especially common among the urban educated. In other cases, each individual change from one language to another symbolizes a negotiation to change the social distance holding between participants. Scotton (1982c; 1983) refers to the switching for this purpose as making marked choices. Thus, when a passenger on a Nairobi bus who fears that the conductor will not give him his change is about to get off, he switches from the unmarked choice for this interaction, Swahili, into English. English is a marked choice in this situation, and its use symbolizes authority and education: the passenger uses it to let the conductor know he is not a person to be trifled with (Scotton and Ury, 1977:12).

SUMMARY

This chapter has outlined current patterns of bilingualism in East Africa and has surveyed the distribution of indigenous languages. While the three nations of East Africa (Uganda, Kenya, and Tanzania) show similarities in their linguistic makeup and in their bilingualism patterns, they show somewhat different official responses to their linguistic and historical identities. In all cases, no single indigenous language is spoken by a significant enough group of native speakers to make it an easy choice as the official language. Therefore, choosing an ethnically neutral language is the alternative all three nations followed. The specific choices, however, were not the same. In opting for Swahili as its sole official and national language, Tanzania has most departed from policies established under colonial rule. Although English is still the medium of post-primary education (and its role was reaffirmed in 1983), its overall position has been reduced. This also applies to the vernaculars. The uniform practice of using Swahili is a symbol of both socioeconomic egalitarianism and national integration, reflecting the nation's socialistic policies.

In making English their choice as an ethnically neutral official language, Kenya and Uganda have chosen the common solution in Africa. In general, colonial languages are the sole or main official languages. Since they maintain modified capitalism, it is not surprising that they carry over the language policies from colonial days associated with socioeconomic stratification. In making English official, but taking no radical steps to make it accessible to the masses, Kenya and Uganda have chosen a policy that keeps the possibility for socioeconomic mobility in the hands of a minority. Again, this is the common pattern in Africa.

Perhaps partly to compensate for this situation, other languages have received varying degrees of recognition. Swahili is the national language in both nations, although in Kenya it is much more used in public, formal capacities and it also has a definite status as a school subject. A limited, but unwieldy, number of vernacular languages are officially recognized as the media of the lower primary grades. Some would argue that this use of vernaculars is pedagogically, not politically, motivated, of course. For an overview on language and education in East Africa, with special reference to pedagogical practices, see Chishimba (1982).

Whether the imbalance between those who have access to the official language and those who do not will be changed in the near future is uncertain. Two solutions seem possible: to continue with English as official but to implement mass schemes to make it more widely known; or to change the official language. Swahili is the most obvious candidate in both Kenya and Uganda, although some problems with this solution have been discussed above.

The general argument when African linguists/educationists speak out on language policy is that indigenous languages must have a more significant official role, especially in education. This argument is at odds with the actual patterns of language use now in place, as described in this chapter, with norms among the educated favoring much public use of English. These patterns, however, could be changed. More of a problem would be to change language policies in the schools. For general statements on African educational language policies, see Afolayan (1978), Ansre (1978), or Bokamba (1981). First, more use of vernaculars or even Swahili while maintaining English as the official language and the medium of school examinations does not seem well motivated. Second, there is the question of logistics: if education is to begin in mother tongues, which mother tongues? Especially in a mobile population, the number of tongues that need to be available if each child is to learn in his or her mother tongue seems unworkable. Finally, there is the investment which the governing elite has in English; a change in language policy would inevitably change the social structure since it would alter patterns of access in the socioeconomic marketplace.

NOTES

1. Thanks to the Ford Foundation-sponsored Survey of Language Use in Eastern Africa, relatively more information is available for this part of Africa than for other areas. The survey volumes, based on data gathered from 1968 to about 1972, have special sections about language in education. The volumes are Bender, Bowen, Cooper, and Ferguson,

eds. (1976) on Ethiopia; Ladefoged, Glick, and Criper (1971) on Uganda; Ohannessian and Kashoki, eds. (1978) on Zambia; Polomé and Hill, eds. (1980) on Tanzania; and Whiteley, ed. (1974) on Kenya.

2. While not all subgrouping issues are settled, a classification of the East African Bantu languages into four groups seems reasonable, following Nurse and Philippson (1980). Two of these groups extend beyond the borders of East Africa.

3. For a case study on the relationship of language and ethnic group identity with reference to the Luyia group, see Angogo-Kanyoro (1980; 1984). Also see Itebete (1974).

4. The Swahili dialect spoken in eastern Zaire is called Kingwana. It is fairly different from East African dialects, but still more or less mutually intelligible.

5. An example of the comments of those who want more official recognition of Swahili in Kenya is found in a feature article on May 21, 1983, in *The Standard*, an English-language newspaper in Nairobi. Under the headline, ''Kiswahili Needs More Respect,'' is an interview with the vice-chairman of the Kenya Kiswahili Association. It is no coincidence that he is a native speaker of a Kenya coastal dialect of Swahili. In addition to arguing for more emphasis on Swahili in the schools and its recognition as the official language, he claims the superiority of Kimvita, a Kenyan coastal dialect, over Kiunguja, the dialect of Zanzibar which was the basis for Standard Swahili.

6. For additional information about language in education in East Africa, see the Ford Foundation survey volumes. Of particular interest are Glick's contribution to Ladefoged et al. (1971:85–151) and Gorman (1974b). Both authors studied reasons for success in English tests. In neither study, however, was English performance found to be significantly related to any variables studied (such as urban/rural residence, age, sex, initial medium or education, father's education).

7. By historical accident, both Kenya's and Uganda's capitals are in the homeland of the largest ethnic group, the Ganda in Uganda and the Gikuyu in Kenya. Thus, if speakers are going to add a vernacular to their repertoire, Luganda in parts of Uganda and certainly in Kampala, or Kikuyu in parts of Kenya and most likely in Nairobi is the obvious choice. In addition, the influence of the largest group is felt elsewhere: reporting on repertoires of sample groups from across Kenya, Whiteley notes, ''Taking all the samples, Kikuyu is reported as a fourth (fifth, sixth, etc.) language more than twice as often as any other language'' (1974b:53).

Parkin's study of language-adding practices in two patron-client groups in Nairobi (1974b) also showed that the patron group was the larger one and that it was the client group which added the larger group's language in the greater numbers. He studied Kikuyu-Kamba and Luo-Luyia pairs.

Scotton (1972) gives additional evidence that large-group members count on others to learn their languages rather than vice versa. While Swahili is heavily used as a lingua franca in Kampala, Ganda claimed to be able to speak much less Swahili than other ethnic groups. In the multiethnic sample (N–223), 55 percent claimed ability to at least ask and answer questions in Swahili, but only 37 percent of Ganda claimed they could do this. Even other Eastern Bantu language speakers (the group containing Luganda) had quite different repertoires, with 63 percent claiming this ability in Swahili.

8. Abdulaziz (1982:107), who also studied Kenyan rural areas, commented, ''In a number of cases the leader in the village or homestead is an ex-soldier, policeman, or urban worker who has some knowledge of Swahili or English, which languages he used in transactional settings.''

9. Still, many Tanzanian parents want their children to learn their mother tongues.

Rubanza (1979:44) found that 76 percent of his sample wished their children to speak Haya as their first language and only 20 percent actually expressed a preference for Swahili in this status. Polomé (1980c:131) also reported that about four-fifths of students interviewed at teacher training colleges (no total number given) in the early 1970s said they would make their children learn their mother language, but would give Swahili preference. "The motivation was most often self-identification, the vernacular being the genuine bearer of traditions," commented Polomé. There was also the practical reason that parents wanted their children to be able to converse with grandparents who might not know Swahili well.

BIBLIOGRAPHY

Abdulaziz, M. H. 1982. "Patterns of Language Acquisition and Use in Kenya: Rural-Urban Differences." *International Journal of the Sociology of Language* 34: 95–120.

Afolayan, A. 1978. "Towards an Adequate Theory of Bilingual Education for Africa." In *International Dimensions of Bilingual Education*, ed. J. E. Alatis. Washington, D.C.: Georgetown University, pp. 330–90.

Angogo-Kanyoro, R. 1980. "Linguistic and Attitudinal Factors in the Maintenance of Luyia Group Identity." Ph.D. diss., University of Texas, Austin. (Published under new title, 1983. *Unity in Diversity, a Linguistic Survey of the Abaluyia of Western Kenya.* Wein: Afro-Pub.).

————. 1984. Personal communication.

Ansre, G. 1978. "The Use of Indigenous Languages in Education in Sub-Saharan Africa: Presuppositions, Lessons, and Prospects." In *International Dimensions of Bilingual Education*, ed. J. E. Alatis, Washington, D.C.: Georgetown University, pp. 285–301.

Barton, H. D. 1980. "Language Use Among Ilala Residents." In *Language in Tanzania*, ed. E. Polome and C. P. Hill. London: International African Institute and Oxford University Press.

Bender, M. L., J. D. Bowen, R. L. Cooper, and C. A. Ferguson, eds. 1976. *Language in Ethiopia.* London: Oxford University Press.

Bokamba, E. D. 1981. "Language and National Development in Sub-Saharan Africa: A Progress Report." *Studies in the Linguistic Sciences* 11: 1–25.

Bujra, J. 1974. "Pumwani: Language Usage in an Urban Muslim Community." In *Language in Kenya*, ed. W. H. Whiteley. Nairobi: Oxford University Press, pp. 217–52.

Chishimba, M. M. 1981. "Language Teaching and Literacy in East Africa." In *Annual Review of Applied Linguistics*, ed. R. L. Kaplan. Rowley, Mass.: Newbury House, pp. 168–88.

Ehret, C. 1980. "The Nilotic Languages of Tanzania." In *Language in Tanzania*, ed. E. Polomé and C. P. Hill. London: International African Institute and Oxford University Press, pp. 68–78.

Fishman, J. A. 1980. "Bilingualism and Biculturalism as Individual and as Societal Phenomena." *Journal of Multilingual and Multi-cultural Development* 1: 3–15.

Gorman, T. P. 1974a. "The Development of Language Policy in Kenya with Particular Reference to the Educational System." In *Language in Kenya*, ed. W. H. Whiteley. Nairobi: Oxford University Press, pp. 397–454.

————. 1974b. "The Teaching of Language Arts Secondary Level: Some Significant Problems." In *Language in Kenya*, ed. W. H. Whiteley. Nairobi: Oxford University, pp. 481–537.

Greenberg, J. H. 1963. "The Languages of Africa." *International Journal of American Linguistics* 29: 1.

————. 1971a. "African Languages." In *Language, Culture, and Communication*, ed. F. H. Greenberg. Stanford, Calif.: Stanford University Press, pp. 126–36.

————. 1971b. "Urbanism, Migration, and Language." In *Language, Culture, and Communication*, ed. F. H. Greenberg. Stanford, Calif.: Stanford University Press, pp. 198–211.

Guthrie, M. 1967–71. *Comparative Bantu*. Vols. 1–4. London: Gregg Press.

Haugen, E. 1972. "The Stigmata of Bilingualism." In *The Ecology of Language*, ed. E. Haugen. Stanford, Calif.: Stanford University Press, pp. 307–24.

Heine, Bernd. 1973. "Zur genetischen Gliederung der Bantusprachen." *Afrika und übersee* 56:164–84.

————. 1980a. "Language and Society." In *Language and Dialect Atlas of Kenya*, ed. B. Heine and W. J. G. Höhlig. Vol. 1. Berlin: Reimer, pp. 60–67.

————. 1980b. "The Non-Bantu Languages of Kenya." In *Language and Dialect Atlas of Kenya*, ed. B. Heine and W. J. Möhlig. Vol. 1. Berlin: Reimer, pp. 53–58.

————. 1980c. "The Non-Bantu Languages of Kenya." In *Language and Dialect Atlas of Kenya*, ed. B. Heine and W. J. Möhlig. Vol. 2. Berlin: Reimer.

Henrici, Alick. 1973. "Numerical Classification of Bantu Languages." *African Language Studies* 14: 82–104.

Heynemann, S. 1975. "Influences on Academic Achievement in Uganda: A 'Coleman Report' from a Non-industrialized Society." Ph.D. diss., University of Chicago.

Hinnebusch, T. J. 1976. "Swahili: Genetic Affiliations and Evidence." *Studies in African Linguistics*, Supplement 6: 95–108.

————. 1979. "Swahili." In *Languages and Their Status*, ed. T. Shopen. Cambridge, Mass.: Winthrop, pp. 209–93.

Hinnebusch, T. J., D. Nurse, and M. Mould. 1981. *Studies in the Classification of Eastern Bantu Languages*. Hamburg: Helmut Buske.

Kashoki, M. E. 1978. "The Language Situation in Zambia." In *Language in Zambia*, ed. S. Ohannessian and M. E. Kashoki. London: International African Institute, pp. 9–46.

Ladefoged, P., R. Glick, and C. Criper. 1971. *Language in Uganda*. Nairobi: Oxford University Press.

Mazrui, A. 1979. *Language Policy After Amin*. African Report. September-October, pp. 20–22.

Möhlig, W. J. G. 1980. "Bantu Languages." In *Language and Dialect Atlas of Kenya*, ed. B. Heine and W. J. B. Mohlig. Vol. 1. Berlin: Reimer, pp. 11–52.

Molnos, A. 1969. *Language Problems in Africa*. Nairobi: East African Research Information Centre.

Neale, B. 1974. *Kenya's Asian Languages*. In *Language in Kenya*, ed. W. H. Whiteley. Nairobi: Oxford University Press, pp. 69–86.

Nurse, D., and G. Philippson. 1980. "The Bantu Languages of East Africa: A Lexicostatistical Survey." In *Language in Tanzania*, ed. E. Polomé and C. P. Hill. London: International African Institute and Oxford University Press, pp. 26–67.

Ohannessian, S., and M. E. Kashoki, eds. 1981. *Language in Zambia*. London: International African Institute and Oxford University Press.

Parkin, D. J. 1974a. "Status Factors in Language Adding: Behati Housing Estate in Nairobi." In *Language in Kenya*, ed. W. H. Whiteley. Nairobi: Oxford University Press, pp. 147–66.

———. 1974b. "Language Shift and Ethnicity in Nairobi: The Speech Community of Kaloneni." In *Language in Kenya*, ed. W. H. Whiteley. Nairobi: Oxford University Press, pp. 167–88.

———. 1974c. "Language Switching in Nairobi." In *Language in Kenya*, ed. W. H. Whiteley. Nairobi: Oxford University Press, pp. 189–216.

Polomé, E. 1980a. "The Languages of Tanzania." In *Language in Tanzania*, ed. E. Polomé and C. P. Hill. London: International African Institute and Oxford University Press, pp. 3–25.

———. 1980b. "Swahili in Tanzania." In *Language in Tanzania*, ed. E. Polomé and C. P. Hill. London: International African Institute and Oxford University Press, pp. 79–102.

———. 1980c. "Tanzania: A Sociolinguistic Perspective." In *Language in Tanzania*, ed. E. Polomé and C. P. Hill. London: International African Institute and Oxford University Press, pp. 103–38.

Rubanza, Y. 1971. "The Relationship Between Kiswahili and Other African Languages: The Case of Kihaya." M.A. Thesis, University of Dar es Salaam.

Scotton, C. M. 1972. *Choosing a Lingua Franca in an African Capital*. Edmonton: Linguistic Research, Inc.

———. 1977. "Linguistic Performance as a Socioeconomic Indicator." *Journal of Social Psychology* 102: 35–45.

———. 1978. "Language in East Africa: Linguistic Patterns and Political Ideologies." In *Advances in the Study of Societal Multilingualism*, ed. J. A. Fishman. The Hague: Mouton, pp. 719–60.

———. 1982a. "An Urban-Rural Comparison of Language Use Among the Luyia in Kenya." *International Journal of the Sociology of Language* 34: 121–36.

———. 1982b. "Learning Lingua Francas and Socio-economic Integration: Evidence from Africa." In *Language Spread*, ed. R. L. Cooper. Bloomington: Indiana University, pp. 63–94.

———. 1982c. "The Possibility of Code-Switching: Motivation for Maintaining Multilingualism." *Anthropological Linguistics* 24: 432–44.

———. 1983. "The Negotiation of Identities in Conversation: A Theory of Markedness and Code Choice." *International Journal of the Sociology of Language* 44: 115–36.

Scotton, C. M., and W. Ury. 1977. "Bilingual Strategies: The Social Function of Code-Switching." *International Journal of The Sociology of Language* 13: 5–20.

Sedlak, Philip. 1983. Personal communication.

Walusimbi, Livingstone. 1984. Personal communication.

Whiteley, W. H. 1969. "Swahili, the Rise of a National Language." London: Methuen.

———, ed. 1974a. *Language in Kenya*. Nairobi: Oxford University Press.

———. 1974b. "The Classification and Distribution of Kenya's African Languages." In *Language in Kenya*, ed. W. H. Whiteley. Nairobi: Oxford University Press, pp. 13–68.

Zaborski, A. 1976. "Cushitic Overview." In *The Non-Semitic Languages of Ethiopia*, ed. M. L. Bender. East Lansing, Mich.: African Studies Center, pp. 67–84.

LINGUISTIC MINORITIES AND THE MOTHER-TONGUE DEBATE IN ENGLAND

British society has developed from, and still retains, a wide diversity of cultural influences, differentiated by regional, socioeconomic, religious, and linguistic factors. In particular, England is now more obviously than ever before a multilingual society, with large sections of the population using more than one language in their daily lives. Italian or Polish or Gujerati, for example, are spoken in the family, in local shops, or in community institutions. Some bilingual children and adults have access to newspapers, books, films, and radio programs in their home language as well as in English. Some children attend lessons to learn more of their home language, or perhaps to learn to read and write another language which is valued by their community (Wilding, 1981).

Yet, there is a lack of research and information on multilingualism in England, a clear reflection of the official invisibility of multilingualism at least until the 1970s. The lack of interest shown by educationalists in England in the research findings and evaluations of bilingual schemes in Wales, Scotland, or Ireland suggests that the experience of bilingualism among indigenous British populations was not perceived to be relevant either to the bilingualism of nonindigenous populations in England or to the debate about modern language teaching.

The lack of any basic statistics on language affiliation in England has contributed to this neglect, but no definite decision has yet been made to include a language question in future censuses in England. The most basic information at least is necessary to inform social policies related to multilingualism, such as the provision of community interpreters and translators, media coverage, and school and adult education policies. The dearth of information may have contributed to the situation we found in 1980, when only a few Local Education Authority (LEA) officers and advisers knew how many bilingual pupils they had in their schools. However, lack of official statistics does not explain the absence of information among many teachers and administrators about the range and type of "mother-tongue" teaching provision organized outside the state school system. In some areas, a high percentage of bilingual pupils attends this parallel form of schooling. But even in the early 1980s, many teachers knew little about this influence on the educational development of their pupils, or, if they did, they did not consider it to be directly relevant to their work (Saifullah Khan, 1980).

One explanation for the relative lack of research and discussion about the policy implications of bilingualism in England is, of course, the particularly important international role of the English language. The other explanation is not simply the converse—the differential and inferior status accorded to all other-than-English languages. We have to remember that attitudes to languages cannot be assessed in isolation from attitudes to the speakers of those languages. The relative status of different minority languages in England is also influenced in large part by the historical relations between England and their countries of origin and by the present socioeconomic status of the speakers. These factors help to explain how the South European languages of migrant workers from European Community countries, and the Eastern European languages of political refugees from World War II have greater prestige than the South Asian languages spoken by settlers from ex-colonial countries.

Two other factors contributing to the relatively slow development of interest in this field help to explain why some of these higher status European languages are taught as modern languages to monolingual English pupils in LEA schools, but often not to children of bilingual families. The first relates to the dominant perspective on minorities in general and on bilingualism in particular. The second links these points with the historical development of policies and practices set up to deal with the new situations created by the presence of pupils from different cultural and linguistic backgrounds.

In England, the terms "immigrant" and "minority" are almost synonymous with "coloured." In presenting the Linguistic Minorities Project, we have always stressed that we were equally interested in the languages spoken by the "invisible" white minorities. As the term "immigrant" is also used in popular debates to include British-born children of immigrants, we have steadfastly avoided using this term altogether. In this context it is not surprising, therefore, that much of the research in England has focused on "black" or "brown" minorities. As these minorities are perceived to be "the problem" rather than the catalyst for the dominant institutions to reconsider the appropriateness of their provision for all categories of the population, attention has been focused, through policy-based research in particular, on difficulties to be solved instead of opportunities to be learned from.

HISTORICAL BACKGROUND

The political refugees from Eastern Europe who settled in Britain after World War II arrived before the issues of immigration and "race" (seen in terms of black-white relations) became closely linked in popular discourse. Most speakers of Polish, Ukrainian, and Latvian, for example, settled in Britain between 1945 and 1950. They were, however, subject to another characteristic response by British institutions, professionals, and laypeople which is often ignored in the literature about the more recent nonindigenous minorities. This is the essentially monolingual perspective of the dominant ethnic group in England. While related to the general assimilative response to the arrival of immigrants, the stress on the acquisition of English without reference to the first language shaped the development of both education policy and practice. Many members of these Eastern European linguistic minorities soon understood that only English was accepted in the public domain and in formal interactions, and their own subordinate languages should be restricted to private, informal, community-based activities.

The 1950s and 1960s were years of economic expansion, and workers were recruited from colonies and ex-colonies to the metropolis to meet the mostly politically defined labor shortage. This apparent shortage could have been tackled through an alternative economic and political strategy, which would have involved greater investment in the renewal of industrial equipment and an improvement in the wages of the lowest paid industrial workers. Instead, the cheap labor provided by the countries of the British Empire was taken advantage of.

Many of the migrant workers from South Asia and the Caribbean settled in the cheapest housing and took on jobs with unsocial hours, poor conditions, and wages.

The condition of the rundown inner-city areas of many British cities became associated in the public mind with the arrival of "alien" outsiders. By the early 1960s, there was rising pressure from local authorities and public opinion to limit immigration. As the increasingly restrictive legislation was introduced, workers and their families arrived to "beat the ban." By the early 1970s, a mythology about the presence of "black people" became pervasive and was reinforced by inflammatory and divisive coverage by the media.

With the intensification of economic recession in the late 1970s, high rates of unemployment developed, particularly in those sectors of the British economy that had previously been dependent on immigrant labor. In these declining or "restructuring" industries, there were many examples of both blatant and subtle forms of institutional racism. Not surprisingly, the 1970s also saw an increase in fascist organization and overt racial hostility on the street.

Other fundamental economic and political realities altered the pattern of migration in the 1970s. The international reorganization of the market economy between north and south by transnational corporations, and Britain's entry into the European Economic Community in 1973, affected patterns of employment and sources of labor. For industrialized Northwest Europe the Mediterranean periphery provided large numbers of workers from, for example, the Maghreb, Portugal, Spain, Greece, Cyprus, Yugoslavia, and Turkey. Most migrant workers of South European origin have come to England since 1950, with the exception of some of the older Italian population which dates back to the nineteenth century. Many of the migrant workers within the European Community have less political and legal security than the ex-colonial settlers in Britain and are found in the least secure, lowest paid, and often least unionized sectors of the economy, especially the service trades such as catering and hotel work. Despite the rapid increase in unemployment in many industrial countries, many descendants of migrant workers and their families are not fulfilling the expectations and convenience of the "host" country by returning to their "homelands."

There are also linguistic minorities of Greek Cypriot and Turkish Cypriot origin in England, who came originally as migrant labor from an ex-colony. Since the 1974 war in Cyprus, some at least can be regarded as refugees. Other political refugees came from East Africa and Southeast Asia in the late 1960s and late 1970s, respectively, and smaller numbers from Latin America.

There are two major dimensions in the classification of the different linguistic minorities in England (Linguistic Minorities Project, 1984). They differ, first, in the main reason of the original migration and settlement (e.g., economic migrant versus political refugee) and, second, in the type of country of origin (e.g., ex-colonial Third World and European countries). Both types of categorization offer important perspectives for an analysis that recognizes the interaction between the economic and political factors behind the migrations. Both remind us, as we have mentioned earlier, that the status of a minority language is closely bound up with the perceived status of its speakers.

THE MAIN LINGUISTIC MINORITIES

The distribution of the South Asian populations across the country is largely a result of the employment opportunities that existed in the 1950s and 1960s, and of the process of chain migration in which information about specific localities and personal contacts in these localities played an important part. The major areas of settlement were the conurbations of Greater London, the Midlands, Yorkshire, and Lancashire. Panjabi-speaking Muslims are strongly represented in Bradford and the Lancashire towns in the textile industries, and to a lesser extent in Birmingham, parts of East London, and many other towns. Panjabi-speaking Sikhs and Hindus together probably form the most numerous linguistic minority and are widely dispersed across the country. The main areas of settlement are Southall and Newham in London; Birmingham, Wolverhampton, Coventry; Leeds, Bradford, Huddersfield; Peterborough, Bedford, Gravesend; and a number of other smaller towns. Members of this linguistic minority tend, especially in the Midlands, to be employed in heavy industry and engineering factories. Gujerati speakers, including some East African Asians, are to be found in large numbers in Leicester, Coventry, East and North West London, and in the northern textile towns. For Bengali speakers, the major settlements are in East London where many work in the clothing industry, with smaller numbers in Birmingham, Manchester, Bradford, Coventry, and several other towns. Other

South Asian linguistic minorities who have settled in small numbers in particular localities include Hindi speakers in several cities, Malayalam and Tamil speakers in parts of London (as secondary migrants from Malaysia and Singapore), and Pushtu speakers in Bradford and Birmingham.

Considerable previous research has been conducted among the South Asian populations in Britain. Much of it has concentrated on issues of discrimination faced by these "visible" minorities in the fields of housing, employment, and education. Often they have been studied alongside people of Caribbean origin who have settled in similar neighborhoods. As a result, even such substantial studies as Rex and Moore (1976), and Smith (1977) have not usually distinguished between the linguistic and ethnic minorities within the South Asian population, although other studies by social anthropologists have focused on specific minorities in particular local settings.

The outstanding feature of the language background of all South Asian linguistic minorities is the wide range of related languages, varieties, and dialects that exists throughout the subcontinent, coupled with the high level of multilingualism involving regional languages, national languages, and English. Although the Indian subcontinent is the home of two major language "families," the Dravidian group in the south and the Indic in the north, the Dravidian languages are scarcely represented in England. The majority of speakers of South Asian languages have origins in rural areas of North India, Pakistan, and Bangladesh, and use one of the local rural vernaculars as the home language. They may also use one of the standard regional languages, especially for formal purposes, including those involving the use of written language. They are likely in the first place to express their language loyalty in terms of the standard taught language rather than the home language. Thus, for example, some people originating from Sylhet in Bangladesh who speak Sylheti are likely to name their language as Bengali, and to seek mother-tongue teaching in that national language. A few are beginning to campaign to raise the status of Sylheti, pointing out the existence of an earlier Sylheti literature in a distinct script, and suggesting that classes for children in England should use and teach Sylheti rather than or in addition to Bengali.

In some cases, the boundary between language and dialect is more complex still. For example, Kutchi (sometimes spelled Kachchi in English orthography) is usually characterized by linguists as a dialect or a variety closely related to Sindhi, one that may have developed out of contact between earlier varieties of Sindhi and Gujerati. However, because of their family origins in Gujerat state and education through the medium of Gujerati, many Kutchi speakers in England will describe themselves as speakers of a variety of Gujerati.

The problem of language naming is of particular interest with reference to speakers of Panjabi and Urdu. In order to understand the problem, it is necessary to appreciate the sociolinguistic history of northern India and Pakistan (LMP, 1984).

Briefly, however, most families in England with origins in the Panjab, whether in India or Pakistan, and whether they are Muslim, Sikh, or Hindu by religion, will use spoken varieties of Panjabi which are likely to be mutually intelligible. Furthermore, languages such as Hindi and Urdu continue to serve the function of lingua franca among speakers of different South Asian languages in Britain. However, Muslims, Sikhs, and Hindus would normally expect tuition in their distinct languages of literacy, for example, Panjabi in the Gurmukhi script for Sikhs; Hindu or Panjabi in the Gurmukhi script for Hindus originating from the present Indian state of Panjab; and Urdu for Muslims from the Pakistani part of Panjab. Obviously, then, for purposes of planning educational support, it is desirable to make a distinction between three linguistic minorities.

Most of the people of East Asian origin who now live in Britain are of Chinese ethnic background and are speakers of Cantonese, Hakka, Hokkien, and Vietnamese. There are also small numbers of people of Malay, Indochinese, and Japanese origin in various parts of the country.

Sizable minorities of Chinese origin have been found in Britain since at least the early part of the twentieth century, particularly in dockland areas of East London and Liverpool. A wave of migration from southern China in this period led to the establishment of communities of overseas Chinese in many parts of the world. However, many of these settlements in England are largely the result of later migrations originating from Hong Kong and the New Territories. Many of these settlers were employed in the catering trade, working either in Chinese restaurants or in takeaways (Watson, 1977). London in particular has a large number of people of Chinese origin who have come to the United Kingdom to further their education. Many of this last group are from Malaysia or Singapore rather than from Hong Kong. The most recent group of migrants are political refugees from Vietnam (Jones, 1983).

With such a varied range of migration histories within this minority in Britain, there is obviously a rich variety of social, ethnic, and linguistic backgrounds. Even the migrants from Hong Kong are by no means a homogeneous ethnic group. Most have origins in the rural New Territories rather than in urban Hong Kong itself. Some have the Hakka language as their spoken vernacular. The Hakka (k'echia or guest) people are believed to have originated in northern China, migrated southwards several hundred years ago, and can now be found settled in widely dispersed pockets in most parts of southern China and in a number of villages in the rural areas of the New Territories. The Cantonese mother-tongue speakers (pun-ti people) are indigenous to southern China. Economic and political pressure in the 1950s and 1960s caused many people from rural parts of southern China to move from the Peoples Republic, to expanding urban areas such as Hong Kong and Macao. So for many Cantonese speakers the move to Britain was a second stage of migration.

Refugees from Vietnam are for the most part "ethnic Chinese," most of them speaking Cantonese as their mother tongue (sometimes with a quite distinctive accent). Many of them have been educated through the medium of Vietnamese, and a few have had contact with French and English as the language of recent occupying powers. People of ethnic Chinese origin who settled in Britain from Singapore and Malaysia are from Cantonese and Hokkien-speaking backgrounds for the most part. However, educational policies in those two countries have tended to promote the learning of English and Mandarin in the case of Singapore, and of Malay in the case of Malaysia, with the result that significant language shift away from Cantonese and Hokkien has already taken place among the educated classes. There are also smaller numbers of people of Chinese ethnic origin who migrated to England from the Caribbean, after their families had been established there for three or more generations. Most of them now have little or no knowledge of any of the Chinese languages.

The major concentrations of speakers of Chinese languages are in London, Liverpool, Birmingham, Glasgow, and Manchester. The remainder are widely scattered around the country, a tendency that has arisen because of the limited market for Chinese food in individual localities. On the whole, it appears that the population of Chinese origin in England is relatively young, probably the result of migration patterns in which young men were the pioneers in the 1960s, and were followed by their wives some years later.

Since 1945, large numbers of people from the less developed southern periphery of Europe have migrated in search of work to the urban centers of many Northwest European countries. The United Kingdom has received a smaller proportion of South European migrants than, for example, West Germany or France. However, significant numbers of Italian, Portuguese, Spanish, and Cypriot people have settled in England. Here we will present some of the sociolinguistic features of a few of these linguistic minorities.

There has been an Italian presence in Britain for several centuries, with trading, banking, and cultural links going back to before the Renaissance. Several thousand Italians were living in the Clerkenwell area of London in the mid-nineteenth century. From then until the first decade of this century, there was a significant increase in migration from northern Italy. By the turn of the century, there was rapid growth and considerable prosperity in the service and catering industries, and after 1911 cafe life flourished in London and elsewhere in Britain. The Italians were the first to move into this sector, and some became very successful entrepreneurs. The period of prosperity for Italians at the beginning of this century was shattered by World War II, when the Italian-speaking minority were classified as "aliens," and many were interned or were deported to Australia or Canada. Others returned to Italy.

The postwar period has been characterized primarily by migration from the south of Italy, from regions such as Campania, Calabria, and Sicily. Initially, this migration was encouraged by the Italian and British governments to meet increasing labor demands in Britain's expanding industries. The initial officially sponsored recruitment later developed into a pattern of chain migration from these same areas of southern Italy. New settlements of Italians were established, principally in the south Midlands, but also in the north and southeast of England. Italian men were recruited for the brick industry, based principally in Bedford

but also in a few other towns. Many other Italians found employment in the
horticultural industry in the Lea Valley just north of London. During the 1950s
and early 1960s, Italian workers were also recruited into the South Wales steel-
works and into the mines.

Women workers were also recruited on a fairly large scale under the "Official
Italian Scheme." They came to work in cotton and wool mills, in rubber and
pottery industries, and as domestics in hospitals, until the scheme was phased
out in 1951. Another dimension of migration in this period was the arrival in
Britain of "war brides," some of whom married Polish army combatants based
in Italy. Since the immediate postwar period, the pattern of employment for
many Italian migrants has changed. Some women in particular have found work
in newer industries (Crisp, 1980). Many Italian men have opted for self-em-
ployment, particularly in the catering industry, opening restaurants, coffee bars,
fish and chip shops, or running ice-cream vans. Others have started small tai-
loring, hairdressing, or grocery businesses.

It was only after the whole of the Italian peninsula, Sardinia, and Sicily came
under a single government in the mid-nineteenth century that the Florentine
literary standard began to be more widely accepted as the national language, *la
lingua italiana*. Other Italian varieties were demoted to the status of *dialetti*—
a status still resented by many of their speakers today.

The development of a public education system in Italy slowly spread the use
of the national language, although in the rural areas regional varieties continue
to be widely used among the older generation, and Standard Italian is still very
much a second language. Standard Italian is used fluently only by the well
educated for reading, writing, and wider communication. The development of
travel, internal migration, and the mass media in particular are currently extending the use of Standard Italian throughout Italy. However, neither Italians
who migrated to the United Kingdom in the immediate postwar period nor their
children have had the benefit of such exposure. They tend to know only the local
rural variety of the region of origin, with important consequences for the mother-
tongue classes organized in England (Tosi, 1984).

The most significant period of migration from Portugal to Britain was during
the 1960s. Individuals and families came in search of work here, some as a
result of economic hardship in Madeira. Others came as a result of the social
disruption and increased demand on resources caused by the arrival in Lisbon
of refugees from the colonial wars. The date of the main period of migration
means that this population was predominantly middle-aged by 1981. About two-
thirds of Portuguese speakers in England are based in the Greater London area,
with smaller numbers in towns to the west of London, in the north of England,
and in some holiday resort areas. Outside London the most important settlement
has been in Jersey and Guernsey, and a seasonal migration comes every year to
the Channel Islands between March and October.

Until the mid–1960s, there was a preponderance of women in this migrant
labor force. Some found work in hotels in London's West End or in resort areas,

but the majority went into hospital and domestic services as cleaners, cooks, and maids. By the mid–1970s, the male-female ratio had evened out, but the pattern of employment remained the same.

It is convenient to treat speakers of Greek and Turkish in Britain together for some purposes. This is so, first, because most of the speakers of these two languages in Britain, in contrast to Germany or Scandinavia, for example, have their family origins not in mainland Greece or Turkey, but in Cyprus. There are therefore many similarities in their cultural backgrounds, as well as in their situation in the United Kingdom. Second, census and other official statistics often provide information on a country of birth basis, which offers no way of distinguishing between Greek-speaking Cypriots and Turkish-speaking Cypriots.

Cyprus became an independent republic within the British Commonwealth in 1960, having been under British control for less than a hundred years. This followed three centuries of Ottoman Turkish rule. The population at the time of independence was approximately four-fifths Greek-speaking, one-fifth Turkish-speaking, with smaller Armenian and Maronite communities and a substantial continuing British presence. It is generally thought that the proportions of Greek and Turkish speakers within the UK population correspond roughly to that ratio (Oakley, 1970; Anthias, 1983).

The settlement from Cyprus can be seen in three main stages: a small pre-World War II migration; the major migration between 1945 and 1962, followed by a sharp reduction after the 1962 Immigration Act; and the most recent major movement after the Turkish intervention of 1974. Both Greek and Turkish Cypriots have settled mostly in the Greater London area.

R. Oakley (1970) reported that in the early stages of migration in the 1950s and 1960s, Greek Cypriots were working in the service sector in catering, in hotels, in the clothing and shoe manufacturing industries, in hairdressing, and in grocery retailing. Turkish Cypriots seem to have followed a similar pattern. The economic activities of Cypriot women in particular have changed quite radically since migration (Anthias, 1983).

From 1967 onwards, many more Cypriot men became self-employed and diversified into different types of small businesses, often providing goods and services primarily for other Cypriots (Constantinides, 1977). Still, comparatively few younger Cypriots are moving into professional occupations such as teachers, social workers, lawyers, accountants, and architects.

Not surprisingly, given their geographical and latterly political separation from the "mother countries," and their different history of language contacts, the varieties of both Greek and Turkish spoken in Cyprus, and subsequently in Britain by those of Cypriot origin, are significantly different from the mainland standard languages. The continued economic interaction between Greek and Turkish Cypriots in Britain, in the context of which Turks more often depend for work and services on Greeks than vice versa is reflected in quite widespread knowledge of Greek among Turks, but rarely of Turkish among Greeks.

Polish and Ukrainian are the two main Eastern European languages spoken in England. There were already a few thousand Poles in Britain in the 1930s, but the main Polish settlement began as a government and armed forces in exile, which arrived in Britain after the fall of France in June 1940.

Of the quarter of a million members of the Polish forces in the West in 1945 about four-fifths came to Britain, although not all of them settled there finally. They were later joined by survivors of the German concentration camps, prisoners-of-war, families of military personnel, and people from the displaced persons camps in Germany. Concentrations of Polish speakers developed around the different camps and hostels set up to provide accommodation in areas where labor was needed. By 1960, regional settlement patterns had crystallized, with the largest Polish settlement in London and other sizable concentrations in the Midlands and the north of England.

From the mid–1950s, the improvement of East-West relations has led to the arrival of a certain number of "new immigrants," two-thirds of them women, which has to some degree alleviated the earlier sex ratio imbalance in favor of men.

The great majority of Ukrainians settled in Britain after World War II. In the mid–1950s up to half of the Ukrainians in Britain were still living in various kinds of hostels, a high proportion of them engaged in agricultural work. Nearly half now live in different areas in the East Midlands and the north of England, and the rest in small numbers have settled in the rest of the country. Many of the older British Ukrainians were born in territory that was then part of Poland, and have a knowledge of Polish.

THE MOTHER-TONGUE DEBATE

In England, the debate about bilingualism and schooling has been restricted, with few exceptions, to the issue of mother-tongue teaching. The term *mother tongue* is particularly unfortunate. In many cases, the language taught as mother tongue is not identical with the home vernacular. In some cases, the language of religion, the language of national origin, or the lingua franca are linguistically close to the so-called mother tongue, and in other cases not. Even where these "community languages" are distinct, there remain social and educational arguments for their support. Some community languages are languages of literacy or of formal school instruction in the parents' countries of origin. But it is also important to remember that many members of linguistic minorities in England are multilingual, using their different languages for different functions, and that the value of different elements in their repertoire is changing with different patterns of ethnic relations.

The only types of bilingual education schemes that have been discussed at all widely in England are those with a transitional objective. The mother-tongue debate has, therefore, focused almost exclusively on the teaching of the newer minority languages as curriculum subjects rather than on their use as media of instruction. The debate has also tended to focus on the teaching of bilingual children, neglecting the potential for monolingual English speakers to participate in bilingual schemes.

Several reasons have already been suggested for this situation. First, the initial response to the language education of bilingual pupils was to concentrate on the acquisition of English as a second language and to ignore the pupils' first-language skills. Given the predominantly assimilationist and monolingual attitudes prevailing in England, it was understandable that few teachers realized the value of, or could provide support for, first-language development as a firmer foundation for second-language acquisition. Second, the two main forces that led to a wider public debate on mother-tongue teaching in the late 1970s did not initially define the issue as one involving all pupils. The demand from minority associations and mother-tongue teachers for support for mother-tongue teaching arose from their existing experience of trying to meet demand with very few resources. Teachers working for an education system that would reflect the multicultural composition of society argued that this involved not only the recognition of linguistic diversity in school, but also the teaching of these languages for bilingual pupils.

Once the fuller implications of the language education of bilingual children were appreciated, more teachers and researchers recognized parallel issues in the language education of bidialectal pupils. Many of these issues had been under discussion for years—for example, the transition from spoken vernacular to standard literacy, and the best methods for teaching modern languages. But this realization did not, of course, solve the practical problems of time-tabling, nor the more fundamental issues of crossing professional subdivisions (English as a Mother Tongue, English as a Second Language, Modern Languages, etc.). The introduction of mother-tongue teaching at the secondary level raised major problems with regard to teacher training, materials development, and appropriate examinations (Reid, 1984). But one of the most fundamental hurdles to be overcome involves the opening up of this provision to all pupils, as part of the response to the arguments for offering a wider range of modern languages.

At the primary level, the introduction of mother-tongue provision necessitates the recruitment of bilingual teachers but, as long as transition to English is seen by schools as the primary objective, support for minority literacy is unlikely to be given high priority. Discussion about provision at the primary level developed in the early 1980s and was enriched by the experience of the MOTET project in Bradford. The arguments for supporting this teaching through the mother tongue included reference to the importance of (1) smoothing the transition from home to school and avoiding the imposition of unfair disadvantage at a critical stage of schooling; (2) encouraging the child's general conceptual development and avoiding a sudden curtailment of academic and cognitive skills because of inadequate English; and (3) providing a sound base in the child's first language to facilitate acquisition of the second language (MOTET, 1981).

Another reason why the debate on mother-tongue teaching focused on provision for bilingual children (rather than bilingual education for all pupils in those schools in England with a high percentage of pupils from a single non-English language background) was that many bilingual pupils were already losing their language skills. Even in areas where bilingual pupils had environmental support for their minority language, many were not becoming literate and few were taking examinations in these languages. Increasing numbers of parents and teachers saw only the urgent short-term needs to rescue their own children's command of their languages which, if met, would make less serious the long-term consequences that might be faced by young adults who had lost their command of a valued personal resource.

In many parts of England today, a high percentage of bilingual pupils are using two or more languages in their daily lives (which seems to be the most socially appropriate definition of being bilingual), but where they are not necessarily fluent speakers of their so-called mother tongue. This means that over time an increasing amount of mother-tongue teaching in secondary schools will be starting from an elementary stage, unless pupils have had a good grounding at the primary level in LEA schools or community-run classes. Although this presents particular problems for curriculum development and teacher training, it also provides all pupils with the opportunity to learn one of the minority languages.

These suggestions presuppose a concentration of speakers from one language background, which is the case in many schools in different parts of the country. They also make the assumption that there are native English-speaking pupils who would want to participate in such schemes. This is a vital factor in the context of considerable prejudice and antagonism felt toward members of minorities in many areas of the country. Already there are cases of native English speakers attending mother-tongue classes during and after regular school hours, but one of the greatest challenges is to ensure that monolingual as well as bilingual parents are given the opportunity to consider the advantages of their children becoming bilingual. This is not an achievement normally expected to emerge from modern language teaching at the secondary school level, but in many areas of England now pupils have the possibility of using these newer minority languages in their daily lives, and there is a range of European and non-European minority languages that are important for professional, business, social and leisure services, and secretarial work within England and abroad. Much of the debate has been so narrowly defined in terms of individual bilingualism, however, that it has assessed these social and economic advantages too narrowly in terms of the needs of international trade and diplomacy.

The increase in community-run language provision in nearly all linguistic minorities over the last ten years is an obvious indication of the vitality of the languages, and of the increasing demand. Some schools started in the 1950s and 1960s, but it was in the 1970s that mother-tongue teachers and organizers became more aware of the range of provision offered within their own population nationally, and by other linguistic minorities. Organizers of some of the first conferences in 1976 came together with other South Asian individuals and institutions and discovered a parallel group that was developing among South European teachers or organizers. Although Embassy-run provision opened up a different set of organizational problems, these groups found many common difficulties and issues that needed to be considered. The two groups merged into the Co-ordinating Committee for Mother Tongue Teaching, which has since become the National Council for Mother Tongue Teaching.

As members of linguistic minorities increasingly articulated their demands for more support from the LEAs, the wider discussions about education for a multicultural society kept the issue alive. When the debate shifted from mother-tongue teaching at the secondary level to the use of the mother tongue at the primary level, more people came to recognize the importance of language in education generally. There have also been signs that more English as a Second Language (ESL) teachers have begun to recognize that mother-tongue teaching is the other side of the ESL coin. (This is also increasingly apparent to teachers working in adult ESL. Some modern language teachers too have come to appreciate the potential—and the practical difficulties—of widening the range of modern languages.)

While all of these initiatives suggest a picture of increasing activity and interest, there have been major constraints on consolidating the expertise and interest generated. Within many minority populations, there is the problem of internal communication and a constant battle for resources to maintain and develop provision. Both these difficulties divert energy away from organization and representation. Within the LEA school systems the lack of appropriate teachers and materials, the built-in resistance of the organizational structure, and the attitudes of key personnel have often discouraged initiatives. Examples of systematic collaboration between LEA and community-run schools are few, but represent some of the most well-developed schemes. Although many of these local initiatives have had little publicity, there has also been very little guidance or encouragement from the central government.

The Bullock report in 1975 stressed the importance of bilingualism:

In a linguistically conscious nation in the modern world, we should see mother tongue as an asset, as something to be nurtured, and one of the agencies that should nurture it is the school. Certainly the school should adopt a positive attitude to its pupils' bilingualism and whenever possible should help maintain and deepen their knowledge of their mother tongue (Chapter 20).

The DES document *The Schools Curriculum* (HMSO, 1981) did not discuss the different curriculum options and implications involved in developing the valuable resource of pupils with first languages other than English or Welsh, although it raised the question:

Far more pupils than in the past have a first language which is not English or Welsh. This constitutes a valuable resource, for them and for the nation. How should mother-tongue teaching for such pupils be accommodated within modern language provision so that this resource does not wither away and the pupils may retain contacts with their own communities?

The Fifth Report from the Home Affairs Committee of the House of Commons on Racial Disadvantage made several inconsistent references to the teaching of minority languages in the school system (Home Affairs, 1981):

We are not convinced either that a local education authority is under any obligation to provide mother tongue teaching or that it is necessarily in the general interest that they should do so. (Para 151)

This does not mean the case is hopeless. For many years education in some parts of Wales has been carried on wholly or partly in Welsh. (Para 150)

. . . we feel that some greater efforts to ensure that the secondary school curriculum responds to the presence of ethnic minority pupils would be advisable, for example by encouraging the teaching of Asian languages within the modern languages curriculum. (Para 115)

The only substantial external impetus to the mother-tongue debate has come not from the central government, but from the European Communities (EC) Directive on the Education of Migrant Workers' Children (EC, 1977). Although the British government successfully objected in 1976 to the inclusion of an individual right to mother-tongue teaching which was written into the original draft of the Directive, it made clear that the Directive should be applied in principle to all pupils, whether or not their families came from other member states. This provided an important extension to the scope of the Directive. One of the most notable features of the debate in the mid–1970s about the draft Directive was the lack of information and understanding of the issue among most of the official bodies who were responding to its formulation. Even now the DES's response to the EC on Article III of the Directive shows the need for a more reliable data base. The submission confuses ethnic and language statistics, and the estimates of numbers of children receiving mother-tongue teaching seem low in comparison with our own figures. (See LMP/CLE Working Paper No. 6, 1984.)

Many parents may at present opt for community-based provision because they do not know of the possibility of introducing mother-tongue provision in LEA schools, or are skeptical about the reasons for proposals to do so. However, this does not mean that they are happy with the quality or focus of the community-run schools. Some mother-tongue teachers in community-based classes are in favor of LEA schools taking over this responsibility—so that it becomes more effective and so that it has an impact on the school system as a whole. For some, this would mean that they could concentrate their work on the cultural or religious provision, or provide supplementary language support beyond the few hours offered in the LEA schools.

There is a need for information for all educationalists involved. The building of a trusting and collaborative link with parents is dependent on the teachers' and administrators' knowledge of the parents' points of view and of the specific languages in question.

THE RESEARCH OF THE LINGUISTIC MINORITIES PROJECT

The main objective of the Linguistic Minorities Project (LMP) was to study patterns of bilingualism in selected regions of the country. Our two main aims were to highlight the educational implications of this societal bilingualism and to provide a baseline for future work on the newer minority languages of England. We hoped to contribute toward theoretical and methodological developments, as well as leave a good example of how research and application can be closely integrated, through strategies for active dissemination and research instruments with built-in pedagogic uses.

When LMP started, there was a notable lack of easily available information about the minority languages of England, and little discussion about the social policy implications of widespread bilingualism in England. Discussion among educationalists focused on a rather narrow range of questions about mother-tongue teaching for bilingual pupils. There has also been little academic work on the sociolinguistic characteristics of linguistic minorities in England, in contrast to the fairly substantial research on the indigenous languages of Wales and Scotland.

The LMP was funded by the Department of Education and Science (DES) and based at the University of London Institute of Education from September 1979 to April 1981.

The initial focus of the DES's interest in linguistic minorities in England was on children and schools. The assessment of immediate policy issues and practical initiatives already underway necessitated some comprehensive data on the range of minority languages known by children in the school-going population, and on the scope of their knowledge. There was also interest in the number of these pupils who already attended some form of mother-tongue teaching and in the content and organization of this provision. The DES thought it was important to gather this information from as large a number of LEAs as possible to ensure that our findings reflected the very different situations in different parts of the country. Policy-makers would then be more likely to recognize their own situation in our overall assessments.

While not denying the need for basic data to inform developments in policy and pedagogy, we thought that data referring to children in the state school system should be complemented with an understanding of language use in the pupils' neighborhoods, including details of adult language use and community-run mother-tongue schools and classes.

From the beginning of the Project, we argued that we should pay full attention to the whole range of linguistic minorities in England. For two of our surveys, this meant working with bilingual interviewers from a range of South and Eastern

European and South and East Asian minorities. For one of these surveys, it meant translating our questionnaire into eleven different languages. Similarly, we were convinced that data on the number of children or adults reporting certain spoken or literacy skills were of little relevance for educational or social policy, without an accompanying understanding of what was happening to the languages in everyday life. For this we needed to know when people were using their other-than-English languages and what value they had for their speakers. Without this basic understanding of the social context, there would be no way in which researchers, policy-makers, or teachers could assess the likely trends of language use among linguistic minorities in the future.

In our early discussions on the aims and content of our research, we frequently returned to two themes. One related to our dependency on survey data, based on adults' or pupils' own reports of their language use or skills, rather than observations of what actually happened. We accepted that this kind of large-scale survey was needed to inform policy and build up data for developing hypotheses for future research. We were well aware of the difficulties of carrying out large-scale surveys in a relatively sensitive field in inner-city areas and among often insecure respondents. We also believed that the only valuable and feasible way of doing the schools-based surveys, which often depended on the cooperation of teachers working under pressure, involved using approaches that would provide immediate interest value for the teachers and longer term value for trainers and advisers.

The second theme that preoccupied us in our early discussions revolved around our sense of social responsibility, and our receptivity to the needs of those who contributed to our findings. We were aware of the attitudes of some teachers toward research whose outcome never appeared to help them in their daily difficulties. We were also conscious of the need to provide tools that LEAs could take over themselves, to inform policy and to use for in-service training. Most of all, we thought we understood the frustrations of so many minority teachers and community workers, who often saw no sign of official recognition of their problems or a willingness to tackle them. While we discussed the relative urgency of these needs, and our most appropriate contributions both short and long term, we knew that a full response to local demands would probably restrict our research to one area only. It was at this stage that we discussed the possibility of setting up a parallel research project and became involved in actively disseminating the findings of our research, in particular to all those who had contributed to the data. The LINC Project was funded by the Commission of the European Communities from January 1981 for four years.

The community-based research strategies which we adopted compensated in some ways for our inability to follow the ideal path—the undertaking of neighborhood-based, in-depth studies *before* we developed our survey instruments. Each of the four surveys which we did develop could have been the focus of an independent three-year project in such a new area of research, so we reluctantly put aside the observational studies projects. The final design adopted for our research does in fact allow an evaluation of the appropriateness of a smaller number of different research methods, but we were not able to use as wide a range as we had initially envisaged.

We established three important principles in the early days of our research. First, we aimed always to counter the prevailing view that our work, and the mother-tongue debate, was about South Asian languages only. Second, we wanted to show that policy decisions need to be based on an understanding of the sociolinguistic context, and not just on the numerical data. Through this wider approach to bilingualism in society, we hoped to remind many teachers, policy-makers, and parents that education is not only a matter of schooling. Finally, we were keen to be responsive to all those involved in the research process. We worked from the principles that all participants have a right of access to the data they help to collect, and that researchers need to develop ways of ensuring that access and of encouraging feedback from participants in the research process to guide future work.

Two of the survey instruments, the Schools Language Survey (SLS) and the Secondary Pupils Survey (SPS), focused on the school-going population, and their administration involved class teachers as well as both bilingual and monolingual pupils in the class.

The Schools Language Survey (SLS) aimed to document the range of linguistic diversity in a Local Education Authority (LEA) and the extent of literacy in each minority language; it was carried out by LMP in five LEAs. The findings show varying proportions of the children surveyed reporting spoken skills in a minority language (from about 7 percent in the Peterborough Division of Cambridgeshire to over 30 percent in the London Borough of Haringey), and a consistent 40 to 50 percent of these pupils in each LEA reporting some literacy skills in a minority language. The combinations of languages found in the school population in different areas vary considerably, but usually the most frequent three or four languages account for at least two-thirds of the bilingual pupils in an Authority (LMP/LINC Working Paper No. 3, 1983). Such findings have important implications for the development of language policies that aim to promote the learning of minority languages by many more pupils, bilingual and monolingual. They indicate the scale of the task and the potential for positive action. A Schools Language Survey Manual of Use now provides the opportunity for the SLS to be used more widely, and offers an encouragement for LEAs to update their findings at regular intervals.

The other school-based survey instrument developed by the LMP was the Secondary Pupils Survey (SPS). The questionnaire was originally developed for use in a sample survey, examining in more detail than was possible with the SLS the language use and perception of linguistic diversity among secondary school pupils. Its potential as teaching material and as a means of promoting language awareness, especially among monolingual pupils and teachers, led to a change of focus in its use. The questionnaire was eventually produced in an illustrated format and was made available for individual teachers to use in the classroom with a set of accompanying teachers' guidelines. In collaboration with the ILEA TV Centre, LMP/LINC produced a video program about one approach to using the SPS with a class: this program is entitled "Sharing Languages in the Classroom" and is now available.

The surveys revealed a clear pattern among bilingual pupils which suggested that English was used most of the time with the younger generation, while the mother tongues were used more often with parents and grandparents. There were also some indications, at least in Bradford, that the minority languages were used more when speaking to females, for example, mothers and sisters, than to males.

The apparent tendency among these younger bilingual adolescents to use more English, or both their languages, with their siblings should not be interpreted as an indication of their language loss, nor indeed of a general pattern of language shift among all British-born members of all linguistic minorities. As children from linguistic minorities grow up, and particularly during their school years, the pressures from the predominantly monolingual monocultural majority, in terms of both language use and more general patterns of behavior, are very difficult to resist. These pressures can take many different forms: absence of reference, or even covert or overt opposition, to their "home" language and culture in and around the school; the all-pervading and compelling influence of the English-medium media within as well as outside their home; and, of course, among their peer group. Moreover, many children from linguistic minorities experience racism and become increasingly conscious of the lower socioeconomic status of many ethnic or linguistic minorities they see around them. In their early teenage years, when most children go through a period of opposition to adults in their immediate environment and tend to look for psychological security in terms of conformity with the peer group, adolescents often find it particularly difficult to resist those pressures, which lead them to consider their grandparents' or parents' language and patterns of behavior as something they do not want to be associated with. Some nevertheless do resist, as the figures show, certainly with less difficulty in places where the relevant languages are widely used outside as well as inside the home, and when, for example, the children's languages are given status in the school by teachers and the school personnel as a whole.

The first of our community-based surveys, the Mother Tongue Teaching Directory Survey (MTTD), was developed to collect information on the existing provision for minority languages teaching in both LEA and community-run schools and classes. Through this survey we established that a very high proportion of the teaching is at present not supported financially in any way by LEAs, or at best receives only minimal support in the form of reduced-cost or free teaching accommodation. This is in spite of the fact that virtually all of the pupils attending these classes are between five and sixteen years old.

The MTTD Survey was developed in close collaboration with the National Council for Mother Tongue Teaching in the expectation that after the end of the LMP they would be able to promote the survey throughout the country, with a data bank set up at the Centre for Information on Language Teaching and Research in London. The MTTD surveys in Coventry, Bradford, and Haringey were carried out with the help of bilingual interviewers from the local linguistic minorities, who provided very important input to the research.

One of the findings from the three MTTD surveys is that the majority of the mother-tongue classes in the three areas taken as a whole (83 percent in Haringey, 74 percent in Bradford, and 32 percent in Coventry) had no support from the LEA for teachers' salaries or accommodation at the time of the survey. Even when schools or classes were receiving partial support, usually it was only in the form of free or subsidized accommodation, and they were still often run by local community organizations or overseas government agencies. Even many of the classes within the curriculum of LEA schools and with teachers paid by the LEA were set up through the initiative and perseverance of a bilingual teacher on the staff of those schools (LMP/CLE Working Paper No. 6, 1984).

The Adult Language Use Survey (ALUS) also involved a community-based research strategy, in which LMP collaborated with over a hundred bilingual interviewers in Coventry, Bradford, and Haringey to conduct some twenty-five hundred interviews in respondents' homes. The interview schedule included questions about language skills, language use at home and at work, and attitudes to language teaching provision. The interviews were based on translations of the ALUS questionnaire into eleven languages, and were conducted with carefully prepared samples in each of the three areas mentioned. From the resulting mass of data (which will be more fully analyzed by the Community Languages and Education Project, one of the successor projects to LMP), only four points are mentioned here:

1. The *multi*lingualism of a high proportion of respondents, not only among the respondents of South Asian origin.

2. The high proportions of those who had a real choice in terms of their reported language skills and who used the minority language in domestic settings.

3. The strong support evident among all the local linguistic minorities for an increased contribution from the LEAs to mother-tongue provision.

4. Important differences between respondents of the same linguistic minority in different cities in terms of language skills and language use, which suggest that it is essential to look in some detail at local historical, demographic, social, and economic factors in order to understand the dynamics of bilingualism.

CONCLUSIONS

Bilingual members of British society, from whatever socioeconomic background, have linguistic repertoires that often consist of several different varieties of English as well as a range of varieties in their mother tongues. New varieties of English and of many of the other languages are emerging among adolescents, reflecting their distinctive patterns of socialization and social interaction. As a consequence, bilingual children often experience the same imposed disadvantage as their monolingual English-speaking peers of working-class or certain regional or Caribbean origins, if the schools they attend promote the exclusive use of Southern British Standard English. Explicit or implicit school language policies still almost always mean that bilingual children in England do not have the opportunity to use the language of their parents at school. Only rarely are these languages considered as aids to learning, as legitimate means of expression, or as examination subjects of equal status with other languages.

The almost total change in patterns of language use from the home to school environment is likely to hold back not only the linguistic and conceptual, but also the general educational development of many bilingual children. Even when the home-school linguistic transition is relatively successfully managed, the monolingual policies in many British schools have at least two damaging consequences. Most bilingual youngsters do not have the opportunity to develop all their early oral skills in more than one language, or to establish literacy in the language other than English. Similarly, monolingual English youngsters miss the opportunity of experiencing the use of two languages as a normal and natural phenomenon and of becoming interested in the study of how language and languages work.

The different balance between the various linguistic minorities in each local area inevitably means differences in detailed policies, and this is facilitated by the decentralized educational system in England. But whatever practices are developed in the near future, there is great educational advantage, even in predominantly monolingual English-speaking schools, in building on whatever linguistic diversity there is in the school. It should be remembered that this may include pupils' English dialects as well as languages other than English. Whatever detailed policies are developed by LEAs in terms of supporting mother-tongue teaching in schools or supporting existing community-run initiatives, for a long time ahead there will be the need to support and link the resources and expertise located in both types of provision. In all cases, there is a need for the development of appropriate teaching materials, for the training of bilingual teachers from linguistic minorities and of monolingual teachers from the English-speaking majority, and for much more information and understanding about language use in general among all the members of our multilingual society.

It seems unlikely that bilingualism in England will disappear in the foreseeable future. Minority languages are of value to their speakers for a range of reasons: social, psychological, and linguistic. The more they are devalued or ignored in certain contexts, the more they are likely to develop as a resource for resisting the domination of English. The same processes that restrict the use and value of minority languages also work against the recognition of regional or class-based dialects among "monolinguals." Many of the educational issues are similar—the consequences of transference from one dialect or language to another as the child enters school, or the problems of an individual's development from oral vernacular skills to literacy in the standard language.

There is, however, a major difference between the phenomena of bidialectalism and bilingualism. While many people of the different regional cultures of England are used to switching from one variety of English to another according to context and company, very few use two quite separate languages in their daily lives. English monolinguals have in general a rather poor record in learning foreign languages at school, and enormous sums of money are spent annually in language learning for adults in, for example, industry, leisure, and the diplomatic services. Yet many of the ethnic minority community languages in England are at present ignored or devalued as an individual and societal resource, when in fact their speakers could with minimal investment have their existing skills developed during their school years, and thus offer the country an educational, economic, and political resource of considerable value. The value of minority languages lies not only in what they offer to the large number of bilingual members of British society. Bilingualism also offers the possibility of changing the narrowly monolingual perspective of many majority institutions and individuals.

ACKNOWLEDGMENTS

This chapter is based on the Reports of the Linguistic Minorities Project, which were written jointly by all the members of the research team (Xavier Couillaud, Marilyn Martin-Jones, Verity Saifullah Khan, Anna Morawska, Euan Reid, and Greg Smith). The researchers would also like to acknowledge the assistance of the Assistant Programmer and of the secretarial colleagues on the team. The Report of the Linguistic Minorities Project (see LMP, 1983) and the book of the project (see LMP, 1984) gives details of the findings and discussion of the sociolinguistic and educational issues referred to in this chapter.

BIBLIOGRAPHY

Anthias, F. 1983. "Sexual Division and Ethnic Adaptation: The Case of Greek Cypriot Women." In *One Way Ticket: Migration and Female Labour*, ed. A. Phizacklea. London: Routledge and Kegan Paul.
Bullock Report. 1975. *Language for Life*. London: HMSO.
Constantinides, P. 1977. "The Greek Cypriots: Factors in the Maintenance of Ethnic Identity." In *Between Two Cultures: Migrants and Minorities in Britain*, ed. J. L. Watson. Oxford: Blackwell.
Crisp, S. 1980. "A Study of the Effects of Migration on a South Italian Hill Village and on the Migrants Themselves." Ph.D. thesis, University of Cambridge.
Davies, N. 1981. *God's Playground: A History of Poland*. London: Oxford University Press.
EC (European Communities). 1977. *Council Directive on the Education of Children of Migrant Workers*: 77/486. Brussels: EC.
HMSO. 1981. *The School Curriculum*. London: HMSO.
Home Affairs. 1981. *Racial Disadvantage*. Fifth Report from the Home Affairs Committee of the House of Commons. London: HMSO.

Jones, P. R. 1983. "Vietnamese Refugees in the UK: The Reception Programme." *New Community* 10. 3.

Linguistic Minorities Project. 1983. "The Schools Language Survey: Summary of Findings from Five LEAs." *LMP/LINC Working Paper No. 3*. London: LMP, University of London Institute of Education.

———. 1984. "The Mother Tongue Teaching Directory Survey of the Linguistic Minorities Project." *LMP/CLE Working Paper No. 6*. London: LMP, University of London Institute of Education.

———. (Forthcoming). *The Other Languages of England*. London and New York: Routledge and Kegan Paul.

Mother Tongue and English Teaching Project (MOTET). 1981. Summary of the Report, Vols. 1 & 2. From Dr. O. Rees, University of Bradford or Dr. B. Fitzpatrick, Bradford College, Bradford, Yorkshire.

Oakley, R. 1970. "The Cypriots in Britain." *Race Today* 2:99–102.

Reid, E., ed. 1984. *Minority Community Languages in School*. London: CILT.

Rex, J., and R. Moore. 1976. *Race, Community and Conflict: A Study of Sparkbrook*. London: Oxford University Press.

Saifullah Khan, V. 1980. "The 'Mother Tongue' of Linguistic Minorities in Multicultural England." *Journal of Multilingual and Multicultural Development* 1, 1:71–88.

Smith, D. J. 1977. *Racial Disadvantage in Britain*. Harmondsworth: Penguin.

Tosi, A. 1984. *Immigration and Bilingual Education: A Case Study of Movement of Population Language Change and Education Within the European Community*. Oxford: Pergamon.

Watson, J. L., ed. 1977. *Between Two Cultures: Migrants and Minorities in Britain*. Oxford: Blackwell.

Wilding, J. 1981. *Ethnic Minority Languages in the Classroom?: A Survey of Asian Parents in Leicester*. Leicester Council for Community Relations and Leicester City Council.

R. N. *Srivastava*

SOCIETAL BILINGUALISM AND BILINGUAL EDUCATION: A STUDY OF THE INDIAN SITUATION

The language scene in India provides a unique mosaic of linguistic diversity and heterogeneity. The age-old coexistence of several mutually unintelligible languages has made India linguistically a complex whole. India's linguistic and ethnic complexity has been discussed from systematic, sociological, and communicational perspectives by Pandit (1972), Southworth and Apte (1974), Kachru (1978), Srivastava (1980a, 1980b), Shapiro and Schiffman (1981), Pattanayak (1981), and Khubchandani (1983). However, the extent of its linguistic heterogeneity and complexity can be gauged from the Indian census which continues to be the primary source of information on the prevalence of multilingualism in the region. While Mitra (1964) provides the picture of linguistic heterogeneity as reflected in the recording of numerous mother tongues in the 1961 census of India, Khubchandani (1978) presents the distribution of contact languages and the nature of contact patterns based on the data made available in the 1961 census.

The number of mother tongues (MTs) as reported by the individuals at the time of 1961 census along with their family affiliation is given in Table 12.1. The table shows that 1,652 MTs were reported by nearly 439 million people—532 belonging to the Indo-Aryan, 148 to the Dravidian, 53 to the Austro-Asiatic, and 227 MTs to the Sino-Tibetan language family. The category ''Others'' includes both unclassified MTs whose affiliation to a language family could not be ascertained and languages of foreign origin. Since these MTs are the names that the census returns give as codes reported by individuals as spoken languages and not the actual languages or dialects spoken by them, an attempt was made in the census to classify different MTs into languages. As a result, nearly two hundred languages are established as MTs—sixty belonging to the Indo-Aryan,

Table 12.1
Number of MTs and Language Families (Source: 1951 Census)

Families	Number of speakers	Mother tongue speakers				
		Less than 1,000	1,000 and above	5,000 and above	10,000 and above	Total
		Number of Mother tongues				
Indo-Aryan	321,721	356	52	26	98	532
Dravidian	107,411	104	14	4	26	148
Austro-Asiatic	6,192	20	10	2	21	53
Sino-Tibetan	3,184	111	43	21	52	227
Others (unclassified)	429	657	17	2	7	683
Sikkim	-					9
	438,937	1,248	136	55	204	1,652

Indo-Aryan, 21 to the Dravidian, 20 to the Austro-Asiatic and 95 to the Sino-Tibetan language family.

twenty-one to the Dravidian, twenty to the Austro-Asiatic, and ninety-five to the Sino-Tibetan language family.

Besides traditionalizing Sanskrit, the classical language which is a constant orthogenetic source of changes in modern Indian languages, the English which is a modernizing heterogenetic source, there are fourteen major Indian languages. Two of these fourteen—Urdu and Sindhi—are nonstate languages as they have no home territory of their own. On the other hand, Hindi has six states—Himachal Pradesh, Haryana, Rajasthan, Uttar Pradesh, Madhya Pradesh, and Bihar. Furthermore, out of 1,652 MTs, nearly 400 are tribal languages.

This pan-Indian linguistic heterogeneity is reflected at all levels of social and political organization. The federal organization of India embraces broadly twelve major language areas, each identified by a distinct language whose speakers form a dominant pressure group. These linguistically identified regions are neither organically homogeneous ethnic regions nor functionally monolingual communication regions. Apart from the dominant regional language, every region is inhabited by speakers of more than one minority language spoken by no fewer than twenty persons per one thousand population (Khubchandani, 1978). The dominant language of Andhra Pradesh, for example, is Telugu, but there are at least twenty other prominent languages in the area.

Although the majority of Telugu speakers reside in their home state, that is, Andhra Pradesh, a sizable number of them have spilled over into contiguous states. The 1961 census reveals that in Tamilnadu, Mysore, Maharashtra, and Orissa, Telugu speakers number thousands, or even millions. Similarly, if we look at the distribution of prominent languages of Andhra Pradesh, we find that apart from Hindi-Urdu, the density of nonnative speakers matches the order of the number of Telugu speakers that have moved over to other states, that is, Tamil (Tamilnadu), Kannada (Mysore), Marathi (Maharashtra), and Oriya (Orissa). (For details, see Srivastava, 1971.) This bidirectional diffusion of speakers of different languages belonging to different language families is attested all over the country. It is common experience that the migrant speech communities of India continue to speak their own language in the home domain of language use. Through their MTs, they endeavor to maintain their ethnic boundaries. At the same time, for the descendants of these migrants the language of the host community begins to serve as a language of wider communication in a matter of a few generations. Since both migrant speech community and the host community agree on limited separation, this results in cultural pluralism. Thus, while the migrant speech community retains its native language as an effective device for ethnic separateness and survival, it may acquire the language of the host community as a job-select language. Such cases of "partial shift" in the use of MT (rather than "total assimilation") are seen all over India, with the result that there is not a single major Indian speech community whose speakers do not employ at least three contact languages. (Appendix 1 provides information about the number of MT speakers of major languages, along with the name of the first three contact languages which they habitually employ during their speech interaction.) The Indian Union at present consists of twenty-two states and nine union territories. Even though the redistribution of state territories was motivated by the idea of reducing the number of linguistic minorities by bringing speakers of a common language together, not a single state of union territory is completely unilingual. (Appendix 2 shows the administrative divisions of India as they existed in 1971, with the population and statistical strength of the three most important languages in each state.)

As migrants do not usually lose their MT in the traditional context of India, we find the presence of linguistic minorities in all states and union territories. Apart from the speakers of tribal speech communities whose concentration is found in Manipur, Meghalaya, Nagaland, Tripura, Andaman and Nicobar Islands, and Arunachal Pradesh, there are minority speakers of scheduled languages distributed all over India. The intensity of minority language speakers varies from one state to another, ranging between 4.96 percent in Kerala to 84.54 percent in Nagaland.

The following have emerged as the most salient features of the language profile of India:

1. Different vernaculars of India fall under four distinct language families of India—Indo-Aryan, Dravidian, Austro-Asiatic, and Sino-Tibetan—but the Indian linguistic scene is dominated by two family groups—Indo-Aryan and Dravidian—with a population covering 97.7 percent of its population.

2. Major languages (i.e., languages specified in the VIII Schedule of the Indian Constitution) cover 88 percent of speakers in the total population. The VIII Schedule includes the following languages: Assamese, Bengali, Gujarati, Hindi, Kannada, Kashmiri, Malayalam, Marathi, Oriya, Punjabi, Sanskrit, Sindhi, Tamil, and Urdu.

3. There appears to be a statewide direct correlation between the degree of heterogeneity in native population and the intensity of bilingualism. There are two official languages of the Union—Hindi (primary) and English (associate)—which together cover more than half of the entire bilingual population.

4. A total of 240 dialects, that is, 12 percent, have ten thousand or more speakers, and 1,248 dialects, or 75 percent, have fewer than a thousand speakers. This indicates that there exist numerous dialects and pockets of tribal inhabitants with distinct ethnic background and that they have not been integrated to form a larger superordinate group.

5. Different states and union territories might have been declared unilingual/bilingual for administrative convenience, but basically each of them is a multilingual and pluri-cultural entity.

SOCIETAL BILINGUALISM AND LANGUAGE CONTINUUM

The successive census reports show that all major languages of India function as contact languages within and/or beyond their home territory. As already pointed out, speakers of different migrant speech communities tend to maintain their ethnic (home) language and also learn to speak the dominant regional language, thus providing a case of societal bilingualism. It should be noted, however, that India's grass-roots bilingualism is much more than this immigrant bilingualism. It is true that migrants do not entirely give up the use of their native language in the social setting of India simply because in such a context "ethnic separateness of home-life is valued" (Gumperz and Wilson, 1971), and language is employed as a functional tool for ethnicity and culture maintenance. But such an instance of cultural pluralism is not restricted to the migrant section of Indian society. We find that speakers of different regional dialects have long showed their allegiance to their supralocal language. For example, linguistically distinct and diverse dialect speakers of Hindi like those of Bhojpuri, Brajbhasa, Awadhi, and Maithili accepted their regional dialects as their primary MT and Hindi as their associate MT. Viewed from the axis of formal linguistics, these dialects are distinct languages because structurally they are different from each other and from standard Hindi. Because speakers of these regionally marked linguistic codes regard themselves as part of the great Hindi tradition, these codes are viewed functionally and sociolinguistically as regional dialects of Hindi. For this reason even those dialect speakers who have marginal competence in Hindi identify it as their MT (Srivastava et al., 1977). Furthermore, if we look at the communicative function of Hindi in its home territory, we find that it serves as a supradialectal norm of verbal behavior for a single intraurban speech community connected by a superregional network of communication (newspapers, books, radio, etc.), which extends from one urban center to another without directly touching the intervening rural areas (Gumperz and Naim, 1960).

Like Hindi, all major regional languages function as a supradialectal norm of verbal behavior and form a single speech community regardless of its dialectal differences. It is not the assimilation/incorporation type of situation where subordinates give up their languages (dialects) in the process of socialization. Instead, it is a kind of cultural pluralism wherein subordinates (dialect speakers) are first given their relative autonomy and then brought into a coordinated compliance with the objectives of the superordinate (language speakers) group. In such a situation, an individual belonging to a given speech community possesses at least a double identity: a personal and local identity (marked linguistically by one's dialect) and superimposed regional identity wherein the ego becomes identified with that of all others within the speech community (marked linguistically by one's regional language). This type of cultural pluralism uniquely accounts for India's societal bilingualism.

Bilingualism is a natural state of verbal behavior in India. Thus, a Gujarati spice merchant settled at Bombay, as pointed out by P. B. Pandit (1972), can simultaneously control five or six languages. Such a merchant will speak Gujarati in his family domain, Marathi in a vegetable market, Hindi with the milkman, Kacchi and Konkani in trading circles, and even English on formal occasions. Such a person may be poorly rated in the area of implicit knowledge of linguistic rules of these languages, but in terms of verbal linguistic ability, he can easily be labeled a multilingual, fairly proficient in controlling different life-situations with ease and skill. An inherent social need turned Indians to grass-roots bilingualism without taking recourse to any formal educational training. For this reason, in spite of mass illiteracy, a societal type of bilingualism has become the life and blood of India's verbal behavior.

The plural character of the nation and the functional configuration of languages in its multilingual setting have also made India's bilingualism concentric in orientation. The spread of different languages as contact languages with varying intensities has assigned different functional loads to them in the Indian linguistic scene. In this context, we find four distributional patterns of major languages (Khubchandani, 1978:557): (1) contact languages confined to their home states (Assames, Kashmiri, Tamil, Oriya, Kannada, Marathi); (2) contact languages spilling over into neighboring states within the linguistic region (Gujarati, Punjabi, Telugu, Malayalam, Bengali); (3) contact languages spreading beyond their home region (Hindi, Urdu); and (4) contact languages not belonging to any region (English, Sanskrit). Patterns of intraregional and interregional communication have thus evolved different kinds of pressure indexes for various languages in the different regions of India. For example, English has emerged as one of the two most important contact languages in the communication matrix of India's urban elite speakers. On the other hand, Hindi is also used as a contact language in the nationwide network of communication matrix by a great majority of people, but its domain is restricted to the nonelite context of verbal interaction. Thus, English elitist bilingualism can be seen functionally at work primarily in the educated section of the speech community, which gives its users power and prestige, while Hindi folk bilingualism is functionally operational basically among people who are not necessarily educated, nor do they achieve power and status through this language.

This distinction between English elitist bilingualism and Hindi folk bilingualism is vital for an understanding of the development of bilingualism in a stratified plural society. First, while elitist bilingualism makes a person competent to enter the learned section of a society and ensures such a person membership in the upper class, folk bilingualism is generally the result of ethnic groups in contact and competition. Second, as C. B. Paulston (1978:311) points out, elitist bilingualism is a matter of choice and, hence, does not pose any serious problem for motivating people to become bilingual through education. On the contrary, folk bilingualism results when people involuntarily learn another language for their survival. Hindustani is learned in multilingual centers such as Bombay, Calcutta, and Madras by people who are not well educated for their occupational security. According to M. L. Apte (1974), this variant of Hindi shares many characteristic features of the languages generally labeled as pidgins and creoles. As an end product of folk bilingualism, this pidginized variety of Hindi, though widely used all over India, is never promoted in the field of education because it is stigmatized in the elite value system as corrupt Hindi.

The official status of Hindi further complicates the situation. The officially sponsored Hindi is highly Sanskritized and uniquely formalized book language meant to provide the base for elitist bilingualism. This variety of Hindi is being legitimatized as the official language of the union and is being placed in competition with English. Thus, in its high Sanskritized form Hindi is a case of elitist bilingualism, and in its low pidginized variety it is a source of folk bilingualism. The first form is being officially sponsored as a language in education, but outside the educational domain it remains totally dysfunctional. In its pidginized form, it is functionally employed all over India as a contact language but is totally excluded from the domain of education.

The same is true for all other major languages of India. Folk bilingualism is primarily responsible for spreading a language beyond its home territory. As revealed by the 1971 census (Appendix 2), except for Assamese, Kashmiri, and Oriya, all the major regional languages occur as either second or third numerically most important languages in one or more states. Nonmajor languages like Dogri and Konkani and tribal languages like Santali and Bhili also occur as one of the three numerically most important languages in more than one state/union territory. The nature and extent of concentric bilingualism force us to hypothesize that the percentage of bilingualism among the speakers is lower for that language which has a higher functional potential for cross-regional speech interaction, that is, lingua franca (Srivastava, 1977:78). This hypothesis is attested by the mean percentage of bilingualism given by Apte (1970:72) for the four categories:

1. Hindi (official language of the union): 5.105
2. Major state languages: 9.569
3. Major nonstate languages: 18.842
4. Minor languages: 42.144

The most relevant characteristic of Indian bilingualism has been the allocation of societal roles to different verbal codes that constitute the verbal repertoire of a given speech community. The noncompeting nature of these roles has sustained the nonconflicting and stable pattern of societal bilingualism. It is precisely for this reason that, despite a high percentage of illiteracy and the absence of any formal teaching program of languages, Indian speech communities have been able to support "folk" multilingualism at the grass-roots level of existence (Pandit, 1972; Khubchandani, 1983; Srivastava, 1977). An Indian speech community regulates the use of the various codes of its verbal repertoire through code-switching and code-mixing and, over and above, by simplifying the structure of one code and assimilating the elements of the other code. On the horizontal axis, languages in India form a continuous chain from Sind to Assam, with mutual intelligibility between adjacent areas (Gumperz, 1964). Similarly, on the vertical axis of speech interaction each major speech community exhibits a continuous chain from the most illiterate variety of local village dialect to the highly specialized English language. Regional and national languages serve as

media of supralocal communication, with reciprocal intelligibility between hierarchically adjacent areas (Srivastava, 1980a).

The horizontal and vertical axes of speech interaction give rise to the concept
of language continuum. Scholars working in the area of English-speaking Caribbean societies have shown that a continuum of language exists: creole at the
one end and Standard English at the other, with an intersecting middle zone of
linguistic mixing (Le Page, 1968; DeCamp, 1971; Bailey, 1973; Bickerton,
1973). According to Srivastava (1984b), this linear aspect of language continuum, in the context of the Indian situation, attests at least the following language
types. (These types form a continuum—national language at the one end and
"in-group" minority languages at the other, with an intersecting middle zone
of major, mediate, and minor types of nationality languages.)

1. National/Official Language: interlanguage for languages of "great tradition"; for example, Hindi in the pan-Indian context.
2. Major Nationality Languages: interlanguage for languages of "little tradition"; for
   example, Bengali, Marathi, Tamil, and Telugu.
3. Mediate Nationality Languages: languages of linguistic minorities in search of their
   own "great tradition"; for example, Santali and Konkani.
4. "Out-group" Minority Languages: languages of linguistic minorities with "little tradition," serving also as languages of wider communication; for example, Halbi and
   Sadari.
5. "In-group" Minority Languages: languages of linguistic minorities with "little tradition" performing exclusively the function of intragroup communication; for example,
   Mishing in Assam, Malto in Bihar, or Juang in Orissa.

Despite the constitutional safeguards for linguistic minorities, certain in-group
minority languages are gradually being excluded from the educational system.
M. G. Chaturvedi and S. Singh (1981:32) point out that, earlier, eighty-one
languages were used as media of instruction in the different states and union
territories. This number decreased to sixty-seven in 1970–71, and by the time
they conducted their Third All India Educational Survey in 1973, there were
only fifty-eight educational languages.

That this shift is symptomatic of a change in the society itself is borne out by
the new pattern of language maintenance and shift discernible in India. Language
maintenance is not a problem for the traditional agrarian society of India. It is
probably for this reason that, unlike the situation in Europe and America where
language shift is the norm and language maintenance an exception, "in India
language maintenance is the norm and shift an exception" (Pandit, 1972:9). A
traditional agrarian society readily accepts any migrant group and its language
without any tension or conflict, provided it is not a threat to the host community
or does not compete with its language in respect of status and power. However,
the situation is rapidly changing. India is experiencing a phase of industrialization
and urbanization. In an industrial urban society, different speech communities

are forced to live with each other in a state of constant competition and conflict. In such a situation, a change is produced in the status relation between different codes of the verbal repertoire of a given speech community. Wherever codes employed by migrant and host communities compete with each other to perform the same function, shift is a fair probability.

Pandit's statement that in India language maintenance is the norm and shift an exception is inaccurate in at least three different contexts. The Hindi belt which attests language-dialect type of restricted cultural pluralism provides the first context. When the indigenous subordinate dialect speakers leave their home region, their descendants give up their primary MT (dialect) in favor of Hindi in a matter of a few generations. The migrant's MT disappears because it is not considered to be an identity marker. The tribal subordinates provide a second context of MT shift. Several tribes in the northeastern zone have given up their highly localized MT in favor of regional language or of an emerging lingua franca. The 1961 census shows that 44.45 percent of Kurux (Oraon) speakers have shifted to the Oriya language in Orissa and that this MT shift to Bengali in Bengal is around 55 percent. The 1961 census also reveals that in this region no less than 63.47 percent of tribal population has shifted to Sadari—an emerging lingua franca—as their MT. Punjabi Hindu speech communities of Punjab and Delhi provide the third context. A. Mukherjee (1980) has shown that, while members of the Bengali speech community show a minimal degree of MT displacement, Punjabi Hindus get completely assimilated to the environing host society. The younger generation shows a 100 percent shift from Punjabi to Hindi. All these instances reveal that, with respect to the question of integration (complete assimilation to the host society), accommodation (part assimilation and part retention of their identity), and retention (maintenance of their exclusive identity), migrant subordinates in India behave differently in urbanized metropolises than those in traditional agrarian settings.

HISTORICAL PERSPECTIVE

India provides an exemplary instance of diffusion of linguistic traits with a remarkable time depth. For several millennia, it has been a multilingual and multicultural country in which speakers of distinct linguistic and ethnic stocks have coexisted and interacted. As a consequence of this coexistence and language contact, India offers a rich example of how linguistic traits become diffused across genetic boundaries. The fusion and diffusion of ethnic, cultural, and linguistic traits among speakers of Aryan, Dravidian, Austro-Asiatic, and Tibeto-Burman families has led, on the one hand, to what S. K. Chatterji (1978) has called the birth of the Indian Man and, on the other, to what Murry B. Emeneau (1956) has described the genesis of India as a "linguistic area." According to Chatterji (1978:63), Aryan and Dravidian speakers, together with other elements of the Indian population, began to miscegenate even before they found themselves in India. The Aryan and Dravidian elements gave birth to the "Indian Man" during the close of the Vedic period. Emeneau recognized that Indian languages belonging to different ethnic stocks developed in mutual interaction and on this basis came up with his notion of "linguistic area" which "includes languages belonging to more than one family but showing traits in common which are found not to belong to the other members of (at least) one of the families" (Emeneau, 1956:16). He accepted India as a "linguistic area" where linguistic areas were shown to be a direct consequence of a contact process instead of common origin. This concept is explicated both by Kuiper (1967) and further by Emeneau (1962, 1974).

There is now ample evidence of a pre-Vedic convergence of Indo-Aryan with Dravidian in the area of vocabulary, sound system, and grammatical structures (Kuiper, 1967; Southworth, 1979; Hock, 1975, 1984). The process of convergence has been global and all-pervasive. There is clear evidence of Indo-Aryanization of Dravidian languages (Sridhar, 1975) and dravidianization of Indo-Aryan languages (Andronov, 1970). The convergence process is also notable in the Himalayan region between Indo-Aryan and Sino-Tibetan (Bendix, 1974). Similarly, tribal areas in eastern and central India attest to the contact situation between Dravidian and Austro-Asiatic (Munda) languages. This contact area can well be defined as Dravido-Mundo-Aryan in nature and scope because speakers of languages belonging to all three language families have converged. There is also a microlinguistic area in the northwest Indian frontier with regard to convergence of traits belonging to Indo-Aryan, Iranian, and Dardic stocks.

The convergence of languages in extended bilingual contact can be seen in India on different levels and in different situations. It is operationally functional internal to a language involving regional dialects (Hindi), caste dialects (Kannada), styles (Tamil and Telugu), and so on which exist in diglossic relationship. The convergence process in a long contact situation between languages of the same and different language families has brought onto the linguistic scene of India even contact (pidgin) languages. They are now being identified as languages in their own right; for example, Halbi (Chattisgarhi + Oriya + Marathi), Malwi (Gujarati + Rajasthani), and Saurashtri (Gujarati + Tamil). There is also an instance of Indo-Portuguese Creole in which nonindigenous languages are involved in creating pidgin and creole in the subcontinent. Studies like Gumperz and Wilson (1971) reveal that languages in India have so integrated themselves that for these languages there exists "a single semiological, a single syntactic and a single phonetic component and alternative set of rules for the relation of semantic categories to morphemic shape" (Gumperz and Wilson, 1971:164). Different languages are identified mainly in terms of their distinct vocabularies. According to M. S. Andronov (1964:13), languages in contact situations have undergone far-reaching convergence, thereby weakening their so-called genetic relationships within the family. The cumulative result of structural changes of contact and convergence is that in many respects Indo-Aryan languages seem to be more akin to Dravidian than to the other genetically related Indo-European languages.

This convergence leads to the notion of the "Indian Man" and makes for similarities in languages that would otherwise belong to genetically unrelated languages. However, this does not preclude the maintenance of distinct local and regional identity by the members of different speech groups. It therefore suggests that ethnicity and culture maintenance is a stable phenomenon for India. As shown by Gumperz and Wilson (1971) and Pandit (1972), despite heavy convergence at all levels of language organization, one aspect (i.e., lexicon) is kept separate as a marker of the local/regional identity.

Linguistic convergence under conditions of stable bilingualism has been a continued process throughout India's history because, on the one hand, members of ethnic minority groups asserted the desirability of preserving their way of life through its language, culture, religion, and so on, and, on the other hand, members of the dominant group showed toleration for these differences. Even though these minority groups have primary sociocultural relations in their own group, they tend to develop secondary relations with the dominant group. This tendency of social participation regulated by institutional roles makes the society culturally plural and socially integrative. It is a unique situation wherein exclusiveness in the area of primary sociocultural relations promotes a maximal degree of enclosure, whereas the active interaction with members of a dominant group controlling both the polity and the economy in the field of secondary socialization provides the minimal degree of enclosure.

This process of integration, which encourages the maintenance of ethnic identities of different groups on one level of social organization and promotion of their merger into a subordinate group on another level, continues even today. For example, in spite of its very low percentage, South Indian speakers in Delhi are not forced to give up their culture and life-style in order to be identified as Delhiwallahs. These people came to Delhi as executives or as correspondents or as teachers, but they brought with them their temples, their schools, their amateur theatre, and their music. Through these sociocultural devices, they never lent themselves to total cultural self-abnegation, but they also never remained isolated in other areas of social participation. Since, in India, the separateness of ethnic relations like dialects of a given language does not usually detract a social group from the wider loyalties to a nation and since language is employed as an effective tool for cultural maintenance as well as for social participation, we find here a condition conducive for the cultural pluralism within a multilingual framework. This also explains why here we find a partial rather than a total language shift.

The change in the social structure of the modern society at the regional and national levels has resulted in incongruent relations emerging between subordinate ethnic minority groups and the superordinate host society. In the past, India's language policy was more liberal, but today it has inadvertently moved toward a strong position of centralization. As a result, the different groups of the society now face tension and conflict. As language is a very transparent cultural symbol, the tension is being manifested in the form of language conflict and language movements. In the attempt at detribalization, the majority dominant group expected minority ethnic groups to give up their native traits. On the other hand, these groups are now creating and perpetuating new boundary markers for their survival and, in many cases, are forming their own "great tradition." Therefore, their position has shifted. Whereas earlier they were engaged in learning the language of the superordinate in order to partake of the administrative and economic benefits (motivation for the MT shift), now they are participating in activities relevant to the maintenance of their own ethnic identity and reshaping of destiny (motivation for the MT maintenance).

LANGUAGE PROBLEMS IN CONTEMPORARY INDIA

The study of organized efforts to solve the persisting language problems of social significance and of national order has been designated by social scientists as an area of language planning. More specifically, it is an area that deals with "conscious governmental efforts to manipulate both the structure and functional allocation of codes within a polity" (Fishman, 1969:186). B. H. Jernudd and J. Das Gupta (1971:197) emphasize the need for a broader identification of problems and believe that a major task of language planning is to identify the concrete areas of society that demand planned action regarding language resources. Language problems are to be seen within the totality or pattern of relations between languages and their environment which E. Haugen defines as "Language Ecology" (1979:243).

Language planning in some of the developing multilingual and multicultural countries of South and Southeast Asia is a kind of entrepreneurial experience that is radically different from that of some of the developed monolingual countries of the West. With a population of over 650 million, 1,652 MTs, and 10 major writing systems, India as a sociolinguistic complex offers a unique challenge for language planners. However, it is not only the multiplicity of languages that makes the task of planners intricate and complex. India has been multilingual from the beginning of recorded history, and for this country bilingualism has been a natural state of verbal behavior. "What is new and significant for political study is the mobilization of language groups for social and political objectives" (Das Gupta, 1970:70). How these processes of mobilization have invariably resulted in the political expressions of language loyalties can be seen through the number of language movements which India has experienced since independence (Annamalai, 1979) and in the political restructuring of some of the states since 1956 when, on the recommendations of the States Reorganization Commission, the boundaries of certain states in India were redrawn on a linguistic basis (Srivastava, 1984b). In 1956, there were only sixteen states, whereas in 1971 the Indian Union consisted of twenty-two linguistically organized states and nine union territories. In 1960, Maharashtra was divided into two states because of the conflict between two prominent speech communities, Gujarati and Marathi, and in 1966, Punjab was divided into two states, Punjab and

Haryana, because of the violence and bitterness between the Hindus and the Sikhs, the Hindus adhering to Hindi and the Sikhs to Punjabi.

The Congress party of India formally accepted the principle of linguistic redistribution of provinces as a clear political and administrative objective at the important Nagpur session of 1920 (Kamath, 1966). The case for the formation of states on a linguistic basis rested on the following factors: (1) enabling the general public to maintain administration in their own language, (2) promoting both the economic and social interests of a particular language group, (3) reducing the number of linguistic minorities and their problems, and (4) strengthening the political unity of India. Two facts were emphasized—one, different linguistic groups were subnations and, two, people speaking a common language could be brought together by declaring these states monolingual.

India's recent history has shown that the scheme for redistributing states on a linguistic basis has increased interstate rivalries and has led to violence, bitterness, and disturbances among members of different speech communities. An objective study of the situation shows that, as the problem of linguistic minorities is *sui generis,* the linguistic reorganization of states in itself is no solution to the vital problem of these subordinated speech communities (Srivastava, 1984a, 1984b). One has to recognize that, while India's language ecology is based on grass-roots bilingualism in which each major language acts merely as a *link* language, the actual formation of linguistic states converts link language into a *dominant* language, that is, language of political power and prestige. As a dominant language, the recognized state *official* language gets impregnated with power and begins to block the upward social mobility of the members of other speech groups. This became the major cause of intergroup rivalries and a ground for the demand for further linguistic fragmentation of the country.

Other features of India's language ecology that have become a concern for policy-makers are as follows:

(1) In a traditional and stratified society like that of India, a network of regional and social identities exists (Srivastava and Gupta, 1982). Consequently, in the manner of sociopolitically organized systems—local (village), regional (state), national, and so on—language identities are also layered hierarchically. It is obvious then that language conflicts may manifest a clash of interests between any two levels of identities. For example, Hindi as the national/official language of India comes into conflict with English (as an *associate* official language of India and as a language for internal communication), with Tamil and Bengali (as developed nationality languages), with Maithili and Bhojpuri (as regional dialects threatening to establish their own local identities), and with Santal and Khasi (as ethnic vernaculars of tribes that are in search of their own great tradition).

(2) India's major languages offer an enormously complex language situation because of all kinds of linguistic variability—regional (dialectal), social (sociolectal), and stylistic (diatypic). Complexities are also caused by the superimposed functional varieties, multigraded assimilation of loan words, and various

kinds of interference and switching of different codes among multilingual speakers of this language. All these factors greatly complicate the task of standardization (codification). Through codification, standardization prescribes an
authentic variant of a language in the face of language variability (Garvin, 1964).
C. A. Ferguson characterizes standardization as "the process of acceptance of
one variety of a language throughout the speech community as a supra-dialectal
norm" (1968:37). Similarly, according to Garvin, a standard language has to
fulfill three distinct functions: unification, prestige, and frame-of-reference (Garvin, 1964:522). Two or more superimposed varieties (microlects) exist for one
and the same language, and these varieties tend to compete with each other for
their preservation and promotion to the status of standardized variant. Thus, in
the Hindi belt, the two major microlects, High Hindi and High Urdu, can be
taken as two literary styles superimposed over a Hindustani-based vernacular.

   Almost all major languages show a sharp cleavage between standardized literary microlect and nonstandard vernacular microlect—for example, Telugu
(Sjoberg, 1962), Marathi (Apte, 1962; Bersten, 1975), Tamil (Shanmugam Pillai,
1960), Bengali (Dimock, 1960), and Kannada (Bright, 1960; McCormack,
1960). Conscientious linguists working in the field of South Asian languages
have supported the proposal of C. C. Fries and K. L. Pike (1949) that languages
in such a context exhibit the coexistence of simultaneous systems that "operate
partly in harmony and partly in conflict" (Gumperz, 1961; Ferguson and Gumperz, 1960; Srivastava, 1969). The gap in terms of comprehensibility and communicability between two microlects can sometimes be almost as wide as the
gap between two languages (Srivastava et al., 1978). How and to what extent
linguistic variability can pose problems for language standardization in India has
been discussed by Krishnamurti (1979) and Southworth (1985). It is apparent
from cross-linguistic comparisons of this process that for these languages more
than one standard norm has emerged. Further, the process is not uniform. Standard Tamil is closer to the written classical variety and is not based on the
contemporary spoken variety of any section of the people, while written standard
norms in Hindi, Bengali, Marathi have their base in the spoken standards of the
metropolitan centers viz. Delhi, Calcutta and Poona respectively.

   (3) With the rule of the British, English became the vehicle of scientific and
technological knowledge, as also the language of administration and prestigious
vocations. The use of regional languages remained confined to areas of expressive
culture. In post-independent India, a constitutional safeguard was provided for
promoting regional languages in the domains of administration and other prestigious vocations. It was sincerely felt that the regional languages must be
equipped with new vocables, terminologics and phrasal expressions in the areas
of discourse in which English had hitherto enjoyed exclusive privilege (Srivastava
and Kalra 1984:43). Modernization is a problem that leads to the process of
elaboration which, according to Ferguson, is "lexical expansion and developing
new styles and forms of discourse" (1968:33). Cross-linguistic comparisons of
the historical processes of code-elaboration in Bengali, Hindi, Kannada, Marathi,

Oriya, Tamil, Telugu etc. (Krishnamurti and Mukherjee 1984) reveal that except for Tamil, the modernization process is characterized by two tendencies: Traditionalization (revivalist), which at the highest subculture makes the style classical by Sanskritization of the language, and *Anglicization* (westernization), which makes the style modern by Anglicizing the language, that is, by constant transfer of linguistic units of all sizes from English to the regional language. The politicization of the Tamil language has been marked by a move toward cultural emancipation of the language. An attempt is being made not only to make an internal translation of proper Sanskrit names into Tamil, but also to Tamilize English technical terms and popular loan words.

(4) In India, code-switching and code-mixing as linguistic phenomena have vital implications for language dynamics and language change. In contact situations with local and regional dialects, they enrich the language with distinctive and colorful traits expressive of local environment, and with noncognative languages like English in a natural and effortless way. They promote among the people the ability for sentence-for-sentence translatability and, by diffusing linguistic traits across linguistic structures, increase the power and mutual adaptability. However, an attitude analysis of people across language areas shows that code-switching and code-mixing are viewed as marking an undeveloped stage of their language development and as indicating poor control of one's own linguistic and literary heritage. An elitist approach to codification and elaboration of regional languages has created the new variant of regional language, which in the past has been a preserve of the educated elites. As Das Gupta points out, the whole process of language standardization and modernization "seems to go contrary to the logic of mass literacy, affective access of new groups to the educated communication arena and to socialization of maximum human resources in general" (Das Gupta, 1970:590).

(5) There seems to be a direct correlation between a region's literacy rate and language ecology. Literacy may be defined as an extension of the functional potential of language with regard to the channel of communication which involves reading and writing skills. It has two distinct aspects however: *orientational* (mathemagenic factors), that is, the ability to control the graphic medium of a language; and *operational* (performance factors), that is, the ability to use a language in a written medium. The second aspect is directly concerned with the variant of a language which is institutionally employed in the ecological setting of writing. It has been shown that the highest rates of illiteracy in India are found where "the written standard variety of a language is far removed in grammar and vocabulary from the local vernacular and home variant of the language" (Srivastava, 1984c:32). DeSilva (1976) has shown a positive nexus between poverty and illiteracy on the one hand and between illiteracy and diglossia on the other.

A survey reveals that there are at least three situations in India in which literary skills are being initiated through a second language. The first situation concerns the tribal or minority language speakers who employ the major language of their region or English for literary skills, even though they use a contact pidgin as the language of interethnic communication (Shreedhar, 1976:371). The second situation concerns dialect speakers who are initiated into literacy through primers written in a standard language, at the cost of linguistically distinct codes in which learners have exclusive proficiency (Srivastava, 1984c; Krishnamurti, 1978). The third situation exists in the English-medium schools where speakers of different major Indian languages "first achieve literacy in English—a language in which their capacity as well as opportunity for use is extremely limited when compared to the native speakers of English" (Sah, 1978:32). This practice of initiating literacy in a second language not only violates the operational efficiency condition that literacy is most effectively achieved in MT, but also downgrades the learner's MT and generates disharmonious relationships between functions of literacy (i.e., what literacy does for learners) and uses of literacy (i.e., what learners do with literacy skills).

LANGUAGES IN EDUCATION AND BILINGUAL EDUCATION

Three main trends characterize the postcolonial phase of African and Asian history: (1) rediscovery of the importance of indigenous languages, (2) recognition of the importance of mother tongues for providing equal access to education, and (3) promotion of unity of polity comprising a large number of heterogeneous ethnolinguistic groups by selection and development of a national/ official language (Srivastava, 1980a). MT teaching is considered of primary importance within the overall development policy because it is the language in which a child first finds expression of self and environment; it gives everyone equal access to educational opportunities; and it helps bridge the gap between the home and the school language. Selection and promotion of national language are considered essential because the access language (1) serves as one of the main unifying factors in the national integration, (2) becomes the means and symbol of national identity and pride, and (3) serves as a competent medium for interethnic communication.

India's educational policy seeks to maintain national unity through its acceptance of linguistic diversity. With the acceptance of the principle of unity within diversity, educational planners have started looking at the problem of relative focus on language as a subject and medium of instruction in the wider context of a child's stages of socialization and an institution's levels of education. Scholars, for example, have visualized three forms of socialization: *primary*, the process wherein children learn to adapt to family and community roles in primary group contexts; *secondary*, the process through which children learn to be members of their larger community; and *tertiary*, the process whereby learners develop operational and professional skills (Singleton, 1973). Similarly, the Report of the Education Commission (1964–66) proposes three levels of education: Level I, which includes preschool and primary education, Level II, which includes lower and higher secondary school, and Level III which includes graduate education, professional degrees, and higher research.

The Three Language Formula was first devised for India's school education by the Central Advisory Board of Education in 1956 and was subsequently modified by the Conference of Chief Ministers in 1961. It is based on three factors: (1) recognition of the right of ethnic minorities to get educational instruction through their MT; (2) promotion of the state official language as a major regional language for bringing the different ethnic groups of the region into the sociocultural mainstream; and (3) development of a pan-Indian official language of the union in order to integrate the country as a polity. The formula recognizes the following languages:

1. The regional language and the mother tongue where the MT is different from the regional language.
2. Hindi or, in Hindi-speaking areas, another Indian language.
3. English or any other modern European language.

Different surveys of the place of languages in the school curriculum (Chaturvedi and Mohale, 1976) and languages as media of instruction in Indian schools (Chaturvedi and Singh, 1981) show that the central government has been unable to ensure the faithful implementation of the formula. Apparently, each of the variables—planning, implementation, population, and situation—contributes in its own way to the failure of its effective realization. For example, a substantial cause of wastage and failure within the schools has been traced to the imparting of education in the early stages in languages other than the mother tongue (Goel and Saini, 1972; Pattanayak, 1981; Roy and Kapoor, 1975). However, several MTs of India neither have writing systems of their own, nor are they employed in the ecological setting in which writing is contextually appropriate. Because many MTs enjoy little prestige in the eyes of their users, no attempt has been made to bring them into the orbit of education. Hence, it is probably for this reason that out of 1,652 MTs or, say, out of 200 classified languages, only 67 languages are presently being employed as educational languages. Other factors responsible for the failure of the formula are: (1) ignorance regarding the nature and function of grass-roots societal bilingualism characteristic of the country, (2) neglect of both the structure and functional allocation of linguistic codes within the framework of India's educational policy, (3) nonavailability of a transfer model in education for a smooth switchover from minor ethnic languages to mainstream regional languages and from these nationality languages to national and international languages as educational languages, and (4) lack of seriousness about developing language pedagogy as a scientific discipline required for making a sound distinction between the functionality of L_1, L_2, and L_3 teaching.

Higher education is plagued by many internal contradictions. With regard to the place of languages in higher education, the following viewpoint is current: as the use of English as such divides the people into two nations—the few who dominate and the many who are dominated—the changeover in the medium of instruction from English to Indian languages has been necessary. The reality, on the other hand, directs us to believe that in the field of higher education English continues to be functionally a very potent language. The reasons advanced for retaining English in higher education are as follows: (1) English is a highly developed language best suited for India's industrial and scientific progress; (2) English is less divisive because of its neutral character; (3) English enables the educated Indian to move about inside and outside the country; (4) English brightens the students' prospects of getting prestigious jobs; and (5) English is still the language of administration (Srivastava and Gupta, 1982:15–16). For a detailed discussion of the topic, see Kachru (1978; 1983).

A statistical examination of the number of languages at the successive stages of education reveals that the higher one moves in education and the more one aspires to professional excellence, the smaller is the number of languages employed as the medium of instruction. This is so much the case that for technical training and scientific research English is the only medium throughout the country. Of a total of sixty-seven educational languages, fifty are used as media of instruction at the school stage; this number progressively decreases, with only twelve languages left at the graduate level of the teaching programs.

When studied from the above viewpoint, the multilingual educational setting seems to provide an excellent condition for bilingual education programs. Viewed from within, however, we find that most educational institutions at the school stage are monolingual in orientation. Almost all rural schools employ a vernacular medium, whereas prestigious schools situated in the urban areas are English medium right from the primary stage. Some schools have a bilingual orientation, but the goal of their bilingual programs is either transitional bilingualism (i.e., the use of learner's native language only during the first few years of primary education, and subsequent transfer to the use of either the major regional language or Hindi or English) or partial bilingual education (i.e., the use of native language in the domain of expressive culture like religion, culture, or literature, as subordinated to the use and development of skills in the second language usually meant to be employed in the domain of progressive culture). The case for a bilingual program that seeks to create full bilingualism is almost missing from the Indian scene. Moreover, India's educational orientation is such that it promotes the cause of one-way bilingual education as the program is generally addressed to minority language users who are encouraged to learn the language of the majority, and not vice versa. Bilingual education as a phenomenon exists on India's educational map simply because its ecological setting is multilingual and multicultural, and not because of any conscious planning or act.

As a result of the situation discussed above, the problem of language in education has to be viewed in a much wider perspective and with a more integrated structure than is found in India. It needs an integrated perspective that accepts language simultaneously as a means of cognition, as a tool of communication, and as an instrument of national development and integration. Apart from being the armory of the human mind (cognitive function) and vehicular function (communicative function), language is also a potentially unifying or disruptive force. An educational policy true to the social condition can organize language education as a key factor in the development of society and nation, which is the main function of education. In contrast, an unrealistic language policy can make education a subversive force that either denies a majority of people the opportunity of participation in transforming the society, or generates a constant source of conflict and tension. The sad part of the story of India is that in its policy formulation for education, it is strikingly silent about the role of language in education and, consequently, its role in the development of human resources.

BIBLIOGRAPHY

Andronov, M. S. 1964. "On the Typological Similarity of New Indo-Aryan and Dravidian." *Indian Linguistics* 25: 119–26.
———. 1970. *Dravidian Languages*. Trans. D. M. Segal. Moscow: Nauka.
Annamalai, E., ed. 1979. *Language Movements in India*. Mysore: Central Institute of Indian Languages.
Apte, M. L. 1962. "Linguistic Acculturation and Its Relation to Urbanization and Socioeconomic Factors." *Indian Linguistics* 23: 5–25.
———. 1974. "Pidginization of a Lingua-Franca: A Linguistic Analysis of Hindi-Urdu Spoken in Bombay." *International Journal of Dravidian Linguistics* 3: 21–41.
———. 1970. "Some Sociolinguistic Aspects of Inter-lingual Communication in India." *Anthropological Linguistics* 12: 63–83.
Baily, C-J. N. 1973. *Variations and Linguistics Theory*. Arlington, Va.: Center for Applied Linguistics.
Bendix, E. H. 1974. "Indo-Aryan and Tibeto-Burman Contact as Seen Through Nepali and Newari Verb Tenses." *International Journal of Dravidian Linguistics* 3: 42–59.
Bersten, M. 1975. "The Variant Model of Language: Some Data from a Study of Marathi Speech." *Indian Linguistics* 36: 227–33.
Bickerton, D. 1973. "The Nature of a Creole Continuum." *Language* 49: 640–69.
Bright, W. 1960. "A Study of Caste and Dialect in Mysore." *Indian Linguistics* 21: 44–50.
Chatterji, S. K. 1978. *Selected Writings*: Vol. 1. New Delhi: Vikas.
Chaturvedi, M. G., and B. V. Mohale. 1976. *Position of Languages in School Curriculum in India*. New Delhi: National Council of Educational Research and Training.
Chaturvedi, M. G., and S. Singh. 1981. *Languages and Media of Instruction in Indian Schools*. [Third all-India educational survey.] New Delhi: National Council of Educational Research and Training.
Das Gupta, J. 1970. *Language Conflict and National Development*. Berkeley: University of California Press.
DeCamp, D. 1971. "Toward a Generative Analysis of a Post-creole Speech Continuum." In *Pidginization and Creolization of Languages,* ed. D. H. Hymes. London: Cambridge University Press, pp. 349–70.

DeSilva, M.W.S. 1976. *Diglossia and Literacy*. Mysore: Central Institute of Indian Languages.

Dimock, E. C. 1960. "Literary and Colloquial Bengali in Modern Bengali Prose." In *Linguistic Diversity in South Asia: Studies in Regional, Social and Functional Variation*, ed. C. A. Ferguson and J. J. Gumperz. Bloomington: Indiana University Press, pp. 43–63.

Emeneau, Murry B. 1956. "India as a Linguistic Area." *Language* 32: 3–16.

———. 1962. "Bilingualism and Structural Borrowing." *Proceedings of the American Philosophical Society* 106: 430–42.

———. 1974. "The Indian Linguistic Area Revisited." In *Contact and Convergence in South Asian Languages*, ed. F. C. Southworth and M. L. Apte. [*International Journal of Dravidian Linguistics*: Special Volume] 3: 92–134.

Ferguson, C. A. 1968. "Language Development." In *Language Problems of Developing Nations*, ed. J. A. Fishman, C. A. Ferguson, and J. Das Gupta. New York: John Wiley, pp. 27–35.

Ferguson, C. A., and J. J. Gumperz, eds. 1960. *Linguistic Diversity in South Asia: Studies in Regional, Social and Function Variation*. Bloomington: Indiana University Press.

Fishman, J. A. 1969. "National Language and Language of Wider Communication in Developing Nations." *Anthropological Linguistics* 11: 3–35.

Fries, C. C., and K. L. Pike. 1949. "Coexistent Phonemic Systems." *Language* 25: 29–50.

Garvin, P. L. 1964. "The Standard Language Problem: Concepts and Methods." In *Language in Culture and Society*, ed. D. Hymes. New York: Harper and Row, pp. 521–23.

Goel, B. S., and S. K. Saini. 1972. *Mother Tongue and Equality of Opportunity in Education*. New Delhi: National Council of Educational Research and Training.

Government of India. 1964–66. *Report of the Education Commission* [Chairman: D. S. Kothari]. New Delhi: Manager of Publications.

Gumperz, J. J. 1961. "Speech Variation and the Study of Indian Civilization." *American Anthropologist* 63: 976–88.

———. 1964. "Hindi-Punjabi Code Switching in Delhi." In *Proceedings of the IX International Congress of Linguistics*, ed. H. Lunt. The Hague: Mouton, pp. 115–24.

Gumperz, J. J., and C. M. Naim. 1960. "Formal and Informal Standards in the Hindi Regional Language Area." In *Linguistic Diversity in South Asia: Studies in Regional, Social and Functional Variation*, ed. C. A. Ferguson and J. J. Gumperz. Bloomington: Indiana University Press, pp. 92–118.

Gumperz, J. J., and R. Wilson. 1971. "Convergence and Creolization: A Case from the Indo-Aryan/Dravidian Border in India." In *Pidginization and Creolization of Languages*, ed. D. Hymes. London: Cambridge University Press, pp. 151–67.

Haugen, E. 1979. "Language Ecology and the Case of Faroese." In *Language and Literary Studies in Honor of A. A. Hill*, ed. M. A. Jazayery, E. C. Polomé, and W. Winter. Vol. 4. The Hague: Mouton.

Hock, H. H. 1975. "Substratum Influence on (Rig-Vedic) Sanskrit?" *Studies in the Linguistic Sciences* 5: 76–125.

———. 1984. "(Pre-) Rig-Vedic Convergence of Indo-Aryan with Dravidian? Another Look at the Evidence." *Studies in the Linguistic Sciences* 14: 89–107.

India Literacy Atlas. 1978. Mysore: Central Institute of Indian Languages.

Jernudd, B. H., and J. Das Gupta. 1971. "Towards a Theory of Language Planning." In *Can Language Be Planned? Sociolinguistic Theory and Practice for Developing Nations,* ed. J. Rubin and B. Jernudd. Honolulu: University Press of Hawaii, pp. 195–215.

Kachru, B. B. 1978. "English in South Asia." In *Advances in the Study of Societal Multi-Lingualism,* ed. J. A. Fishman. The Hague: Mouton, pp. 477–551.

———. 1983. *The Indianization of English: The English Language in India.* Delhi: Oxford University Press.

Kamath, V. B. 1966. *Linguistic Vivisection of India: Why not stop it still?* Bombay: Bharatiya Vidya Bhawan.

Khubchandani, L.M. 1978. "Distribution of Contact Languages in India: A Study of the 1961 Bilingualism Returns." *Advances in the Study of Societal Multilingualism,* ed. J. A. Fishman. The Hague: Mouton, pp. 553-585

———. 1983. *Plural Languages, Plural Cultures.* East-West Center:University of Hawaii Press.

Krishnamurti, Bh. 1978. "Problems of Language Standardization in India." *Language and Society,* ed. W. McCormack and S. A. Wurm. The Hague: Mouton, pp. 673–692.

Krishnamurti, Bh. and A. Mukherjee, eds. 1984. *Modernization of Indian Languages in News Media.* Hyderabad: Osmania University.

Kuiper, F. B. J. 1967. "The Genesis of a Linguistic Area." *Indo-Iranian Journal* 10, 81–102.

LePage, R. B. "Problems of Description in Multilingual Communities." *Transactions of the Philological Society,* pp. 189–212.

McCormack, W. 1960. "Social Dialects in Dharwar Kannada." *Linguistic Diversity in South Asia: Studies in Regional, Social and Functional Variation,* ed. C. A. Ferguson and J. J. Gumperz. Bloomington: Indiana University Press, pp. 79–81.

Mitra, A. 1964. *Census of India—1961.* Vol. 1. Delhi: Government of India.

Mukherjee, A. 1980. Language maintenance and language shift among Punjabis and Bengalis in Delhi: A sociolinguistic perspective. (Ph.D. dissertation, Delhi University).

Pandit, P. B. 1972. *India as a Sociolinguistic Area.* Poona: University of Poona.

Pattanayak, D. P. 1981. *Multilingualism and Mother-Tongue Education.* Delhi: Oxford University Press.

Paulston, C. B. 1978. "Education in a Bi/Multilingual Setting." *International Review of Education* 3: 309–28.

Roy, P., and J. M. Kapoor. 1975. *The Retention of Literacy.* Delhi: Macmillan Co.

Sah, P. P. 1978. "Literacy, Language Use and Modes of Thought." *Language Forum* 4: 31–44.

Shanmugam Pillai, M. 1960. "Tamil—Literary and Colloquial." In *Linguistic Diversity in South Asia: Studies in Regional, Social and Functional Variation,* ed. C. A. Ferguson and J. J. Gumperz. Bloomington: Indiana University Press, pp. 79–81.

Shapiro, M. C., and H. F. Schiffman. 1981. *Language and Society in South-Asia.* Delhi: Motilal Banarsidas.

Shreedhar, M. V. 1976. "Standardization of Naga-pidgin." *Anthropological Linguistics* 18: 371–79.

Singleton, J. 1973. "Cross-cultural Approaches to Research on Minority Group Education." *Anthropology and Language Science in Educational Development*. [Educational Studies and Documents, No. 11.] Paris: UNESCO, pp. 17–21.

Sjoberg, A. F. 1962. "Coexistent Phonemic Systems in Telugu: A Sociocultural Perspective." *Word* 18: 269–79.

Southworth, F. C. 1979. "Lexical Evidence for Early Contacts Between Indo-Aryan and Dravidian." In *Aryan and Non-Aryan in India,* ed. M. Deshpande and P. Hook. Ann Arbor, Mich.: Center for South and Southeast Asian Studies, pp. 191–233.

―――. 1985. "The Social Context of Language Standardization in India." In *Language of Equality,* ed. N. Wolfson and J. Manes. Berlin: Mouton, pp. 225–39.

Southworth, F. C., and M. L. Apte, eds. 1974. *Contact and Convergence in South Asian Languages*. [Special volume of *International Journal of Dravidian Linguistics*] 3, pp. 1–20.

Sridhar, S. N. 1975. "Linguistic Convergence: Indo-Aryanization of Dravidian Languages." *Studies in the Linguistic Sciences* 8: 197–215.

Srivastava, R. N. 1969. Review of A. R. Kelkar, *Studies in Hindi and Urdu* [Poona: Deccan College] *Language* 45: 913–27.

―――. 1977. "Indian Bilingualism: Myth and Reality." In *Indian Bilingualism,* ed. P. Gopal Sharma and S. Kumar. Agra: Central Institute of Hindi, pp. 57–87.

―――. 1980a. *Language Teaching in a Bi- or Pluri-lingual and Multicultural Environment* (Academic Report). Paris: UNESCO.

―――. 1980b. "Societal Bilingualism and Problems in Organizing Language Teaching in India." *Indian Journal of Applied Linguistics* 6: 13–37.

―――. 1984a. "Literacy Education for Minorities: A Case Study from India." In *Linguistic Minorities and Literacy,* ed. F. Coulmas. Berlin: Mouton, pp. 39–46.

―――. 1984b. "Linguistic Minorities and National Languages." In *Linguistic Minorities and Literacy,* ed. F. Coulmas. Berlin: Mouton, pp. 98–114.

―――. 1984c. "Consequences of Initiating Literacy in the Second Language." In *Linguistic Minorities and Literacy,* ed. F. Coulmas. Berlin: Mouton, pp. 29–37.

―――. 1984d. "Literacy in South Asia." *Annual Review of Applied Linguistics* (1982–83) 4: 93–110.

Srivastava, R. N., et al. 1978. *Evaluating Communicability in Village Settings*." Delhi: Delhi University [2 parts].

Srivastava, R. N., and R. S. Gupta. 1982. "Media of Instruction in Higher Education in India." *Indian Journal of Applied Linguistics* 8: 1–22.

Srivastava, R. N., and A. Kalra. 1984. "Modernization of Hindi in News Media." In *Modernization of Indian Languages in News Media,* ed. Bh. Krishnamurti and A. Mukherjee. Hyderabad: Osmania University, pp. 41–53.

Appendix 12.1

Major Language Profile (Source: Census 1961; based on Apte, 1970, and Khub-chandani, 1972)

Major languages	Native (MT) Speakers (in millions)	Native (MT) ratio/1000 to total population	Contact (Speaker) (in thousands)	Contact ratio/1000 among non-native population	Native Contact ratio/1000 (3+5)	Name of first three contact languages	Number of Speakers (of 7) in thousand
1	2	3	4	5	6	7	8
Hindi	129.2	294	9.363	50	324	English Urdu Punjabi	3,315 783 415
Telugu	37.7	86	3.279	8	94	Tamil Kannada English	2,328 1,056 855
Bengali	33.9	77	1.907	5	82	English Hindi Assamese	1,563 615 557
Marathi	33.3	76	2,724	7	83	Hindi English Kannada	2,018 528 474
Tamil	30.6	70	3,759	9	79	English Telugu Kannada	1,252 583 285
Urdu	23.4	53	2,006	5	58	Telugu Hindi Kannada	1,036 1,021 831
Gujarati	20.3	46	558	1	47	Hindi English Marathi	774 424 146

Major languages	Native (MT) Speakers (in millions)	Native (MT) ratio/1000 to total population	Contact (Speaker) (in thousands)	Contact ratio/1000 among non-native population	Native Contact ratio/1000 (3+5)	Name of first three contact languages	Number of Speakers (of 7) in thousand
1	2	3	4	5	6	7	8
Kannada	70.4	40	3,551	9	49	Telugu Tamil Marathi	775 563 460
Malyalam	17.0	39	218	0.5	39	English Tamil Hindi	762 168 81
Oriya	15.7	35	1,075	3	38	Hindi English Telugu	252 209 245
Punjabi	11.0	25	465	1	26	Hindi English Urdu	726 402 235
Assamese	6.8	16	1,649	4	20	Bengali English Hindi	236 158 150
Kashmiri	2.0	5	25	0.1	5	Urdu Hindi English	158 15 8
Sanskrit	25 (thousand)	-	149	0.5	-	-	-
English	224 (thousand)	-	10,915	27	-	-	-
INDIA	439.2	...	42,536	97	...	...	...

Appendix 12.2

**Language Profile of Indian by State (Source: Census 1971; based on India Literacy
Atlas 1978)**

S.No.	State/Union Territory	Capital	Population	Three numerically most important languages
1	2	3	4	5
	INDIA	Delhi	548,159,652	
	STATES			
1.	Andhra Pradesh	Hyderabad	43,502,708	1. Telugu - 85.37 2. Urdu - 7.59 3. Hindi - 2.28
2.	Assam	Dispur	14,625,152	1. Assamese - 59.54 2. Bengali - 19.44 3. Hindi - 5.34
3.	Bihar	Patna	56,353,369	1. Hindi - 79.77 2. Urdu - 8.86 3. Bengali- 3.46
4.	Gujarat	Gandhinagar	26,697,475	1. Gujarati - 89.39 2. Bhili/Bhilodi - 2.83 3. Sindhi - 2.28
5.	Haryana	Chandigarh	10,036,808	1. Hindi - 89.42 2. Panjabi- 8.34 3. Urdu - 1.95
6.	Himachal Pradesh	Simla	3,460,434	1. Hindi - 86.87 2. Panjabi - 4.75 3. Dogri - 3.57
7.	Jammu & Kashmir	Srinagar	4,616,632	1. Kashmiri - 53.14 2. Dogri - 24.68 3. Hindi - 15.06

1	2	3	4	5		
8.	Kerala	Trivendrum	21,347,375	1. Malayalam	–	96.02
				2. Tamil	–	2.37
				3. Konkani	–	0.38
9.	Madhya Pradesh	Bhopal	41,654,119	1. Hindi/	–	83.03
				2. Bhili/	–	3.12
				Bhilodi		
				3. Gondi	–	2.87
10.	Maharashtra	Bombay	50,412,235	1. Marathi	–	76.61
				2. Urdu	–	7.26
				3. Hindi	–	5.02
11.	Manipur	Imphal	1,072,753	1. Manipuri/	–	63.24
				2. Meithei		
				2. Tangkhul	–	5.37
				3. Kabui	–	4.06
12.	Meghalaya	Shillong	1,011,699	1. Khasio	–	45.18
				2. Garo	–	32.48
				3. Bengali	–	9.29
13.	Mysore (Karnataka)	Bangalore	29,299,014	1. Kannada	–	65.97
				2. Urdu	–	9.0
				3. Telugu	–	8.18
14.	Nagaland	Kohima	516,449	1. Ao	–	14.26
				2. Konyak	–	14.01
				3. Angami	–	13.22
15.	Orissa	Bhubaneswar	21,944,615	1. Oriya	–	84.15
				2. Telugu	–	2.28
				3. Santali	–	1.72
16.	Panjabi	Chandigarh	13,551,060	1. Panjabi	–	79.49
				2. Hindin	–	20.01
				3. Urdu	–	0.21

1	2	3	4	5		
17.	Rajasthan	Jaipur	25,765,806	1. Hindi	–	91.13
				2. Bhili/	–	3.25
				Bhilodi	–	
				3. Urdu	–	0.21
18.	Sikkim	Gangtok	209,843	1. Gorkhali/	–	63.97
				Nepali		
				2. Lepcha	–	10.63
				3. Sikkim	–	5.19
				Bhotia		
19.	Tamil Nadu	Madras	41,199,168	1. Tamil	–	84.51
				2. Telugu	–	8.75
				3. Kannada	–	2.56
20.	Tripura	Agartala	1,556,342	1. Bengali	–	68.79
				2. Tripuri	–	22.72
				3. Hindi	–	1.48
21.	Uttar Pradesh	Lucknow	88,341,144	1. Hindi	–	88.54
				2. Urdu	–	10.5
				3. Panjabi	–	0.57
22.	West Bengal	Calcutta	44,312,011	1. Bengali	–	85.52
				2. Hindi	–	6.13
				3. Santali	–	3.18
	UNION TERRITORIES					
1.	Andaman & Nicobar Islands	Port Blair	115,133	1. Bengali	–	24.12
				2. Hindi	–	16.07
				3. Nicobarese	–	15.06
2.	Arunachal Pradesh	Itanagar	467,511	1. Nissi/	–	24.4
				Dafla		
				2. Adi	–	21.06
				3. Gorkhali	–	6.61
				Nepali		

1	2	3	4	5
3.	Chandigarh	Chandigarh	257,251	1. Hindi - 55.96 2. Panjabi - 40.67 3. Urdu - 0.66
4.	Dadra & Nagar Haveli	Silvassa	74,170	1. Bhili/ - 83.01 Bhilodi 2. Gujarati- 12.07 3. Marathi - 2.29
5.	Delhi	Delhi	4,065,698	1. Hindi - 75.97 2. Panjabi - 13.04 3. Urdu - 5.68
6.	Goa, Daman & Diu	Panaji	857,771	1. Konkani - 64.87 2. Marathi - 19.71 3. Gujarati- 7.07
7	Laccadive, Minicoy & Amindivi Islands (Lakshadeep)	Kavaratti	31,810	1. Malayalam - 83.9 2. Tamil - 0.36 3. Hindi - 0.19
*8.	Mizoram	Aizawal	332,390	
9.	Pondicherry	Pondicherry	471,707	1. Tamil - 89.0 2. Malayalam- 5.43 3. Telugu - 3.69

*Figures for Assam include those of Mizoram also.

13   *Moshe Nahir*

LANGUAGE PLANNING AND LANGUAGE ACQUISITION: THE "GREAT LEAP" IN THE HEBREW REVIVAL

The revival of Hebrew as a vernacular and a standard language, an unprecedented sociolinguistic phenomenon, completed as it was in less than a generation (approximately 1890–1916) and described at times as "miraculous," has drawn the attention of writers and scholars for decades. Language planning practitioners and theoreticians and linguists in the field of second-language acquisition have shown interest in it since it is expected that understanding the processes involved may be beneficial in explaining the failure of past similar experiments and the prospect of success, not only in language planning and attempts at language revival, language spread, and language reform (Nahir, 1984), but also in applied linguistics, particularly second-language acquisition and bilingual education.

Perhaps because of the Hebrew revival in Palestine at the turn of the century, much of the relevant literature has been popular, emotionally oriented, or even romanticized (e.g., St. John, 1952; Tur-Sinai, 1960). Literatures associated with similar struggles, political or other, often feature a tendency to romanticize the respective movement and its achievements as well as myths and legends focusing on the heroic leader(s). The Hebrew revival movement is no exception. Its initiation and success have for decades been almost exclusively attributed to or identified with Eliezer Ben-Yehuda and his Hebrew Language Committee (later Academy). While he undoubtedly had an important role in the movement as a visionary and a prophetic voice and a codifier of modern Hebrew, it has been recently recognized that not only could such an accomplishment not be performed by a single individual but the revival was a collective effort carried out mostly by a group with which he had little contact, viz., the school teachers in the rural Jewish communities ("settlements") of Palestine. Several significant relevant facts have been brought out: (1) In 1914, when the revival was virtually completed in the country generally (i.e., in both the urban and rural regions), only 4 percent of the population spoke Hebrew in Jerusalem, where Ben-Yehuda and his committee were located and which was their center of activity (on the 1914 census, see Bachi, 1956; the ratio was similar, incidentally, in most other urban areas). (2) The committee was altogether inactive during the revival's most critical period, between 1891 and 1904. Therefore, it could have little or no role in the process.

This study seeks to explain the Great Leap in the revival of Hebrew.[1] Specifically, it focuses on how, within one generation, the shift took place from the use of Yiddish, which was almost universally spoken in rural Palestine, and of numerous other languages spoken in its urban regions, into Hebrew.

Several attempts have been made to discover what made the revival possible. Among these, "the will of the people" has been frequently mentioned as the sole or major factor. According to Karl W. Deutsch (1942), for example, the Hebrew revival (which he erroneously equates with language planning in Norway and Ireland; see Nahir, 1978a:99) resulted from "an act of the political will." Furthermore, he asserts that now "it is possible to revive . . . any ancient language sufficiently known to history, if it should so suit any group's desire for separate identity" (Deutsch, 1942:604). The historical evidence, however, does not support this optimism: political will was abundant in most past attempts at linguistic revival, yet all but Hebrew have virtually failed (Haugen, 1966), including that of Irish, one of Deutsch's own examples.

CONDITIONS AND FACTORS IN LINGUISTIC REVIVAL

Language (or speech) revival has been defined as "the attempt to turn a language with few or no surviving native speakers back into a normal means of communication in a community" (Nahir, 1984:30).[2] A distinction has been made between "conditions" for and "factors" in the success of speech revival (Nahir, 1977b, 1978a). Two conditions have been identified: (1) *Need,* that is, the existence of a sociolinguistic situation, usually some type of multilingualism, in which a community has no common speech and, therefore, lacks a means of communication. This situation usually presupposes a chain of historical events that have brought together people of different linguistic backgrounds. (2) *Code,* that is, the availability of a revivable language—a written language for speech revival, or an old, "dead," historical, or even artificial language for other forms of language revival—to resort to and revive.

Although these conditions are prerequisites for linguistic revival, several factors may, to varying degrees and in various combinations, contribute or even be crucial to a revival's success. The existence of one or more factors, particularly if powerful, may at times even substitute for "need" as a condition when it is missing or if only a partial state of multilingualism exists. It will be seen further, for example, that one of the factors affecting the Hebrew revival was the attitude of Palestine's Jewish community to the Hebrew language which derived from their attitude to the national-revival movement. This factor was so powerful that it compensated for a partial absence of "need": Yiddish, the Jewish language imported from Eastern Europe, was almost generally spoken in the rural "settlements," and yet, as above, it was there that the revival occurred first. Finally, there is a major distinction between "conditions" and "factors": the *conditions* must be met prior to a linguistic revival, while the respective *factors* can contribute to its success, as they have in the case of Hebrew. When conditions have been met, different revival attempts may be affected by either the same *or* different factors, in various degrees and combinations.

SOCIOCULTURAL FACTORS IN THE HEBREW REVIVAL

The uniqueness of the Hebrew revival and the effectiveness of the status planning that brought it about were overwhelmingly due to the background that existed in Palestine during and even prior to the relevant period. A recent study (Nahir, 1983) has listed and investigated the three major sociolinguistic and sociocultural factors at work, viz., the communicative factor, the national-political factor, and the religio-educational factor.

The Communicative Factor

As noted briefly above, linguistic needs are now viewed as crucial for success in language planning in general and language spread and acquisition in particular (e.g., Haugen, 1966; Rubin, 1971; Nahir, 1984; and Paulston this volume). Similarly, observation of the historical examples indicates that a critical condition for the successful revival or restoration of a vernacular is the community's need for a means of communication. Such a need presupposes, however, a historical chain of events, albeit unfortunate, that has brought together people who share their past and have similar cultural, economic, or other objectives, but different linguistic backgrounds. Palestine's Jews in the late nineteenth century were the only such case on record. Furthermore, this community was in possession of an old, historical language, Hebrew, still in use in written form, which it could now attempt to revive and use in spoken form as well. In all other known revival attempts a communicative need did not exist, as the respective communities had a common "new" language, such as English in Ireland (Macnamara, 1971). The languages to be revived were usually intended to be used only as second languages, with bilingualism the ideal. Thus, speech revival can only succeed if the prospective language is to fill a communicative vacuum.

Such a communicative vacuum prevailed at least in the urban sections of Palestine's Jewish community. A unique historical progression, begun when the Romans exiled the largely Hebrew-speaking Jews from Palestine in the first and second centuries C.E., ended toward the close of the nineteenth century with the advent of the Jewish national movement and resettlement in Palestine. The latter were motivated by a combination of developments—widespread persecutions and programs directed against many Eastern European Jewish communities, the rise of nationalism in Europe, and calls by a growing number of contemporary literary and other European Jewish leaders for a return to the ancient homeland—and culminated in 1893 in the establishment of the political Zionist movement and the beginning of significant Jewish immigration to Palestine. This resulted in turn in an acute state of societal multilingualism. Originating mostly from several Eastern European countries, immigrants could not communicate with other immigrants who spoke different languages or with the small local Jewish population itself consisting, linguistically and to some extent culturally, of scores of subgroups. When Eliezer Ben-Yehuda, a leader of the revival, arrived in Palestine in 1882, he found that its thirty thousand Jews "were not a community united by their language. This was truly a Babel Generation, each group [speaking] in the language of the country it had come from" (Ben-Yehuda, 1917/18:95).[3] When the Hebrew Language Committee, the first Hebrew-language planning agency, was formed in 1890, one of its major objectives was "to clear from the Jews living in the Land of Israel the jargons, Ashkenazic, Cephardic, etc., that . . . make them behave as if they belonged to different nations. . . . And these jabbers . . . bring about hatred, jealousy and resentment among the various [Jewish] communities" (*Collection of Documents*, 1970:20). According to another contemporary source, "there was no common language in Jerusalem. . . . The Sephardics . . . spoke Judeo-Spanish. . . . The Musta'arabin (local Jews) spoke Palestinian Arabic, the Maghrebines (North African Jews) spoke Arabic in the North African dialect, the Caucasians spoke Georgian, the Crimeans spoke Tatar and the Ashkenazics . . . spoke different dialects of Yiddish" (Peres, 1964:19).

Even in the more linguistically homogeneous rural villages usually referred to as "the settlements" a visiting educator found that "the jargon was still predominant, and wherever I went I heard children speak mostly [foreign] languages at home and in the streets" (Zuta, 1929:114).[4] Still, the state of multilingualism that prevailed in the settlements was not as severe as in the urban centers, since they consisted of Eastern European immigrants, most of whom spoke Yiddish (usually in addition to Russian, Ukrainian, Polish, etc.). Yet, at least in the Jewish community at large, linguistic fragmentation posed a serious problem. The communicative factor is thus clearly evident throughout, yet its impact is seen to have been by and large the most powerful in the urban center. In the settlements, on the other hand, it was largely the national-political factor that prevailed in the entire period.

Finally, it ought to be noted that Yiddish, spoken by most settlers, or even Arabic, French, or German, spoken by other, smaller, groups, could have been selected for adoption and spread. Owing to the other existing factors, however, Hebrew was the preferred choice.

The National-Political Factor

An increasing number of case studies in recent decades has resulted in the recognition that national-political feelings and aspirations can constitute a powerful motivator in linguistic behavior and language planning (e.g., Heyd, 1954; Haugen, 1966; Fishman, 1971; Bourhis, 1984). The case of Hebrew is no exception. In Palestine's agricultural "settlements," comprising as they did a substantial part of the country's Jewish population, the national-political factor probably played the most important role as background to the transition into Hebrew from the dominant Yiddish. It was also the most crucial factor in the "code-selection" process, in which Yiddish, the vernacular spoken by most settlers, and Hebrew, the ancient language of the Bible, used in written form for two millennia, were the only two serious contenders. It is instructive, therefore, to compare current attitudes to both languages by members and leaders of the community as well as by some influential intellectuals.

Many early immigrants-settlers strongly resented the need to use Yiddish, since it constituted a constant reminder of their people's prolonged exile and persecution in the "diaspora" and of their own life previously in pogrom-ridden Eastern Europe, with its abuse, suffering, and misery. At the same time, Yiddish was considered even by contemporary educators as a "vulgar" language, "unfit for use in the schools as a vehicle for matters of science" (Azaryahu, 1929:62). This attitude may at least partly explain the results of a sociolinguistic study carried out decades later in Israel which found Yiddish to be undesirable and "derided as a symbol of the unpleasing aspects of a diaspora existence" (Herman, 1968:499).

On the other hand, the case for Hebrew as the Jews' literary and national language, in spite of the widespread use of Yiddish as a vernacular by Eastern Europe's Jewry, had many advocates. It was led by Asher Ginzberg (better known by his pseudonym Aḥad-Ha'am), a prominent essayist and a highly influential exponent and theoretician of Jewish nationalism. For him, Yiddish was merely a "Jewish-German Jargon, spoken by our people in the northern countries for several centuries [but] no more significant for them than the other exile-languages, using it . . . only when compelled to, for the sake of those unlettered in Hebrew" (Aḥad-Ha'am, 1903:1979). Hebrew, on the other hand, was for the Jewish people its national language, in which "it had created a great, respectable literature . . . and in which it had realized the full scope of its national spirit [since] the threshold of history. . . . Its place in the depths of our spirit has not been, and never will be taken over by any other language. . . . This language alone has been and will ever be our national language" (Aḥad-Ha'am, 1903:179f.). In another major essay, "A Conflict of Languages," Aḥad-Ha'am passionately asserts that "a nation is only one that has a national capital', a [language] accumulated from one generation to the next, which serves as a basis for its national life" (Aḥad Ha'am, 1910:406).

Aḥad-Ha'am's views on the national and political role of Hebrew clarify several aspects of the revival: (1) They explain the motivation to preserve and maintain written Hebrew for two millennia. The rise in European nationalism and the decline in Jewish religious practice in recent centuries led many to substitute the maintenance of Hebrew for Jewish nationalism, which also explains the exclusive use of biblical Hebrew by pre-revival "secular" writers and rejection of varieties developed after the Jews' exile from Palestine by the Romans. (2) They explain the motivation behind the choice of Hebrew as the language to be revived both as a national language and as a vernacular. (3) They demonstrate the national-political-linguistic attitudes at work as a factor during the revival itself. Aḥad-Ha'am's contribution to it was most crucial, however, in that, highly esteemed and influential as he was, his views had a profound impact on Palestine's Jewish intelligentsia and educators, who were in the forefront of its implementation. His writings thus accelerated the process considerably.

While Aḥad-Ha'am, who still lived in Europe through most of this period, was the foremost proponent of the preservation of Hebrew as a national language, most of the drive to use it as vernacular was carried out in Palestine's Jewish community by local leaders and intellectuals who viewed a linguistic revival as a crucial condition for national revival in the ancient homeland. One of the first of these leaders was Eliezer Ben-Yehuda, a visionary and the first codifier of modern Hebrew, who insisted on the indivisibility between renewed Jewish nationhood and the Hebrew language: "If I did not believe in the redemption of the Jewish people, I would have no use for the Hebrew language. . . . Let us revive the nation, and its language will live too! . . . Such a miracle is not impossible for it to accomplish." (Ben-Yehuda was still confident that "this great miracle . . . was due to the idea of [our] national revival in the land of the fathers" (1918:233). Similarly, a contemporary educator recalled that the combination of the national and the linguistic revivals was "greatly instrumental in bringing our dispersed people closer and mending the pieces of our nation in our gathering of the exiles and tongues" (Azaryahu, 1929:57).

Finally, it should be noted that the national-political factor prevailed more intensely in the settlements consisting as they did of recent immigrants whose very move to Palestine was motivated by national considerations and for whom national revival without a concurrent linguistic revival was inconceivable. The intensity of national-sociolinguistic attitudes in the community at large may be seen as a continuum between the general urban population at one extreme and the rural school system (see next section), where the intensity was the greatest, at the other, with the diverse urban school systems and the rural populations floating between the poles. As will be seen in the next section, a direct correlation existed: where the national-political factor was more intense, the implementation process was most effective.

The Religio-Educational Factor

Compared with languages that have survived in written form and been used by small elite groups (e.g., Latin) and "dead" languages (e.g., Hittite, Akkadian), we may designate pre-revival Hebrew as a "living written language." For two millennia, since its demise as a vernacular, it was uninterruptedly used in writing religious, liturgical, philosophical, and other works by a long line of authors, sages, scribes, rabbis, philosophers, spiritual and communal leaders, liturgical poets, and, in recent centuries, "secular" poets and novelists. The large number of both authors and readers, an enduring reality throughout Jewish history, stemmed from the fact that virtually all males had a considerable knowledge of written Hebrew. This, in turn, was the result of a fundamental cornerstone of Jewish law which required that all males participate in daily services and regularly study the Bible and the Talmud, and at least some of their numerous interpretations. With the exception of the Aramaic parts of the Talmud, these were all written in Hebrew. Thus, the study, passive knowledge, and regular use of written Hebrew constituted a major integral component of all males' education and way of life (see Rabin, 1976).

Despite a sizable departure from religious observance in recent centuries, the European Jews' knowledge of Hebrew was not affected substantially. The rejection of religion usually resulted from or was accompanied by the adoption of Jewish "enlightenment" or, in the late nineteenth century, secular Jewish nationalism. Both developments, often occurring within the same groups, encouraged the study of Hebrew and its adoption, now as a national language and a symbol of Jewish national aspirations (see Pelli, 1981). Furthermore, the rejection of religion usually took place when individuals had reached adulthood and had completed their formal, almost universally religious education. This is evident in the biographies and autobiographies of Palestine's early leaders, virtually all of whom were well versed in Hebrew language and religious and secular literature. Finally, throughout the Jewish exile an important byproduct of general literacy in Hebrew and its "living written language" status was its general use as a lingua franca among Jews. Most, if not all, of Palestine's Jewish males were thus well prepared linguistically for the acquisition of Hebrew in spoken form too. This, too, accelerated the process considerably.

THE GREAT LEAP: FOUR COMPONENTS IN THE TRANSITION TO HEBREW

Identification of the three factors at work during the revival—the communicative, the national-political, and the religio-educational factors—is crucial not only for an understanding of the revival itself, but also for drawing from it any possible generalizations relevant to both language planning and large-scale second-language acquisition. In itself, however, it does not fully explain the great leap, or the actual transition of Hebrew from a status of a written language to that of a native and only or major vernacular of the largest single segment of the community. The critical question then still remains, namely, how the selection of Hebrew as the language to be revived was actually implemented, or how Hebrew was nativized. This question is particularly intriguing since, as noted earlier, Yiddish as a native language was almost universally spoken in the settlements, while it was there where the revival, or the transition, was fastest and most effective (Bachi, 1956).

With few exceptions (e.g., Bar-Adon, 1977), this question has hardly been given the attention it deserves, possibly because of the revival's unprecedented nature or because the transition involved seemingly insignificant local activities, with little or no success immediately noticed and with almost no centralized coordination, all resulting in scanty first-hand contemporary documentation.

Researchers of other language revival attempts (e.g., in Irish, Cornish, and Welsh) have found that, as a rule, despite the authorities' persuasion or rulings, people will speak either their native language or whichever other language will help them to meet their communicative needs most effectively. In the final analysis, "it is the population-at-large who decide the fate of a language" (Edwards, 1977:100; cf. Macnamara, 1966, 1971; Green, 1966; James, 1977) probably because, as in all behavior, immediate reward and reinforcement are critical for communication as well. In rural Jewish Palestine prior to the revival, Yiddish would promise such a reward. There had to exist, therefore, an extremely unique situation that would constitute an exception to this behavior principle in which, more specifically, native speakers of Yiddish would speak Hebrew. It will be seen that such an exceptional situation indeed prevailed in Palestine's Jewish community in this period.

Recent studies (e.g., Fellman, 1973; Haramati, 1979) have asserted that the revival was carried out by "the schools" rather than by Ben-Yehuda, the "father of the revival" and his associates in the Hebrew Language Committee who have been traditionally credited and identified with it by oral folklore and even by writers and scholars (e.g., St. John, 1952; Tur-Sinai, 1960). Recognizing the schools' role, however, still provides only a partial account of the process. Even the most effective, successful teaching methodology or school, including the recently popular language immersion programs, will produce bilinguals at best. Because of the above behavior principle, even under ideal conditions the education system alone cannot replace its students' native language with another and has never done so. Though crucial to the revival process, Jewish Palestine's schools were no exception.

In one of the few studies dealing with the process of the actual nativization of Hebrew, Bar-Adon (1977) attributed it to "the children" and their language: "*By definition, only children* could, as they indeed did, carry out the very process of *nativization* in Modern Hebrew from its inception. This process resulted in a *native linguistic competence,* not possessed by any adult before them" (1977:489; Bar-Adon's emphasis). As in the process involved in the nativization of creolized languages, Hebrew became the community's major native language only after the first generation of children had been "born into it" and spoke it as its first language. Bar-Adon suggests the notion of "mini-generations" for children, "somewhat like a 'school year'," including partially overlapping generations of siblings and peers, to explain the intensity of the process and its completion within two or three decades. Though valid and interesting, this thesis still fails to explain *why* the "mini-generations" of children would speak Hebrew, even though their native language and that of the rest of the community was Yiddish.

Nor does it explain what caused the linguistic behavior of the children seemingly to contradict a basic behavior principle in speaking a nonnative language which was not expected to result in a direct, immediate reward in the form of effective communication with their interlocutors. The following will attempt to answer this question and will propose a schematic framework to explicate the process.

The transition from Yiddish into Hebrew, begun and by and large carried out in the "settlements" from which it spread to the rest of the community, seems to have involved, a process of implementation that consisted of a series of four steps or components: (1) The community's children are instilled with desired linguistic attitudes, (2) the children are presented with and acquire the linguistic model, Hebrew, (3) the children speak and transfer Hebrew as a second language out of the schools, and (4) the newly born receive and speak Hebrew as a first language. These steps, viewed here schematically, often overlapped. Furthermore, they involved activities that were not necessarily consciously aiming at achieving the revival of Hebrew.

The First Component: The Community Children Are Instilled With Desired Linguistic Attitudes.

Intensely favorable attitudes to the Hebrew language were an integral ingredient of the Jewish national revival, as is evident in numerous contemporary reports and literary works (e.g., Ben-Yehuda, 1881, 1918; Ravnitsky, 1989; Yudelovitz, 1929). In his report on the proceedings of the first conference of the Palestine Hebrew Teachers Association, for example, Yudelovitz records a call by Israel Belkind, a leading early settler, to students everywhere to study Hebrew "with all their vigor, and cause it to be spoken by the entire new generation so that it will then be spoken throughout [the country]" (Yudelovitz, 1929, p. 94).

In the absence of any political power and with little or no impact on their collective destiny, the settlers viewed a linguistic revival as the one area completely under their own control and consequently a major channel into which their national aspirations could be directed. Therefore, the linguistic revival was generally conceived of as a condition and a temporary substitute for national, if not political, revival. If the language of the Bible, spoken by their forefathers in their ancient free and independent homeland and used in written form by generations, could only be spoken again as a fully legitimate national language, a major battle, both real and symbolic, would be won in the struggle for national revival. Thus, the strength of the linguistic attitude toward Hebrew in late-nineteenth-century Jewish Palestine cannot be overemphasized.

Such attitudes among the settlers, one of the factors in the background to the language revival, eventually found their way into the schools in which, according to contemporary reports, the prestige of Yiddish vis-à-vis Hebrew was very low indeed. In his memoirs, a contemporary student recalled, for example, how even as early as 1891, when the process was just making its debut, he discovered the comparative status of the two languages: "[The Teacher] announced in the very first session, 'Hebrew in Hebrew', that is, forget Yiddish which we spoke at

home and listen to and speak his language, Hebrew'' (Neiman, 1963:22). In
1907, a visitor to schools in several settlements reported of the Hebrew teachers'
achievements in instilling their young students with the right attitudes to Hebrew.
In Gedera, one of the early settlements, for example, he observed a teacher
"teaching all subjects in Hebrew only, while implanting the Hebrew spirit in
the hearts of the little ones" (R.Z.L., 1902).

The combination of favorable and unfavorable attitudes to Hebrew and Yiddish, respectively, produced an atmosphere in which children could not help
knowing or sensing which language was more prestigious and should thus be
preferred if and when it was acquired. A situation existed, in other words, in
which communicating in Hebrew constituted a most powerful reinforcer. The
communicative tool, or the linguistic model, however, was yet to be acquired.
This was done in the schools.

*The Second Component: The Children Are Presented With And Acquire The
Linguistic Model.*

This was carried out mostly by teachers (often referred to as ''teacher-leaders'')
in the ''settlements,'' particularly where they or other interested activists were
successful in establishing Hebrew as the medium of instruction in the schools,
often following considerable resistance by some teachers, administrators, parents, and other skeptics. The ''teachers-leaders'' and other proponents of the
revival increasingly recognized that teaching all subjects in Hebrew was a crucial
condition to its success. In this, however, these teachers and the cooperating
schools encountered some formidable pedagogical and linguistic barriers, of
which probably the most serious was the need to teach the students the non-
Hebrew subjects in a language they did not yet know.

In order to overcome this barrier, several schools established ''preparatories''
that would prepare their students for concept-learning in Hebrew by devoting
one or two years prior to entry into elementary school at age six to total exposure
to Hebrew speech. This was to be the preparatories' only objective, and no
attempt would be made to teach the students other subjects. Once they had
acquired proficiency in Hebrew, they would enter first grade where they could
be instructed in this language (Azaryahu, 1933). It was expected, as stated by
a contemporary educator, that in these preparatories, ''children will get used to
speak in Hebrew about things they see from an early age and they will use the
language naturally. And then, when they enter school, they will be prepared to
read books and understand what they read'' (Hovav, 1902).

The preparatories seem to have had significant success. Ben-Yehuda's son,
Itamar Ben-Aviv, reported in 1902 of one in Jaffa in which, only months after
it had opened, Hebrew could be heard ''loud, real, and alive. . . . They speak
Hebrew . . . , and in three months!'' (Ben-Aviv, 1902:110) The impact of this
approach on the preparatories' graduates entering school was noted by another
observer who had visited a school in Zichron Ya'akov, one of the early settlements: ''In the first grade I could not believe what I heard. Boys and girls aged

seven and eight read Hebrew and showed what they knew in grammar, history, arithmetic and geography—all in Hebrew'' (Hazichroni, 1902:242).

In his survey of Palestine's Jewish schools in the revival period, Joseph Azaryahu later summarized the preparatories' overall contribution:

As to their effect on the revival of the language among the children . . . the kindergartens did wonders. Thanks to them alone Hebrew became the language the youngsters used almost regularly, and when they entered school they could continue to develop their potential naturally and persistently. Moreover, now these children became the most effective vehicle for spreading Hebrew speech amongst their families (Azaryahu, 1933:79).

Another leading contemporary educator similarly concluded that these kindergartens were "the very [tool] that made Hebrew spoken both by our children and by the next generation" (Zuta, 1929:121).

These Hebrew preparatories may be viewed as an early, successful version of "language immersion" programs, initiated and popularized in recent years in the field of second-language acquisition and adopted particularly where governments or language agencies attempt to advance individual bilingualism. It is widely accepted that such programs may prove to be the most effective, viable instrument for achieving widespread individual and, eventually, group bilingualism in countries such as Canada, where this has been a prime national objective. The one difference between the preparatories of the revival period and modern immersion programs is that in the immersion programs all subjects are taught in the target language, while the revival period has attempted to teach no specific subject. In these, the sole objective was to develop the students' communicative proficiency in the target language as preparation for future study in it. Such study would then ideally be similar to present-day immersion programs.

The settlements' elementary schools and, to some extent, their secondary schools also had a critical role in the implementation process via their teachers. According to numerous reports in the contemporary press, these teachers presented their students with the linguistic model and insisted on its use in their classrooms ever since 1888 when the first school (in Rishon-Letsiyon) established the "Hebrew in Hebrew" approach and introduced Hebrew as the language of instruction for "elementary science" subjects (Yudelovitz, 1929:151). A teacher who visited this school three years later recalled his reaction: "I could not have believed it until I went there and saw . . . high-school students speak simple, fluent Hebrew led by expert, thoroughly devoted teachers. . . . Hebrew was the dominant, spoken language" (Grazovsky, 1891:3).

Reports on the situation in the rest of the country were similarly favorable, or at least promising. A visitor to Palestine in 1908 found, for example, that the schools in both the cities and the settlements "keep improving . . . due to the influence of our culture carriers'—the Hebrew teachers. In most settlements . . .

the Hebrew teacher is the only channel through which flow the new currents in literature and in life'' (Ben-Moshe, 1908:85).

Another important, if indirect, indicator of the teachers' and schools' achievements is the rapid growth in the number of Hebrew schools during the transition to Hebrew, at the expense of non-Hebrew schools. Between 1903 and 1913, this number grew from a total of seventeen schools (sixteen in the settlements), to 60. They now included 20 kindergartens (10 in the settlements), thirty-four elementary schools (twenty-eight in the settlements), two secondary schools (in the Tel-Aviv, Jaffa, and Jerusalem), two teachers' colleges (in Jaffa and Jerusalem), one vocational school (in Petach-Tikva, Palestine's first Jewish settlement), and an art school (in Jerusalem) (Azaryahu, 1929).

As indicated above, students' inability to speak Hebrew was the major barrier to its use as a medium of instruction, which led to the establishment of the preparatories. There were several other severe handicaps, however: (1) An acute shortage of qualified teachers (Yudelovitz, 1929; Azaryahu, 1929; Zuta, 1929). In the absence of teacher training schools early in the transition period, some qualified teachers were imported, yet even most of these knew little or no Hebrew. Other teachers, mostly immigrants, were unqualified even in non-Hebrew subjects, but frequently their Hebrew proficiency was also poor, acquired as it was from the book (Zuta, 1929). (2) A severe shortage of adequate texts and other teaching materials. (3) An acute inadequacy of the lexicon reflected mainly by a paucity of terms for everyday concepts such as newspaper, train, match, flowers, and office, and of terms required in teaching the various school subjects (see Nahir, 1978a). These and other handicaps constituted one of the chief reasons for the establishment in 1982 of the Teachers' Assembly (Yudelovitz, 1929) and, in 1903, the more ambitious and active Hebrew Teachers Association (Kimhi, 1929).

Contemporary evidence leaves no doubt, then, that children were receiving the linguistic model and acquiring Hebrew in the schools. It ought to be noted, however, that their parents, notably their fathers, often contributed somewhat to the process, too. As indicated earlier (see ''The Religio-educational Factor''), most males had a solid if usually passive knowledge of Hebrew, albeit its biblical or Talmudic varieties (Rabin, 1976; Nahir, 1983). Thus, upon becoming parents, they could often be helpful in providing the linguistic model to their offspring, complementing or reinforcing the teachers' efforts.

The Third Component: The Children Speak And Transfer Hebrew As A Second Language Out Of The Schools.

This seems to have been the most critical, complex, and probably unprecedented step of the transition. It has also been the most difficult to account for or fathom. Having been instilled with the desired linguistic attitudes (step 1), and having acquired the linguistic model (step 2), it was now critical that children transfer the use of Hebrew out of the schools, viz., that they speak it, albeit as a second language, in *and* out of the schools—in the street, with friends, and eventually in their homes. Then, upon reaching adulthood, speaking Hebrew with their own children would come naturally, and the cycle would be completed. This, however, proved to be much more difficult to accomplish than the revival activists expected, as a contemporary writer found in 1891: "Even the Hebrew school graduates, who were already more or less fluent in the language, mostly stopped speaking Hebrew when they were away from school, especially at home" (Smilansky, 1930:9).

Nevertheless, as contemporary evidence indicates, children gradually began to transfer Hebrew out of the schools. They realized, consciously or otherwise, that, although the use of Yiddish, their native language, would result in an immediate, tangible reward in the form of effective communication, using Hebrew, even inadequately, as a second language would result in a much more powerful reward: (1) it was the socially desirable, prestigious language, and (2) speaking it was an important, vital contribution to national revival (see above, "The National-Political Factor"). Yiddish had no such prestige or promise. As the children were constantly reminded, it belonged to an ugly past in forced exile which they all ought to forget. As it may be behaviorally expected, they chose to use Hebrew with its clearly superior social and political status.

Such a choice by the children is abundantly evident in contemporary accounts and has led to an interesting dichotomy between the "children's tongue" and the "children's mother tongue": "While [Hebrew] is not yet the children's mother-tongue, it has already become throughout the country the children's tongue" (Azaryahu, 1910:137). A contemporary writer whose son had attended school in Rehovot later recalled his progress which must have resulted in such a dichotomy: "The language of instruction was Hebrew and naturally it became the language spoken among the students. . . . The school was well organized, and the children made such good progress that Hebrew became like a native language to them" (Levin-Epshtein, 1932:210). Similar developments were taking place in other settlements as well. In Rishon-Letsiyon, for example, an observer found that "all the youngsters who attended school speak and write Hebrew. In the streets and homes one can hear much Hebrew spoken. Everything formal is carried out in Hebrew only" (Haviv, 1910:3). According to a report from another settlement, Zichron-Ya'akov, "at last our teachers have now prevailed and Hebrew is dominant in our settlement. [You] will find speakers of Hebrew not only among the students at school but among the settlement's young men and women as well, although they did not know the language before; I was one of them" (Hazichroni, 1902:242).

The bridging between the schools and the homes was probably most effectively done by the younger students. The acquisition of Hebrew was at times proceeding in what may seem a reverse direction or order, that is, from children to adults, which is not uncommon in immigrants' linguistic behavior. (The case in point is distinct, however, in that Hebrew was not the community's dominant language. Furthermore, it was still the native language of few or none of its members): "The children influenced their parents and forced them to learn Hebrew. . . . The Kindergarten students brought Hebrew into the home. The mothers would then take evening classes in Hebrew . . . and in this way a single language was created—the mother-child language'' (Feinsod-Sokenick, 1929:266). A press report on Zichron Ya'akov's younger students observed that they ''study every-thing in Hebrew. . . . It is a joy to see the boys and girls speak Hebrew amongst themselves. They . . . want to show everyone that instead of [Yiddish] which they used to speak they now speak the Hebrew language'' (Haškafa, 1902:130).

Although the transition in the urban centers was, as indicated earlier, relatively slow and sporadic, a similar bridge existed in these between Hebrew use in the schools and in the homes, a children-to-adults direction in the language acqui-sition process, as reported in a ''letter to the editor'' in 1905: ''I saw my friend's daughter, two years and three months old, speak only Hebrew and sing beautiful songs. Yet she did not only learn how to speak Hebrew at school; she has also been teaching her parents whatever she knows'' (Pirhi, 1905:5).

An indicator, albeit somewhat indirect, of the growth in the number of those who acquired Hebrew as a second language was the rapid rise in the popularity and circulation of the Hebrew press (Kressel, 1964). Although many of the readers were new immigrants who, as indicated, had reasonable Hebrew-reading proficiency as part of their (often religious) education prior to their arrival in Palestine, most acquired Hebrew, still as a second language, in Palestine's Hebrew schools. Already in 1912, it was observed that ''there is almost no [young] man or woman who cannot read a Hebrew newspaper'' (Klausner, 1915:256).

The third component of the transition, the use of Hebrew as a second language outside the schools, culminated and was reflected in the gradual formation of Hebrew-speaking ''islands'' (Haramati, 1979:252), in which Hebrew as a second language was generally spoken by the young. Zichron-Ya'akov in 1902, for example, was such an ''island,'' according to an enthusiastic observer: ''Let . . . all those who doubt the revival of our language come to Zichron Ya'akov . . . and see little girls and older girls walk hand-in-hand . . . singing and playing in Hebrew'' (Haškafa, 1902:236). The number and size of such ''islands'' grew as the partially overlapping fourth component was in progress and the transition process was nearing its completion.

The Fourth Component: The Newly Born Receive Hebrew As A First Language.

This is the conclusion or culmination of the transition process. Having spoken Hebrew as a second language in and out of the schools for several years, usually between one and two decades, children now reached adulthood, married, and had their own children. Since the national and linguistic attitudes that had been instilled in these new parents when they were children still prevailed and were sufficiently powerful, probably with national-political aspirations even strength-ened, the language spoken in the new homes with the newly born was naturally to be Hebrew. To this new generation Hebrew was now a native and often only language, spoken naturally and in all aspects of life.

At this stage, when a growing number of children speak Hebrew as a native language, while many older children and young adults and some older adults speak Hebrew but still as a second language, a clear children-to-adult direction is seen to have developed in the acquisition and spread of the language. A newspaper article in 1907 reports, for example, that when Zichron-Ya'akov's new physician was to deliver his first public lecture, his decision to do so in Hebrew was somewhat surprising, since only children were expected to fully master the language: "The public here is used to hearing school-children chatter in Hebrew, but they did not expect a learned physician to use it" (Haškafa, 1907:3). It seems that at least to some observers the distinction between the generations' linguistic behavior was even sharper. An educator visiting Palestine's Jewish communities in 1910 found that "the young generation . . . speaks Hebrew, and the old—almost all speak Yiddish" (Berkman, 1911:31). Finally, Haim Brenner, a prominent writer, who had serious doubts about the revivability and viability of Hebrew as a vernacular, later recalled what had changed his view: "What won me over to the Hebrew language [were] the school children. They were the critical factor" (Kushnir, 1944:143).

As in the previous steps, the move to this fourth step cannot be precisely demarcated or delineated. The native use of Hebrew by the newly born was taking place concurrently and in an overlapping fashion in an ever-increasing number of new families. When the number of such families was sufficiently large to constitute an observable, significant speech community, Hebrew can be considered to have been revived as a vernacular. The final component of the transition may be deemed to have taken place approximately between 1905 and 1915. In this period the first sizable age groups of children who spoke Hebrew as a second language matured and had their own children, now speakers of Hebrew as a first language.

At this point a significant Hebrew speech community was observed and even quantified, and the transition process, or the revival, completed. According to the 1916 census, 40 percent of Palestine's Jews (thirty-four thousand of eighty-five thousand aged two and over) spoke Hebrew as an "only or first language" (*Census,* 1918; Bachi, 1956). It is even more significant, however, that this percentage was considerably higher among the young—approximately 75 percent in the settlements and in the town of Tel-Aviv, founded a few years earlier, where the Hebrew school system was most firmly established. Roberto Bachi, a leading statistician of the revival, asserted that by World War I "the future of Hebrew was guaranteed . . . due to the fact that it had become the younger generation's major language" (Bachi, 1956:80).

THE REVIVAL AND PLANNING AGENCIES

The restoration of Hebrew to vernacular status was by and large the result of a combination of steps taken by small groups of highly motivated, extremely determined teachers particularly, though not exclusively, in Palestine's Jewish agricultural settlements. As asserted by a leading contemporary educator, "This great miracle . . . was performed by the Hebrew schools. The schools were not one of the factors in the revival. . . . They were the tool . . . which carried out the great revolution—the transformation of a literary language into the language of the people, the language of life'' (Arnon, 1947:40).

While the discussion above concurs with this statement, it ought to be noted that throughout the revival period certain other bodies were also involved. Some of their activities accelerated the process somewhat, thus probably reducing the time required to complete its cycle. The major participating groups were the Hebrew Language Committee, the Hebrew Teachers' Association, and the newly formed labor movement.

The Hebrew Language Committee (transformed in 1953, following the establishment in 1948 of the State of Israel, into the government-sponsored Hebrew Language Academy) was founded in Jerusalem in 1890 by Eliezer Ben-Yuhuda and his associates, C. Hirshenson and C. Calmi, with the objective of reviving Hebrew as a vernacular and as a medium for all communication. Despite its reputation as the ''reviver of Hebrew,'' however, most of the Committee's impact was in planning the corpus rather than the status of the language (see Fellman 1973; Nahir 1978a, in press). In fact, even this impact was very limited since, due to various difficulties, the Committee was wholly inactive during the critical years and was disbanded almost as soon as it had been formed, regrouping only in 1903, when the Revival was well under way. As to Ben-Yehuda, the ''father of Modern Hebrew,'' ''a close observation . . . will reveal that his failure was in his implementation efforts while his impact on the revival was in his codification work'' (Nahir, 1978c), primarily the expansion of the Hebrew lexicon. His role in the status planning aspect of the revival was at best that of a visionary or a grand prophet. In this, as in his lexical work, he made extensive use of his weekly newspaper *Hatsvi*, in which he repeatedly called for support of the Revival. To be sure, his codification activities did have some indirect, complementary impact on the implementation aspect of the Revival and the spread of Hebrew, too, in that it facilitated somewhat communication in the language, thus making its study, acquisition and use not only more effective but more feasible as well.

The Hebrew Teachers' Association was established in 1903, after an attempt at organizing the Hebrew teachers a decade earlier had ended in failure four years later. Most of its activities included both professional improvements in the quality of its members' performance and attempts to solve the countless difficulties they were constantly facing in teaching a language, or in a language which was still lacking terms for numerous basic modern concepts. Its declared objectives were ''(a) to improve Jewish education in Palestine and to make its schools Jewish national-Hebrew oriented.   (b) The revival of the Hebrew language and the Jewish spirit in the schools.   (c) To improve conditions for the teachers'' (Azaryahu 1929:72f). The Association's activities during the revival and since have included organizing professional conferences, various courses, workshops, and intensive teacher training programs. It also published a journal, *Hahinuch (Education),* and other professional literature (Kimhi, 1929; Chomsky,

1957). Although much of this activity during the revival aimed at the codification of modern Hebrew, it also had an impact, both direct and indirect, on its status, that is, its implementation and acceptance by the children through their teachers and by adults as well, both in the settlements and in the rest of the country.

Finally, the then emerging labor movement contributed to the revival, particularly through its influence on its fast-growing membership. This, however, began only after the turn of the century, with the arrival of a new (second) wave of immigrants following pogroms in Eastern Europe and the subsequent new rise in Jewish nationalism, when the transition was already nearing its completion. Nevertheless, the numerous adult Hebrew courses offered and organized by the movement and the many-faceted encouragement it gave to the acquisition and use of Hebrew by its members and other adults served as an impetus to the entrenchment and further acceleration of an ongoing process.

CONCLUSIONS

A schematic presentation of a four-component cycle has been used in this study in an attempt to explain the processes that at the turn of the century led to a transition from the use of Yiddish and other languages to Hebrew in Jewish Palestine. Viewed broadly, the process may also be seen as mass language acquisition as a way to achieve a language planning goal—speech (or language) revival. It has also been shown that the transition would have been virtually impossible without the crucial contribution of the prevailing sociocultural and sociolinguistic factors, during and even prior to the beginning of the process. The community's children, for example, could not have been instilled with the required linguistic attitude (Component I), nor could Hebrew have been transferred out of the schools to be spoken by the children universally as a second language (Component III), had it not been for the prevalence of the national-political factor. Similarly, without the religio-educational factor, introducing the linguistic model and the acquisition of Hebrew as a second language by the children (Component II) would have been inconceivable. There seems to be no doubt, therefore, that the revival as a whole was possible only because, once certain conditions have been met, the actual transition was taking place while several sociocultural factors were concurrently at work. The revival was so complex, and has been viewed as an inexplicable phenomenon, just because a combination of both these forces was required for it to be accomplished. No similar combination is known to have been produced by history.

As indicated, the transition to Hebrew was a collective effort by a small, highly motivated community spearheaded by a decentralized, yet devoted group, of Hebrew school teachers. It has been seen, however, that activities by several bodies—the Hebrew Language Committee, the Teachers' Association, and the Labor Union—accelerated the process and somewhat reduced the time required to complete its cycle. Finally, having been revived, standardized, and lexically modernized, Hebrew in today's Israel has a virtually monolingual status. To the extent that bilingualism exists, it is with few exceptions individual. Its impact on the current status of Hebrew or its corpus is probably marginal. Thus, the cycle which within less than a century has transformed a small, partly multilingual and partly Yiddish-speaking community of several thousand into the present-day Hebrew speech community of 4 million seems to have run its course.[5]

NOTES

1. I have borrowed this term from Wilga M. Rivers, "Talking Off the Tops of Their Heads," *TESOL Quarterly* 6 (1972): 71–81. Reprinted in W. M. Rivers, *Communicating Naturally in a Second Language* (Cambridge: Cambridge University Press, 1983), pp. 41–54.

2. For the distinctions between language revival and speech revival, see Nahir (1977a).

3. Translation from Hebrew, like all others in this study, are by the writer.

4. These "settlements" (*mošavot*) must not be confused with the much better known Kibbutzim (collective farms), of which the first, Kineret, was established only in 1909, when the revival was close to completion.

5. It should be mentioned that Arabic is also one of Israel's two official languages, spoken by about ten percent of the population. Arabic-Hebrew bilingualism has so far not been investigated by sociolinguists.

BIBLIOGRAPHY

Ahad-Ha'am (Asher Ginsberg). 1903. "Thiyat Haruach" [The Revival of the Spirit]. In *Kol Kitvey Ahad-Ha'am (Ahad-Ha'am's Writings)*, ed. H. Roth. Tel-Aviv: Dvir, 1946; rpt. 1961.

Arnon, Avraham. 1947. "Sixty Years of the Hebrew School in Palestine." *Hed-Hahinuch* 21, 9 (Hebrew): 8–40.

Azaryahu (Ozrakovsky), Joseph. 1910. "Batey Hasefer Be'erets Yisrael" [The Schools in the Land of Israel]. *Hahinuch* 1, 2.

———. 1929. "Hahinuch Ha'ivri Be'erets Yisrael" [Hebrew Education in the Land of Israel]. In D. Kimhi, ed., pp. 57–112.

———. 1933. "The First Kindergarten in the Land of Israel." *Bitaon* (Chicago) 3, 3–4 (Hebrew). Rpt. in *Joseph Azaryahu's Writings*, Vol. 3. Tel-Aviv: Massada, 1954.

Bachi, Roberto. 1956. "A Statistical Analysis of the Revival of Hebrew in Israel (and Palestine)." *Scripta Hierosolymitana* 3: 179–247.

———. 1974. *The Population of Israel*. Jerusalem: Hebrew University of Jerusalem.

Bar-Adon, Aaron. 1977. "On the Nativization of Modern Hebrew and the Role of Children in the Process." In *Studies in Descriptive and Historical Linguistics: Festschrift for Winfred P. Lehmann*, ed. P. J. Hopper. Amsterdam: John Benjamins B.V.

Ben-Aviv I. 1902. "The Hebrew Kindergarten in Jaffa." *Haškafa* 3:14.

Ben-Moshe Y. 1908. "A Letter from the Land of Israel." *Ha'olam* 2, 6.

Ben-Yehuda, Eliezer. 1881. "Mixtav Leven-Yehuda" [A Letter to Ben-Yehuda]. In R. Sivan, ed., 1978, pp. 49–54.

————. 1917/18. "Hahalom Vešivro" [The Dream and Its Fulfillment]. In *Ben-Yehuda*: *Selected Writings* (Hebrew), ed. R. Sivan, pp. 55–132.

————. 1918. "Teḥiyat Tsibur Ivri Be'erets Yisrael" [The Revival of a Hebrew Community in the Land of Israel]. In R. Sivan, ed., 1978, pp. 232–38.

Berkman, Y. 1911. *Be'erets Hatikva—Masa Le'erets Yisrael* [In the Land of Hope—A Journey to the Land of Israel]. Warsaw: Hatikva.

Betts, C. 1976. *Culture in Crisis: The Future of the Welsh Language*. Upton, Wirral: Ffynnon Press.

Bourhis, Richard Y. 1984. "Introduction: Policies in Multilingual Settings." In *Conflict and Language Planning in Quebec,* ed. R. Y. Bourhis. London: Multilingual Matters, pp. 1–28.

Census of Palestine Jews. 1918. Jaffa: Palestine Zionist Organization (Hebrew).

Chomsky, William. 1957. *Hebrew: The Eternal Language*. Philadelphia: Jewish Publication Society of America.

Collection of Documents (Leket Teudot). 1970. Jerusalem: Hebrew Language Academy.

Deutsch, Karl W. 1942. "The Trend of European Nationalism—The Language Aspect." *American Political Science Review* 36: 533–41. Reprinted in *Readings in the Sociology of Language,* ed. J. A. Fishman. The Hague: Mouton, 1968, pp. 598–606.

Domhnallain, Thomas O. 1977. "Ireland: The Irish Language of Education." *Language Problems and Language Planning* 1, 2: 83–95.

Edwards, John. 1977. Review of P. B. Ellis, 1974; Mackinnon, 1974; C. Betts, 1976. *Language Problems and Language Planning* 1, 2: 97–102.

Ellis, P. B. 1974. *The Cornish Language and Its Literature*. London: Routledge and Kegan Paul.

Feinsod-Sokenick, H. 1929. "The Development of the Kindergarten." *Hed-Hahinuch* 3: 14–15.

Fellman, Jack. 1973. *The Revival of a Classical Tongue: Eliezer Ben-Yehuda and the Modern Hebrew Language*. The Hague: Mouton.

Fishman, Joshua A. 1971. "The Impact of Nationalism on Language Planning: Some Comparisons Between Early Twentieth-Century Europe and More Recent Years in South and Southeast Asia." In *Can Language Be Planned?*, ed. J. Rubin and B. H. Jernudd. Honolulu: University Press of Hawaii, pp. 3–20.

Grazovsky, Y. 1891. "Letters from the Land of Israel." *Hamelits* 31:86.

Green, David. 1966. *The Irish Language*. Dublin: Cultural Relations Committee of Ireland.

Haramati, Shlomo. 1979. *The Role of the Hebrew Teacher in Reviving the Hebrew Language: 1882–1914*. Jerusalem: Rubin Mass (Hebrew).

Haškafa. 1902. "From the Settlements—Zichron-Ya'akov" 3: 17, 31.

————. 1907. "Zichron-Ya'akov," 8, 52.

Haugen, Einar. 1966. *Language Conflict and Language Planning: The Case of Modern Norwegian*. Cambridge, Mass.: Harvard University Press.

————. 1983. "The Implementation of Corpus Planning: Theory and Practice." In *Progress in Language Planning,* ed. J. Cobarrubias and J. A. Fishman. The Hague: Mouton, pp. 269–89.

Haviv D. (Laubman). 1910. "On Yiddish—A Further Response to Ben-Yehuda." *Ha'or* 1: 128.

"Hazichroni." 1902. "Letter to the Editor." Haškafa 3:32.

Herman, Simon R. 1968. "Explorations in the Social Psychology of Language Choice."
    In *Readings in the Sociology of Language,* ed. Joshua A. Fishman, The Hague:
    Mouton, pp. 492–511.
Heyd, Uriel. 1954. *Language Reform in Modern Turkey.* Jerusalem: Israel Oriental
    Society.
Hoffman, John E., and Haya Fisherman. 1971. "Language Shift and Maintenance in
    Israel." *International Migration Review* 5, 2:204–26. Reprinted in *Advances in
    the Sociology of Language,* ed. J. A. Fishman. Vol. 2. The Hague: Mouton,
    1972, pp. 342–64.
Hovav, H. 1902. "Some Comments on Educating the Children." Haškafa 3:14.
James, Carl. 1977. "Welsh Bilingualism—Fact and Friction." *Language Problems and
    Language Planning* 1, 2: 73–82.
Katz, Elihu, Michael Gurevich, et al. 1972. *Tarbut Yisrael (The Culture of Israel),* 2
    vols. Jerusalem: Israel Institute of Social Research and the Communications In-
    stitute of Hebrew University.
Kimhi, David, ed. 1929. *Sefer Hayovel Leagudat Hamorim (1903–1928) (The Teachers'
    Association Jubilee Book [1903–1928]).* Jerusalem: Teachers' Association.
Klausner, J. 1915. *Olam Mithave (A World Being Formed).* Odessa.
Kressel, G. 1964. *Toldot Ha'itonut Ha'ivrit Be'erets Yisrael (History of the Hebrew
    Press in the Land of Israel).* Jerusalem: Hasifriya Hatsiyonit.
Kushnir, M., ed. 1944. *Yosef Haim Brenner—Mivḥar Zichronotay (Joseph Haim Brenner:
    Selected Memoirs).* Tel-Aviv: Hakibutz Hameuhad, p. 143.
Levin-Epshtein, A. Z. 1932. *Zichronotay (Memoirs).* Tel-Aviv: Levin-Epshtein.
Macnamara, John. 1966. *Bilingualism and Primary Education: A Study of Irish Exper-
    ience.* Edinburgh: University Press.
———. 1971. "Success and Failures in the Movement for the Restoration of Irish." In
    Can language Be Planned? eds. J. Rubin and B. H. Jernueld. Hawaii: University
    Press of Hawaii, pp. 65–94.
Nadel, Elizabeth, and Joshua A. Fishman. 1977. "English in Israel: A Sociolinguistic
    Study," *The Spread of English,* ed. Joshua A. Fishman et al. Rowley, Mass.:
    Newbury House, pp. 137–67.
Nahir, Moshe. 1977a. "Language Revival versus Speech Revival: A Question of Ter-
    minology." *Language Planning Newsletter* 4:7.
Nahir, Moshe. 1977b. "The Five Aspects of Language Planning: A Classification."
    Language Problems and Language Planning 2, 2, 89–102
Nahir, Moshe. 1978b. "Normativism and Educated Speech in Modern Hebrew." *Inter-
    national Journal of the Sociology of Language* 18:49–67. Rpt. *Hebrew Teaching
    and Applied Linguistics,* ed. M. Nahir. Washington, D.C.: University Press of
    America, 1981, pp. 355–82.
Nahir, Moshe. 1978c. Review of *The Revival of a Classical Tongue: Eliezer Ben-Yehuda
    and the Modern Hebrew Language,* by Jack Fellman. *Language Problems and
    Language Planning.* 2, 3:177–81
Nahir, Moshe. 1979. "Lexical Modernization in Hebrew and the Extra Academy Con-
    tribution." *National Language Planning and Treatment,* ed. Richard E. Wood.
    Special Issue, *Word* 30, 1–2. Pp. 105–116.
Nahir, Moshe. 1983. "Sociocultural Factors in the Revival of Hebrew." *Language
    Problems and Language Planning* 7, 3, 263–84.

————. 1984. "Language Planning Goals: A Classification." *Language Problems and Language Planning* 8, 3: 294–327.

————. In press. "Status Planning and Corpus Planning in Modern Hebrew." In *Comparative Language Planning*, ed. Jacques Maurais, Quebec: Conseil de la langue francaise.

Neiman, D. 1963. *In the Beginning—the Nation, the Language and the State 1881–1961.* Tel Aviv: Author's Publication.

Paulston, Christina B. 1985. "Bilingualism and Bilingual Education: An Introduction." This Volume.

Pelli, Moshe. 1981. "Revival of Hebrew and Revival of the People: The Attitude of the First Maskilim to the Hebrew Language." In *Hebrew Teaching and Applied Linguistics,* ed. M. Nahir. Washington, D.C.: University Press of America, pp. 97–123.

Peres, Isaiah. 1964. *Mea Šana Birušalayim (One Hundred Years in Jerusalem).* Jerusalem: Rubin Mass.

Pirhi, J. 1905. "A Question to the Founders of the Kindergarten." *Haškafa,* 6:21.

Population and Housing Census. 1961. Jerusalem: Israel Government Publications.

R.Z.L. 1902. "Letter to the Editor." *Haškafa* 3:23.

Rabin, Chaim. 1976. "Liturgy and Language in Judaism." In *Language in Religious Practice,* ed. W. J. Samarin. Rowley, Mass.: Newbury House, pp. 131–55.

Ravnitsky, Yitshak. 1890. "A Simple, Clear Language." *Kaveret* (Odessa): 27–32.

Rosenbaum, Yehudit. 1983. "Hebrew Adoption Among New Immigrants to Israel: The First Three Years." *International Journal of the Sociology of Language* 41: 115–30.

Rubin, Joan. 1971. "A View Towards the Future." In *Can Language Be Planned?,* ed. J. Rubin and B. H. Jernudd. Honolulu: University Press of Hawaii, pp. 307–10.

St. John, Robert. 1952. *Tongue of the Prophets: The Life Story of Eliezer Ben-Yehuda.* New York: n.p.

Sivan, Reuven, ed. 1978. *Eliezer Ben-Yehuda—Hahalom Vešivro: Mivhar Ktavin Be'inyeney Lašon (Eliezer Ben-Yehuda—The Dream and Its Fulfillment: Selected Writings on Language Issues).* Jerusalem: Bialik Institute.

Smilansky, Ze'ev. 1930. "Letoldot Hadibur Ha'ivri Be'erets Yisrael" [On the History of Hebrew Speech in the Land of Israel]. *Hapo'el Hatsa'ir* 23, 7.

Tur-Sinai, N. H. 1960. *The Revival of the Hebrew Language.* Jerusalem: Hacohen Press.

Yudelovitz, David. 1929. "Zichronot Rišonim" [Early Reminiscences]. In D. Kimhi, ed., pp. 150–56.

Zuta, Haim. 1929. "Bema'ale Hahar" [Up the Mountain]. In D. Kimhi, ed., pp. 112–29.

Dennis R. Craig

CREOLE ENGLISH AND EDUCATION IN JAMAICA

HISTORICAL AND DEMOGRAPHIC BACKGROUND

Jamaica, originally colonized by the Spanish, was captured by the English in 1655. Within a few years, all the Spanish settlers had left, most of them going to Cuba, and with them their language, except for a few place names: Rio Cobre, Mount Diablo, Rio Bueno, Ocho Rios, and so on, which survive until today. The memory of the Spanish presence is also indicated today by references such as Spanish Town for the old Spanish capital of the island then named St. Jago; Spanish wall: a type of wall built of stones and mortar; Spanish jar: a large earthenware jar originally designed for storing water; and a few other similar references.

Preceding the coming of the English, the original inhabitants of the island, tribes of Arawak Indians, had been rapidly exterminated by the Spaniards, and the Arawak language had suffered the same fate that Spanish would later suffer. Like Spanish words, a few Arawak words still survive: Mamee (*Maima*) Bay; "buccaneers," from the Arawak pirates' practice of barbecuing meat (*boucan*) on sticks over a fire; and the word "Xaymaca," the name of the island (said to mean, "land of wood and water") now modified, via Spanish, into Jamaica.

With the rapid disappearance, through war or disease, of the indigenous Indian population, the Spaniards, like all colonizing nations at that time, imported African slaves for work on the plantations that were established. When the Spaniards left, they took their slaves with them, but a number of escaped slaves, Maroons, in this case Spanish Maroons, said to have numbered about three hundred, remained living in the hills where they had established themselves. The language of these Spanish Maroons must have resembled the original Spanish/Portuguese-based pidgin language that has survived today as the creole language Papiamentu, spoken in the Netherlands Antilles; but nothing much, with any certainty, is known about the actual language of the Spanish Maroons in Jamaica. These Spanish Maroons would subsequently have been joined by the much larger numbers of escaped slaves from the English plantations over the next two centuries after 1655. This influx of new English-influenced Maroons evidently established in the Maroon settlements an older, and more African-influenced, form of the English-lexicon language, now known as Jamaican Creole.

F. Cassidy (1961) quotes Bryan Edwards who, describing the Maroons in 1776, said: "Their language was a barbarous dissonance of the African dialects, with a mixture of Spanish and broken English." But Cassidy continues:

"was" is significant; for Dallas, who knew the Maroons intimately, wrote only seven years later: "The Maroons in general speak, like most of the other Negroes in the island, a peculiar dialect of English, corrupted with African words; and certainly understood our language well enough to have received (religious) instruction in it."

R. Dallas' account fits well with that of E. Long (1774) who, speaking of the native population in general, said, "The language of the Creoles is bad English larded with the Guinea dialect."

The comments of early writers like Dallas and Long concerning what is now known as Jamaican Creole indicate the dominance of lexical considerations in attempts to describe the language. That dominance persisted for at least the next century and a half, and resulted in Jamaican speech being generally regarded as a careless form of English, since the Jamaican lexis consists largely of English words. However, apart from a small number of clearly African-derived words, the influence of African languages on Jamaican Creole is probably to be seen in the syntactic and semantic aspects of the language which differ significantly from English, and which will be outlined below. We say "probably" with reference to African influences because there is a continuing controversy as to whether the suggested syntactic and semantic aspects derive from a medieval European-based lingua franca, or from African-language influences, or from language universals that manifest themselves whenever human beings have to create language anew. See, for example, the initial arguments in D. Bickerton (1981).

After 1655, the number of African slaves imported for work on the English plantations over the next century was so large that it became a subject of concern to the British government because of the constant threat of slave rebellions and the diminishing proportions of white people in the country, apart from the plantation owners and overseers. By the 1730s, the number of Maroons had grown to the point where the British were forced to fight a number of wars against them, ending in a treaty that permanently established the Maroon settlements in Jamaica. Afterwards, the British government actively encouraged British subjects (Irish, Scottish, etc.) to settle in the island, so that the proportion of the white, as distinct from the black, population might be increased. Nevertheless, the proportion of whites continued to remain small over the next century. R. LePage (1960) gives a detailed account of the importation of people into Jamaica; the most reliable early histories of the island are those of E. Long (1774) and B. Edwards (1793).

In 1838, the end of the apprenticeship period after the abolition of slavery in 1834, most of the labor on the plantations was still performed by blacks of African descent. At that time, these former slaves celebrated their new freedom by moving in large numbers away from the plantations and establishing independent villages of their own. As a result, for the next half-century, the plantation owners imported a number of indentured laborers from India first, then from China, and, in addition, some laborers (though not a significant number) from Portugal. These Indians, Chinese, and Portuguese immigrants did not prove effective laborers in Jamaica, and their numbers never became significant. They survive as small minorities today, so small that their respective languages have had no appreciable impact on the mainstream of Jamaican speech. The numerical dominance of the black, African-descended, and former slave population therefore persists up to the present: of a total population of 1,797,399, 90 percent (1,634,686) consists of the original African population, 17 percent is of East Indian origin, while only 0.7 percent (11,926) is of European and North American background. The Chinese account for 0.7 percent, and the rest are racially mixed or "other."

It can be expected that all persons born and brought up in Jamaica are, in casual, everyday speech, speakers of Jamaican Creole. Depending on education and social class, however, probably about 20 percent of such persons would be accustomed, in everyday living, to switch from Creole into a local variety of Standard English, which has sometimes been referred to as Standard Jamaican English; the remaining 80 percent or so of Jamaican Creole speakers can also, when social occasions demand it, switch from the more extreme forms of Jamaican Creole into a form of language, a mesolect, that is intermediate between Creole and English. More will be said later about these types of Jamaican speech.

SOCIAL STRUCTURE AND LANGUAGE ATTITUDES

One early legacy from plantation slavery in Jamaica was a society with sharp divisions in terms of race and color. Being white automatically meant being of an upper social class, whether rich or poor; being mixed or of brown complexion meant being next in the social hierarchy; and being black meant being of the lowest social class. However, the numerical dominance and the often fierce militancy of the black Jamaican population meant that the race-and-color situation was forced to begin changing soon after about 1900. Marcus Garvey (1887–1940), born in Jamaica, is only the most internationally famous of the blacks in Jamaica who voiced early objections to the traditions of privilege which had been passed on from the eighteenth and nineteenth centuries. By the end of the

1930s, there was a strong trade-union movement in Jamaica which subsequently gave rise to political parties that strove for the social and political equality of all persons. By the 1950s, the numerical dominance of the black Jamaican population meant that race and color, as factors in social and economic activity, had almost completely disappeared, persisting probably only in certain small and covert pockets of endeavor. They had been replaced by material wealth and education as the determinants of social class. Some insightful discussions of this situation are available in Clarke (1966), Henriques (1968), Kuper (1969), Nettleford (1970), Norris (1962), and Manley (1974), to mention just a few of the relevant references.

The importance of education at this time underscored the importance of the traditional official language: English. From the earliest times, the viewpoint had existed, even among upwardly aspiring habitual speakers of Jamaican Creole, that Jamaican Creole was a form of "bad" and "broken" English, a "patois" caused by the carelessness and slovenly habits of the lowest social class. The chief contributor to this view is the fact that Jamaican Creole and English largely share a common vocabulary; consequently, it is easy for the illusion to develop that phonological differences between Jamaican Creole and English are not the manifestation of different phonological systems, but simply the result of bad habits on the part of Jamaican Creole speakers. The same illusion applies, and even more so, to morphological and syntactic differences, again because of the largely common lexicon.

Under the influence of the viewpoint referred to, and facilitated by the common vocabulary, Jamaican Creole-speakers had always tended to represent themselves as speakers of English. Such representation was supported by the fact that most Creole-speakers, merely by being "careful," were capable of shifting their speech, as mentioned earlier, away from their most characteristic forms of Creole into a "mesolect" that at least in its sounds and morphology more closely resembled English. More will be said subsequently about both Creole and the mesolect, but the point at the moment is that the way upwardly aspiring Creole-speakers regarded their language, together with the common features shared by that language and English, made it possible for an educational policy to persist in which English was regarded as the mother tongue of all Jamaican children entering school. At least up to the 1950s, it was still possible to find schools in Jamaica where children were forbidden, under threat of punishment, from being heard speaking Creole in the classroom. One saving factor to such children, however, was that many teachers themselves, being exclusively Creole-speakers at some earlier phase of their lives, often lapsed into Creole themselves, and consequently were not always conscious of their children's lapses.

In this situation, it is not surprising that the educational system constantly complained about the deficiencies of school leavers' English. As early as 1946, an educational commission under L. L. Kandel, appointed by the British colonial government of that time, pointed out that the need for alarm about English proficiency in Jamaica was much greater than it was in Britain itself where complaints were also being voiced. Even so, the policy of the educational system, in being merely negative to Creole, continued as before.

B. Bailey (1964) summed up the Jamaican-language attitude situation as follows:

It is possible to move from one social class to another by changing one's linguistic norm. This is of course due to another factor, the correlation between a good education and acceptable English, which makes it possible to assume that ability to manipulate SJE (Standard Jamaican English) is indicative of a good education, in addition, of course, to birth in a higher caste or "class."

Despite this early stigmatizing of Jamaican Creole, Jamaican society possesses a rich heritage of folk tales, songs, and oral culture, generally in Creole. The best examples are perhaps to be seen in the writings of Louise Bennett (e.g., 1942, 1943, 1950) and in the subsequent collection of Bennett's original poems in Creole (Bennett, 1966). Preceding these works are the examples of popular humor and comment which still continue to appear every day in the country's newspaper, *The Gleaner*—for example, the items under the pseudonym of "Quashie" in the 1940s and 1950s, and the present-day Creole-language cartoons of Leandro. It is only a short remove from this creativity in Jamaican Creole to that which has become known worldwide in present-day popular entertainment: "rock-steady" and "reggae" music, as in the recordings of Bob Marley, "D.J." songs as in the records of "Yellow Man" (Winston Foster), and "Dub" poetry as in the poems of Linton Kwesi Johnson (born in Britain of Jamaican parentage) and Michael Smith (see Johnson, 1974, 1975; Smith, 1979).

Before the 1960s, the thinking was that Jamaican Creole—in the context of English being the only official language of the society and of the Creole remaining oral and unstandardized—would gradually decline in use and disappear with the progress of education in English, as the country developed. This feeling has proven to be very mistaken. Since 1962 when the country became independent of Britain, Jamaican Creole has become identified as an integral part of national sentiment. Although it remains unused as a spoken or written language for formal purposes (it has no standard spelling system), its use has actually increased within the society, for popular oral entertainment of all kinds, in commercial advertising, and in the electronic media generally. However, neither the parents of school children nor the country's Ministry of Education have evinced any interest in using Jamaican Creole as a written language, even in early education. English remains the only language for all formal purposes.

JAMAICAN CREOLE, MESOLECT, AND STANDARD ENGLISH

The English of native Jamaicans is characterized by a distinctive accent and peculiarities of lexis and idiom that justify its being regarded as a variety of

Standard English that is different from Standard British English or any other standard variety. This Standard Jamaican English is intelligible to speakers of any other standard variety and is, therefore, a part of internationally accepted English. The distinctive features of Standard Jamaican English derive from features of Jamaican Creole in pronunciation, lexis, and idiom, which are transferred to the English of speakers educated in Jamaica. There are no formally published descriptions of Standard Jamaican English, but its distinctive characteristics, in accordance with what has already been said, are perceivable in those phonological and lexical features of Jamaican Creole which do not have morphological or syntactic implications. Without attempting any further comment on Standard Jamaican English, therefore, it would be best to say something about Jamaican Creole. After that, because there is a significant linguistic variation between what can be termed Jamaican Creole and what can be termed Standard Jamaican English, it will be necessary to examine this variation which has become known in studies of Caribbean language since W. Stewart (1962) as mesolect.

The grammar, lexis, and phonology of Jamaican Creole have been described in Bailey (1966), LePage and DeCamp (1960), and Cassidy (1961), and have been the subject of further discussion in several studies since.

A wide difference exists between Jamaican Creole and English in the pronunciation even of words that are common to both languages. The result is a mutual unintelligibility, despite the largely common lexicon. The differences are based on contrastive features such as the following: English consonant clusters tend to be reduced to single consonants in Creole. The sound /h/ tends to be absent in fluent Creole in words where it is present in English. Post-vocalic /r/ tends to be absent in Creole in words where it is present in English. Midcentral and back vowels in English tend to be lowered in Creole. These are not the only phonemic contrasts, but even these few, in combination, are sufficient to create unintelligibility between Creole and English speakers, as may be noticed, for example, in the following pronunciations:

Jamaican Creole	English
/an/	hand
/tanop/	stand (up)
/aas/	horse
/bos/	burst
/kuos/	course
/gyal/	girl
/gwaan/	go on

Purely at the level of the morpheme and word, therefore, the mutual unintelligibility of Jamaican Creole and English can be appreciated when it is realized that it is not even the whole of the Creole lexicon, but only a majority portion of it that is common to English as illustrated above. There is a substantial set of other lexical items that do not correspond, either totally or in part, in the two languages. For example:

Jamaican Creole	English
/wan/	a, an
/gat/	have
/ikni/	children
/nyam/	eat
/lik/	hit
/wepaat/	where?
/wentaim/	when?
/juk/	prick; stick

The changes in word form allowed in Jamaican Creole are very few, giving the language a very simple morphology compared with that of English. In particular, there are no inflectional changes in nouns, verbs, and pronouns as in English. The invariable pronoun forms, regardless of case relationships, are the Creole-pronounced forms of the English: *us, we, you, him, it,* and a special form (unu) meaning *you* (plural).

There are many different morphological devices, of which the following are just some examples:

1. The suffixes /-a/ and /-is/ are used to form the comparative and superlative of adjectives. Even the English-derived suppletive forms such as *good, better,* and *best* are not exempt from such suffixation. For example: /haad, haada, haadis/, for *hard, harder, hardest*; but also /gud, guda, gudis/ and /gud, beta, bes (besis)/ for *good, better, best.*

2. The suffix /-nis/ may be added to adjectives to form abstract nouns. For example: /badnis/ from *bad,* to mean *evil* or *wrong-doing*; /chupidnis/ from *stupid,* to mean *stupidity.*

3. The device of reduplication is used very creatively in order to vary the meanings of words. For example: /waak-waak/ from *walk,* to mean *walk about* or *walk up and down*; /piis-piis/ from *piece,* to mean *in several bits.*

4. The suffix /-i/ is used as a diminutive, sometimes in combination with reduplication. For example: /baiti-baiti/ from *bite,* to mean *nibbled* or *bitten here and there.* These devices are a part of the daily communicative capacity of all Creole speakers. They are used creatively and spontaneously, as discussed, for example, in D. Craig (1982), to assist speakers to coin new lexical items in daily discourse. By this means, the Creole-speaker compensates for the lexical limitations of Creole. The devices are not used as freely as this in the English language where they also exist.

From what has been said, it will be obvious that all morphological devices in Jamaican Creole are directed toward lexical creation, and not toward the marking of grammatical relationships. For the marking of grammatical relationships, a number of particles are employed, of which the following are some examples:

/dem/   Plurality and distributive marker. For example: /di buk dem/, *the books*; / Jaan dem/, *John and his associates*. It may be specially noted that the generic plural, as well as the generic singular, of nouns is totally unmarked. For example: /daag bait/, *dogs bite,* or *'The dog (is an animal that) bites.* In addition, the plurality marker is not used if the noun is preceded by a quantifier. For example: /trii buk/, *three books.*

/a/   Continuative aspect marker used before verbs and adjectives. For example: /im a ron/, *he/she is running*; /di kaafi a kuol/, *the coffee is getting cold.*

/en/; /di/   Past marker used before verbs and adjectives. For example: /im en ron/, *he/she ran.*

/de/   Locating marker. For example: /di buk de pon di tiebl/, *The book is on the table.*

/no/   Negative marker. For example: /no waata no de/, *There is no water*; /di jab no iizi/, *The job is not easy.*

Apart from the use of such particles, grammatical relationships are unmarked except by word order and a rising intonation contour to indicate questions in sentences or question tags.

From the illustrations given thus far, it can be seen that word order in Jamaican Creole is the same as that in English declarative sentences, regardless of whether the Creole sentence is affirmative, negative, or interrogative. All word-order types of Creole sentences, with two exceptions, can therefore be found in English, although with different internal conventions relative to grammatical marking.

Creole has a preferred style of discourse consisting of very short sentences with frequent coordinate linkages. For example, English sentences of the form

He went outside although it was raining.

will tend to be rendered in Creole in the form

It (was) raining and still him (he) go (went) outside.

A fuller discussion of these discourse characteristics of Creole is given in Craig (1984).

Over the years that Creole and English have been coexisting in Jamaica, what L. Selinker (1972) termed "an interlanguage" has developed between the two. This interlanguage has previously been referred to as the mesolect. Mesolectal speech is generally characterized as retaining some Creole features while having more English features than Creole has, and by having some interlanguage fossilizations of its own.

Some Creole lexical items like /lik/ and /juk/ remain in the mesolect; such items might even continue to persist in what would have to be regarded as Standard Jamaican English.

These same mesolectal speakers, in the same way as Creole-speakers, are likely to continue to use the morphological devices. However, they would tend to partially replace the Creole particle system (except for the modals which they will retain) by the occasional use of the appropriate English inflections, tense forms, and so on. The tense forms, however, will tend to persist as a problem. Even though the Creole tense/aspect particles might not appear, the English verb inflections to show tense might not appear either. Moreover, the uninflected forms of verbs might regularly appear without both the Creole markers and the required English inflections. Finally, in mesolectal speakers, the use of intonation and Creole discourse characteristics will persist.

The preceding account of the linguistic form of Jamaican Creole and mesolect provides a basis for considering the nature of the educational problem in the teaching and learning of English within this specific context.

LANGUAGE EDUCATION

The contrasts that exist between Jamaican Creole and English as languages obviously create a bilingual situation, despite the core of common lexis. Even if most Creole speakers can shift into being mesolectal speakers when the occasion demands, the mesolect itself is only superficially closer to English than Creole is, as has been shown in Craig (1978). The much discussed Creole-English continuum that is occupied by mesolectal language must therefore be considered as a range of interlanguage phenomena, full of variation but indicative of failure of individuals and, diachronically, of a majority of the society to achieve a full command of English.

As far as the educational system of Jamaica is concerned, therefore, once the ignorance that originally led to the denial of Creole was removed, there was little question that a policy of bilingual education was justified for a majority of children—those coming from the low socioeconomic masses of the society who are habitual Creole-speakers. The question has really been about the most appropriate type of bilingual policy.

The attitudes to language in the society, the aspirations of Creole-speaking parents to have their children grasp the opportunities which English affords, the migrant characteristics of the rapidly expanding Jamaican population which have created significant Jamaican communities in English-speaking countries overseas and strengthened the already pervasive influence of English at home—all of these factors dictate that, while some type of bilingual educational policy is necessary, a policy involving the use of Creole as a written language in education will not be tolerated by the majority of parents, even Creole-speaking parents, in the society.

Possible models for educational policies in Creole-speaking communities have been discussed in Craig (1980), where it is shown that depending on the details

of the sociolinguistic situation, a Creole-speaking community may opt for one
of several different educational models. The type of model for which Jamaica
seems to have opted, quite informally and without a deliberate decision at any
point in time, seems to be one of *monoliterate bilingualism*. In this model,
Creole is never used as a written language in schools, and English is the only
written language.

Apart from a few intellectuals who would like to see Jamaican Creole become
an officially written language in the society, so that the sovereignty of the
indigenous Jamaican may thereby be clearly asserted, the Jamaican Creole-
speaking masses themselves, as might be expected, have given tacit acceptance
to a monoliterate bilingual policy in schools. Creative writers of all kinds find
no difficulty in transferring their English literacy skills to the writing of Creole
when the need arises. There is no pressure whatsoever on the school system for
literacy in Creole.

Because of the continued vitality of Creole and its creative use, without doubt
the community would benefit if the orthography earlier illustrated should be
adopted for common usage among writers. In this respect, there can be no
problem in teaching such an orthography to persons who are already literate in
English, including trainee teachers and literate children in schools. The fact that
it has not yet been done must be attributed to ignorance and inertia rather than
to any deliberate policy decision, since it would not affect the monoliterate-
bilingual goal of initial literacy in English.

Whether or not Jamaican Creole is allowed to be a written language of education, the special problem in the Jamaican situation would be that of teaching
English to speakers of a lexically related creole language. This is a special
problem, recognized since the 1960s as being different from that of teaching
English either as a native language (ENL) or as a foreign language (EFL). It
has since then become characterized as a specific type of the problem of teaching
Standard English as a second dialect (SESD) and has been extensively discussed
in Craig (1976, 1977, and 1983). The educational aspects of that discussion will
be summarized here.

To begin with, the fact that the Creole-speaking learner of English has a
vocabulary that is substantially English, and probably also can shift into a mesolect that superficially resembles English (at least more than Creole does), means
that, from the learner's viewpoint, the English language can be regarded as
consisting of four sets or strata of linguistic features as follows: A, features
common to both English and Creole and, therefore, within the production repertoire of the learner; B, features not usually produced in the informal Creole
of the learner, but known to the learner and produced under stress in prestige
social situations; C, features which the learner would recognize and comprehend
if used by other speakers (especially in a meaningful context), but which the
learner would be unable to produce; and D, features totally unknown to the
learner. It is sometimes convenient to regard features in sets A and B as forming
a single class, and similarly those in C and D as forming a single class. Even

when regarded in this way, the four sets show that in the class of target language already known to the learner, there is a set of features that would be used only in unusual and very formal situations. In the class of target language not within the production repertoire of the learner, there is a set of features that can be recognized and comprehended. The implications of these sets or strata of features, as outlined in Craig (1976) (with reference to nonstandard speakers generally), are summarized in the following.

The special implications of this stratification of language vis-à-vis the Creole or non-Standard learner of English has been discussed in Craig (1971:378). There it is shown that, because of the B and C strata, the learner often fails to perceive new target D elements in the teaching situation, unlike the learner of a foreign language. As a result, the reinforcement of learning which derives from the learner's satisfaction at mastering a new element and knowing he or she has mastered it is minimal, unlike that accruing to the learner of a foreign language. Because of the ease of shifting from Standard English to Creole or other non-Standard speech and vice versa, the learner (again unlike the learner of a foreign language) resists any attempt to restrict his or her use of language exclusively within the new language elements being taught.

It is therefore not surprising if many non-Standard speakers taught by foreign language methods continue to show a very low rate of acquiring Standard Language. T. Kochman (1969:87) felt that the "efficiency quotient" of Standard Language teaching, that is, the result that comes from an input of time and effort, is so negligible that the wisdom of attempting to teach the Standard under conditions such as those relevant here has to be questioned. The reasons for such poor results have usually been ascribed completely to social factors and the unfavorable attitudes of learners as in, for example, R. Fasold (1968) and R. Abrahams (1970). Social and attitudinal factors are exceedingly important and obviously play a part, but slow or negligible acquisition of the Standard is not restricted to poorly motivated learners or to learners below the age of social awareness (see Labov, 1964:91). The question that therefore needs to be studied is whether the very nature of bidialectal situations does not produce strictly linguistic and nonattitudinal factors that have some additional bearing on the poor results of language teaching.

The teaching program dictated by the suggested stratification of language, vis-à-vis the learner, and by the considerations related to that stratification is structured as follows:

(1) Topics for treatment in language are selected so as to reflect the interests, maturity, and immediate cultural environment of the learners, but at the same time so as to permit adequate use of the specific linguistic structures that form the goal of teaching at the specific point in time.

(2) The learners are led by the teacher to explore the topic fully in whatever language the learners possess. The teacher may either speak the vernacular or speak some other

type of language closer to the Standard, or speak the Standard itself, as long as the learners are able to comprehend easily. The teacher accepts whatever language the learners choose to respond in, including such new language as is infiltrating into the learners' competence. This part of the program is completely oral and may be designated "free talk." The purpose of this part is to promote normal growth and development of the learners in whatever language medium is most natural to them.

(3) The teacher uses the selected topic, or aspects of the topic, as the basis of systematic quasi-foreign language practice. Because of the high rate of recognition and comprehension in the bidialectal situation, through the learners' possession of the language strata A, B, and C, teaching procedures do not usually call for a very intensive use of imitation drills. Rather, the call is more for substitution and transformation practices, controlled dialogues and dramas, and a heavy reliance on simulated situations for forcing learners into creative use of the specific linguistic structures that are aimed at. This part of the program may be designated "controlled talk," and only Standard Language is used.

(4) For teaching in (3), linguistic structures are selected so that, relevant to the A, B, C, D classification of structures already discussed, the learners are forced to use a target structure or target structures selected from C and D (which for practical purposes may be combined into a single class). At the same time, they are forced to use incidental structures that come fortuitously from A and B (which, again for practical purposes, may also be combined into a single class).

(5) Language learners who are also learning to read use material consisting only of such linguistic structures as at each given stage they have already learned as at (3), and that are relevant to the topics discussed at (2). Language learners who can already read may use materials that are linguistically unstructured (and the more such learners can be saturated with reading, the better). The purpose of this set of measures is to ensure that the acquisition of and interest in reading are not hampered by Standard Language deficiencies, and that reading and language-learning should reinforce each other. Once reading is firmly acquired, however, there is no longer any point in linking it to the formal learning of language structure.

(6) For all learners, use is made in writing only of those linguistic structures that have already been learned as at (3), and in most cases the content of the writing is restricted to topics treated as at (2). By this means, writing is closely linked to proficiency in speech, and one reinforces the other.

(7) The various subject areas of the total school curriculum enter into the section of topics explained as at (1), so that aspects of these areas get reworked in controlled speech, reading, and writing in the same way as all other experiences.

The difference between what is outlined here and strictly foreign language teaching procedures lies in what has been termed free talk and the way in which controlled talk, reading, and writing are linked to it and to one another. The different parts of the program have to be planned together and be well integrated. In this way, the learner gets the kind of stimulating education that ought to be present in a first-language program. At the same time, linked to this stimulation and arising out of it, there is a concentration on the ordered and sequenced teaching of new language elements. The built-in resistance of the second-dialect learner to such teaching is countered by the carryover of his or her free-talk interests into other activities, by the constant reinforcement passing from one activity to another, and by the encouraged possibility of newly learned language gradually infiltrating into free talk, becoming a part of it and becoming gradually augmented. This last-mentioned possibility is more than just a possibility since it has been shown, as already discussed, to be the inevitable way in which language learning proceeds in this situation, that is, as a gradual mixture and replacement of items along the continuum. This mixture and replacement occasioned by new language learning, as already explained, does not mean that the learners lose their original vernacular. They retain their original vernacular for such occasions as it is needed in their home and peer-group environment. At the same time, they acquire an increasing ability to shift their formal speech into the Standard Language end of the continuum until they achieve an acceptable proficiency in Standard speech. On the way toward the achievement of such proficiency, many compromises are inevitable: some learners might persist in retaining certain of their original speech characteristics in the most nearly Standard Language they learn to produce. Others might achieve good native proficiency in reading and writing the Standard Language but also persist in their original non-Standard speech even on the most formal occasions, and so on. Bidialectal education ought not to expect more than this. J. Fishman and E. Lueders-Salmon (1972) have shown that German dialect-speakers react to the necessity as well as the experience of learning High German in some of the characteristic ways that are now well known in the United States of America and the West Indian language situations. It would thus seem that the factors discussed here are to be found universally in many different bidialectal situations.

The principles and procedures sketched in the preceding paragraphs will not be found in uniform application in Jamaican schools, because of the relative newness of those principles and procedures and also because the influence of the Ministry of Education on the syllabuses of schools is nonauthoritarian and indirect. The Ministry merely issues suggestions and guidelines to teachers. However, indications of the stated approach will be noticed in Ministry of Education syllabuses and guidelines where "an integrated approach" to language teaching is described. Since 1978, this approach has been embodied especially in a series of pupils' materials and teachers' guides for the first three years of primary education. These materials—Primary Language Arts—are published by Heinemann Educational Books for the Jamaica Ministry of Education (see Wilson, Craig, and Campbell, 1978), and are issued by the Ministry of Education, free of cost, to schools. The materials involve an oral program of "free talk" in Creole, and a program of "controlled talk" in English designed to teach English as a second dialect, with parallel programs for the teaching of reading and writing in English. The materials envisage that, after three years, learners will be able to move into a regular fourth-year primary school program.

Children who have already passed through the primary school and are in secondary schools, beginning at age eleven plus show all the English-language deficiencies that may be expected from earlier uninformed language-education approaches. A recent estimate of the Ministry of Education is that 52 percent of such children leave the primary school without being able to read functionally. There are no specific programs as yet for such children at age eleven, but a strong adult literacy program (the Jamaica Movement for the Advancement of Literacy—JAMAL) has been operating in the country for many years with some success. It serves to assist adults who have passed out of the school system and recognize the need to be literate in English.

An adaptation of the English-teaching approach that has been outlined has been designed for children, starting at the secondary school level, who have acquired reading but whose command of spoken and written English and proficiency in listening and reading comprehension of English are inadequate. This adaptation involves the following: first, a precise determination of the syntactic and lexical targets, and the communication tasks that students need to learn; second, habit-formation and communicative practices that will result in the required learning. Again, these procedures borrow from the methodology of foreign language teaching, but they differ from foreign language teaching because they are effected by means of a gradual modification of the learner's already-possessed, formal language repertoire, and encourage creativity in that repertoire at each stage. They differ from native-language teaching because they have very specific linguistic elements as targets at each stage. The secondary school materials that embody the stated procedures are Craig and Walker-Gordon (1981) and Craig (1983b).

These secondary school materials, or others with the same aims, are not yet widely used in those secondary schools that need them most. The reason is that the nonselective secondary schools, which are largely populated by the Creole-influenced children of the lower social classes, are not well provided for within the educational system, although 80 percent of the secondary school-age population is to be found in these schools. Textbooks and materials have not in recent years been issued free of cost to these schools, and parents on the whole cannot afford to buy such books and materials. In addition, working conditions for teachers in these schools are very poor, and the better qualified teachers seek jobs in a number of selective, high-prestige, secondary "high schools" which cater for the 10 percent of the better educated, less Creole-influenced, secondary-age population that is selected annually for these schools by means of an eleven plus examination. The result is that educational levels in the nonselective secondary schools are very low and will remain so until the government of the country is in a position to provide for such schools on a more ample scale. In the meantime, the "bi-loquial" nature of Jamaican society continues to pose a significant educational problem.

BIBLIOGRAPHY

Aarons, B., and W. Steward, eds. 1969. "Linguistic-Cultural Differences and American Education." *The Florida FL Reporter,* Anthology Issue.

Abrahams, R. 1970. *The Advantages of Black English*. Southern Conference of Language Learning, Florida.

Alatis, J., ed. 1978. *International Dimensions of Bilingual Education*. Washington, D.C.: Georgetown University Press.

Bailey, B. 1964. "Some Problems in the Language Teaching Situation in Jamaica." In *Social Dialects and Language Learning,* ed. R. Shuy. Champaign, Ill.: National Council of Teachers of English.

———. 1966. *Jamaican Creole Syntax: A Transformational Approach*. London: Cambridge University Press.

Baratz, J., and R. Shuy, eds. 1969. *Teaching Black Children to Read*. Washington, D.C.: Center for Applied Linguistics.

Bennett, L. 1942. *Jamaica Dialect Verse*. Compiled by George R. Bowen. Kingston: Herald Ltd.

———. 1943. *Jamaica Humour in Dialect*. Kingston: Gleaner Co.

———. 1950. *Anancy Stories and Dialect Verse*. Kingston: Pioneer Press.

———. 1966. *Jamaica Labrish*. Kingston: Sangster and Co.

Bickerton, D. 1981. *Roots of Language*. Ann Arbor, Mich.: Karoma Publications Inc.

Cassidy, F. 1961. *Jamaica Talk: Three Hundred Years of the English Language in Jamaica*. London: Macmillan Co.

Cassidy, F., and R. LePage. 1967. *Dictionary of Jamaican English*. London: Cambridge University Press.

Cazden, C., V. John, and D. Hymes, eds. 1972. *Functions of Language in the Classroom*. New York: Teachers College Press, Columbia University.

Clarke, E. 1966. *My Mother Who Fathered Me*. London: Allen and Unwin.

Craig, D. 1971. "Education and Creole English in the West Indies: Some Sociolinguistic Factors." In *Pidginization and Creolization of Language,* ed. D. Hymes. New York: Cambridge University Press.

———. 1976. "Bidialectal Education: Creole and Standard in the West Indies." *International Journal of the Sociology of Language* 8:93–134.

———. 1977. "Creole Languages and Primary Education." In *Pidgin and Creole Linguistics,* ed. A. Valdman. Bloomington: Indiana University Press.

———. 1978. "Creole and Standard: Partial Learning, Base Grammar, and the Mesolect." *In Georgetown University Roundtable on Languages and Linguistics,* ed. J. Alatis. Washington, D.C.: Georgetown University Press.

———. 1980. "Models for Educational Policy in Creole Speaking Communities." In *Theoretical Orientations in Creole Studies,* ed. A. Valdman and A. Highfield. New York: Academic Press.

———. 1982. "Compensation for Limited Lexis in Creole English." Paper presented in the Fifth Biennial Conference of the Society for Caribbean Linguistics, Mona, Jamaica, U.W.I.

———. 1983a. "Teaching Standard English to Non-Standard Speakers: Some Methodological Issues." *Journal of Negro Education* 52, 1:65–74. Washington, D.C.: Howard University Press.

———. 1983b. *New World English, Books 3 and 4*. London: Longman Group Ltd.

———. 1984. "Communication, Creole and Conceptualization." *International Journal of the Sociology of Language* 45:21–39.

Craig, D., and G. Walker-Gordon. 1981. *New World English, Books 1 and 2* (with Teachers Guides). London: Longman Group Ltd.

Dallas, R. 1803. *The History of the Maroons*. London: Strachan for Longman and Reese.

Edwards, B. 1793–1801. *The History, Civil and Commercial, of the British Colonies in the West Indies, Vols. I, II and III*. Dublin: Luke White (1793) and London: John Stockdale (1801).

Fasold, R. 1968. "Isn't English the First Language Too?" NCTE Annual Conference, Wisconsin.

Fishman, J., and E. Lueders-Salmon. 1972. "What Has the Sociology of Language to Say to the Teacher?" In *Functions of Language in the Classroom*, ed. C. Cazden, V. John, and D. Hymes. New York: Teachers College Press, Columbia University.

Henriques, F. 1968. *Family and Colour in Jamaica*. London: McGibbon and Ree.

Hymes, D., ed. 1971. *Pidginization and Creolization of Language*. New York: Cambridge University Press.

Johnson, L. 1974. "Voices of the Living and the Dead." *Race Today* (March).

———. 1975. *Dread Beat and Blood*. United Kingdom: Bogle L'Ouverture.

Kandel, L. 1946. *Report of the Secondary Education Continuation Committee*. Jamaica: Government Printery.

Kochman, T. 1969. "Social Factors in the Consideration of Teaching Standard English." In *Linguistic-Cultural Differences and American Education*, ed. B. Aarons and W. Stewart. *The Florida FL Reporter*, Anthology Issue.

Kuper, A. 1969. *Changing Jamaica*. Jamaica: Kingston Publishers.

Labov, W. 1964. "Stages in the Acquisition of Standard English." In *Social Dialects and Language Learning*, ed. R. Shuy. Champaign, Ill.: NCTE.

LePage, R. 1960. "An Historical Introduction to Jamaican Creole." In *Jamaican Creole*, ed. R. LePage and D. DeCamp. London: Macmillan Co.

LePage, R., and D. DeCamp, eds. 1960. *Jamaican Creole*. London: Macmillan Co.

Long, E. 1774. *The History of Jamaica*. London: Lowndes.

Manley, M. 1974. *The Politics of Change*. London: Andre Deutsch.

Nettleford, R. 1970. *Mirror, Mirror: Identity, Race and Protest in Jamaica*. Kingston: Collins-Sangster.

Norris, K. 1962. *Jamaica: The Search for an Identity*. London: Oxford University Press.

Rice, F., ed. 1962. *Study of the Role of Second Languages in Asia, Africa and Latin America*. Washington, D.C.: Center for Applied Linguistics.

Selinker, L. 1972. "Interlanguage." *IRAL* 10:209–31.

Shuy, R., ed. 1964. *Social Dialects and Language Learning*. Champaign, Ill.: NCTE.

Smith, M. 1979. "Three poems: 'Dread', 'Caan believe it', 'Roots'." In Savacou 14/15, Kingston, Jamaica.

Statistical Yearbook of Jamaica. 1981. Jamaica: Department of Statistics.

Stewart, W. 1962. "Creole Languages in the Caribbean." In *Study of the Role of Second Languages in Asia, Africa and Latin America*, ed. F. Rice. Washington, D.C.: Center for Applied Linguistics.

———. 1964. *Non-Standard Speech and the Teaching of English*. Washington, D.C.: Center for Applied Linguistics.

Valdman, A., ed. 1977. *Pidgin and Creole Linguistics*. Bloomington: Indiana University Press.

Valdman, A., and A. Highfield, eds. 1980. *Theoretical Orientations in Creole Studies*. New York: Academic Press

Wilson, D., D. Craig, and H. Campbell. 1978. *Primary Language Arts*. Kingston, Jamaica: Heinemann Educational Books (Caribbean Ltd.).

PUBLIC BILINGUAL EDUCATION IN MEXICO

Conditions affecting the lives and languages of Mexico's Indians have changed dramatically since the arrival of the Spaniards. Both historical and linguistic data make it clear that the various Indian groups had considerable contact with one another in pre-Columbian times, especially in the realms of economics, politics, and warfare. Virtually all of these contacts were wiped out by the catastrophic conquest by the Spanish. This was as true for the small nomadic bands, such as those of Baja California, as for the highly complex nations like the Aztec and Mixtec.

One of the very early rulings of the Spanish clergy and civil governments was to move all the people into compact settlements, surrounded by farmlands, isolated from one another, and placed at the disposal of the Spanish settlers for their economic exploitation (see, for example, Farris, 1983; Foster, 1961; Gibson, 1964, Roldán, 1675; Sherman, 1979, Taylor, 1972; Wasserstrom, 1983). Pre-conquest treaties were automatically nullified and self-governance above the village level disallowed, never to be recreated. All contact was to be Spanish-Indian, with the language of the Spanish axiomatically recognized as the only official one. This situation continued, with minor variations, until the middle of the twentieth century.

Bilingual education has existed in Mexico since at least the time of the Spanish conquest and possibly before (Heath, 1972; Stross, 1983). However, it was limited strictly to the elite until 1951, when the federal government inaugurated a program for the other end of the social spectrum, the Indians, most of whom could not speak the national language.

With the establishment of the first field station of the National Indian Institute in the state of Chiapas, the federal government in 1951 began to enact policies designed to benefit the aboriginal population, estimated to be at least 10 percent of the nation (Nolasco, personal communication). Not only was bilingual education to be a cornerstone of its programs, but in time the Institute would also support the reunification of the Indians into a single political pressure group (Nahmad Sittón, personal communication). Although the National Council of Indian Peoples (Consejo Nacional de Pueblos Indígenas) does not yet seem to wield much political clout, at the national level it has managed to maintain critical independence of its founders and has received considerable press coverage for the presentation of its clients' needs and views.

THE INDIAN POPULATION TODAY

Today Mexico is a babel of tongues, just as it has been throughout its history. How many languages are spoken is a matter of debate; within the past two decades, linguists have counted anywhere from twenty-two to ninety-one (Arana de Swadesh et al., 1975; Kaufman, 1974), while representatives of the federal government speak in terms of fifty-six (Nahmad Sittón, 1982). The count varies so much because some authors include within a given language what others consider to be several languages (as in the cases of Mixtec and Zapotec); in others cases the reverse occurs, with what some consider to be one language listed as several (as with most of the languages of Baja California). Currently, an estimated one hundred idioms (languages and their major mutually unintelligible dialects) are being spoken.

Linguists generally agree that there are three major language families among the aboriginal tongues: Uto-Nahua, found primarily in the northern and central parts of Mexico; Oto-Mangue in the center; and Mayan, in the central and southern regions. However, the relationship of a number of idioms not only to each other but also to these families is still being debated. For example, in addition to the three major families, T. Kaufman (1974) lists five isolated languages and one grouping of three (Mixe-Popoluca-Zoque). On the other hand, M. Swadesh and E. Arana (1975) admit only one of Kaufman's isolates (Kikapu) and place all the others within the Mayan family.

With the number of languages unclear and with the defining characteristic of "Indian" based on language usage, the size of the Indian population is at least equally difficult to determine with any precision. Moreover, as in the case of so many countries, the Mexican census is generally considered to be rather inaccurate, especially in the counting of nonmainstream groups. Both in practice and in official rhetoric, Mexican culture combines its Indian and Spanish antecedents, both cultural and genetic. Since the attribution of "Indian" as distinct from "mestizo" (mixed-blood) cannot be genetically determined, a mixture of cultural markers have been used in the past to determine who will be counted as Indian in the census and who as mestizo. Language usage has always been included among these markers and has proven to be the most robust over time. The 1980 census enumerates those who "speak some Indian language", which is defined as "the name by which the different languages spoken by the Indian

groups whose ancestors date back to the pre-colonial epoch, are identified''
(Secretaría de Programación y Presupuesto, 1983:206, 247).

According to the 1980 census, 6.4 percent of the national population over the
age of five fit this description. But with many Indians "invisible" to the census
takers, the actual numbers are probably much higher. The numbers proposed by
the Office of Indian Education of the Secretariat of Public Education, based in
part on the 1970 census, are higher than those of the 1980 count, although still
inaccurate. Stories of parents hiding their children from the enumerators are still
quite frequent. In one Chiapas community, municipal authorities listed 38,000
heads of families in 1977 for purposes of internal taxation, but the 1980 census
lists a total population of only about 32,500 (Mendez Gomes, personal communication; see Table 15.1).

Indians are found living in every state of the nation and in sizable groups in
twenty-one of the thirty-one (Ruíz Velasco and Bonilla Castillo, 1982), from
northwestern Baja California to the Yucatan Peninsula. They are to be found in
each of the major ecological niches—desert, tropical highlands, and humid lowlands. There is also a large Indian population in the environs of Mexico City,
composed primarily of descendants of the Nahuas who lived there at the time
of the conquest.

Because of the great diversity of languages, habitats, and world-views, relatively little can be said to characterize the Indian population as a whole, except
that it is overwhelmingly rural and poverty stricken. The poverty is due largely
to the economic exploitation that has been its lot ever since the arrival of the
Spanish. Another commonality is that, although the various cultures do contain
more aboriginally derived traits than the majority one, they also include myriads
of elements derived from the Spanish, principally in the realms of technology,
religion, and dress.

In addition to language usage, the principal criteria for differentiating the
various groups from one another at the local level, as well as from the majority
culture, are some of these very same Spanish-influenced traits, as adapted and
modified over time. After language, uniqueness in dress is one of the major
identifying criteria in many regions. Unique religious practices are also found
in most groups, the most notable centering on the agricultural cycle, especially
rainfall, sowing, and the harvest. Beyond distinctive dress, many groups continue
to manufacture craft items for their own use and sometimes for sale to outsiders.
Often these locally made items are used because commercially manufactured
substitutes are too costly, but there are also those who take pride in their arts
and strive to maintain them. It is especially these crafts and the distinctive dress
of many groups that give Mexico much of its unique color, which can be seen
in tourism advertisements such as posters of the "Flying Dancers" (Voladores)
of Papantla, a Mayan woman standing next to an ancient ruin, or participants
in the dance festivals of Oaxaca.

In discussing differences between Indians and mestizos, Eric Wolff (1959)
has centered more on world-view, taking as his primary distinguishing criterion

Table 15.1
Speakers of Indian Languages (estimated for 1980)

Language	# of Speakers	Language	# of Speakers
Nahua	1,007,430	Amuzgo	17,496
Maya	573,001	Tojolobal	16,765
Zapotec	357,083	Chatino	14,837
Mixtec	293,933	Cuicatec	12,844
Otomi	278,592	Huave	9,379
Totonac	157,329	Yaqui	8,928
Mazahua	131,984	Huichol	8,663
Mazatec	127,966	Popoluca	8,178
Tzeltal	125,283	Cora	7,866
Tzotzil	120,206	Tepehuan	7,079
Chol	92,917	Tepehua	6,988
Huastec	83,291	Pame	4,605
Purepecha	76,133	Pima	3,838
Mixe	68,561	Chocho	3,838
Chinantec	68,261	Guarijio	3,838
Chontal (Tabasco)	59,522	Chontal (Oaxaca)	2,419
Tlapanec	38,821	Chichimec	1,535
Mayo	35,095	Papago	921
Popoloca	35,057	Pai Pai	569
Zoque	34,203	Cucapa	307
Tarahumara	32,110	Seri	228
Drique	23,565	Cochimi	115

Other Languages

Chuj:	currently spoken only by Guatemalan migrants
Ixcatec:	counted in Mazatec
Jacaltec:	currently spoken only by Guatemalan migrants
Kikapu:	currently spoken only by Oklahoman migrants
Kiliwa:	similar to other Baja Californian languages
Kumiai:	similar to other Baja Californian languages
Lacandon:	counted in Maya
Mame:	spoken primarily by Guatemalan migrants
Matlazinca:	virtually no living speakers
Motozintlec:	virtually no living speakers
Ocuiltec:	virtually no living speakers

Sources:	Ruíz Velasco and Bonilla Castillo (1983)
	México Indígena (May, 1977)
	Personal Communications

the fact that while the mestizos see themselves as a part of a nation, perhaps even of a world population, the Indians' chief interests are their local community, which to them represents the "center of the universe." This is true even for those who have to migrate great distances in order to earn a living. To what extent this is due to a carryover from colonial times, to more recent isolation, or as a means of ego defense against the mistreatment so commonly received from outsiders has never been determined, although all of these factors do influence cultural conservation or change.

During the colonial period, people were classified socially according to their genetic and geographical antecedents; some of these classifications were given official recognition in documents such as tax lists and censuses. Among the terms most commonly used were Indian, Spaniard, White (Blanco, which included the children of Spaniards born in the Americas), Black (Negro), Mulatto, Servant (Naborio), and Mestizo. In time, this last term came to absorb all the others except the first. During the colonial period, officially sanctioned and differing demands and standards of behavior were expected of each social group (Roldán, 1675).

After the War of Independence of 1810, Indians as such were no longer afforded distinctive treatment in the eyes of the law, but were to be treated like all other citizens. Given the differences in their history and especially in the nature of their landholdings, which were communal, many of the new laws worked to their detriment. This became painfully obvious during the presidential regime of Benito Juarez, himself an Indian, who pushed for the "legalization" of all landholdings, a difficult and expensive proposition for most Indian communities. As a result, many groups lost much of their ancestral lands to *hacendados* (hacienda owners) who later recruited them and their descendants into peonage. During the lengthy presidency of Porfirio Diaz (1876–1911), the Indians' economic base became ever more precarious and many groups that had survived until then virtually disappeared as they were absorbed into a mestizoized semi-slave class, their members bound by the debts incurred by previous generations.

After the Revolution of 1910, definite attempts were made to ease the plight of the peasantry, but policies were always worded in general terms, with no differentiations made between mestizos and Indians. Only the national mestizo culture and its Spanish language were recognized. Not only did this apply to labor laws but to all legislation as well, including that concerning schooling.

At this time a new model for rural schooling was developed, in which the teacher was seen as a missionary, bringing the light of all that was new or better in the world to the peasantry. These missionary-teachers did accomplish many community development projects in the villages, introducing, among other things, health services, sanitation, and improved communications. Some of them are still recalled with great warmth and appreciation in mestizo communities. But when these teachers found themselves in Indian villages, the situation was different, for they could barely communicate with the adults and even less with the children.

During the 1930s, a few pilot projects were undertaken using the local Indian language as a medium of instruction and literacy. The Otomi and Tarascan projects, both located in the central part of the country, were to bear unexpected fruit some twenty years later.

During the l930s, the federal government also began to recognize the special legal needs of the Indians. A corps of idealistic lawyers was organized into the Office of Indian Affairs (Asuntos Indígenas), but it was not to fare well over time. Shortly after its inception in 1936, it was reorganized for the first of many times, always with diminished scope and power, until it was completely absorbed into the Office of Indian Education upon the founding of that office in 1978 (Gonzáles G., 1982).

In 1940, an Inter-American Conference was held in Patzcuaro, in the heart of the Tarascan region. It was attended primarily by anthropologists and other non-Indian professionals. One of the concluding statements of the conference was a very strongly worded recommendation to the effect that all the countries that did not yet have one immediately organize a federal office to deal with all aspects of life in which Indians had received unfair treatment. In Mexico, this recommendation was not carried out until 1948, at which time the National Indian Institute was created. In 1951, its first field center began operations in Chiapas, staffed by some of the very same people who had participated in the Otomi and Tarascan projects a decade earlier. Bilingual education, with literacy first taught in the mother tongue, was a major cornerstone of the program.

Over the years, the Institute expanded the scope of its operations, gradually coming to cover all but the most numerically insignificant of Indian enclaves in the country. During the l970s several attempts were made to give legal validity to the Indian languages. For example, the Secretariat of Public Education, as part of its official policy, stated in 1973 that one of its goals was to create a common language for all Mexicans but "without giving less prestige to the use of the aboriginal languages." At the same time, it officially approved bilingual education as a means of supporting both the national and local languages and of meeting some of its other educational goals (Diario Official de la Federacion [September 11], 1978:16).

What does the future hold for the Indian population? A best-scene scenario would put an end to economic exploitation. Every family and every community would have the wherewithal to amply meet all of its needs. Youngsters would be able to elect whether to remain in the community or to prepare for nonrural careers without ever taking into consideration economic remuneration. Moreover, each group would be able to freely decide whether to further develop its own culture, adopt the majority one, or accept and improve on elements of both.

A worst-scene scenario would begin with an intensification of the current economic crisis, bringing with it starvation and widespread illness. In many ways history would repeat itself, with the people selling themselves into debt peonage again, dispersing, finding themselves immersed in the national culture, and denigrating or denying their Indian heritage. In a couple of generations, the vastly diminished Indian cultures would largely disappear.

A more realistic scenario would follow more along the lines of recent history, with opposing tendencies toward satisfying basic economic needs (generally far away from the home community) and toward the further development of a few cultural traits. In time, the national culture would come to dominate; among other effects, many crafts would give way to cheaper commercial alternatives. Housing, health, diet, and communications would improve somewhat, both within the home communities and in the areas to which the surplus population would move. (Until recently, the annual growth rate was 3.5 percent, nationally, with the Indians not far behind, truly a demographic explosion.) Crafts, costumes, beliefs, and customs will largely wend their way into museums and libraries, but not at the expense of the people's well-being.

THE PROGRAM OF BILINGUAL EDUCATION

The program of formal education for Indian children currently in effect under the policy indicated above is housed in the Office of Indian Education (Direccion General de Educación Indígena) of the Secretariat of Public Education. All the Office's personnel, with the exception of a few social scientists, are considered to be Indians, from the Director to the newest recruits for classroom teachers. As such, all are expected to speak at least one Indian language as well as Spanish; a sizable but undetermined proportion of the personnel are fluent in more than one Indian language.

The major concern of the Office is to provide bilingual and bicultural instruction of a caliber equal to or better than that for mestizos, in grades kindergarten through six, for Indian children throughout the nation. At present, seventeen thousand teachers and nearly half a million children are involved in the system. These latter represent about a quarter of the total Indian school-aged population (Ruíz Velasco and Bonilla Castillo, 1983:180). Primary schooling is not universal for Indian children, nor for mestizos living very far from settled communities. Although the Secretariat generally does claim that primary schooling is now virtually universal for nonexceptional children, occasional spokespersons dispute this, sometimes stating that as many as 3 million are not yet provided for. Enrollments vary from one community to another, from very close to 100 percent, as in Oxchuc, Chiapas, to less than 50 percent in Chamula, also in the state of Chiapas.

Steps taken to implement official policy include the following:

1. The establishment of over four thousand kindergarten centers with a total enrollment of about one hundred and fifty thousand children, aged five to seven, attended by nearly six thousand teachers. These are located in both bilingual and nonbilingual schools. The kindergarten program, designed primarily by Indian teachers, does not differ markedly

from other programs for this age group, especially as they are conceived in Mexico. The children's tongue is the only medium of instruction, with Spanish introduced at the end of the school year via some songs and common greetings. Teaching is rather formal, but the children generally appear to feel free to express their needs and interests. The teachers are encouraged to use the physical surroundings of the school as much as possible. The kindergarten teachers are the only ones to be supplied with a modicum of curriculum materials other than textbooks.

2. The preparation of some seventy-three reading primers and teacher's manuals in as many idioms. Of these, twenty-six have been printed and distributed at least once, thirty-one are being prepared for printing, and the rest are in revision and awaiting the evaluation of the books currently in print before being processed. All of these books were written by Indian teachers under the guidance of curriculum specialists and linguists.

3. The selection and preparation of a program for oral Spanish as a second language, with a teacher's manual and student's picture book designed to serve as the basis for pattern practice.

4. The preparation of a teacher's manual and children's workbook for the other areas of the first grade academic program. In order to save costs, one large edition has been prepared rather than myriad smaller ones. The children's books consist solely of illustrations, numbers, and the mathematical symbols commonly used at this level. The teacher's book is written in Spanish and includes detailed instructions for each of the lessons suggested, as well as the use of each of the pages in the children's book. Although written in the national language, it is expected that the teachers will translate and use only the local Indian language with their students. In order to help them with terminology new to the language, a listing of all mathematical terms to be used was included with their translations in the primer manual, the only one specific to the local language. So far no term has defied translation, although some, such as "number line" and "quadrangle" did present some difficulty to the translators; "zero" was easier to handle, always being translated as "nothing, naught."

5. The overall goals of the six-year primary program are essentially the same as those of the national program and not markedly different from those of other countries. It is unique only in that the children are expected to become thoroughly bilingual by the end of the sixth grade, in both conversational and academic Spanish, a language rarely heard in their communities.

Since the books for Indian-language instruction have been distributed in only a minority of schools and then only to first graders, the overwhelming majority of the children find themselves using Spanish-language textbooks. Therefore, the bilingual aspect of the program, as it is applied in most classrooms, consists of the translation of the content of the books by the teachers and responses in the Indian language by the children, until such time as they can handle the material directly in Spanish. With little or no instruction in the national tongue as a second language and few Spanish speakers among the students, the language is learned very slowly and imperfectly; the same is true for the academic content. Almost all the students repeat a grade at least once but more commonly twice. The dropout rate is correspondingly high, especially after the children are old enough to make a viable contribution to the family economy. Only one of every hundred beginning first graders is likely to successfully complete the six-year course of studies (Ruíz Velasco and Bonilla Castillo, 1983:96–97).

Where the bilingual program has been put into effect in the first grade the picture varies somewhat. It is much easier for the children to learn the academic material, leading to lower rates of retention and desertion. (As of this writing there were no statistics available.) The Office of Indian Education planned to evaluate the existing materials during the 1984–85 school year, to be followed by whatever modifications were indicated and then by the massive production of all the necessary materials for at least the first grade. Finally, materials for the other grades will be developed, one at a time. Since these plans could not be accomplished within one presidential regime (in a country where every new presidency implies major policy shifts and massive personnel changes), the most that was anticipated for the foreseeable future was the preparation of an integrated second grade program, as well as language arts materials for grades three through six in both languages.

PROBLEMS AND ATTEMPTED SOLUTIONS

The major problem facing Indian education is the lack of funds to accomplish what is needed, especially in regard to the production of curriculum materials. Since this funding depends on the economic health of the nation, which is now very precarious, this problem may not be solved for many years. Meanwhile, the schools, teachers, and students continue to muddle along as best they can.

Teacher morale is another area of serious concern. The teachers are caught between two worlds. One is that of their natal communities, which generally stress cooperation within small bounded groups, public service, and limited adult roles and behavior patterns. The other, to which they have been exposed since at least the beginning of secondary school, has pressured them to denigrate their people and join the majority culture. On the job this pressure continues, especially in their contacts with mestizo teachers and union organizers. Most of the Indian teachers tend to lean toward the national culture, although almost all express considerable ambivalence about their ethnic identity. The response of the Office of Indian Education has been to stress pan-Indian values in all encounters between the Mexico City leadership and the people in the field, while recognizing that more must be done to improve morale.

The academic program is poorly related to the needs of the communities and is not very successful in preparing the children for secondary and higher education. Less than half of the few who graduate from elementary school continue their education (Ruíz Velasco and Bonilla Castillo, 1983:96–97). This situation has been stressed over and over again by the National Council of Indian Peoples and the Professional Association of Indian Professors (AMPIBAC), a teachers' organization. At each of their national conferences, both agencies have called for ''education designed by Indians for their development, for their ethnic identification, for their cultural renewal and participation in (national) politics'' (AM-PIBAC, 1981:6).

The Office of Indian Education is trying to develop and implement a program to satisfy these demands. The teachers, however, are poorly prepared to carry out such a job. In 1951, the first teachers were chosen from among the most bilingual and literate of community leaders; none could boast even a sixth grade education. Since then, as the number of potential teachers has outstripped the number of available jobs, academic requirements have risen. At present, they include a minimum of secondary schooling (ninth grade) in most regions; nationally, the elementary certificate is the absolute minimum. But leadership qualities have been given less and less emphasis.

Preservice training has been accomplished through special courses, which have varied from two weeks to one year in length. During recent years, inservice training has included short courses for all personnel and special normal school training for those lacking professional certification. (The federal government has just decreed that henceforth all new teachers will require the equivalent of the U.S. B.S. degree, but this does not affect persons currently enrolled in normal schools.) Today, slightly over half of the Indian teachers have earned their professional certificate, while only about 5 percent have not yet gone beyond primary school (Ruíz Velasco and Bonilla Castillo, 1983:25).

The students, too, have their problems. The principal one, as indicated above, is the competition for their participation in the economic activities of the family. One of the older teachers tells of his father's profuse apologies for letting him waste his time going to school rather than teaching him what was important: farming (Santis Gomez, personal communication). Another tells of how she begged a man to leave his son in school instead of taking him off to a coffee plantation. Replied the father, "Then how will he eat?" (Arias Perez, personal communication). In the case of girls, the picture is often further complicated because there are relatively few female teachers and schools are seen as the province of men. According to the standards of most communities, the girls are not sufficiently protected, especially as they grow toward pubescence and marriageability.

Another problem for many students is the long distances between home and school; it is not at all unusual for them to walk two hours in each direction. For those who live very far away, there is often the opportunity of attending a part-time boarding facility (*albergue*), returning home on weekends and vacations, or a full-time boarding school (Centro de Integración Social), but these, too, have their drawbacks. The principal one, these days, is that the food budgets, never fully adequate, have been ravaged by inflation. Despite frequent adjustments, the children often go hungry, and a nutritionally adequate diet is beyond the reach of even the most ingenious meal planner. In addition, at the higher (colder) altitudes, there may not be enough blankets to give each child more than one. In some areas the water supply is insufficient or sporadic; medical care is often not readily available. Only the most dedicated of students seem to use these boarding facilities with enthusiasm. Many of them figure among the few who continue their schooling beyond the sixth grade.

Perhaps the greatest problem faced by the children is the clash in values and behavior patterns between those they learn at home and those rewarded by the schools. Although these clashes are considerably lessened in the schools with Indian teachers, they still exist, pulling the children between their homes and the outside world.

The Office of Indian Education is fully cognizant of all these problems and is trying to resolve them as best it can with insufficient funding and a dearth of professional specialists who are as familiar with Indian communities as with their areas of expertise. Until now these specialists, be they curriculum developers, linguists, psychologists, anthropologists, or sociologists, have shown that when they cannot work within the conditions and cultural settings of life in the Indian communities or when their contributions remain couched in the world-view of their own culture, the results of their efforts are virtually nil. Until recently, few outsiders have been willing or able to comprehend the intimacies of Indian life, and, to date, there have been no Indians with sufficient academic training. The Office of Indian Education therefore decided that the more efficient route would be to train Indian teachers and then have them translate their professional preparation to the cultural world of their people. It would also be much fairer for them to have more opportunities to advance professionally than to have more "experts" foisted on them. Therefore, two programs have been developed for advanced teacher training. In one, a group of teachers is studying curriculum development at the National Pedagogical University; they are now in their second year of classes. In the other, the area of concentration is cultural linguistics; the second group is now going through this two-year program.

Another thrust of the Office of Indian Education has been to attempt to develop its own six-year course of study for the elementary school, one that would better meet the needs of the communities while not denying adequate academic preparation to those wishing to continue formal education beyond this level. This project, like so many others, is hampered by the lack of adequately trained Indian personnel, but even more by the lack of funds for pilot testing its proposals.

Another major goal, as indicated above, has been to raise the awareness of the teachers, reinforcing the positive elements of their natal cultures as a means of building pride in their cultural inheritance, which they often equate with poverty and deprivation. This has been an uphill and continuing battle. The hope is that once a truly bilingual program is in place the teachers will see for themselves the advantages of this approach and come to reaffirm their ethnic backgrounds.

In relation to the problems faced by the students, in addition to the attempts to improve the curriculum and the constant struggles to increase the budgets of the boarding facilities, more and more women are being given teaching positions. This helps to feminize the schools to the degree that girls can now feel comfortable there and their parents less anxious. However, since only a handful of schools have more than one class per grade and the teachers generally find handling more than one group in a classroom overly difficult, the logical step of organizing sex-segregated classes is almost impossible to take.

All educational authorities agree that other than making schooling compulsory by force (it already is, legally, through the sixth grade or the age of fourteen), the competition with child labor will be won only if and when parents and children alike see in schooling a more viable solution to their economic problems. That moment still lies in the future.

RESEARCH STUDIES

The quantity and quality of educational research have improved markedly in the past few years (Modiano, 1984). Basic studies, especially those related to the Indian languages, prevail. The majority of those published during the past decade have emanated from the Summer Institute of Linguistics, with the various sectors of the Secretariat of Public Education (including museums, the National School of Anthropology, and various research institutes) in second place. Combined, these works include a total of nine bilingual dictionaries (in Spanish and Ch'ol, Huave, Mixtec, Nahua, Otomi, Popoloca, Popoluca, Tepehuan, Tojolobal, Trique, Tzotzil or Zoque) and a number of detailed grammatical descriptions.

Several evaluations were also conducted, especially in the area of language usage in and out of the schoolhouse. All showed the ambivalence of the teachers toward their own ethnic group, to the detriment of the children's well-being or academic achievement (Chavez Bernal, 1982; López, 1982; Ros Romero, 1981). A more traditional evaluation, of a program designed to teach oral Spanish to kindergarten children in one year, demonstrated that none of the educational objectives were reached (Modiano, 1984). Based on these results, the Office of Indian Education introduced the Indian-language kindergarten program as rapidly as it could. A subsequent evaluation showed that with all the instruction in a language the children understood and Spanish relegated to some introductory lessons at the end of the school year, all the educational goals were achieved (Tovar and Cabrera, 1982).

Another investigation, more traditional in design, examined kindergarteners' perception of colored (as opposed to black and white) illustrations (Modiano et al., 1982). Most of the items, taken from the national first and second grade textbooks, were correctly interpreted, but those that implied movement in space (such as a flickering fire) were misinterpreted by most of the subjects regardless of the medium of presentation (drawings or photographs).

Action research, incidental to the preparation of curriculum materials, was another fruitful approach, although only one descriptive study resulted (Modiano, 1982). Indian teachers, in consultation with curriculum specialists and linguists, prepared a total of seventy-three reading primers for as many dialects of twenty-six languages. Another thirty-one, covering as many variants of six languages, are under development, as are about a dozen titles of supplementary reading materials in very elegant editions. The Summer Institute of Linguistics, using primarily foreign linguists with native informants, published sixty-four primers for twenty languages and 250 supplementary reading pamphlets by native authors, generally in very limited trial editions. Several teaching grammars were also prepared by the Secretariat and the Institute alike; six of these have been published so far. While the Secretariat's materials are generally designed for classroom use, those of the Summer Institute are confined largely to adult education in Protestant church-related groups.

A major problem in carrying out research at this time is the lack of adequate funding. With the nation in a severe economic crisis, monies for educational research, all of which comes from the federal budget, have all but disappeared. Nonetheless, some studies, especially evaluations, are being conducted. One notable aspect of educational research in Mexico, especially in Indian education, is the alacrity with which results are applied to planning and programs, even though not all of these changes have yet reached the schoolhouse level.

SOURCES OF INFORMATION

There is no one central place either in Mexico or elsewhere where additional data on the programs of public bilingual education are stored. Moreover, some materials, including many referred to above, are not generally available, being either out of print or having never been given general circulation. The most fruitful places to begin an exhaustive search of materials related to these programs are in the libraries of the National Indian Institute (Avenida Revolución 1279, Colonia Los Alpes, 01010 Mexico, D.F.) and the Office of Indian Education (Azafran 486–4 Piso, Colonia Granjas Mexico, 08400 Mexico, D.F.).

SUMMARY

The history of Mexico's Indian population is one of exploitation and poverty. Their languages number anywhere from about twenty to one hundred depending on who does the counting and how. Educational policies have taken the unique circumstances and needs of the Indians into account only during the past thirty-four years. The major section of this chapter describes the official program for bilingual and bicultural Indian education for grades K–6. The program has grown from forty-six teachers and some fourteen hundred children in 1951 to over seventeen thousand teachers and close to half a million children as of this writing. Not surprisingly, the program has all the problems common to large bureaucracies, as well as some related to the unique characteristics of the population served. The results of research and evaluation studies are being employed as a basis for policy and program modifications.

The Office of Indian Education would like to do much more to raise the quality of the schooling it offers, but the economic crisis gripping the country has caused

restraint in all domestic funding, including that vital to bringing about the changes
so badly needed. This situation affects all aspects of research and development,
especially the preparation of curriculum materials and teacher training.

BIBLIOGRAPHY

AMPIBAC. 1981. *Instrumentación de la educación bilingüe y bicultural*. Oaxaca: SEP/
    DGEI.
Arana de Swadesh, E., et al. 1975. *Las lenguas de México*. Vol. 1. Mexico City: SEP/
    INAH.
Diario Official de la Federación. 1978. Mexico.
Chavez Bernal, J. P. 1982. "Un resumen de la evaluación para la reorientación de los
    albergues escolares." In *Hacia un México pluricultural: de la castellanización a
    la educación indígena bilingüe y bicultural*, ed. A. P. Scanlon and J. Lezama
    Morfin. Mexico City: SEP/DGEI, pp. 419–41.
Farris, N. M. 1983. "Indians in Colonial Yucatan: Three Perspectives." In *Spaniards
    and Indians in Southeastern Mesoamerica*, ed. M. MacLeod and R. Wasserstrom.
    Lincoln: University of Nebraska Press, pp. 1–39.
Foster, G. M. 1961. *Culture and Conquest: America's Spanish Heritage*. New York:
    Wenner Gren/Viking Fund.
Gibson, C. 1964. *The Aztecs Under Spanish Rule*. Stanford, Calif.: Stanford University
    Press.
González, G. E., et al. 1982. "Fundamentos jurídicos, teóricos y metadológicos de la
    educación bilingüe-bicultural en México." Unpublished manuscript.
Heath, S. B. 1972. *Telling Tongues: Language Policy in Mexico, Colony to Nation*. New
    York: Teachers College Press.
Kaufman, T. 1974. *Idiomas de Mesoamérica*. Guatemala City: José de Pineda Ibarra,
    Ministerio de Educacion.
López, G. 1982. "Castellanización y la práctica pedagógica en escuelas bilingües del
    Valle del Mezquital." In *Hacia un México pluricultural*, ed. A. P. Scanlon and
    J. Lezama Morfín. Mexico City: SEP/DGEI, pp. 367–95.
Mexico Indigena. 1977. *Grupos indígenas de Mexico*. Mexico City: Instituto Nacional
    Indigenista (May), Centerfold.
Modiano, N. 1982. "Salid y escribid: el proceso de elaboración de material didáctico
    para la enseñanza de la lecto-escritura en lenguas indígenas." In *Hacia un México
    pluricultural*, ed. A. P. Scanlon and J. Lezama Morfín. Mexico City: SEP/DGEI,
    pp. 223–31.
———. 1984. "Bilingual-Bicultural Education in Mexico: Recent Research." *Contem-
    porary Educational Psychology*.
Modiano, N., P. Maldonado, and S. Villasana B. 1982. "Accurate Perception of Colored
    Illustration: Rates of Comprehension in Mexican-Indian Children." *Journal of
    Cross-Cultural Psychology*. 13:490–95.
Nahmad Sittón, S. 1982. "Indoamérica y educación: ¿etnocidio y etnodesarrollo?" In
    Hacia un México pluricultural, ed. A. P. Scanlon and J. Lezama Morfín. Mexico
    City- SEP/DGEI, pp. 21–44.
Roldán, J. 1675. *Ordenanzas*. Oxchuc, Chiapas: unpublished manuscript. (Popularly
    known as the *Libro Sagrado*.)

Ros Romero, M. C. 1981. *Bilingüismo y educación: un estudio en Michoacán*. Mexico City: Instituto Nacional Indigenista.

Ruíz Velasco, E., and F. Bonilla Castillo. 1983. *Estadística educativa indígena*. Mexico City: SEP/DGEI.

Secretaría de Programación y Presupuesto. 1983. *X censo general de población y vivienda, 1980*. Vol. 2. Mexico City: SPP/Instituto Nacional de Estadística, Geografia e Información.

Sherman, W. L. 1979. *Forced Native Labor in Sixteenth Century Central America*. Lincoln: University of Nebraska Press.

Stross, B. 1983. "The Languages of Zuyua." *American Ethnologist* 10:150–64.

Swadesh, M., and E. Arana. 1975. "Clasificación de las lenguas de México (1962–1964)." In *Las lenguas de México*, ed. E. Arana de Swadesh et al. Vol. 1. Mexico City: SEP/INAH, pp. 84–88.

Taylor, W. B. 1972. *Landlord and Peasant in Colonial Oaxaca*. Stanford, Calif.: Stanford University Press.

Tovar, E. C., and M. A. Cabrera. 1982. "La evaluación en el preescolar indígena dentro del marco de la educación bilingüe y bicultural." In *Hacia un México pluricultural*, ed. A. P. Scanlon and J. Lezama Morfín. Mexico City: SEP/DGEI, pp. 403–18.

Wasserstrom, R. 1983. *Class and Society in Central Chiapas*. Berkeley: University of California Press.

Wolff, E. 1959. *Sons of the Shaking Earth: The People of Mexico and Guatemala—Their Land, History and Culture*. Chicago: University of Chicago Press.

16

ASPECTS OF BILINGUALISM IN
MOROCCO

With its geographical position at the juncture of two continents, at the north-ernmost tip of Africa, the most western point of the Arab world, and yet only a twenty-minute flight away to Europe, it is hardly surprising that Morocco should be a multilingual country with a long history as a meeting-point for contrasting cultures. Within its present population of over 20 million, of whom almost 9 million are urban dwellers (figures from the National Census, 1982), we can distinguish a number of different categories of monolingual and bilingual speakers, though unfortunately there are, to my knowledge, no precise figures available concerning the membership of these categories.

It is perhaps necessary to mention here that the term *bilingual* has been variously used; some include among bilinguals those who have a very limited, possibly purely receptive knowledge of one of their two languages (e. g., Die-bold, 1961), while others restrict the term to those whose proficiency in each of two languages is comparable to that of native speakers (e.g., Bloomfield, 1933; Christophersen, 1948). As we will see below, Moroccans include speakers of both types as well as all the range in between. In what follows, the term *bilingual* will, for the sake of convenience, be used in a broad sense to describe not only those who are familiar with two and only two languages, but also the many Moroccans who might elsewhere be termed multilinguals, since they have a knowledge of three or more languages.

In the first place, Morocco has a large group of monolinguals whose only language is Moroccan Arabic, the colloquial variety of Arabic which is the mother tongue of probably the majority of Moroccans. Such monolinguals tend to have had no education, and thus probably constitute a majority of the older generation. The various colloquial dialects of Arabic form a continuum, so that the dialect spoken in Morocco, at the extreme western edge of the Arabic-speaking world, is fairly similar to that used in Algeria and Tunisia, but diverges considerably from those of the Middle East; thus, a speaker of, say, Iraqi Arabic would have considerable difficulty in understanding a speaker of Moroccan Arabic. (On the other hand, in recent years many Moroccans, including the monolinguals identified above, have acquired some familiarity with the Egyptian Arabic dialect by watching the many Egyptian films shown on Moroccan television and in the cinema.)

A second group of Moroccans consists of those whose mother tongue is not Moroccan Arabic but Berber. The term *Berber* is used to cover a number of widely differing dialects that are not entirely mutually comprehensible. In Morocco, three major dialect areas can be identified. Tarifit is the dialect of Berber used by inhabitants of the Rif Mountains, in the north of Morocco; Tamazight is spoken in areas of the Atlas Mountains, in central and southeast Morocco; and Tashelhait is the dialect of the southwest. Only those Berber speakers who live fairly remote lives in predominantly Berber-speaking areas are at all likely to remain monolinguals. The majority of Berber speakers, even if they receive no formal education, also learn Moroccan Arabic at an early age, once they begin to explore the world outside their immediate family. A third category of Moroccans, then, consists of those who are bilingual in Berber and Moroccan Arabic.

Neither Berber nor Moroccan Arabic has any standardly recognized written form. Hence, in order to obtain even the most elementary education the Moroccan has to acquire some knowledge of Classical Arabic, which differs considerably from Moroccan Arabic at all levels: in phonology (some phonemes in Classical Arabic have no equivalent in Moroccan Arabic, and vice versa), lexis (there are very extensive differences in vocabulary between the two), morphology, and syntax. Given the extent of the differences between the two, one might wish to maintain that knowledge of both Moroccan and Classical Arabic constitutes another category of bilingualism; however, in Morocco those who know only Moroccan and Classical Arabic are conventionally described as monolinguals. Thus, all Moroccans who have received some degree of education possess at least some knowledge of Classical Arabic, but there are many degrees of proficiency, ranging from those whose education was limited to a study of the Koran and who are thus familiar with its verses, parts of which they may incorporate into their own speech in formal and religious contexts, to those who have studied Classical Arabic to the level of higher education. Those who have received their education entirely through the medium of Arabic are known in Morocco as "Arabisants" and include members of some professions such as lawyers and teachers.

The majority of educated Moroccans are also proficient in French because they have received part or all of their education through this language. In addition, there are many relatively uneducated Moroccans, especially in the towns, who have some knowledge of spoken French, usually acquired through their work. This is the case for retired soldiers, shopkeepers working in the modern areas of the towns, hotel porters and cleaners, and many others whose jobs bring them into contact with foreigners. Again, one can distinguish many degrees of Arabic-French bilingualism. A. M. Blondel and F. Décorsière (1962) proposed a classification identifying several categories of bilingual speakers, exhibiting different degrees of proficiency and acculturation, ranging from the intellectual who is a perfectly balanced bilingual, able to participate in and profit from two cultures, to those for whom Arabic is dominant and French is merely an instrument used at work, with, somewhere in between, a category of speakers who are not fully proficient in either language and who suffer a lack of confidence and loss of identity.

To add to the complexity of the Moroccan language situation, in the north of the country many inhabitants use Spanish rather than French as a second language, especially in towns such as Tangier, Tetouan, Larache, Nador, and El Houceima. Again, some of these have acquired a high degree of proficiency in Spanish through formal education in the language, while others have simply picked up the language through their dealings with Spanish people. There are also Moroccans who are proficient in both Spanish and French.

The presence of a small Jewish community in Morocco adds further diversity to the language situation. The Jews living in Morocco can be divided into two main groups on the linguistic level. The first consists of those whose native language is Spanish, who are found only in the northern cities mentioned earlier, and who are descendants of the Jews who were banished from Spain in the fourteenth and fifteenth centuries. The second group is found in the other parts of Morocco and has dialectal Arabic as a first language; these include the descendants of the Spanish Jews who settled in areas away from the strongly Hispanicized towns of the north, together with the original Moroccan Jews, whose ancestors had lived in Morocco long before the emigration from Spain began. Members of both groups are likely to become bilingual through education and through contacts with other Moroccans. Thus, the native Spanish speakers learn Moroccan Arabic, and both groups acquire some proficiency in Hebrew, which is taught in connection with religious instruction in the Jewish school system. Moreover, as is noted by H.Zafrani (1980), since the period of French colonization the Arabic-speaking Jews have wholeheartedly adopted French as a second language, so that young Jews nowadays often seem to prefer to use this language, with its associations with European culture. A third group of Jews, those whose first language was Berber and who lived mainly in the south of Morocco, has, according to H. Zafrani, now vanished completely through mass emigrations to Israel, which have also considerably reduced the size of the other groups.

To summarize, then, Morocco has a large number of different types of bilinguals, speaking Moroccan Arabic, Berber, or both, along with any combination of Classical Arabic, French, and Spanish. Only Moroccan Arabic and Berber are acquired as native languages, whereas Classical Arabic, French, and Spanish are typically first encountered in a formal educational setting. French and, in the north of Morocco, Spanish have the status of second languages, in that they are used in interactions within the Moroccan speech community. They can be contrasted with English, which is introduced at a later stage of secondary education. Although many Moroccans go on to achieve considerable proficiency in English, it is not naturally used in interactions among Moroccans, and thus has the status of a foreign language. The concern here is not with this or other foreign languages.

HISTORICAL BACKGROUND

The present highly complex language situation is the product of a number of distinct historical developments. The original inhabitants of Morocco were the Berbers, and it was not until the seventh century that the Arabs invaded from the east and conquered the area, bringing with them the Arabic language and the religion of Islam. The Berbers living in the plains near the Arab settlements soon found it useful to learn Arabic for trading puposes. Indeed, according to B. G. Hoffman (1967), large numbers of these Berbers became completely arabized, abandoning the Berber language altogether, while there were also Arabs who learned Berber and abandoned Arabic. Thus, the Arabic monolinguals in Morocco today include descendants of Berbers, and the Berber speakers include descendants of Arabs—language is not altogether an accurate indicator of ethnic origin.

Even the Berbers living in remote areas of the mountains eventually became familiar with Arabic through contact with Muslim preachers, who succeeded in converting them to Islam. Thus, from the very outset, in the minds of Moroccans Arabic was closely linked with religion, and this factor may help explain why it was so rapidly accepted and respected by the Berbers. As is demonstrated in A. Bentahila (1983a), the link between Arabic and religion has remained strong to this day. E. Gellner (1973), in his study of Arabs and Berbers in North Africa, also emphasizes the religious impact of Arabic on the Berber individual, who "sees himself as a member of this tribe or that tribe, within an islamically-conceived and permeated world—and not as a member of a linguistically defined ethnic group, in a world in which Islam is but one thing among others" (Gellner, 1973:13). The fact that Berber is in perpetual contact with Arabic means that its vocabulary has been greatly influenced by Arabic. As L. Brunot (1950:16) observes, "nombreaux sont les mots arabes que ces dialectes ont du adopter, concernant surtout la religion, l'administration et les transactions commerciales." To a lesser extent, Moroccan Arabic has also borrowed from Berber.

The second major historical factor in the creation of the present language situation was the French Protectorate, which lasted from 1912 to 1956 and extended over the whole of Morocco except for a northern strip under the control of Spain. The policy of the French colonizers was to inculcate Moroccan society with the cultural values and tastes of French civilization, and this, of course, entailed convincing Moroccans of the superiority of the French language. R. Bidwell (1973:6) observes that "it has always been a cardinal belief of Frenchmen that there is only one valid culture in the world, that it is their duty to lead all men towards it and that where adaptation is necessary it is for the non-French to give way.'' This assumption seems to have been the basis for the ''mission civilisatrice'' to which the French in Morocco were committed. The major tool of this concept was a French education system that was introduced alongside the long-standing traditional Moroccan one. One result was the creation of an opposition between traditional and modern which still remains in evidence in the attitudes of Arabic-French bilinguals toward the two languages (see Bentahila, 1983a).

The traditional system of education in Morocco, dating back to not long after the Arab invasion, was organized on three levels. Primary education was provided in the /msi:d/ or Koranic school, where children learned the Koran by heart, at the same time acquiring basic skills in reading and writing Classical Arabic. Only the sons of the wealthy continued their education to the secondary level, where they studied other aspects of Islamic scholarship, as well as grammar, logic, and literature. The highest studies were carried out at the University of Karaouine in Fez, founded in 859 A.D., where students graduated as *oulema* (Islamic scholars) and where the branches of study included philosophy, philology, theology, astronomy, algebra, and medicine.

The new French system of education which was introduced beside this traditional one created considerable diversity. The new schools set up included European schools intended mainly for the children of the French colonizers themselves, although some upper class Moroccan children were also admitted. On a wider scale, they set up Franco-Islamic schools, where French was the main language of instruction, Classical Arabic being used only for the teaching of religious studies. Here pupils were taught more about French history and culture than about their own. There were also Franco-Jewish schools differing only in the kind of religious instruction provided, with Hebrew being used instead of Classical Arabic. Higher education was open to only a very small number of Moroccans, and most of these were obliged to complete their studies in France.

In 1930, the French took a further step toward diversification with the ''Dahir Berbère'' (Berber Decree), which set up another category of schools, reserved for Berbers, where Berber and French were taught, but not Arabic. This step had the aim of weakening the links between Arabs and Berbers and emphasizing the distinction between the two ethnic groups, which had never been reflected in the traditional education system. At the same time, it represented a determined attempt to integrate the Berbers into the Christian culture of the French, bypassing Arabic with its indissoluble links with Islam. Apparently, the French in Morocco believed that ''the Berbers, having no culture of their own, would not resist French culture'' (De Caix, quoted in Bidwell, 1973:53). The Moroccans did not accept this policy of divide-and-rule, however, a policy that became one of the key factors leading to an upsurge in nationalistic feeling and a return to traditional values. One result of this reaction was the setting up of private schools, sponsored by Islamic scholars, which were intended to rival the various categories of French schools, while using Arabic as the medium of education. As will be seen, relics of these schools still remain.

In 1956, the Protectorate came to an end. Independence brought with it the possibility of radical changes in the language situation, particularly with regard to the educational and administrative sectors. A five-year plan was set up for the reorganization of the education system, and four main objectives were established: unification, universalization, Moroccanization, and Arabization. (For more discussion, see Zartman, 1964; Moatassime, 1974; and Bentahila, 1983a). The first of these objectives involved a reduction in the diversity of schools introduced by the French (not forgetting that, in the north, further diversity had been created through the establishment of schools using Spanish as the main language of instruction). A unified system of primary schools was set up, but these still led to a choice of types of secondary school: between the bilingual ones where both French and Arabic were used as media of instruction and the less numerous arabized schools. The arabized schools derived from the private schools set up by the nationalists in response to French policies, where Arabic was made the medium of instruction for all subjects. Side by side with these schools were schools offering the "original" education, of the type that had existed before the Protectorate, linked very closely to Islamic scholarship.

The second objective, universalization, was concerned with making education accessible to a larger proportion of the Moroccan population. Under the French system, which was highly competitive and selective, the number of Moroccans attending school was extremely limited, while even fewer managed to obtain useful qualifications. Considerable efforts were therefore made to increase attendance figures, and schooling was for some years made compulsory between the ages of six and fourteen. However, because of serious practical difficulties, in 1963 the period of compulsory education was reduced to age seven to thirteen. The percentage of children in this age group attending school, which increased rapidly from 17 percent in 1956, when independence was declared, to 47 percent in 1964–65, fell after this point, reaching only 33 percent in 1972–73 (Baina, 1981). Indeed, despite continued rapid expansion in the number and size of schools, the aim of universal education in this age group has never yet been achieved, simply because the population has continued to increase at an extremely high rate. At the other end of the scale, alongside the University of Karaouine, the modern University Mohamed V was opened in Rabat, followed by others in Fez and Marrakech. More recently, other new universities and faculties linked to the first universities have been set up, as well as various institutes of higher education, bringing the total number of students in universities and other institutes to over ninety thousand in 1982–83 (figures from *Le Maroc en Chiffres*, 1982).

The large-scale expansion achieved in accordance with this second objective posed some problems for the achievement of the third, which sought to replace the large proportion of foreign teachers by Moroccan nationals. At first, an attempt was made to reduce the number of staff of French nationality and to replace them by staff from the Middle East, especially Egypt. This, it was hoped, would also facilitate the fourth objective—to replace French by Arabic as a medium for education. This project was soon abandoned, for the Middle Eastern teachers did not seem to adapt well to the Moroccan system; the teaching methods they used did not accord with the French-style methods to which the Moroccans had become accustomed. They also faced linguistic difficulties, inasmuch as their lack of knowledge of either French or Moroccan Arabic made it difficult for them to integrate with the other teachers—and indeed with the wider community in which they found themselves. The number of French expatriate teachers had to be increased considerably after 1963 in order to cope with the vast expansion in numbers. At the present time, the process of Moroccanization has been completed in the primary schools, where all staff are now Moroccan, and the proportion of foreign teachers left in secondary schools is decreasing year by year. In 1976–77, there were 7,872 foreign teachers in secondary schools, in 1979–80, 4,954, and in 1982–83, the figure had been reduced to 3,624 (figures from *Le Maroc en Chiffres*, 1976, 1980, and 1982). On the other hand, the number of foreigners teaching in higher education is still increasing every year, though recently the rise seems to be leveling off. (Again according to *Le Maroc en Chiffres*, in 1975–76, there were 374 foreign teachers in Moroccan universities; in 1979–80, 860, and in 1982–83, 934.)

The fourth objective, Arabization, was to restore Arabic to its former position as the sole medium of instruction for all levels of education, and thereby also to establish it as the working language for all spheres of activity. This aim was obviously a reaction against the situation that had prevailed during the Protectorate, when Moroccans had been obliged to adopt an alien language, imposed on them from the outside and bearing no relation to their own culture and heritage. There were also more practical, financial reasons why Arabization seemed desirable, for, as A. Moatassime (1974) notes, a bilingual administration, involving the production of all documents in two languages, was far more costly than one using a single language. In aspiring to the aim of Arabization, people recalled the Middle Ages when Arabic had been a successful vehicle for scholarship in both arts and sciences. However, although about thirty years have now passed since independence was declared, Arabization has still not been completed, and it probably remains the aspect of Morocco's language situation which provokes most debate and discussion today. To see why, after all this time, the role of French in Morocco is still of some importance, we need to consider in more detail some aspects of the present situation.

THE PRESENT SITUATION

Considerably complicating the present language situation in Morocco is the diglossic relationship that holds between Moroccan Arabic and Classical Arabic. Diglossia can be defined as the coexistence in a speech community of two distinct varieties of a language, where each variety has quite separate functions and the two contrast sharply in status. One, usually referred to as the high variety, is regarded as prestigious and is associated with education and refinement, while the other, a low variety, is regarded as inferior and looked on negatively. (For some general discussion of diglossia, see Ferguson, 1959; Marçais, 1930; and Lecerf, 1954. See also Elgibali, this volume.) Moroccan Arabic, as the low variety, is the language used in everyday informal exchanges, and the only language of illiterate Arabic speakers, while Classical Arabic, the high variety, is the only written one, also used in formal speeches, lectures, and news broadcasts. Literate Moroccans are thus faced with a dichotomy, since they cannot easily write down what they might say or utter in an everyday situation things they might write or read.

Along with these functional differences goes a very sharp contrast between people's attitudes to the two varieties. Moroccan Arabic is regarded as an inferior form unworthy of serious attention, whereas Classical Arabic is revered for its richness and beauty. (See, for instance, the results of a survey described in Bentahila, 1983a.) As a standard language, Classical Arabic, unlike Moroccan Arabic, has been codified in dictionaries and grammars. In contrast, the only such descriptions of Moroccan Arabic are those written for nonnative speakers wishing to learn the language, and not intended for use by Moroccans. The prestige of Classical Arabic is further enhanced by its associations with religion, since it is believed to be the very language through which God communicated the Koran to Muhammad. This special religious significance has made Classical Arabic almost unique as a language preserved practically unchanged over many centuries. Other languages are, of course, in a state of constant change. In contrast, Moroccan Arabic has been subject to the influence of French and Spanish, as well as Berber, and has borrowed extensively from both of them. Classical Arabic, however, has been artificially protected from such influences. Finally, Classical Arabic also receives importance because of its role as the language that unites the various Arabic-speaking nations (whose colloquial dialects, as we noted earlier, are not always mutually comprehensible), as a symbol for the Arabs' common culture, and as the vehicle for their literary and scholarly heritage.

Alongside these two contrasting varieties of Arabic, French has maintained a significant role in the life of a large proportion of educated Moroccans. Outside the education system, it continues to be widely used in many spheres. It is without doubt still the language *par excellence* of all scientific and technological matters in Morocco, although changes are being introduced, as we will see. It also plays an important role in the economic and commercial sectors, being the major language used in the operations of banks, building societies, and many other businesses. It is important to realize, however, that its functions are not limited to such professional domains, but that it also plays an important part in the field of leisure activities and entertainments.

Morocco has one radio station which broadcasts only in French and another which is bilingual, switching back and forth between Arabic and French at frequent intervals throughout the day. The single television channel provides programs in French as well as Arabic, and many of the television advertisements are also in French. Several of the daily newspapers published in Morocco are in French, and there is also a wealth of weekly and monthly publications in this language. It is interesting, too, that a local newspaper like *Le Journal de Tanger* uses both Arabic and French in each edition, with columns in Arabic and French mixed together, side by side on the same page. Some other newspapers and magazines, such as *Al bayane* and *Al Assas*, produce two separate versions of each issue, under the same name, one in Arabic and the other in French, to appeal to all sections of the reading public. As for outside entertainments, in the major cinemas in the towns films in French (which include American and other European films dubbed into French) seem to be far more popular than those in Arabic, as can be seen from a glance at the cinema advertisements in the national newspapers. Moreover, films in Egyptian Arabic are often provided with French subtitles when shown in Morocco, in order to facilitate their understanding by Moroccans.

In a survey described in detail in Bentahila (1983a), it was found that a sample of Moroccan bilingual informants liked radio and television programs in French better than those in Arabic, and preferred to read newspapers and books in French rather than in Arabic. The major reasons given for these preferences were in all cases that the materials presented in French were felt to be more up to date, varied, sophisticated, and lively. On the other hand, the small number of informants who said they preferred materials in Arabic tended to justify their choices simply by mentioning the fact that Arabic was "their" language, or suggesting that for reasons of patriotism Moroccans *ought* to prefer material in Arabic. The differences between the kinds of justification given for each choice thus present an interesting contrast. Arabic seems to be favored for idealistic reasons almost as a matter of principle, whereas those who prefer French material have strong instrumental motivations, being influenced by what they themselves can gain, whether in information or entertainment value, from the materials itself.

Moroccans who have received a bilingual education in Arabic and French are thus still likely to find themselves using both of these languages in the course of their everyday lives. However, in certain domains they will probably find it more convenient or appropriate to use one rather than the other. An investigation reported in Bentahila (1983a) found that the kind of interlocutor, type of setting, and topic of conversation all influence the choice of language by such bilinguals, and that generally French tends to be used more than Arabic in situations involving a certain degree of formality, while Arabic is favored in situations of intimacy. A third pattern of language use is the tendency to use, not French alone or Arabic alone, but a mixture of the two involving constant code-switching between Arabic and French, which could almost be identified as another separate variety in the repertoire of Arabic-French bilinguals. (On this subject, see Bentahila, 1983a; Bentahila, 1983b; and Bentahila and Davies, 1983).

Evidence has been obtained through a variety of tests, designed to investigate conscious and unconscious attitudes, to show that French, Classical Arabic, and Moroccan Arabic each have their own distinct images and associations in the minds of Moroccan bilinguals, and that each is felt to be useful for different purposes (see Bentahila, 1983a, for details). These tests found that French, in contrast to Arabic, is consistently associated with modernity, education, and sophistication and is perceived as a means of social advancement. In a matched guise test, Moroccans were judged to be more important, educated, and generally more favorably perceived by other bilinguals when speaking French than when speaking Moroccan Arabic. Moroccan Arabic, on the other hand, is judged to be an indispensable means for everyday communication with ordinary people, but of no other inherent value, whereas Classical Arabic seems to be most prized not for its utility but for what it symbolizes: religion, patriotism, and the Arab identity.

THE EDUCATION SYSTEM AND ARABIZATION

We may now return to look at the way Arabization policies have influenced the present education system. So far, progress toward making Arabic the medium used in all domains has been rather erratic, with frequent reversals of policy and inconsistencies of planning, and some projects have been abandoned. Problems in assembling sufficient numbers of teachers qualified to work through the medium of Arabic, which were compounded by the huge expansion in pupil and student numbers, have hindered the progress of many schemes. In the early years after independence, evening classes were organized in order to prepare teachers to teach through the medium of Arabic. Some other Arabic-speaking countries also helped to establish institutes for the training of teachers. Yet despite all these efforts, progress toward Arabization has been halting, and has led to certain discontinuities, where pupils who began the study of certain subjects in Arabic were afterwards obliged to switch to French in order to continue their studies in the same field. There have also been fluctuations in the support for Arabization among planners and administrators over the years; even those who expressed verbal support for Arabization policies have not always aided their implementation.

Despite these setbacks, the Arabization of primary education is now complete, with even arithmetic and science, which used to be taught in French, now conducted through the medium of Arabic. It is only the French language itself which is now presented through the medium of French, and this is now introduced only in the third year of primary education, instead of from the very beginning, as used to be the case during the Protectorate. At secondary level, Arabization plans are progressing well, with work ongoing toward the preparation of suitable textbooks but at the moment French is still used for some science courses. At the university level, French remains the sole medium of instruction for all scientific and technological subjects. Outside education, many sections of the government administration have now been Arabized, but again French has not been eradicated from the domains of technology. However, there has been progress in developing adequate materials, through the work of the Arabization Office in Rabat, which works in cooperation with similar organizations in other Arab countries in establishing glossaries of Arabic technical terms in various domains.

These attempts to influence the Moroccans' language use through legislation have undoubtedly had some effect, especially on those now passing through the education system. However, while the policy of Arabization is clearly based on an idealistic concern that Morocco should assert its identity as an Arab country and throw off all vestiges of colonial influence, its application has raised a number of practical difficulties. One problem is that, while pupils are now introduced to French at a later stage instead of from their first day at school, and use it far less than was previously the case in their early years at school, they are nevertheless still expected to be able to work through the medium of French if they wish to pursue scientific studies to a higher level. A general lowering in the degree of proficiency achieved in French means that today many students experience real difficulty in coping with university studies through this medium. The problem would, of course, be resolved if Arabization could be extended to cover these higher levels too, but there are still difficulties to be overcome before this can be achieved.

At the purely linguistic level, there have been complaints about the impracticality of the Arabic writing system, with its large number of symbols and diacritics which makes printing in Arabic expensive. A move toward resolving this problem has been brought about by G. A. Lakhdar's development (see Lakhdar, 1976) of a simplified system for printing and typing, which preserves the principles of Arabic calligraphy while reducing the total number of characters required. Application of this system has made the production of material in Arabic more economical, for instance, by reducing the number of keys required on a typewriter. Even on this point, however, there is disagreement, and the system has not been widely adopted outside Morocco. Another problem concerns the absence of short vowel indicators in written Arabic, which means that considerable time and effort are required to acquire fast reading skills. This has often been cited as a serious hindrance to the use of Arabic, by, for instance, Marçais (1930), Lakhdar (1976), Lecerf (1954), Monteuil (1960), Moatassime (1974), and Benyakhlef (1979).

More seriously, there have been difficulties in equipping Classical Arabic with the large set of precisely defined new technical terms required to deal with modern scientific advances. Among the reasons suggested for this have been claims that the morphological structure of Arabic does not lend itself to borrowing from other languages (Lakhdar, 1976), that the language contains large numbers of imprecisely defined synonyms and, more generally, that it is somehow an inherently vague and imprecise language (Monteuil, 1960; Shouby, 1951). The difficulties have been compounded by the lack of coordination between the different Arabic-speaking countries, which has made even a simple exchange of textbooks impractical. Many countries seem to have devised their own sets of terms without regard for those used by others, so that, ironically enough, at a conference of the Arab School on Science and Technology, held in Rabat in 1983, it was felt necessary for all contributions to be presented through the medium of either English or French, but not Arabic! However, the organization of such a conference does show that recently considerable progress has been made with regard to cooperation between different countries, and that interesting research is being carried out in attempting to apply the latest developments in computing and information processing to Arabic materials and to machine translation into Arabic.

Despite some of the claims mentioned in the preceding paragraph, it can be argued that the most serious obstacles to Arabization policies are not so much linguistic as psychological (see Bentahila, 1983a, and forthcoming for this argument). It is not the nature of the Arabic language itself which prevents the establishment of terminology and the preparation of precise scientific texts, but rather the very deeply entrenched attitudes to the language which were mentioned earlier: the fact that Classical Arabic is associated with the past and is felt to be something that should be preserved as it was and protected from external influences. These attitudes are strengthened through the traditional way in which Arabic is taught in school, which involves much memorization, copying, and the study of historical rather than modern texts, with the focus always on written material and a corresponding neglect of oral skills. Moreover, the approach used lays greater emphasis on style and eloquence, the way ideas are expressed rather than the ideas themselves. This excessive concern with *how* to use Classical Arabic makes many Moroccans hesitant to use it at all when they merely want to express something in the simplest and most direct way.

Unfortunately, planners have rarely attempted to make an objective evaluation of the attitudinal factors lying behind current problems. On the contrary, the arguments advanced for Arabization itself, as frequently debated in the press and the media, tend to be couched in subjective and emotive terms, appealing to idealistic notions such as patriotism and national integrity rather than practical concerns such as convenience and economy. However, any ultimately satisfactory resolution of Morocco's language problems, in education or elsewhere, will depend on attitudes to the languages as much as on the languages themselves.

A recent study of the attitudes of a sample of educated bilinguals toward Arabization (Bentahila, 1983a) found that, while most of the respondents did express sympathy with the ideals of promoting the use of Arabic and thereby reinforcing Morocco's true identity as an Arab and Muslim country, and rejected overt criticisms of the policy of Arabization, their answers nevertheless revealed a strong attachment to the bilingual Arabic-French system through which they themselves were educated. While firmly rejecting the idea that science could not be taught in Arabic, they nevertheless indicated their own preference that it should be taught in French. A majority favored the maintenance of bilingual education and felt that knowing both Arabic and French was a source of enrichment which enabled them to express themselves better than would otherwise be the case; only 8 percent claimed to regret their bilingualism. Strikingly, they strongly endorsed the suggestion that Moroccans feel closer to Europe than to the Middle East. There would thus seem to be something of a conflict in the minds of such bilinguals—between their theoretical support for Arabization, as an ideal, and their strong awareness of the practical advantages of bilingualism. Given that this kind of Arabic-French bilingual represents a majority of the educated younger generation (the number of Moroccans pursuing a monolingual Arabic education in state schools is relatively small: only 23,660 in 1982–83, as opposed to 878,574 pupils in bilingual state schools—figures from *Le Maroc en Chiffres*, 1982), their views should be given careful attention.

Findings such as these suggest that the planners should not simply pursue the goal of eradicating French from every domain, regardless of the consequences. The policy to be pursued should be seen as one of enrichment rather than of reduction, with the focus on developing the usefulness of Arabic rather than too hastily discarding the advantages offered by a knowledge of French. One step that would contribute to this goal would be a reduction of the distance between Moroccan Arabic and Classical Arabic.The development of a more practical, unified form of Arabic which can readily be both spoken and written, and which can cope with all the varied needs of its users, would do more than anything else to establish Arabic as the primary language of Moroccans in all domains, Meanwhile, it would seem that many Moroccans are understandably reluctant to abandon the benefits to which their bilingualism gives them access. A decisive move toward Arabic monolingualism, however appealing on ideological grounds, would mean sacrificing these practical advantages and moving against the trends of the space age world, where international communication is becoming ever more important. Thus, while efforts should be concentrated on developing the potential of Arabic to become a truly practical tool with an up-to-date image, it would seem appropriate, in the meantime, to preserve for Moroccans the advantages of bilingualism, while ensuring that the bilingualism that they are offered is of what Lambert (1977:19) calls the "additive" rather than the "subtractive" sort.

SUMMARY

The language situation in Morocco today is a complex one involving several different languages and many different categories of bilingual speakers. Berber and Moroccan Arabic are spoken as first languages; Classical Arabic is the high variety standing in a diglossic relationship to colloquial Moroccan Arabic; and French and, to a lesser extent, Spanish are used as second languages. The elements of this present situation can be traced to the country's geographical position and to the historical contacts between peoples to which this position contributed: notably, the Arab conquest of the seventh century and the French Protectorate of the first half of the present century. Since 1956 when the French left, numerous plans have been proposed to restore Arabic to its former position

as the only medium of instruction and administration. Despite these efforts to
achieve Arabization, French still plays an important role in many domains,
especially in the fields of science and technology, as well as being used in
everyday life by large numbers of Moroccans. The problems encountered by
language planners attempting to implement Arabization programs have often
been attributed to the nature of the Arabic language itself, but it is suggested
here that the greatest obstacles arise rather from people's attitudes toward their
languages. Research suggests that Moroccans who know French are very conscious of the advantages they gain from this bilingualism. Although in theory
they tend to sympathize with the ideal of Arabization, they are reluctant to
abandon the benefits to be derived from a knowledge of French unless convinced
that Arabic is practical enough to cope with all their twentieth-century needs.

BIBLIOGRAPHY

Baina, A. 1981. *Le système de l'enseignement au Maroc*. Casablanca: Editions
     Maghrebines.
Bentahila, A. 1983a. *Language Attitudes Among Arabic-French Bilinguals in Morocco*.
     Clevedon, England: Multilingual Matters Ltd.
———. 1983b. "Motivations for Code-Switching Among Arabic-French Bilinguals in
     Morocco." *Language and Communication* 3, No. 3.
———. Forthcoming. "Language Attitudes as an Obstacle to Arabisation." *Proceedings
     of the Arab School on Science and Technology, 1st Fall Session*. Washington,
     D.C.: Hemisphere Publishing Corp.
Bentahila, A., and E. E. Davies. 1983. "The Syntax of Arabic-French Code-Switching."
     Lingua 59, 4.
Benyakhlef, M. 1979. "Propositions pour une arabisation de niveau." *Lamalif*, No. 104.
Bidwell, R. 1973. *Morocco Under Colonial Rule*. London: Frank Cass.
Blondel, A. M., and F. Décorsière. 1962. "Une possibilité d'enrichissement." *Esprit*,
     October-December: 787–91.
Bloomfield, L. 1933. *Language*. London: Allen and Unwin.
Brunot, L. 1950. *Introduction à l'arabe Marocain*. Paris: Maisonneuve et Cie.
Christophersen, P. 1948. *Bilingualism*. London: Methuen.
Diebold, A. R. 1961. "Incipient Bilingualism." *Language* 37: 97–112.
Ferguson, C. A. 1959. "Diglossia." *Word* 15:325–40.
Gellner, E. 1973. "Introduction." In *Arabs and Berbers: From Tribe to Nation in North
     Africa*, ed. E. Gellner and C. Mimcaud. London: Duckworth.
Hoffman, B. G. 1967. *The Structure of Traditional Moroccan Rural Society*. The Hague:
     Mouton.
Lakhdar, G. A. 1976. *Méthodologie générale de l'arabisation de niveau*. Rabat: Institute
     d'Etudes et de Recherches pour l'Arabisation.
Lambert, W. E. 1977. "The Effects of Bilingualism on the Individual: Cognitive and
     Sociocultural Consequences." In *Bilingualism: Psychological, Social and Edu-
     cational Implications*, ed. P. A. Hornby. New York: Academic Press.
Lecerf, J. 1954. "Esquisse d'une problématique de l'arabe actuel." *Afrique et Asie* 26:31–
     46.

Marçais, W. 1930. "La diglossie arabe." *L'enseignement public* 97:401–409.
Maroc en Chiffres, Le. 1976, 1980, 1982. Casablanca: Banque Marocaine du Commerce Exterieur.
Moatassime, A. 1974. "Le bilinguisme sauvage au Maroc." *Revue du Tiers Monde* 15:619–70.
Monteuil, V. 1960. *L'arabe moderne*. Paris: Librairie C. Klincksieck.
Shouby, E. 1951. "The Influence of the Arabic Language on the Psychology of the Arabs." *Middle East Journal* 5:284–302.
Zafrani, H. 1980. *Litteratures dialectales et popularies juives en occident musulman*. Paris: Geuthner.
Zartman, J. W. 1964. *Morocco: Problems of New Power*. New York: Alberton Press.

17

Adebisi Afolayan

BILINGUALISM AND BILINGUAL
EDUCATION IN NIGERIA

Nigeria is a multilingual, multicultural, and multinational polity. Hence, multilingualism, or at least bilingualism, is a necessary condition for the country's
development and growth. But the nature of bilingualism required for the Nigerian
socio-politico-economic context is not matched by the patterns of its bilingual
education. For Nigeria to achieve an optimum level of development, therefore,
there should be a new direction in its bilingual education program. More importantly, that new, dynamic, and development-oriented program must be effectively and efficiently executed in order to produce the desired growth and
development not only of individual Nigerian citizens but also of the entire geopolitical unit as a socio-politico-economic community.

MULTILINGUALISM AND MULTICULTURALISM IN
NIGERIA

Although the exact population of the Federal Republic of Nigeria today is
unknown, it is an indisputable fact that the country is multilingual and multicultural. The last census of the country was undertaken in 1963, and because a
political interpretation is always given to any census by its citizens, it has not
been possible to hold any other reliable census since. The nature of the ethnic
groups represented in the 1963 census figures is provided by a breakdown quoted
in West Africa in August 1966, as follows:

Ten Component Parts of the Nigerian Population

1. Hausa Fulani: 13.6 million people (two different intermingled ethnic groups)
2. Yoruba: 13 million

3. Ibo: 7.8 million

4. Efik/Ibiobio: 3.2 million

5. Kanuri: 2.9 million

6. Tiv: 1.5 million

7. Ijaw: 0.9 million

8. Edo: 0.9 million

9. Urhobo: 0.6 million

10. Nupe: 0.5 million

There are forty-one minor component units.

The total population given for Nigeria by the 1963 census was 55 million. Since then, the population has increased tremendously, and at the same time, more information about the linguistic nature of the country has also become available. It is generally accepted that over two hundred languages are spoken in the country, and some scholars (Ikara, 1984) already suggest that the languages number over four hundred.

From the historical point of view, Nigeria is a multilingual, multicultural, and multinational polity brought together as a geopolitical unit by the British colonial power in 1914. Prior to the amalgamation of the two Protectorates of Southern and Northern Nigeria in 1914, the various peoples lived as separate sociocultural units within differently administered political-economic units. On the one hand, as a sociocultural unit, the various peoples had their different languages, but the socio-politico-economic units were not in one-to-one correspondence with the different languages. Neither were the various sociocultural units or even the socio-politico-economic units of the same texture. Thus, although African historians have produced sufficient evidence showing that it was not the British colonial power that initiated socioeconomic interactions among the various peoples, it was clear that it was the British colonial power that brought all the people together in successive stages under the same single political administration. First, it was the people around Lagos Colony and other coastal places that were brought together under the same administration; then the peoples in the immediate neighboring hinterland areas, although as looser units; and finally, the entire country.

Since different ethnic groups were involved, historically different kinds of sociocultural, political, and administrative patterns of living characterized the various peoples. For example, the southwestern part of the country was noted for its strong organization and monarchical form of government. The political administration was dominated by obas and chiefs who were in charge of various political units. In contrast, the southeastern part of the country tended to be primarily a republic. It was also not characterized by large-scale organization. In further contrast, the northern part of the country had fallen under the unifying force of Islam. This Islamic influence was superimposed upon a traditional monarchical administrative setup. Thus, in a way, the political organization of the north and the southwest resembled each other. However, the southwest and southeast (or the West and the East, as they were known politically) also resembled each other from the point of view of religion. In each of the two places, African traditional religion was being replaced by Christianity. This was understandable inasmuch as these areas were closest to the coast and therefore constituted the first natural points of contact with the Christian missionaries who had come into the country by boat across the Atlantic. On the other hand, the diverse forms of traditional African religion were more easily influenced and replaced by the Christian religion than Islam was. In contrast, the northern part of the country was farthest from the missionary's initial points of call in the country. Moreover, the pervading Islamic religion was more powerful in resisting the influence of the Christian religion.

From the very beginning, therefore, there was a disparity between the way the north and the south received Western Christian influences. This disparity was heightened by the informality of the British colonial policy. The British colonial power always liked to be as little involved in the local administration as possible, primarily in order to cut down the total costs of colonial administration. The British colonial power, therefore, was inclined to utilize the local people's machinery of government. Thus, it tried to perfect its practice into what became known as the system of Indirect Rule or Native Administration. Nigeria happened to be the part of the British colonial empire where this system was finally evolved and most fully implemented.

The British colonial power, in bringing the various peoples together as a geopolitical unit in 1914 (and even in the earlier successive stages of amalgamating various peoples since the conquest of Lagos in 1861 and its annexation in 1863), deemed it necessary to introduce the English language into the already multilingual situation as the linguistic tool of administration for Nigeria. Although it is erroneous to believe, as many still do, that these various peoples were totally uneducated and that it was the Christian missionaries and the British colonial power that introduced education into their midst, it cannot be denied that the various peoples were generally at the preliterate level of existence. Thus, they enjoyed traditional or nonformal education. The level of traditional education was impressive and strong, but formal education to inculcate literacy and modern scientific ideas was introduced by the Christian missionaries and the colonial authorities. Of course, earlier a form of literacy education had developed around Timbuktu and was spread through the influence of Islam. Undoubtedly, the effect of that education was then limited both in the scope of the curriculum and the extent of its patrons or clients. In any case, it was through that means that another foreign language was introduced into the area, namely, Arabic. However, since the educational processes were very limited in scope, the influence of the Arabic language was yet more restricted. The borrowing of Arabic words by the indigenous local languages of the area and the survival of many of those borrowed words in the languages today bear eloquent testimony to this contact between Arabic and the local Nigerian languages either directly or through Hausa. Apart from those borrowings, the influence of Arabic has been more or less confined to the field of religion, where Islam has been the main channel of introducing the language to the various Nigerian peoples.

The dominating influence of the colonial administration made the English language stand out from other languages available to the Nigerian peoples. It was the most prestigious, and the mastery of it conferred great social, political, and economic power on its speakers. Thus, it could be said that the many languages of the total Nigerian population fell largely into two groups. The larger group was made up of all indigenous languages of the people, and the other group was made up of only English. As noted above, Arabic has had its domain only in religion. Hence, bilingualism rather than multilingualism was required of individual Nigerian citizens in order to function as competitive and successful members of the Nigerian nation from its inception.

PATTERNS OF BILINGUALISM IN NIGERIA

From what has been said so far, it is clear that the pattern of bilingualism could not have been uniform. There were both historical shifts and different phases from the geo-sociocultural point of view. We have already mentioned certain aspects of the historical phases of bilingualism in Nigeria, but there are at least two other important features to note. The first is marked by the successive stages of infiltration of the English language, through the successive stages of expansion of British colonial administration, over the entire geopolitical unit. The second was the nature of the changes in the pattern of bilingualism that occurred within each location or administrative unit.

Other Important Historical Features

There was a lack of uniformity in the practice of bilingualism, particularly as it involved the use of the English language. Understandably, English as an instrument of bilingualism was first imposed and established in Lagos and other places very close to the coast. The English language was in effect first introduced by the British traders to their Nigerian counterparts. The Portuguese, and not the British, were the first European nation to come to the west coast of Africa, and a simplified secondary language emerged from the language-contact situation. Thus, commercial interactions have been responsible for the growth of Pidgin English. This kind of secondary language is not the same as the language of the British trading visitors, which later became entrenched among the people through educational processes. The greatest links between them are provided by the fact that the same locality was immediately involved and the peoples and languages that had come into contact in both commercial and educational situations were virtually the same. The earlier commercial situation was more complex in terms both of the peoples and the languages involved. That is why there are some words of Portuguese origin in Nigerian Pidgin English.

The spread of the English language as the second language available to the bilingual Nigeria, which began at the coast, can be said to have extended over the entire federation by the Act of Amalgamation of the country into one political unit in 1914. From that time until Nigerian independence in October 1, 1960— that is, for the remaining period of Nigerian colonial history—distinct regions could be recognized in identifying patterns of bilingualism. These formed the political basis of the administration of the country, and at first they were three: East, North, and West.

A kind of north-south differentiation was established. The East and the West were most alike with regard to the pattern of bilingualism. Not only was English used in the two regions, but also a dominant Nigerian language existed in each. Both Nigerian languages belonged to the same Kwa family. Thus, for most citizens, the linguistic problems of learning and using the English language were not very dissimilar in the two regions, and a fairly similar kind of dialect of English tended to emerge in both. However, there were two major differences between the two regions. In the Western Region, a greater proportion of citizens were native speakers of the dominant Yoruba language, whereas Igbo was the dominant language of the Eastern Region. To further accentuate this difference between these two regions, the minority areas within the Western Region were later carved out into a fourth political region, the Midwest Region. This left the Western Region monolingual while the Eastern Region remained multilingual, though with a dominant majority language.

The carving out of the Midwest Region further complicated the pattern of bilingualism in the South, making it yet more unlike the pattern in the North. On the one hand, the Midwest Region became the most multilingual of all the regions, and, in addition, it was the smallest. Thus, of all the regions it most favored the spread and use of the English language (or its counterpart, Pidgin English) as a lingua franca.

The second event that separated the Western Region from the Eastern Region occurred toward the end of the colonial era. Both regions took advantage of the opportunity offered by the British colonial government for any region that so desired to assume some measure of autonomy. In 1955, the Western Region embarked on a Universal Free Primary Education Scheme. Soon after, the Eastern Region followed. The Western Region's plan succeeded and still survives, but the Eastern Region had to severely modify its scheme. Thus, this distinction further separated the pattern of bilingualism in the two regions. Every young citizen of the Western Region, particularly after the carving out of the Midwest Region, could embark not only on bilingualism but also on a diglossia involving the mother tongue, Yoruba, and English. In contrast, only a percentage (although still perhaps a majority) of the citizens of the Eastern Region could similarly embark on both bilingual-ism and diglossia involving Igbo and English. The number of those citizens of the Eastern Region who could embark on diglossia was further reduced by the need to communicate with non-Igbo speakers of the region. This meant that the English language served as a language of everyday communication, as a lingua franca, among many citizens of the region.

The Midwest Region, the youngest and the most short-lived region, was the most complex in terms of multiplicity of languages. Of the ten ethnic groups earlier listed for the country, three (Ijaw, Edo, Urhobo) belong to this region. Therefore, multilingualism, rather than bilingualism, was the normal practice there. Everyone would normally begin by learning and using their own mother tongue. Another language, either an indigenous language of the wider locality or Pidgin English, was needed to communicate with neighbors located either within the same local government or the adjoining local government. Once in school, they had to learn the English language, which was the official language of government. In contrast, in the rest of the South, bilingualism and even a tendency to diglossia prevailed.

The Northern Region presents a contrasting pattern to the South in general, and the East and the West or later Midwest in particular. Two different ethnic groups, the Hausas and the Fulanis, had so intermingled that they all virtually used the Hausa language as their mother tongue. That does not mean that Fulani is no longer an independent language. Of the ten major ethnic groups, three others, besides the Hausa-Fulani group belong to the Northern Region: the Kan-uri, the Tiv, and the Nupe. Only the Nupes numbered under a million. The other two constituted the fifth and the sixth most populous groups in the country—about two and three million, respectively. Hence, although Hausa was a major language of the region, speakers of other languages within the region outnum-bered those with Hausa as their mother tongue. Because of the importance of Hausa and its status as the language of everyday use as the means of disseminating and sustaining the Islamic religion that was widespread over the entire area, many speakers of the minority languages learned Hausa as their second language. The North and East therefore had something in common in respect of bilin-gualism: a certain percentage of the citizens were bilingual in their mother tongue and the major language of the region (Igbo for the East and Hausa for the North). Only in the Midwestern Region, particularly when it was part of the Western Region, were there bilinguals who had their mother tongue and Yoruba as their two languages. The majority of the total population of the Western Region were monolingual rather than bilingual. Initially at least, the majority of the citizens in any of the regions, simply because of the limitation in the spread of the English language as an effective tool for communication, were monolingual in their mother tongues. As socio-politico-economic interactions within each region strengthened and formal educational processes became more established, of the four only in the Western Region were the majority of the total population monolinguals.

Current Patterns of Bilingualism

Following J. Fishman (1968), we would like to recognize the ambiguity in the English word "nation," and attempt to analyze the "successive stages of sociocultural integration" taking place within the Federal Republic of Nigeria to produce different "stages of nationalisms" and the "successive stages of politico-geographical integration" resulting in different "stages of nationism." The Nigerian languages were the instruments of sociocultural integration, whereas political and constitutional provisions were the instruments of geopolitical integration.

Three stages of sociocultural integration have taken place within the Federation of Nigeria: monolingualism, bilingualism, and multilingualism. The overall situation is actually more complex because each stage can take different forms, and there is some measure of overlap between any two stages of integration. This situation of overlap is easy to conceive in view of the general fact that all language matters are issues of "more or less" rather than of "all or none."

The first stage of sociocultural integration, marked by monolingualism-monoculturalism, takes place within three different sociocultural contexts and three different forms: primarily within an ethnic or sociocultural group; secondarily within an ethnic or sociocultural group into which its immediate neighbors have been incorporated; and among different types of speakers of the same language (mother tongue, second language, and even foreign language speakers of the language, particularly the first two).

The first and primary context of integration based on monolingualism-monoculturalism within the same ethnic or sociocultural group is a natural process, particularly within a multilingual community. That a group of people speaks the same language and shares other allied cultural features lead members of that group to act in common in relation to members of other groups. This has largely been misconceived in Nigeria as tribalism but should properly be regarded as nationalism. The negative connotation evoked by the use of "tribalism" has its roots in certain feelings of racial superiority. For the use of "tribe" to refer to each ethnic group in Africa is matched by the use of "nation" for each of such groups in Europe. Thus, it is customary to refer to the "Welsh nation," the "Scottish nation," and the "English nation" within the United Kingdom in contrast with references to the "Yoruba tribe," the "Hausa tribe," and the "Igbo tribe" within Nigeria. When the elements of racial superiority and antagonism are removed, it is the same or comparable process of sociocultural integration that results in the strong feelings of nationalism among the Welsh, the Scottish, or the English within the United Kingdom and the feelings of nationalism among the Hausas, the Igbos, and the Yorubas of Nigeria. This point needs to be emphasized, particularly because of its inevitable intermediate status within the positive development of an overall feeling of nationalism common to all Nigerians in the Federal Republic of Nigeria and to which all local or component "nationalisms" are subordinated. Like any other process of recognizing the individual in contrast with others, this "nationalism" based on each ethnic group has its negative aspects that may be rooted in insularity, sectionalism, and unhealthy rivalry. The "nationalism" based on each ethnic group, characterized by monolingualism and monoculturalism, is a natural stage within the sociocultural integration of different peoples within a multilingual-multicultural polity.

This stage of sociocultural integration, based on a single language or culture, may operate within different geopolitical units within the Federal Republic of Nigeria. When the language is a minority one, it may just function at the village level. A majority language such as Hausa, Igbo, or Yoruba may function at the local government, state, or even national level.

When the domain of monolingualism-monoculturalism is the local government, it is common to find in Nigeria today that the people involved belong to the same ethnic group. Sometimes, however, if the local government area itself is multilingual with a majority language and a satellite of minority languages, we may have a situation where the sociocultural integration is found within a group comprising the mother-tongue speakers of the language and minority groups of second-language speakers of the language. This same kind of integration may be found at the state level. The first form occurring within a single ethnic group will be found only within monolingual states of Nigeria, such as Kano, Imo, and Oyo. The second form, occurring within a group larger than a single ethnic group, will be found in each multilingual state with a majority language and a host of minority languages, the speakers of which have learned to use the majority language as a second language.

The second stage of sociocultural integration is effected by bilingualism-biculturalism. This stage overlaps the first stage of sociocultural integration, whereby speakers of a minority language have acquired the majority language of their local government or state as their second language. Such individuals are not monolinguals but bilinguals. Thus, in a very real sense, that situation constitutes a form of the second stage of sociocultural integration: the incorporation of a member of a minority group into that of a majority group. The enlarged group is based on one language and one culture, but, as an integrated group, it possesses some bilingual-bicultural elements.

The status of the majority language within the entire Nigerian political unit affects the domain at which it operates. We have already mentioned the local government and the state levels. If that majority language is one of the three major Nigerian languages recognized by the Nigerian Constitution (Hausa, Igbo, and Yoruba), then the integrated group may operate at the national level. Indeed, such a bilingual-bicultural individual may even have another majority Nigerian language, instead of a minority language (which we have earlier identified) as the mother tongue.

As an alternative to an indigenous Nigerian language, the English language may be the second language of the bilingual-bicultural person. When that happens, the bilingual person can effectively operate not only on local and state levels, but also on the national level. This fact is supported by the two relevant provisions, Paragraphs 51 and 91 of *The Constitution of the Federal Republic of Nigeria 1979*:

51   The business of the National Assembly shall be conducted in English, and in Hausa, Ibo and Yoruba when adequate arrangements have been made therefor.

91   The business of a House of Assembly shall be conducted in English but the House may in addition to English conduct the business of the House in one or more other languages spoken in the State as the House may by resolution approve.

The level of sociocultural integration tends to be both looser and stronger in the second stage involving English and an indigenous Nigerian language than that based on two indigenous Nigerian languages. That is paradoxical but perhaps not too difficult to understand. Normally, this second stage of sociocultural integration is also marked by some element of diglossia. The specialization of the roles of the two languages involved in the bilingualism-biculturalism provides the necessary explanation. At the personal and intimate cultural levels, a bilingualism-biculturalism that is based on two indigenous Nigeran languages is bound to be stronger than that based on an indigenous language and the English language. After all, any two Nigerian languages are bound to be more culturally related than an indigenous language and the English language. On the other hand, when national and less personal or official matters are concerned, the involvement of the English language in the bilingual process tends to signal a stronger tie between the members of the bilingual group than that existing among members of the group whose bilingualism involves just two indigenous languages. In this connection, when the involvement of two indigenous Nigerian languages in a bilingual process becomes the tool of a stronger tie among members of a group in the consideration of national or official matters, paradoxically such a stronger tie is indicative of a looser level of national integration. It is indicative of sectionalism at the national level, which means that the effective sociocultural integration has taken place at the second stage which operates at the state, rather than at the national, level. Undoubtedly, that stage of sociocultural integration has been most effectively attained in Nigeria today.

The third stage of integration is characterized by multilingualism-multiculturalism. Again, as is in the two other stages, there is an overlap between the second and third stage. We have seen how the bilingual may also be able to operate at the national level instead of being restricted to the state level. We have also seen how the integration promoted by a bilingualism involving two indigenous Nigerian languages can only be a pseudonational one. This means that the most usual instrument for the Nigerian national integration is multilingualism. Hence, for a Nigerian today effective sociocultural integration at the national level will have to be found within a group using several languages in order for it to be a strong form of integration. The weaker form of national integration is usually maintained by bilingualism. This is because the indigenous language component will tend to introduce some weakening element of social disintegration through the promotion of sectional interests of the sociocultural group attached to that language. The exception is when the evidence for the national sociocultural integration is produced by fighting a common national enemy. Otherwise it requires several languages and several sociocultural groups to be involved in the consideration of a national matter, and without any superior power or backing for any of the languages or groups, before evidence of socio-cultural integration at the national level can be naturally produced.Thus we can conclude that today multilingualism-multiculturalism is a necessary condition for the development of sociocultural integration at the overall Nigerian national level.

This now brings us to the consideration of the "successive stages of politico-geographical integration" within Nigeria, producing various "successive stages of nationalism." This is best discussed within the three-tier system of political administration existing within the country: the local government, the state government, and the federal government.

The geopolitical structure of the country provides a framework within which the politico-geographical integration could take place in successive stages. This administrative structure is organized at three levels. First, there is the *local government level* with monolingualism and monoculturalism as its dominant agent; at this level the highest form of integration has taken place. Second, there is the *state level*. As has been noted earlier, prior to the creation of states, there were three and later four regions. The regional basis of administration provided a basis for politico-geographical integration marked by two characteristics. (1) Each of the regions was dominated by one of the three main Nigerian languages. Consequently, the politico-geographical integration that was achieved tended to be based on the three major ethnic groups of the country and therefore was conducive to a great deal of unhealthy rivalry that eventually culminated in the civil war between 1966 and 1970. (2) The integration was also characterized by the agitation of minority groups. The minorities claimed their right to self-determination and individual recognition. Thus, there was a great deal of tension within whatever had been achieved as evidence of politico-geographical integration. This tension was, among other means, signaled by the agitation for independent states for various minority groups. This agitation, coupled with the effects of political alignments, first resulted in the creation of the Midwest Region out of the old Western Region. Later, it resulted in the division of the country into twelve states in 1966 and the establishment of the current nineteen-state structure of the country in 1975. One of the major activities of the Second Republic between 1979 and 1983 was the consideration of creating more states. If the people's wishes had been met, the total number of states today would be no less than fifty. Although the present economic situation prevents any further action in that direction, it seems valid to conclude that this agitation for states has arisen from the belief that the state level constitutes the most potent force for politico-geographical integration in the country today. Although this level of integration has, as has earlier been described, bilingualism-biculturalism as its agent generally in the country, it has tended to develop most effectively on monolingualism and monoculturalism.

Finally, there is the *federal or national level* of politico-geographical integration. This level of integration which, as has earlier been described, thrives best on multilingualism-multiculturalism, seems to be the least developed so far.

National unity and national divisiveness have interesting correlations with the occurrence and utilization of monolingualism, bilingualism, and multilingualism in Nigeria today. On the one hand, as Joshua Fishman (1968:45) has remarked:

The general point here is that differences do not need to be divisive. *Divisiveness is an ideologized position* and it can magnify minor differences; indeed, it can manufacture differences in languages as in other matters almost as easily as it can minimize seemingly major differences or ignore them entirely, whether these be in the realm of language, religion, culture, race, or any other basis of differentiation.

Conscious and even ideologized language differences need not be divisive, whether at the national or at the international level. Thus the pattern of national diglossia has its international counterparts as well.

On the other hand, the ideologized positions that are tantamount to divisiveness and unity, respectively, are stimulated, fostered, and maintained by the language situation existing within a geopolitico entity such as Nigeria. There is, therefore, some justification in the provisions found in Paragraph 8 of *The Federal Republic of Nigeria National Policy on Education* (1977):

8.   In addition to appreciating the importance of language in the educational process, and as a means of preserving the people's culture, the Government considers it to be in the interest of national unity that each child should be encouraged to learn one of the three major languages other than his own mother-tongue. In this connection, the Government considers the three major languages in Nigeria to be Hausa, Ibo and Yoruba.

Undoubtedly, the assumption behind that provision is that the less linguistically diversified or the more linguistically unified the Federal Republic of Nigeria can become, the greater the level of unity that can be attained. There is some measure of validity in that assumption. This assumption seems to be supported by the people's wish for states that are more or less based on monolingualism and monoculturalism. In any case, failure to implement the provisions of that paragraph indicates the measure of politico-geographical integration or lack of it that has taken place effectively in the country at the federal or national level.

BILINGUAL EDUCATION IN NIGERIA

The nature of language development and language use in Nigeria has a high degree of correlation with its level of sociocultural integration and politico-geographical integration. Essentially, we have shown that bilingualism-bicul-turalism characterizes the emergent Nigerian. In order to promote bilingualism and its immediate sibling, diglossia, education must be invoked. Indeed, the amount of bilingualism and diglossia now found in the country is the product of education. Moreover, it seems inevitable that education should be effectively and efficiently bilingual-bicultural and even multilingual-multicultural if the re-quired level of sociocultural and political integration is to be attained. In that connection, we have already shown that multilingualism-multiculturalism is re-quired for the highest level of sociocultural integration and politico-geographical integration at the national or federal level. We have also shown that bilingualism-biculturalism could effectively operate at the national level as an alternative.

The current educational system is not sufficiently and efficiently bilingual-bicultural, let alone being multilingual-multicultural. As has been shown, ef-fective participation at the national level requires bilingualism-biculturalism based on the individual Nigerian citizen's mother tongue and the English lan-guage. The efficacy of bilingualism-biculturalism based on the individual Ni-gerian's mother tongue and another majority Nigerian language has to await the emergence and mass acceptance of an indigenous Nigerian language as the official and national languages of the country. Unfortunately, the indigenous Nigerian languages have been largely neglected, and the English language has been both underrated and overrated. The individual citizen's mother tongue ought to be the basis for full primary education if permanent literacy and permanent numeracy are to be the minimal goals of primary education. The *National Policy* demands those goals, and they seem to be reasonable and valid demands.

Recent events have indicated that primary education will for some time at least remain the only level of formal education that can be made available to all citizens of Nigeria. In 1976, the federal government embarked on a Universal Free Primary Education Scheme for the entire nation. Primary education is not yet universal or compulsory for all children in the nation because the rampant worldwide economic regression has made it impracticable. Indeed, the economic situation is forcing a considerable reduction or shrinking of opportunities for secondary and tertiary levels of education. It has therefore become increasingly important that primary education be effective. It has also become increasingly clear that the lack of adequate emphasis on the utilization of the individual citizen's mother tongues for primary education signals the ineffectiveness of current primary education.

Similarly, the English language has not been made to play its proper role within the educational system. As has been shown elsewhere (Afolayan, 1984), besides the enigmatic process of both underrating and overrating it, there has also been a game of self-deception behind the utilization of English within the educational system of the country. The effective use of English as the medium of primary education is falsely assumed to have been achieved. At the secondary school level, the specialized subject areas are overemphasized at the expense of the English-language medium, which has been so deemphasized that what passes for secondary education is generally mere memorization and regurgitation of notes. At the tertiary level of education, the level of English required is also underrated, while at the same time the corresponding amount of English already acquired by the students is overrated. Consequently, the level of bilingual-bicultural education given in the country is ineffective and inadequate, being incapable of inculcating in the recipients a positive self-image, originality of thought, or independent initiative in action.

If Nigeria is to have an educational program that is maximally development-oriented, bilingual-bicultural education must be reorganized. Similarly, multi-lingualism-biculturalism will have to be effectively promoted in order to foster and maximize the nation's level of sociocultural integration and politico-geo-graphical integration. In addition to making adequate provisions for the use of the individual citizens' mother tongues and the English language in all forms and levels of education, there will also be the need to implement the type of provisions found in Paragraph 8 of the current National Policy. This means that, for example, within the new 6–3–4 system of education envisaged for the country, the first six years of primary education will have the child's mother tongue as the medium and both the mother tongue and the English language as subjects; the first three years of secondary education will have the child's mother tongue, one of the three Nigerian major languages (Hausa, Igbo, and Yoruba) and English as subjects and also English as its medium; and the last three years of secondary education, as well as the subsequent tertiary education, will have at least English as a subject and as a medium, and the other languages (the student's mother tongue and any other Nigerian languages) may then be studied optionally or as the need arises.

At the same time, it should be possible for continuing education programs to exist vigorously for those whose formal education has terminated at the primary level. In such an event, their mother tongues should be the necessary tools for such life-long educational processes. Resources, such as specialized books, should therefore be made available to ensure the success of such programs. Similarly, the execution of mass literacy programs and the maintenance of effective nonformal education at all levels should be based on indigenous Nigerian languages. In addition, informal educational programs and facilities should be provided in Nigerian languages as well as in the English language. When all the languages in Nigeria have been properly utilized in their appropriately specialized roles, all forms of education (formal, informal, and nonformal) at all levels (fundamental, secondary, and tertiary or elementary, intermediate, and advanced) can be fully harnessed for the development of individual citizens and the country as a whole. It is then that maximum sociocultural integration and politico-geographical integration will be attained in the country and that a true "unity in diversity" model of bilingual-bicultural education (Afolayan, 1978) will be found to be in efficient operation in Nigeria.

Certain difficulties now stand in the way of successful implementation of a bilingual educational program. The indigenous Nigerian languages are yet to be reduced into writing. Moreover, technical terms and necessary metalanguage for use in educational and noneducational formal contexts are yet to be available for virtually all of them. Not only textbooks and other instructional materials, but also the teachers required for various forms and levels of education in the languages or through their media are yet to be produced both qualitatively and quantitatively. Such a program is too expensive, particularly as so many languages are involved. It is not just that the entire country is multilingual-multicultural, but that certain states, many localities, and even an appreciable number of cosmopolitan centers are extremely diversified linguistically and culturally. Above all, there is no rallying national ideology; consequently, the political will to launch and implement such a program is lacking.

Fortunately, all of these problems are surmountable and once it is fully realized that such a program holds the key to future social, political, intellectual, scientific, and technological development, and the growth and progress of the modern Nigerian nation, the necessary machinery can be set in motion. The required national ideology can be adopted and backed by the necessary political will. Then the Nigerian nation can achieve the bilingual educational program to attain the desired development and growth in this present-day scientific and technological age.

BIBLIOGRAPHY

Afolayan, A. 1978. "Towards an Adequate Theory of Bilingual Education for Africa." In *International Dimensions of Bilingual Education*, ed. J. E. Alatis. Washington, D.C.: Georgetown University, Round Table on Languages and Linguistics 1978.
———. 1984. "The English Language in Nigerian Education as an Agent of Proper Multilingual and Multicultural Development." *Journal of Multilingual and Multicultural Development* 5: 1.
The Constitution of the Federal Republic of Nigeria. 1979. Lagos: Federal Ministry of Information.
The Federal Republic of Nigeria National Policy on Education. 1977. Lagos: Federal Ministry of Information.
Fishman, J. 1968. "Nationality-Nationalism and Nation-Nationism." In *Language Problems of Developing Nations*, ed. J. A. Fishman, C. A. Ferguson, and J. D. Gupta.
Ikara, B. 1984. "English as a Communicative Medium and a Cultural Dilemma in Nigeria." A key-note address delivered at the Conference on English Studies in Higher Education in Nigeria, Bayero University, Kano, September 24–28, 1984.

BILINGUALISM IN PARAGUAY

THE NATIONAL LINGUISTIC COMMUNITY

In recent years, the traditional perspective from which the study of bilingualism in Paraguay was approached has been significantly broadened and enhanced. This concern has manifested itself as an effort to affirm the value of bilingualism as a distinctive element of the nation and, hence, as a significant factor in its unity and survival.

The persistent glorification of Guarani, which in certain historical moments prepared the way for a confrontation with tendencies restricting the use of the native language, has generated a series of materials, documents, and studies—of varying worth and scope—that permit us to appraise the strength of this effort. This task was fundamentally sustained through the use of the native language—as is usually the case among folklorists—rather than through an integral and dynamic perception of the bilingual process itself. Today this process is conceptualized as an expression of the merging of two societies as a comprehensive historical phenomenon.

This chapter will attempt a systematic and evaluative overview of the traditionally recognized aspects of Paraguayan bilingualism. In addition, it will offer a critical, contemporary perspective from which we may assess both the implications of the two contact languages for formal education and the sociolinguistic attitudes of Paraguayans toward this situation.

Ethnic Groups and Linguistic Families

Within the national linguistic community, Spanish and Guarani are the two languages *par excellence*. However, other languages exist in the country, spoken

Translated from Spanish by Lee Puig-Antich.

to a lesser extent by small but diverse indigenous groups still remaining. Comprising 10 percent of the total Paraguayan population, these groups are located in areas somewhat distant from urban centers and have limited interaction with *paraguayos*, a term used to indicate non-Indians.

In order to describe the Paraguayan linguistic situation as precisely as possible, we will reproduce the data furnished by the first *Censo y Estudio de la Población Indigena del Paraguay* (Census and Study of the Indigenous Population of Paraguay), taken in 1981 by Paraguayan Institute for Indian Studies and the Bureau of Statistics and the Census.

Owing to its territorial range and function, Guarani is the most important—although not the only—language of the seventeen indigenous tribes that make up the ethnic configuration of Paraguay. These languages can be classified into five linguistic families.

Tupi-Guarani Linquistic Family. This family is represented in the Chaco region by the Guarayos and Tapiete, and in the Eastern Region by the Pai-Tavytera, Chiripa-Guarani, Mbya-Guarani and Ache-Guayaki. Today the members of all these ethnic groups, except for the Ache, speak Paraguayan Guarani. However, they have retained their own vocabulary, which they use among themselves when outsiders are not present. Still unavailable are reliable studies that would clarify the relationships among the different dialects of Guarani used by indigenous groups. Nor is it clear to what extent these dialects have fallen into disuse.

The marked cultural and linguistic differences among the Ache-Guarani have convinced some scholars that they do not belong to the Tupi-Guarani stock but have simply adopted many Guarani lexical items. Nevertheless, the most recent information available suggests a close relationship between the Ache language and the traditional Guarani of the Chiripa.

Zamuco Linguistic Family. This family is represented by the Moros Ayoreos and the Chamacocos, ethnic groups located in the northeastern part of the Chaco. The two languages are mutually unintelligible, and dialectal differences are found within each group. These differences are minimal in Ayoreo; however, concerning Chamacoco, the river Indians (from Fuerte Olimpo and Puerto Diana) consider the dialect of the Tomaraxa (the group from the interior) to be purer than their own, which includes words from Guarani and Spanish.

Mataco-Mataguayo Linguistic Family. In Paraguay, this family is represented by the Chulupi (or Nivacle), the Mak'a, and the Manjuy, and in Argentina and Bolivia by the Mataco. The ethnic groups have distinct languages, and Chulupi and Manjuy possess various dialects.

With respect to the people referred to here as the Manjuy, there exists some uncertainty as to whether they comprise a single ethnic group and what their relationship to the Choroti of Argentina is. Chase Sardi (1972) refers to two ethnic groups—the Manjuy and the Eklenjuy. (The information and terms were provided by Chulupi informants.)

Two large ethnic and dialectal divisions of the Choroti may be identified. The first, the Yojwaha, live along rivers and are divided into three subgroups—the

Nootiniwk, Ikiowej Thiele, and IsiemThele. Today they are found in Argentina or Bolivia. According to Ciriaco Perez and Walter Flores (Nivacle informants), the Chulupi call this group Eklenjuy. The second division, the group designated as Manjuy by the Choroti, refers to itself as Jobwjwa; these are the "Montaraces" Choroti. They are divided into two subgroups—the Thlawaa Thlele and the Wikina Wos—both located in the Paraguayan Chaco.

Guaicuru Linguistic Family. In Paraguay, this family is represented solely by those referred to here as "Toba-Qom," a subgroup of the Toba and Pilaga, which extends from the Argentine Chaco to Bolivia. The Toba-Qom of Paraguay speak their own dialect but have no difficulty understanding the Argentine dialects. Apparently, their language is also intelligible to the Caduveos (Mbaya) of the Brazilian Mato Grosso region. Some authors (Susnik, 1965; Chase Sardi, 1972) assert the existence of a Toba Lengua group which designates itself "Emok" and which is characterized by Toba (Guaicuru) and Lengua bilingualism. However, in spite of Toba-Lengua marriages, few people currently speak Lengua in the main community of Cerrito. Similarly, the term *Emok* is unknown as a self-designation, and some believe that this word comes from Mak'a.

It must be mentioned that the term *Toba-Qom* is likewise not in common use and is simply composed of the usual term *Toba* and the self-designation *Qom* in order to distinguish it from the "Toba-Maskoy," whose language belongs to the Maskoy linguistic family.

Lengua-Maskoy Linguistic Family. This linguistic family is comprised of the Lengua, Angaite, Sanapana, Guana, and Toba-Maskoy peoples. The Lengua constitute the largest ethnic group in the country (a total of 8,121 were counted) and are divided into at least two distinct subgroups with their own dialects.

The other ethnic groups in this linguistic family have languages, which to a certain extent are mutually intelligible and may therefore be classified as dialects of Lengua. All of these groups refer to themselves as Enlhit or Enenlhit, and probably were territorial groups of the Lengua which split off relatively recently.

The Indians belonging to these ethnic groups are among the most decultured in the country (owing, above all, to their long history of labor in the workshops and factories of the tanning industry). In many cases, they have abandoned their language in favor of Paraguayan Guarani. The tanning industry is the oldest industry situated in the Paraguayan Chaco and operated by Argentine landowners.

Each ethnic group generally has its own term with which it designates itself and its members. This term can almost always be translated as "gente" [people] or "hombre" [man], since in the life of traditional cultures all over the world, the concepts of "ethnic group" and "people" are the same. As a point of reference, the idea of belonging to an ethnic group receives much less emphasis among indigenous people than that of belonging to a local or territorial group. The latter represents the sociopolitical unit of highest order, and it is difficult to ask Indians to which ethnic group they belong without resorting to such Spanish words as *etnia, nacion, raza, tribu* [ethnic group, nation, race, tribe, respectively], and so on. According to the context of the situation, some of the self-designations may mean "varon" [male]. The Chulupi, for example, call themselves "Nivacle," a term contrasting with "Samto" (Paraguayan or Argentine *criollo*), "Ele" (gringo) [foreigner], or the names of the other ethnic groups which they know (the Manjuy, Ja'nono, Guarayos, Juutshinaj, Toba, etc.). In another context, however, "Nivacle" means "varon" and contrasts with "Navatch'e," meaning "mujer" [woman]. Similarly, the Ayoreo refer to themselves as "Ayoreode" (pl.), which in one context contrasts with "cojñone" ("whites" and members of other ethnic groups) and in another, with "Ayoredie" (mujeres) women.

Today there are Indians who deny that these terms refer exclusively to members of their own group and think that the translation should be "indigena" [Indian, native] or "gente." Among some indigenous groups, the term "gente" is used only in reference to Indians, a usage adopted from the Paraguayan population, which uses the word exclusively for non-Indians. The Chamacocos of Puerto Diana insist that the word "Ishior" includes the Sanapanas and other neighboring groups as well as members of their own group. Likewise, some Tobas assert that "Qom Lyk" may indicate any "cristiano" [Christian].

The dialectal differences give rise to rather curious linguistic situations. For example, in the Emok tribe the masculine and social language is Toba, whereas, the language used among women is Lengua. Not all of these tribes formerly spoke the present language. Some belonged to other linguistic families, and others adopted Guarani; still others maintain as a secret language the language they used prior to adopting the present one (Chase Sardi, 1972). Most of these dialects are in the process of extinction since they are reduced to their respective indigenous cores, which are decreasing in number.

In some communities, for example, Cerrito, home of the Emok-Toba, Toba/Guarani/Spanish trilingualism is found. To deal with this situation, Guarani has been adopted as a medium of instruction for oral communication. All of the documents presented contain requests to the Ministry of Education to implement educational plans that address the linguistic problem as part of an ongoing process.

Although Paraguay has never been characterized by massive waves of immigration, there are presently significant communities of foreigners who have retained their native language in varying degrees. The largest of these are the Mennonite, German, Japanese, and Korean. However, except among Mennonites, Spanish is already the predominant language among first-generation speakers. In rural Japanese settlements, the use of Guarani as a second language predominates.

Of recent concern in Paraguay is the expansion of Portuguese in areas bordering on Brazil. Because of large hydroelectric projects and a penetrating Brazilian political presence, Paraguay sees its "cultural independence" threatened by the process of cultural assimilation initiated by Brazil.

According to the *Censo Nacional de Problacion y Vivienda* (National Census of Population and Households), the 1982 percentages of Spanish and Guarani speakers were distributed as follows:

Paraguay	Guarani only	Spanish and Guarani	Spanish only
Rural	60.08	30.91	5.39
Urban	15.00	70.21	12.50
Total	40.10	48.16	6.43

The data indicate that 88.26 percent of the total population of the country speak Guarani. Although other languages spoken in Paraguay are not included here, it is evident that these figures are significant for an appreciation of the extent of Spanish/Guarani bilingualism in Paraguay today.

GUARANI IN THE CULTURAL PROCESS OF PARAGUAY

"Mestizaje" and Bilingualism

The arrival of the conquistadors led to constant and intense interaction between the Spanish and the aboriginals and, hence, between their respective languages, Spanish and Guarani. Because Paraguay never had a massive influx of either Spaniards or other immigrants, it eventually developed into an isolated socio-cultural milieu, giving rise to the birth of a type of bilingualism which developed and expanded throughout nearly four centuries of independent national life. It is precisely this point which helps explain the social, cultural, and linguistic differences between Paraguay and the other Latin American countries.

Many features bore upon the fusion of the two languages and cultures. The Spaniards needed the aboriginal language for their relationships with the Indians, a fact that was reinforced by the union between Spaniards and native women in an unattractive geographic area. This unusual type of polygamy was encouraged and increased as the Spaniards gained power over the Indian. The absence of precious metals led to a rural economy based on cattle, which was sustained by the native women. These women, working cheaply and in great numbers, constituted the most important force in productive labor. The economic value attached to the possession of Indians was compared to the worth of Andean silver and gold. Thus, one reads, "At the beginning the wealth of the settlers was measured by the number of Indians they held in *encomienda* or in servitude" [Translated from Moreno, 1959]. The aboriginal woman became not only the most important element in the incipient and precarious economy of the Spaniards, but also the base on which the powerful and rapid process of *mestizaje* was founded.

Perhaps the most important factor in the history of Paraguayan bilingualism was the missionary work of the Society of Jesus.

In Paraguay there began an audacious experiment in government—erected on a theocratic base—which was unlike any the world had known before and which would endure until the expulsion of the Order in 1767. For more than a century and a half the Jesuit fathers ruled the vast Guarani collectivity entrusted to their care for purposes of evangelization and social, political and economic organization, according to canons which differed radically from those which regulated life in the rest of the province. . . . The Jesuits imposed rigid, strict and minute regulations upon the lives of the Guarani Indians, unlike any known by other aboriginal nations. [Translated from Cardozo, 1959]

Language was the most important factor during this period of acculturation, since the Jesuits required the use of Spanish. Spanish was the indispensable means of sociopolitical affirmation, whereas Guarani was associated with three conditions: cultural isolation, conservatism in norms of conduct, and social limitation. In the colonial period, this sociolinguistic setting was identified with Indian, mestizo, and *criollo* poverty, creating the awareness of a "distinctive intimacy" [Translated from Susnik, 1965].

The influence of the Jesuit Fathers and their intense educational labors enriched the Guarani language at the same time that Spanish was being taught to the Indians. In 1624, the Jesuit priest, Antonio Ruiz de Montoya, produced the first Guarani dictionary and grammar. Thus, Guarani, which for so long had been only oral, came to be a written language.

The intellectual training of the Jesuits, together with the desire to proselytize, formed the basis for the important literary, educational, and religious output, which would appear and later increase. Most of the literature consisted of instructional texts, books, and religious materials translated into Guarani and used primarily for religious instruction. Of the numerous linguists belonging to the Order, Father Ruiz de Montoya produced the most important basic works on the native language. The attempt to standardize Guarani using some of his works as a basis began in 1722 with the publication of *Vocabulario de la Lengua Guarani* (256 pp.). This was followed by other works, notably, *La Gramatica del Idioma Guarani* by Fray Juan N. Alegreso and—of particular interest to contemporary readers—*Gramatica Guarani*, published by Father Antonio Guasch in 1959. Publication in the native language ceased in 1730. In addition to more important works, "sketches, primers and catechisms for elementary instruction, 'treatises' in Spanish and Guarani, and seven works on astronomy, meteorology, calendars and astronomical tables by Father Buenaventura Suarez" were published [Translated from Kostianovsky, 1975]. With the expulsion of the Jesuits in 1767, the production and diffusion of written works in the native language fell into a lethargy that would last a long time.

The almost natural isolation of the country increased considerably with the rise to power of Dr. Gaspar Rodríguez de Francia. In spite of creating enormous obstacles to political, social, and economic development, this regime strengthened the ever increasing contact between the two cultures with their respective languages, values, and attitudes. "Isolation under Francia halted immigration and economic development, obstructed channels of communication, and closed the door to capital and technology; but socially, it contributed to the homogenization of the population" [Translated from Benitez, 1955]. During this period, the country returned to the isolationist spirit that had prevailed in the time of the missionaries. External contact and influence were reduced to a minimum; mistrust of things foreign was created; and family life and social relations were permeated by secretiveness under Francia's administration.

From then on, the bilingual process proceeded slowly even though the governments that succeeded Dr. Francia tried to encourage education in Spanish. Existing historical documents show a marked rejection of the use of Guarani in educational institutions and in middle- and upper-class social circles. Thus, Paraguay backed Carlos Antonio Lopez in an intensive campaign for Spanish literacy and mass education. With the abolition of Indian towns, the subsequent conversion of indigenous surnames to Spanish, and the hiring of professional teachers and technicians from abroad, the Spanish language began a major expansion (A.N.A., S.H., 1848).

The War of the Triple Alliance (1865–70) broke the increasing expansionism of the language and of all else that was Spanish. "The collective opinion was impressed once again by the values which bore on the situation and which were in essence part of the original historical stratum—the impulsivity, aggressivity and telluric wisdom of the Indian; the irreductibility" [Translated from Pla, 1970]. In the need to mobilize the sentiments of the people during the great struggle, Guarani reappeared with greater strength than before. These emotions were expressed in the periodicals of the trenches—*El Cabichi, El Centinela*, and *El Cacique Labmare*—which carried sections in Guarani and Spanish and published verse and rudimentary prose. In 1867, Marshal Lopez ordered the unification of the spelling system.

After such a bloody war, which resulted in domination by the neighboring countries and in the reduction of the population to women and children, the predominant cultural environment became virtually Spanish. Some time later there appeared some intellectuals who defended the Guarani language with the fervor that springs from intuitive knowledge of the roles played by each of the languages. In 1911, an author wrote that to Guarani

have been attributed the dulling of the intellectual apparatus and the difficulty seemingly experienced by the masses in adapting themselves to European methods of labor. The argument commonly presented is that for every language, there is a mentality which—so to speak—defines and portrays itself in that language; and since Guarani is so radically different from Spanish and other Aryan languages, not only in lexicon . . . but also in the very construction of words and sentences, there must exist, therefore, serious obstacles to the work of civilization in Paraguay. The remedy is obvious: kill Guarani. Attacking the language, one hopes to modify the intelligence; teaching European grammar to the people, one hopes to Europeanize them. . . . The economy is invoked and Spanish will be adopted, each one for its purpose." [Translated from Barret, 1943]

With the Chaco War (1932–35) came the emergence—primarily for political reasons—of a clear conception of Guarani as a symbol of nationality. However, its use never acquired popularity or prestige in some social circles in Asunción, owing to a "conviction" that the use of Guarani erected an insurmountable barrier against the proper learning of Spanish. Nevertheless, this reappraisal of the native language has gained adherents in the last two decades through public and private initiatives and especially through the government's decision to require the teaching of Guarani at all levels of education.

Historical reports on the use of Guarani in the social and political spheres have been the object of much reflection on the part of historians and politicans. J. Pla (1970:7) reminds us that partisan manifestos are written in Spanish, but speeches made in times of emergency are delivered in Guarani. In periods of cultural expansion, Spanish advances; in periods of upheaval, Guarani returns. Emotion seeks the vernacular route; the intellect seeks the Hispanic one.

Language and Education

The High School for the Humanities, founded in 1944, was the first institution to incorporate the teaching of Guarani into its curriculum. Four years later, this school was converted into the Faculty of Philosophy and Letters of the National University of Asunción, where Professor Decoud Larrosa began the arduous task of promoting the aboriginal language and incorporating it into university teaching. These efforts were directed toward providing university training for Guarani teachers in order to prepare them for primary and secondary teaching.

Before these teachers could be hired, the Ministry of Education needed to incorporate Guarani into the educational curriculum. In 1971, in the conclusions of new studies by the Planning Committee for Secondary Education, provision was made for the addition of two hours of Guarani instruction per week to the three-year sequence of the Basic Curriculum. In 1961, the Institute of Guarani Linguistics was created. One of its purposes is to educate and train teachers in short courses offered at intervals. In 1972, the Institute for Advanced Language Study of the National University of Asunción established the university degree in Guarani, thereby granting university status to the study of the aboriginal language. This gave greater impetus to the process of standardization begun in the early 1960s.

The fast-growing awareness of the value and role of the native language was reinforced by television and radio programs in Guarani, religious sermons, and the popular masses in Guarani, as well as by journalism. In general, a socio-cultural environment has been evolving in which the contact languages are acquiring a functional niche of their own. However, this complementary distribution in usage is still unrecognized by many of their speakers and even by scholars.

The Bilingual Situation in Paraguay Today

The almost complete lack of knowledge about the Paraguayan sociolinguistic situation has prompted various foreign scholars—of varying repute—to develop theoretical frames of reference that do not accurately reflect actual conditions. Today as in the past, it is common for linguists and sociolinguists to analyze and, even worse, to generalize from findings after no more than a two-week stay in the country. On the other hand, it is also true that for a number of reasons that cannot be dealt with here little research has been carried out within the country. In the mid–1970s, a marked interest in bilingual research developed among Paraguayan scholars, which resulted in a number of publications here and abroad (Corvalán et al., 1982). The remainder of this chapter will treat the implications of bilingualism and the formal system of education for the contemporary era, as well as the present attitudes of the Paraguayan people toward their languages—Spanish as the official language, and Guarani as the national language (as provided by the National Constitution of 1967).

The roots of the Paraguayan linguistic situation lie in the existence of an indigenous language, Guarani, which competed openly with a standard European language, Spanish, and which achieved a status equal to Spanish instead of being eliminated (as was the case in most of the other Latin American countries) (Corvalán, 1977).

Today Paraguayan bilingualism reflects "cultural duality." Given that the linguistic situation reflects the merger of the culture of the conquistadors with that of the Guarani Indians, it would appear that owing to the long passage of time since colonization, "cultural duality" is now represented by the two major population distributions—urban and rural—and not by the traditional white/Indian dichotomy. Other factors contributing to this particular cultural duality are: (1) the extremely homogeneous social, geographic, and climatic characteristics of Paraguay; (2) the uniform racial traits; and (3) fluid boundaries in the distribution of socioeconomic strata.

It has been frequently repeated that the role of the vernacular in Paraguay is intimately related to the well-known dichotomy between "power and solidarity" (Rubin, 1968) in all sectors of the national society. This theoretical perspective applies to the rural areas, whereas in urban centers it must be related to the concept of "national identity" (Corvalán et al., 1982).

Once the transition from the "folk" language to the urban language—Guarani to Spanish—has been completed and the bilingual process has begun, the native language changes its role in the urban sector: it becomes symbolic of the country and the object of increasing loyalty. The position taken here is that factors such as the expanding awareness of the cultural value of bilingualism, a greater use of Guarani outside the family, and the uniqueness of the national scope of the bilingual situation have contributed to Paraguayan pride. This is seen most clearly among bilinguals and, hence, among the urban population.

The Outlook for Paraguayan Bilingualism

Although public and private initiatives have given great impetus to the study and use of Guarani, they have not been sufficient to produce coordinate bilinguals in urban areas. Nor have they done so in rural districts where Spanish is infrequently used and precariously taught. In other words, the complexity of the situation requires treating the problems from two different perspectives, which are related to the two sociographic categories characterizing the population distribution, that is, the urban and the rural. It is necessary to remember that the capital of the country has approximately six hundred thousand inhabitants, and the next largest urban center after Asunción has only fifty thousand, according to the 1982 census. Of the total population, 57.2 percent belong to the rural sector.

This disproportion in the population distribution affects the quality and quantity of services, including education. The aspects of bilingualism of specific interest here are the needs and attitudes of the people in regard to the use and/or teaching of the two languages. At this point it is necessary to introduce the notion of Jopara, which resulted from the contact between the languages in question. Jopara has serious implications for both usage and education. For greater clarity in the following exposition, Jopara will be described from two perspectives—the social and the linguistic.

Attitudes of the Speaker. Although the attitudes of the speaker toward use of the languages have been explored (Rubin, 1968), mention should be made of the attitudes toward Jopara. That is, while loyalty and pride exist with respect to Guarani, there exists, paradoxically, a certain deprecatory attitude with respect to the usage norms of the two linguistic codes. G. de Granda accurately states that "it is feasible to find the roots of the complex of attitudes which concern us in a specific, easily individualized event: the erroneous choice of the linguistic reference model with respect to which the characteristic varieties of contemporary Spanish and Guarani are judged" [Translated from de Granda, 1981]. Indeed, it is common to hear judgments—whether positive or negative—regarding Paraguayan speech in any type of linguistic situation, social strata, subject for discussion, and so on. In other words, the idiolect of the native speaker is always subject to what is commonly called *la picota publica* [the town pillory].

The current sociolinguistic situation in Paraguay is extremely odd. We are rapidly retreating from the ignorance and/or indifference which for a long time characterized this sociocultural phenomenon. It would seem that the Paraguayans have suddenly awakened from their lethargy and are confronting a new situation in which they are overly concerned about what is "correct" or "incorrect" in each language. Several factors enter into this process: the purists of both languages, a "new" perception of what it means to be a bilingual country, greater exposure to the use of the codes through mass media, and an increase in research and publication on Paraguayan bilingualism. The gravity of this new situation stems mainly from the rise of a "collective linguistic inferiority complex" [Translated from de Granda, 1961], if the steps necessary for serious and viable linguistic planning are not taken.

Jopara as the Result of Guarani-Spanish Contact. The long, intense contact between the two national languages of Paraguay has given rise to profound interferences between the respective linguistic systems on the morphosyntactic, lexical, and phonemic levels. The linguistic result of this interference is commonly known as Jopara. Consequently, the structural convergence is much more obvious and serious in the written mode. Notwithstanding, Paraguayan Spanish is usually compared to formal Hispanic linguistic usage—and not even with the various types of Spanish currently used in Spain. Jopara is characteristic of incipient bilinguals and is found, to a lesser degree, among coordinate bilinguals. In the main, Jopara is typically restricted to urban areas, and, of course, to the capital. On the other hand, the use of ''pure'' Guarani is more common in rural areas. The choice of linguistic variety is determined by the speaker's sex and age.

Bilingual Education

Many authors have proposed different models of programs for bilingual development. Factors considered are: language, length of instructional time, type of curriculum, socioeconomic characteristics of the students, trained teaching staff, and finally, short- and long-term goals. In other words, the type of bilingual education must be directly related on one hand to educational goals, and on the other to the objective of maintaining and expanding Spanish/Guarani bilingualism as the most relevant and unique characteristic of the Paraguayan sociolinguistic context.

A glance at the teacher's manual, *Manual de Educacion Bilingüe* [Manual for Bilingual Education], reveals that the objective of the bilingual program in primary school is for the child ''to appreciate the national languages, to express himself confidently in them, and to develop the basic skills of listening, speaking, reading and writing in Spanish, and of *listening and speaking in Guarani*''' (Corvalán's emphasis). This decision is based on ''the necessity for the child to develop a positive self-image and affirm his identity as a Paraguayan, by offering him the opportunity to express the values of the national culture in their true equality'' [Translated from Paraguay MEC, 1981].

The most striking feature about the objectives of the national language policy is that different linguistic goals are set for each language. For the standard language, it is recommended that the four stages in the language acquisition process be obtained. In the case of Guarani, we continue to confine it to its traditional role as a language for oral communication, thereby exposing it sooner or later to the certain danger of stagnation and/or extinction. It is very difficult to maintain and enrich a living language which is neither read nor written, especially when its community of speakers are subject to outside linguistic and cultural influences. In time we will no longer speak of the Guarani language, but rather of what is commonly called "badly spoken Spanish"—when the level and kind of interference in either language becomes uncontrollable because corrective educational measures have not been taken.

In order to understand the problems that confronted the educational system, it is necessary to consider two important aspects of that system: its centralized character, and the fact that instruction is in Spanish regardless of the pupil's sociographic milieu or level of competence in Spanish. In short, a single type of instruction existed throughout the country. However, a few years ago, the Program for Bilingual Education was approved for use on the national level. This program

takes into consideration the use of both Spanish and Guarani in the teaching/learning process, with emphasis on one or the other language depending on the linguistic ability of the child. At the primary level Spanish and Guarani are used for oral communication (listening and speaking), while for reading and writing, only Spanish is used. As the Guarani monolingual acquires proficiency in Spanish, the use of Spanish is intensified. The *Programa de Educacion Bilingüe* [Program for Bilingual Education] is thus a program of transition [Translated from MEC, 1981].

In actual practice, Guarani is still used in the traditional way in the primary schools of rural areas and lower class urban areas, that is, for translating the educational content from Spanish. It is also used to aid schools that have implemented the Program for Bilingual Education, which at this time has not established a curriculum for the maintenance and improvement of Guarani. This program is clearly in its initial stage; there is still much that needs to be adjusted, changed, and tried out in terms of bilingual methodology and types of instruction, and hence in the use of native language in the classroom. Although guidelines for the implementation of the method have been established, there is no doubt that a certain margin of freedom should be left to the teacher with respect to the various situations arising from classroom interaction (Corvalán, 1983).

Much effort is being devoted to the preparation and publication of texts for the teaching of Guarani structure (Canese, 1984). Also under development is a teacher's guide on the kinds of interference already analyzed, especially the interference of Guarani with Paraguayan Spanish. These endeavors are oriented toward the goal of standardizing the native language and thereby increasing the prestige it acquires as a result of conversion to a standard language (Corvalán, 1985).

This brings us to another question with political overtones—the adoption of a uniform spelling system for Guarani. If Paraguay is going to continue to be bilingual, the controversy over the few disputed symbols should not be allowed to obstruct the efforts toward standardization. It must not be forgotton that an oral language can neither maintain its vitality nor augment the number of its speakers if it is threatened by the compulsive use of a standard language that is also the official language of the country.

The emphasis on so-called language unification leads to the atrophy of creative forces that have historically shaped Paraguayan national identity through the Guarani language. It is possible that the process of Hispanicization will lead to a crisis of identity in which one loses one's sense of belonging to a unique nation.

If, however, instruction were parallel—on one hand, literacy, so that the transition from the rural to the urban world could be made through use of the native language, and on the other hand, the gradual and progressive teaching of Spanish throughout the higher grades—then the doors to a world of knowledge would be opened and it would be possible to obtain the tools necessary for full social participation. In short, what is being proposed here is a gradual and systematic program of "immersion" in the second language without neglecting the native language. The native language would be maintained throughout the curriculum, not merely as an aid for learning the second language, but also as a language to be *taught*—together with the whole set of rules governing its internal structure.

In the case of indigenous tribes with different languages, Guarani is the most effective medium of both communication and instruction. This task is mainly undertaken by numerous groups of German, American, and other missionaries seeking to proselytize. The effort has led to the preparation and publication of reading/writing texts and primers in Guarani, so that it may serve as a lingua franca among the different indigenous groups.

With the important exception of the first National Census of the Indian, taken in 1982, governmental concern for these questions has been small. The most important initiatives are taken by the private sector, especially the Committee of Paraguayan Churches, which is involved with both the fight for land and the educational process.

Sociolinguistic Research in Paraguay

Without attempting to offer an exhaustive, state-of-the-art description of Paraguayan bilingualism, let us devote the last part of this study to milestones in the research on the linguistic situation under consideration.

Different theoretical positions have been taken by foreign researchers which, "although quantitatively abundant [are] not always acceptable in terms of scientific adequacy" (de Granda, 1982). Thus, we have a continuum of theoretical positions concerning the relativity of bilingualism (Rona, 1973)—going from "a unique pattern of bilingualism on a national scale in the world" (Ferguson, 1959) to the view which holds that to consider "Spanish and Guarani as separate languages is to appeal to abstractions" (Melía, 1973).

Others consider it possible to place the complex linguistic situation of Paraguay into a conceptual framework in which both languages are polarized between the concepts of power and solidarity (Rubin, 1968). This view emphatically rejects (de Granda, 1981) the characterization of the Paraguayan linguistic community as predominately diglossic (Melía, 1973). To these theoretical conceptions must be added one of recent appearance in which the fundamental aspect regarding Spanish/Guarani use is considered to be the urban-rural continuum (Corvalán, 1981). Because of a lack of research by Paraguayans, many of the studies by foreign authors have been cited so often that in some cases their original meaning has been distorted. This has clearly been the case with the work of Rubin (Wood, 1981). In recent years, a critical reexamination of these studies has been undertaken for the purpose of evaluating them under perspectives that are more objective and more in line with Paraguayan sociolinguistic reality (de Granda, 1979; Corvalán, 1982).

In the past, most of the literature of Paraguayan bilingualism consisted of long descriptions of the origin and development of Guarani. A kind of romantic and almost "supernatural" aura concerning the existence and survival of Guarani through time enveloped these works. Their naivete contributed to the emergence of the pronounced linguistic awareness of the Paraguayan—a characteristic that distinguishes the Paraguayan from speakers in other Latin American bilingual settings (de Granda, 1981). Since the 1970s, there has been more emphasis on scientific rigor. However, the level of production has not filled the gaps still existing in basic, empirical data—information that is so essential for the application of more complex theoretical and interpretative frames of reference.

In 1963, the American anthropologist, Joan Rubin, began publishing data for her doctoral thesis, "Bilingualism in Paraguay" which would have a strong influence in a scientific area little known until then.

At the beginning of the 1940s, a certain stereotype of the role of Guarani in Paraguayan society had been formed. The majority of authors, mainly prominent politicians and literary figures, were in agreement that "the population uses Guarani or Spanish indiscriminately, in greater or lesser degree according to the circumstances or particular social sectors" in which communication takes place (Insfran, 1942).

Perhaps it has been in the field of Paraguayan literature—today as in the past— that the positive and negative features of bilingualism have been debated the most. These traits became the theme of a lengthy polemic, ill-defined until now, and resulted in writers taking a stance either for or against the use of the vernacular in literary works. Thus, many authors feel that bilingualism is one of the major obstacles confronting the development of Paraguayan fiction. Roa Bastos poses this dilemma when he asks what would happen if an author wrote only in Guarani. This would "limit his work to the local area. . . . As we know, when one writes in Spanish but thinks in Guarani, translation is carried out during the very process of literary creation. This cannot but affect the integrity of the work" (Roa Bastos, 1957). This position has changed over time into an assertion that bilingualism should be present in Paraguayan literature even though it is restrictive (Roa Bastos, 1982).

In 1964, the work on bilingualism began to acquire different characteristics, and Rubin's strong influence was felt on the specialized literature. A Paraguayan journal commented that bilingualism "follows a typically Paraguayan system of alternation between two social forces—power . . . and solidarity . . . , explaining the combination of the forces in addition to the curious cases in which one of the two forces temporarily reigns" (Codas, 1964).

On a theoretical plane, the question has been raised about whether "Paraguay has entered into a stage which is neither a tendency toward monolingualism nor an affirmation of bilingualism, but rather a slippage into alingualism"—a concern based on modern structural linguistics in which "the individual is spoken by the language"(Melía, 1973). This view is analyzed from the standpoint of the social factors that bear on the potential existence of alingualism, i.e. lack of language, a possibility that has produced some consternation, and even surprise, in Paraguayan intellectual circles. The pros and cons of Melía's argument led to immediate discussion, with great differences of opinion.

The wide diffusion of knowledge, interpretations, and, to some extent, distortion of the bilingual problem in Paraguay began with the "discovery" of this situation by foreign researchers (Corvalán, 1982). Paraguayan bilingualism began to occupy a prominent and "exotic" place in the classic literature on bilingualism (Fishman, 1967). Paradoxically, the obscurity surrounding the subject increased.

Owing to the few studies produced by Paraguayans, the more or less reliable findings of foreigners came to be taken as "the explanation," in spite of certain weaknesses in methodology and in the samples chosen for purposes of generalization to the national level (Rona, 1966).

An opposing view holds that the bilingual situation in Paraguay is not so sharply delineated, except in relation to other Latin American countries. The concern is with the dissension existing among Paraguayans over the establishment of Classical Guarani on the one hand and Jopara on the other. This indicated that both languages—Guarani and Spanish—could coexist without danger of degradation or extinction (Pottier, 1969).

The first specialized bibliography on Paraguayan bilingualism appeared in the mid–1970s and was republished in succeeding years. This, along with another bibliography on bilingualism in Latin America, became the most exhaustive reference material published to date on Paraguayan bilingualism (Corvalán, 1982, 1984).

The interference between the two contact languages has been studied through the analysis of a written corpus furnished by a sampling of students from a vocational-technical school (Welti, 1979). This is one of the few studies that bring into focus the limitations of a bilingual community from a structural perspective. Loan words between the two languages also arouse interest among scholars. However, the problem posed by Jopara is criticized, even though a systematic analysis of the contact languages has not yet been carried out (Herreros, 1976; Dominguez, 1978; de Granda, 1979, 1980; Morinigo, 1931). The extent and use of the linguistic codes existing in the repertory of bilingual communities (Rubin, 1968; Melía, 1973; de Granda, 1980) as well as the interpretation of structures and the processes of linguistic convergence (Melía, 1973; Morinigo, 1959; Tovar, 1964; Cassano, 1973) are important contributions to the understanding of Paraguayan bilingualism.

The findings of some of these studies made considerable impact on some deeply rooted ideas in Paraguayan society, that is, certain archaisms in Spanish that had been thought to be Guarani loan words, and the influence of Argentine speech. These are clarified and discussed more objectively in these studies (de Granda, 1979).

Also of interest to foreign scholars for a long time has been everything pertinent to the attitudes of the people toward each language (Rubin, 1978; de Granda, 1981; Rona, 1966; Garvin and Mathiot, 1960). This concern, together with the development of more qualified researchers, has led to the emergence of a Paraguayan body of literature which analyzes specific segments of the population, for example, the attitudes of primary teachers and parents with respect to the use of Guarani (Corvalán, 1982; MEC, 1976; Pérez Maricevich et al., 1978).

In the mid–1970s, the first study was published which analyzed linguistic interaction in the classroom based on the use of nonparametric statistics. The main objective was to explore the incidence of bilingualism in the school performance of primary children and their teachers (Rivarola et al., 1978).

The Ministry of Education surveyed the opinions of parents and teachers with respect to the use of the languages and also made the first attempt to measure the linguistic competence of first grade children (Pérez Maricevich et al., 1978). This line of research was repeated with fourth grade students who had finished the program called "Bilinguismo" offered by certain schools (Corvalán, 1982). Both studies are the first of their kind and shed substantial light on the measurement not only of the oral and written linguistic competence of children but also of the teacher/student interaction in the classroom.

Contribution to knowledge about the Paraguayan linguistic situation was the publication of the two volumes of *Sociedad y Lengua: Bilinguismo en el Paraguay* (Corvalán et al., 1982), which bring together the most representative and widely known works on the subject. The importance of this work lies not only in the inclusion of out-of-print or inaccessible studies, but also in the Spanish translation of several works originally written in English which have long been the most important and well-known conceptual frames of reference. At the beginning of 1985, there was published some research focusing specifically on the implications of bilingualism for formal education (Corvalán, 1985).

CONCLUSIONS

Both the public and private sectors have shown a growing concern and interest in the influence of bilingualism on the teaching/learning process. Starting in 1985—for the first time ever—the idea of literacy in the native language was considered in Paraguay. This will result in the production of texts and primers for experimental use.

The accumulation and spread of scientific knowledge about Paraguayan bilingualism has contributed to the increase in the pride and identity of the native speaker with respect to the two major languages of Paraguay—Spanish and Guarani.

The principal objective of this overview is to achieve efficient and viable linguistic planning within the formal educational system and to raise the awareness of the Paraguayan linguistic community with respect to the standardization of Guarani, for purposes of maintaining and/or expanding bilingualism on the national level.

BIBLIOGRAPHY

Asunción, National Archives, S. H. 1848. "Decreto declarando ciudadanos libres a los indios naturales de toda la republica." Vol. 282, No. 24.

Barret, R. 1943. *Obras completas*. Buenos Aires: America Lee, pp. 151–53.

Benitez, J. P. 1955. *Formacion social del pueblo paraguayo*. Asunción: America-Sapucaia, p. 26.

Canese, K. de. 1984. *Sobre la unificacion del alfabeto de la lengua guarani*. Asunción, 37 p. (a máquina).

Cardozo, E. 1959. *El Paraguay Colonial*. Buenos Aires: Niza, pp. 126–27.

Cassano, P. V. 1973. "The Substrate Theory in Relation to the Bilingualism of Paraguay. Problems and Findings." *Anthropological Linguistics* 15, 9: 406–25.

Chase Sardi, M. 1972. "Esquema étnico del Paraguay." *Revista Diálogo* 1, 14:30.

Codas, C. 1964. "El bilinguismo en el Paraguay." *Ybytyrusú. Revista Guaireña de Cultura* 2, 8: 21–23.

Corvalán, G. 1977. *Paraguay Nación Bilingüe*. Asunción: Centro Paraguayo de Estudios Sociológicos, p. 18.

———. 1981. "La educación bilingüe y el contexto socio-cultural: El caso del Paraguay y los Estados Unidos." Paper presented at the XVI *Seminario Internacional*, Asociación Argentina de Estudios Americanos, Buenos Aires, 18–21 September 17 p.

———. 1982. "El bilinguismo en la educación en el Paraguay: es creativo u opresivo?" In *Sociedad y Lengua: Bilinguismo en el Paraguay*, ed. G. Corvalán and G. de Granda. Asunción: Centro Paraguayo de Estudios Sociológicos, p. 191.

———. 1983. *Que es el bilinguismo en el Paraguay?* Asunción: Centro Paraguayo de Estudios Sociológicos, 56 p.

———. 1984. "Enseñanza en lengua materna y rendimiento educativo en el Paraguay." *Perspectivas* 14, 1: 97–108.

———. 1985. *Lengua y educación: Un desafío nacional*. Asunción: Centro Paraguayo de Estudios Sociológicos. 136 p.

De Granda, G. 1979. "El español del Paraguay, temas, problemas y métodos." *Estudios Paraguayos de la Universidad Católica* 7, 1: 9–145.

———. 1980. "Lengua y sociedad. Notas sobre el español del Paraguay." *Estudios Paraguayos de la Universidad Católica* 8, 1: 9–140.

———. 1981. "Actitudes sociolinguisticas en el Paraguay." *Revista Paraguaya de Sociología* 18, 51: 7–22.

———. 1982. "Calcos sintácticos del guaraní en el español del Paraguay." In *Sociedad y Lengua: Bilinguismo en el Paraguay*, ed. G. Corvalán and G. de Granda. Asunción: Centro Paraguayo del Estudios Sociológicos, pp. 701–32.

Dominguez, R. 1978. "Glosario del Yopará." *Suplemento Antropológico de la Universidad Católica* 13, 1–2: 261–74.

Ferguson, Ch. 1966. "Discusión sobre el estudio de Rona." *Sociolinguistics*: 293–97.

Fishman, J. 1967. "Bilingualism With and Without Diglossia; Diglossia With and Without Bilingualism." In *Problems of Bilingualism*, ed. John Macnamara. *Journal of Social Issues* 23, 2: 29–38.

Garvin, P. and M. Mathiot. 1960. "The Urbanization of the Guarani Language: A Problem in Language and Culture." In *Men and Cultures*, ed. Anthony F. C. Walance. Selected papers of the Fifth International Congress of Anthropological and Etnological Sciences. Philadelphia: University of Pennsylvania Press, pp. 783–90.

Guasch, A. 1944. *El idioma guaraní: gramática, vocabulario doble, lecturas*. Asunción: Imprenta Nacional, p. 322.

Herreros, B. U. de. 1976. "Castellano paraguayo. Notas para una gramática contrastiva castellano-guaraní." *Suplemento Antropológico de la Universidad Católica* 1–2: 29–123.

Insfran, P. M. 1942. "El Paraguay, país bilingüe." *Revista del Ateneo Paraguayo* 1, 5–6: 59–61.

Instituto Paraguayo del Indígena. 1982. *Censo y estudio de la población indígena del Paraguay, 1981*. Asunción: Paraguayan Institute for Indian Studies, pp. 29–33.

Kostianovsky, O. M. de. 1975. *La instrucción pública en la época colonial*. 2d ed. Asunción: Escuela Tecnica Salesiana, pp. 132–33.

Melía, B., S.J. 1973. "El guaraní dominante y dominado." *Suplemento Antropológico de la Universidad Católica* 8, 1–2: 119–28.

———. 1974. "Hacía una tercera lengua en el Paraguay." *Estudios Paraguayos* 2, 2: 31–71.

Moreno, F. R. 1959. *La ciudad de Asunción*. pp. 60, 121.

Morinigo, M. A. 1959. "Influencia del español en la estructura linguística del guaraní." *Boletín de Filología*. 5, 3: 235–47.

Paraguay. Ministerio de Educación y Culto. 1981. *Educación bilingüe en el Paraguay. Manual para el Maestro*. Asunción: M.E.C., p. 171.

Pérez-Maricevich, Francisco et al. 1978. *Algunos aspectos del rendimiento escolar relacionados con el bilinguismo*. Ed. Héctor A. Macchi. Buenos Aires, p. 220.

Pla, J. 1970. "Español y guaraní en la intimidad de la cultura paraguaya." *Caravelle* 14: 17.

Pottier, B. 1969. "Aspectos del bilinguismo paraguayo." *Suplemento Antropológico de la Revista del Ateneo Paraguayo* 4, 1: 189–93.

Rivarola, D., et al. 1978. *Determinantes del rendimiento educativo en el Paraguay*. Asunción: CPES/ECIEL, p. 224.

Roa Bastos, A. 1957. "Problema de nuestra novelística." *Alcor* 7: 6–8.

———. 1978. *Las Culturas Condenadas*. Mexico: Siglo xx.

Rona, José Pedro. 1966. "The Social and Cultural Status of Guarani in Paraguay." In *Sociolinguistics: Proceedings of the UCLA Sociolinguistic Conference*, ed. H. Bright. The Hague/Paris: Mouton, pp. 277–98.

———. 1973. "La relatividad del bilinguismo y su realización social." Paper presented at the Simposio sobre sociolinguistica y planificación linguistica, Mexico, D.F., June.

Rubin, J. 1968. "Bilingualism in Paraguay." *Anthropological Linguistics* 4, 4: 52–58.
———. 1978. "Toward Bilingual Education for Paraguay." *Georgetown University Round Table on Languages and Linguistics.* Ed. James E. Alatis. Washington, D.C.: Georgetown University Press, pp. 189–201.
Susnik, B. 1965. *El Indio Colonial del Paraguay.* Vol. 1. Asunción: Museo Etnográfico "Andrés Barbero," p. 26.
Tovar, A. 1964. "Español y lenguas indígenas, algunos ejemplos." *Presente y Futuro de la Lengua Española.* Actas de la Asamblea de Filología del I Congreso de Instituciones Hispánicas. Madrid: Cultura Hispánica, pp. 245–57.
Welti, M. C. de. 1979. "Bilinguismo en el Paraguay. Los límites de la comunicación." *Revista Paraguaya de Sociología.* 16, 46: 63–97.
Wood, R. E. 1981. "Current Sociolinguistics in Latin America." *Latin American Research Review.* 16, 1.

BILINGUALISM IN PERU

An account of the peoples and languages of Peru must begin with a sketch of the sources of information concerning the speakers and languages in question as well as the degree of bi- or multilingualism. For the twentieth century, reference can be made to the national population censuses of 1940 (of particular interest), 1961, 1972, and 1981. By drawing on various sources, it has been possible to reconstruct figures for the nineteenth century, for the years 1828, 1836, 1861, 1862, and 1873, which can be combined with the more recent data.

Owing to the influx of migrants and the concentration of economic power in Lima, the capital city has outdistanced the rest of the country, especially since the end of the last century, achieving an unparalleled growth equal to one-quarter of the total population in 1981 (Table 19.1).

It is not the intent here to call attention to the relative disagreement of researchers concerning the aims of the censuses. Rather, as one investigator recently noted (Suarez, 1979:66–67), there are obvious reasons for questioning the way in which the Peruvian population has been enumerated and the methodology used, particularly in the latest censuses. That is, the total population actually counted, the total counted plus the omitted, and the total counted plus the omitted and the estimated (the Selva population) appear under different hypotheses, according to whether comparison is made between the censuses of 1940 and 1961 on the one hand and between those of 1972 and 1981 on the other. There is more than one hypothesis for the methodological changes, and, of course, those changes will have an effect on the degree of contrast between the urban and rural populations. The rural is apparently linked with "Indian-

Translated from Spanish by Lee Puig-Antich.

Table 19.1
Population of Peru

	1940	1961	1972	1981
Total population (in thousands)	6 208	9 907	13 538	17 518
% of urban population	35.4	47.4	59.5	65.1
% of rural population	64.5	52.6	40.5	34.9
Rate of annual growth		2.3	2.9	2.6
Rate of growth				
Urban population		3.7	5.1	3.6
Rural population		1.3	0.5	0.9

Source: Censos Nacionales de Poblacion. Peru.

ness,'' while the urban is associated with modernism. It is similarly acknowledged that the degree of illiteracy, schooling, decrease in the use of languages other than Spanish, and attitudes toward the indigenous culture (attachment, rejection, scorn) are rooted in the urban-rural dichotomy.

Recently, a group of social scientists from the IEP (Instituto de Estudios Peruanos—Institute of Peruvian Studies), directed by J. Cotler, has advanced the study of the urbanization process and the popular sectors. By adjusting the census calculations, the IEP has concluded that Peru is not as urbanized as generally believed and that migration is primarily affecting Lima (Cotler et al., 1984; Galin et al., 1985).

For the subject under consideration here, the importance of the adjustments made to the statistical instruments used in recent years is that the rate of urbanization experienced by the country in the last forty years has not been so explosive and that the era in which the majority of Peruvian settlements were considered rural is not so long ago. That is, as important as migration is in quantitative and psychosocial terms, it has not caused the sudden conversion of a basically rural country with few urban nuclei in the interior into an urbanized, modern, and homogeneous land that has shaken the symptoms of cultural plurality and provincial multilingualism.

Table 19.2 shows the progression in the figures as they emerge from the census documents at hand (prior to analysis). It is necessary to realize that we are faced with a problem that is crucial to the understanding of the world and of contem-

Table 19.2
Population by Department, Peru (in thousands)

	1828	1838	1881	1862	1873	1961	1972	1981
Peru	1,250	1,374			2,699	10,420	14,121	17,032
Lima	149	152	331	181	223	1,682	3,086	4,738
Arequipa	137	137	184	122	134	407	561	702
Cuzco	216	216	530	800	310	648	751	829
Ayachucho	160	160	230	130	236	430	479	501
Junin	200	144	332	210	278	546	720	849
Puna	156	156		246		727	813	894
Libertad	231	162	143	80	183	609	808	961

Source: Data from Basadre, 1961:1, 167 y 11, 513; Baldomero, 1861; Paz Soldan,
         1982; Cabello, 1873. Table taken from Muwaken, Pieter, Lima, 1970-1890:
         a reconnelsance, mns., pp. 14-15. Data from 1972 Census. Alberto
         Escobar, "Lima y el Proyecto Nacional: Lengua, Sociedad y Culture."
         In Lima dans realite peruvienne. A.F.E.R.P.A. Grenoble, 1975, p. 33.
         (Escobar 1983:322)

porary Peru, and that this unintentional distortion has effects that must be taken
into consideration.

To speak of bi- and multilingualism in a society that has polarized the urban
and rural requires recognizing the existence and use of the aboriginal languages
as well as their appropriateness for different roles in the culture and in the behavior
of individuals and social groups as urban or rural mono- and bilinguals.

HISTORICAL ANTECEDENTS

The distinctive character of the formation of modern states in this part of the
world is a result of what is termed the ''discovery, conquest and colonization''
of the New World by Europeans, especially Spaniards. Of obvious concern here
is the encounter between pre-Hispanic cultures and the Spanish soldiers who
settled in these lands after the invasion. The course of that encounter (in terms
of cultures, languages, material goods, and semiotic codes) has been well covered
by Peruvian and other South American historians. What needs to be emphasized
is that during the arrival of the Spanish language in America (the sixteenth
century), a form of that language began to be consolidated and extended throughout the Iberian Peninsula by the Castillian people. The reconquest of the peninsula
had occurred, solidifying the kingdom of Ferdinand and Isabella. In the same
year that the Moors departed (1492), Columbus' ships set forth to discover new

routes to the Orient, and the first grammar of a language derived from Latin was printed—*Grammatica Castellana* by Antonio de Nebrija. From the beginning, differentiation began to be noticeable on American soil. The circumstances in which the Spaniards established themselves on the land varied widely according to whether ancient cultures and societies (such as the Mesoamerican and the Andean) were involved. That is, in some areas the presence of aboriginal man and culture was tenuous and disappeared rapidly. In other regions this presence was almost nonexistent, while in still others it not only existed but has maintained itself for centuries, even to the present day (Escobar, 1968; Suarez, 1968; Heath and Laprade, 1982:132; Ugarte Chamorro, 1961).

In spite of the colonial and republican periods, ethnic groups still exist which appear to preserve a cultural link with the ancient, pre-Hispanic peoples and languages. This type of contact has led to various outcomes in terms of integration (total or partial) into national society. Furthermore, if one recalls the numerous linguistic families that have become extinct (e.g., along the coast, to mention the obvious), it is possible to imagine the diversity in each era and the factors contributing to the treatment of the indigenous peoples. The interaction between the human groups, resulting in the restriction of the aboriginals to the southern Sierra and the Amazon Selva, has been a misfortune that explains the appearance of monolinguals in languages frequently thought to be exotic "dialects." However, even Quechua and Aymara, which have become familiar through the study of Peruvian history, have not escaped being regarded as signs of inferiority (Cerrón Palomino, 1982a).

The preceding suggests that an account of the present situation needs to take the past into account in order to overcome attitudes still prevalent among middle-class monolingual speakers of Spanish. By virtue of speaking any kind of Spanish whatsoever, they lack the social perspective necessary for understanding the processes involved in the formation of the Peruvian nation and the productiveness of the changes made in the last twenty-five years. During this time bilingualism, peasant Spanish or interlanguage, and regional accents have acquired a fundamental role—that of increasing the ways of making oneself understood. In other words, reality and social change are rapidly but imperceptibly attaining the status of semiological codes, among which languages, music, and polychrome art raise an issue that has been of great concern since the War of the Pacific—the problem of national identity (CEDEP, 1979).

The language question is linked to the development of educational thought and intellectual history in the new society. It is formulated and then either supported or forgotten, according to trends, governments, individuals, and frames of reference—and this in a society whose sense of nationhood depends on recognition of its identity and of a common purpose, that is, communicating by means of a language, Spanish, which is a general language but hardly the only one. This is obviously a problem for both the sociology of language and sociolinguistics. It is necessary to realize that we have repeated opinions, figures, and materials without contrasting historical fact with contemporary trends in the ethnography of rural-urban communication (Escobar et al., 1975).

The relationship between speakers and their position in society shows the role of the languages on both the local and national levels. The linguistic outcome— in terms of social stratification, numbers of speakers, language roles, and language loyalty—offers a topography of the functions and roles of the different languages. Until recently, both the national and regional upper classes of the country exercised political, economic, and international power. Therefore, mastery of Spanish has been an indispensable requirement for admission to positions of responsibility at the height of social power. At the base of the pyramid are the Amerindian monolinguals, above them the interlanguage speakers (ranging from incipient to subordinate bilinguals), and then the provincial speakers of regional Spanish (with the coastal variety being somewhat higher on the scale than the Andean). At the apex one expects to find a Lima model, and beyond that, a pan-Hispanic standard, understood to be an adjusted variety of American and peninsular Spanish (Escobar, 1975:33–43; Burga and Flores Galindo, 1979:155–266).

THE PRESENT SITUATION

Colonial society laid the foundations for republican society, with the result that until recently the leadership has had a distorted and biased view of the languages of non-Spanish speakers. Obviously, the colonial structure would be called into question after the War of the Pacific and after this statement by Gonzalez Prada: "The real Peru does not consist of the groups of *criollos* and foreigners who inhabit the strip of land between the Pacific and the Andes; it is the great numbers of Indians scattered across the eastern band of the cordillera who constitute the nation." This has provided the impetus for studies by social scientists and educators in the last twenty years (Bonilla, 1981; Cotler, 1978; Spalding, 1974).

The growth in urban areas has confirmed the idea that the southern mountains in Peru were thought of as the "Indian blot." This meant that there was a dichotomy between the areas dominated by modernism (represented by the cities, and particularly the coast) and the indigenous areas (mainly in the mountains and countryside). As a result, the group known as the Centenario Generation arose in opposition to the so-called Novecientos Generation. Although this clash was simplistic, it provided the turning point in the transition from a Hispanist to a more indigenist or integrationist attitude. That is, in contrast to such names as José de la Riva Aguero, Julio C. Tello, or Víctor Andrés Belaunde appear those of Luis E. Valcárcel, José Uriel García, and Jorge Basadre who undertook the task of describing the national reality and, within that reality, the Andean role in which the Sierra is seen as the actualized expression of a culture and languages in a regional and republican framework. The concerns of the Centenario Generation were carried over into contemporary political currents by Víctor Raúl Raya de la Torre and José Carlos Mariátequi.

Therefore, languages such as Quechua (in its several varieties) and Aymara (with fewer speakers and varieties, and more restricted geographically) began to be of interest to others besides European and North American travelers. In addition, they began to be studied from the perspective of what has been called contemporary descriptive linguistics. Similarly, the inventory and description of the ethnic groups of the Selva were originally undertaken by the missionaries, and only after the 1950s were they studied with modern linguistic methods. These changes, along with developments in Peruvian society and the appreciation of Peru by students of history and other social sciences, including linguistics, as an object for reflection and study, led to a watershed in the 1960s, which included political action. Not surprisingly, at that point the old dualist line of thought was called into question, and theories of domination, marginalism, and the concept of the internal colony were examined in addition to the various Marxist lines of thought (Cerrón Palomino, 1981).

Since then, the definition of the language problem has been linked to the entire social context as well as to the mother-tongue/second-language difference (particularly Spanish versus the vernacular). In this regard, it is important to point out that linguistics as a discipline specially committed to the recognition of the non-Spanish speech systems of the country has increasingly demonstrated the significance of its findings for education, both in the teaching of second languages and in the comprehension of their role in the mosaic of South American languages and their usefulness in bilingual education—as an element that reinforces a new model of understanding the national identity through a prudent and careful perception of the language problem in the Andean region. (Here the term ''Andean region'' refers to the central area of the Andes, that is, Ecuador, Peru, and Bolivia.) (''Mesa Redonda sobre el Monolingüismo Quechua y Aymara y la Educación en el Peru,'' sponsored by Casa de la Cultura del Peru, chaired by José María Arguedas, November 20–24, 1963. The proceedings were published three years later.)

The achievements made in bilingual education will be outlined later in this chapter. What needs to be mentioned here is that from a marginal scientific and pedagogical position, everything related to languages as a factor in identity, from the 1960s on, has acquired a well-deserved significance and has provided the impetus for a series of legal changes. These changes created an explicit linguistic policy in 1972 and a national policy for bilingual education. This policy—with its variations—can be traced to the present time through the new Constitution and a series of legal, political, and social indicators that demonstrate how social change is attracting the attention of politicians and scholars. Urbanization and the spread of nationwide communications (print media, radio, and television) have given an importance to linguistic phenomena and semiotic codes which has helped discredit the long-established opinion that Peru was monolingual or at least the official culture and that disregarded the emerging strength of those peoples who expressed themselves in other languages and who could include bilinguals or monolinguals in some areas of the country. For them, Spanish was not the maternal language, and the type of Spanish accessible to them was not compatible with academic standards or with norms supposedly established by Liman Spanish.

The explosive growth of Lima and some of the provincial cities has highlighted the importance of "cholofication." There is no longer any debate on the increasingly clear importance of the popular strata. Originating mainly in the hinterlands, they have incorporated themselves into urban life with all the trappings of a regional culture which is fostering a kind of new articulation in music, food, the economy, language, and dance. Contrary to previous beliefs, this culture supports the use of a model of diversity as a possible way to conceptualize national unity. This model would include an attitude of respect not only toward Amerindian languages, but also toward regional standards of Peruvian Spanish, as well as a more flexible written standard for Spanish. It would reflect a society in which Spanish speakers coexist with speakers of other languages and in which—except for a nondominant group—the teaching of Spanish is, in the final analysis, the teaching of a second language. From this standpoint, bilingual education should be viewed as the usual way to teach Spanish in the elementary and public schools of Peru.

BILINGUAL EDUCATION

The current Constitution of Peru (1979) indicates that Spanish is the official language of the Republic. It recognizes Quechua and Aymara as languages that may be used officially in the areas and ways established by law, and it declares the remaining aboriginal languages to be the cultural patrimony of the nation (Ballón, 1983). This curious article of the Peruvian Carta Magna (Article 83) undeniably separates Spanish, Quechua, and Aymara from the remaining languages, that is, those of the Selva. In Article 35, the state declares that it will promote the study and knowledge of the aboriginal languages, and it guarantees to Quechua, Aymara, and other native communities the right to a primary education in the native language. Besides containing other wording, Articles 83, 35, and 34 did away with the national official status granted to Quechua by Decree-Law No. 21156, promulgated on May 27, 1975, by the military government of General Velasco Alvarado.

Therefore, the present Constitution recognizes that Peru seeks to achieve integration by means of a general language, Spanish, but that other languages also exist, among which Quechua and Aymara are of historical and quantitative importance. It acknowledges their place within the context of a contact situation in various Andean areas of the country. When other languages are referred to as aboriginal, the languages of the Selva or Amazon, rather than Quechua or Aymara, come to mind. Consequently, even with respect to language, it has not been possible in the long run to suppress the recognition of Peru's cultural and linguistic pluralism. There seems to be an admission that Peru is not a unilingual country. Although Spanish is the most widespread language and offers the widest scope for national and international communication, there is greater awareness that many people speak a language other than Spanish as their maternal language and that there still exist monolinguals who know the oral use of Spanish. Obviously, bilingual education is recognized and sanctioned, but curiously there is no policy for bilingual education, nor has there been a change in the regulations of the former law, also decreed by the military government.

In contrast, bilingual education has been given special consideration in the Amazon region, perhaps because of its antiquity. An agreement signed by the Ministry of Education with the Summer Institute of Linguistics (1979), and later with the Work of the Vicariate of San José de Amazonas and the CAAAP (Centro Amazonico de Antropologia y Aplicacion Practica—Amazon Center for Anthropology and Practical Application) has been in existence in this region since 1952. Subsequently, experiments were carried out in the Sierra by the University of San Marcos and in Puno after an agreement between the Peruvian government and the Office of German Technical Assistance. A commentary on these projects will be offered below. What they have in common is their experimental character and their connection (in part) to the normal system of the country, although they differ somewhat within their respective geographic areas. In addition, they focus on the school and education, and, most of all, on community development.

For understanding the ethnic and linguistic diversity of the Amazon region, a pertinent reference is the *Atlas de comunidades nativas* (Chirif and Mora, 1977). This work gives an idea of the history and location of the various groups of native communities, as well as the fluvial context (the most suitable means of representing their location in the Selva). Also useful is a work by D. Ribeiro and M. R. Wise, *Los grupos de la Amazonía Peruana* (1978), in which the years 1900 and 1975 are compared for population and degree of contact with, or isolation from, mestizo groups and the institutions of national society. It concludes that the ethnic groups of the Peruvian Selva belong to twelve linguistic families—Arahuaca, Cahuapana, Harakumbet, Huitoto, Jibaro, Pano, Peba-Yagua, Quechua, Tacana, Tucano, Tupi-Guarani, and Zaparo. The statistics pertaining to the aboriginal population of the Selva are, as already noted, the least reliable of the national census data. However, the 1972 census prepared by the Bureau of Analysis of the Ministry of Education estimated that for 1981, 5 percent (i.e., 250,229 persons) of the total population speaking a vernacular language would speak one of the languages from the Selva.

With respect to the linguistic families of the Sierra, two are recognized— Proto-Quechua and Proto-Aru (or Jaqi). The types of Quechua presently spoken in Peru are descended from these reconstructions. Both G. Parker (1963) and A. Torero (1964, 1974) have concluded that the dialectal diversity of Quechua can be explained in terms of a distinct historical axis which was originally situated in the central zone and which displaced the Aru family toward the south. This is proved by the survival of the small islands of Jaqaru and Kawki in the

Department of Lima, far removed from the larger Aymara areas in southern
Peru, around Puno and Tarata (Hardman, 1975, 1983; Briggs, 1976) and from
the Aymara center in Bolivia. Cerrón Palomino (1982b:213–42) presents a detailed picture of the various hypotheses concerning the assumed common origin
of the two families. However, his arguments leave no doubt that a relationship
between Quechua and Aymara must be rejected, even though structural similarities evidently exist and semantic and lexical borrowings can be explained on
the basis of the ancient contact between the languages.

As for the bilingual projects implemented in the Quechua area, the best known
and most distinguished have been the experiments lasting several years, in contrast to short-term projects now remembered only in specialized articles and
reports (Ministerio de Educación, 1966. 1972, 1973). Of current interest is the
experiment carried out in Huamanga, and resumed periodically with varying
objectives and results in the ongoing project sponsored by the University of San
Marcos through CILA (Centro de Investigación de Lingüística Aplicada—Center
for Research in Applied Linguistics) in the Department of Ayacucho (Zúñiga,
1982; Burns, 1971). Apart from this effort, which was initiated by a Peruvian
university with foreign help and in collaboration with the Ministry (since 1963),
the most innovative and extensive undertaking—in terms of duration, diversity
of languages, and number of participating schools, students, and teachers—is
the Puno Project, which at this writing extends to the sixth grade. This project
has been carried out in collaboration with INIDE (Instituto Nacional de Investigación y Desarrollo de la Educación—National Institute of Educational Research and Development and the German government since 1978 (Aranda and
Sanchez, 1982; López, 1984).

CONCLUSIONS

It would appear that bilingual education in Peru, fragmented by region and
by school, has not fulfilled the expectations of its founders, who, in different
times and places, undertook this improbable task. That is, the results of bilingual
education are not completely satisfactory and depend, in great degree, on psychosocial, political, and economic conditions and their relationship to the public
system of the state. As a theory, bilingual education is indeed worthy of defense,
but in terms of achievement it is not totally justifiable. The same has occurred
in the areas of social and sexual discrimination. These are ancient and universal
problems of humankind, which defy reason in the face of the irrational.

However useful and advantageous the results may be, the outcome in both
the Selva and the Sierra (including Puno, in spite of its trilingual publications,
teacher manuals, and ethnoliterary studies) does not conceal the enormous difference between the bilingual school and the unilingual school (either public or
private). In addition, it is evident that in countries like Peru, the private school
performs a significant portion of the educational work, and that the rural-to-
urban migration has resulted in a substantial deficiency in the use of the official

language by lower and middle classes, and by teachers as well as students. This is not a situation that affects only small areas or a few thousand people, but is widely diffused throughout the country, from bottom to top. This problem is distinct from the problem of bilingual education. As pointed out by this author in 1963 and more recently by I. Pozzi-Escot (1984), when Spanish is said to be the most widespread language in Peru and to encompass the highest percentage of speakers, it is utopian to overlook the fact that for many of those speakers, it should be taught as a second language. As long as a way to transform the teaching of Spanish in the *entire* country is not found, language instruction will meet with diminishing returns, for two reasons: it will not be able to draw the most appropriate pedagogical conclusions; and it will accentuate the differences created by a hollow social scale which values certain individuals over others.

In this writer's opinion, the small amount of study allotted to American and Peruvian Spanish is not due simply to the technical deficiencies of our specialists, but to the ideology which derived from the colonial era and which dominates Peruvian national society and the ruling classes (Escobar, 1978). As long as bilingual education is directed only to monolingual indigenous groups of the Selva and the Sierra, there will be keen competition to abandon bilingual schools in favor of regular, nonbilingual schools, and a concomitant high dropout rate. Although many children and adults at various levels can benefit from instruction in language and other subjects (both in and out of the classroom), it must be realized that educational content hinges on political alternatives—and these alternatives involve decisions regarding educational and linguistic planning. Neither a law nor an educational policy can change the social reality of a country, but they can undoubtedly open the way for fundamental changes in the structure of society, thereby making it more amenable to the idea of greater access to material goods and rights in the contemporary world. Therefore, in order to be understood in regions such as the Andean, bilingual education must be transformed into the standard way of teaching language on a national scale. If this is not done, it is doubtful—as demonstrated by the completed studies and evaluations—that it will divest itself of the experimental and inconsistent quality that has characterized it to date (Pozzi-Escot, 1972a and b, 1984; Engle, 1973; Dutcher, 1982; Escobar, 1983).

BIBLIOGRAPHY

Aranda, E., and R. Sanchez. 1982. "Experiencias de Educación Bilingüe en problemas quechuas y aymaras de las áreas rurales de Puno." *Cuadernos de información educacional*. INIDE, pp. 11–40.

Ballón, E. 1983. "Multiglosia y poder de expresión en la Sociedad Peruana." *Educación y Lingüística en la Amazonía Peruana*, comp. A. Corbera. Lima: CAAAP, pp. 17–27.

Bonilla, H. 1981. "Clases populares y Estado en el contexto de la crisis colonial." *La independencia en el Perú*. 2d ed. Lima: Instituto de Estudios Peruanos, pp. 13–69.

Briggs, L. T. 1976. "Algunos rasgos dialectales del aymara de Bolivia y del Perú."
      Notas y Noticias Lingüísticas 3 (July-August):7–8. La Paz: Instituto Nacional de
      Estudios Lingüísticos, pp. 1–19.
Burga, M., and A. Flores Galindo. 1979. *Apogeo y crisis de la república aristocrática.*
      Lima: Rikchay Peru, pp. 155–266.
Burns, D. 1971. *Cinco años de educación bilingüe en los Andes del Perú 1965–1970.*
      Lima: Instituto Linguistico de Verano.
Casa de la Cultura del Perú. 1966. *Mesa redonda sobre el Monolingüismo quechua y
      aymara y la educación en el Perú.* Lima.
Centro de Estudios para el Desarrollo y la Participación (CEDEP). 1979. *Perú: Identidad
      Nacional.* Lima.
Cerrón Palomino, R. 1981. "Aprender castellano en un contexto plurilingüe." *Lexis* 5,
      1 (July): 39–51.
———. 1982a. "La cuestión lingüistica en el Peru." *Aula Quechua.* Lima: Signo Univ-
      ersitario, pp. 105–23.
———. 1982b. "El problema de la relación quechua-aru: Estado actual." *Lexis* 6, 2:
      213–42.
Chirif, A., and C. Mora. 1977. *Atlas de comunidades nativas.* Lima: SINAMOS.
Cotler, J. 1978. *Clases, estado y nación en el Perú.* Lima: IEP.
Cotler, J., et al. 1984. "Características sociales de los sectores populares de Lima." Ms.
      Proyecto de investigación urbanización y sectores populares urbanos. Lima: In-
      stituto de Estudios Peruanos.
Dutcher, N. 1982. *The Use of First and Second Languages in Primary Education: Selected
      Case Studies.* Washington, D.C.: World Bank Staff Working Paper No. 504.
Engle, P. L. 1973. "The Use of Vernacular Languages in Education: Revisited." Ms.
      University of Illinois at Chicago Circle.
Escobar, A. 1968. "Present State of Linguistics. Current Trends in Linguistics." *IV:
      Ibero-American and Caribbean Linguistics.* The Hague: Mouton, pp. 616–27.
———. 1975. "La educación bilingüe en el Perú." *Proceedings of the First Inter-
      american Conference on Bilingual Education.* Arlington, Va.: Center for Applied
      Linguistics, pp. 34–42.
———. 1978. *Variaciones sociolingüísticas del castellano en el Perú.* Lima: Instituto
      de Estudios Peruanos.
———. 1983. "Fundamentos lingüísticos y pedagógicos de la enseñanza de una segunda
      lengua en poblaciones indígenas." *Educación, Etnías y Descolonización en Amér-
      ica Latina. Una guía para la educación bilingüe intercultural.* Vol. 2. México:
      UNESCO, pp. 315–339.
Escobar, A., comp. 1972. *El reto del multilinguismo en el Peru.* Containing essays by
      Escobar, Hardman, Torero, Parker, Pozzi-Escot, Cerron Palomino, d'Ans, Wolck,
      Gonzales-Moreyra, Aliaga, and Escribens. Lima: Instituto de Estudios Peruanos.
Escobar, A., et al. 1975. *Perú¿ pais bilingüe?* Lima: Instituto de Estudios Peruanos.
Galin, P., O. Castillo, and J. Carrión. 1985. "Clases Populares y Asalariados en Lima."
      Ms. Lima: Instituto de Estudios Peruanos.
Hardman, M. 1975. "El jaqaru, el kawki y el aymara." *Actas del Simposio de Monte-
      video, Enero de 1966.* México, pp. 185–92.
———. 1983 (1966). *Jaqaru: compendio de estructura fonológica y morfológica.* The
      Hague: Mouton.
Heath, S. B., and R. Laprade. 1982. "Castilian Colonization and Indigenous Languages:

The Cases of Quechua and Aymara.'' *Language Spread: Studies in Diffusion and Social Change*. Bloomington: Indiana University Press, pp. 118–47.

Instituto Lingüístico de Verano. 1979. *Educación Bilingüe. Una experiencia en la Amazonía Peruana*. Lima: Ignacio Prado Pastor.

López, L. E. 1984. ''Tengo una muñeca vestida de azul.'' *Autoeducación*, Nos. 10–11: 45–50.

Ministerio de Educación. 1972. *Primer Seminario Nacional de Educación Bilingüe, Algunos Estudios y Ponencias*. Lima.

———. 1972. *Política National de Educación Bilingüe*. Lima.

———. 1972. *Reglamento de Programas de Promoción Educativa para las Areas Rurales*. Lima.

:———. 1973. *Reglamento de Educación Bilingüe*. Lima.

Parker, G. 1963. ''La classificación genética de los dialectos quechuas.'' *Revista del Museo Nacional* 32: 241–52.

Pozzi-Escot, I. 1972. ''La situación lingüística en el Perú y su repercusión en la enseñanza del castellano en la zona andina.'' Ph.D. diss., National University of San Marcos, Lima.

———. 1984. ''El castellano como segunda lengua en el Perú.'' *Cielo Abierto* 10, No. 30: 37–46.

Ribeiro, D., and M. R. Wise. 1978. *Los grupos de la Amazonía Peruana*. Lima: Instituto Linguistico de Verano.

Spalding, K. 1974. *De indio a campesino*. Lima: Instituto de Estudios Peruanos.

Suarez, J. 1968. ''Classical Languages. Current Trends in Linguistics.'' *IV: Ibero-American and Caribbean Linguistics*. The Hague, Paris: Mouton, pp. 254–74.

Suarez, R. 1979. ''Población y fuerza laboral en el Perú: revisión metodológica e implicancias.'' *Economía* 2, 4: 65–146.

Torero, A. 1964. ''Los dialectos quechuas.'' *Anales científicos de la UNA*, No. 2: 446–478.

———. 1974. *El quechua y la historia social andina*. Lima: Universidad Ricardo Palma.

Ugarte Chamorro, M. A. 1961. ''Lucha en torno a la oficialización del castellano en el Peru.'' *Sphinx* 2, 14: 101–25.

Zúniga, M. 1982. ''Un programa experimental de educación bilingüe quechua-castellano en Ayacucho.'' *Aula Quechua*. Lima: Signo Universitario, pp. 257–77.

BILINGUALISM AND BILINGUAL
EDUCATION IN SINGAPORE

Singapore, situated at about 1 degree north of the equator, lies at the center of
Southeast Asia. Denied any significant natural resources except a strategic geographical location and enterprising migrants, this small republic has emerged in
recent years as a major regional, financial, commercial, communication, and
tourist center. Although the physical dimensions are paltry—Singapore has a
land extent of only 570.4 square kilometers and a population of 2.5 million—
the political and economic indicators are impressive. Singapore is often quoted
as an example of political stability and administrative efficiency. Its per capita
gross national product (GNP) at US 5,900 is second only to that of Japan in
Asia, it is the world's second busiest port, it has a registered unemployed rate
of 0.6 percent of the workforce, and its financial reserves rank it as the eleventh
"richest" country in the world.

The truly remarkable thing about the Singapore success story is that it could
so easily have gone wrong. Singapore began its march toward success as a plural
society with racial groups which, when not ignorant of one another were hostile
to one another. When Stamford Raffles founded the settlement in 1819, there
were fewer than two hundred inhabitants. Extensive settlement began only in
the mid-nineteenth century when a thriving entrepot economy under British
control attracted migrants from near and far. Today, Singapore's population
continues to be ethnically mixed with the Chinese at 76.7 percent, Malays at
14.7 per cent, Indians at 6.4 percent, and others at 2.2 percent. Singapore's
migrant history is reflected in the 20 percent of citizens who were born outside
Singapore. A new phenomenon is the presence of nearly one hundred and fifty
thousand "guest workers," single men and women from such areas as Korea,
the Philippines, Thailand, India, Sri Lanka, and Malaysia.

As might be expected, Singapore's migrants come from a variety of countries and regions. The Chinese come from a number of southern Chinese provinces, with the Hokkiens at 43 percent, Teochews at 22 percent, and Cantonese at 17 percent predominating. For the Indians, Tamils from Tamil Nadu predominate at 63.9 percent, Malayalis are 8.1 percent, and Punjabis 7.8 percent. The vast majority of Malays (69 percent) are from Peninsular Malaysia, while the Javanese and Boyanese make up 18 and 11 percent, respectively.

The pattern of languages used in Singapore reflects this diversity of origin. C. Y. Kuo (1980:40) uses Dankwart Rustow's characterization of "a variety of unrelated languages each with its own literary tradition" as being appropriate for Singapore, and notes that the 1957 census identifies thirty-three specific mother-tongue groups, with twenty reported to have more than one thousand speakers. A 1978 estimate of the population aged fifteen and over noted that Hokkien, Teochew, and Cantonese could be understood by 77.9, 59.7, and 63.2 percent of the population, respectively. However, Mandarin (see Chapter 9), the school language, is spoken by less than 1 percent of the population. The figure claimed for Malay was 67.3 percent and for Tamil 6 percent. English was understood by 61.7 percent of the population. The figures for Malay and English are high for different reasons. Malay is widespread because of its function as a lingua franca, used to varying degrees of competence by all three ethnic groups; the increased competence in English is more recent and is attributable to the postwar spread of English-medium schooling.

Adding to the complexity caused by language variety are other factors. With the Chinese the problem lies with the degree of incomprehensibility between dialects, although the written script gives the language unity. However, as we noted earlier, the school dialect is Mandarin, spoken as a mother tongue by less than 1 percent of the Chinese population. The Indians have to cope with several distinct languages with different writing systems, but the school language is Tamil. The Malays face the problem of a rapidly evolving language, with extensive borrowings from English, but the use of the Roman script may be said to lessen the educational burden. English, as the metropolitan language, was treated as another official language in the 1950s but has now emerged as the *de facto* "national language" displacing the *de jure* national language, Malay.

HISTORICAL BACKGROUND

As noted earlier, Singapore is a migrant society. The 1871 census showed that migration had been extensive, for there were already 54,572 Chinese, 26,148 Malays, 11,501 Indians, 2,000 Eurasians, and a sprinkling of Arabs, Siamese, and Filipinos. The ratio between the ethnic groups tended to fluctuate—the Malays were 26.9 percent of the population in 1871—but it seems from early on that the Chinese would predominate. The immigration flows were also affected by colonial government interventions, as, for example, via the assisted repatriation scheme during the 1930 depression and the Aliens Ordinance of 1933 which the British used to control the flow of immigration. The pull factors encouraging migration were strong, however. Singapore's status as a free port led rapidly to economic growth. The growth of the rubber and tin industries in Malaya and Singapore's role as a processor of raw materials were important factors.

Prewar Singapore has been characterized as a plural society whose primary characteristic was "cultural distinctiveness associated with extensive social and spatial segregation" (Chiew, 1983:30). British colonial policies, by practice rather than by design, kept the plural society intact. The vertical cleavages were both sharp and distinctive. The three major ethnic groups were divided in terms of language, religion, economic specialization, and habitation. English-medium education, available only to a small number, was a further dividing factor, splitting the Chinese community down the middle; the Malays in their turn shunned English-medium education which was largely church-sponsored for fear of religious conversion.

The census reports for 1931 and 1947 provide some insight into the degree of linguistic communicability. The 1931 census showed that only 28.2 percent could speak English, the administrative language; the Indians at 14.1 percent made up almost half the total. The percentages were little improved in 1947 when 33 percent claimed the ability to read and write a simple letter in English. Census data for 1931 also showed the degree of economic specialization. The Chinese were concentrated in clerical and professional occupations at 31.2 percent and in commerce and finance at 23.6 percent; the Malays in transport and communications at 31.2 percent and in agriculture at 30.5 percent; while almost half the employed Indians, 50.3 percent, were in clerical and professional services (Chiew, 1983:30). Participation in education also reveals a similar pattern of segregation. By this time a four-stream system of education had emerged; English, Chinese, Malay, and Tamil schools. The English and Chinese schools were the most extensive with both elementary and secondary divisions; the Malay and Tamil streams were weakest in terms of pupils, resources, and standards. Statistics are somewhat spotty, but it is estimated that in 1938 there were thirty-three English-medium schools with an enrollment of 14,592 students. It was estimated that there were 215 Chinese-medium schools with an enrollment of 13,315 students. There were apparently five Tamil schools with an enrollment of 156 pupils (Wilson, 1978:52–54, 64).

As the above suggests, there existed a link between ethnic pluralism and societal differentiation. In colonial Singapore, there was an unequal distribution of access to wealth, status, and power. Education—particularly the medium of instruction—and the consequences arising from access and achievement in the different media, had considerable impact on life chances. Consequently, colonial education policy and the evaluation of the segregated system were central factors in the increasingly hostile relationship between the English- and the vernacular-educated. British education policy was in favor of English-medium education and minimal Malay-medium education. Chinese-medium education, ignored by the colonial government and only community-supported, fell to the influence of radical social reformists from China. In the early decades of the twentieth century, Chinese-medium education became a political weapon to be used against the colonial authority—the Chinese language became a symbol of ethnic solidarity and of cultural superiority and English the language of oppression. When the British authorities in the 1920s sought to supervise Chinese education, it was political control rather than pedagogical improvement they had in mind. This politicization of education was one of the most serious and immediate problems that postwar governments had to face.

THE CONTEMPORARY SCENE

Before we examine Singapore's bilingual education policies in detail, it is important to understand the context within which education policies are formulated and implemented. As in many developing countries, education is highly valued in Singapore, both from the government perspective that stresses both personnel considerations and the maintenance of cultural and linguistic heritages, and from the individual's perspective of education as an invaluable avenue of social mobility. Education is currently the second largest expenditure item in the Singapore budget, and nearly half a million students are enrolled in educational institutions.

The government, having achieved a measure of political stability and economic growth and diversification, seeks primarily to ensure the continuance of such trends. The principal strategy is increased centralization of authority, an emphasis on rationalization and cost-effective management, and a steady erosion of the legitimacy of subgroups, clans, castes, and so on. On the political front, there is a search for suitable second-echelon leaders and a concern that the disruptive communal politics of the 1950s and 1960s will not be repeated. The current leadership, for instance, deems the issues of medium of instruction, cultural identity, and interethnic relationships as settled questions. On the economic front, the government is seeking to move Singapore into high-technology industries, to promote Singapore as a regional center for banking, oil-refining, and communications, and to increase the range and depth of Singapore's international connections.

Education, talent, and an openness to international ideas and knowledge are thus heavily stressed. Increasing emphasis is placed on the scientific content of tertiary education and on technical-vocational education—opportunities for postsecondary education, for instance, are being expanded. At the same time, it is felt that Singapore needs to recruit skilled talent from abroad; at home, socially controversial policies are in place to ensure the reproduction of talent and its identification in schools. Access to global developments in turn is said to be possible only through English which has now lost its colonial identity and has become the nationally significant language.

The government is also concerned that in the rush for modernization Singaporeans might lose a sense of themselves as Asians and become "deculturalized." Thus, mother-tongue competence is stressed, and the importance of language to a proper understanding and appreciation of cultural traditions is a prominent rationale for bilingual education (Gopinathan, 1979, 1980). In the last couple of years, the government has begun to implement an extensive program of moral education in elementary and lower secondary classes; at the upper secondary level, students are to be offered a choice of religious education curricula.

BILINGUALISM: SOCIETAL DIMENSIONS

The goals for language policy in Singapore can best be understood by keeping in mind the societal imperatives the government of the day faced. Two key factors stand out. First, as a consequence of colonial rule, Singapore developed as a plural society and had a history of interethnic tension. Second, there was need for rapid economic and social development to meet the needs of a young and growing population. Both challenges were met by a political system that had a pronounced degree of centralization and was prepared to engage in extensive social engineering to bring about orderly social change. The strategy was to win legitimacy to an achievement-oriented, nonparticularistic elite, to build new institutions and institute new processes to entrench supportive brokers, and to isolate those seen as overly committed to ethnic-based loyalties. Crucial to this strategy was language policy, both in and out of education. As described below, in Singapore language was to be a uniquely fruitful instrument in the process of molding the Singapore identity.

The first goal, given the multilingual nature of Singapore society, was for a language policy that would contribute to integration by promoting interethnic communication. There was some awareness during colonial rule that some means for linguistic interaction must be found, and it was assumed that English had most potential as a link language. This policy was doomed to failure, however, because the colonial authority was not prepared to expand English-medium schooling and because, after 1920, a sizable proportion of the Chinese preferred Chinese-medium education. The government then faced, and succeeded, in building Chinese secondary schools, training teachers, and the like. It was not until 1956 when *The Report of the Committee on Chinese Education* was issued that the principle of equal treatment for all school languages and societal bilingualism was accepted. Thus, a policy of societal and educational bilingualism is one response to the problem of linguistic pluralism. Though there was broad agreement for this policy, it has not always been easy to translate policy into practice, and it was not until the late 1960s that bilingualism began to be entrenched in the educational system.

A second aspect of the policy of societal bilingualism can be said to be the use of language as a societal resource. It is clear from the literature that in many multilingual societies language-bred hostility is a major source of social tension and weakness. In Singapore's case, the emphasis has largely been on making virtue out of necessity. English, a colonial language, an object of suspicion during the interwar years, has now been transformed into a "national" language. This transformation has been achieved by identifying English as a "neutral" link language between the various ethnic groups, a strategy in which the national government succeeded where the British had failed. A crucial element in the government's strategy has been the identification of English as a major source of economically valuable knowledge and technology. Singapore's possession of a metropolitan language, it is argued, is an asset which some countries have squandered but in Singapore is to be nurtured and reproduced so as to enable access to world markets and greater integration into the world economy. As the Prime Minister Lee Kuan Yew put it: "the deliberate stifling of a language (English) which gives access to superior technology can be damaging beyond repair . . . [and] tantamount to blinding the next generation to the knowledge of the advanced countries" (cited in Chan and Evers, 1978).

The position as regards the mother tongues can also be said to illustrate the notion of language as resource, though the reasons for retaining them are differently stated. Two strands may be identified. One strand is what C. Pendley (1983) terms the function of language as "moral integrators and sources of symbolic identification." This may be said to have great significance at the individual level, and in a recent speech the Prime Minister underlined this dimension:

To have no emotionally acceptable language as our mother tongue is to be emotionally crippled. We shall doubt ourselves. We shall be less confident. . . . This [Mandarin] is a deep and strong psychic force, one that gives confidence to a people to face up to and overcome great changes and challenges . . . to look at Chinese characters, see them as mysterious hieroglyphics is to be psychologically disadvantaged (*Straits Times*, September 22, 1984).

One could argue as well for societal-level significance. As noted earlier, over the years the government has sought to shape a vision of Singapore as a rational, modernizing society but without losing a sense of its origins in the East and its fundamental nature as an Asian society. Singaporeans are often told that Western countries have lost a sense of moral purpose, that societal integration is eroding, and that Singapore should avoid that path and look instead to countries like Japan. Thus, the use of ethnic heritage, and particularly language, is seen as a bulwark against vices that international contact and the extensive use of English might bring.

A second aspect worth noting is that rapid social change brings with it loss of confidence, power, and influence for groups as much as for individuals. As Singapore moves toward a more bureaucratic and centralized administrative structure with an economy dominated by multinationals and power in the hands of an English-educated technocratic elite, traditional power brokers like family firms, clan associations, newspapers, and language teachers unions, previously powerful, are likely to feel isolated and suspicious of such trends in society. The retention and promotion of mother tongues at this time is likely to ensure that these groups will have something to hold on to and, if not support, at least acquiesce in large-scale social engineering. Language is thus a valuable tool for managing the effects of social dislocation brought about by modernization.

A third aspect of the mother tongue as resource concept is economic. Here one may see Mandarin as playing a role similar to English. Just as English is to be retained to ensure access to international markets, Mandarin—and this is part of the reason for encouraging the shift from dialects—is seen as valuable in providing access to markets in Mainland China.

We move now to examining the translation of the rationales for policy, both at the national level and in the education system. In legislative terms, Singapore is a multilingual society. Four official languages are recognized for use in the republic: Chinese, Malay, Tamil, and English. In addition, Malay has the status as the sole national language. In the Republic of Singapore Independence Act of 1965, the status of Malay as the national language is limited as follows:

(a) that it be in the Roman script

(b) no person shall be prohibited or prevented from using or from teaching or learning any other language, and

(c) nothing in this section shall prejudice the right of the Government to preserve and sustain the use and study of the language of any other community in Singapore.

In practice Malay has largely symbolic and ceremonial functions. All four languages may be used in Parliament, in the legal system, over the national broadcasting system, and in the press.

BILINGUALISM IN THE SCHOOLS

At the school level, educational bilingualism is now well entrenched. All students are required to take a second language, and that second language is most often a mother tongue. Concern with poor levels of bilingual attainment led in 1979 to the introduction of different tracks, primarily characterized by differing language competence requirements in the first and second language. Such tracking begins as early as the third year of elementary school. The stress on minimum levels of competence reaches right up to university entrance. Over and above suitable academic qualifications, students are required to possess minimum levels of bilingual competence or to attain it before graduation. In general, the trend seems to have been toward lowering requirements for mother-tongue competence while holding standards for English high.

A second significant feature of the language policy in education is that parents have free choice in the medium of instruction. Although this choice was exercised most extensively in the 1960s, today most parents are opting for English-medium schools where the mother tongues are offered as second languages. It is expected that by 1987 there will be a single national stream using English as the medium of instruction. This is an unexpected outcome of a policy of equal treatment, but large-scale economic changes have made English the most valued language. It must also be noted that free choice has meant not only a general shift toward English, but also that the Indian ethnic group in particular has exercised its choice in a way that defeats the government's objective of wishing ethnic groups to retain their mother tongues. According to one estimate in the early 1980s, less than 50 percent of Indian pupils offered Tamil as a second language at the elementary level. Caught in a situation where Tamil has neither political nor economic significance, a large number of Indian parents have opted for their children to be taught either Mandarin or Malay as their "mother tongue." The problem is aggravated by the logistics of implementing a bilingualism policy. Too few Indian students means that it is sometimes not feasible to offer instruction in Tamil during regular school hours; rather than opt for after-school hours in another school, students choose available languages (Gopinathan and Mani, 1983).

BILINGUAL ATTAINMENT

In spite of a general consensus over the significance and direction of Singapore's language policies, in the mid–1970s there was widespread criticism of changes in policies, levels of attainment, exposure time, and the like. Changes in economic performance and opportunity, and in particular a need to ensure minimum levels of numeracy and literacy, created the conditions for a review of education policy. This was undertaken in 1978 by a team led by the Deputy Prime Minister, Dr. Goh Keng Swee. *The Report on the Ministry of Education, 1978* provided the most explicit and authoritative critique of Singapore's language policies as they related to education. Among its findings, the following are of special importance:

(1) Low Literacy: At least 25 percent of the Primary Six population did not attain minimum literacy levels. For early secondary school leavers in the armed forces, only 11 percent of recruits were able to handle English competently.

(2) Between 1975 and 1977, 62 percent of those who sat for the Primary School Leaving Examination and 66 percent of those who sat for the GCE "O" level examination (General Council on Education, "Ordinary" as opposed to "Advanced" level) failed either in the first or second language.

(3) On various measures of pupil performance—examinations, newspapers, and book reading—students fared badly.

(4) The report reviewed various strategies devised to improve language levels and found several to be ineffective (Goh Report, 1979).

The principal finding was that too much was being demanded of too many in terms of language competence; in the Report's words, "the policy of bilingualism has not been universally effective.'' The principal recommendations were tracking, differentiated curricula, and different examinations.

BILINGUALISM—REASONS FOR INEFFECTIVENESS

The problems of bilingual achievement in Singapore can be traced to a variety of causes: multiracial population of diverse cultural and linguistic backgrounds; a stressful learning environment in which language competency is all important; a poor understanding of the pedagogical implications of policies; and a failure to recognize the persistence of dialects. Besides, most pupils were learning two languages which they often did not speak at home. Finally, children of different language abilities were being subjected to the same education program.

The realization and acknowledgment of these inherent differences of varying aptitude for language learning and Singapore's linguistic complexity has led to the recognition that effective bilingualism cannot be achieved by, and thus cannot be expected of, all Singaporeans. As a result, the emphasis in the bilingual policy has shifted. In 1978, the policy was modified, with increased emphasis on proficiency in English. "The new education system which will evolve over the years will be one in which great prominence is attached to English at the cost of some reduction in standards in the mother tongue, be it Mandarin, Malay or Tamil.'' The reason for this emphasis is that ''Generally pupils from the non-English medium schools lose out to those from the English medium schools in job opportunities due to their lack of proficiency in English'' (Goh Report, 1979).

This shift in concern can be attributed to the changed status and role of English in Singapore. As Kuo (1976) notes, English has gained ground in Singapore, becoming the most prestigious language and the vehicle for upward social mobility. This elevated status for English is due to Singapore's emergence as the regional center of banking, trade, and commerce. English is clearly the key to economic modernization and development.

Two other features unique to Singapore need mention, for they illustrate the problems of setting objectives in societal terms and then having to deal with their pedagogical implications. Recent reforms in the education system following a recognition that bilingualism made too many demands has resulted in streaming after the third year of elementary schooling. The weakest group was streamed into a monolingual stream, and the initial policy was to make them competent in their mother tongue. Today, however, the demand for English competence is so great that these students will now be taught a simplified curriculum in English, their weaker language. At the secondary level, a problem has emerged over the languages to be used for teaching moral and religious studies. An earlier rationalization for bilingualism stressed the importance of indigenous languages in transmitting cultural and moral values. Language was seen as the most important element of culture, and subjects such as history, civics, and social studies were marked out for teaching in the mother tongue. However, while religious studies are being introduced into the curriculum so as to enable students to maintain their cultural and religious traditions, the government seems to have reversed its policy and is pushing for these subjects to be taught in English, much to the dismay of language teachers associations.

SPECIAL ASSISTANCE PLAN (SAP)

The Ministry has not given up hope that some students may be able to manage two languages at first-language level. Of special importance is the Special Assistance Plan schools project. This plan, which saw the conversion of nine established Chinese schools into bilingual institutions, was conceived after Nanyang University had elected to use English as its medium of instruction as a result of the steady decline in enrollment in the Chinese-medium primary schools. SAP schools, aimed at "preparing our brighter pupils to be effectively bilingual" (Ministry of Education, 1980), was targeted at the top 8 percent of those passing the Primary School Leaving Examination.

In the context of the SAP schools, effective bilingualism is defined as communicative competence to speak, understand, respond, and read and write in English and Mandarin at first-language level (Prime Minister Lee Kuan Yew, 1978). The SAP schools are provided with financial assistance, special incentives, and options. Yet, pupils in the top 8 percent have generally been reluctant to opt for these schools. An evaluation of the SAP program shows that the objective of effective bilingualism has yet to be attained. English still remains the weaker language among these students. Thus, based on the results of the first batch of SAP students and comments pertaining to the burden of learning two languages at first-language level, it has been decided that students be given the option of doing one language at first-language level and the other at second-language level.

THE "SPEAK MANDARIN" CAMPAIGN

While reviews and rethinking of school policies were coming to the fore in the late 1970s, the government was also preparing to intervene at the national level, to move language development in a new direction. The "Speak Mandarin Campaign" was launched in April 1978, and the Prime Minister has argued that the persistence of dialect use among school children explains why Mandarin has failed to become the more widespread language among the Chinese. A second reason for the campaign was that dialect use fragmented the Chinese community and prevented the common language, Mandarin, from playing its legitimate unifying role.

Once again, the societal-level issue of language status is intertwined with the school-level problem of effective attainment. The Prime Minister was right in asserting that the time and effort invested in teaching and examining Mandarin in the schools would be wasted if steps were not taken to ensure the use of Mandarin rather than dialects in a variety of domains. However, the timing of the campaign may be viewed within a larger context. The campaign was launched at a time when Nanyang University, the bastion of Chinese tertiary education, was slowly switching over to English. From this perspective, it is possible to understand the campaign as a balancing move to reassure the Chinese community that their cohesiveness, cultural identity, and language claims still remained the primary concern of the government. The move can also be understood in more pragmatic terms. It was clearly inefficient and "irrational" to use a multiplicity of dialects when a high-status variety was available and being taught in the schools. Rational social and language planning called for the elimination of such contradictions; such a view would be consistent with the model of language planning which the government has adopted.

The implementation of the campaign has not been without attendant controversies. Among measures taken have been the gradual phasing out of dialect programs over radio and television, the introduction of conversational Mandarin lessons over radio, the organization of forums, panel discussions, seminars on the Speak Mandarin theme, and a publicity blitz aimed at those involved in the more common everyday occupations, hawkers, taxi drivers, bus conductors, government service personnel like postmen, public utilities, clerks manning government counters, and the like. Since 1980, there has been a continuing effort to get children to give up their dialect names when registering for school. There is also the clear requirement that government-citizen transactions, if they are done in Chinese, should be conducted in Mandarin, by all those deemed to be proficient in language. At a later stage, it was realized that the family domain was important, and so the family's linguistic habits became the target for change.

Complaints over the campaign have come from various quarters. Many dialect speakers objected to the claim that dialects were somehow less Chinese and incapable of communicating high-status culture; the withdrawal of many very popular dialect programs over television was strongly criticized. An interesting effect of the Speak Mandarin Campaign is the awareness and concern it generated among other ethnic communities regarding their mother tongues. For a short while, it was feared that the Mandarin Campaign was aimed at all ethnic groups, though this was very clearly not the intention. Nevertheless, the notion of a common unifying language caught on in the Indian community, which saw a short-lived upsurge of interest in promoting Tamil as a common link language and the organization of various competitions and seminars to encourage the use of another tongues.

What of the campaign's success? It is clear that the earlier anxieties about the campaign from the dialect groups and the other ethnic groups have been overcome. In addition, the Prime Minister noted that the percentage of new primary one pupils from predominantly Mandarin-speaking families increased from 26 percent in 1980 to 59 percent in 1984. Within the same period, the percentage of pupils from mainly dialect-speaking families dropped from 64 percent to 27 percent. The Prime Minister has stated his conviction that persisting with the campaign for another ten years would mean that "we should succeed in speaking

Mandarin as a matter of habit'' (Singapore Government, Press Release, September 4, 1984). It seems clear that in the long term the effort to change language preferences will result in some significant changes. However, it needs to be remembered that the large numbers already out of the school system, still high levels of early school leavers, and a simplified Mandarin curriculum in the schools may not make the goal of having all Chinese use Mandarin much more extensively feasible. Thus, while there is acceptance of Mandarin and its legitimacy, in some domains dialect use is likely to remain strong.

THE STATUS OF ENGLISH

English, while not the target of any campaign, has succeeded beyond the dreams of its early promoters. The role and status of English in Singapore today are marked by several features. The first is the remarkable acceptance of English as a *de facto* national language, particularly when we remember that for much of the 1950s it was regarded, principally by the Chinese-educated, as the language of an alien oppressor, and policy efforts in the 1960s and early 1970s were centered on making the mother tongues vital educational languages. A second feature has to do with the ambivalence with which English is regarded by both the political establishment and the ethnic groups, especially the Chinese. English is, on one hand, seen as the carrier of desirable modernizing influences and thus an indispensable part of Singapore's plans for the future. At the same time, it is regarded as a carrier of the ''fads and fetishes'' of the West which Singapore needs to avoid. This constant stress on the shortcomings of English as a culturally valuable language probably explains the Singaporeans' instrumental attachment to the language, and accounts for the pockets of resistance to the use of English in private and familiar domains among some Singaporeans. The home is in many instances a barrier to the complete acceptance of English, and the government's rationalizations about language functions have contributed to this.

One final observation may be made. In the 1950s and earlier, restricted access to English meant that competence in English was highly rewarded. Today the major challenge to Singapore's bilingual policy is the fact that widespread access to English-medium schooling has not led to equitable levels of attainment of English competence. Not only is such disparity in attainment likely to be a major source of societal tension and disagreement, but it also puts at risk Singapore's plan to be a major high-technology and information center. What is ''fortunate'' is that all groups seem equally handicapped in the pursuit of English-language competence (Kuo, 1977).

CONCLUSIONS

In spite of the problems already evident in attempting a bold bilingual program in a multilingual society with a history of language-generated hostility, Singapore's language policies can be termed successful. First, language-related issues are no longer politically contentious. Disagreements over policies and consequences remain, but in contrast to many other multilingual states Singapore has reached a consensus as to what is desirable in terms of a national language policy. All important sectors in society subscribe to the policy of bilingualism; in more informal situations, the ease with which speakers switch from official languages to dialect demonstrates the lack of tension over appropriate language choice and use.

Second, in spite of the shortcomings identified earlier, there has been a slow growth in the numbers. The general literacy rate for persons aged ten and above was estimated to be 84.8 percent in 1982. However, the magnitude of the task faced is seen in the statistic that about 60 percent of literate persons were literate in only one official language, mainly Chinese. Nevertheless, a comparison of census data for 1970 and 1980 indicates that, whereas in 1970 only 19.1 percent were bilingual in two or more official levels, within a decade that figure had risen to 37.9 percent. With the changes made to language strategies, it can be predicted that by 1990 a majority of those over ten and above would be bilingual. It would then have taken about three decades to have achieved a 40 percent increase in bilingual school leavers, a considerable achievement by any criterion and especially noteworthy given the troubles that plague other bilingual systems.

ACKNOWLEDGMENTS

I wish to acknowledge the assistance of Mahalakshmi Sripathy in the preparation of this chapter.

BIBLIOGRAPHY

Chan, H. C. and H. D. Evers, 1978. ''National Identity and Nation Building in Singapore.'' In *Studies in ASEAN Sociology*, ed. H. C. Chen and H. D. Evers. Singapore: Chopman Enterprises.

Chiew, Seen-Kong. 1983. ''Ethnicity and National Integration. The Evolution of a Multiethnic Society.'' In *Singapore Development Policies and Trends*, ed. Peter S. J. Chen. Singapore: Oxford University Press.

Gopinathan, S. 1979. ''Singapore's Language Policies: Strategies for a Plural Society.'' In *Southeast Asian Affairs*. Singapore: Institute of Southeast Asian Studies.

———. 1980. ''Moral Education in a Plural Society: A Singapore Case Study.'' *International Review of Education* 26 2:171–85.

Gopinathan, S., and A. Mani. 1983. ''Changes in Tamil Language Acquisition and Usage in Singapore: A Case of Subtractive Bilingualism.'' *Southeast Asian Journal of Social Sciences* 2, No. 1.

Kuo, C. Y. 1976. ''A Sociolinguistic Profile.'' In *Society in Transition*, ed. Rias Hassan. Kuala Lumpur: Oxford University Press.

———. 1977. ''The Status of English in Singapore: A Sociolinguistic Analysis.'' In *The English Language in Singapore*, ed. W. Crewe. Singapore: Eastern Universities Press.

———. 1980. ''The Sociolinguistic Situation in Singapore: Unity in Diversity.'' In

Language and Society in Singapore, ed. E. A. Afrendas and C. Y. Kuo. Singapore: Singapore University Press.

Ministry of Education. 1980. "Education in Singapore." Singapore: Government Printer.

Pendley, C. 1983. "Language Policy and Social Transformation in Singapore." *Southeast Asian Journal of Social Science* 2, 2:46–58.

Wilson, W. E. 1978. *Social Engineering in Singapore: Educational Policies and Social Change.* Singapore: Singapore University Press.

Douglas Young

BILINGUALISM AND BILINGUAL EDUCATION IN A DIVIDED SOUTH AFRICAN SOCIETY

Bilingualism is constitutionally established in South African (SA) society. The economy, industry, the media, education, the law, and government all function within statutory requirements that Afrikaans and English, the two official languages, be used with equality and due recognition of the rights of the respective speakers. In many spheres of employment, particularly public administration, the civil service, law, and education, demonstrable bilingualism is a prerequisite for appointment and career advancement. This bilingualism is enforced in successive Acts of Parliament dated 1910, 1926, and 1961.

Afrikaans and English are, however, the mother tongues of the white minority, many Asians, and the coloured community only. ("Coloured" is a person of mixed blood.) In all, no more than about 30 percent of the SA population of about 30 million have these languages as their mother tongues. Some 67 percent of the total population is black (African), comprising seven official ethnic groups speaking at least ten Bantu languages. The balance of 3 percent of the populace comprises Indian-language speakers and various European tongues, for example, German, Italian, French, and Portuguese.

BILINGUALISM VERSUS MULTILINGUALISM

In the white SA community, bilingualism is understood to mean fluency, in varying competencies, in the use of both Afrikaans and English only. In the specific sense that bilingualism means the measurable competence that individuals have to use more than one language in a contact situation, SA is indeed a bilingual society. But its complexity extends far beyond that; in reality, SA is a heterogeneous, multilingual, pluralistic society with strong conflicts between the forces of particularism and globalism, in J. Fishman's (1977) terms. The very nature of SA society places a high premium on communication across legally established socioethnic and group demarcations by means of a lingua franca, usually English. Very few white South Africans are bilingual in the sense that they use a black language, while large numbers of blacks, of whom some 40 percent are illiterate (SAIRR, 1984:436), use one or both official languages effectively out of the need to subsist in an employment market controlled by white capital. Indeed, most blacks command their own and other Bantu languages plus Afrikaans and/or English, with some facility in daily communication. The dominant mode of bilingualism is thus transitional and unilateral for the majority of SA's people. This position has not been reached without significant language conflict rooted in ideological tensions centered on issues of race and group identity, as will be discussed below.

RACE, LANGUAGE, AND SEPARATISM

South African preoccupation with race, color, and group identities, embodied in the apartheid ideology of the Nationalist government, is inextricably tied to language and language planning. It results, for example, in offensive and socially divisive nomenclature such as "black," "coloured," "Indian," and "white," as has unavoidably been done herein, in order to characterize SA's social complexity. The term "Bantu" used here denotes only its linguistic classificatory sense. Until the mid–1970s, it was used by the government to classify all blacks, or nonwhites. Prior to that, in British colonial times, the label was "Native." The use of the term "African" by white SA liberals was unacceptable to Afrikaners, perhaps because of the translatability of African to mean Afrikaner. The conflict between particularism and globalism dates back to the nineteenth century, with roots in the Dutch and English colonists' successive attempts to control indigenous peoples. The rapid emergence of Afrikaans out of Dutch in the early twentieth century led, in 1948, to Afrikaans becoming the dominant language of political control by the white majority. The tensions flowing from these developments spawned sensitivities that inhibited widespread research into bilingualism.

Only E. G. Malherbe's classic 1925 and 1977 studies analyze the phenomenon in depth, though recent tentative work done by the Human Sciences Research Council (HSRC) redresses this neglect. Internationally, the pariah status of SA, because of its repugnant apartheid policies, has perhaps blunted foreign motivation to conduct research and publish on a topic so well covered in other countries. For example, E. Glyn Lewis' (1982) standard work on the topic devotes scant attention to SA in a tome of over four hundred pages. Similarly, J. Miller's (1983) study omits SA completely. The challenge to put right these omissions and neglect remains as powerful as ever. This chapter will outline some of the imperatives to inquiry in a country where the complex interrelationship of language, ideology, nationalism, and education need much fuller understanding.

LINGUISTIC DEMOGRAPHY

The heterogeneity and diversity of SA's multilingualism are shown in the data below. In overview, SA consists of the following racially classified groups:

Blacks, excluding "independent" homelands: 17,741,000

Blacks in the homelands: 4,987,998

Whites: 4,748,000

Coloureds: 2,765,000

Asians: 870,000

   Total: 31,111,998

These figures derive from the 1980 official census, which does not classify in terms of mother-tongue identities. Estimates of the distribution of mother-tongue speakers of the various languages of SA are as follows:

Official Languages

Afrikaans (Whites): 2,581,080

English (Whites): 1,763,220

Both, as spoken by coloureds: 2,765,000

   Total, official languages: 7,156,000

Official Ethnic, Bantu Languages

Nguni Group

Zulu: 5,709,000

Xhosa: 3,002,000

Swazi: 858,000

S. Ndebeli: 394,000

N. Ndebeli: 267,000

Sotho Group

Tswana: 1,364,000

N. Sotho: 2,358,000

S. Sotho: 1,750,000

Tsonga: 1,011,000

Venda: 191,000

Foreign: 117,000

(These figures exclude some of the above languages as spoken in the homelands, e.g., Sotho, Xhosa, and Zulu.)

Indian Languages

Tamil: No data available
Gujerati: No data available
Urdu: No data available
Hindi: No data available
Telegu: No data available
  Total Indian: 870,000

Immigrant Lanugages

German: 40,240
Portuguese: 57,000
Greek: 16,780
Italian: 16,740
Dutch: 11,740
French: 6,340
Other: 35,000
  Total Immigrants: 183,840

Pidgin

FANAKOLO, a pidgin used in the work situation, particularly in the mines on the Witwatersrand, connotes master-servant relations. It comprises a vocabulary of 70 percent Zulu, 24 percent English, and 6 percent Afrikaans, with a highly simplified syntax closer to English than to Bantu. It is used in a labor contact situation, particularly between migrant mine workers from neighboring states (Lanham, 1978:26).

HISTORICAL BACKGROUND

Bantu Languages

Three major language families in contact form the basis for present-day South African society: (1) Khoi-san, or Hottentot [Khoi or Khoin] and Bushman [San]; (2) Bantu (represented by the ten ethnic languages already outlined), and (3) Indo-European (represented by Afrikaans, based on Dutch as spoken by Dutch settlers in the Cape in the seventeenth century, and English, brought to the Cape Province by British settlers in the nineteenth century).

San languages initially appeared in the late Stone Age. Now in danger of

extinction, San speakers number about fifty thousand, confined mainly to the
Kalahari Basin in Namibia and to Botswana. The fragmentary nature of these
San communities has led to linguistic dissimilarities and decreasing interintel-
ligibility between many small San groups. L. W. Lanham (1978) asserts that
the San languages have "little place in the patterns of multilingualism in Southern
Africa. Very few whites or blacks in Southern Africa control more than a restricted number of San words and expressions. San speakers usually learn a
language of Whites only to the limit of the contact situation; most control the
Bantu language of the area" (Lanham, 1978:14). Literacy is extremely low
among San speakers.

The Khoi, or Hottentot, has little archaeological support for a firm location
in time, but evidence suggests a separate identity from as early as the sixteenth
century. Khoi languages, like the San, have survived poorly, following absorp-
tion by Bantu-speaking tribes and through assimilation with coloureds in the
Cape Province since the eighteenth century. Nama is a significant Khoi survivor,
today spoken by an important group in Namibia, with widespread bilingualism
with the local Afrikaans community. Lanham suggests that Nama, a developed,
literate language in the Namibian school curriculum, is nevertheless giving way
to Afrikaans as an urban lingua franca (Lanham, 1978:15). Apparently, contact
with English dates back to the seventeenth century. N. J. Parsons quotes the
example of a young Khoisan leader who was taken to England to learn the
English language and European trading practices. When Jan van Riebeeck landed
at the Cape in 1652, he was greeted on the beach by a Khoi leader who spoke
to him in English (Parsons, 1982:78).

The Bantu languages are central to the development of Southern and particularly South Africa, evinced by the vast majority of their speakers in the de-
mography of the region. Archaeology places the presence of the Bantu languages
in South Africa from at least the fifth century A.D., and firm evidence exists to
place the Nguni group speakers on the east coast of South Africa. Lanham argues
that Nguni and Sotho, as the two major Bantu language clusters, "have strong
circumstantial evidence to support their presence in South Africa for at least half
of the 15 centuries of the Iron Age" (Lanham, 1978:16). Originating in the
Niger-Congo region of Africa, and descended from the Proto-Bantu of which
there are some four hundred similar linguistic descendants, Bantu languages in
Southern Africa had early contact with Khoi-san, mainly San speakers, as evinced
in the click consonants and in the lexicon. Approximately 15 percent of Xhosa
vocabulary is Khoi. Of the Sotho languages, only Sesotho is extensively influenced by Khoi-san (Lanham, 1978:16).

The history of Bantu languages is largely oral until the nineteenth century,
when, in about 1860, scriptures were translated into vernaculars. Increasing
contact with Dutch and English colonists and missionaries over at least two
centuries resulted in the widespread coinage of loan words in all Bantu languages.
In Xhosa, for example, Afrikaans and English influence resulted in nouns such
as *itafile* = table; *ihempi* = hemp in Afrikaans = shirt; *itispuni* = teaspooon;

ifayidukwe = *doek* in Afrikaans = cloth; *ifenstile* = *venster* in Afrikaans = window.

Mother-tongue interference at the syntactic level sometimes results in miscommunication in cross-cultural settings; for example, by saying "the cup it broke" a black housemaid is seemingly disclaiming responsibility for having broken the cup. In fact, the Nguni syntax omits the ergative, agentive form. Similarly, "the train left me" means "I missed the train." English fixed expressions, assimilated into Nguni languages, result in expressions such as "Doctor, the patient is late," used by black nurses, meaning "Doctor, the patient is dead," from the English 'the late Mr. Smith'.

A rich indigenous literature exists in all the official languages. Textbooks abound in these at all levels of schooling. Technical terminologies have been coined by the Department of Education and Training in charge of black education, though some educationists argue that a more fundamental induction of concepts is needed in the natural and physical sciences. The controversy engendered by such assertions has obvious Whorfian overtones, needing research.

Both Zulu and Xhosa speakers have major daily newspapers, and radio programs are transmitted in all official ethnic languages. TV channels now exist for Zulu and Xhosa speakers and are widely viewed by all groups, who also have access to the white channel. The Xhosa and Zulu channels are widely viewed by whites, and this augurs well for a move away from the unilateral bilingualism discussed above.

Afrikaans

With over 4 million speakers today, white and coloured, representing some 13 percent of the entire population, Afrikaans is unquestionably established as a national language. Its direct identification with the language of government by a white minority group has led to it being perceived as the language of the oppressor, resulting in some alienation from its public use by many coloured and black people. Historically and linguistically, Afrikaans is the product of a remarkable language development and change over a relatively short period of three hundred years.

Afrikaans as it is now spoken had its public foundation at a meeting of the Fellowship of True Afrikaners in Paarl in the Western Cape in 1875. Their aim was to "create an awareness amongst the speakers of Afrikaans that Afrikaans, not Dutch or English, was their mother tongue and ought to be their written language" (Combrink, 1978:69). Fifty years later, in 1925, Afrikaans was constitutionally legalized as one of the two official languages of the then Union of South Africa. Though *de jure* equal with English at the time, it was *de facto* an unequal partner, heavily overshadowed by English as a national language, which was then endorsed by the might of Britain, the colonial overlord. In 1975, a monument, perhaps unique in linguistic history, was erected in Paarl to commemorate the founding of the Afrikaans a hundred years before.

Now, in 1985, Afrikaans is *de facto* and *de jure* at least equal to English as a national language, though some Afrikaner academics have expressed doubts about its continued survival, given its identification with the language of oppression and its lack of widespread use beyond the confines of South Africa. Consideration of the historical development of Afrikaans is relevant to an understanding of how it has so rapidly become a catalytic force in strenuous efforts at maintaining white group identity and language parity, for this endeavor lies at the root of the present South African sociopolitical dilemmas. The ensuing overview draws heavily on J.G.H. Combrink's 1978 analysis.

There are two main hypotheses about the origin of Afrikaans. The one asserts that Afrikaans developed spontaneously out of certain Dutch dialects on foreign soil, in the absence of the constraints of schooling and literacy. The other hypothesis is that Afrikaans is the product of contact between (1) Dutch and indigenous languages, for example, Khoi and Bantu; (2) Dutch and English, French, and other European languages, especially German; and (3) Dutch and immigrant creoles, for example, Portuguese in the seventeenth century and Malay in the eighteenth. Combrink calls the latter "heteroglossist." He poses the question of whether Afrikaans was born of an immaculate conception or as a result of some dirty trick played on Dutch. After evaluating the evidence, particularly since 1940, he concludes that "we are now in a position to declare that Afrikaans was born of a polygamous shotgun marriage involving several Dutch dialects, albeit under pressure of various foreign influences" (Combrink, 1978:70).

The layman's tendency to dismiss Afrikaans as a mere dialect or simplification of Dutch, without verb inflections in the present indicative, is refuted by the strong evidence marshalled by Combrink. The spontaneity and symbiotic development of Afrikaans out of the dominant Dutch used in the sparsely populated settlement at the Cape in the early eighteenth century led to a rapid demise of the use of other languages such as French and even Khoin, the speakers of Khoin surrendering their mother tongue as a result of contact with the Cape Dutch language.

To use Combrink's conclusions:

more than ninety percent of the structure of Afrikaans is of Dutch vernacular descent. In the process of development up to 1800 a few items of Malay, Portuguese, Khoin, German and French descent entered the language. After 1800, i.e., when Afrikaans was already in existence, a small lexical influence was exerted by the southern Bantu languages. English has also had a pretty strong lexical, semantic and syntactic influence since 1800 (Combrink, 1978:84).

More recent changes in Afrikaans (since the 1920s) are the result of sustained contact with English, especially in the workplace, through the media and education. English is a dominant second language for most Afrikaners.

Afrikaans in the Coloured Community

The Coloureds' use of Afrikaans, which for many is traditionally a mother tongue, is a complex issue, little researched. It is characterized by frequent code-switching between Afrikaans and English, with a rich variety of dialects. The increasing use of English to replace Afrikaans is politically inspired and often motivated by a wish for upward social mobility, rather than out of an appraisal of English as a superior language per se.

K. McCormick (1983) interviewed sixty-five students at the (coloured) University of the Western Cape, near Cape Town, to gauge their language preferences. All her subjects regarded themselves as bilingual in English and Afrikaans in varying competencies. Her findings included the following: English was the language of the middle class, and Afrikaans that of the working class in Cape Town, though not in outlying rural areas. In terms of political affiliation, some of her subjects said they would refuse to use Afrikaans to a white, since such use required standard Afrikaans. Similarly, Standard English was seen as that spoken by the dominant social class, symbolizing oppression. Educationally, her subjects reported having started schooling in Afrikaans and finishing it in English, the latter being perceived as the language of higher education. Urbanization of rural coloureds would result in switching to English to symbolize urban assimilation. Similarly, English was the language of meetings, even if most attending were more comfortable in Afrikaans. However, the language of intimacy was unquestionably Afrikaans. The "language of religion" showed no clear pattern of preferences, perhaps because of the Christian/Muslim dichotomy among the coloured people, the Muslims needing Arabic for formal worship or Malayan words mixed with Afrikaans. McCormick draws significant comparisons between Chicano code-switching and that of the Coloured community.

The common origin of Afrikaans and coloured people has long been discussed widely in South Africa, and H. Heese's 1985 findings, which show that many white Afrikaans surnames have a common ancestry with those of coloured people living in the Western Cape in the eighteenth and nineteenth centuries, has launched a heated public debate. Some white Afrikaners have attempted to repudiate these findings, claiming "pure" white origins, free of blood mixing with people of color. The outcome of this controversy could well be increased linguistic tolerance shown by Afrikaans-speaking whites toward Afrikaans-speaking coloured people, once the inevitable acknowledgment of such common ancestry leads to a blurring of ethnic purist attitudes among conservative Afrikaans-speaking whites.

English

The history of English in South Africa is more widely known than that of Afrikaans. This is partly because it is recorded naturally in English in international publications to a greater extent than has been the case with Afrikaans, with its limited intelligibility outside of South Africa.

English was formally introduced into the Cape Province as a result of the first British occupation of the Cape in 1806. Cape Town rapidly became English-speaking, with close British links. But the major initial development of English as a language of Africa followed the settlement, in 1820, of five thousand British government-sponsored settlers. Similar, slightly later settlements occurred in Natal. English soon came under the direct influence of Cape Dutch, later Afrikaans, Zulu, and Xhosa, resulting in the emergence of South African English (SAE), which has a vocabulary rich in evidence of this early cross-cultural contact. Branford's recent (1983) *Dictionary of South African English* is an excellent, comprehensive inventory of the ways in which SAE has grown and changed as a result of this contact. Standard British English was maintained as an accent, reinforced by strong colonial and Commonwealth ties until the early 1960s, after which, with South Africa's exit from the Commonwealth, the prestige value of Southern British English declined rapidly. SAE is now widely acceptable as an accent with a distinctive vocabulary and idiom. Structurally, however, SAE differs only slightly from Standard British English. The most significant work on the role and function of English, particularly as a spoken language in South Africa, is that of Lanham. P. Trudgill's 1982 work on international English, drawing as it does on Lanham's research, gives a useful analysis of SAE in relation to other varieties of world English.

For all its strength as a lingua franca and education medium in South Africa, English is spoken as a mother tongue by only about 8 percent of the population. It is the most widely used second language, with wide functional and sociopolitical value, especially for Bantu speakers and an increasing number of coloured people, as discussed above. All the independent homelands as well as the national states have opted for English as a medium of instruction from the fourth year of schooling through to tertiary education, while most black schools within the republic have decided similarly. The origins and implications of these decisions are discussed later in this chapter.

Historically, English as a second language is crucial in the development of policies of bilingualism and bilingual education. In 1922, the British Governor of the Cape proclaimed English the only official language, with subsequent governors following a policy of anglicizing the Dutch colonists. English rapidly became the language of government, education, and cultural life, even though in 1860 only 20 percent of the white population in the Cape was English. English became the language of public discourse, and Afrikaans that of private and religious life. Afrikaners of the period 1850 to the early 1900s were in many respects mother-tongue English speakers. Even negative attitudes toward British Imperialism did not deter Afrikaners from promoting Afrikaans-English bilingualism and regular use of English in the learned professions, business, and education. Antipathy toward English as a language emanated from the hostilities between Boer and Briton, culminating in the Anglo-Boer War at the turn of the century, coupled with the growth of Afrikaner nationalism and group identity. But British victory, pyrrhic in a sense, resulted in policies of anglicization in government, law, and public affairs. Afrikaans leaders redoubled their efforts to secure the identity and public status of Afrikaans. The taalstryd (language struggle), lasting well into the 1960s, had its roots in the period immediately following the Anglo-Boer War.

Afrikaner nationalism and the powerful drive to maintain Afrikaans soon led, following World War II, to Afrikaner dominance in political, educational, administrative, and many spheres of public life. At the same time, there was growing apathy by English speakers toward maintenance of their language. This situation caused some alarm to a small group of academics and educationists in the 1960s, who successfully attempted to alert public attitudes to the growing decline in standards of English use by English speakers. One of the significant outcomes of this concern was the establishment of the English Academy of Southern Africa, charged with the task of maintaining standards and critical attitudes toward the use of English. Since the early 1970s, English-medium universities have shown increasing concern over declining levels of undergraduate communicative competence in English. The resulting projects include academic support programs to raise the level of competence in the use of English as a second language, particularly among black students.

The sociopolitical tensions flowing from the taalstryd of the midcentury are now on the wane in some respects, partly because white South Africans, regardless of their mother tongue, are increasingly, though belatedly, becoming aware of the need to meet the political and social aspirations of the black majority if a violent confrontation is to be avoided. This has resulted, to some extent, in language interdependence and a semblance of unity of purpose.

THE PRESENT SITUATION

Bilingualism in SA today should be seen in the context of two fundamental events. The first is the exit of SA from the British Commonwealth in 1960, followed by the enactment of legislation transforming SA into a republic in 1961. Second, the tragic unrest in Soweto in 1976 resulting in the deaths of hundreds of blacks, many of whom were school children had, as one of its major causes, the language-medium issue in black primary schooling (see the section on "Black Education" below). The advent of republican government led to clarification of bilingual policies and a subsequent slight dissipation in the taalstryd; the Soweto riots forced a rapid rethinking on the SA government's language planning and medium policies in black schools, with consequences of major import, particularly relating to mother-tongue instruction and English second-language teaching.

Bilingualism and the Republic

In terms of the Constitution of the Republic of South Africa, May 31, 1961, Part X, language policy is stated as follows:

108. Equality of official languages. (1) English and Afrikaans shall be the official languages of the Republic, and shall be treated on a footing of equality, and possess and enjoy freedom, rights and privileges.

(2) All records, journals and Proceedings of Parliament shall be kept in both the official languages, and all Bills, Acts and notices of general public importance or interest issued by the Government . . . shall be in both official languages.

(3) Notwithstanding the provisions of subsection (1), an Act of Parliament, whereby a Black area is declared to be a self-governing territory in the Republic, or a later Act of Parliament or a later Proclamation of the State President . . . may provide for the recognition of one or more Black languages for any or all of the following purposes, namely

(a) as an additional official language of that territory; or

(b) for use in that territory for official purposes prescribed by or under that Act or later Act by such proclamation . . . (RSA, 1961).

Freed from the constraints of British dominance and remote monarchical rule, this policy particularly sought to secure the Afrikaner's right to full, legalized participation in public life, using his or her own language. It may be argued that the recognition given to black languages in self-governing territories anticipated the controversial establishment of the Transkei and other independent homelands, according rights already exercised *de facto* therein.

Duplication of Effort

This protection of the rights of English- and Afrikaans-speakers has led, inevitably, to massive duplication of effort and cost in the issue of public documents and in the output of the mass media, particularly television. Introduced at the late hour of 1976 in SA, the initial and only (white) channel was transmitted in strict accordance with the policy of language equality. The result is news bulletins, often in direct translation—one at 6:00 P.M. and the other at 8:00 P.M. Interviews with politicians, which are always the forefront of newscasts, have to be in both languages. Only one interviewer, usually Afrikaans-speaking, is used. As a result, in spite of admirable bilingualism in many cases, the quality of English used by interviewer and interviewee is suspect and there is regular public outcry about declining standards of English used by the South African Broadcasting Corporation (SABC). On the other hand, the unavoidable constant use of international news agency telexes, often exclusively in English, places Afrikaans at a disadvantage, translation being essential and a point of major language interference. There is much evidence, which as yet is unresearched formally, that as a result of this unavoidable use of English source material Afrikaans is under major threat of change.

Afrikaans is not always syntactically as economical as English regarding the precision of timing needed in newscasting; hence, there is a clearly detectable anglicization of Afrikaans syntax. The power of television in South Africa is so great that this must be seen as an interesting case of language change. On the other hand, having a single television channel for both languages has had a very positive effect on public attitudes, especially children's, resulting in greater language tolerance.

An example of the absurdity of this duplicated effort is often heard in airports: when someone approaches the information desk to ask for a broadcast calling a person who is obviously, say, Afrikaans, the request over the PA system to report to the information desk will be in both languages, regardless. Similarly, the hateful "whites only / slegs blankes" signs in public places, which were once so common, often omitted the probibition's expression in the black language of those it sought so unjustly to exclude!

BILINGUAL EDUCATION

Given the policy of institutionalized bilingualism in the official languages, SA's education systems in broad outline aim to ensure that bilingualism is achieved in white and coloured schools, while pupils in black schools are required to be fluent in their mother tongue and one, and preferably both, of the official languages as a second language. The principle of mother-tongue instruction is followed strictly in white and coloured schools from Sub A (first grade) through Standard 10 (twelfth grade), with the other official language studied as a second language for the same period.

In black schools, the mother tongue of the pupil's ethnic group is the medium of instruction for the first four years of primary school, whereas one of the official languages (in most cases, English) becomes the medium of instruction to Standard 10, with the mother tongue retained as a first-language subject. Both Afrikaans and English are studied as second/third languages until Standard 7. In the final three years of high school, one of the official languages is studied, usually as a second language on the higher grade. This applies equally to both state and private (public) schools, the latter being nonracial. There are ten examination boards which administer public examinations in these languages within the school curriculum, with superordinate moderation of standards by the Joint Matriculation Board, representing the universities.

Until the early 1980s, black school pupils were required to study three languages from Standards 3 to 10, whereas whites were required to study Afrikaans and English only, with the option of a third, usually European, language. This anomaly, now rectified, placed blacks at a great disadvantage, particularly in terms of meeting university entrance requirements, which stress diversity of choice in subjects offered at matriculation level: to study three languages as subjects out of a six-subject curriculum for university entrance seriously weakened the chances of blacks wishing to offer a range, for example, of science-based subjects. In any event, blacks are seriously disadvantaged in competing for places in predominantly white universities that are now nonracial, in that they have been taught English in black schools by teachers undertrained, underqualified, and far from competent in the English they teach. Academic support programs and what might be named compensatory bilingualism stressing English for academic purposes are included in English-medium university curricula for "disadvantaged" students. Most of these students will take four years over a three-year undergraduate degree as a result of deficient schooling in the black education system.

Teacher training courses at all levels, college and university, require that their graduates have language proficiency endorsements certifying ability to teach in both official languages. Research by E. G. Malherbe (1938), corroborated by C. J. Kitching (1984), shows that the competence of white teachers in the second language, especially in rural areas, is lamentably poor. In many cases, at primary school levels, it is no higher in the target language, particularly English, than that of the learners at that target level.

Teacher Shortages

The De Lange Commission on the Provision of Education for the RSA (De Lange et al., 1981), estimated a shortage of 250,000 teachers in all SA schools in 1990, 80 percent of that shortage being in black schools. Given a total black school population of over 5 million in 1985 and an average teacher:pupil ratio of 42.7:1 in black schools (white schools 18.2:1) (SAIRR, 1983:421), the formidable task of teaching any language effectively in a black society with a high school dropout rate, for economic reasons, and high illiteracy and regression from literacy as a result of dropout, the results achieved by teachers and pupils in language learning are remarkable, even though the failure rate at school-leaving stages is high.

Only about 35 percent of all black teachers are qualified beyond Standard 8 (tenth grade), while only about 3 percent have bachelor's degrees (SAIRR, 1983:440). The SA government has progressively increased expenditure on black education since 1977, but this still lags far behind the provision for white, Indian, and coloured education systems on a per capita basis (black per capita expenditure 1982/3:R146,44; white R1,211,00) (SAIRR, 1983:420).

Education, Language, and Social Division

South Africa is the only society that uses its schools to divide its people into sociolinguistic-ethnic groupings. Any attempt to characterize bilingual and multilingual education within this form of social engineering is inevitably trapped, however reluctantly, as has been so in this chapter, into such analysis using the group and ethnic labels generated by apartheid.

No brief overview like this can but scratch the surface of language teaching in SA. Only two issues can be examined in finer detail in terms of each sociolinguistic group: mother tongue/medium of instruction and English second-language teaching.

Black Education

The 1953 Bantu Education Act placed all black education under central government control. The medium of language teaching was the mother tongue up to the end of Standard 8, with Afrikaans and English as obligatory subjects only. In the 1970s, attempts were made to introduce the teaching of certain primary school subjects in Afrikaans, others in English. This resulted in growing tensions which, despite repeated unheeded warnings to Pretoria of imminent conflict, erupted into massive violence in Soweto schools in June 1976. Other political causes were evident too, but the language-medium protest articulated black anger at the obvious effects of the policy of enforcing ethnicity so as to divide Zulu from Xhosa from Sotho from Venda and so on. There was strong resentment toward Afrikaans because it symbolized oppression by its speakers. English was and is the desired lingua franca, the access language to a wider world. Government response was swift: by 1979 a new policy was enacted, initiating free choice of medium from Standard 3 on. In nearly all cases except some in the Free State and far Northern Transvaal, the elective was English, following the example of the newly "independent" Transkei, which already had English as medium. The consequences of this switch to English medium were predictable— teachers comfortable in the primary school teaching in the vernacular lacked competence in English. Pupil performance declined. English as a second language became English as medium, and many of the problems of Africa north of SA were echoed but for different reasons. The teaching of English as a second language has thus become an even more dramatic and urgent imperative for research and problem-solving. Massive preservice and in-service teacher education is underway, both from within the Department of Education and Training controlling black education and from the private sector.

Coloured Education

The Coloured community, disenfranchised in 1952 and now, in terms of the new SA Constitution, reenfranchised after a fashion, live in the Cape Province and metropolitan Transvaal. As with other racially classified groups, Coloured education is separately controlled by a government department, presently the Department of Education and Culture.

Traditionally Afrikaans-speaking and before disenfranchisement regarded as one with Afrikaners, Coloureds, particularly in Cape Town, have abandoned loyalty to Afrikaans in increasing numbers. As a result, in schooling it is difficult to identify the mother tongue of pupils at all levels in the system. The 1976 Soweto riots and subsequent, related school boycotts and unrest in the Western Cape in 1980 highlighted this alienation from Afrikaans.

There is a high degree of Afrikaans-English bilingualism and dynamic, regular code-switching in all subjects in the curriculum. Within any one school, one finds pupils studying the official languages at mother-tongue or at second-language level, though those pupils taking English as a second language tend to be stigmatized by class-conscious peers. English is often identified as a language of upward social mobility and with political opposition to apartheid. Mc-Cormick's 1984 research characterizes the complexity of language attitudes held by Coloured pupils. In her interviews with pupils, she found that

A lot of people become bi-dialectal [in Afrikaans] either if their work demands the use of the standard variety of the language, or if they reach upper levels of secondary or tertiary education . . . people with tertiary education used English when discussing ideas and issues, and Afrikaans for intimate or domestic matters. Regardless of the level of education of participants, English is seen as the language appropriate for gatherings . . . meetings held at schools by boycotting pupils in 1980 were conducted in English even when most of the pupils were Afrikaans-dominant and not fluent in English.

There are Labovian echoes in attitudes toward the use of standard official languages. My own graduate education students strongly resist any form of assessment, as teacher trainees, of their Afrikaans and English in terms of standard criteria of communicative competence in the classroom. They argue that their pupils speak dialects and nonstandard forms and that a teacher attempting to impose a standard language faces certain discreditation. As far as mother-tongue use at home is concerned, tentative personal research shows that many Afrikaans-speaking parents pressure their children into using English at home.

As in black education, there are serious inequalities in the provision of education; teacher training in the official languages remains a key issue.

Indian Education

The Indian community, living in Natal and the Witwatersrand, is effectively English-speaking. SA Indian English (SAIE) has largely displaced Indian languages in the home. The present population of over eight hundred thousand dates back to settlement in Natal in 1860. Schooling is entirely in the English medium, with pupils achieving a high degree of fluency in speaking rather than in writing the language. D. Bughwan (1970) observes that few young Indians have any competence in their vernacular Indian tongues. The requirements of bilingual education are in force in Indian schools, though there is little natural use of Afrikaans outside the classroom.

White Education

Bilingual education is at its most definitive in the most affluently provided, privileged system of education—that for whites. All white schooling from pre-primary to secondary is conducted in one or other of the official languages, with the minimal exception of some schooling in German and Greek. Schools are predominantly state schools within the provinces of the Cape, Orange Free State,

Natal, and Transvaal, and are classified as either Afrikaans or English medium. There remains a small number of dual and parallel medium schools in the Western Cape, a relic of earlier attempts to promote natural rather than artificial bilingualism (Malherbe, 1925) that tends to result from single-medium schooling. Dual medium, wherein instruction takes place in both official languages on a rota or subject-based scheme, was once the desired school system for parents aiming at natural bilingualism and interlanguage tolerance. Politically motivated language planning coupled with fears that interlanguage contact at school would dilute language purity and socioethnic group identity led to a phasing out of these schools. Those remaining tend to be single medium, usually Afrikaans because the cachment, usually rural area is invariably Afrikaans-dominant. For the same reasons, parallel medium schooling, wherein pupils of both language groups received teaching in separate language streams according to mother-tongue classification and then mixed freely in the playground, is virtually extinct in SA.

In all white schools, the nonmother-tongue language is taken at second-language level, or equivalently at first-language grade where motivation and competence suggest this. Parents may choose, in many instances, as to which language-medium school to send their children. Those who have high motivation to achieve full bilingualism elect to send their children to, say, an Afrikaans school at primary level and to an English school at the secondary stage, though peer group conformity and language loyalty often militate against such freedom. Private schools, exclusively English medium, nevertheless follow bilingual education policies in that Afrikaans is offered at first- or second-language level as a subject. An increasing number of state and private schools now offer a Bantu language from about Standard 4 upwards, as a third language. Apartheid presently precludes the use of blacks to teach these languages in provincial schools.

That the mother-tongue medium of instruction is so entrenched in a society where more flexibility of choice would arguably have led to greater commonality is well rooted in the history of Afrikaans already discussed. The effect of anglicization policies, especially under the Milner regime (ca. 1900), spurred Afrikaner quests for greater exclusivity, closely related to religious dogma, translated into the educational philosophy and policy that now dominate white education, known as Christian National Education. The Afrikaner reaction to attempts at anglicization, amply discussed by Malherbe and Kroes (1978), was epitomized in the oft-quoted ''the language of the conqueror in the mouth of the conquered is the language of slaves'' (of Flemish origin). This followed on the defeat of the Boers by the British in the Anglo-Boer War. The insistence on single-medium schools flowing from this reaction also resulted in the English community's introduction of private, usually Anglican Church schools. These schools initially sought to preserve and replicate the values and processes of British public schools, sometimes to the point where they became anachronisms, not in step with their original models' changing values in Britain. The products of these and state schools, in turn modeled on them, served to produce English elites, tending to speak conservative SAE, who rapidly rose to the leadership of white commerce and industry, forming part of the capitalist ideology maintaining white privilege. This leadership is still held by products of a select group of about two dozen English-medium schools (Ashley, 1974:39–60). P. Randall (1984) calls this phenomenon "Little England on the Veld."

English-speaking South Africans have, in general, remained apathetic about educational standards in state schools. There is a great shortage of English-speaking teachers, especially of English, in state schools, particularly in the heavily populated metropolitan areas of Johannesburg and Pretoria. It is estimated that about 75 percent of the teaching of English to English mother-tongue pupils is done by Afrikaners in those areas, for example. Parents electing private schooling for their children claim that they are avoiding the risks of exposing the children to English taught badly by non-English (i.e., Afrikaans-speaking) teachers, who, for ideological reasons, did not have the interests of English-speakers at heart. It needed voices such as those of the Afrikaner academic Malherbe to sound repeated warnings to the English community about such risks (Malherbe, 1966) to revive concern and action over falling standards in English-medium education.

White universities (now largely nonracial in admissions policy except for some Afrikaans-medium examples) are either English or Afrikaans medium or both (in the case of the universities of Port Elizabeth and South Africa). Attendance at all of these universities by no means follows the pattern of that at schools; there is significant integration of language identities, attendance following ideological and pragmatic considerations rather than those of medium exclusivity.

Ideological control is exerted at school level through language, particularly Afrikaans, by means of curriculum content in Afrikaans and English literature. Controversies rage about the listing of authors whose works transmit conservative or alien values, not those felt essential to effect urgently needed political and social change (Volbrecht, 1984, and Esterhuyse, in progress). T. Volbrecht, examining the teaching of English as first language in SA schools, presents a convincing argument that the "Great Tradition" of liberal humanism embodied in the teaching of English literature in the Leavisite mode underpins racial capitalism, coexistent with apartheid. Thus, the social formation of SA society is in part a reactionary outcome to the sociopolitical values transmitted through the study, in this case, of English.

J. Esterhuyse, in a similar study of the effects of prescribed literature and language textbooks in the Afrikaans curriculum, shows how ethnocentrism results in ideological control over the study of the Afrikaans mother tongue. Such control seriously inhibits free access to radical or liberatory literature in the curriculum. He shows how the selective word use and new word coinage of Afrikaans in school texts reflects tendencies toward white supremacist world-views being inculcated in the Afrikaans classroom.

Language Education: Quo Vadis?

In spite of the above portents of continued white supremacy being maintained through the teaching of the official languages, there is other, more heartening evidence of a sense of urgency resulting in change in the teaching of language. In the wider social context, the long-held prejudices and clinging to language-group exclusivities appear to be diminishing. Much has resulted from concerted black and coloured protest in the past ten years. The De Lange Commission (1981) made significant proposals for change, and its subcommittee on Language Education, hastily and belatedly convened, has recommended major changes in language education policies and praxis. There has been widespread development in the introduction of applied linguistics courses at universities, and teacher education programs include significant components on language, particularly second-language teaching. Traditional habits of trying imported solutions to nonexistent problems have given way to inspired local questioning and critiques leading to positive, creative action, materials writing, and teacher reeducation in situ.

RESEARCH

Research into bilingualism per se in SA has been scant, as shown. Effort has concentrated, especially since 1976, on the teaching of English as a second language, though this label has lately been questioned by some black and coloured educationists (Mphalele, personal communication), who resent the implicit equation with the second-class status accorded blacks and coloureds. TESOL (Teaching English to Speakers of Other Languages), following the U.S. model, is increasingly preferred. In TESOL research, the dominant mode has been Action Research, understood herein to mean interventionist work aimed at involving teachers/learners in the writing and production of their own materials, or, simply, in some cases, to use research in an applied mode to influence change in classroom processes. The listing of such projects is an invidious task, however. There are, for example, some seventy TESOL-related projects presently functional in SA, with seventeen publications listed reporting work in progress (Vale and Young, 1985).

The Molteno Project

The Molteno Project is probably the largest and most significant TESOL project in SA. Based at Rhodes University, Grahamstown, its main thrust is work led by Lanham on the ''Bridge to Literacy'' in black schools at the primary level. This involves Bantu mother-tongue language enliteration into English as the medium of instruction. It is showing major success in Transkei and Ciskei.

SACHED (South African Committee for Higher Education)

SACHED is an alternative, distanced learning program which has produced two major TESOL courses (Stacey and Kretchley, n.d.; SACHED, 1984).

Teacher Opportunities Programmes (TOPS)

TOPS is a primary school teacher upgrading project. The TESOL methodology component is being produced in the Language Education Unit, Department of Education, in the University of Cape Town. The Afrikaans equivalent is produced at the University of the Western Cape, Belville, Cape.

Adult Education Centres

These are very active in TESOL-related work, particularly at St. Francis Adult Education Centre, Guguletu, Cape Town; the Department of Adult Education in the University of Cape Town; and the Centre for Continuing Education, University of the Witwatersrand, Johannesburg. Many of these projects center on basic literacy and teacher upgrading.

English Language Teaching Information Centre (ELTIC)

Based in Johannesburg, ELTIC researches in-service teachers' needs, runs in-service courses, and produces materials and a quarterly journal, *ELTIC Reporter*.

Institute for the Study of English in Africa

Based in Grahamstown, the Institute collates and does widespread research into the function of English in Africa, particularly in language-teaching contexts.

Human Sciences Research Council

The major national coordinating research body is the Human Sciences Research Council in Pretoria, which funds, commissions, and itself conducts significant sociolinguistic, linguistic, and applied linguistic research. Two of its recent publications are of import in the bilingualism field. In his sociolinguistic survey on black attitudes to language, G.K.A. Schuring found that English was a prestige language among blacks, whereas Afrikaans had more pragmatic value. T. Hauptfleisch conducted a survey of trends relating to language loyalty and language shift among white adults in urban areas, finding a major language shift away from Afrikaans to English where marriage to an English speaker took place. This finding, based on a very small sample, links with other HSRC projects concerning the attitudes of Coloureds to language. The HSRC has played, and continues to play, a role in ongoing research flowing from the De Lange Commission's work. As a government-funded council, it has nevertheless acquired a strong reputation for objective and independent research. Much of its work focuses on language teaching/learning in black education.

Academic Programs

Nearly all SA universities offer graduate and higher degree research programs in applied linguistics, linguistics, and TESOL: Natal, Rhodes, South Africa, Witwatersrand, Cape Town, and the Rand Afrikaans University, Johannesburg. The last two mentioned have Language Education Units that conduct Afrikaans second-language and TESOL projects in black and coloured communities. A materials-writing project in the Language Education Unit in the University of Cape Town involving teachers in the writing of their own TESOL materials, now published (Cornell, 1985), is of great interest as an example of action research. Using role play and dramatization, it shows ways of markedly improving spoken English communication skills. The Language Education Unit in the Rand Afrikaans University has done significant work on Afrikaans as a second language in Soweto. It also conducts Afrikaans programs for English-speaking businesspeople. The Institute for Language Study (INTUS) in Stellenbosch University does work on the teaching of black languages. Work is also done in the black universities: the University of the North has a Language Bureau that teaches and researches languages. Some work is also done at the University of Fort Hare. The universities of Bophuthatswana and Zululand are also beginning work on applied linguistic themes.

Research Associations

SA has numerous language-oriented associations and societies, of which the following seem relevant herein.

SAALA (South African Applied Linguistics Association) holds an annual conference on themes related to language teaching.

SAALT (South African Association of Language Teachers) has similar conferences and publishes a regular journal, the *SAALT Journal*, based in the Rand Afrikaans University.

LSSA (Linguistic Society of South Africa) also holds annual conferences on linguistic theory themes. It publishes a journal, *Taalfasette*, annually.

ALASA (African Languages Association of South Africa) holds similar meetings on African language themes.

Language Committee of the FAK (Afrikaans Cultural Association) is committed to promoting the Afrikaans language and its culture. It publishes a magazine, *Handhaaf*.

The English Academy of Southern Africa, based in Johannesburg, is committed to maintaining standards of English usage and use, particularly in English-language teaching, this teaching being functionally achieved through ELTIC, listed above.

SACEE (South African Council for English Education) promotes the teaching of English and awards bursaries for teacher training in this field.

Research Directions

The urgency of the need to provide practical solutions to overcome language-learning problems in a multilingual society has largely overridden the temptation to do more theoretical research. One direction for a synthesis of pragmatics with theory is found in the work now being done by K. Chick in the University of Natal, Durban. Inspired by a stay at the University of California at Los Angeles, working under Gumperz, Chick asserts that apartheid is interactionally accomplished in, for example, Zulu-English communication, by means of English speakers' discriminatory use of prosodic features in English, in intonation contours, revealing such attitudes as patronization, or "talking down" using foreigners talk. Chick's thesis is that political change away from racial discrimination cannot be solely structural, but must attend to the social dynamic of black-white interaction at verbal and nonverbal levels as well (Chick, 1983).

The Human Sciences Research Council, Pretoria, is perhaps the best contact address for information relating to any of the above research bodies and activities.

CONCLUSION

No attempt has been made in this chapter to locate SA bilingualism on the international spectrum of bilingual societies and communities, such as the Soviet Union, the United States, Canada, or Wales, nor has there been a classification of the SA phenomenon in terms of the typology suggested by E. Glyn Lewis (1982:3–41). The lack of detailed research to date on this topic in SA, grounded in political sensitivities and overzealous group loyalties, limits the base of objective data on which to build such conclusive statements. Few attitudinal surveys have been conducted except in the limited projects of the HSRC discussed above.

Objectivity is thus elusive, since being a white writer not even representative of a minority culture, in a multicultural society where the majority black culture is unenfranchised and politically powerless, discredits one's essay in that one cannot speak on behalf of that majority.

Bilingualism in SA is associated with politically motivated aims to preserve the language rights of speakers of Afrikaans and English and to ensure the free use and education in the mother tongue, the mother tongue defined as "the language with which they are most familiar." But the resistance to extended education in the mother tongue or vernacular beyond early primary schooling is strong in black education and has resulted in the adoption of English as the medium from the fifth year of schooling, in keeping with many other independent African countries, for example, Ghana, Kenya, Lesotho, Uganda, Malawi, Nigeria, and Swaziland, all of which introduce English-medium instruction from about the fourth year of schooling (HSRC, 1981). But unlike the position in any of these countries, the decision to adopt English was reached in SA only after violent political conflict and black protest against a perceived attempt to maintain ethnicity as part of the policy of apartheid. It can be argued that language planning policies have been used to divide SA society into ethnic units, though these attempts have failed; there is a powerful drive for a common SA language, English, albeit that spoken as mother tongue by only about 8 percent of the population. This is not necessarily out of great love for English, which is also identified with colonization and jingoism, but out of a reluctance by the majority to use Afrikaans because of its use by a government enforcing oppressive racial segregation.

   Apologists for the SA government will argue that significant rapid change and reform are now underway. Relative to the status quo, there is some truth in their rejoinder, but in terms of language planning and bilingual policy-making, provision needs to be made for a system that will erase demarcations based on linguistic ethnocentrism, so that the official languages are no longer perceived as instruments of power and control of the black majority by a white minority. There are firm pointers to widespread interlanguage tolerance not evident ten years ago. Therein lies some measure of hope for the emergence of a common South African society, free of unilateral bilingualism, but rather rich in multilingualism.

BIBLIOGRAPHY

Ashley, M. J. 1974. "Socialization and Education." In *White South African Elites*, ed. H. W. van der Merwe, M. J. Ashley, N.C.J. Charton, and B. J. Huber. Cape Town: Juta and Co., pp. 39–60.

Branford, J. 183. *Dictionary of South African English, 1980*. Oxford: Oxford University Press.

Bughwan, D. 1970. "An Investigation into the Use of English by Indians in South Africa with Special Reference to Natal." Ph.D. diss., University of South Africa, Pretoria.

Chick, K. 1983. "The Interactional Accomplishment of Discrimination in South Africa." Unpublished paper, University of Natal, Durban.

Combrink, J.G.H. 1978. "Afrikaans: Its Origin and Development." In *Language and Communication Studies in South Africa*, ed. L. W. Lanham and K. Prinsloo. Cape Town: Oxford University Press, pp. 69–95.

Cornell, C. 1985. "English Through Role Play and Dramatization in the Classroom." University of Cape Town: Language Education Unit.

De Lange, P. 1981. "Languages and Language Instruction: Report of the Work Committee." Pretoria: Human Sciences Research Council, pp. 1–252.

Esterhuyse, J. 1985. Unpublished M.Ed. Dissertation. Department of Education, University of Cape Town.

Fishman, J. 1977. *Bilingual Education, an International Perspective*. Rowley, Mass.: Newbury House.

Hauptfleisch, T. 1979. *Language Loyalty in South Africa*. Vols. 1–4. Pretoria: Human Sciences Research Council, Report TLK/L–10.

Heese, H. 1985. *Groep Sonde Grense: Die Rol en Status van die Gemengde Bevolking aan die Kaap, 1652–1795*. Cape Town: Nasionale Boekhandel.

Kennedy, C., ed. 1983. *Language Planning and Language Education*. London: George Allan and Unwin, pp. 4–16.

Kitching, C. J. 1984. "The Communicative Competence in English of Afrikaans Speaking Teacher Trainees." M.Ed. diss., Department of Education, University of Cape Town.

Kroes, H. 1978. "Afrikaans in Education." In *Language and Communication Studies in South Africa*, ed L. W. Lanham and K. P. Prinsloo. Cape Town: Oxford University Press, pp. 169–86.

Labov, W. 1969. "The Logic of Non-standard English." In *Language and Social Context*, ed. P. Giglioli. Harmondsworth: Penguin.

Lanham, L. W. 1978. "An Outline History of the Languages of South Africa." In *Language and Communication Studies in South Africa*, ed. L. W. Lanham and K.P. Prinsloo. Cape Town: Oxford University Press, pp. 13–52.

Lanham, L. W., and K. P. Prinsloo, 1978. *Language and Communication Studies in South Africa*. Cape Town: Oxford University Pres.

Leschinsky. C.C.J. 1985. *South African Language Review*. Pretoria: HSRC, pp. 1–64.

Lewis, E. Glyn. 1982. *Bilingualism and Bilingual Education*. Oxford: Pergamon Press.

Malherbe, E. G. 1925. *Education in South Africa*. Vol. 1: 1652–1922. Cape Town: Juta and Co.

————. 1938. *Examinations in South Africa*. The Year Book of Education. London.

————. 1966. *Demographic and Social Factors Determining the Position of English in the South African Republic*. Johannesburg: English Academy of Southern Africa, pp. 1–22.

————. 1977. *Education in South Africa*. Vol. 2: 1923–75. Cape Town: Juta and Co.

McCormick, K. 1983. *Attitudes to the Official Languages and Their Dialects in Cape Town*. Cape Town: University of Cape Town Centre for African Studies, pp. 4–10.

Miller, J. 1983. *Many Voices: Bilingualism, Culture and Education*. London: Routledge and Kegan Paul.

Parsons, N. J. 1982. *A New History of South Africa*. London: Macmillan Co., pp. 5–25, 98.

Randal, P. 1984. *Little England on the Veld*. Johannesburg: Ravan Press.

Republic of South Africa (RSA). 1961. Constitution. Pretoria: Government Printer.

————. 1980. Census. Pretoria: Central Statistical Services.

South African Institute for Race Relations (SAIRR). 1984. *Race Relations Survey, 1983*. Johannesburg: SAIRR.

Schuring, G.K.A. n.d. *Multilingual Society: English and Afrikaans Amongst the Blacks in the RSA*. Pretoria: HSRC, Report TLK/1–7.

Stacey, J., and G. Kretchley. n.d. *Read Well*. Johannesburg: SACHED.

Stacey, J., and G. Kretchley. n.d. *Write Well*. Johannesburg: SACHED.

Trudgill, P., and J. Hannan. 1982. *International English, A Guide to Varieties of Standard English*. London: Arnold.

Vale, L., and D. Young. 1985. *A Directory of TESOL Projects in South Africa*. Cape Town: University of Cape Town, Language Education Unit.

van Wyk, E. B. 1978. "Language Contact and Bilingualism." In *Language and Com-*

munication Studies in South Africa, ed. L. W. Lanham and K. P. Prinsloo. Cape
 Town: Oxford University Press, pp. 29–52.
Volbrecht, T. 1984. "The Articulation of the Social Formation with the Teaching of
 English as a First Language in the Cape Education Department." M. Phil. diss.,
 Department of Education, University of Cape Town.
Young, D. N. 1978. "English in Education." In *Language and Communication Studies
 in South Africa*, ed. L. W. Lanham and K. P. Prinsloo. Cape Town: Oxford
 University Press, pp. 187–214.

BILINGUAL EDUCATION IN SOVIET CENTRAL ASIA

The Soviet Union is the largest country in the world, and it is also one of the most linguistically varied. Few countries have devoted as much time discussing and analyzing the problems associated with multilingualism as the USSR. In order to solve these problems, especially those in the fields of education and communication, the USSR formulated many policies, plans, and programs and implemented them by various means, ranging from coercion to cooptation. However, the efforts of the central government have not always met with favor with the non-Russian nationalities of the country.

In 1980, the USSR had a population of about 265 million (*Narodnoe Khoziaistvo SSSR v 1980 godu*:7), constituting more than one hundred linguistically varied people. These people are also different in terms of their religion and other attributes that ordinarily mark the ethnic boundaries of a group.

The USSR federation comprises fifteen republics. Each republic is named after the people who, with the exception of the Kazakh people, constitute the majority (sometimes only barely) of the population in that republic. Starting from the Baltic and going counterclockwise on the Soviet Union's map, we encounter the Estonians, Latvians, Lithuanians, Belorussians, Ukrainians, Moldavians, Georgians, Armenians, Azerbaijanis, Turkmans, Uzbeks, Kirgiz, Tajiks, and Kazakhs.[1] The so-called Great Russians, who at present constitute a little more than 50 percent of the country's population, also occupy the largest union republic.

These statistics give some idea of the complexity of the linguistic scene in the USSR. The problem gets even more complicated when we attempt to analyze the linguistic nationalism of the various nationalities on the one hand and the ideological imperative of the country on the other.

The USSR is officially committed to the creation of a proletarian society with a homogenized proletarian culture. Apparently, this system also includes a language. Although no one has clearly stated what that language would be (as the discussions that follow will illustrate), the socialist notables of the USSR have left little doubt in their utterances about the primacy of the Russian language in this multilingual country. This ideological imperative has created political problems for the Soviets. Apparently, not all peoples of the USSR see the existence of a homogenized Soviet proletariat culture as a good thing. They fear the russification of their languages, as well as other aspects of their cultures. The Russian peoples' monopoly of power over the distribution of resources in the USSR implies this russification.

The anxiety of the non-Russian people has not been lost on the Soviet government and the Communist party of the USSR. From the beginning, they have tried to come to terms with two mutually exclusive policies. On the one hand, the Soviets try to tolerate (and at times encourage) the nationalism of various minorities, and, on the other hand, they try to integrate the people toward the realization of the homogeneous proletariat culture.

Understandably, almost all of the central government's attempts to create a standardized Soviet culture have been interpreted by the minorities as a ploy for russification of their cultures. In order to reassure the non-Russians, the USSR proclaimed its nationality policies as "nationalism in content and socialism in form." This meant that various ethnic groups in the USSR can use their own mother tongues and the literature that goes with them, provided they reflect the Soviet brand of socialism. As a consequence, the Soviets have the laborious task of trying to find the "appropriate" passages from literature, as well as policing the everyday conversations of the people for signs of deviance. Only recently, for example, have some of the Russian classics like those by Fyodor Dostoyevsky been published in the USSR.

The multipronged conflict between the state and its ideological imperative which pushes for integration and the nationalism of ethnic groups (which in turn leads to greater differentiation) continues to persist in the USSR. The conflict that continues between different nationalities also exists, such as the enmity between the Russians and most other national minorities. A good example of this conflict-ridden scene is Soviet Central Asia. The language policy of the USSR seems to be one of the major contributors to this clash.

Central Asia is the southernmost part of the USSR. It borders the People's Republic of China (PRC) in the east and Iran in the west. It has its linguistically and culturally identical groups straddling the common boundaries it shares with Afghanistan, Iran, and the PRC. It is composed of more than a dozen nationalities, some of which (e.g., the Slavs) are newcomers in the area, while others have been there for centuries. The major indigenous groups (in contrast to the European newcomers) are the Uzbeks, Kirgiz, and Turkman peoples. These peoples speak Turkic and occupy the union republics bearing their names. The other important Central Asian group with its own republic are the Tajiks who speak an Indo-Iranian language.

Historically, these people have always considered their own Islamic heritage and the languages articulating it as superior to those offered by their colonizers, the Russians. As a result, they have perceived their learning the Russian language as a prelude to their own acculturation to the Russian way of life. The Islamic religion encourages learning, including the learning of languages. Apparently, the Central Asians, who consider themselves oppressed, are reluctant to learn the Russian language because it is the language of the oppressors.

This attitude of the indigenous people has in part been a response to the Russians' crass and overtly racist attitudes toward the Central Asians (Wimbush and Alexiev, 1980), and has in turn hampered the programs of Teaching Russian as a Second Language (TRSL). The Russians have ruled for more than a century and have made conscious efforts to acculturate the Central Asians, first under the auspices of the Orthodox Church and later, up to the present time, through the efforts of the Russian government of the USSR. In spite of these efforts, Central Asians lag behind other Soviet ethnic minorities in their acquisition of the Russian language.

This study is an assessment of the theories and practices of teaching Russian to the indigenous Turkic- and Iranian-speaking people of Soviet Central Asia.[2] More specifically, it describes the processes by which the TRSL programs are implemented in the classrooms of Central Asia.

Language acquisition, like other forms of learning, is influenced by many factors, not all of which are present in the school environment. The present study assumes that schooling is important in the acquisition of a second language. It is important as an apparent ''best'' alternative to nonformal types of education like on-the-job training alone. It is also clear that the ''best'' alternative by itself does not lead to the best results. For this to happen, the discovery and development of supportive economic, social, cultural, and political institutions are necessary. Another factor signifying the importance of the school is that the demand for language learning, like the demand for other forms of learning, is derived. The more one learns and becomes educated, the more one wants to continue learning. This demand becomes more clear when the society attaches various reward packages to various levels of education and different types of competency credentials. To learners, theoretically successive levels of education provide greater numbers of options among alternative futures. One of the most important options seems to be the ability to be socially and spatially mobile in the USSR. In Central Asia, learning some Russian permits one to move into the urban centers of the area where there are more opportunities to move up the occupational structure and augment one's level of linguistic competence. In spite of this potential advantage, the proportion of Central Asians fluent in Russian lags behind the average of all other non-Russians fluent in that language (as census data show).

It is difficult to isolate the factors that may be contributing to this lag. Some of these factors are discussed here, and others may be anchored in the people's cultures, traditions, and social psychological makeup, some of which was mentioned earlier.

Soviet Central Asia is composed of the republics of Tajikistan, Uzbekistan,

Turkmenistan, and Kirgizistan. In 1979, the titular people living in these republics composed about 20 million persons scattered over 1.2 million square kilometers (*Narodnoe Khoziaistvo SSSR v 1980 G*:24). The area has had experiences with numerous alphabets prior to the introduction of the Cyrillic script in the late 1930s (Gibb, 1928; Bashakov, 1967; Shorish, 1984). The most important alphabets prior to the present one seem to have been those of Arabic and Latin. The Arabic alphabet came into the area after Central Asia was overrun by the Iran-Islamic armies in the eighth century. This alphabet continued as a means of communication and instruction in the schools until the latter half of the 1920s when it was replaced by the Latin alphabet. In 1938, the Cyrillic alphabet was introduced in Central Asia, where it replaced the Latin alphabet almost totally in all printed material by the early 1940s. In addition, on March 13, 1938, by a decree of the Central Committee of the Communist party of the USSR, the teaching of the Russian language became compulsory in the schools of the non-Russian people, including those residing in Central Asia (Shukurov, 1957:76).

By the middle of 1938, almost all of the Central Asian republics had adopted similar decrees on the compulsory teaching of the Russian language. The task of preparing the Russian teachers fell to the Commissariat of Education of each republic. Owing to the extreme scarcity of such teachers at the time in Central Asia, the republics started importing many teachers from the Slavic-speaking areas of the USSR. Many Russian teachers for the secondary and incomplete secondary schools were provided by various other union republics, especially the RSFSR (Russia proper). In 1938, for example, Tajikistan received 368 teachers from the Russian republic mentioned above, and Central Asians started massive Russian-language teacher training programs. By the end of 1939, almost five thousand teachers of the Russian language for grades two through four were trained in Tajikistan alone (Shukurov, 1957:76ff).

Numerous conferences and meetings to legitimize the conversion to the Cyrillic alphabet and to legitimize and expand the teaching of Russian in Central Asia have taken place over the past several years. One of the most important of these meetings took place in Alma Ata in 1962. It was titled the "Conference on the Development of Literary Languages" and had as its main concern the creation of common lexical stocks for the languages of the USSR. However, as E. G. Lewis points out, in actuality the conference was to investigate the relationships of all these languages to that of Russian (Lewis, 1974:58). The results of all these relationships have been a continuous inflow of Russian words, often at the expense of local terms in almost all non-Russian languages of the USSR. The reactions of the indigenous people to this situation have been varied. (Pool, 1976; *Tojikistoni Soveti*, henceforth *TS*, March 6, 1966:4.

The first interrepublican conference on the study of Russian in these Muslim republics took place in Tashkent in August 1965, following the reorganization of the Soviet schools under the provision of the so-called Khrushchev Reforms. Similar conferences have taken place since then to discuss various aspects of teaching Russian as a second language. The results of these conferences have been to increase significantly the number of hours devoted to the Russian language and Russian-language-related materials in the non-Russian schools (*Rahbari Donish*, 1930:13; King, 1936:312–14; Uzbek SSR, 1939:13–16; *Central Asian Review*, henceforth *CAR*, 1961:27; *Maorif v Madanivat*, henceforth *MvM*, May 19, 1970:4, June 7, 1957:4, September 10, 1974:4).

A conference of teachers of the Russian language was held in Dushanbe on March 28, 1968, in which the role of the Russian language in the "bringing together" (*nazdikshavi*, *sblizhenie*) of the socialist nations was discussed. The meeting was addressed by one of the secretaries of the Communist party of Tajikistan, I. Rahimova, who declared that the learning of the Russian language was the "greatest weapon at the hand of our party in the process of unification of all Soviet people" (*MvM*, March 30, 1968–3). Other conferences on various pedagogical aspects of TRSL have been taking place over the past decades at the republican and federal levels (Baskakov, 1968). In all of these Russian-language conferences and related material appearing in the Soviet press, there seems to be one consistent and concurrent theme: the glorification of the Russian language and the rationalization of its dominant position in government and commerce.

The theses of the Central Committee of the Communist party of Soviet Union (CC of CPSU) and the Council of Ministers of the USSR, *Regarding the Strengthening of the Relationship of School and for the Further Development of the System of Public Education in the USSR*, were published on November 16, 1958. This document presents the official view. The nineteenth clause reads as follows:

In the Soviet schools, instruction is conducted in the native language. This is one of the more important achievements of the Leninist national policy. At the same time in the union and autonomous republics is also studied the Russian language which is a great means of international communication, of strengthening of friendship among the peoples of the USSR and of introducing them to the treasures of Russian and world culture (Kolasky, 1968:26).

Studying the Russian language is important not only because it is a "window" to the outside world, but also because it is the vehicle of international communication and friendship among people. Few would want to undermine such an arrangement by not opting for the study of the Russian language. Moreover, at the present time, without knowledge of the Russian language it would be impossible to become a Soviet leader. Thus, Russian is a prerequisite for upward social, political, and economic mobility.

There are still other stimuli for learning Russian. For example, "[the] Russian language is the most important means in the making of a Communist; one can learn ethical behavior, patriotism, etc., by reading Gorkii, Turgenev, and ... stories by Gogol makes one selfless in defense of the motherland" (Zhuravleya, 1968:4). A. K. Kanimetrov, a former Minister of Education of the Kirgiz SSR, claims that those who learn Russian become better students and adjust better in life (*TS*, November 10, 1972:4). Another example is, "The children must be prepared to fulfill their duty to the motherland, to study arduously the Russian language, in which are written the regulations, military orders, and instructions in which their comrades and commanders will speak" (*Russkii Iazyk i Literatura v Azerbaidzhanskoi Shkole*, henceforth *RIILASH*, 1973, No. 8:5). A last example shows that Russian

is the language of Lenin, Gorkii, the Communist Party . . . Maiakovskii; it is the language of kosmonauts; it is the language of the country. . . . Moreover, the great literary figures of the Tajik literature such as Rudaki, Ibni-Sino, Fidausi, Nosir Khisrav, Umar Khayyom, Sa'di, Hofiz, Jomi, Bedil, and Ahmad Makhdum Donish were competent in more than one language (Asrori, 1966:4).

Another area that gets a great amount of emphasis for the learning of Russian is science and technology and the cultural development of the non-Russians. For example:

Learning Russian makes one moral; it makes one grasp scientific and technical knowledge; it brings people together; increases one's social and political mobility; leads to the development of the socialist person; leads to the economic development of the country; increases friendship among the large and small peoples; it gives needed ideological and political content to the development of the young; it reflects the level of knowledge and the spirit of internationalism and socialism of an individual (Uspenskaia, 1975:2).

All of these qualities are, of course, empirical questions that have not been validated. That is, the authors (both indigenous and Europeans) seem to have some sort of faith in the power of the Russian language to cause behavioral changes in individuals to the degree that is mentioned above. Some of the rhetoric in these statements is reminiscent both of the rhetoric once espoused by General K. P. von Kaufman when he was Governor General of the Russian Turkistan, and of the preaching of V. I. Il'minskii. Both believed that the Russia and the Russian culture, including the Orthodox Church, of the second half of the nineteenth century was a reference culture that would draw non-Russians to it and thereby elevate their cultural level (Pierce, 1960).

Can Russian become the language of the people of the USSR? To answer this question, one has to look carefully at the Soviet linguistic policies in which some of the above statements are anchored, and at the programs and plans that have been designed for their implementation.

The ultimate aim of (Soviet) social and linguistic policy was stated by Stalin as early as the XVIth Congress—"the fusion of nations, languages and cultures" and this ultimate objective has never been abandoned or even modified except to the extent that was originally set out as a declaration of intent is now progressively articulated as a maturing program (Lewis, 1972:54).

But statements by Lenin and Stalin do not leave any doubt about the virtues of centralization and the suitability, if not the superiority, of the Russian language as a means of communication and instruction (Lenin, 1968:2). The idea of merging nations into a single socialist people, apparently sharing one single language among many other things, was for decades the overt linguistic policy of the USSR and has now been modified somewhat. In addition, the element of coercion has been replaced by sets of apparently superior stimuli, some of which were listed above. These new stimuli are products of the present relatively high levels of economic, educational, political, and social development of the USSR. They put a degree of pressure on the creation of Russian as the language of the country.

It is a push-pull situation. One is pushed to learn Russian by one's peers, the mass media, and the Soviet cultural and political institutions. One is also pulled by unparalleled rewards in the form of spatial and social mobility. All of these forces are apparently exerted without making a sacrifice in the form of losing the allegiance of the members of one's community or one's language (Rashidov, 1975:1–3).

Some opinions differ markedly from those expressed by the late Sharaf Rashidov (former First Secretary of the Uzbek Communist party and a Candidate Member of the Political Bureau of the USSR Communist party). These opinions have been expressed by those who look at him as a "russified" native, a "cosmopolitanist" (Shorish, 1981: Carrére d'Encausse, 1980). It is also necessary to realize that probably very few languages other than Russian have inspired such intensive propaganda. Printed and electronic media, scholarly journals, and books have all focused on the cause of the Russian language in recent years. Wherever one goes in Central Asia, one feels the pressure for learning the Russian language.

No one can work effectively in any of the urban centers of this area without some knowledge of the Russian language. Almost all of the street signs and those describing means of transportation are in Russian. Television and radio programs are dominated by the Russian language. Random weeks of television programs (from 1974 to 1985 in *MvM*, *Komsomoli Tojikistan*, and *TS*) revealed that the materials about and in the Russian language amounted to more than 75 percent of total broadcasting time. As for radio, Russian-language-related programs consumed more than 55 percent of the total broadcasting time of Radio Dushanbe. Of course, there is always the possibility that some people will tune in to radio and TV programs other than those originating in the USSR.

In spite of all these efforts, Central Asians still lag behind the rest of the non-Russian population of the USSR in the acquistion of Russian. This fact has not been lost on the Soviet authorities, who have been complaining about the poor quality of TRSL in Central Asia (Besemeres, 1975; Murtazoev, 1984:4–5). As early as 1950, the most common cases of failures in schools in Mordavia, Bashkiria, and Tataristan at the elementary level was failure in the Russian language (Valitov, 1952:67). Even though the problem cited was for the RSFSR, it is equally true for the very high rate of failure of the non-Slavic children elsewhere in the USSR. The problem of failure in Russian constitutes one of the major educational problems of the Soviet Union.

From the standpoint of Soviet educators, several major problems seem to have contributed to student failures and have persisted in TRSL in Central Asia over several decades. These perennial problems fall into two general categories. The first concerns the students and problems associated with the linguistics and pedagogy of second-language learning. The second concerns the teachers of Russian, their training and the logistics required for Russian-language teaching.

When learning Russian, Central Asian students experience great orthographic and pronunciation problems. The orthographic mistakes associated with incorrect pronunciation also suggest that teachers should pay closer attention to the students' mother tongue to see if some of the problem of pronunciation may lie there (Kliueva, 1952:77).

One of the most important concerns of educators over the years has been the very low lexical stocks of non-Slavic children, who often memorize words without being able to perceive their meanings, as some of these words were absent from their languages (Mokhov, 1952:64-j3–64; Kissen, 1952:61–62; Tarzimanov, 1952:65–566; Boitsova and Varkovitskaia, 1952:66–69). The problem of pronunciation, orthographic mistakes, grammatical errors, and inability to distinguish between consonants and vowels all lend themselves to poor syntax for the children of local Central Asians (*CAR*, 1953:43–44, 1954:187–89). The problem is nowhere more apparent than among rural children who are unable to speak and write a simple Russian sentence after ten years of in-class instruction (*CAR*, 1957:38; Medlin, Cave, and Carpenter, 1971:105).

One of the most controversial and conflict-ridden aspects of the TRSL program in Central Asia has been the role and place of the mother tongue in the process of learning Russian. In the context of Soviet linguistic policy, the politics of language has often overshadowed valid pedagogical and linguistic discussions of the subject. The non-Slavic Central Asians have frequently blamed the Russian teacher's lack of knowledge of the student's mother tongues as one of the more important inhibitors of the successful teaching of Russian, thereby causing the failure of Central Asian children to score higher in Russian-language classes (Makhmudova, 1974:6–20). The following represents a Kazakh's reaction:

Ignorance of the Kazakh language on the part of the teacher reacts unfavorably on his teaching. The teacher often wastes much time and effort explaining some words and constructions of sentences through the medium of Russian, which is not fully understood (by the students) by the end of his discussion (*Kazakhstankaia Pravda*, 1956:2).

The argument against the mother tongue as the medium of TRSL takes place on apparent social-psychological and linguistic grounds. Simply stated, some Soviet educators think that, in isolating the learner from the impact of the mother tongue and developing a ''Russian only'' environment, one can increase the rate of acquisition of the Russian language. A. M. Dzhafarzoda, in a study of bilingualism (Russian-Azeri), found higher frequencies of bilinguals in urban and workers' villages than in places that could not afford the type of infrastructures (media, other means of communication, factories, and so forth) conducive to bilingualism (Dzhafarzoda, 1973:82–87). These debates do not take into account the function of the mother tongue in the overall educative process of the young. Instead, a great many Russians and some non-Russian scholars and politicians insist on a program of TRSL which makes Russian the "second mother tongue" of the non-Russian people. Apparently, the term "second mother tongue" is meant to imply the ability of the learner to think in Russian as well as in the mother tongue (Radzhabova, 1973:3–11).

Many writers insist on using Russian as a medium of TRSL. "The present method of teaching Russian in National schools requires limitations, as much as possible, of the influence of the mother tongue" (Uspenskaia, 1975). Such statements are often made without clear and adequate substantiation, and too many of them are documented by appealing to authorities who are either unknown to the reader or not authorities in the area of specialization. Appeals to people like Ibrahim Altynsarin (1841–1889, Kazakh protege of the Tsarist missionary worker Il'minskii), Marx, Engels, and others, whose interests in linguistics and second-language teaching have been tangential, is an all too common strategy.

This does not mean, however, that serious discussions of this topic are not taking place at other levels in the USSR's academic circles. The question of language policy and problems in linguistics have been discussed in this part of the world with much more intensity, at a higher level of sophistication, and over a much longer period of time than in most countries in the world. What has been discussed in this chapter up to this point are the pedagogical problems of second-language teaching from the standpoint of the practitioners in the class-rooms of the Soviet Union—the teachers, the inspectors, the language specialists, and other educators (Lewis, 1974; *MvM*, March 5, 1968:1).[3] These people have been taking widely divergent views in discussing the role of the mother tongue in TRSL. Generally, the Russians have advocated no role for the mother tongue, and the local Central Asians have advocated a great role for the mother tongue. Frequently, these views are expressed without any linguistic or pedagogical justification, even though, from a pedagogical point of view, the positive role of the mother tongue in children's cognitive and affective learning is unassailable.

Language specialists at a UNESCO meeting agreed that it was essential for learners to start schooling in their mother tongue in order to minimize both the problem of conceptualization and the break between the home and the school. The specialists also agreed that teachers of the second language should know the mother tongue of the pupils and that the transfer to the second language should be postponed as long as possible (UNESCO, 1952). S. M. Makhmudova, an Uzbek educator, relies on comparative grammar as one of the best methods in TRSL. In this method, the use of the mother tongue becomes essential. The economy embedded in comparative grammar makes it an attractive method.

Since many children know about some aspects of the grammar of their language before coming to school, it is not necessary to give lengthy definitions or explanations of those aspects which the two languages have in common (Makhmudova, 1974).

According to S. M. Makhmudova, the contrastive linguistics approach (which by necessity relies on the teacher's bilingual ability) includes the comparison of the phonetics and grammatical phenomena of Russian and the native languages, and translations from Russian to the native language and from the native language to Russian. In this undertaking, materials can be grouped according to: (1) phenomena similar or identical in both languages, which need not be time consuming; (2) phenomena characteristic of both languages, but not identical, which need explanation and clarification by the teacher because of native language interference; (3) phenomena particular to Russian and absent from the student's native language, which makes this area completely new to the learners and free from interference by the mother tongue. The learners' experiences in learning are relatively (to (2) above) less ambiguous (Makhmudova, 1974:6–20; Abdulloeva, 1971:18).

The non-Russian educators of Central Asia have also been taking a leaf from the Russian educators' book in their defense of the mother tongue and the pedagogical value assigned to it. They have turned some of the arguments advanced by Russian writers for TRSL around to describe the usefulness of the mother tongue, not only as a facilitator in TRSL, but also, in its own merits, as conducive to learning (Asrori, 1966). The importance of the native language in the flowering of human culture and civilization is mentioned over and over by these non-Russian writers.

There are, in general, two types of teachers of Russian in Central Asia—native Russian speakers and non-Russian teachers. Many of the native Russian speakers and other Russian-language teachers (mostly other Slavs) have come from areas outside Central Asia. Many of them come from RSFSR and some from the other two Slavic republics, the Ukraine and Belorussia. In addition, many graduates of pedagogical institutes of these Slavic republics, specializing in the teaching of Russian, spend their student teaching assignments in the Central Asian republics. Almost all of these expatriate Russian-language teachers settle in the urban centers, and rarely do they venture into the rural areas. Since more than 75 percent of schools in Central Asia are located in the rural districts, many of these schools have no Russian teachers (Dodoboev, 1975:1–2; Tojieva, 1968:1; *MvM*, November 23, 1971:1; Khudoidodov, 1975:2; Editorial, *RIILASH*, No. 12, 1973:3).

According to most observers, the effectiveness of both rural (generally non-Slavic) and Slavic Russian teachers in TRSL constitutes the Achilles heel of the Russian-language program in Central Asia. Both of these groups suffer some degree of ineffectiveness. Because of their ignorance of the local languages and cultures and a poor grasp of the TRSL methodology, the Slavic-speaking teachers cannot teach productively. On the other hand, the non-Russian teachers, trained in Central Asian educational institutions, have poor training overall (*TS*, April 2, 1968:1).

As previously noted, most Slavic-speaking Russian teachers stay in the cities of Central Asia where the infrastructure is not too different from the cities of their home regions. Most local Central Asian graduates of teacher training institutes also prefer to stay in urban centers. Therefore, the scarcity of qualified Russian teachers in the rural areas of Central Asia remains unchanged. Apparently, the establishment in the early 1960s of branches of the pedagogical institutes which supposedly specialize in the training of Russian teachers for the rural area has not been able to reduce this shortage. Since these branches enrolled almost exclusively students from the rural areas, it was argued that upon graduation these students would remain in the rural districts to teach their own relatives the Russian language. It is not clear how many of these graduates, the so-called special groups (*Guruhoi Makhsus*), choose to stay in the rural areas upon graduation. In any case, the quality of these branches seems to have remained low, in part because of the poor preparation of their students (graduates of rural elementary and secondary schools) and the teachers (Personal interviews; *CAR*, 1965:310–22). Poor lesson plans and poor understanding of the systematization of curriculum material according to age of students augment the list of problems in TRSL in Central Asia. Each practitioner in the classroom and others who are concerned with the program are encouraged by officials to innovate methods in TRSL. As a result, a hodgepodge of approaches for TRSL are used in the classrooms and pedagogical institutes of the Central Asian republics.

The teaching of Russian as a second language in Central Asia, aside from ideological anad political contradictions noted earlier, is marked by other difficulties peculiar to second-language pedagogy. First, teaching a language is different from teaching other subjects. As C. Cazden has observed, "language poses multiple problems for education because it is both curriculum content and learning environment, both the object of knowledge, and a medium through which other knowledge is acquired" (Cazden, 1973:135). Second, the teaching of a particular second language, Russian in this case, should not be standardized for all students. Their mother tongues differ not only linguistically and in terms of concept from the second language being taught, but also from each other's. TRSL in Central Asia suffers from poor understanding of both of these phenomena.

The problem of curriculum content for Russian teachers in non-Russian schools illustrates not only the confusion in TRSL, but also the absence of any theoretical foundations. For example, a program for the "special groups" (Uzbeks and Tajiks) in the special branch of Leninabad (Khujand) Pedagogical Institute had the following courses: (1) a special seminar on out-of-class work on the Russian language and literature; (2) a special practical course of writing and composition; (3) a special practical course on the development of visual aids, and (4) a special course of Russian and Tajik literature. A Russian-language week was eventually added, during which students were apparently to become imbued with Russian culture (Sevost'ianova, 1968:2; Karakulakov, 1968:3).

A professor from the same institute has argued that knowledge of Old Church Slavonic is essential in the training of teachers of Russian, for "without it one cannot claim to know the present Russian language, and the thirty hours devoted to it in the program is extremely inadequate" (Rusakova, 1968:3). One probably cannot argue against teaching Old Church Slavonic to future linquists, but one can question the wisdom of its inclusion in the curriculum of the "special groups" in the Central Asian pedagogical institutes. The extremely poor preparation of the local students at the time of entrance to higher educational establishments (*Vuzy*) of Central Asia, and the very poor training that the students receive while enrolled in the pedagogical institutes, make it infeasible. On similar pedagogical grounds, one can argue against the inclusion of nineteenth-century Russian classics in the "special groups" curriculum (Liubana, 1968:4).

The major logistical problem in TRSL in Central Asia has been finding qualified Russian teachers. In general, most teachers of Russian are badly trained but there are not even enough of these badly trained teachers to satisfy the needs. As a result, many schools, especially those in the rural areas of Central Asia, have no teachers at all, or have teachers initially trained for other subjects such as biology and physics, who end up teaching Russian (Birashk, 1975; *MvM*, 1971, November 23:1). Furthermore, statistics often quoted above on the percentage of Russian teachers with training in higher educational establishments have to be evaluated in the light of the poor quality of training given these teachers in the *Vuzy* of Central Asia (Khodoidodov).

Aside from the chronic shortages of qualified Russian teachers, there are chronic shortages of good instructional materials (among them textbooks) and other supportive facilities (including, perhaps, social and cultural institutions) for TRSL in Central Asia. Over the years very few books have been published on TRSL, and those that have been published are deficient in terms of methodology and pedagogy (Khodoidodov; Rubenshtain, 1974:107–14). The problem of poor-quality textbook production persists even today. Deficiencies in this area, from the point of view of teachers and students, seem to be poor-quality paper, very small print (which makes reading difficult), and poor reproduction of illustrations. The shortage of materials designed for out-of-class reading is especially acute. Because of this scarcity of reading materials and the poor production of the materials that can be obtained by the students, the out-of-class TRSL program in Central Asia, especially in the rural areas, has been a failure (Rubenshtain; *CAR*, 1957, V). Interestingly, almost all textbooks in TRSL are authored by non-Central Asians, and the best teachers in the TRSL program are non-Central Asians, judging by the names of teachers who have received "best Russian teacher" awards (Editorial, *MvM*, April 6, 1968:1).

There are probably as many proposals for teaching methods for TRSL in Central Asia as there are teachers. This is partly because the Soviets encourage individual teacher innovations in teaching methods, but the idiosyncrasies of particular teachers, the composition of the student body in terms of ability, ethnicity, mother tongue, and social class background, and the urban or rural location of the schools are also important factors.

In general, formal education and its language-teaching component in the USSR are teacher-centered. Formal language teaching, in particular, requires a transmitter (such as a teacher or a machine) which systematically transmits to the learner new information about new words, sentences, and aspects of the culture of which the language being taught is a part. The TRSL teachers in Central Asia have often been faulted not only for their poor training in the art of TRSL, but also for their inability to make linkages between the language being taught and the political, economic, and ideological dimensions of the Soviet social system (*MvM*, 1971:1). Apparently, policy-makers believe that a good teacher in TRSL is one who, in addition to good academic qualifications, has a desirable political and ideological orientation (*MvM*, 1971:1). The empirical evidence on teachers' political orientations in the educative process of the young is sketchy and often contradictory, especially concerning the teachers' role in the process of political socialization of children (Merelman, 1972:34–166; Prewitt, 1975:105–14). But there is no doubt that a teacher's qualifications and professional commitment are significant in children's achievement. This role is probably most obvious in the teaching of a second language, where the teacher's awareness of the child's stages of cognitive development and of the role of social class in the process of acquisition of knowledge and its retention are crucial.

The methodology of TRSL remains basically partisan. The non-Russian Central Asian educators largely believe in the superiority of comparative grammar (which permits teachers to talk about both languages and requires them to be bilingual). The native Russian teachers and other Slavs interested in the topic insist that increasing and developing the student's vocabulary is the best method of solving the present TRSL problems. This proposal prohibits talking about the languages involved and has long been favored by the Russians.

The early 1960s witnessed activities on the part of teachers in Central Asia for the implementation of some of Khrushchev's reforms, which in TRSL were vocabulary development, sentence construction, and development of skills on speech narratives (Nazarova, 1962:3–4). All of these were to take place with minimal usage of the mother tongue. The purpose of this program was to enable seventh and eighth grade students to develop their skills in written and oral Russian. The method was actually the drilling of each word and sentence until it was memorized and pronunciation was perfected. Teachers were also concerned about the development of sets of superior stimuli outside and inside school to motivate children to learn Russian.

This method, however, failed to increase the children's (especially rural children's) level of achievement in Russian, and the rate of failure of Central Asian children in Russian-language courses continued to rise. This rise has been somewhat blunted by increases in the level of investment in TRSL in the late 1970s and early 1980s. To the dismay of many educators, among them the Central Asian Russian teachers, the methodology described above still persists, and there is nothing in the party program for the near future heralding change (*Gazetai Muallimon*, October 26, 1985:1–7). The results of the 1979 census, which again showed the relative lag of Central Asians in the acquisition of the Russian language, once again triggered the discussion on teaching method and curriculum development (*Narodnoe Khoziaistvo SSSR v 1980 a*:24). The dramatic increase in the number of Uzbeks speaking Russian (49.3 percent) is incongruous and cannot be explained by available TRSL data.

The Central Asian Russian language teachers continue to improvise methods. Some, like the one developed by a Kazakh teacher, combined formal and non-formal educational activities. Classroom instruction was supplemented by listening to radio programs in Russian and broadcasting over the local radio station in that language. Students were required to join the Russian language clubs where they read newspapers printed in Russian and discussed the material with each other. Other gatherings, such as student parties and excursions during which students spoke only Russian and gave speeches on various topics, were encouraged. In all of these activities, the role of the teacher was to be that of the facilitator and a somewhat passive transmitter (Chandirli, 1972:83–88). To many people outside and inside the USSR, this method indeed looks innovative and refreshing. Most classes, however, are still conducted in the transmitter-reciprocal method where the teacher is the sole source of knowledge and information about the language.

Another innovation was the teaching of Russian in some of the kindergartens (*Russkii Iazyk v Natsional'noi Shkole*, 1972). But this program is not uniformly administered in the USSR. The amount of "Russian only" hours per year varies greatly from republic to republic. It is anticipated that the number of hours devoted to the Russian language in kindergartens will increase as part of the overall early education program envisioned in the 1985 Education Reform (*Gazetai Muallimon*, 1985:1–7).

It is difficult to assess the results of these programs in early teaching of the Russian language. The argument of A. K. Kanimetrov (former Minister of Education of Kirgiz SSR), who in 1972 convinced the USSR's Ministry of Education to accept his proposal for the teaching of Russian in the kindergartens, is interesting not so much for its appeal in the 1970s (it did not spread beyond a few republics), but for its being in harmony with the present educational policies of the USSR. Then, Kanimetrov argued, "there were about 100 different ethnic groups in the republic in 1970 and sometimes 7–12 different nationalities in the same classroom." The only language instruction that could be carried out, according to the former Kirgiz Minister, "was that of Russian, because this is the language in which most parents want their children to be taught." He went on to say that "those who studied Russian in kindergarten became the best students in later years and also were well adjusted" (*TS*, Novemer 10, 1972:4). It is hard to figure out how the Minister was able to establish this relationship between the learning of Russian language in kindergarten and the later achievement of these children. The 1985 Education Reform, although still far from implementation, does have personnel and educational explanations that are different from the Kirgiz Minister's apparently intuitive insights.

These proposals are apparently made with little consideration for their implementation. What is the purpose of non-Russians reading in Russian materials originally written in non-Russian languages? If the purpose is anything other than merely augmenting the student's stock of Russian words, it has never been articulated or demonstrated. If the proposal to teach Soviet literature—for Russian-speaking children this means Russian literature and a few pieces from Western sources, rarely anything by a non-Russian writer—is implemented, whatever is gained in Russian vocabulary is more than offset by the loss in understanding the literature, as well as the loss of aesthetic quality that often accompanies translations. More important, however, is the overwhelming evidence opposing such a policy on pedagogical grounds (UNESCO, 1952; Cazden; Cohen, 1975).

Depending on how one views the teaching of Russian as a second language in Central Asia, the program has been either a failure or a success. It has been successful in making, over the past fifty years (according to Soviet census data), one out of every three urbanites and one in ten ruralites able to speak some Russian. Many of these people speak Pidgin Russian.

But the TRSL program has not been successful if one compares it to similar programs elsewhere in the USSR. In this comparison, the proportion of Central Asians who are fluent in Russian falls below the average of other non-Russians with similar levels of competency in the Russian language. Almost all of those who have acquired some level of competency in the Russian language are fluent in their own mother tongues (Silver, 1976). Officially, this bilingualism is a desirable outcome of TRSL. However, this sentiment may not be similarly perceived by those who see in bilingualism a threat to the development of a genuine monolithic "Soviet culture," a culture that apparently has as a main component one language—most certainly the Russian language. These attitudes toward bilingualism have influenced the methodologies of second-language pedagogy in Central Asia.

As noted earlier, the practitioners of TRSL can be grouped into two general categories: those relying on "total Russian" environment—mainly Slavs—which forbids discussions about the mother tongue, and those relying on comparative grammar—mainly Central Asians—which require bilingual teachers and the knowledge of the learner's culture. At present, both of those methods are used in TRSL in Central Asia. The perennial problem of scarcity of qualified Russian teachers still exists, but it is expected to be ameliorated somewhat once the Education Reform of 1985 is put into practice. This refom also seeks to break up the vicious circle of incompetency, in which incompetent teachers train incompetent students to become incompetent teachers ad infinitum.

NOTES

1. Transliteration keys detailed in E. Allworth's edition of *Nationalities of the Soviet East: Publications and Writing Systems* (New York: Columbia University Press, 1971), have been used for the indigenous Central Asian languages.

2. This is an updated and expanded version of an article in *Slavic Review* 35, 3 (1976):443–62. I am grateful to Jamsheed Shorish for his help.

3. A. M. Dzhafarzoda, "Kratkaia Lingvisticheskaia Kharakteristika Azerbaidzhanskogo—Russkogo Dvuiazychiia," *RIILASH* No. 4 (1973):82–87. For a study of Soviet efforts in bilingualism, see D. E. Bartley, *Soviet Approaches to Bilingual Education* (Philadelphia: Center for Curriculum Development).

BIBLIOGRAPHY

Abdullaeva, M. 1971. "Zaboni Russiro Boz Behtar Omuzem," *Zanoni Tojikiston* (June):18.

Askarov, Iu. 1969. "Zaboni Duimi Modarii Mo. *Maorif v Madinivat*," (*MvM*), December 20:2.

Asori, V. 1966. "Zabodoni Fazilati Odamist." *Tojikistoni Soveti*, henceforth, *TS*, March 6:4.

Babaev, S. 1973. "O Prochinakh Nedochetov Russkoi Rechi Uchashchikhsia Karakaipakskoi Shkoly." *Russkii Iazyk v Natsional'noi Shkole*, No. 1:70–72.

Bartley, D. A. 1971. *Soviet Approaches to Bilingual Education*. Philadelphia: Center for Curriculum Development.

Bashakov, N. A. 1967. "O Sovremennom Sostoianii i Dal'neishem Sovershestovovanii Alfabita Dlia Tiurkikh Iazykov Narodov SSSR." *Voprosy Iazykoznaniia*, No. 5:33–46.

Besemeres, J. F. 1975. "Population Politics in the USSR." *Soviet Union* 2, Nos. 1 & 2.

Birashk, A. 1975. "Didari az Shuravi va Sukhani Chand dar Bara'i Amuzish va Parvarishi Shuravi." *Pavami Navin.* 2

Boitsova, A. F., and L. A. Varkovitskaia. 1952. "Pochemu Neobkhedim Predvaritel'nyi Ustnyi Kurs Russkogo Iazyka." *Russkii Iazyk v Shkole*, No. 3:66–69.

Carrére d'Encausse, H. 1980. *Decline of an Empire*. New York: Newsweek Books.

Cazden, C. 1973. "Problems for Education: Language as Curriculum Content and Learning Environment." *Daedlus* 102, 3:135.

Central Asian Review (CAR). 1953. "Tadzhikistan." Vol. 1, No. 1:43–44. 1957. Vol. 5, No. 1:38–40. 1954. Vol. 2, no. 2:187–89. 1961. "Organization of Education," Vol. 9, No. 1:27, 1965. Vol. 13, No. 4:310–22.

Chandirli, S. M. 1972. "Nasha Pochta." *Russkii Iazyk i Literatura v Azerbaidzhanskoi Shkole (RIILASH)*, No. 1:83–88.

Cohen, A. D. 1975. *A Sociolinguistic Approach to Bilingual Education: Experiment in American Southwest*. Rowley, Mass.: Newbury House.

Dmitrieva, I. M., ed. 1974. *Voprosy Metodiki Prepodavaniia Russkogo Iazyka v Uzbekskoi Shkole: Sbornik Statei*. Tashkent: "Uchitel'."

Dodoboev, R. 1975. "Vaz'iyati Ta'limi Zaboni Rusi va Tadbirhoi Behter Kardani On." *MvM*, April 5:1–2.

Dzhafarzoda, A. M. 1973. "Kratkai Lingvisticheskaia Kharakteristika Azerbaudzhan-skogo-Russkogo Dvuiazychiia." *RIILASH*, No. 4:82–87.

Gazetai Muallimon. 1985. "Programmai Partiiai Kommunistii Ittifogi Soveti." October 26:1–7.

Ghaniev, Gh. 1971. "Ba'zi Mas'alahoi Ta'limi Zaboni Rusi." *TS.* January 26:4, June 25:2.

Gibb, H.A.R. 1970. *The Arab Conquests in Central Asia.* London: James G. Forlong Fund.

Ioshonjonov, A., M. Shukurov, and M. Rahmanov. 1964. *Metodikai Ta'limi Zaboni Tojiki dar Maktabi Ibtedoi.* Dushanbe: Irfon 42–47.

Kanimetrov. A. K. 1972. "Zaboni Rusi Zaboni Man-Zaboni Mo." *TS*, November 10:4.

Karakulakov, V. V. 1968. "Dar Bara'i Tayyori Kardani Muallim." *MvM*, March 5:3.

Katz, Z., R. Rogers, and F. Harned. 1975. *Handbook of Major Soviet Nationalities.* New York: Free Press.

Kazakhstanskaia Pravda. 1956. March 27, quoted in *CAR*, 1957, Vol. 5, No. 1:39.

Khodoidodov, B. 1975. "Ba'ze Mas'alahoi Ta'limi Zabon va Adabiyoti Rus Dar Mak-tabhoi Tojiki." *MvM*, March 20:2.

King, Beatrice. 1936. *Changing Man: The Education and System of the U.S.S.R.* London: Victor Gollancz, Ltd.

Kissen, I. A. 1952. "O Razgovornykh Urokakh Bez Cheteniia i Pis'ma." *Russkii Iazyk v Shkole*, No. 3:61–62.

Kliueva, V. N. 1952. "Ustnyi Kurs v Programakh po Russkomu Iazyku Dlia Nerusskikh Shkol." *Russkii Iazyk v Shkole*, No. 2:77.

Kolasky, J. 1968. *Language Policy: Education in Soviet Ukraine.* Toronto: Peter Martin, 26.

Kommunist Tadzhikistana. 1956. April 5.

Komsomoli Tojikiston. 1973. February 7:4, 1974, January 20:4.

Lenin, V. I. 1968. Quoted in O. Shukurov. "Zaboni Lenini." *MvM*, March 5:2.

Lewis, E. G. 1972. *Multilingualism in the Soviet Union.* The Hague: Mouton, p. 181.

———. 1974. *Linguistics and Second Language Pedagogy: A Theoretical Study.* The Hague: Mouton, p. 58.

Liubana, B. S. 1968. "Mashghuliuyoti Amali." *MvM*, March 5:4.

Makhmudov. A. R. 1973. "Tverdye i Milagkie Soglasnye Russkogo Iazyka." *RIILASH*, No. 11:49–56.

Makhmudova, S. M. 1974. "Iz Opyt Ispol'zovaniia pri Izuchenii Russkogo Glagola v Uzbekshoi Shkole." In *Voprosy Metodiki Prepodavaniia Russkogo Iazyka v Uz-bekskoi Shkole i Sbornik Statei*, ed. I. M. Dmitrieva, pp. 6–20.

Mal'tseva, K. V. 1975. "Problemhoi Muhimmi Ta'limi Zaboni Rus." *MvM*, April 5:2; June 7:4; February 16:4; August 2:4.

Maorif va Madaniyat, MvM. 1968. March 10:4; March 30:3; April 6:1. 1970. May 19:4. 1971. November 23:1. 1974. September 10:4. 1975. February 16:4; June 7:4; August 2:4.

Ma'rufova, S. 1968. "Rohohi Takmili Tal'im." *MvM*, August 20:2.

Medlin, W. K., W. Cave, and F. Carpenter. 1971. *Education and Development in Central Asia: A Case Study on Social Change in Uzbekistan.* Leiden: E. J. Brill, 105.

Merelman, R. M. 1972. "The Adolescence of Political Socialization." *Sociology of Education* 45:134–66.

————. 1975. "Social Stratification and Political Socialization in Mature Industrial Societies." *Comparative Education Review* 19, 1:13j-j30.

Mokhov, A. 1952. "O Razgovernykh Urokakh." *Russkii Iazyk v Shkole*, No. 3:63–64.

Murtazoev, B. 1984. "Paivandi Maktab va Hayot." *Adabiyot va San'at*, February 23:4–5.

Nazarova, M. A. 1962. *Razvitie Richi Uchashchiskhsia v Sviazi s Izucheniem Russkogo Sintaksiasa v 7–8 Klassakh Turkmenskoi Shkoly.* Ashkabad: Turkmenskkoi gosudarstvennoe Ucheno Pedagogicheskoe Izdatel'stvo, 3–4.

Niyozmohammedov, B. 1970. *Zabonshinosi tojik.* Dushanbe: Donish.

Piatina, N. A. 1974. "Rabota nad Oshibkami na Urokakh Russkogo Iazyka v II-IV Klassakh Uzbekskoi Shkoly." In *Voprosy Metodiki Prepodavaniia Russkogo Iazyka v Uzbekskoi Shkole: Sbornik Statei*, ed. I. M. Dmitrieva, 33–39.

Pierce, R. 1960. *Russian Central Asia, 1867–1917.* Berkeley: University of California Press.

Pool, J. 1976. "Developing the Soviet Turkic Tongues: The Language of the Politics of Language." *Slavic Review* 35, 3:425–42.

Popova, G. I. 1973. "Rabota nad Ortografiei v Protsesse Usvoeniia Obshchei Leksiki Dlia Russkogo i Azerbaidzhanskogo Iazykov." *RIILASH*, No. 2:26.

Prewitt, K. 1975. "Some Doubts About Political Socialization Research." *Comparative Education Review* 19, 1:105–14.

Radzhabova, T. M. 1973. "Nekotorye Voprosy Prepodavaniia Russkogo Iazyka v Nachal'nykh Klassakh Azerbaidzhanskikh Shkol." *RIILASH*, No. 2:3–11.

Rahbari Donish. 1930. August-September:13, Arabic script.

Rashidov. S. 1975. "Zaboni Rusi-Zaboni Robita va Hamkori Millitho va Khelghoi Ittifoqi Soveti." *MvM*, November 27:1–3.

Rubenshtain, F. L. 1974. "Iz Opyta Primeneniia Diafil'mov na Urokakh Russkogo Iazyka i Literatury v VI Klasse Uzbekskoi Shkoly." In *Voprosy Metodiki Prepodavaniia Russkogo Iazyka v Uzbekskoi Shkole: Sbornik Statei*, ed. I. M. Dmitrieva, 107–14.

Rusakova, B. M. 1968. "Grammatikai Ta'rikhi Zaboni Rusi." *MvM*, March 5:3.

Russkii Iazyk i Literatura v Azerbaidzhanskoi Shkole. 1973. No. 8:5, No. 12:3.

Russkii Iazyk i Literatura v Natsional'noi Shkole. 1972. No. 1:77–79.

Sevost'ianova, T. E. 1968. "Khonishi Ifodanok-Kalidi Komiyobiho." *MvM*, March 5:2

Sharikova, L. Z. 1971. "K Voprosy Izucheniia Katergorii Vida Tiurkoizzychnoi Shkole." *Voprosy Teorii i Metodi Izycheniia Russkogo Iazyka(glagoi).* Kazan: Ministerstvo Proveshcheniia RSFSR Kazanskii Gosudarstvenny i Pedagogicheskii Institut:3–26.

Shneidman, N. N. 1973. *Literature and Ideology in Soviet Education.* Toronto: D. C. Heath.

Shorish, M. M. 1981. "Dissent of the Muslims: Soviet Central Asia in the 1980s." *Nationalities Papers* 19, 2:184–94.

————. 1984. "Planning by Decree: The Soviet Language Policy in Central Asia." *Language Problems and Language Planning* 8, 1:35–49.

Shukurov, M. R. 1957. *Revlutsivai madani dar Tojikiston.* Stalinabad: Irfon.

Shukurov, O. Sh. 1968. "Zaboni Lenini." *MvM*, March 5:2.

Silver, B. 1976. "Bilingualism and Maintenance of the Mother Tongue in Soviet Central Asia." *Slavic Review* 35, 3:406–24.

Sovetskaia Kirgizia. 1956. April 18.

Tarzimanov, F. V. 1952. "O Razgovernykh Urokakh v Pervom Klasse Nerusskoi Shkole." *Russkii Iazyk v Shkole*, No. 3:65–66.

Tojieva, B. 1968. "Ta'limi Zaboni Rusi dar Tojikiston." *MvM*, January 16:1.

Tojikistoni Soveti (TS). 1968, April 2:1. 1972, November 10:4. 1975, August 3:4; August 5:4; November 7:4; November 18:4.

Tsentral'noe Statisticheskoe Upravlene pri Sovete Ministrov SSSR. 1981. *Narodnoe Khoziaistvo SSSR v 1980 Godu*. Moscow: Finansy i Statistika.

UNESCO. 1952. *Report of the Mission to Afghanistan*. Paris: UNESCO.

———. 1968. "The Use of Vernacular Languages in Education: The Report of the UNESCO Meeting of Specialists." *Readings in the Sociology of Language*, ed. J. Fishman. The Hague: Mouton.

Uspenskaia, L. V. 1975. "Roli Zaboni Modari dar Omuzishi Zaboni Rusi." *MvM*, April 5:2.

Uzbek SSR, Narodnoe Komissariat Prosveshcheniia. 1939. *Instruktsiia o Provedenii Soveshcheniia Uchitelei v Avgusta 1939*. Tashkent: Izdat. Narkompros:13–16.

Valitov, A. M. 1952. "Nasushchnye Zadachi Pervonachel'nogo Obucheniia Russkomu Iazyku v Natsional'noi Shkole." *Russkii Iazyk v Shkole*, No. 2:67.

Wimbush, S. E., and A. Alexiev. 1980. *The Ethnic Factors in the Soviet Armed Forces: Preliminary Findings*. Santa Monica, Calif.: Rand Corp.

Yusofbekov, R. 1974. "Talaboti Zamon va Tadbirhoi Minba'd Behtar Namudani Ta'limi Zabon va Adabiyoti Tojik." *MvM*, January 10:2–3j.

Zakharova, E. V. 1974. "Tvorcheskii Diktant v Shkole s Tadzhikskim Iazykom Obucheniia." In *Voprosy Metodiki Prepodavaniia Russkogo Iazyka v Uzbekskoi Shkole: Sbornik Statei*, ed. I. M. Dmitrieva, 47–48.

Zhuravleya, A. 1968. "Roli Zabon va Adabiyoti Rus dar Tarbiai Kommunistii Khonandagon." *MvM*, June 4:4.

Miguel Siguan

BILINGUAL EDUCATION IN SPAIN

A MULTILINGUAL COUNTRY

Spanish, or Castilian, is the official language of Spain and the mother tongue of the majority of its inhabitants. It is also the language through which the political and administrative unity of the Spanish nation has been established. Nevertheless, other languages in Spanish territory continue to be the mother tongue of a considerable portion of the population. Although official data are lacking, the approximate figures given below suggest the importance of these languages.

In Catalonia (population 6 million), a region located in the northeastern part of the Iberian Peninsula, the language spoken is Catalan, a language derived from Latin as are Spanish, French, and Italian. Fifty percent of the population of Catalonia have it as their mother tongue, and another 30 percent speak or at least understand it. A variety of Catalan, sometimes called Valencian, is spoken in Valencia, located south of Catalonia on the Mediterranean coast; other local varieties are spoken in Valenica, located south of Catalonia on the Mediterranean coast; other local varieties are spoken in the Balearic Islands (population five hundred thousand). In both cases, between 50 and 70 percent of the population can be considered to speak Catalan as their native language, although it is usually restricted to purely family use. Galician, another Romance language, similar to Portuguese, is spoken in Galicia (population 3 million), in the northwestern part of the peninsula. Galician is spoken or understood by 80 percent of the population, although it is used in predominantly rural and family settings. Lastly, Basque (or Euskera) is spoken in the Basque provinces (Euskadi). It is perhaps

Translated from Spanish by Lee Puig-Antich.

the oldest European language spoken today and has no known relationship to any of them. Twenty-five percent of the 2 million inhabitants of the Spanish Basque provinces currently speak Basque, as do 10 percent of the population in neighboring Navarre (population four hundred and fifty thousand).

Since the reestablishment of a democratic government in Spain, this linguistic pluralism has been reflected in an educational system that takes the various minority languages into consideration and that can be characterized as extremely liberal and progressive. This system is described in this chapter, but first some information on the historical background and sociocultural components of the situation will be presented.

HISTORICAL ROOTS AND THE CONTEMPORARY SITUATION

The occupation of the Iberian Peninsula by the Romans at the beginning of our era (second century B.C.) resulted in the substitution of Latin for the indigenous languages, except in the western part of the Pyrenees, where Basque, an ancient language of unknown origin, continued to be spoken. Centuries later, the disintegration and transformation of Latin into the Romance languages coincided with the invasion of the peninsula by the Arabs (tenth century). The Christians were left in control of only a narrow, mountainous strip on the northern coast of the peninsula, from where they launched the Reconquest, protracted over the next five centuries. In this mountainous strip, several languages descended from Latin were crystallized and ultimately reduced to three: Galician in the west; Castilian in the central area; and Catalan in the east. The development and later expansion of these three languages were determined by the political fortunes of the groups of people who spoke them and by the success of those people in the struggle to reclaim territory from the Arabs.

In the thirteenth century, the linguistic map of the Iberian Peninsula was already definitively fixed. The Basque enclave did not constitute a political entity, and even though Basque was maintained, it did not expand. Catalonia conquered Valencia and the Balearic Islands, and planted its language there. Galicia did not succeed in establishing political power, but as a result of demographic pressure, its language expanded southward to what is now Portugal. The Castilian nucleus, situated in the central part of the peninsula, advanced steadily toward the south, spreading throughout the southern half of the peninsula.

From the twelfth to the fourteenth centuries, the three languages experienced literary development. Galician was largely limited to lyric poetry in the twelfth century; however, during the thirteenth and fourteenth centuries, both Catalan and Castilian inspired literary movements of extremely high quality, which were among the most outstanding in Europe.

In the fourteenth century, the equilibrium between Catalan and Castilian was broken. The Kingdom of Aragon, which included Catalonia, Valencia, and the Balearic Islands, was united with the Kingdom of Castile. Although its autonomy was respected, Aragon lost its political initiative. The discovery of America and the imperial efforts of Charles I and Phillip II assured the ascendancy of Castilian. Catalonian literature consequently entered into a decline, and the official use of Catalan waned.

In the eighteenth century, with the establishment of the Bourbon kings on the Spanish throne, the French model of a strongly centralized, linguistically unified state was adopted. Languages other than Castilian were actively repressed; their use declined and was progressively restricted to family and rural settings. In the mid-nineteenth century, however, the Romantic movement burst forth with a glorification of ancient cultures and nationalities. The movement was strongly felt in regions that had preserved their indigenous languages, but each area exhibited distinct characteristics depending on its history and, in particular, its socioeconomic situation.

In Catalonia, the revival of Catalan as a literary language occurred simultaneously with a substantial economic and industrial development which transformed Catalonia into the most advanced region in Spain. The middle class supporting this development promoted political *catalanismo* as a way of safeguarding this progress against the central government. At the beginning of the twentieth century, Catalonia acquired a few years of political autonomy. Some years later, with the advent of the Republic, the experiment was repeated, oriented this time from the Left. In the meantime, a very important literary and cultural renaissance took place, and the language was modernized (grammar, orthography, lexicon).

In the remaining Catalan territories (Valencia and the Balearics), which underwent neither industrial development nor the arousal of political consciousness, the linguistic and cultural movement produced other kinds of effects, as it also did outside the Spanish borders in French Catalonia (incorporated into France in the eighteenth century) and in the Occitan-speaking areas of southern France.

As in Catalonia, considerable industrial development also occurred in the Basque provinces, but the middle class that emerged identified itself only slightly with Basque nationalism. Because both a literary tradition and cultural institutions were lacking, the literary and cultural rebirth was weak. Thus, despite the nationalism which has been active since the beginning of this century and the political autonomy achieved during the Republican era, there is little hope that Basque will again become the first language of the majority of the population.

Finally, in Galicia there was neither industrial nor economic development; hence, Galicia continues to be a poor region whose population is forced to emigrate in large numbers. The rebirth of Galician was exclusively literary; it did not gain political strength, and it has remained a purely rural language.

The regime of General Francisco Franco, established at the end of the Spanish Civil War (1939), exalted national unity, and not only eliminated the autonomous regions but also suppressed the use of languages other than Spanish. Although definite progress was made in this respect—going from actual persecution in the first years to broad tolerance in the last—the glorification of Spanish unity continued, together with distrust of those who defended linguistic and national pluralism. The latter were, of course, always found among the most active elements of anti-Franco opposition.

With the establishment of the democratic government after the death of General Franco, this situation changed completely. The new Spanish Constitution (1978) affirms that Castilian—or Spanish—is the official language of the country, but that the large number of languages existing on Spanish soil is a common good that must be preserved and encouraged.

At the same time, the Spanish nation was organized into a group of autonomous regions, each with a relatively broad statute of autonomy, providing for a parliament and a government, and in the autonomous regions with a local language, for the possibility of that language attaining official status along with the national official language, Spanish. Since the autonomous regions administer the educational system, the statute of autonomy makes provision for the local language to occupy an important place in education also.

Even before the statutes of autonomy went into effect, the Spanish Ministry of Education enacted the Decree on Bilingualism (1979), which established that in the areas with their own language, all levels and grades of Basic General Education [*Enseñanza General Basica*] ages six to fourteen should include at least three hours of instruction in this language per week and that this minimum could be increased in schools that requested it.

Throughout the transitional stage, from the adoption of the Constitution (1978) to the implementation of the statutes of autonomy, the Decree on Bilingualism was the pivot around which all the linguistic changes in the educational system revolved. Afterwards (1981), when the statutes of autonomy had already been put into effect and the regional governments had therefore taken over responsibility for the educational system in their respective areas, the Ministry of Education issued some recommendations on the subject, which, in the section of interest here, reads as follows:

As has already been stated, in the territories with their own languages, the objective proposed by the school system must be that the pupils possess a full command of both languages upon completion of the compulsory program of education. This means that they must be able to use the languages correctly and effectively in any situation and for any purpose.

To attain such an objective, the following measures are necessary:

1. The program at all levels must include instruction in both languages to the extent needed to ensure success.

2. Each language must, in addition, be used as a medium of instruction in the school curriculum. The time starting and the degree to which each language is used as a language of instruction must be determined in each case according to a set of factors bearing upon both learning and linguistic knowledge, for example, the extent to which each language is used in the surrounding environment. The diversity of these factors allows for considerable flexibility in this regard, provided that the ultimate objective of full command of both languages is maintained.

3. If, as a result of this flexibility, an area should contain schools with different linguistic models, then parents shall be able to choose among them insofar as possible.

4. In principle, education shall be initiated in the pupil's mother tongue, with instruction in the other language being introduced subsequently. However, where feasible, and subject to parental approval, the mother tongue can be used to introduce the other language from the beginning of schooling. In such an event, pupils will, in all likelihood, be acquainted with both languages by the second year of Basic General Education.

5. The attention given to the mother tongue does not imply the establishment of a dual educational system based on the linguistic origins of the pupils. Any primary school must be prepared to admit children irrespective of their mother tongue.

6. Bilingual education must not neglect the fact that during their schooling, pupils also need to acquire a foreign language, as required by law.

7. It is necessary to carry out research projects which will permit objective evaluation of different teaching and organizational approaches for attaining mastery of both languages. Such studies must reflect the differences arising from real-life situations.

8. In areas where the language spoken by the indigenous population is different from that of the autonomous community to which it belongs, democratic principle demands that the ultimate goal—bilingualism—not be forgotten, and that to achieve this goal, it is necessary to proceed with tact and flexibility during the course of both short- and long-term planning.

CATALONIA

Some of the characteristics that make Catalan a unique and privileged case within the panorama of European minority languages have already been indicated. Catalan is a language that is supported by an old and significant literary and academic tradition. It is completely standardized, with a system of lexical, grammatical, and orthographic norms accepted without question, and it can currently rely on strong political backing to ensure its official use, as well as on broad popular support. However, this extremely favorable situation is circumscribed by the simultaneous existence of Spanish and the greater influence of the Spanish language. This occurs not only because Spanish is the official state language, and, hence, the language of greatest political and economic power, but also because the number of Spanish speakers both within and outside Spain is much greater than the number of Catalan speakers.

In spite of the efforts of the autonomous government of Catalonia to foster Catalan culture through the mass media, the volume of written and audiovisual materials produced and consumed in Catalonia (books, magazines, newspapers, radio and television programs, films) is much greater in Spanish than in Catalan.

There is yet another factor. As a result of its industrial and economic development, Catalonia has attracted immigrants from other regions, especially from the south of Spain, in such numbers that today nearly half of its population was born outside Catalonia. The great majority of these immigrants are, of course, Spanish-speaking.

It is well known that when a politically and socially strong language exists alongside of a minority and, hence, weaker language in the same region, a language hierarchy known as diglossia is usually produced. In Catalonia, however, the social stratification of the two languages is unique. In relation to Spanish, Catalan is a minority language, hence weaker, and in a subordinate position. But at the same time, it is the language of a large part of the economic and intellectual middle class, as well as the language of local political power. Spanish, on the other hand, is the language of immigrants and the lower strata of the population. That is, even if Spanish is, in principle, the stronger language, from certain perspectives it is also the less prestigious. This situation might be characterized as double or cross-diglossia. However, the fact that the people of Catalonia speak different mother tongues has not separated the two communities along linguistic lines. Despite the extraordinary changes that have occurred in recent years in the status of the two languages, Catalonians have remained united, and the changes have been assimilated practically effortlessly.

Since the Generalitat (Autonomous Government) of Catalonia (1931–36) took over the administration of the education system, it has publicly affirmed that its express objective is that all pupils will have mastered both languages and will be able to use them effectively by the end of basic schooling. The government acknowledges that this objective can be attained through school models that differ with respect to the presence of each language in the instructional program. On the other hand, it has refused to allow different school models to be established on the basis of pupils' linguistic origins. That is, it has not permitted the establishment of different schools for children whose mother tongue is Catalan and those whose mother tongue is Spanish. Any educational institution in Catalonia must be able to accept children from either language background. When the dominant school language is different from the new pupils' mother tongue, the school must initially teach the children in their native language and introduce them only gradually to the second one.

As far as attainment of the objectives is concerned, until the change in regime, instruction had been given exclusively in Spanish. Hence, the efforts of the Generalitat since assuming responsibility have been directed toward the following goals:

1. To ensure that the minimum requirement for Catalan (three to five hours a week) is fulfilled at all levels of instruction in all schools. Subsequently, this requirement was broadened to mean not only the teaching of the Catalan language, but also the instruction, in Catalan, of some of the school subjects.

2. To assist those educational establishments that want to set up the instructional program partly or primarily in Catalan, offering them not only the administrative means to do so, but also other kinds of encouragement. The Catalonian government has also fostered the production of teaching materials in Catalan, which in turn has stimulated the carrying out of pedagogical experiments, etc.

Despite some important historical precedents for instruction in, and of, Catalan, the process of change initiated by the government has encountered numerous obstacles. The first and most serious obstacle—as is usually the case when a change in the linguistic basis of education is attempted—has been with the teaching personnel. For various reasons, the number of teachers born outside Catalonia and who therefore did not know Catalan either at all or only superficially was very high. Even those born in Catalonia who could speak Catalan had insufficient knowledge and no experience in teaching it. In order to augment knowledge of the language and adapt it to instructional needs, the institutes of educational science of the three Catalonian universities inaugurated a program of Catalan courses for teachers who were already employed, which by 1983 had reached more than fifteen thousand trainees. The problem has been steadily declining, especially with respect to the future. This is because it is now necessary to demonstrate some knowledge of Catalan in order to enroll in primary and secondary teaching programs. Furthermore, the seven teachers' colleges (Escuelas de Formacíon del Profesonado) for Basic General Education offer their students an adequate knowledge of Catalan, and some of them even use Catalan as the instructional language in the majority of courses.

A major difficulty at the time of implementing the new language policy was the extraordinary variety in the linguistic background of the pupils and their families, since, in general, the school population of Catalonia is distributed equally between Catalan-speaking and Spanish-speaking children. This proportion varies greatly according to location—from areas and schools where Catalan-speakers are completely predominant, to places dominated by Spanish-speakers. This demands the use of quite diverse teaching approaches, and, consequently, the same school program can produce different linguistic results according to the location of the school.

Finally, in order to explain the changes in educational organization which have taken place to date, it is necessary to recall that in Catalonia, as in the whole of Spain, two types of schools exist: public schools, supported and administered by the government (in this case by the government of Catalonia), in which the teachers are government employees and the programs established by the educational authorities are strictly adhered to; and private schools, supported by parents, but subsidized with public funds, in which broad administrative autonomy is maintained despite being subject to inspection by educational authorities. As a result, linguistic practices vary more in private schools than in public shools. It was the private schools which, even before the advent of the democratic government, introduced the Catalanization of instruction and which remain in the forefront of this process today. Conversely, some private schools are solidly founded on the Spanish language by the express desires of their supporters. In public schools, on the other hand, a greater fidelity to prevailing governmental directives understandably occurs.

Types of Educational Institutions According to Languages

As a consequence of the current policy, teaching establishments may be classified into three main types or models according to language of instruction:

1. Schools with instruction mainly in Catalan (Catalan schools).

2. Schools with instruction mainly in Spanish.

3. Schools with instruction in both languages in varying degrees.

A typology of bilingual schools must reflect not only the language of instruction but also the internal and external language of communication used by the school, the cultural implications of the school's linguistic practices, and the habitual and family language of the pupils. But at least as far as Catalonia is concerned, classification by language of instruction highlights the fundamental differences, while the remaining features fulfill a complementary role.

Schools with Instruction Mainly in Catalan. In these schools, Catalan is the medium of instruction for most or all of the school subjects, with the sole exception of courses in Spanish language and literature. In the majority of these schools, both internal and external communication also takes place primarily in Catalan, and many activities attempt to integrate the pupils into specifically Catalonian traditions and culture.

Public schools of this type are typically found in rural areas where a Catalan-speaking student body predominates, while private schools tend to be found in urban areas, where they attract Catalan-speaking families eager to promote their language. Nevertheless, all "Catalan" schools have a small percentage of pupils whose family language is Spanish. This type of school also exists in areas where Spanish-speaking pupils predominate, although such schools are few and somewhat experimental.

Although no official data are available, it is estimated that as of the 1983–84 academic year schools of this type admitted between 20 and 25 percent of the school population in Catalonia.

Schools with Instruction Mainly in Spanish. These schools remain faithful to the traditional linguistic model of instruction in Spanish, even though, as required by current law, they offer the minimum amount of instruction of and in Catalan (at least five hours weekly in all grades). A significant number of Catalan-speaking pupils attend these schools. Since most of the schools have more Spanish-speakers, however, Spanish becomes the interstudent language of communication. With respect to the schools' internal and external communication, both languages, or mainly Spanish, are used. It is estimated that schools of this type currently admit between 50 and 60 percent of the school population of Catalonia.

Schools with Instruction in Both Languages. This category includes schools whose language programs lie somewhere between the two previous types but which nevertheless differ considerably among themselves. They comprise: (1) schools whose objective is to furnish a real bilingual education, with the initial schooling differentiated according to the family language of the pupils, and the school subjects subsequently divided between the two languages; (2) schools basically similar to Type 2, with instruction mainly in Spanish, but which consider the minimum legal requirement for Catalan to be insufficient and therefore give it a larger place in the curriculum and in cultural and extracurricular activities; (3) schools that are gradually becoming "Catalan" schools but have not yet finished this process; and (4) schools that have not arrived at a consensus concerning language policy, so that the presence of the two languages reflects a compromise or simply a lack of agreement. Although these schools spring from diverse motives, the intermediate character of this linguistic practice—more Catalan than in Type 2 but less than in Type 1—corresponds to the middle position also occupied by Catalan in the administrative and extracurricular activities of these schools. Likewise, pupils attending them are recruited from both Catalan-speaking and Spanish-speaking families. It is estimated that schools of this type admit between 20 and 25 percent of the school population.

After Basic General Education

The period of common instruction for the whole population ends at age fourteen. From then on, pupils can choose between vocational and academic programs, the latter of which lead to the university. The schools offering these programs could be described in general as following the same guidelines and corresponding to the same types indicated above for basic education, although Catalan occupies a greater place in the academic program than in the vocational.

In both programs, however, teachers frequently feel free to use the language that they prefer or the language in which they best express themselves, it being assumed that their students, after having finished basic education, are capable of using both languages. At the university level, this assumption becomes the general rule.

Since the establishment of autonomy in Catalonia, the three universities located there have declared their support for Catalan culture and consider Catalan the first of their official languages within a legal framework that permits the existence of both. The university assumes that all its members understand both languages, even if not everyone can speak them, and that all members of the university have the right to use either language in any given circumstance. As a result of this policy, it is estimated that almost half the university courses are now given in Catalan and nearly a third of the doctoral theses and other scientific papers are written in that language. Administrative documents and information are usually produced in Catalan but may also appear in the other language. At any formal or informal university gathering, participants speak the language that they prefer, that is, the one they normally use, on the assumption that the other people present can understand them. This assumption is usually correct since everyone at the university who has Catalan as his or her first language is also able to speak Spanish, and everyone whose first language is Spanish understands Catalan even if he or she does not speak it. The only exceptions are the students and professors who have recently come to the university from outside Catalonia.

Evaluation of the Results

Linguistic Competence. As early as 1970, before the change of regime, the Institute of Educational Sciences (Instituto de Ciencias de la Educación) of the University of Barcelona had begun, under the newly enacted Education Law (Ley de Educación), an experimental bilingual education project in various schools, which was based on the following approach: children would learn to read and write in their mother tongue but would be introduced to the other language at the same time, so that thereafter they could share the same classrooms and the same lessons. Subsequently, both Catalan and Spanish would be used as languages of instruction, with the subjects in each yearly sequence being divided between the two languages. The results showed that the introduction of Catalan as a language of instruction considerably improved the pupils' competence in Catalan and did not adversely affect either their scholastic achievement or their competence in Spanish.

Since then, various attempts have been made to evaluate the results of the changes introduced, although in general they have been limited to assessing the linguistic outcomes. The most recent, and also the most ambitious and scientifically rigorous, of these studies was carried out by the Bureau for the Teaching of Catalan (Servei d'ensenyamente del catala) of the Catalonian Department of Education (Departamento de Enseñanza) and coordinated by N. Garolera. Its purpose was to evaluate the competence in Catalan and Spanish of the pupils in Catalonia who were studying the fourth year of Basic General Education (average age ten) in 1982, and who were the first to have received some type of education in Catalan since the beginning of their schooling.

The survey included fifteen hundred pupils from fifty-four schools, chosen so as to constitute a representative sample of schools in the region, both because of their location (according to areas having greater or lesser numbers of Catalan speakers) and the amount of attention given to Catalan. The latter was calculated according to the language of instruction at each school, the mother tongue of the teachers and pupils, and the language used in the daily operation of the school. It was then possible to classify the schools into three types based on the importance given to Catalan. These types were similar to the ones described here previously. By means of a questionnaire distributed to pupils and parents, each child was evaluated in terms of a set of factors that might affect the results, for example, the geographic origin of the parents, their social level, the language used in the home, the linguistic environment within and outside the family, and the attitudes toward each language. At the same time, each child was evaluated by the teachers and assigned a score for general learning capacity.

Lastly, linguistic competence was assessed by two parallel series of tests, in Catalan and Spanish, respectively, and consisting of oral comprehension (words, texts), reading comprehension (words, texts), oral expresssion (vocabulary, communicative skill), written expression (composition), interferences (lexical, morphosyntactic), spelling, and phonetics. The reliability and statistical consistency of the tests were checked, and a later analysis confirmed that both series were parallel as measurement instruments.

The results obtained can be summarized as follows:

The pupils achieved greater mastery of Spanish than of Catalan in the sample as a whole and in each of the groups comprising it, with the sole exception of children whose mother tongue was Catalan and who attended very "Catalanized" schools, referred to earlier as Type A schools. Even in this case, however, the level of competence in Spanish was high.

The statistical dispersion in the results obtained for Spanish is much less than that shown by Catalan. This means that, while most Catalan-speaking children acquire an acceptable command of Spanish, a sizable group of Spanish-speaking pupils makes little progress in Catalan. This is especially apparent in oral expression, for almost all Catalan-speaking children are capable of expressing themselves in Spanish, although the opposite does not prove to be the case.

The dispersion in the results for Spanish correlates directly with the general learning capacity of the pupils and only slightly with other variables in the sample, such as mother tongue, linguistic environment, or type of school. This means that in Catalonia neither linguistic origin nor the type of school attended (in terms of the amount of Catalan used) has a significant effect on the probability that pupils will achieve good command of Spanish. On the other hand, the dispersion in the results for Catalan is related to the language, the linguistic environment of the subjects, and the type of school attended. Only when the influence of these factors is eliminated do the outcomes obtained for Catalan show any correlation with learning aptitude.

The conclusions of the study just summarized can also be stated another way: In predominantly Catalan schools where Catalan is the main language of instruction and where the majority of teachers and pupils speak Catalan as their first language, pupils whose mother tongue is Catalan acquire a high level of proficiency in Catalan as well as a satisfactory level in Spanish. Spanish-speaking pupils, who attend these schools in much fewer numbers, also acquire a satisfactory knowledge of Spanish and Catalan. In contrast, in schools where the Spanish language and Spanish-speakers predominate, Catalan-speaking pupils maintain Catalan and acquire good oral and written skills in Spanish, but the Spanish-speakers, even though they come to understand written and spoken Catalan, are generally not able to use it actively, either orally or in writing.

Scholastic Achievement. In an educational system in which two languages are used, it is necessary to examine not only the results pertaining to the competence achieved in each language, but also the influence of the dual language situation on the results of the school learning process. As indicated earlier, until now no rigorous studies on this subject have been carried out in Catalonia—an omission that indeed merits some comment.

Let us consider first the pupils whose mother tongue is Catalan. For a long time these children were taught exclusively in Spanish, a situation that led to vigorous protests on the part of some Catalan educators. At the well-known

Seminar on Education and Bilingualism organized by the International Bureau of Education (Bureau International d'Education) in Luxembourg in 1928, R. Gali, one of the main driving forces behind educational reform in Catalonia, joined the chorus of those who condemned bilingual education or, more precisely, education in a language different from the mother tongue. Gali attributed to it not only negative effects on intellectual development, which was the theory advocated by Saers, but also on moral development. Today we are more cautious in assessing the possible consequences of this experience, for we know that they depend on many factors. In any case, it is obvious that with appropriate teaching techniques, Catalan-speaking children can be educated in their own language without suffering adverse effects, and that, in fact, the results will be favorable. What remains to be investigated is whether these pupils, all social and pedagogical factors being equal, obtain better school results than Catalan-speakers who continue to receive most of their education in Spanish.

The most important problem is posed by pupils whose mother tongue is Spanish and who are taught mainly in Catalan. The available data indicate that in these cases no unfavorable outcomes occur in scholastic achievement. However, until now Spanish-speaking pupils who are educated in Catalan are not only fewer in number, but are also usually from schools with high-quality instruction, where education in Catalan is of a somewhat experimental nature. It is well known that any innovation in pedagogical practice can be successful, at least initially, simply owing to the enthusiasm of the people carrying out the innovation. In order to obtain conclusive results, education in Catalan needs to be more widespread, and broader, more systematic evaluative studies must be conducted. In analyzing the results, it will have to be remembered that there are more Spanish-speaking pupils among the lower social strata of Catalonia, and their greater incidence of school failure upon receiving their education in Catalan could be due, above all, to their social background, which may hinder them even if they receive a monolingual education in Spanish—and this deficiency could be worsened by a change in language. As we know, a number of contemporary studies purport to show that identical systems of bilingual education may have quite different effects according to the social and cultural level of pupils for whom it is provided.

Outlook

To the extent that the current situation continues—that is, the existence of an autonomous government that supports Catalan nationalism and in which the political parties agree as to language policy—one would expect the presence of Catalan in the educational system to be strengthened and progressively broadened, although without abandoning the educational goal of attaining comparable skill in each language. However, one is led to believe that the progress of Catalan will be slower from now on since a large part of the population of Catalonia speaks Spanish as its mother tongue and customary language. In addition, the families and schools most interested in education in Catalan have already seen a number of their aspirations fulfilled. What remains to be seen is whether the future progress of Catalan will increase the number of truly bilingual schools, or whether the present dichotomy between primarily Spanish-language schools and primarily Catalan-language schools will persist. What does seem evident is that even if the latter situation continues, the school system will not produce a split in the Catalonian population along linguistic lines.

VALENCIA

In Valencia and the Balearic Islands (Majorca, Minorca, and Ibiza), various dialects of Catalan—Valencian, Majorcan, Minorcan, Ibizan—have been spoken since the thirteenth century. However, in these places the relationship between the local language and the official Spanish language is very different from the situation in Catalonia.

There is one section of the Valencian region where Catalan has never been spoken. In the remaining area, although the language achieved brilliance in the Middle Ages, the cultural and literary renaissance of the past century was hardly noticed, nor was it accompanied by a political movement pressing for autonomy. The linguistic situation was therefore diglossic, with Spanish as the strong, literary language and Catalan as the rural, family-based language. Only during the struggle against Franco was a certain awareness of the cultural roots of the indigenous language produced. This awareness had limited effects, first because it was restricted to a few university groups, and, above all, because the identification of the local language with Catalan seemed to suggest that a condition of cultural dependency had been established with respect to Barcelona, the capital of Catalonia and center of Catalan influence—and this would be detrimental to the Valencian sense of identity. Taking advantage of this feeling, certain political groups fostered "Valencianism," as opposed to "Catalanism." The linguistic consequence was an attempt to standardize Valencian and to include rules, particularly orthographic ones, which were distinct from Catalan norms. The effort met with little success, and gradually the opinion that Valencian and Catalan were the same language despite superficial variations gained ground. Nevertheless, these disputes and the political controversies arising from them slowed the development of education in Valencia, so that it was not until 1983–84 that the autonomous government of Valencia was able to propose the teaching of the Valencian language in schools and to begin training courses for teachers. For some time, however, there have also been several private attempts at instruction not only of, but also in, Valencian. Thus, it is reasonable to assume that the revival of the language in Valencian education will follow a path similar to the one taken in Catalonia, but at a much slower pace.

THE BALEARIC ISLANDS

Catalan has been used chiefly in domestic and rural settings in the Balearics, even though the last century witnessed something of a literary and cultural renaissance. The linguistic situation can be characterized as diglossic, although distinctive traits can be found on each island. Minorca exhibits the highest cultural level and the greatest literary use of the local language, whereas Ibiza, until a few years ago, had remained at an extremely primitive level with a high rate of illiteracy. These three islands, however, have become centers for international tourism. This change has affected the language situation in that the knowledge of foreign languages, especially English, is now highly valued.

Unlike the situation in Valencia, there has never been any doubt in the Balearics that the native language, despite the local variations, is Catalan. Neither has there been an excessive distrust of the cultural capital, Barcelona—and if this feeling has occurred, it has not posed a problem. Given these conditions, the autonomous government of the Balearic Islands has had no difficulty in winning compliance with the legal requirements concerning the teaching of Valencian (the previously mentioned Decree on Bilingualism of 1979). The difficulty that has arisen has been due to the relative lack of interest shown by the autonomous government in this subject and, in the final analysis, by the people affected by it.

The currently available data for the school year 1982–83 show that 50 percent of the pupils in Basic General Education (ages six to fourteen) receive the minimum three hours a week of Catalan instruction required by law. The remainder either receive less than the minimum or no Catalan instruction at all. In the vocational and university-preparatory programs, the ratio is even more unfavorable.

Here as everywhere, the major obstacle is the lack of teachers qualified to undertake the new kind of education. As in Catalonia, the Institute of Educational Sciences has concerned itself with offering training courses to teachers, which so far have been taken by nearly half the teachers in the islands. In addition, the Teachers' College (Escuela de Formacion) sees to it that the new teachers know Catalan so that they may teach it. This permits us to predict that the situation will undergo change, albeit slowly, and that eventually all pupils in the Balearics will receive sufficient Catalan instruction.

Some experimental attempts to use Catalan as an instructional language also exist, but as of now, neither the autonomous government nor the population in general seems interested in expanding them. The ubiquitous tourists and the appeal of foreign languages may explain this diminished interest in mother-tongue instruction. Only at the university do we find any attempt to strengthen the use of Catalan in teaching, and these efforts are conerned with university-level education.

THE BASQUE PROVINCES (EUSKADI)

Although Basque nationalists consider that the five territories of Guipuzcoa, Biscay, Alava, Navarre, and the French Pays Basque constitute an indissoluble entity, here we will treat the Spanish Basque region (Biscay, Alava, and Guipuzcoa) and Navarre separately since these areas comprise two autonomous territories, each with its own government, within the framework of the Spanish nation. Only brief reference will be made to the French Pays Basque, included within France.

As previously mentioned, the Basque language is very old. It is probably the oldest language in Europe, and it has resisted every type of invasion, and political and cultural annexation. Nevertheless, the penetration of Spanish and French into its historical territory has been powerful, although unequally distributed, as shown by the figures in the accompanying tabulation:

Basque speakers (in thousands)

Area	Population	Basque Speakers	Percentage
Guipuzcoa	682	307	45
Biscay	1,152	174	15
Alava	238	18	8
Basque provinces	2,072	449	25
Navarre	483	53	11
French Pays Basque	227	78	34

Source: M. Siguan, ed., *Lenguas y educación*, University of Barcelona, 1983, p. 23.

When a nationalist movement emerged in the nineteenth century during the industrialization of the Basque provinces, the Basque language was, of course, strengthened as a symbol of nationality. Its situation was so precarious, however, that few thought it could once again become the common language of the Basques. Throughout the centuries, Basque had scarcely been nurtured from a literary or academic standpoint, nor had it been unified and, hence, standardized. As we have seen, the number of speakers was small, and, unlike Catalonia, where there had always been many bilinguals, in the Basque provinces the contrary occurred. Those who spoke Spanish had lost the use of Basque, while those who still spoke Basque lived in isolated, rural districts and did not know Spanish. The proposal that the majority of the Spanish-speaking population learn Basque seemed to demand the impossible.

But during the years of struggle against Franco, Basque nationalism regarded the language not only as a symbol of national identity but also as the necessary condition for attaining cultural identity. In order to achieve this objective, it was necessary to carry out a great educational effort directed toward the younger generations, since the adults—including militants from the nationalist movement—found it difficult to learn Basque.

Hence, the *ikastolas* came into being. These are Basque-language schools committed to educating the children of Spanish-speaking families who think that their children should be able to express themselves in Basque, and that the only way to do so is to acquire the language in early childhood.

The first *ikastolas* were established around 1967, while General Franco was still in power. Despite problems of every kind—lack of legal recognition, economic difficulties, and so on—plus the fact that teachers often had no other qualifications than their patriotic enthusiasm, the number of *ikastolas* and their pupils continued to grow.

In 1978, the Statute of Autonomy of the Basque provinces was approved, and the Basque Parliament and government began to function. As in the case of Catalonia, the Basque government assumed all responsibility for educational matters and for the language policy, which was aimed at introducing and strengthening the Basque language in the educational system.

Types of Schools

The Basque area, like the rest of Spain, has both public schools, supported and administered by the state, and private schools—a dual system to which the previously mentioned *ikastolas* must be added. The *ikastolas* are Basque-language schools which were originally private since they had come into being outside of, and even in opposition to, the governmental administration. However, they have since been subsidized and are currently in the process of being integrated into the public system.

The figures in the following tabulation indicate the relative importance of these various types of schools in the Basque region (Euskadi):

Elementary school pupils (Basic General Education) according to type of school (in thousands), school year 1981–82

Area	Public Schools	Ikastolas	Private Schools
Guipuzcoa	40	23	39
Biscay	116	11	77
Alava	23	2	12
Euskadi	179	36	128
%Euskadi	42	10	37

Source: M. Siguan, ed., *Lenguas y educación*, University of Barcelona, 1983, p. 52.

As in Catalonia, the Basque government's policy has been designed, first, to implement in all schools the Decree on Bilingualism (which established that all pupils from regions with an indigenous language must receive at least three to five hours of instruction in that language per week), and second, to assist schools wishing to grant greater curricular importance to that regional language. The implementation of this policy has proved to be extremely difficult for a number of reasons (to be discussed later), one of which was the small number of teachers initially capable of teaching Euskera (Basque) or in Euskera.

Public Schools. After three years of administration by the Basque government, the situation in the public schools can be summarized as follows:

Percentage of pupils in Basic General Education (6 to 14 years old) in Euskadi, according to amount of Basque-language instruction

No Basque instruction	30%
Basque as a school subject (3–5 hours per week)	59%
Bilingual education in Spanish and Basque	6%
Education primarily in Basque	5%

Source: M. Siguan, ed., *Lenguas y educación*, University of Barcelona, 1983, p. 87.

Ikastolas. The *ikastolas* have grown very rapidly, as the figures in the accompanying tabulation show.

School Population in the *Ikastolas*

Area:	1969–70	1980–81	1981–82
Guipuzcoa	5,770	37,145	39,128
Biscay	1,958	17,175	19,107
Alava	171	5,086	5,509
Spanish Basque provinces	8,899	54,302	58,235
Navarre	348	5,369	5,727
French Pays Basque	8	506	564

(The above figures include preschool and Basic General Education pupils.)

Source: M. Siguan, ed., *Lenguas y educación*, University of Barcelona, 1983, p. 40.

As the Spanish political situation changed, the economic and administrative problems of the *ikastolas* decreased, even though the number of schools and pupils attending them grew. Their pedagogical problems, however, increased. In its original form, the *ikastola* admitted Spanish-speaking children, and from the first, the only language of instruction was Basque. The argument for this procedure was that it was the only way for children from non-Basque-speaking homes to acquire mastery of the language. Pedagogical justification was provided by the so-called immersion method. It soon became clear, however, that premature immersion in a strange language brought about numerous problems in adaptation and learning. In addition, the acquisition of Euskera proved to be less rapid and thorough than had been believed, and the scanty pedagogical preparation of some of the first teachers in the *ikastolas* complicated the situation further. Because of these difficulties, numerous discussions were held among those reponsible for the *ikastolas*. As a result, while some of these schools have remained faithful to the original concept, others have chosen to provide a gradual introduction of Euskera to Spanish-speaking children, leading in some cases to true bilingual education.

After the formation of the Basque government, the *ikastola* movement as an education system outside the authority of the government administration lost its reason for being. Today the *ikastolas* are not only generously subsidized; they are also in the process of being integrated into the public school system while still retaining their individuality

Private Schools. The importance of private schools—which in the Basque region account for 37 percent of the school population—has already been indicated. Since it was formed, the Basque government has been urging these schools to introduce the Basque language and to comply with at least the minimum requirements of the Decree on Bilingualism. Although statistics on the results have not been published, most families who want their children to learn Basque in childhood send them to the *ikastolas*. It is therefore likely that interest in the Basque language among the remaining private schools is considerably less and that Basque occupies a smaller place in their curriculum than it does in that of the public schools.

Evaluation of the Results

Although studies parallel to those cited for Catalonia are in progress, their findings have not yet been published. But one might readily assume—and some less rigorous studies do confirm it—that, as in Catalonia, the outcomes differ according to the language origins of the pupils. Basque-speaking children, even with less Spanish in the educational system, acquire Spanish fairly easily, whereas Spanish-speaking pupils learn to express themselves comfortably in Basque only if they attend a school with a large amount of Basque instruction. The greater use of Spanish in the public and social life of the Basque region explains this discrepancy.

As in Catalonia, there are no published studies that relate the language of instruction to scholastic achievement, despite the discussions held in certain *ikastolas* on this subject. But given the great similarity between Catalan and Spanish, and the striking differences between Basque and Spanish, one might assume that in the case of Basque and Spanish it is more difficult to transfer the knowledge acquired in one language to the other, and that it is therefore more probable that education imported in the second language will have an influence on academic achievement. In any event, the need to investigate this topic is quite evident.

Teaching Staff. As pointed out earlier, the main difficulty in expanding the amount of Euskera in education has been the lack of competent teachers.

At first, the University of the Basque Region was not able to prepare teachers in this field, and it was only after the establishment of the Basque government that teacher training courses began to be organized. It must not be forgotten that providing adult teachers with training in Basque is much more difficult than training them in Catalan—so much time and effort are required that few people are able to attain the goal.

The only possible solution is, of course, that prospective teachers gain sufficient ability in Euskera during the course of their study to be able to use it in teaching. Some years ago, the public teachers' colleges were not prepared to offer this training, and the task was undertaken by a church-related teachers' college as it already offered most of its instruction in Euskera. Since the Basque government took over the management of the education system, the three public teachers' colleges located in the Basque area also ensure students' competence in Basque.

Texts and Teaching Materials. As a result of the absence of a tradition in the instruction of, and in, Basque, fifteen years ago not only were there few teachers capable of undertaking this instruction but also there was a total lack of textbooks and other teaching materials in Basque. Within a few years, however, an extraordinary effort was carried out, despite the lack of precedents and many other difficulties, among them economic problems resulting from the limited market that could absorb such materials. Today all the materials needed to cover Basic General Education as well as a large portion of secondary education can be found.

The University

As the Basque region acquired political autonomy, its university also received a large measure of self-determination. It has attempted to introduce Basque into the university milieu not only as an object of study, but also as a language of communication and education. To an even greater extent than with primary education, this represented a complete innovation since university instruction in Basque had never before existed. Even university education in Spanish was very recent as no university at all had existed in the Basque region until a few years ago.

The ultimate goal is for all university disciplines to be taught in both Spanish and Basque. Even though attainment of this objective is still in the distant future, significant progress in this direction has already been made, and perhaps 20 percent of all university courses can be taken in both Spanish and Basque. For this to occur, it was necessary to engage in a great effort to extend the Basque language among faculty and students, establish a scientific vocabulary, and prepare textbooks in different disciplines.

Problems and Prospects. From the data presented above, it can be concluded that the juvenile population of the Basque region is distributed approximately as follows:

- About 15 percent speak Euskera as their mother tongue and are taught primarily in Spanish but receive some Euskera instruction.
- Nearly 10 percent speak Spanish as their mother tongue and are taught primarily or partly in Euskera.
- About 33 percent speak Spanish as their mother tongue and are taught in Spanish, but receive some Euskera instruction. Of those, it can be estimated that 5 percent of the population will continue to expand their knowledge of Euskera and will be able to speak

it with facility. The remaining 30 percent will only achieve various other levels of oral
and written expression.

• Lastly, about 30 percent of the population does not yet receive any systematic Euskera
instruction.

Thus, it can be anticipated that within a few years, nearly 40 percent of the
population will be able to speak Euskera on a habitual basis, in addition to
another 30 percent who will be able to understand it to some extent. The significance of these figures becomes evident if we recall that the proportion of
Basque speakers in the general population is currently 25 percent. Even more
important is the fact that until a few years ago Basque was a language in complete
regression, used almost exclusively in rural and family settings. Now, for the
first time in many centuries, the number of Basque speakers, instead of decreasing, is increasing, as is the official and urban use of the language.

It is impossible to predict just how far this expansion will go; however,
alongside the encouraging data, it must be remembered that there are also difficulties and limitations. For example, the great linguistic distance between Euskera and Spanish makes the process of learning or reviving Euskera against a
Spanish background quite difficult—much more difficult than learning Catalan
and Galician from Spanish (and vice versa). A Spanish-speaker who goes to
Catalonia with no knowledge of Catalan will probably be able to understand
Catalan at the end of a year—even if only on an elementary level—provided he
or she brings a minimum of good-will, concentration, and effort to the task.
This makes it not unreasonable to suggest in any public gathering that each
person speak the language he or she prefers, on the assumption that everyone
more or less understands the other language. Such assumptions are not possible
in the Basque region. To learn—and even merely to understand—Euskera from
Spanish requires a systematic effort that must be sustained over a long period
of time.

There are other difficulties intrinsic to the Basque language, first and foremost
of which is its internal cohesion. In order for a language to be used as a medium
of instruction, and indeed even to be taught, it must be standardized, that is, it
must have a lexicon and a single set of grammatical and orthographic rules that
define the ''normal'' use of the language. As a result of an almost exclusively
oral transmission, Basque exhibits great dialectal variety. Even though an agreement was reached some time ago on language unity, the influence of the various
dialects continues to be very strong.

Even more serious is the problem of modernizing the vocabulary. In order
for a language to have official and literary uses, in order for it to be used as a
medium of communication in universities, government, and business, it must
have at its disposal a vocabulary comparable to that of languages with a long
tradition of use in these endeavors. The traditional Basque language is obviously
lacking in this respect, and the modernization of its vocabulary will necessitate
great effort. At this point, a still unresolved conflict remains between those who

defend the incorporation of Greek and Latin roots (which form the basis of the learned vocabulary in most of the languages of our cultural milieu) and those who, on the contrary, advocate that indigenous Basque roots be fully utilized.

But the major difficulty in the revival and expansion of Euskera is the presence of Spanish (and French in the Pays Basque), with the influence it wields through its long literary and cultural history, its large number of speakers, and its use in the international arena. Even in the hypothetical situation of complete political independence, it is difficult to imagine Euskera as the only language of the Basques. It would have to coexist with an international language of communication, which in the Basque region would logically continue to be Spanish.

The limitations imposed by this situation are easy to envisage, but let us point out another one, hardly observed until now, but which will become increasingly important. Unlike the past, when most Basques were either Spanish or Basque monolinguals, the pervasiveness of Basque in education is producing a generation of bilinguals capable of expressing themselves in both languages. Obviously, this phenomenon is going to influence the evolution of the Basque language, which for centuries had owed its strength and originality to the isolation and the monolingualism, of its speakers. But from now on, Basque will increasingly be used by people who also know Spanish, a language richer than Basque at present, and they will use Basque in situations where Spanish is more suitable. Bilinguals speaking Basque will surely use Spanish idioms that Basque does not possess, and they will also cease using inherently Basque forms that have no counterpart in Spanish. Therefore, it may happen that the more Basque spreads, the more it will be altered—losing its purity and individual characteristics, and drawing nearer to Spanish.

Even if these limitations are acknowledged, it cannot be denied that thanks to a great educational push, the Basque language has passed from a state of regression to one of expansion.

NAVARRE

Basque continues to be a living language in northern Navarre, on the French border, although the number of its speakers does not represent more than 10 percent of the total population.

In the area where Basque is maintained, it is in a situation similar to the one described for Euskadi, and the strengthening of Basque nationalism and the renewed interest in the Basque language as a symbol of national identity will undoubtedly have repercussions in Navarre. A good example of such influence is seen in the establishment of *ikastolas* at various locations in Navarre, even where history has left no record of Basque ever having been spoken there.

As already indicated, some six thousand pupils are educated in *ikastolas* in Navarre, which represents somewhat more than 10 percent of the school population. These *ikastolas* have the same pedagogical problems as those in the Basque provinces, and they look to that region for solutions.

The expansion of education in Basque and, in general, the cultural revival of the Basque language have encountered a major obstacle in Navarre: Basque nationalism regards Navarre as an integral part of the Basque nation, but in the political institutions of Navarre—the regional Parliament and the government— the advocates of this position represent a small minority.

The perfectly predictable result of this situation is that, even though the local government has affirmed its desire to extend knowledge of Basque to all sectors— especially to the educational domain, insofar as parents desire it—the progress achieved to date has been quite limited. The *ikastolas* remain a private movement facing economic and administrative difficulties. As far as public schools are concerned, it is only in the Basque-speaking areas that the Decree on Bilingualism is carried out—and this with difficulty, owing to the lack of trained teachers. In order for instruction of, and in, Basque to be established on more solid footing, we must wait for political relations between Navarre and the Basque provinces to be clarified.

GALICIA

Sociological studies are in agreement that between 70 and 90 percent of Galicia's 3 million inhabitants speak Galician to a greater or lesser extent. They also agree that the linguistic situation is typically diglossic: Galician is spoken primarily in rural areas, while Spanish predominates in the city; Galician is used above all in the family circle and in daily life, while Spanish is the language of public and official affairs. This is equivalent to saying that, even though most Galicians are able to speak both languages, they consider Spanish to be superior. To appreciate this situation, it is necessary to bear in mind that, unlike Catalonia and the Basque region, Galicia has not experienced industrial and economic development but, rather, has continued to be an impoverished agricultural region, even relative to the average Spanish level of development.

This situation is slowly changing. First, certain intellectual groups, especially at the University of Santiago de Compostela, have brought pressure to reestablish the literary use of the language, and, in particular, its use in education. A number of courses are given in Galician at the university itself.

In addition, in recent years Galicia has received a statute of autonomy providing it with a regional government having authority over the educational system. Unlike Catalonia or the Basque region, where the power in the respective governments is occupied by the nationalist parties, in Galicia there is no important nationalist movement. It is thus a fair assumption that the regional government is less interested in the promotion of the local language.

Nevertheless, the presence of Galician in the educational system—nonexistent a few years ago—has increased considerably, even if much more slowly than in Catalonia and the Basque provinces. In 1981, 50 percent of the school pupils in Galicia were taught Galician, and this proportion has probably increased since then. To make such instruction possible, the university has organized training courses for teachers who are already employed, while prospective teachers are now able to receive this training during the course of their studies.

Very little has been done, on the other hand, to utilize Galician as a medium of instruction in primary or secondary education. Several attempts have been made to use Galician as the initial language of instruction for Galician-speaking pupils, and somewhat fewer attempts have been made to use it as the exclusive language of instruction, but none of these has received much support. The regional government has decided that if Galician is to be used as the language of instruction in a school, it must be formally requested by the pupils' parents— and, on the whole, parents have not shown much interest in such an innovation. The current objective of the Galician government seems to be restricted to extending the teaching of Galician as a school subject to all pupils, except for the previously mentioned case of the university.

The teaching of Galician, together with its use as a vehicle of culture, presents difficulties similar to those encountered in other languages. The standardization of the language—vocabulary, grammar, orthography—theoretically does not present a problem, since dialectal differences are small and Galician does have a relatively important literary tradition. Likewise, problems concerning the modernization of vocabulary ought not to arise in principle, owing to the fact that Galician is a Romance language and most of the contemporary technical and cultural vocabulary is from Greek and Latin roots. However, an unusual controversy has arisen in connection with the issues of standardization and modernization. The expansion of the Galician people to the south in the Middle Ages was accompanied by the extension of the language, but soon afterwards the territory where this expansion took place became an independent country, Portugal. This prompted the spoken language to evolve into a literary language with international influence. Thus, it would appear that there is a simple solution to the problem of the modernization of Galician, that is, to adopt Portuguese as a model. But curiously, neither the Portuguese nor the Galicians want to recall their common beginnings. The Portuguese do not want to be reminded that their language originated in one of the poorest rural areas of Spain, and the Galicians think that to identify themselves with Portuguese—or to simply approach it— would be equivalent to submitting to Portuguese culture and accepting the intellectual leadership of Lisbon. As a result, the modernization of Galician has provoked considerable controversy between the advocates and opponents of drawing on the Portuguese model.

As with all minority languages, the major obstacle to the extension of Galician is the small size of the Galician-speaking population (which has economic and various other consequences) and the position of inferiority which the minority language occupies with respect to the languages existing alongside it. But in the case of Galician we must add the diglossic situation referred to above. While in Catalonia or the Basque region the language has become a symbol of identity and collective pride, and in certain circumstances can be a means of obtaining prestige and social advancement, in Galicia the native language is associated

with the poverty of peasant life. Neither social advancement nor emigration—
the fate of many Galicians—will follow from the learning of another language.
While this situation continues, it is unlikely that Galician families will view
education in Galician as a right that is worth claiming.

OTHER TYPES OF BILINGUAL EDUCATION

Prior to the 1970 General Law on Education (Ley General de Educación), the
Spanish educational system separated children at the age of eleven into those
who began secondary education and those who continued at the primary level
until the age of fourteen. Pupils entering secondary education immediately started
the study of a foreign language, usually French, and later they could begin
another. The General Law on Education unified the educational system for all
pupils up to the age of fourteen and established that the introduction to a foreign
language would begin for everyone at age eleven. But in consideration of the
magnitude of the change required by the unification of the educational system,
it was recognized that the general expansion of foreign language instruction
should be accomplished gradually and according to the available means, in
particular, the teachers.

The fact of the matter is that despite the passage of time, this expansion has
not yet taken place. Although there are some very interesting attempts, including
the early introduction of a foreign language, a substantial number of pupils finish
Basic General Education at the age of fourteen without having received any
foreign language instruction.

At the same time, social demand for foreign language study during the school
years has grown noticeably, and insofar as it has not been satisfied by the public
schools, private initiatives have emerged to fulfull this function. Among the
measures taken are supplementary classes outside the normal school hours, as
well as private institutions that offer early bilingual education, beginning with
the preschool stage, in either French or, more often, English. In addition, there
are the foreign schools, mainly French and German, which are old and well-
regarded schools that offer authentic bilingual education of high quality in various
Spanish cities.

The social demand for foreign language study is particularly strong in some
of the areas with an indigenous language, especially in Catalonia and the Basque
region, border regions with a high economic and cultural level where the knowledge of foreign languages is quite widespread. In these places, the introduction
of the local language has made it necessary to take into account the presence of
three languages in the educational system: the native language, Catalan or Basque; the official language of the country, Spanish; and a foreign language.

This problem is not insoluble. Barcelona has at least one school at this level
which combines bilingual instruction based on the two native languages (Catalan
and Spanish) with the early introduction of French and the later study of English
in order to fulfill the requirements of the European baccalaureate. This school

is obviously of high quality and pedagogically superior to the average public or private school. But of all the regional governments, it is evident that those of Catalonia and the Basque region and, generally speaking, of all the areas with their own language have taken up the challenge of offering foreign language instruction and bilingual education to all their pupils. If this goal is not achieved, the impression would be given that the introduction of the regional languages would prevent or diminish the learning of a foreign language. As a result, the inclusion of the native language in the school program would be unpopular, at least among certain social groups.

BIBLIOGRAPHY

Bureau International d'Education. 1928. *Le bilinguisme et l'education.* (Travaux de la Conference de Luxemburg.) Geneva.

Diex, N. 1981. *Las lenguas de España.* Public. del Ministerio de Educación. Madrid.

Entwistle, J. W. 1969. *The Spanish Language, Together with Portuguese, Catalan, and Basque.* London: Faber and Faber.

Generalitat de Catalunya. 1983. *Cuatre anys de català a l'escola.* Barcelona, 1983.

Revista de Educación (Madrid), No. 268 (dic. 1981). Número monográfico: *"Educación y bilinguismo."*

Revista de Occidente (Madrid), 1982. No. 10–11 (February). Número monográfico: *"El bilinguismo: problemática y realidad."*

Siguan, M. 1984. "Language and Education in Catalonia." In *Prospects.* (UNESCO). Paris 1984.

Siguan, M., ed. 1983. *Lenguas y educación en el ámbito del estado español.* Publicaciones de la Universidad de Barcelona.

BILINGUALISM AND EDUCATION OF
IMMIGRANT CHILDREN AND ADULTS IN
SWEDEN

Sweden is sometimes said to have been an ethnically homogeneous society up until the European labor migration changed the situation radically in the 1960s. Such a claim overlooks the fact that Sweden houses two indigenous minorities within its present borders: the Saame or Lapps, who are considered to be the original population of northern Scandinavia, and the Finns in the Swedish part of the Torne Valley at the Finnish border. It also disregards the migration of various ethnic groups to Sweden during the past centuries, some of whom have been totally absorbed into the majority population, while others have maintained their ethnic identity. Nonetheless, the claim as to Sweden's ethnic homogeneity is not totally unfounded. Compared with a number of European and other countries, the majority population of Sweden is composed primarily of one ethnic group with few foreign elements.

Since ethnicity or mother-tongue affiliation is not registered in Swedish census statistics, it is difficult to obtain figures concerning the size of the indigenous minorities. According to some estimations, the total Saame population does not exceed fifteen thousand (SOS, 1984:147). The 1980 Populations and Housing Census registered only seven hundred persons who supported themselves by means of reindeer herding, the Saame's traditional occupation. (This figure was estimated at twenty-five hundred by Arnstberg and Ehn in 1976.) The Saame language spoken in Sweden is divided into three dialects that are mutually incomprehensible. It belongs to the Finno-Ugric group of languages.

Although the population of the entire Torne Valley is ethnically Finnish, in 1809 when Sweden ceded Finland to Russia, the valley was divided along the Torne River, forming the Swedish-Finnish border. The population in the Swedish part of the valley was subsequently subjected to a massive assimilation campaign, although this campaign did not begin until the late nineteenth century when nationalistic notions concerning the idea of one people speaking one language living in one country began to gain popularity in Europe. Yet, Finnish has been maintained until the present time. The present linguistic situation in the Swedish Torne Valley has been described as a diglossic one. Finnish is considered the "low" variety—for everyday oral use, but also for use in the special type of religious sect that is widely spread in the area, the so-called Laestadianism—and Swedish the "high" variety—used in more formal or official situations, at school, in business, and in communication with the authorities (Jaakola, 1973).

The most important ethnic groups that have migrated to Sweden in historical times are the Germans, mainly an elite group of merchants and public officials who came from the twelfth to the sixteenth centuries; the Finns, farmers who settled in remote and uninhabited areas of Sweden during the sixteenth and seventeenth centuries; the Walloons, iron manufacturers and iron workers from Belgium, during the seventeenth century; the Jews from the seventeenth century onwards; and the Gypsies from the sixteenth century on. Among these groups, only the Jews and the Gypsies have maintained their ethnic identity, the situation being similar to that found in many other countries. The present number of Jews in Sweden is approximately fourteen thousand. The number of Gypsies is estimated at three thousand to three thousand five hundred (cf. Arnstberg and Ehn, 1976).

Following World War II, Sweden became an "immigration country." The first immigration wave can be characterized as refugee immigration. During the last two years of the war, a large group of refugees from the Baltic countries, numbering approximately thirty-five thousand people, arrived in Sweden. To a large extent, members of this group have remained in the country. The Estonians, who comprise the greatest number, have especially succeeded in maintaining their linguistic and cultural heritage until the present day; a number of third-generation children speak Estonian. During World War II, a large number of Danes and Norwegians also fled to Sweden, but many returned home when the situation became normalized in the home countries. The same was true for many of those refugees who were temporarily transferred to Sweden from the continent.

Labor market immigration began in the 1950s, initially with a group of Italians who were employed in Sweden in accordance with a bilateral agreement between the two countries. In these early years of labor market migrations, workers from West Germany, the Netherlands, and Austria were the most predominant groups aside from the Italians. During the 1960s, when the demand for labor could not be fulfilled within Sweden, the annual number of immigrants increased from approximately 25,000 to a peak of 73,500 in 1970 (Widgren, 1980:21). The largest groups during these years came from Yugoslavia, Greece, and Turkey.

In 1967, demands from the Swedish trade-union movement led to governmental restrictions on labor market immigration from outside the Nordic countries, resulting in requirements that work and living arrangements had to be made prior to entry into the country. (The Nordic countries have had an agreement concerning a common labor market since 1954.) As a result, immigration decreased during the 1970s, during which time the annual number of immigrants has ranged from twenty-five to forty thousand (in 1982 it was 25,100 [SOS, 1984:14]). Another effect was a change in the constellation of the immigrant group as a whole. Soon after the restrictions were enforced, the proportion of immigrants from the Nordic countries increased drastically, and during a short period in the late 1960s, it comprised approximately 75 percent of total immigration. This proportion has declined since 1975, in 1981 consisting of 36 percent (Statistics Sweden, 1983:10). It also meant that labor market immigration came to a halt and was replaced by what has been referred to as consequential or "family-related" immigration, that is, immigration involving next of kin to already established immigrants. Aside from this group, refugees, who either have come to Sweden independently or as a result of Swedish political initiatives, comprised a substantial proportion. Waves of refugees have continuously entered Sweden, both during the labor market immigration period (from Hungary in the 1950s and Czechoslovakia and Poland in the 1960s) and during later periods (from Latin America, Turkey, Vietnam, Uganda, Iran, Poland again, and Lebanon).

Since 1980, there has been a continuous decrease in the annual number of immigrants; in 1983, the number was 22,291, which is the lowest figure since 1962 (Hammar and Reinans, 1984:3). In 1984, however, the trend was reversed when a 14 percent increase in relation to 1983 was registered.

Table 24.1 (from Widgren, 1980:24) shows the structure of alien immigration to Sweden during 1977. At this time, the immigration peak of the 1970s was reached. The proportions in the various backgrounds of the non-Nordic immigrants have remained approximately the same since that time.

If we look at those foreign nationals residing in Sweden, a characteristic feature is the enormous heterogeneity as regards nationality, a development that has become increasingly typical during the last decade. Table 24.2 (Statistics Sweden, 1983:12) shows a rank listing of the foreign nationals according to their country of origin.

As can be seen, a large proportion of the immigrants come from Finland. As a consequence, the opportunities for bilingual education programs and social services have been greater both in number and in variety for the Finnish group than for other immigrant groups. The fact that the remainder of the immigrant population is comprised of many small groups—some 150 nationalities—has had important consequences for both the development of educational programs and the direction of research, as will be seen in a later section.

At the end of 1983, the number of foreign citizens residing in Sweden was slightly below four hundred thousand. With the inclusion of naturalized immigrants, the foreign-born population in Sweden amounted to 637,463 persons, which is 7.7 percent of the total Swedish population of approximately 8.3 million. About 50 percent of the foreign-born population was born in one of the Nordic countries, a majority of these in Finland (Hammar and Reinans, 1984:19ff).

Table 24.1

Composition of the Immigration to Sweden by Foreign Citizens during 1977

Category	Number	% of the total immigrant population	% of the non-Scandinavian immigrant population
Scandinavians	19 640	51	
Non-Scandinavians:	19 070	49	
family members	9 230	24	48
refugees transferred to Sweden on Swedish initiative	930	2	5
other refugees	3 360	9	18
labor market immigrants	1 650	4	9
adopted children	1 920	5	10
guest students	790	2	4
"humanitarian" cases	240	1	1
returning Swedes (with foreign citizenship)	190	1	1
Others	760	2	4
Total	38 710	100	100

THE PRESENT SITUATION

The distinction between indigenous minorities and immigrants will not be maintained throughout the present section. Rather, the focus will be on the immigrant situation; the indigenous minorities will be mentioned when possible but without too great detail.

Language

As mentioned above, no census data are available concerning which languages are spoken among the immigrant population in Sweden—or among naturalized or native Swedes, including the indigenous minorities. Therefore, figures on the language situation are based on estimations only. As regards the situation for school children, however, the information available is more reliable, since ''home language other than Swedish'' is registered for all pupils.

It is difficult to estimate the number of speakers of Saame, since those Saame who are not reindeer herders are dispersed throughout the country. In an interview study of language and culture among present-day Saame, H. Johansson (1975) investigated a sample of 233 nonreindeer-herding and 113 reindeer-herding Saame. This sample was estimated to represent every seventeenth adult person

Table 24.2
Foreign Nationals in Sweden at 31st December, 1981, by Citizenship and Percentages of All Foreign Nationals

Country of citizenship	Total	Percentage of all foreign nationals
Finland	171 994	41.5
Yugoslavia	38 771	9.4
Denmark	28 305	6.8
Norway	25 352	6.1
Turkey	19 493	4.7
Greece	13 820	3.3
West Germany (BDR)	13 337	3.2
Poland	10 703	2.6
UK	8 828	2.1
Chile	7 904	1.9
USA	5 781	1.4
Italy	4 524	1.1
Iceland	3 698	0.9
Iran	3 344	0.8
Spain	3 287	0.8
Austria	3 243	0.8
Hungary	2 836	0.7
Vietnam	2 734	0.7
France	2 355	0.6
Netherlands	2 256	0.5
Switzerland	2 155	0.5
Uruguay	1 965	0.5
Argentina	1 738	0.4
India	1 661	0.4
Syria	1 647	0.4
Portugal	1 573	0.4
Bolivia	1 562	0.4

Table 24.2 (*continued*)

Country of citizenship	Total	Percentage of all foreign nationals
Lebanon	1 557	0.4
Ethiopia	1 392	0.3
Morocco	1 376	0.3
Thailand	1 186	0.3
Czechoslovakia	1 146	0.3
Japan	1 026	0.2
USSR	1 003	0.2
Tunisia	969	0.2
Iraq	890	0.2
China	844	0.2
Pakistan	784	0.2
Israel	727	0.2
Colombia	701	0.2
Sri Lanka	649	0.2
Romania	622	0.2
Oceania	608	0.1
Algeria	569	0.1
Canada	569	0.1
Brazil	529	0.1
Korea (South)	516	0.1
Australia	501	0.1
Stateless and unspecified	2 845	0.7
Other countries	8 126	2.0
All countries	414 001	100.0

Table 24.3
Knowledge of Saame among Reindeer Herding and Non-Reindeer Herding Saame

	Cannot understand	Cannot speak	Cannot read	Cannot write
Reindeer herding	5 %	20 %	45 %	80 %
Non-reindeer herding	20 %	40 %	65 %	85 %

Table 24.4
Self-Rating of Bilingual Proficiency among the Torne Valley Finnish Minority by Age Groups

Age	Know Finnish best	Know Finnish and Swedish equally well	Know Swedish best	%	(N)
55-64	55	25	20	100	(69)
45-54	48	25	27	100	(59)
35-44	46	28	26	100	(63)
25-34	31	21	48	100	(48)
15-24	20	19	61	100	(107)

in the entire population. Johansson's investigation gives a picture of the decreasing knowledge of Saame among the younger generation; 50 percent in the reindeer-herding group and 90 percent in the nondeer-herding group stated that none of their children knew Saame. Table 24.3 shows the knowledge of Saame in the two groups. (The figures are based on Johansson, 1975:121.)

The Finnish-speaking indigenous minority of northern Sweden is presently estimated to consist of between thirty thousand (SOS, 1984:120) and forty thousand (Wande, 1982:2) persons. In an interview survey of the Torne Valley Finnish minority (Jaakola, 1973), bilingual subjects were asked to rate their level of proficiency in both of their languages. Table 24.4 from Jaakola (1973:63) shows that Finnish plays a less important role among the younger generation than among the older; the situation seems to be similar to that of the Saame minority. On

Table 24.5
Estimated Number of Speakers of Certain Languages in Sweden

Finnish	270 000
Serbo-Croatian	34 000
Greek	21 000
Estonian	20 000
Spanish	19 800
Polish	18 800
Hungarian	16 900
Italian	8 800
Turkish	8 500

the other hand, 96 percent of those interviewed (N = 347) considered themselves to be bilingual, at least to some degree (Jaakola, 1973:61).

In a study of Torne Valley school children (ten year olds) and their parents, where language proficiency among the children was assessed both through self-rating and testing (Rönmark and Wikström, 1980), results very similar to those of Jaakola were found. For example, only 20 percent of the subjects were more proficient in Finnish than in Swedish. Rönmark and Wikström's interpretation was an obvious one, that is, that a language shift was taking place.

Estimations regarding the size of the different languages among immigrant groups have been made from time to time. For example, the Swedish Immigration Board (SIV) carried out a survey in the early 1980s in order to establish a basis for the planning of so-called multilingual social services (SIV, 1982:79). Table 24.5 shows the results concerning nine immigrant groups.

Languages other than those presented in Table 24.5 also have substantial numbers of speakers, however. The statistics as of December 31, 1981, for "persons born abroad," which can be used for a rough estimation for the number of speakers of certain languages, included approximately forty-two thousand persons from Denmark and Norway, respectively; sixteen thousand from North America; eighty-five hundred from Great Britain; thirty-eight thousand from West Germany; and seven thousand from Austria (Statistics Sweden, 1983). It should be recognized that the figures in Table 24.5 represent a rough approximation only. For example, figures for speakers of Estonian have ranged from sixteen thousand to twenty-five thousand according to various sources (cf. Raag, 1983:18).

Table 24.6
Self-Rating of Proficiency in Estonian among Estonian Immigrants in Sweden

Alternative responses	Distribution of responses		
	G e n e r a t i o n		
I know Estonian:	Ia	Ib	II
- better than Swedish	80	4	0
- as well as Swedish	15	11	0
- somewhat worse than Swedish	5	28	53
- considerably worse than Swedish	0	46	44
- rudimentarily	0	11	3

Ia: Persons born -1930, i.e., who were above the age of adolescence at the time of immigration

Ib: Persons born 1931-1944, i.e., persons who arrived in Sweden as children

II: Persons born 1944-, i.e., persons born in Sweden

Little research has been conducted on the maintenance of immigrant language beyond the first generation. R. Raag (1982), however, asked ninety-eight first- and second-generation Estonians to rate their proficiency levels of Estonian. Table 24.6 shows the result from this study.

Ongoing research (Boyd, 1984) has investigated the use of Finnish, as well as other immigrant languages, among second-generation fifteen year olds. Table 24.7 from S. Boyd (1984), which concerns children from families where both parents speak either Finnish ("fifi") or languages other than Swedish or Finnish ("anan"), shows that a majority of the children use the minority language with their parents, while Swedish dominates in contacts with siblings and friends, even when these are bilingual.

As Boyd points out, however, these results may not be generalizable in all respects. One reason is that the subjects studied had grown up prior to the period during which the Home Language Reform, which provides students with mother-tongue instruction in the schools, was enacted. It may also be the case that the group of fifteen year olds is not representative of other age groups owing to possible age-specific attitudes regarding minority/majority group membership among teenagers.

Table 24.7
Language Use among Second-Generation 15-Year-Olds from Monolingual Non-Swedish Homes when Communicating with Various Bilingual Interlocutors

Language used with	Mother	Father	Siblings	Boy-/girl friend	Best friend	"Most friends"
Only or mostly Swedish	26 %	30 %	74 %	67 %	79 %	84 %
Only or mostly the minority language	68 %	61 %	15 %	15 %	8 %	6 %
Both languages	6 %	9 %	11 %	17 %	13 %	10 %
(N)	250	235	212	65	153	166

Religion

Sweden has an Evangelic-Lutheran so-called state church, where most Swedish citizens are members; in 1980, only 4 percent were not members, although there has been an increase in nonmembership during the last years. (In 1976, the number of nonmembers was 2.8 percent.) Aside from the Swedish state church, there have traditionally been a number of so-called free churches. Swedish children whose parents are members of the state church automatically become members. Those who do not wish to become members must renounce their membership.

The immigration to Sweden of people who embrace other churches and religions has resulted in religious diversification in the country. The Roman Catholic Church, which in Sweden was gradually replaced by the Lutheran Church during the sixteenth century, was reestablished at the end of the eighteenth century when Catholic foreigners domiciled in Sweden were allowed to practice their religion. Its members were few, however; until the 1930s, there were only about five thousand members. Today the number of members exceeds one hundred and five thousand (SOS, 1984), consisting mainly of immigrants but also of a substantial number of Swedes. The same pattern is true for the Mosaic and Orthodox churches. Islam, Hinduism, and Buddhism are also practiced in Sweden.

Within the Swedish state church, there are also Finnish and German congregations. Unilingual congregations are not the rule, however. For example, the members of the Roman Catholic Church of Gothenburg include approximately fifty nationalities. The mass is conducted in ten different languages within a month's period (SOS, 1984:126).

Table 24.8
Immigrants' Income in Proportion to the Income for Corresponding Groups in the Total Population

Age	Foreign citizens		Naturalized citizens born abroad	
	Men	Women	Men	Women
20-24	96	94	101	98
25-34	85	100	97	104
35-49	84	102	99	106
50-59	88	101	104	108
60-64	91	109	110	115
16-64	87	99	108	113

Economic and Social Conditions

In general, in Sweden as in other immigrant countries, the economic and social situation for the immigrant population is inferior to that of the majority population (cf. SOS, 1984:79–96). The unemployment rate is higher among immigrants than among Swedes; immigrants typically work in manufacturing or service branches and are more frequently employed in less well-paid jobs than are Swedes. Proportionally more immigrants than Swedes work shift hours; in addition, immigrants work in environments considered less healthy than those of Swedes. Nonetheless, the differences in income between immigrants and the majority population are small, as can be seen from Table 24.8 where the income of immigrants is given as a proportion of the income for the corresponding groups of the total population (from SOS, 1984:93, based on Ekberg, 1981).

In particular, there is a difference between men who are foreign citizens and majority group members, whereas many women and immigrants who have become naturalized have levels of income that exceed those of comparable groups among the majority population. A partial explanation for this difference is that working hours are not considered in the comparison. For example, the comparatively positive income situation for immigrant women is due to the fact that they, on the average, have longer working hours than Swedish women.

As regards housing conditions, immigrant households, more often than Swedish households, are considered overcrowded; 16 percent versus 4 percent (SOS, 1984:97). The criterion used in Swedish statistics for overcrowdedness consists of more than two persons per room, exluding kitchen and living room. Those who are considered overcrowded according to this criterion do not necessarily have a similar opinion themselves (SOS, 1984:98). Statistics show, however, that there are no differences in the standard of dwellings, between immigrants and Swedes.

As regards social relations between immigrants and Swedes, an interesting trend is the rate of intermarriage. Approximately 50 percent of immigrant women and 40 percent of immigrant men cohabit with Swedes. Among these, 84 percent of the women and 77 percent of the men are married. These figures can be compared with the figures for marriages or cohabitation among persons from the same country, consisting of 45 percent of the women and 50 percent of the men (SOS, 1984:99). Such conditions undoubtedly have important consequences for the future maintenance of linguistic and cultural diversity in the country.

Interview studies have been carried out in both 1969 and 1981 regarding the attitudes toward immigrants among Swedes. The main result was that the feeling of "apprehension of" and "dislike for" immigrants was more frequent among older persons, those with less education, and those who had had little contact with immigrants. A comparison between the two investigations showed, however, that the negative attitudes toward immigrants had decreased during the period between 1969 and 1981 (Westin, 1984).

The Political Situation

From 1968 to 1974, public measures taken on behalf of immigrants and ethnic minorities were investigated in the governmental Commission on Immigrants and Ethnic Minorities (SOU, 1974). The Commission's suggestions that immigrants be allowed a real opportunity to retain their ethnic identity was accepted by the government, and in 1975 Parliament passed a bill establishing new guidelines for policies regarding immigrants and ethnic minorities. Three main objectives were emphasized:

1. Equality between immigrants and Swedes.
2. Cultural freedom of choice for immigrants.
3. Cooperation and solidarity between Swedes and ethnic minorities.

With regard to the goal for equality between Swedes and immigrants, it was suggested that the ethnic minorities should have the same access to information, education, and culture as Swedes. In order to achieve this goal, it was seen as essential that immigrants be helped to develop adequate skills in Swedish; the development and maintenance of skills in the home language was also an essential part of the "equality" principle, however. With regard to the second goal, that is, freedom of choice, the immigrants' right to choose concerning the extent to which they wished to maintain their own language and cultural identity or to adopt a Swedish language and cultural identity was recognized. The third goal emphasizes the importance of the development of tolerance and community of spirit between immigrants and Swedes achieved through increased information and education aimed at improving intercultural understanding (see SOU, 1983).

Aside from the above-mentioned overriding goals, which have also had important implications for educational policy (these will be discussed in the next section), concrete measures have been taken concerning the political status of immigrants. Since 1976, foreign citizens domiciled in Sweden have been allowed to vote in local and regional elections, provided that permanent residence in Sweden has been maintained for at least three years prior to the election. Evaluations of the extent of participation among immigrants in the elections of 1976, 1979, and 1982 show that immigrants have participated to a lesser degree than Swedes (in 1982, 52 percent for immigrants versus 90 percent for Swedes) (SOU, 1984). Nevertheless, the figure of 52 percent is not regarded as discouraging, considering that immigrants, especially those who have not been in the country for a long period of time, are faced with a number of obvious difficulties in connection with exercising their right to vote (cf. Hammar and Reinans, 1984:60). Furthermore, the figure of 90 percent voting participation is extremely high compared to what is common in many other countries.

The question of whether voting rights for immigrants should be extended to national elections has been considered by a special parliamentary commission (SOU, 1984). The majority of the commission (Social Democratic and Communist party members) suggested that voting rights be extended for Nordic citizens only, while a minority (nonsocialist party members) voted for unaltered regulations. The commission's suggestion has met with harsh criticism and is unlikely to be the object of governmental proposals to the Parliament (cf. Hammar and Reinans, 1984:62).

Many immigrants are members of various ethnic organizations, the national boards of these organizations serving as interest groups with regard to political questions concerning immigrants. Aside from their political importance, the local chapters have an especially vital cultural role to play. Immigrant organizations are entitled to public financial support.

BILINGUAL EDUCATION

Goals and Policies

The general political goals mentioned above have played an important role in shaping policy for the education of immigrants. In this section, we will focus on the education of immigrant children. To some extent, however, the adult education of immigrants will be considered, too, because this area has been an important component of the general educational policy for immigrants in Sweden.

The right of immigrant children to maintain and develop their mother tongue in school was first recognized in Sweden in 1962. It was not until a number of years later, however, that mother-tongue instruction became widespread and that its importance for the child's social, emotional, and intellectual development began to receive greater recognition.

The Commission on Immigrants and Ethnic Minorities (operating from 1968 to 1974), although lacking a specific educational focus, made a number of suggestions that were directly related to the education of minority children. Based on research findings concerning language development and bilingualism and the importance of the mother tongue for the child's emotional and intellectual development as well as for the development of a harmonious relationship between parent and child, the goal for the education of minority children should be to promote active bilingualism.

On recommendation from the Commission, a special working group was formed within the Department of Education to investigate issues related to the education of minority children. This group suggested that the general political goals of equality, freedom of choice, and cooperation and solidarity should also be applied to the educational sphere and, in agreement with recommendations from the Commission, that a special goal with regard to the education of immigrant children should be to develop active bilingualism (SOU, 1983). The government accepted the majority of the working group's suggestions, resulting in passage of the Home Language Reform which went into effect in 1977. The Home Language Reform makes it the responsibility of the municipalities to provide home language instruction for all students who desire it and for whom the home language represents a living element in the child's home environment. Home language instruction includes both instruction in the home language per se and tutoring in subject matter through the medium of the mother tongue. State subsidies are provided for this instruction. In addition, the Home Language Reform stipulates that all students in need of support teaching in Swedish be allowed to receive this information.

Since the enactment of the Home Language Reform, the special needs of immigrant children have been given increasing attention. Educational goals for immigrant children are described in the centrally framed curriculum for primary school education now in force (Lgr, 1980). Two recent government commissions have investigated the situation of immigrant children: one with regard to children of preschool age (SOU, 1982) and the other with regard to the situation for language and cultural maintenance among immigrant children in primary and secondary school (SOU, 1983).

With regard to adults, a functional command of Swedish and knowledge of the Swedish society has been recognized as necessary for carrying out the general political goals with regard to immigrants (SOU, 1974). To this end, Swedish-language instruction has been offered to adult immigrants as one of the most important societal tools for enhancing the immigrants' participation at all levels of Swedish society (cf. SO, 1979; Hammar, 1979).

Organizational Forms

The municipalities are given a great deal of freedom with regard to the organizational forms for instruction in the home language, and a number of models have been developed. This has also resulted from the fact that the number of immigrant children, their ages and ethnic identity, parental preferences, and the availability of bilingual staff have varied considerably in the local municipalities. Before describing the various models, the Swedish educational system as a whole will be briefly described.

The educational system in Sweden comprises a compulsory, comprehensive nine-year school, an integrated upper secondary school designed to accommodate all sixteen-year-olds, a system of municipal adult education, and a higher education system, which in principle, is open to everyone with qualifications corresponding to two years' upper secondary schooling (Swedish Institute, 1984). In addition, all children are entitled to preschool education for at least one year before beginning compulsory schooling at age seven. Preschools, however, are part of the public child care programs and are administered separately from the regular school system by the National Board of Health and Welfare. Guidelines concerning both the preschool and school programs are highly centralized in Sweden, resulting in the establishment of uniform educational standards throughout the country.

Preschool Programs for Immigrant Children. Immigrant children, as well as Lapp- and Finnish-speaking children in northern Sweden enrolled in the Swedish preschool system, are offered the opportunity to receive support in the home language if they desire such instruction and if this language constitutes a living element in the home environment. Since 1977, state subsidies have been provided for all six-year-olds, and since 1979, for all five-year-olds. A number of organizational models have resulted. These include mother-tongue groups (in which lessons in Swedish may also be given by peripatetic teachers), combined groups consisting of approximately 50 percent immigrant children from one language group and 50 percent Swedish-speaking children, and placement of the child in a regular Swedish group with home language training being provided by a peripatetic teacher approximately four hours per week. Permanent employment of bilingual staff is preferred over the use of peripatetic teachers because it provides the opportunity for integrating language learning in the regular program. Although few provisions are made for immigrant children cared for at home by their parents, in some municipalities open preschools are also organized which parents can attend with their young children and which have specific open hours for certain language groups.

At the New Year, 1982, 17,300 children with a home language other than Swedish were enrolled in Swedish preschools, comprising 7.4 percent of the total enrollment. Approximately 60 percent received some form of home language training. The highest percentage of those receiving home language instruction were five- and six-year-olds, for whom state subsidies are available. Quantitatively speaking, home language training is best provided for children who speak Spanish, Finnish, Turkish, and Greek. The provision of home language training for children belonging to one of the smaller minority groups is more problematic (Statistics Sweden, 1983).

Statistics concerning the specific type of home language instruction being provided are not available for years later than 1980. At that time, home language groups numbered 365 in the entire country (SOU, 1982). Approximately 60 percent of these groups were for Finnish-speaking children. This meant that approximately 40 percent of the children participating in home language instruction attended home language groups, the remainder being placed in integrated groups or in regular Swedish groups, with home language instruction being given by a peripatetic teacher (the latter form being far more common).

Primary and Secondary Education Programs for Immigrant Children. The way in which instruction for primary school immigrant children is organized in Sweden has taken a number of forms. Four main organizational models are used (Statistics Sweden, 1983).

Most immigrant children are placed in ordinary Swedish classes from which they may be temporarily "pulled out" for home language instruction and/or Swedish as a second-language instruction. A second model consists of integrated classes consisting of approximately 50 percent Swedish-speaking children and 50 percent immigrant children from the same language background. The immigrant children are taught for part of the time in their own group and part of the time together with their Swedish classmates. The amount of Swedish use increases successively from grades one to three, and often the children are placed in a regular Swedish class at the beginning of the fourth grade.

In the so-called home language class, the third model, all instruction, at least initially, is carried out through the medium of the home language. Swedish as a second language is introduced during the second or third grades. The amount of Swedish used in instruction increases successively from grades one to six and is introduced at the latest in grade four (see Virta, 1983). By grade six, instruction is carried out equally in both languages. Although technically speaking home language classes do not exist beyond the sixth grade, but since classes from earlier grades are sometimes kept intact at higher grade levels, this allows for the continuation of some home language instruction even at the junior high school level. Finally, a fourth model consists of preparatory classes in which students from a variety of language backgrounds are instructed together on a temporary basis (see below). It should be recognized, however, that the above description represents "the ideal" and that in reality programs within any particular model type can vary considerably (cf. Källstrom, 1982).

The Central Bureau of Statistics has carried out annual surveys of immigrant pupils and immigrant instruction in compulsory comprehensive schools since 1974. In the fall term of 1982, 992,700 children were attending municipal compulsory schools in Sweden. Of these, 86,700, or 8.7 percent, had a home language other than Swedish. This percentage has been relatively stable since 1979. Approximately 43 percent of primary school immigrant children had Finnish as a mother tongue. In upper secondary school approximately 4.9 percent of the enrolled children had a home language other than Swedish.

The percentage of children participating in some form of home language instruction in primary school was approximately 65 percent and in secondary school approximately 41 percent (Statistics Sweden, 1983). The number of home language classes in primary school during the school year 1982–1983 was 561, which represented a decrease of 39 from the previous year. Seventy-eight percent of these classes were for Finnish-speaking children. During the same period, there were 298 integrated classes and 86 preparatory classes (Statistiska meddelanden, 1983). According to the above source, approximately 16 percent of the children participating in home language instruction received this instruction in the form of home language classes. Virta (1983), however, based on statistics from a study by the National Board of Education, places this figure at only 9 percent. Nevertheless, these figures show that the majority of immigrant children are not attending any type of bilingual class and are placed in regular Swedish classes. As Källström (1982), Virta (1983), and others have pointed out, the ongoing debate in Sweden concerning the benefits of home language versus integrated classes for immigrant children has, unfortunately, diverted attention from this group.

Swedish Instruction. With regard to special instruction in Swedish for immigrant pupils, although much less emphasis has been placed on this component than on the home language component in the public debate concerning the education of immigrant children (researchers such as Tingbjörn [1981] and Paulston [1983] speak of a downright neglect in this area), supportive Swedish lessons have been given since 1966.

In compulsory school, 43,434 children received supportive Swedish lessons in 1982; this was 50 percent of all pupils with home language other than Swedish (Statistics Sweden, 1983:41). Only those children who are judged by the school to be in need of supportive Swedish lessons are entitled to receive this instruction. One of the problems in providing this education is that in some areas where the proportion of immigrant children is high, resources are not adequate to meet the needs (Ekström, 1983:34). Thus, 59 percent were judged in need of supportive Swedish lessons in 1982 (Statistics Sweden, 1983:38) as compared to the 50 percent who actually received them. The figures for upper secondary school for 1981 as regards supportive teaching are as follows: 26 percent required support, while only about 15 percent received such instruction (Statistics Sweden, 1983:61–62).

In addition to the supportive Swedish instruction, so-called preparatory classes with pupils from one or more language backgrounds can be set up as a temporary arrangement in schools with a large number of immigrant children. The aim of such classes is to introduce recent immigrants to the Swedish school and, in particular, to prepare the pupils for subject matter instruction in Swedish.

In order to facilitate the transition from compulsory school to upper secondary school, especially for those immigrant children who have arrived just prior to entry into upper secondary school, so-called introductory courses have been developed (SÖ, 1977). Emphasis is on Swedish as a second language, but other subjects relevant to preparation for secondary school studies are also included.

Adult Education. Since 1965, adult immigrants have been offered Swedish courses free of charge. The most reliable statistics relating to participation in these courses are based on teaching hours rather than number of participants. These statistics show a steep increase in the 1970s, followed by a slight decrease in the 1980s in the number of teaching hours: 100,000 hours in 1965–66; 780,000 in 1971–72 (cf. Hammar, 1979); and 675,000 in 1981–82 (Statistics Sweden, 1983:84).

In 1973, the so-called Swedish Lessons Act was enforced, stating that immigrant employees without basic knowledge of Swedish were entitled to 240 hours (in some cases 160 hours) of Swedish instruction during paid working hours. In other words, some of the costs for this statutory education were imposed on the employer. For various reasons, the Act has been much less of a success than expected. It is even considered as having had the effect of excluding immigrants from employment, thus contributing to a higher percentage of unemployment among immigrants without basic knowledge of Swedish (SOU, 1981a).

A substantial portion of the total amount of Swedish instruction has been arranged by state-approved adult education associations, which were also the first to organize this type of education. Beginning in 1971, Swedish instruction has also been given within the framework of labor market training for unemployed immigrants (the so-called AMU courses). The proportion of Swedish instruction within AMU has been much larger than was expected in the early 1970s, a development that should be seen in relation to the general unemployment situation for immigrants and the problems related to the Swedish Lessons Act mentioned above.

To complete the picture, it should also be mentioned that Swedish instruction is given at refugee reception centers at so-called folk high schools and within the university system, for foreign students.

Suggestions concerning the future organization for adult immigrants have been presented by a parliamentary commission on Swedish for Immigrants, the SFI Commission (SOU, 1981a and b). In 1984, a government bill on the issue was presented to the Parliament. The final parliamentary decision involves important changes in relation to the present situation among other areas that place greater responsibility on the local municipalities. In addition, centrally framed syllabuses and other guidelines, for example, concerning teacher training requirements, have been suggested.

Apart from language instruction, adult immigrants who are illiterate or lack basic knowledge in certain subjects, for example, mathematics, are offered basic education in these areas in the so-called GRUNDVUX program. This educational form is also offered to Swedes whose knowledge of reading, writing, and/or mathematics is rated as below the average for pupils completing grade four of the compulsory school. The number of participants in GRUNDVUX totaled 10,181 in March 1982, 63 percent of whom were immigrants (Statistics Sweden, 1983:95). A total of 30 percent of the immigrant pupils were taught in their mother tongue to some extent (Statistics Sweden, 1983:95).

As mentioned above, Swedish instruction for adults is seen as one of the major tools in attaining the objectives of Sweden's official policy with regard to immigrants and ethnic minorities, in particular the principle of equality between immigrants and Swedes. The relation between immigrants' proficiency in Swedish and general living conditions has been investigated in a study by I. Municio and T. Meisaari-Polsa (1980).

Teacher Training. Teacher training programs for home language teachers were initiated in 1977. The training consists of a two-year program. So far, only a few languages have been involved, and the number of students has been small in relation to the needs. A number of those employed as home language teachers, however, already have teacher training from their countries of origin. Although efforts have thus been made to employ trained teachers, the majority of the present home language teachers do not have adequate teacher training. In 1981, the number of home language teachers totalled approximately four thousand (Statistics Sweden, 1983:102).

As regards teachers of Swedish as a second language, full teacher training programs were begun as late as 1983. This teacher training aims specifically at supplying upper primary schools and secondary schools with teachers. In 1984, special positions and eligibility conditions were established for teachers of Swedish as a second language at these levels. Similar measures have not yet been taken concerning teachers of children at grades one through six. As regards teachers in adult education, the situation is similar in that no specific teacher training requirements have been established except in one of the organizational forms for such teaching, the AMU courses (see above). The number of teachers of Swedish as a second language, including all educational levels, is estimated at approximately seventy-five hundred (Tingbjörn, 1983:16). Although there has been no regular teaching training for those teachers now in the field, a large number have nevertheless followed university courses in Swedish as a second language, which began in 1973. Although these courses are given outside the regular teacher training program, they are, both quantitatively and qualitatively, quite on a par with other subjects leading up to degrees in the teaching profession (Hammarberg, 1981).

Problems and Suggested Solutions

Problems and suggested solutions related to the education of minority children have been discussed, in among other sources, in the reports from the two governmental commissions investigating the situations for preschool and primary secondary school immigrant children (see SOU, 1982; SOU, 1983; see also SOS, 1984). Problems also have been considered in connection with several investigations of the actual implementation of educational reforms among specific interest groups or at various levels of the educational system:

- Preschool: Municio (1983).
- Comprehensive school: Ekström (1982); Enström (1982); Enström and Tingbjörn (1982); Källström (1982).

- Upper secondary school: Edberg and Holmegaard (1982).
- Home language teachers: Enström (1984).
- Introductory courses: Edberg, Hagelin, and Holmegaard (1980).

Major areas discussed include information needs, teacher training, and organizational issues.

With regard to information needs, despite great strides made in this area in the past decade, there remains a lack of understanding among certain groups concerning the goals of the home language program and, consequently, of the need for home language instruction. As a result, inappropriate language placements are sometimes made in preschool or school programs, or programs are not developed for immigrant children at local levels. There is a need for increased attention to immigrant issues in basic and in-service education for various personnel categories who work directly with immigrant children and families. Parents also need more information; many parents lack an understanding and knowledge of the basic goals and philosophies of the different bilingual education models as well as of their own role in developing active bilingualism in the home.

Another problem in Sweden, as in many countries, concerns teacher training. Although, as was mentioned earlier, educational programs have been developed for teachers at various stages of the educational system, many problems remain, for example, concerning the recruitment of qualified home language teacher candidates, especially at the preschool level, the availability of teachers in certain parts of the country as well as for certain language groups, the lack of training among many teachers already employed in the field, and the need to update existing educational programs as new experiences emerge from the field. The various commissions investigating these areas have made a number of suggestions, for example, better statistics so that more accurate planning for the number of teachers needed in the future can be carried out. Especially worth mentioning is the recent recognition of the need to include a multicultural component in the education of *all* teachers in the future, both Swedish and home language, as well as a greater emphasis on teacher training in the area of Swedish as a second language.

With regard to organizational issues, many preschool children receive home language instruction for only four hours per week. For many, this instruction begins too late, that is, not until the child is five or six. This, in addition to the difficult working situation for home language teachers working on a peripatetic basis, has led to recommendations concerning the placement of bilingual preschool children in home language or integrated groups whenever possible. A further suggestion made by the commission investigating the preschool area was that all immigrant children be allowed two years' home language training during preschool which could begin at any stage. This is seen as an improvement from waiting until the child is five or six. Whether or not this recommendation will be adopted by the government is unclear at present.

In many situations in which children receive home language instruction, they must be pulled out of their regular classes in order to receive this instruction; as a result many children choose not to participate in the program. It has been suggested that children be allowed to receive home language instruction after school hours if they desire it.

A remaining problem concerns the many children who are mainstreamed in Swedish classes, many of whom belong to very small language groups and who, thus, may not be able to receive home language lessons. Although recommendations have been made concerning ways to help Swedish teachers incorporate the cultures of immigrant pupils in their classrooms, one would also hope to see more attention placed on language-related issues in the future. Through such means as developing parallel curricular materials or the use of parents or paraprofessionals who speak the home language in the classroom, even immigrant children who come from the "smaller" language groups could be helped to develop their mother tongue.

Increased recognition has also been given to the need for some type of long-range "linguistic planning" for each child. Too often immigrant children are placed in home language groups at the preschool level for whom no followup placement is available in primary school. If such is the case, it may be important to introduce Swedish as a second language at the preschool level. There is also a need for the development of some type of language assessment program in conjunction with this linguistic planning.

Finally, problems related to the lack of curriculum materials have led to the suggestion that a national center for the development of curriculum materials be established.

RESEARCH

Before describing results with regard to evaluation of different types of bilingual education programs at the preschool and primary and secondary school levels, a brief history of the debate concerning the role of the mother tongue in the education of immigrant children will be given. Sweden has taken a rather unique position with regard to mother-tongue teaching, which has had important implications for research and policy-making on an international level.

The Swedish Debate

The Swedish debate on the role of the mother tongue in the education of immigrant children can be traced back to the work of N. E. Hansegård (1968) who described the language situation for Finnish-speaking children in the Torne Valley. According to Hansegård, the early introduction of Swedish in the schooling of these children often led to poor knowledge of both the first and second languages; thus, the term "double semilingualism" was introduced. Hansegård (1968) emphasized the role of the mother tongue in the child's communicative, intellectual, and emotional development, suggesting that the child's early school experiences be carried out in this language.

Although the notion of "semilingualism" has played an important role in drawing attention to the situation of immigrant children, as especially evident in the work of T. Skutnabb-Kangas (e.g., 1981), much criticism has been directed toward the concept as such as well as toward its use. B. Loman (1974), one of the first researchers to investigate semilingualism, found no empirical support of it. Hansegård's results were criticized for their lack of consideration of social factors. When social factors were controlled for, no differences in Swedish skills were found between residents of the Torne Valley and those in other areas of Sweden (Loman, 1974). Hansegård (1977), however, claims that the empirical research undertaken by Loman investigates only superficial, formal aspects of language, disregarding the important intellectual and emotional functions. He thus contends that the existence of semilingualism is by no means disproved by Loman's investigations.

More recently other linguists have also criticized the use of the concept for its lack of empirical support, among other reasons (Wande 1977; Stroud 1978; Oksaar 1980; Öhman 1981; Hyltenstam and Stroud 1982). Wande (1977) who himself grew up in the Torne Valley, has pointed out that several interpretations are possible of the original data on which Hansegård based his assumptions; also suggested was the need for an interpretation of the data in a wider linguistic and societal/cultural perspective than that originally taken. Stroud (1978) has carried out an analysis of the concept as a theoretical construct, suggesting that there are three senses in which the notion of semilingualism can potentially be used depending on the strength of the language-thought relationship which is assumed. One reason for the somewhat vague nature of the discussions surrounding the semilingualism concept is thus that one or another of these interpretations often is implicitly assumed by various writers without their always being conscious of this fact. Stroud also suggests that a number of other tacit theoretical assumptions upon which the concept is based are either questionable or difficult to settle.

Öhman (1981) discusses the diffusion of the concept in society and strongly urges proponents of the term to consider seriously the negative consequences it has had for immigrant children both in terms of low self-esteem and decreased expectations from the wider environment. Hyltenstam and Stroud (1982) point out the negative connotations which the notion semilingualism, as well as other terms such as "linguistic facade," also used to describe the speech of immigrant children, have had. As these authors suggest, the use of such negatively loaded labels can often have certain self-fulfilling effects (Rosenthal and Jacobson, 1968). Moreover, the term *semilingualism* is misleading, for, by focusing on linguistic issues, it has diverted attention from the cluster of factors that contribute to immigrant children's poor school achievement which, in addition to linguistic factors, also involves social, cultural, cognitive, and emotional factors (Hyltenstam and Stroud, 1982). These authors, Paulston (1983) and others, have thus recommended that the term *semilingualism* no longer be used.

The term *semilingualism*, with its heavy emphasis on the necessity of developing mother-tongue skills, has often been a major factor in educational and political arguments for mother-tongue classes. Actual research concerning the effects of mother-tongue instruction, however, was not initiated until the 1970s.

Especially important is Toukomaa's study of Finnish-speaking children in two Swedish cities (see Skutnabb-Kangas and Toukomaa, 1976). Among other findings, the results showed that children who had immigrated to Sweden at age ten learned Swedish more easily than those who had immigrated at age seven to eight. The authors, therefore, suggested that it was important to allow the mother tongue to develop to "an abstract level" before introducing Swedish. Results concerning the importance of the mother tongue were also supported by Canadian research findings concerning the developmental interdependence hypothesis (see Cummins, 1979), that is, that the level of L2 competence which a bilingual child attains is partially a function of the competence developed in L1 at the time L2 exposure begins.

On the other hand, a number of researchers in Sweden and elsewhere have strongly criticized the idea that the child must first learn the mother tongue "to an abstract level" before the second language is introduced. P. Ouvinen-Birgerstam and E. Wigforss (1978) attack P. Toukomaa's results (see Skutnabb-Kangas and Toukomaa, 1976) on methodological grounds. M. Pienemann (1977) argues that results from children who have immigrated at various ages cannot be generalized to immigrant children born within a country, for the learning conditions for the two groups are inherently different. L. H. Ekstrand, in a number of literature surveys (see, e.g., 1981a and b), has found no support for the "mother-tongue hypothesis" and suggests that children can easily learn two languages during early childhood. With regard to the superior performances of the older learners in Toukomaa's study (see above), this could as well be due to an age factor as to a causal relationship between the two languages (Ekstrand, 1979).

J. Allwood, M. MacDowall, and S. Strömqvist (1982), repeating arguments that have been presented earlier in the debate, have suggested a number of factors explaining the lack of consensus among researchers with regard to the education of immigrant children. First, there has been rather little recent basic research in the area, especially concerning the theoretical concepts on which the debate rests. For example, researchers have had very different points of departure with regard to the relationship between language, thought, and emotion which has led to confusion in the practical context (see also Stroud, 1978). Definition of some of the dependent variables involved, such as "active bilingualism," is fraught with difficulties, as is the construction of tests that measure those variables. Other factors suggested concern with such phenomena as researchers' views about assimilation versus cultural and linguistic pluralism, as well as how they view the process of second-language learning.

If one holds the belief that Swedish can be easily learned through mere exposure in the natural environment, home language models are not seen as impeding the child's acquisition of Swedish. Recently, however, more attention has been paid to the complexity of the second-language acquisition process and, consequently, to the need to provide exposure to the second language in a variety of contexts. Finally, a wide variety of methods have been used in the various research studies. In some cases, empirical studies have been carried out, whereas in other cases arguments have been based on secondary sources such as literature surveys.

Bilingual Education at the Preschool Level

Research projects dealing with bilingual education at the preschool level are summarized in SOU (1982). Most of the projects have been initiated by the National Board of Health and Welfare in answer to the enormous need for information in the local municipalities with regard to the development of day care forms for preschool immigrant children.

In order to increase knowledge concerning ways of organizing programs, a pilot scheme administered by the National Board of Health and Welfare was carried out between 1971 and 1973 in eighteen municipalities. The study focused on children in kindergarten groups, that is, six-year-olds. Initially, different ways of organizing training in Swedish were studied. The findings showed that the desired results with regard to Swedish were not achieved and that greater emphasis should be placed on the development of the children's mother tongue. The permanent employment of bilingual staff in the groups was also suggested as being important both for the children's language development and for ensuring a link between the preschool and home.

A study of six-year-olds enrolled in two organizational models was carried out by B-I Stockfelt-Hoatson (1978). In one model, children from several immigrant groups were placed together with Swedish children, and the immigrant children received home language training by a peripatetic teacher. The second group consisted of Finnish-speaking children taught by a bilingual teacher. Observations in the two groups showed that the Finnish-speaking group functioned better, as in the mixed group aggressive behavior frequently occurred when the children could not make themselves understood. The test results showed a normal development in nonverbal tests. The children performed at below-average level in verbal tests, however, and there were no significant differences between children from the two groups. Results from teacher ratings and interviews with parents also showed that adults often overrated the children with regard to their language abilities.

The above studies involved six-year-old children; a study of younger immigrant children in a day care setting was carried out by G. Schyl-Bjurman (1975). Finnish children between the ages of three and seven placed in Swedish-speaking groups and receiving home language training six hours per week were studied. The results from language testing of the children showed the effects of the program to be positive, considering the limited number of hours per week the children received home language training. Behavioral observations of the groups supported the need for organizational methods in which children of similar ages and language backgrounds are placed together in groups staffed by bilingual teachers.

A project studying Latin-American children (see Malmö socialförvaltning, 1980) was one of the few studies employing a control group. The study involved forty-five children placed in four Swedish groups. Latin-American personnel were also employed in the groups. The control group consisted of Latin-American children placed in Swedish-speaking groups for whom no special measures had been taken with regard to enhancing the children's linguistic and cultural development. Language testing of the children showed that the project children performed better than the control group children in both languages.

G. Svensson (1979) studied the situation of very young immigrant children (age six months to three years) when placed in an environment in which they did not have access to personnel or other children who understood their language. This age period appeared to be especially critical with regard to a language switch. This is supported by other findings (see Gardell, 1978; Smith, 1935). Svensson suggests the placement of young immigrant children in either home language or integrated groups whenever possible.

Recent studies have focused not only on the different bilingual models themselves but also on factors influencing the functioning of the models and on the preschool as a language-learning environment for immigrant children. K. Naucler (1983) carried out a questionnaire study in thirty-two municipalities as well as a pilot study consisting of observations in twenty-five preschools. The preschools were selected in order to represent a variety of models—home language, integrated, mainstream Swedish with home language training provided by a peripatetic teacher. The focus was on how the two languages were used in the program and on what factors steered language choice.

The results showed a great variation even within the same model type with regard to how much home language and Swedish were being used. Possibly the most important factor was education of staff. In cases where both bilingual and Swedish staff were employed and where Swedish personnel had higher education, the language of the group could be Swedish even in groups where all the children shared a language other than Swedish. Naucler (1983) suggested the importance of the prestige and status of the minority language in the preschool and society, attitudes of bilingual and Swedish teachers toward the majority and minority groups, and the consciousness with which goals and methods with regard to the use of the two languages within the program had been established and were being carried out.

Further studies have focused on the language-learning milieu in the preschool. Andersson and Naucler (1984) and Naucler (1984) intensively studied the language environment in a bilingual preschool for thirteen three- to six-year-olds where four of the children were native Swedish-speakers and the remainder had Spanish as a mother tongue. In Andersson and Naucler (1984), interactional patterns between children and adults were studied in relation to their effects on the development of children's communicative skills. Large individual differences were found among adults with regard to the ways in which they communicated with children, and factors were isolated which were felt to be especially positive in fostering children's communicative development.

Naucler (1984) focused on the use of Spanish and Swedish in the preschool. Despite attempts to regulate language use by means of a one person:one language strategy (that is, personnel each of whom uses his or her native language only when interacting with the children and associating certain activities with specific languages), it was found difficult to maintain the use of Spanish, the minority language. Approximately 75 percent of all language activities were carried out in Swedish. One reason for this situation, as Naucler pointed out, was that Swedish was the common language of communication (i.e., the Swedish-speaking children were not expected to learn Spanish). Other psychological and communicative factors also served to break down the above principles concerning language use.

Studies such as the above are extremely important in shedding light on the language-learning environment of the preschool and on factors that can mediate the effects of various organizational models.

Finally, L. Arnberg (1984a) carried out an evaluation of mother-tongue play groups for mothers and toddlers meeting once a week. The results indicated that the benefits of the group were more related to the socio-affective aspects of bilingualism than the linguistic ones, owing to the frequency with which the group met. However, the groups were felt to have an important support function for parents raising their children bilingually.

Conclusions. As has been pointed out in SOU (1982), only limited conclusions can be drawn from the studies carried out thus far. The importance of the mother tongue for the child's security and development has been demonstrated, as well as the positive results from programs where permanent staff are employed who are familiar with the child's language and cultural background. The results have also shown that programs which focus on the special needs of immigrant children give better results with regard to both languages than merely placing the child in a regular Swedish group without any attention being paid to the child's language and cultural background. This is supported by results from the literature (see Arnberg, 1983).

On the other hand, earlier research has told us little about how to organize programs so as to best ensure the child's development in the home language and Swedish. No well-controlled studies in which various models have been compared have yet been carried out at the preschool level. Although recent research findings show that the different models do not always function in the way in which they are intended, there remains a need for research concerning how the use of the two languages should be structured in the preschool setting, especially with regard to individual children. The lack of such research is undoubtedly related to the recent nature of the problems involved, the need for immediate solutions, and the enormous complexity of the area.

Bilingual Education at the Primary and Secondary School Levels

With regard to the evaluation of bilingual education programs at the primary school level, a major literature survey has been carried out by Virta (1983). The present discussion focuses mainly on this report, although other sources are also cited. The majority of the studies have involved Finnish-speaking children.

Immigrant Children Placed in Swedish Classes. Studies of immigrant children placed in Swedish classes have shown that in many cases the children function on a par with their Swedish classmates (see Wennerström, 1967). Often, however, the results indicate that the children are no longer bilingual; for many, a language shift to Swedish has occurred, even in the home domain.

In a study sponsored by the National Board of Education (see Liljegren and Ullman, 1981, 1982; Liljegren, 1981a and b), the importance of differentiating results with regard to individual immigrant groups was shown. Seven thousand immigrant children who completed primary school in 1979 were studied with regard to grades in Swedish and the percentage of children continuing with further education. When the group was considered as a whole, there were no major differences between the immigrant children and their Swedish classmates. Nonetheless, the results were much less favorable with regard to certain specific immigrant groups.

Toukomaa (1977) carried out a study of 687 Finnish children from grades one to six attending Swedish classes. The purpose of the study was to investigate:

1. Language development in Finnish and Swedish.
2. The relationship between L1 and L2.
3. The children's school achievement.

The children's showed normal development in nonverbal tests but were below average in language tests in both languages. In general, school achievement was poor. School grades were highly correlated with language skills in both Finnish and Swedish. Finally, children with good skills in the mother tongue often had good skills in Swedish. Although some evidence for a causal relationship was indicated, other factors must be considered, for example, underlying variables related to general intelligence factors.

Immigrant Children Attending a Transitional Bilingual Model. Thirty-four children attending a transitional bilingual model were studied by H. Löfgren and P. Ouvinen-Birgerstam (1980). Most of the children had attended a Finnish-speaking preschool for two years. In language tests in both languages, the children performed at approximately one standard deviation below the norms. The authors attributed this finding in part to the overrepresentation of children from working-class backgrounds among the project children. In school grades and with regard to standard test results in Swedish and mathematics, however, the children performed as well as their Swedish-speaking classmates and children from the same residential area. The results were also compared to those of Finnish-speaking children attending a mother-tongue model in a study by K. Lasonen (1978). Although the children performed equally well in a Finnish-language measure, in several regards the two groups were not fully comparable. The children in the bilingual model had attended a two-year Finnish-speaking bilingual preschool, whereas the children participating in the mother-tongue model had not.

Immigrant Children Attending Mother-Tongue Classes. With regard to children attending mother-tongue classes, surprisingly few results are available. Lasonen (see Lasonen and Toukomaa, 1978) studied 340 Finnish children who had attended mother-tongue classes from grades one to three. Two control groups were used consisting of a group in Finland and fifty-three Finnish children who had attended Swedish classes. The results were as expected. Finnish children attending Finnish classes performed better than those attending Swedish classes in language measures in Finnish, although still below norms for the Finnish control group. In the Swedish-language measure the results were in the opposite direction, that is, although both groups performed under the norms for Swedish children, the children attending Finnish classes performed worse.

More long-range results are available from a study by G. Hanson (1982) who studied the school grades of 163 Finnish-speaking children who had attended mother-tongue classes from grades one to six. The children's school marks at grades seven to nine were found to be similar to those of Swedish students in parallel classes, including those in Swedish. In addition, the children had maintained the mother tongue to a much greater extent than Finnish children attending other models. Although comparisons with Finnish children attending Swedish classes were carried out, the generalizations that can be made are limited owing to the small number of subjects. The results indicated, however, that children who had attended mother-tongue classes showed better results with regard to school achievement than those attending Swedish classes and performed equally well in Swedish. The results concerning Swedish are surprising, and it is unfortunate that more background data are not available. This would shed light on whether the results were due to factors related to language transfer, the positive self-identity of children attending mother-tongue programs, or sample selection.

Comparison of Mother Tongue and Bilingual Models. The Swedish debate has focused mainly on the advantages and disadvantages of mother-tongue versus integrated or bilingual classes. A study comparing these two models was carried out by H. Löfgren and E. Ericsson (1982). The results are of limited generalizability, however, owing to the large dropout rate as well as the exploratory nature of the study (e.g., with regard to the language measures used).

Finnish-speaking children in grades five and six from nine mother-tongue and six integrated classes were studied. The results from the language tests showed that children participating in mother-tongue classes performed somewhat better in Finnish, whereas those participating in integrated classes performed somewhat better in Swedish. As the authors point out, however, this could as well have been attributed to differences in background variables between the two groups as the organizational model itself. Children in the mother-tongue group were also more likely to view themselves as "less Swedish" than children in the integrated classes. The authors also suggested that the debate in Sweden regarding the effects of organization models is far too restricted, as other factors such as length of residence and social factors are highly important in determining the educational outcomes of immigrant programs. Another factor related to organizational models was that, in many cases, bilingual models were established for organizational reasons (e.g., too few children to form a home language class) rather than for "philosophical" ones (Löfgren and Ericsson, 1982). It is difficult to imagine that such a factor will not influence program content and quality.

Löfgren and Ericsson (1982) thus suggest that the role of the individual organizational model should not be exaggerated. If there is a strong desire for mother-tongue classes among parents and teachers, there is no reason why these classes should not be established. On the other hand, such programs demand that greater attention be paid to the subject of Swedish as a second language than has earlier been the case in order to take advantage of the benefits of early bilingualism. However, bilingual models should not be discouraged either, for no negative effects have been found to be associated with them.

Conclusions. With regard to research concerning the education of immigrant children in Sweden, two main questions seem important: (1) whether or not the mother tongue should be used in instruction and, if so, (2) what forms mother-tongue instruction should take: bilingual or mother-tongue classes. Most of the studies carried out have involved Finnish-speaking children. Because of the particular circumstances of the Finnish-speaking minority group in Sweden, the results concerning this group cannot always be generalized to other groups (see e.g., Paulston, 1983). Nevertheless, some general trends will be described.

With regard to the first question, a number of studies have shown the benefits of mother-tongue instruction. Most of the studies have involved Finnish children in which the children are compared with Finnish children mainstreamed in Swedish classes. On the other hand, some research findings have shown that many immigrant children appear to manage well when placed in regular Swedish classes. Thus, an important task for future research is to attempt to isolate those factors that contribute to the differential results so that we can better understand the effects of mother-tongue instruction, especially in relation to its benefits for children from a variety of cultural, social, and linguistic backgrounds. Apart from pedagogical issues alone, however, mother-tongue instruction has been shown to play an important role in the maintenance of the minority language.

With regard to the second question, that is, the form in which mother-tongue instruction should be given, researchers have differed as to how much importance they should attribute to the bilingual versus mother-tongue educational model. Researchers such as Löfgren and Ericsson (1982) seem to suggest that the role of model is minor in relation to other outside factors. They also point out that, in practice, mother-tongue and bilingual models may often not be that different.

Other writers, however, suggest the importance of mother-tongue models for language maintenance, or for psychological or pedagogical reasons (Skutnabb-Kangas, 1981; Virta, 1983). Many of those researchers who recommend a mother-tongue model, however, do not ignore the need for instruction in Swedish as a second language which it is felt should begin as early as possible.

Other Research on Bilingualism

Other research has focused on various aspects of bilingualism rather than on bilingual education per se. L. Arnberg (1981, 1984b) has studied children's language development in the context of the mixed-lingual family as well as the patterns of use of the two languages in such families (1979, 1981). The code-differentiation process in children acquiring the two languages simultaneously (Arnberg and Arnberg, in press) has also been studied. K. Aronsson (1978, 1981a and b, 1983) has investigated bilingualism and concept formation, as well as metalinguistic awareness in the bilingual child. Also of interest are studies of information processing and bilingualism (Dornic, 1979, 1980) and of memory functions in bilinguals (Mägiste, 1979, 1980, 1982).

Linguistically Oriented Research on L1 and L2

Public debate and governmental concerns about immigrant education in Sweden have, to a large extent, considered organizational questions such as which model should be preferred in the teaching of immigrant children; when the second language, Swedish, should be introduced; how many hours of instruction should be devoted to the home language and how many to Swedish; and how many hours of Swedish instruction should be given to adult immigrants. Many of the arguments offered in the discussion of these issues are based on educational and psychologically oriented research into bilingualism and second-language acquisition. Unfortunately, far less emphasis has been placed on discussing issues related to the content of both home language instruction and Swedish instruction in this debate. It seems to be difficult for those who are not actively involved in the actual teaching—be they politicians, school administrators, or researchers—to take an active interest in the content questions. The view that many organizational questions are dependent on content issues such as what is achievable, and what can and what should be carried out in the classroom, has thus had difficulty gaining a hearing (cf. Hyltenstam, 1981).

At the individual teacher level, however, the focus has been on content questions for quite some time. As regards the linguistic component of the content area, the need for information about the developmental aspects of both first and second languages has been increasingly recognized. Similarly, general norm data for bilingual development where Swedish is one of the languages are necessary. The underlying assumption behind the desirability of this kind of knowledge has been that language support and training need to take the pupil's actual linguistic

and communicative situation as a starting point, further guiding the child's L1/
L2 development or the adult's L2 development from there. Such a diagnostic/
supportive teaching approach must, naturally, be based on knowledge about
normal monolingual and bilingual development. Recent research has attempted
to meet these information needs, both with regard to immigrant children's first
and second languages and the acquisition of Swedish by adults.

Studies of immigrant children's L1 and L1 development are presently being
carried out among children who speak Finnish (Nesser, 1981, 1982); Hungarian
(Dugantsy, 1983); and Serbo-Croatian (Stankovski, Durovic, and Tomasevic,
1983). These studies show that features from Swedish are transferred to the L1s
of the children. One example is the development of an indefinite article in Finnish,
which lacks such a structure, through the use of the Finnish numeral *yksi* ("one"),
or the overuse of the indefinite article in Hungarian. Another example of differences between immigrant children's use of their first language and its standard
variety is the reduced phonological system employed by children who speak
Serbo-Croation (Stankovski, 1978). Results from this kind of empirical investigation should shed light on "normal" L1 development in a minority language
situation of the type immigrant children face in Sweden.

Apart from these studies of the language development of immigrant children,
more general studies of immigrant languages in Sweden (Swedish-Estonian, e.g.,
Oksaar, 1972; Raag, 1982; Maandi, 1984; Swedish-Finnish, Wande, 1982, Lainio, 1984) provide norm data of relevance for the home language teaching of
these languages in Sweden.

As regards Swedish as a second language, most studies have analyzed data
from adult learners or have used a contrastive/typological methodology without
empirical learner data. A characteristic feature of Swedish second-language acquisition research is its typological/comparative focus. This can be seen as having
both a theoretical and practical explanation, the practical one being based on the
variety of languages spoken by immigrants in Sweden. Thus, a number of studies
have investigated and compared learners of Swedish with various mother tongues
either in order to survey and estimate learning problems that may occur (Johansson, 1973; Hammarberg and Viberg, 1977a; Tingbjörn, 1976; Gårding and
Bannert, 1979; Bannert, 1980), or in order to give a detailed account of certain
linguistic phenomena that have surfaced as being problematic for speakers of
various languages (Hammarberg and Viberg, 1976a, 1976b, 1977b; Hyltenstam,
1977, 1978, 1984).

The most important exception to the concentration on adult learners is the so-
called SPRINS project (Tingbjörn, 1976), where school children's learning of
Swedish has been investigated (see, for example, Tingbjörn, 1977; Andersson,
1981).

While many of the above-mentioned studies have focused on syntax or phonology, lexical-semantic aspects of Swedish as a second language have also been
studied in a typological comparative framework by Å. Viberg (e.g., 1980, 1984a,
and in various other studies). Viberg's results concern verbs in a number of

semantic fields such as perception, verbal communication, and cognition. They show that, although the differences between languages may be considerable in the ways in which they structure certain semantic fields, there are also certain restrictions on such structuring.

U.-B. Kotsinas (1982 and in various other studies) has investigated untutored adult learners of Swedish, mainly from Greece, with low educational background. The research primarily concerns vocabulary use and communicative strategies used by learners with a highly restricted L2. The results indicate unexpected regularities in semantic overextensions and in other "strategic" means of expression in language production which, on the surface, appear to be quite disorganized.

Although a typological perspective has been pervasive in Swedish research, studies have also been carried out on learners from one particular background, for example, Hyltenstam and Magnusson (forthcoming) on Finnish learners; Budmar (1983) on Polish learners; and Hammarberg (1986) on German learners of Swedish.

More recent, ongoing projects concern classroom input target-language variation as a learning problem and native language attitudes toward foreign accents (Bannert and Hyltenstam, 1981; Håkansson, 1982; Dahlbäck, 1983); longitudinal studies of untutored adult learners (Allwood, Strömqvist, and Voionmaa, 1983; Strömqvist and Allwood, 1985); and longitudinal studies of tutored adult language learners (Viberg and Axelsson, 1984). For more detailed overviews of research into Swedish as a second language, see Hammarberg (1984) and Viberg (1984b).

SUMMARY

In this overview, we have sought to give a comprehensive picture of the Swedish solutions for the education of immigrant and other minority group students. We have also chosen to include adult education, as this educational sector, along with programs for children, has been considered an important means of fulfilling the political goals with regard to Swedish policies for immigrants, especially the attainment of equal opportunity and participation in society.

As a background for the description of the education of immigrant children and adults, a brief survey is given of the demographic, linguistic, social, political, and religious characteristics of the immigrant and indigenous minority populations. A historical description of a number of factors that have led to the present situation is also given.

An attempt has been made to explicate the reasons as to why the Swedish government made the decisions that led to the so-called Home Language Reform for school children, mother-tongue teaching at the preschool level, and Swedish instruction for immigrant children and adults. We have also reviewed the research that has been carried out in order to evaluate, or in other ways shed light on, educational issues for these groups. In order to make the picture more comprehensive, we have also included a section on research bearing on the linguistic content of the various programs, particularly research into first-language development in immigrant children, second-language acquisition studies carried out among adults and children, and investigations into the characteristics of the minority languages as spoken in Sweden.

BIBLIOGRAPHY

The Swedish letters "å", "ä", and "ö" appear in the English alphabetical order for "a" and "o".

Allwood, J., M. MacDowall, and S. Strömqvist. 1982. "Barn, språkutveckling och flerspråkighet—en kritisk översikt. *Utredning om Språkminoriteten i förskoleåldern*. Socialdepartementet.

Allwood, J., S. Strömqvist, and K. Voionmaa. 1983. "Ecology of Adult Language Acquisition. A Psycholinguistic Research Project. *Gothenburg Papers in Theoretical Linguistics* 45. University of Gothenburg, Department of Linguistics.

Andersson, A-B. 1981. "Diktamensundersökningen." In *Invandrarbarnen och tvåspråkigheten*, ed. G. Tingbjörn and A-B. Andersson. Stockholm: Liber Utbildningsförlaget och SO, pp. 58–96.

Andersson, A-B., and K. Naucler. 1984. "Språklig interaktion i en tvåspråkig förskolegrupp." *SPRINS-projektet*, 25. University of Gothenburg, Department of Linguistics.

Arnberg, L. 1979. "Language Strategies in Mixed Nationality Families." *Scandinavian Journal of Psychology* 20:105–12.

———. 1981. "Early Childhood Bilingualism in the Mixed-Lingual Family." *Linköping Studies in Education Dissertations* 14. Linköping University.

———. 1983. "Bilingual Education for Preschool Children." Report LiU-PEK-R–73. Linköping University, ED 245–535.

———. 1984a. "Mother Tongue Playgroups for Pre-school Bilingual Children." *Journal of Multilingual Multicultural Development* 5:65–84.

———. 1984b. "Remaining Bilingual: A Follow-up Study of Four Children Exposed to English and Swedish in the Home up to Age Seven and a-Half." Paper presented at the Fourth Scandinavian Conference on Bilingualism, Uppsala, June 1984.

Arnberg, L., and P. Arnberg. In press. "The Relation Between Code Differentiation and Language Mixing in Bilingual Three- to Four-Year-Old Children." Accepted for publication in *Bilingual Review*.

Arnstberg, K-O., and B. Ehn. 1976. *Etniska minoriteter i Sverige förr och nu*. Lund: LiberLäromedel.

Aronsson, K. 1978. "Language Concepts and Children's Classification Strategies." Dissertation Series. Lund University, Department of Psychology.

———. 1981a. "Nominal Realism and Bilingualism: A Critical Review of Studies on Word:Referent Differentiation." *Osnabruker Beitrage zur Sprachtheorie* 20.

———. 1981b. "The Bilingual Preschooler as Grammarian. Children's Paraphrases of Ungrammatical Sentences." *Psychological Research Bulletin* 21:10–11.

———. 1983. "Rim, vitsar och språksinne." In *Tal och tanke*, ed. U. Teleman. Lund: LiberFörlag.

508   Kenneth Hyltenstam and Lenore Arnberg

Bannert, R. 1980. "Svårigheter med svenskans uttal: inventering och prioritering."
    Praktisk lingvistik 5. Lund University, Department of Linguistics.
Bannert, R., and K. Hyltenstam. 1981. "Swedish Immigrants' Communication: Problems
    of Understanding and Being Understood." *Working Papers* 21:17–27. Lund Uni-
    versity, Department of General Linguistics.
Boyd, S. 1984. "Den andra generationens språkliga situation." (Manuscript.) Gothenburg
    University, Department of Linguistics.
Budmar, S. J. 1983. *Brytning hos svensktalande polacker*. Uppsala: Almqvist and Wiksell
    International.
Cummins, J. 1979. "Linguistic Interdependence and the Educational Development of
    Bilingual Children." *Review of Educational Research* 49:222–51.
Dahlbäck, H. 1983. "Vowel Variation in a Swedish dialect as a Problem of Intelligibility
    of L2 learners." In *Papers from the Seventh Scandinavian Conference of Lin-
    guistics*, ed. F. Karlsson. 2:506–20. Publication No. 10, University of Helsinki,
    Department of General Linguistics.
Dornic, S. 1979. "Information Processing in Bilinguals: Some Selected Issues." *Psy-
    chological Research* 40:329–48.
———. 1980. "Information Processing and Language Dominance." *International Re-
    view of Applied Psychology* 29:119–40.
Dugantsy, M. 1983. "Ungerska i Sverige. Analys av språkliga drag i sverigeungerska
    barns skoluppsatser." *Fuskis/Fidus* 7. Uppsala University, Finn-Ugric Institute.
Edberg, L., K. Hagelin, and M Holmegaard 1980. "Rapport från två års försöksverk-
    samhet med introduktionskurser för invandrarelever i Göteborg läsåren 1977/78,
    1978/79." *SPRINS-projektet* 4. Gothenburg University, Department of
    Linguistics.
Edberg, L., and M. Holmegaard. 1982. "Invandrareleven i gymnasieskolan. Faktorer
    som påverkar studiesituationen samt förslag till försöksverksamhet." *SPRINS-
    projektet* 16. Gothenburg University, Department of Linguistics.
Ekberg, J. 1981. "Invandrarnas inkomstförhållanden." *Statistisk tidskrift* 3.
Ekstrand, L. H. 1979. "Replacing the Critical Period and Optimum Age Theories of
    Second Language Acquisition with a Theory of Ontogenetic Development Beyond
    Puberty." *Educational and Psychological Interactions* 69. Lund: Malmö School
    of Education.
———. 1981a "Unpopular Views on Popular Beliefs About Immigrant Children: Con-
    temporary Practices and Problems in Sweden." In *Educating Immigrants*, ed. J.
    Bhatnagar. London: Croom Helm.
———. 1981b. "Theories and Facts About Early Bilingualism in Native and Immigrant
    Children. *Grazer Linguistische Studien* 14:25–52.
Ekström, L. 1982. "Invandrar/minoritetsundervisning på grundskolans lag- och mellan-
    stadier. 3 Invandrarundervisningen och läromedlen." *SPRINS-projektet* 11. Goth-
    enburg University, Department of Linguistics.
———. 1983. "Invandrarbarnens skolsituation." *Svenska i skolan* 16:29–35.
Enström, I. 1982. "Invandrar/minoritetsundervisning på grundskolans lag- och mellan-
    stadier. 2 Lärarundersökningen." *SPRINS-projektet* 10. Gothenburg University,
    Department of Linguistics.
———. 1984. "Hemspråkslärarna." *SPRINS-projektet* 22. Gothenburg University, De-
    partment of Linguistics.
Enström, I., and G. Tingbjörn. 1982. "Invandrar/minoritetsundervisning på grundskolans

låg och mellanstadier. 4 Invandrarkonsulenterna." *SPRINS-projektet* 2. Gothenburg University, Department of Linguistics.

Gardell, I. 1978. *Internationella adoptioner.* En rapport från Allmänna Barnhuset.

Gårding, E., and R. Bannert. 1979. "Projektrapporter Optimering av svenskt uttal." *Praktisk lingvistik* 1. Lund University, Department of Linguistics.

Håkansson, G. 1982. "Quantitative Studies of Teacher Talk." *Scandinavian Working Papers on Bilingualism* 1:52–72. Stockholm University, Department of Linguistics.

Hammar, T. 1979. "Språkutbildningen som medel att nå invandrarpolitiska mål i Sverige." In *Tvåspråkighet*, ed. A. Stedje and P. af Trampe. Stockholm: Akademilitteratur, pp. 149–57.

Hammar, T., and S. A. Reinans. 1984. *SOPEMI Report on Immigration to Sweden in 1983 and 1984.* Stockholm: Commission for Immigrant Research, Sweden, English Series Report No. 9.

Hammarberg, B. 1981. "Utbildning av lärare i svenska som främmande språk." In *Språkmöte*, ed. K. Hyltenstam. Lund: LiberLäromedel, pp. 96–117.

———. 1984. "Forskning kring svenska som målspråk: fonologi." In *Nordens språk som målspråk. Forskning och undervisning*, ed. K. Hyltenstam and K. Maandi. Stockholm University, Department of Linguistics, pp 46–60.

———. 1986. "Learnability and Learner Strategies in Second Language Syntax and Phonology." In *Modeling and Assessing Second Language Acquisition*, ed. K. Hyltenstam and M. Pienemann. Clevedon: Multilingual Matters.

Hammarberg, B., and A. Viberg. 1976a. "Anaforiska processer i svenskan i invandrarperspektive—några utgångspunkter." *SSM Report*, 3. Stockholm University, Department of Linguistics.

Hammarberg, B., and A. Viberg. 1976b. Reported speech in Swedish and ten immigrant languages. *SSM Report*, 5. Stockholm University, Department of Linguistics.

Hammarberg, B., and A. Viberg. 1977a. "Felanalys och språktypologi. Orientering om två delstudier i SSM-projektet." *SSM Report*, 1. Stockholm University, Department of Linguistics.

Hammarberg, B., and A. Viberg. 1977b. "The Place-Holder Constraint, Language Typology, and the Teaching of Swedish to Immigrants." *Studia Linguistica* 31:106–63.

Hansegård, N. E. 1968. *Tvåspråkighet eller halvspråkighet?* Stockholm: Aldus/Bonniers.

———. 1977. "Loman och halvspråkigheten." *Invandrare och minoriteter* 2:36–51.

Hanson, G. 1982. "Finnkampen. Om finska invandrarbarn i tvåspråkig hemspråksklass." Stockholm University, Psychology Department. (Stencil.)

Hyltenstam, K. 1977. "Implicational Patterns in Interlanguage Syntax Variation." *Language Learning* 27:383–411.

———. 1978. "Variation in Interlanguage Syntax." *Working Papers* 18. Lund University, Department of General Linguistics.

———. 1981. "Invandrarinriktad språkundervisning och interimspråkforskning. En inledning." In *Språkmöte*, ed. K. Hyltenstam. Lund: LiberLäromedel, pp. 9–20.

———. 1984. "The Use of Typological Markedness as Predictor in Second Language Acquisition: The Case of Pronominal Copies in Relative Clauses." In *Second Languages*, ed. R. W. Anderson. Rowley, Mass.: Newbury House.

Hyltenstam, K., and E. Magnusson. Forthcoming. "Typological Markedness, Contextual Variation, and the Acquisition of the Voice Contrast in Stops by First and Second

Language Learners of Swedish." In *Progression in Second Language Acquisition*, ed. T. Bhatia and W. Ritchie. Special Issue of the *Indian Journal of Applied Linguistics*.

Hyltenstam, K., and C. Stroud. 1982. "Halvspråkighet—ett förbrukat slagord." *Invandrare ocb minoriteter* 3:10–13.

Jaakola, M. 1973. *Språkgränsen. En studie i tvåspråkighetens sociologi*. Stockholm: Aldus/Bonniers.

Johansson, F. A. 1973. *Immigrant Swedish Phonology. A Study in Multiple Contact Analysis*. Lund: Gleerup.

Johansson, H. 1975. *Samernas språk och kultur. En intervjuundersökning rörande kulturella, sociala och psykologiska frågor*. Umeå University, Pedagogical Institute.

Källström, R. 1982. Invandrar/minoritetsundervisning på grundskolans låg-och mellanstadier. 1. Rektorsområdesundersökningen. SPRINS-projektet 9. Gothenburg University, Department of Linguistics.

Kotsinas, U.-B. 1982. *Svenska svårt. Några invandrares svenska talspråk. Ordförrådet.* MINS, 10. Stockholm University, Institute for Nordic Languages.

Lainio, J. 1984. Finsk dialektutveckling i en svensk industristad. Slut-rapport 1. Språksociologisk del. *Fuskis/Fidus*, 8. Uppsala University, Finn-Ugric Institution.

Lasonen, K. 1978. Routsin suomalaiset siirtolaisoppilaat. Osa 2: Empiirinen tutkimus. (Finska invandrarbarn i Sverige. Del 2: Empirisk studie.) *Research Reports No. 66.* University of Jyvälskylä, Department of Education.

Lasonen, K., and Toukomaa, P. 1978. Linguistic development and school achievement among Finnish immigrant children in mother tongue medium classes in Sweden. *Research Reports No. 70.* University of Jyväskylä, Department of Education.

Liljegren, T. 1981a. "Elever, med annat hemspråk än svenska, som gick ut grundskolan 1979," delrapport 2, Skolöverstyrelsen.

————. 1981b. "Elever, med annat hemspråk än svenska, som gick ut grundskolan 1979," delrapport 3, Skolöverstyrelsen.

Liljegren, T., and L. Ullman. 1981. "Elever, med annat hemspråk än svenska, som gick ut grundskolan 1979," delrapport 1, Skolöverstyrelsen.

Liljegren, T., and L. Ullman. 1982. "Elever, med annat hemspråk än svenska, som gick ut grundskolan 1979," delrapport 4, Skolöverstyrelsen.

Löfgren, H. and E. Ericsson. 1982. "Undervisningsmodeller för barn med annat hemspråk än svenska. Utvärdering av modersmålsklasser kontra sammansatta klasser." *Pedagogiska rapporter* 22. University of Lund.

Löfgren, H., and P. Ouvinen-Birgerstam. 1980. "Försök med en tvåspråkig modell för undervisning av invandrarbarn." *Pedagogiska rapporter* 22, University of Lund.

Loman, B., ed. 1974. *Språk och samhälle 2. Språket i Tornedalen*. Lund: Gleerups.

Maandi, K. 1984. "Language Change. Estonian in Sweden." Paper presented at the Eighth Scandinavian Conference of Linguistics, Cophenhagen.

Mägiste, E. 1979. "The Competing Language Systems in the Multilingual: A Development Study of Decoding and Encoding Processes." *Journal of Verbal Learning and Verbal Behavior* 18:79–89.

————. 1980. "Memory for Numbers in Monolinguals and Bilinguals." *Acta Psychologica* 46:63–68.

————. 1982. "Automaticity and Interference in Bilinguals." *Psychological Research*, 44:29–43

Malmö socialförvaltning. 1980. "Latinamerikanska projektet." Avdelningen för barnomsorg, 4:e distriktet.

Municio, I. 1983. *Hemspråk i förskolan. En undersökning av genomförande.* Stockholm: Expertgruppen för invandrarforskning. Rapport nr. 21.

Municio, I., and T. Meisaari-Polsa. 1980. *Språkkunskaper och levnadsförhållanden.* Stockholm: Expertgruppen för invandrarförskning. Rapport nr. 12.

Naucler, K. 1983. "Hemspråket i förskolan." *SPRINS-projektet* 19. Gothenburg University, Department of Linguistics.

————. 1984. "Språkväxling i en tvåspråkig förskolegrupp." *SPRINS projektet* 26. Gothenburg University, Department of Linguistics.

Nesser, A. 1981. "Finska barns språkutveckling—fonologi och morfologi." *Fuskis/Fidus* 2. Uppsala University, Finn-Ugric Institution.

————. 1982. "Subjekt. objekt och predikativ i Sverigefinska barns uppsatser." *Fuskis/Fidus* 5. Uppsala University, Finn-Ugric Institution.

Öhman, S. 1981. "Halvspråkighet som kastmärke." I *Att leva med mångfalden.* Stockholm: LiberFörlag.

Oksaar, E. 1972. "Spoken Estonian in Sweden and in USA: An Analysis of Bilingual Behavior." In *Studies for Einar Haugen,* ed. E. S. Firchov et al. The Hague: Mouton, pp. 437–49.

————. 1980. "Tvåspråkighet i teori och praktik." *Invandrare och Minoriteter* 5–6:43–47.

Ouvinen-Birgerstam, P., and E. Wigforss. 1978. "Pertti Toukomaas undersökningar saknar vetenskaplig täckning." *Invandrare och minoriteter* 2:16–23, 31.

Paulston, C. B. 1983. *Swedish Research and Debate About Bilingualism.* Stockholm: Skolöverstyrelsen.

Pienemann, M. 1977. "Zur bilingualen Schule für ausländische Arbeiterkinder." *Studium Linguistik* 4:87–91.

Raag, R. 1982. *Lexical Characteristics in Swedish Estonian.* Acta Universitatis Upsaliensis, Studia Uralica et altaica Upsaliensis, 13, Uppsala.

————. 1983. "Estniskan i Sverige." *Fuskis/Fidus* 6. Uppsala University, Finn-Ugric Institution.

Rönmark, W., and J. Wikström. 1980. *Tvåspråkighet i Tornedalen. Sammanfattning och diskussion.* Umeå University, Pedagogical Institution.

Rosenthal, R., and L. Jacobsson. 1968. "Self-Fulfilling Prophecies in the Classroom: Teacher's Expectations as Unintended Determinants of Pupils' Intellectual Competence." In *Social Class, Race and Psychological Development,* ed. M. Deutsch, J. Katz, and A. Jensen. New York: Holt.

Schyl-Bjurman, G. 1975. "Rapport om försöksverksamheten i Borås med hemspråksträning för invandrarbarn i förskola." Socialstyrelsens försöksverksamhet inom barnstugeområdet (FIB).

SIV. 1982. *Flerspråkig samhällsservice.* Norrköping: Statens invandrarverk.

Skutnabb-Kangas, T. 1981. *Tvåspråkighet.* Lund: LiberLäromedel.

Skutnabb-Kangas, T., and P. Toukomaa. 1976. "Teaching Migrant Children's Mother Tongue and Learning the Language of the Host Country in the Context of the Socio-cultural Situation of the Migrant Family." *Tutkimuksia Research Reports* 15. University of Tampere, Department of Sociology and Social Psychology.

Smith, M. 1935. "A Study of the Speech of Eight Bilingual Children of the Same Family." *Child Development* 6:19–25.

SÖ. 1977. *Introduktionskurs för invandrarungdom.* Läroplan för gymnasieskolan. Supplement Nr S2, 77:2. Skolöverstyrelsen.

———. 1979. *Invandrarna och utbildningsväsendet. Handlingsprogram för SÖ's arbete med invandrarfrågor.* Stockholm: Skolöverstyrelsen.

SOS. 1984. *Tema invandrare.* Levnadsförhållanden. Rapport 38. Stockholm: Statistiska centralbyrån.

SOU. 1974. "Invandrare och minoriteter." *Statens offentliga utredningar* 69.

———. 1981a. "Svenskundervisning för vuxna invandrare. Överväganden och förslag" *Statens offentliga utredningar* 86.

———. 1981b. "Svenskundervisning för vuxna invandrare. Kartläggning av nulaget." *Statens offentliga utredningar* 87.

———. 1982. "Språk- och kulturstöd for invandrar- och minoritetsbarn i förskoleåldern." *Statens offentliga utredningar* 43.

———. 1983. "Olika ursprung—Gemenskap i Sverige." *Statens offentliga utredningar* 57.

———. 1984. "Rösträtt och medborgarskap. Invandrares och utlandssvenskars rösträtt." *Statens offentliga utredningar* 11–12.

Stankovski, M. 1978. "Procesi redukcije fonoloskoj sistema srpskohrvatskog kod djece doseljenika u svedskoj jezicnoj sredeni." *Slavica Lundensia* 6. Lund University, Slavic Institution, pp. 21–49.

Stankovski, M., L. Durovic, and M. Tomasevic. 1983. "Development Structures in the Family Language of Yugoslav Immigrant Children in a Swedish Language Environment." *Slavica Lundensia* 9. Lund University, Slavic Institution, pp. 11–20.

Statistics Sweden. 1983. *Immigrants and Immigrant Teaching in Sweden.* Stockholm: Statistics Sweden.

Statistiska meddelanden. 1983. "Förskolor, fritidshem och familjdaghem den 31 december 1982." S 1983:18.

Stockfelt-Hoatson, B-I. 1978. "Training of Immigrant Children in Pre-school in Norrköping." *Linköping Studies in Education Dissertations* 8. Linköping University.

Strömqvist, S., and J. Allwood. 1985. "Ecology of Adult Language Acquisition. A Psycholinguistic Research Project." *Scandinavian Working Papers in Bilingualism* 4. Stockholm University, Department of Linguistics.

Stroud, C. 1978. "The Concept of Semilingualism." *Working Papers* 16. Lund University, Department of General Linguistics, pp. 153–72.

Svensson, G. 1979. "Små invandrarbarn på daghem." Familjestödsutredningen vid Socialdepartementet.

Swedish Institute. 1984. "Primary and Secondary Education in Sweden." *Fact Sheets on Sweden.*

Tingbjörn, G. 1976. "Språkutvecklingen hos invandrarbarn i Sverige (SPRINS)." In *Papers from the First Nordic Conference on Bilingualism*, ed. T. Skutnabb-Kangas. Helsingfors University, Institution for Nordic Philology, pp. 84–91.

———. 1977. "Invandrarsvenska." *Svensklärarföreningens årsskrift 1977*, pp. 35–51.

———. 1981. "Svenska som främmande språk i ungdomsskolan." In *Språkmöte*, ed. K. Hyltenstam. Lund: LiberLäromedel, pp. 66–95.

———. 1983. "Svenska som andraspråk." *Svenska i skolan* 16:9–23.

Toukomaa, P. 1977. "Om finska invandrarelevers språkutvekling och skolframgång i den svenska grundskolan. Expertgruppen för invandrarforskning (EIFO)." Stockholm: Arbetsmarknadsdepartementet.

Viberg, Å. 1980. "Tre semantiska fält i svenskan och några andra språk. 1. Kognitiva predikat. 2. Perceptionsverbens semantik. 3. Emotiva predikat." *SSM-Report* 7. Stockholm University, Department of Linguistics.

———. 1984a. "The Verbs of Perception: A Typological Study." In *Explanations for Language Universals*, ed. B. Butterworth, B. Comrie, and O. Dahl. Berlin: Mouton, pp. 123–62.

———. 1984b. "Forskning kring svenska som målspråk: grammatik och ordförråd." In *Nordens språk som målspråk. Forskning och undervisning*, ed. K. Hyltenstam and K. Maandi. Stockholm University, Department of Linguistics, pp. 3–45.

Viberg, Å., and M. Axelsson. 1984. "The Acquisition of Swedish as a Second Language in the Classroom. Some Preliminary Findings." Paper presented at the Fourth Scandinavian Conference on Bilingualism, Uppsala, June 1984.

Virta, E. 1983. *Språkligt tänkande, tvåspråkighet och undervisning av minoritetsbarn.* Ds U 1983:17. Utbildningsdepartementet.

Wande, E. 1977. "Hansegård är ensidig." *Invandrare och minoriteter* 3–4:44–51.

———. 1982. "Finskan i Sverige." *Fiskus/Fidus*, 3. Uppsala University, Finn-Ugric Institution.

Wennerström, G. 1967. "Språklig anpassning och studieframgång hos barn till utländska föräldrar." Rapport nr 18 från Pedagogisk-psykologiska institutionen, Lärarhögskolan i Stockholm.

Westin, C. 1984. *Majoritet om minoritet. En studie i etnisk tolerans i 1980-talets Sverige.* Stockholm: Liber.

Widgren, J. 1980. *Svensk invandrarpolitik.* Lund: LiberLäromedel.

Gottfried Kolde

LANGUAGE CONTACT AND
BILINGUALISM IN SWITZERLAND

SOME STEREOTYPES ABOUT SWISS-LANGUAGE CONTACT

Switzerland is one of the best known and most frequently cited multilingual countries in the world. This does not prevent foreign or native observers from oversimplifying. One widely held opinion shows up clearly in the following statement by W. B. Simon (1969:18): "The case of Switzerland need only be mentioned in passing because it is well known as the classic example of harmonious multi-lingualism." One only has to read U. Weinreich (1952) thoroughly to realize that at least the "dynamic situation" in the Grisons is a situation of conflict. More recently, books have appeared with revealing titles such as *A Crisis in Swiss Pluralism* (Billigmeier, 1979), *Der Tod des Romanischen, der Anfang vom Ende Für die Schweiz* [The Death of Romansh: The Beginning of the End of Switzerland] by J. J. Furer, 1981, or *La Romandie dominée* [French Switzerland Oppressed], by A. Charpilloz and G. Grimm-Gobat (1982).

A second stereotype concerns the individual multilingual competence of the Swiss. To quote F. Kainz (1965:353, my translation): "Every Swiss citizen knows, apart from his mother-tongue, the two [*sic*] other national languages ("Staatssprachen") at least well enough for makeshift communication." Perhaps Kainz's personal experience was limited to communication with lift boys in Swiss hotels who, among others, served P. André (1944:87–88, my translation) as warning against "the ruinous effects of bilingualism on the innermost and most delicate qualities of personality (. . .) Look at the polyglot: he likes to think of himself as a citizen of the world but remains a vagabond forever." Swiss language law and the methods of teaching the other Swiss languages at school have always aimed at separating the language communities and keeping the languages separate in the minds of speakers, especially in the areas of intense language contact (Kolde, 1981).

A third and very astonishing opinion, to be found quite frequently among German laypeople, is that Switzerland is not a multilingual country at all. This error, ridiculous though it may be, corresponds closely to the serious reproach of numerous French Swiss against their German-speaking confederates: that they too often simply forget the other language communities in their own country. But even German linguists sometimes make rather careless formulations: P. Kühn (1980:536, my translation) finds that "language development in Switzerland (*sic*) is still on the road from diglossia to bilingualism," a statement which, as we will see, makes no sense at all for French Switzerland.

During twelve years at Geneva I have come to recognize the complexity and variety of language contacts in this country. These contacts resist generalization. As I will dare to treat rather extensively the highly controversial questions of language politics and ethnic identity, I would like to stress once and for all that I have learned to admire the Swiss way of handling the problems in these fields. Over many centuries effective patterns of coexistence have been developed, which, unfortunately, cannot be simply taken over by other multilingual countries with more problems and another history.

Throughout this chapter, emphasis is on the sociolinguistic aspects of language contact. The effects of this contact on the languages and language varieties in contact will only be mentioned occasionally. No exhaustive description of interference phenomena and the resulting peculiarities of the languages is intended.

BASIC DESCRIPTION OF THE SWISS LANGUAGES, LANGUAGE COMMUNITIES, AND LANGUAGE BORDERS

The four national languages of Switzerland are German, French, Italian, and Romansh (Federal Constitution, Art. 116). The following terms are used throughout this chapter to denote languages, without any political implications. The German-speaking Swiss are called "German Swiss" (*Deutschschweizer*), and the regional variety(ies) of German they speak, "Swiss German" (*Schweizerdeutsch*). The corresponding terms are used in the case of French and Italian, and for the speakers of Romansh, U. Weinreich's term "Retoromans" is used.

Concerning the degree of standardization and inner variation of these languages, two well-known facts must always be borne in mind: (1) The standard varieties of Swiss German, French, and Italian are more or less identical with great European languages of high practical and cultural value, whereas a common standard form of Romansh does not yet exist, but rather only four distinct regional forms, each of them spoken and written. (2) For oral communication within the group, the German and Italian Swiss use exclusively local or regional dialects, while the French "patois" are practically extinct on Swiss territory.

Switzerland's respective language communities are of very different size, ranging from the two-thirds German majority to the 0.8 percent Retoroman minority. During the last hundred years, the proportions have remained nearly stable. In view of considerable internal migration and immigration, the definition of mother tongue given in the explanations to census questionnaires must be kept in mind: it is the language "in which one thinks and which one knows best"—a clearly assimilation-orientated definition.

If we only take Swiss citizens into consideration, the Italian-speaking proportion of the population in 1980 drops by more than half because foreign workers from Italy far outnumber native Italian Swiss. The great majority of the 6 percent of "other languages" are foreign workers, too, mainly from other southern countries, whereas political refugees are not crucial.

The Swiss German, French, and Italian language areas are "only" appendages of much greater language areas, while the small Romansh area is isolated from its nearest linguistic and cultural relatives, all of whom are also minorities. Moreover, the Romansh area is interspersed with German islands, as a large-scale map would make apparent, "like a piece of Roman purple that was caught and torn off by the Alpine peaks" (Weinreich, 1952:268). The great central German Swiss area extends, like a huge wedge, with the northern Swiss frontier as base, far into the Romance territory, thus dividing the latter into a Western (French) and an Eastern (Italian and Romansh) area, an impressive visualization of the historical "invasion" of the Alemannics.

The different Swiss-language areas are defined on the basis of the official language of each commune, which, in turn, is always the principal language of the majority of its population according to census data. Therefore, all communes are officially unilingual, with Biel/Bienne as the sole exception, but the language areas are not as homogeneous as they might seem. Furthermore, the political (i.e., cantonal) borders do not coincide totally with the language borders. In view of the great autonomy of the cantons in language legislation and politics, it is worth mentioning that seventeen (of twenty-six) cantons (and half-cantons) are unilingual German, four unilingual French (Geneva, Vaud, Neuchatel, Jura), and one unilingual Italian (Ticino), whereas three have a German- and a French-language area: Berne a tiny French, and Fribourg and Valais a one-third German minority with differing legal status. According to the cantonal constitution, Berne and Valais are bilingual, but not so Fribourg. Finally, one canton is even trilingual: the Grisons have Romansh, German, and Italian as cantonal languages. It is quite evident that the plurilingual cantons are areas of intense language contact. But even the "unilingual" ones are not homogeneous according to the mother tongue of their inhabitants and show interesting differences owing to asymmetrical patterns of internal migration.

The language borders are sharply defined according to the official local language. "Natural borders" hinder direct language contact on 90 percent of them, according to Weinreich (1952:103), but extremely different population density and the development of telecommunications reduce this impact of Swiss geography. From west to east, the following segments of the language borders can be distinguished. In the Jura south of Basel, the French-German border is now rather stable, after the assimilation of the Swiss German immigrants of former centuries to their French-speaking neighbors (Buchmann, 1963). In the "Mittelland" between the Jura and the Alps, the two bilingual cities Biel/Bienne and Fribourg/Freiburg are situated on the language border, marked by no natural barrier, and there exists a strip of linguistically mixed population which is much broader on the French side of the official language border than on its German side (Kolde, 1981:85–95), because of the permanent immigration (and subsequent rapid assimilation) of German Swiss. The central alpine part of the language border follows almost entirely the main ridges of the Alps. The only place where it can move easily is the valley of the Rhone, and there the French area has enlarged during recent centuries. Finally, in Eastern Switzerland, the language border between the German and the Romansh area is rather unstable and confused, with growing German-speaking minorities even in the center of the Romansh areas.

HISTORICAL BACKGROUND

The present-day territory of Switzerland has probably been the scene of intense culture and language contact for at least three millennia, but we know very little about the times before the arrival of the Romans. In the valleys of the Western Alps and their foothills, the Roman armies found a Celtic population that has left few traces of its language (some place names and terms for farm implements), to say nothing of the non-Indo-European peoples who had been assimilated by the immigrating Celts many centuries earlier. Under the rule of the Romans, the population of the Western Alpine provinces developed, on the substratum of their native Celtic idioms, some sort of a "Latin pidgin" called "Gallo-Romance." From the third century A.D. Germanic tribes, the Alemanni, repeatedly invaded the region between the Alps and the Jura, destroying Roman castles far to the south, but they regularly withdrew after their invasions. When in 436 A.D. the Burgundians were nearly annihilated by the Huns, the Roman commander Aëtius settled the rest of this Germanic people in the region south of Geneva in order to stabilize this strategically important area. There, they founded a kingdom, which lasted about a century, and built up a well-functioning administration for the region up to the Lake of Biel. But as they assimilated very quickly into the indigenous Gallo-Roman population, their language has not left many traces in the local dialects, aside perhaps from -ens as the suffix of place names.

At the beginning of the sixth century, the Alemanni definitely crossed the Rhine, without meeting much resistance. They settled down permanently in the open country between the Alps and the Jura, more gradually, in the lower parts of the mountain valleys. These areas had been more or less depopulated during the turmoil of the decline of Roman power, whereas the towns and castles remained Gallo-Roman somewhat longer. In the northern parts of present-day Switzerland, the indigenous Gallo-Roman population gradually assimilated with the Germanic newcomers, but the more the Alemanni advanced to the south, the more they themselves became assimilated, especially in the region of former Burgundian administration. During the seventh century, parts of the Lake District between the Lakes of Neuenburg, Biel, and Murten were inhabited by Gallo-Romans, Burgundians, and Alemanni, apparently living in peaceful coexistence. In 750, the River Aare became the border between the dioceses of Lausanne and Constance. On the one hand, this church administrative border no doubt followed the first stretches of a Germanic-Romance language border between the Alps and the Jura, and, on the other hand, it stabilized them. But there remained, for many centuries, long segments where the two language groups were separated from each other by uninhabited regions.

By about 1,000 A.D., a rather continuous language border dividing the present western part of Switzerland into a northern and a southern portion was established in more or less its present form.

The early history of the eastern part of present Switzerland was quite different. During the five centuries of Roman occupation, on the basis of their original, probably non-Indo-European language, the indigenous Raets developed a Roman pidgin named "Romansh." At its maximum extension, the area of this language (or group of languages) extended from the Danube to the Adriatic. But as a result of Alemannic and Bavarian immigration, this area diminished to three isolated language islands: the eastern Friulian group in the present Italian Province of Udine, the central Dolomite group in present South Tyrol, and the western "Prima Raetia" group which was incorporated, after 806, into the Frankish Empire and the diocese of Mayence. Its subsequent Germanization began among the ruling classes and in the towns, particularly at Chur, which has been a totally German town since the fifteenth and sixteenth centuries. Today the Retoromans have no center—more of them live in Zurich than Chur! The movement of the Germanic Walsers had already reached the Retoroman territory in the thirteenth century, and after long periods of conflict the Retoroman, Bündner German, Walser, and Italian regions were rather well defined from the sixteenth to the nineteenth century. Today we are witnessing what may be the final phase in the Germanization of this region.

The small area south of the central alpine chain west of the Retoroman territory, actually Italian Switzerland, belonged to the kingdom of the Longobards from 570 to 774, but only some place names in Ticino recall this period of contact with Germanic peoples. After one century of Carolingian rule, the region became part of the Dukedom of Milan, and, since the movement of the Walsers reached only the northwestern edge of it (Bosco-Gurin), the St. Gotthard Pass remained the Alemannic-Italian border.

The Swiss Confederation, founded in 1291, contained for many centuries only German-speaking cantons as full members. Freiburg was admitted as a German-French bilingual canton in 1481, but only on the condition that there should be a marked Germanization of its administration and school system (Kolde, 1981:101). During the following period and up to 1798, several cantons concluded treaties of mutual assistance with nonconfederate towns and territories, which thus became "indirect" allies ("Zugewandte Orte") of the Confederation. Other territories were subject lands ("Untertanenländer") of the original cantons. Many of the allies (like Geneva or parts of Valais) and of the subject lands (like Vaud or Ticino) were entirely Romance-speaking. Even in the case of the subject lands, the masters apparently did not interfere with regional language practices. However, this "tolerant" language politics does not reflect the liberal principles of the German Swiss master cantons, but simply the fact that until the eighteenth century language was not considered an important political factor. Some problems did arise, for instance, in Ticino when the vernacular languages came to replace Latin as the language of the courts, or when many German Swiss immigrated, for denominational and economic reasons, into the French Jura during the eighteenth century. But in all these situations the Swiss were able to develop procedures and traditions for dealing with language (and other) minorities. Unfortunately, there are still great gaps in our knowledge of historical language contact patterns and problems in Switzerland.

We also need to know much more than we do about another very important historical process—the radically different dialect development. On the one hand, there was a complete language shift of the "French" Swiss population from the patois to standard (Paris) French. (Rousseau, born in 1712 in Protestant Geneva, did not understand a word of the local patois, and at the present time one can find only a few old women in remote Catholic valleys who still speak patois.) On the other hand, we have witnessed the development, in German and Italian Switzerland, of a dialect-standard diglossia, and finally there exist four different varieties of Swiss Romansh, each of them spoken and written. Efforts to make up a unified standard Romansh for a limited range of written use have only just begun.

Strictly speaking, the Confederation remained, as a political body, unilingual German until 1798. The French and Italian territories became independent cantons only during or after the Napoleonic era—Ticino and Vaud in 1803, Neuchatel, Valais, and Geneva in 1815. But the Constitution of the Helvetic Republic (1798) had already given to the French and Italian languages equal rank with German as official languages of the new state (Kohn, 1956:47). The liberal federal Constitution of 1848 provides in Article 109 that German, French, and Italian are the national languages of Switzerland. During World War I, the slow-to-develop Swiss national identity, already weakened by language conflicts between French and German Switzerland around the turn of the century (Müller, 1977, and several contributions in du Bois, 1983) went through a difficult period. Then, by a referendum in 1938 the Swiss citizenry adopted an amendment to the federal Constitution recognizing Romansh as the fourth national language and, at the same time, splitting the concept of "national language" into "national" and "unofficial" (for federal affairs), the unofficial status not being attributed to Romansh. This decision, a "typical Swiss" compromise in view of the 1 percent of Retoromans, was partly the Swiss reaction to the Italian irridentist claim that Romansh was only an Italian dialect and that the Retoromans should consequently join the new fascistic Italy (Weinreich, 1952:107).

As the result of sometimes violent separatist activities and after a long legal procedure, including voting at all political levels, the northwestern part of the French-speaking Jura became independent from Berne in 1978, as the twenty-third and one of the smallest (and poorest) cantons of the Confederation. Since the economically more important southern part of the Jura decided to remain Bernese, the notorious Jura conflict has not yet been definitely settled. Even if this conflict was not primarily a language conflict, but an economic and denominational one (Keech, 1972), the ethnic notion of "romand" (see below) and thus, indirectly, language, played an important role as a symbol of identity and separation.

THE PRESENT CONTACT SITUATION

As opinions about the actual degree of harmony in the interrelations of the four Swiss-language groups are extremely controversial, it is impossible to give, in brief, a comprehensive and coherent report. Instead, we will examine only general factors that are often supposed to reduce conflicts.

The Territorial Principle

The long-standing democratic and federalist tradition, with its marked cantonal and local autonomy in language policy, has no doubt helped reduce the number of potentially damaging language contact situations and favors individual assimilations. In addition, the basic territorial principle means that, with the unique exception of Biel/Bienne, all communes are officially unilingual, and even in this town schooling at least is unilingual. But as the functional and the individual principle must also be taken into consideration, at first glance legal and administrative decisions sometimes do not appear to be fully coherent. Recently, the federal government has rejected, for instance, the demand of a Jurassian politician that the Confederation should protect the language borders, the immediate cause of this demand being the presumed Germanization of the Southern Jura. The grounds for this rejection were that the Constitution guarantees the existence of the national languages, but not the precise borders of their respective areas. To create "national language parks," possibly against the will of the population concerned, would go against the individual liberty. On the other hand, the federal Supreme Court has repeatedly decided against German Swiss inhabitants of Retoroman communes who did not want to send their children to Romansh primary school. In this case, the territorial principle wins over the individual one because the "existence" of the language is in danger. For R. Viletta (1978), a Retoroman expert in language legislation, the territorial principle is "the philanthropic and progressive notion of protecting language communities in their historical territory," whereas, in the name of the Jurassians, C. Merkelbach (1978:35) surprisingly criticizes the rigid application of this principle, because it does not prevent the language borders from shifting. Furthermore, the territorial principles cause great school problems in the case of migration across the language border (Lüdi, 1981:132) and cannot prevent the formerly inconceivable multiplication of language contact situations owing to the ever-growing industrial and economic complexity and the power of the mass media.

In our day, political and commercial standardization on a national Swiss level even results in a growing number of "national words" (or semantic variants) common to—and typical for—the Swiss varieties of all four national languages. For example: Swiss French *action*, Swiss German *Aktion*, Swiss Italian *azione*, and Romansh *aczuin* have the same meaning, just as do *offre speciale* in the French of France, *Sonderangebot* in the German of Germany, *offerta speciale* in the Italian of Italy, and *special offer* in English.

Lack of Congruence of Linguistic and Social-Cultural Divisions

One of the major reasons for the well-known Swiss "language peace" is the lack of congruence between language and other social divisions such as the denominational, cultural, or rural-urban division (Weinreich, 1953:97, following Meyer, 1939). This description is rather idealized, however. First, one must recall that during many centuries only German cantons were full members of the Confederation. Furthermore, political, administrative, and economic power is more and more concentrated in the great German Swiss cities of Zurich, Basel, and Berne. Thus, the feeling of being colonized and exploited is most often expressed in the peripheral French, Italian, and Romansh territories, although many German Swiss regions are in the same situation. Finally, other social criteria, like religious denomination, education, profession, and rural versus urban residence, are losing much of their former impact in modern egalitarian society, and the language often is the most important attribute of social identity in a world of "total information," the individual members of which are no more polyglot than they were before.

An interesting counter-example to Weinreich's idealized view is the case of Fribourg. In this city, during many centuries German was associated with "manual work," "rural origin," "reactionary," "narrow-minded," "living in the oldest section of the city," and French with "urban," "educated," "well-to-do," "liberal-democratic, progressive," and "living in the upper city." Today all these stereotypes can still be met—and (partly) falsified statistically (Kolde, 1981:108–15).

The Principle of Proportional Representation

All Swiss minorities enjoy the strict application of this principle, from the top positions in federal politics and administration to the mass media. But the problems with the magic formula for federal staffing begin with the definition of "top position": using different criteria, German as well as French Swiss observers may feel that their own language group is underrepresented, while for the 1 percent Retoromans this principle cannot work at all. In some cases, the most appropriate candidate for a specific task might not have the "right" mother tongue, and thus his or her choice will disturb the linguistic equilibrium.

It is common practice in Swiss linguistically mixed official bodies for all to speak their own language, the interlocutors' understanding competence in other national languages taken for granted (Kolde, 1981:237–40). But this principle works only for German and French, and even there surely not in all social classes. The federal translation service, which is responsible for the immediate and accurate translation of the increasing flood of political and administrative texts into the two other official languages, cannot always meet the high requirements of oversensitive minorities.

The press poses problems only for the Retoromans because the regional Romansh papers suffer from the offensive marketing strategies of powerful German Swiss editors. Moreover, the Retoromans must content themselves with a few hours weekly of radio and TV programming incorporated into the German Swiss channel. On the other hand, the German Swiss, French Swiss, and Italian Swiss radio and TV programs can be received everywhere in Switzerland. Recent private local radio stations in Biel and Fribourg broadcast in the two local languages, in the exact demographic proportions. The public clamor for equal treatment of the different language communities is so vigorous that recently the use of one television channel for special sports programs provoked a flood of protest letters, even appeals to the Supreme Court, because in German Switzerland it was always the Italian program (in French Switzerland, the German or Italian one) that was sacrificed.

The Swiss National Consciousness

The Swiss national consciousness is based on shared values such as neutrality, tolerance, cultural pluralism, and national institutions like the citizen army. The Confederation is regarded by each of its various groups as the guarantor of its own way of life (territorial nation as "Willens-nation," Weilenmann, 1925). The necessity to define the Swiss nation in contrast to neighboring nations with the same cultural background and nearly the same standard language as one of the Swiss-language communities, but often with rather different political systems and recent history, has no doubt strengthened internal Swiss coherence and solidarity. C. Schmid (1982:73) finds a "sense of shared national identity . . . especially among the younger groups," although the feeling for the cultural kin "is stronger for the French minority than for the German minority." However, the general European stereotypes concerning the "Romance-Germanic" opposition and the "cultural gradient" from west to east exist in Switzerland, too, and are sometimes even reinforced: in the eyes of the French Swiss, the German

Swiss are even "more typical Germans" than the Germans themselves, and vice versa.

The Disputed Four Swiss Ethnic Groups

We have just touched on the central and most controversial question of Swiss pluralism: that of national versus "ethnic" identity. As we have seen in the historical outline, one cannot speak of different Swiss ethnic groups in a racial-anthropological sense: the mixture of "Celtic," "Romance," and "Germanic" is nearly the same in all parts of Switzerland, and the family names in Geneva phone books reflect the intense inner migration and immigration over recent centuries. But common history, religious affiliation, economic interests, and cultural traditions (from dialects to carnivals) have created marked local (communal) and regional (cantonal) identities. Consequently, in the general opinion Swiss citizens display the following three hierarchically ordered identities. First, they argue and act as members of a commune, second as inhabitants of a canton, third as Swiss citizens, whereas the common language does not constitute a well-defined identity. It is true that, for example, the Genevois and the Vaudois, both Protestant French Swiss, are at least as different from each other in many respects as the Genevois and the Balois: "La Romandie n'existe pas" (Pichard, 1978). It is part of the ideology of Swiss pluralism that the weakness of language-based ethnicity is one of the major reasons for Swiss "language peace."

But during the last few decades a word seems to be used more and more frequently in French Switzerland. The word frightens the historian Denis van Berchem, as he said in an interview published by the *Journal de Genève* on December 22, 1982, because it denotes a "false institution without deep roots": the word *romand, romandie*. These fears are well founded: the amateur historian and Valaisan clergyman Clovis Lugon calls for a modification of the federal Constitution to create a "Conseil des Etats romands." Moreover, several movements and associations in French Switzerland propose to "wake up" the "romands" and to defend their interests and their language, such as the "Association romande de solidarité francophone" in Geneva and the "Mouvement populaire romand" in Lausanne. They have even invented a common romand flag, blue-white-red with six stars (symbolizing the six at least partly French cantons) and the Swiss cross.

The language distinction is reinforced by "secondary" qualities, including ascribed preferences in eating, drinking, dressing, hairstyle, games, sports, and political and ideological orientation. R. Anliker and V. Schmid (1980) found important differences in German and French history textbooks for primary schools. H. Fischer and U. P. Trier (1962), using the semantic differential technique, state the same thing regarding the auto- and hetero-stereotypes of these two language communities. In federal votes on questions that have nothing to do with language, the Romance cantons are frequently outvoted by the German

Swiss majority. But the fact that the original cantons often join the Romance regions advises caution—perhaps the anti-centralist orientation of both regions is more important than the language.

A. Charpilloz and G. Grimm-Gobat (1982:70) cite the answers on the attitudinal research question as to whether the informants define themselves primarily as inhabitants of their commune, the region (canton), the language area, or of Switzerland as a whole. Twenty-nine percent of the French Swiss informants named exclusively or inter alia the language community, 16 percent of the German, and 14 percent of the Italian Swiss informants. The same authors quote (p. 3 following) numerous results of marketing-orientated opinion research as evidence for the existence of ethnic differences between the Swiss-language communities. For example: 47 percent of the German Swiss but only 27 percent of the French Swiss claim to spend their vacations in Switzerland; 44 percent of the French, 33 percent of the German, and 26 percent of the Italian Swiss use deodorants; and 42 percent of French Swiss women use eyeshadow versus 22 percent of their German Swiss peers. On the other hand, 7.8 percent of the Lucerne post office workers were likely to call in sick, as against 14.15 percent at Geneva and 18 percent in Ticino. Finally, 55 percent of the German Swiss find that the army is necessary, but only 22 percent of their French confederates.

The comprehensive comparative study of second-language use, proficiency, and attitudes of high school students in the two "bilingual" Swiss cities of Biel and Fribourg (Kolde, 1981) confirms the views quoted above.

When Zurich high school students were asked by a Genevan student working on a control test to choose from an unordered list of adjectives denoting positive and negative social features, those which they regarded as typical for French or German Swiss, one student refused to comply, giving the following comment (my translation): "In this list I find only negative words for the German Swiss, and positive ones for the French Swiss. Therefore I marked only the latter," namely: *sociable, tolerant, liberal minded, emancipated, artistic, dynamic, voluble, lively, socially conscious*, and, in brackets, *politically on the left*. This implies that, in a long and unordered list of adjectives this German Swiss student finds only negative features for her own group and only positive ones for the "others." She protests against an "unfair" assignment: a striking example of projected negative hetero-stereotypes. (She knew that this list had been established in Geneva!)

The different language and ethnic attitudes would also show up very clearly in a comparative study of lexical interferences and borrowing in both directions, especially in contact areas like Biel and Fribourg. Swiss German contains more Romance elements than vice versa, and, even more revealingly, different domains, lexical fields, and socio-stylistic levels are affected. Compare the Germanisms *poutzer* (to clean), *schlaguer* (to beat), *peteler* (to beg), *snapser* (to booze) in Swiss French, versus *touchiere* (to touch), *remplaciere* (to replace), and *defraichiere* (to fade) in Swiss German (Kolde, 1981:157–59). The situation of Romansh is totally different insofar as the interference with and borrowing from German via tourism, industrialization, the mass media, and schooling has attained a level that is regarded by many observers as a real danger for Romansh.

The mass media are often criticized for exaggerating, even "creating" the problems, by presenting issues in a polemical and consciously biased form and by stressing the shortcomings and conflicts instead of mentioning the numerous positive examples of mutual understanding, tolerance, and national solidarity. Indeed, the harshness and biasedness of a caricature published repeatedly under the title "Grüezi viol" can hardly be surpassed: the outline of Switzerland is filled with four tangled figures: the brutal German Swiss doing violence to the innocent and shocked "Romande," sitting on the head of the groaning Italian Swiss and his heavy paw on the defenseless Retoroman. Even though the strength of the Swiss national identity is unquestionable, these interlingual or interethnic tensions are not taken lightly. For many years, national institutions like Pro Helvetia have been supporting cultural activities that promote mutual under- standing across language borders. In 1980 a great conference was organized at Montreux under the patronage of the federal government on the question: "One or four Switzerlands?" At the moment, an impressive project of the National Research Agency (Nationalfond) on "cultural pluralism and national identity" is in preparation, the warning example of Belgium often being quoted as an effective bugbear.

Two caveats should conclude the observations made in this section:

1. The tendency to attribute all social conflicts solely to the "language" factor is wide- spread in all multilingual societies but should not be followed uncritically by the linguist.
2. In keeping with a widespread human attitude (*laudatio temporis acti*), the current situation is normally interpreted as a time of increasing interlingual tensions and ethnic awareness. This view is not necessarily correct. H. H. Kerr (1974:22), comparing the sense of "cantonal, linguistic and Swiss identity by language and age cohort," comes to the optimistic conclusion "that nation-building in Switzerland had only begun to take root at the turn of the century and is still underway."

The German Swiss Diglossia or Internal Bilingualism

All German Swiss use their very different local (or regional) Alemannic di- alects, even in formal situations where fifty years ago only the use of standard German was conceivable. Formerly, German Switzerland was regarded as one of the best examples of diglossia, with three determining factors: the medium (spoken versus written), communication within the group or with foreigners, and formal versus informal situation (Schwarzenbach, 1969). Today we are witnessing a clear trend toward "oral bilingualism" (Ris, 1979:56) or, at least, an exclusively medium-determined diglossia (Haas, 1978:106), a trend with far- reaching consequences in several respects:

1. The oral use of dialect in situations that are strongly determined by written language use (administration, science, etc.) favors syntactic and lexical interference. As a result, utterances are, in extreme cases, dialectal only in their phonetics, but full of syntactic and lexical elements of Standard German, a trend that meets loud disapproval from dialect purists.

2. Formerly, two German Swiss speaking rather different dialects could avoid the risks of interdialectal communication (reduced mutual intelligibility and, perhaps, evocation of negative interdialectal attitudes; see Werlen, forthcoming) by the choice of Standard German as the lingua franca. Today the speakers of marginal Swiss dialects must either acquire a second "subsidiary" dialect for interdialectal communication, or they simply avoid their extreme dialect forms (Haas, 1982:110). At any rate, the marginal Swiss dialects are undergoing important changes. This does not mean that a more or less uniform "national dialect" is coming into being (Haas, 1978, versus Zimmer, 1977), but nevertheless the German Swiss have already coined a highly pejorative name for this nonexistent variety: "Oltenbahnhofschwytzerdütsch."

3. The most serious consequences of this development no doubt concern the oral communication of German Swiss with interlocutors from other German-speaking nations, especially with non-German confederates who learn only Standard German at school.

There are, of course, several historical reasons for this recent advance of dialect use, for example, the "Geistige Landesverteidigung" (national defense with cultural weapons) during the Third Reich, but actually the following three reasons are no doubt most important (Schwarzenbach and Sitta, 1983):

First, the general relative decrease of writing in private and print in mass communication favors the use of dialects as the traditional oral varieties to the detriment of the written forms: radio, TV, and telephone are partly replacing newspaper, book, and letter. Furthermore, Haas (1982:107) observes a "universal" historical tendency toward the "lower," "more informal," "more oral" style even in written language use. Second, since the *Schwytzerdütsch* dialects are the symbol of German Swiss identity, the real "mother" tongues, their use creates a warm, intimate atmosphere, and their regional diversity symbolizes the federalist structure of Swiss social and political life. Finally, dialect is taken to be "democratic" because the German Swiss are simply not aware of the existing social stratification of their dialects, and their marked phonetic structure is even related to the positive auto-stereotype of the German Swiss "rough diamond" (Mörikofer, 1836; Greyerz, 1933:246). On the contrary, Standard German is, for the German Swiss, the language of cold rationality and the foreign, frightening world. Third, especially for many young German Swiss, dialect use is an instrument of social politics, a symbol of progressiveness, whereas Standard German stands for the establishment, constraints, institutions, and authority. It is the "father tongue" of school, church, and court.

As a result of this extremely high prestige of dialect, the northern Swiss boundary has become a "pragmatic language border" (Ris, 1978): nearly the same Alemannic dialect is used on the two banks of the Rhine, but the conditions of its use are totally different. Even the Swiss variety of Standard German, the so-called *Schweizerschriftdeutsch*, differs clearly from the other regional varieties of Standard German in phonetics, morphology, semantics, and, most strikingly, in its lexicon. These peculiarities are even cultivated as another symbol of German Swiss identity, whereas, revealingly enough, the French Swiss term *français fédéral* is used to mock the bad French of the predominantly German-speaking federal administration. The French patois has no prestige value at all for the French Swiss: "Patois is good for staying at the tail of a cow," quotes Weinreich (1952:162).

The attitudes of the *Italian Swiss* to their standard variety furnish an instructive analogy to the German Swiss situation. In his very critical pilot study entitled "Lingue matrigna, Italiano e dialetto nella Svizzera italiana" (stepmother language: Italian and dialect in Italian Switzerland), S. Bianconi (1980) demonstrates how Standard Italian acts (or is treated) as a stepmother, not accepted by its Italian Swiss speakers. At first glance, the facts reported in this chapter seem only to complicate Swiss-language contact. But when one looks again, one realizes that they also increase the value of French as a means of interlingual communication and thus help to stabilize Swiss multilingualism.

SECOND SWISS-LANGUAGE PROFICIENCY AND SCHOOLING

F. Kainz' (1965) high overall evaluation of individual bilingualism among the Swiss has already been quoted and questioned in the introduction. W. B. Simon (1969:18) has more precise ideas: "The German-, French-, and Italian-speaking citizens of the Swiss nation simply take it for granted that the educated Swiss have to become fluent in languages other than their own, especially if they aspire to a career in the service of their government or in their school system." H. Kloss (1966/67:11) is more skeptical and assumes that, apart from the diglossia of the German Swiss, the individual Swiss is no more bilingual than the Dutch or the Scandinavian, and perhaps even less so. Television practice confirms Kloss's view: whenever in German Swiss television news a personality is interviewed in French, after a few French words a simultaneous translation into German begins, to the great irritation of listeners with some knowledge of French. Fluent proficiency in a second national language is not a necessary condition for high positions in federal politics, as is revealed when members of the federal government dare to speak it publicly.

Even at Biel, the Swiss bilingual city *par excellence*, there is no bilingual newspaper. An advertising sheet with editorial, bearing the ambitious title "Biel/Bienne" and published with the explicit intention of promoting the mutual understanding of all coexisting language communities, contains many articles twice, in German and in French, because this advertiser is not only distributed in the city, but also in the officially unilingual suburbs. This is at least the explanation given by a responsible journalist. Several years ago, the programs of a little progressive theater at Biel were bilingual in such a way that they presupposed a bilingual reader. But this was a much-cited exception.

A representative survey (Scope, 1973) revealed that 22 percent of the German Swiss with only primary schooling claimed "some proficiency" in French, and 73 percent of those who have attended high school. The overall average was 67 percent, as opposed to 52 percent of the French Swiss who claimed some knowledge of German. Of course, results of such self-assessment must be interpreted carefully. The differences between the groups may also be due to different implicit norms of "proficiency": fewer informants with a university degree pretended to "know" another language than those with only secondary schooling.

"Proficiency in other national languages" means, for the majority of German and French Swiss, some knowledge of one other national language in addition to the mother-tongue French, respectively, German. This is the only linguistic condition for federal recognition of final high school examinations (Maturität). As this obligatory foreign language is normally German in French Switzerland and French in German Switzerland, Italian is rarely taught as a foreign language in Swiss schools, and Romansh nowhere. Only the Italian (and Retoroman) Swiss must learn two foreign national languages at school, which presents another serious handicap for the "real" Swiss minorities. As German is the general language of instruction in all Grison high schools, the Retoroman students are even forced to practice Romansh-German bilingualism.

English, with its high prestige as a world language, is gaining ground (often criticized) as a lingua franca, even for internal Swiss-language contact, and easily pushes Italian out of favor among the non-Italian Swiss. The Genevois would far prefer English as their first foreign language to the very unpopular German (Allal et al., 1978:46), but such a demand goes against the principles of Swiss-language politics and has therefore always been rejected up to now.

Even in the French-German bilingual city of Biel, the second language is taught to the respective other language group, in exactly the same way as any foreign language: where the territory principle does not work, the strictly unilingual school must play the "isolating role": "In the unilingual situation it [the school] helps maintain a conservative, standardized language; in the bilingual situation it supports, in addition, the norms of the language against unchecked foreign borrowing" (Weinreich, 1953:88). In language contact areas, everything is done to prevent the children from becoming "coordinate" bilinguals and from developing bilingual norms. The extremely negative attitude toward balanced individual bilingualism as a "pathological state" causing mental disorientation (*anomie*) (Epstein, 1915) is still rather widespread. The nearer to the language border, the stronger the official resistance to all types of "bilingual education" (von Greyerz, 1928; Baumgartner, 1932). It is at Einsiedeln, far from the language border, that Pater Jungo argues in favor of a bilingual education—for the children of foreign workers (Jobin, 1979).

Much is done, on the other hand, to promote mutual understanding of the language communities by school exchange. The Director of the Swiss Conference of Cantonal Education has recently created a team of experts called "Landessprache 2" in order to promote the teaching of a second national language, because D. Borel (1973:3) is not correct when he states that in general in the primary schools of all cantons a second national language is taught from the fifth grade on. Even in 1984, this was not yet the case at Geneva, for example, where formerly German began in the seventh grade. This intensification of foreign language learning has even aroused minority fears in Geneva. Sometimes Rousseau is cited in support of this attitude because he argues in *Emile* that foreign languages should not be learned before the mother tongue is really consolidated— at the age of thirteen. In six cantons of inner Switzerland, the planning for the earlier introduction of second national language teaching had not yet begun at all in 1982.

As a consequence of the high prestige of dialect in German Switzerland discussed above, many German Swiss teachers cannot resist the temptation to use it with their pupils not only during recess, but more and more during lessons too. In that way they can benefit from its positive effects on the social atmosphere in the classroom, even against the explicit orders of the education authorities. In the longer term, they will thus reinforce the isolation of the German Swiss, who will have more and more difficulties in discussions with German peers from Germany, for example (Thomke, 1978), and with French or Italian confederates who learn only Standard German at school. The motivation of the latter to learn this supposedly difficult language is surely not reinforced by the frequent experience that German Swiss partners prefer to speak to them, if not their "incomprehensible" dialect, rather English or French, but on no account Standard German, the unbeloved "semi-foreign language" (Max Frisch). The idea of teaching *Schwytzerdütsch* at French Swiss schools instead of, or, more realistically, in addition to Standard German, runs into numerous problems, even if limited to the most modest aim, to "habituate the ear" to understand the main Alemannic dialects (Müller and Wertenschlag, 1984). M. Zwicky (1978) goes much further and proposes teaching the active use of a normalized koine-dialect, a method that is rejected by most German Swiss (Merkt, 1981).

RESEARCH

In this final section, some major trends in the history of Swiss-language contact research and some desiderata for future studies will be pointed out, without any claim to completeness for either.

For a long time, Swiss contact linguistics stood in the shadow of the great tradition of alemannic dialectology and its pioneering enterprises, the *Schweizerisches Idiotikon*, the *Sprachatlas der deutschen Schweiz*, and numerous specialized studies (for a general survey, see Lötscher, 1983). The three other national dialect dictionaries are currently at different stages of realization. The title of

F. J. Stalder's book *Landessprachen der Schweiz* [Regional Languages of Switzerland, 1819] is misleading because it is actually a description of German Swiss dialects only, with some Romansh, French, and Italian dialect texts in the appendix. Thus, the first important work on our subject dates from 1891 and 1899. In two volumes, J. Zimmerli gives a detailed description of the situation on the French-German language border in Switzerland at that time, based on personal observations. Just after the turn of the century, E. Tappolet compared the dialect situation of French and German Switzerland. H. Weilenmann's work of 1925 can be considered a reaction to the interlingual tensions before (Müller, 1977) and during World War I (du Bois, 1983). Before and during World War II, peaceful Swiss coexistence was called up in several small popular articles by Swiss authors (Burckhardt, 1938; Meyer, 1939; von Wartburg, 1940; Thilo, 1941), followed later by von Planta (1957), Bernhard (1968), and Vouga (1978). At first glance, the tone may seem to have become more polemic and aggressive in recent years (Charpilloz et al., 1982; Lugon, 1983), but as André (1944) shows, this tradition is rather old.

Swiss-language rights and jurisdiction have been treated, under different aspects, by Hegnauer (1947), Schäppi (1971), and Viletta (1978), and the important document of the *Charte des langues* (1969) can only be mentioned. Several foreign sociologists and political scientists have studied the "case of Switzerland," among them Kohn (1956), McRae (1964), Keech (1972), Kerr (1974), and Schmid (1982).

Weinreich's doctoral dissertation of 1952 is still unsurpassed: since Weinreich, no other author has described the sociological, psychological, and linguistic effects of language contact in Switzerland so thoroughly and rigorously, and his bibliography remains a treasure trove even today. The aims of Heye's (1970) investigations in Ticino multilingualism were more limited, whereas Cathomas (1977) was the first to study individual bilingualism in Chur on a sound linguistic basis, followed by Furer (1981) with a more explicit political orientation. The comparative study of Kolde (1981) and the project of Lüdi and Py (Lüdi, 1981; Lüdi and Py, 1984) to compare Swiss German and Spanish immigrants to Neuchatel complement one another in many methodological respects.

The standard work on *internal* language contact in German Switzerland is still that of Schwarzenbach (1969); Ris (1978, 1979) elucidated the sociopsychological background of the unique position of Swiss German dialects. The latest monograph on Swiss Standard German is that of Panizzolo (1982), while the Romance elements in this idiom were collected by Schilling (1970). No comparable studies exist for Swiss French, but only small articles (Tappolet, 1913; Jaberg, 1917; Bodinier, 1960; Schliessl, 1965; Burger, 1979; Knecht, 1979, 1982). The only book that has been recently published (Hadacek, 1983) is more popular and journalistic than scientific. Two relevant research projects are underway: the comparison of the attitudes of Swedish immigrants to Norway and of German immigrants to German Switzerland (Koller, 1980), and another about the present use of Swiss Standard German in public domains (Schwarzenbach and Sitta, 1983). The problems of internal language contact in Italian Switzerland were treated by Lurati (1976), and Bianconi (1980).

Different historical aspects of Swiss-language contact were studied by Sonderegger (1963, 1977, 1982), Berner-Hürbin (1974), and Billigmeier (1979).

Finally, two very different recent collections should be mentioned. The one (Schläpfer, 1982), published only in German, with a French translation in preparation, is more comprehensive and systematic, with a more popular orientation. The other (du Bois, 1983), published only in French, contains several specialized and partly historical articles.

In spite of this impressive list of names and titles, a lot of open questions and data gaps are waiting for persistent investigation, especially in the following three fields:

1. The description of historical language contact in former subject territories (Vaud, Ticino), and of the origin and formation of language and ethnic attitudes and awareness during the last two centuries.

2. The comparative study of current proficiency in, use of, and attitudes to the varieties of the national language in all language areas.

3. Longitudinal analyses that should permit us to find out whether interlingual relations and attitudes are currently changing, and, if so, in which direction.

Currently, a "Swiss Center for Interdisciplinary Research on Languages and Cultures in Contact" is on the point of being founded. The provisional accommodation address is as follows: Prof. Georges Lüdi, Romanisches Seminar der Universität, CH–4051 Basel, Stapfelberg 7.

FINAL REMARKS

In this survey, the common problems of the four national language communities of Switzerland have been described. Therefore, in conclusion the extreme variety of their respective situations should be stressed once more: from the French minority which is, in some respects, a "hidden majority," to the Retoromans and the paradoxical task to preserve their language against the vital interests of many of its speakers who tend, for practical reasons, to shift to German: "To save Romansh against its own will" (Grisons: pour sauver le romanche malgré lui) was a revealing headline in the *Journal de Genève* (October 21, 1980).

Nothing has been said about the 15 percent of the present population who are not Swiss citizens and nearly entirely foreign workers. Their large Romance majority strengthens the third national language community only numerically. Those among them who live in German-French contact areas and who assimilate in the second generation thus enlarge the local French community because their children are normally schooled in this language. But such local shifts cannot affect the overall statistical German-French stability on a regional and national scale.

ACKNOWLEDGMENT

I am grateful to my colleagues Liliane Haegeman-de Pauw and Neil Robert Forsyth for their help in preparing this chapter.

BIBLIOGRAPHY

Allal, L. K., C. Davaud, and A. Fete-Padlina. 1978. *Attitudes à l'égard de l'apprentissage de l'allemand. Enquête auprès des élèves des trois dégrés du Cycle d'orientation*. Genève: Département de l'instruction publique.

André, P. 1944. *Silence obligé*. Neuchâtel, Paris.

Anliker, R., and V. Schmid. 1980. "Frei und auf ewig frei! Politische Identität im Schweizer Geschichtsbuch der Volksschule." *Bulletin des Soziologischen Instituts der Universität Zürich*. Sondernummer.

Baumgartner, H. 1932. "Ein zweisprachiges Gymnasium?" *Bieler Jahrbuch* 6:92–102.

Berner-Hurbin, A. 1974. *Psycholinguistik der Romanismen im älteren Schweizerdeutsch: Die Entlehnungsmechanismen in Quellen des 15. und 16. Jahrhunderts*. Frauenfeld, Stuttgart: Huber.

Bernhard, R. 1968. *Alemannisch-welsche Sprachsorgen und Kulturfragen*. Mit Beiträgen von F. Dürrenmatt und A. Richli. Frauenfeld: Schriften des deutschschweizerischen Sprachvereins, 3.

Bianconi, S. 1980. *Lingua matrigna. Italiano e dialetto nella Svizzera italiana*. Bologna: Il mulino.

Billigmeier, R. H. 1979. *A Crisis in Swiss Pluralism*. Oxford: Holdan Books.

Bodinier, C-P. 1960. "Le français face aux germanismes en Suisse romande." *Vie et langage* 97:182–87.

Borel, D. 1973. "Essai sur les questions linguistiques en Suisse." *Revue militaire suisse* 118:1–10.

Buchmann, W. 1963. "Die deutsch-französische Sprachgrenze im Schweizer Jura im Zeitraum 1860–1950. Regio Basiliensis." *Hefte für jurassische und oberrheinische Landeskunde* 4:2.

Burckhardt, W. 1938. "Das Verhältnis der Sprachen in der Schweiz. Deutschschweizerischer Sprachverein." *Jahrliche Rundschau* pp. 24–36.

Burger, M. 1979. "La tradition linguistique vernaculaire en Suisse romande: les patois." In *Le français hors de France*, ed. A. Valdman. Paris: Honore Champion, pp. 259–69.

Camartin, I. 1982. "Die Beziehungen zwischen den schweizerischen Sprachregionen." In *Die viersprachige Schweiz*, ed. R. Schläpfer, pp. 301–51.

Cathomas, B. 1977. *Erkundungen zur Zweisprachigkeit der Rätoromanen. Eine soziolinguistische und pragmatische Leitstudie*. Bern, Frankfurt: Lang.

―――. 1981. "Die Einstellungen der Rätoromanen zum Schwyzertütsch." *Bulletin CILA* 33, 105–117.

Charpilloz, A., and G. Grimm-Gobat. 1982. *La Romandie dominée*. Lausanne: Favre.

Charte des langues. Sprachencharta. 1969. Fribourg, Suisse.

Davaud, C., and L. Allal. 1979. *Effets de facteurs scolaires et extrascolaires sur les attitudes des élèves a l'égard de l'apprentissage de l'allemand.* Genève: Département de l'instruction publique.

Dicziunari Rumantsch Grischun. (1939 foll.) Chur.

Dörig, H. R., and Chr. Reichenau. 1982. 2½ sprachige Schweiz? Zustand und Zukunft des Rätoromanischen und des Italienischen in Graubünden. Abklärungen und Empfehlungen einer Arbeitsgruppe. Bern, Dissentis.

du Bois, P. 1983. "Mythe et réalité du fossé pendant la Première Guerre mondiale." In *Union et Division des Suisses: Les relations entre Alémaniques, Romands et Tessinois aux XIXe et XXe siècles,* ed. P. du Bois. Lausanne: Editions de l'Aire, pp. 65–91.

Epstein, I. 1915. "La pensée et la polyglossie. Essai psychologique et didactique." Ph.D. diss., Lausanne: Librairie Payot.

Fischer, H., and U. P. Trier. 1962. *Das Verhältnis zwischen Deutschschweizer und Westschweizer. Eine sozialpsychologische Untersuchung.* Bern, Stuttgart: Huber.

Furer, J-J. 1981. "Der Tod des Romanischen, der Anfang vom Ende für die Schweiz." Chur.

Glossaire des patois de la Suisse romand. (1924 foll.). Neuchâtel, Paris/Genève.

Greyerz, O. von. 1928. "Sprachkultur. Gedanken über die Sprachpflichten des Deutschschweizers in zweisprachigem Gebiet." *Bieler Jahrbuch,* pp. 89–100.

———. 1933. *Sprache, Dichtung, Heimat.* Bern.

Haas, W. 1978. "Wider den 'Nationaldialekt'." *Zeitschrift für Dialektologie und Linguistik* 45:62–68.

———. 1981. "Entre dialecte et langue: l'example du Schwyzertütsch." *Bulletin Cila* 33, 22–41.

———. 1982. "Sprachgeschichtliche Grundlagen, die deutschsprachige Schweiz." In *Die viersprachige Schweiz,* ed. R. Schläpfer, pp. 21–160.

Hadacek, C. 1983. *Le suisse romand tel qu'on le parle. Lexique Romand-Français.* Lausanne: Favre.

Hegnauer, C. 1947. *Das Sprachenrecht der Schweiz.* Zürich.

Heye, J. B. 1970. "A Sociolinguistic Investigation of Multilingualism in the Canton of Ticino, Switzerland." Ph.D. diss. University of Michigan.

Hunt, J. A. 1980. "Education and Bilingualism on the Language Frontier in Switzerland." *Journal of Multilingual and Multicultural Development* 1:17–39.

Jaberg, K. 1917. Die alemannischen Lehnwörter in den Mundarten der französischen Schweiz. Sonntagsblatt des 'Bund.' Bern 50.1.

Jobin, J. F. 1979. "Entretien avec le père Michael Jungo." *Zomar* 12:40–42.

Kainz, F. 1965. "Psychologie der Sprache." Vol. 5, 1. *Psychologie der Einzelsprachen.* Stuttgart, Ferd. Enke.

Keech, W. R. 1972. "Linguistic Diversity and Political Conflict: Some Observations Based on Four Swiss Cantons." *Comparative Politics* 44:387–404.

Kerr, H. H., Jr. 1974. *Switzerland: Social Cleavages and Partisan Conflict.* London, Beverly Hills. (Sage Professional Papers in Contemporary Political Sociology, 1:06–002).

Kloss, H. 1966/67. "Types of Multilingual Communities: A Discussion of Ten Variables." In *Exploration in Sociolinguistics,* ed. S. Lieberson. Bloomington, Ind., pp. 7–17.

Knecht, P. 1979. "Le français en Suisse romande: aspects linguistiques et sociolinguistiques." In *Le français hors de France*, ed A. Valdman. Paris: Honoré Champion, pp. 249–258.

———. 1982. "Die französischsprachige Schweiz." In *Die viersprachige Schweiz*, ed. R. Schläpfer, pp. 161–210.

Kohn, H. 1956. *Nationalism and Liberty: The Swiss Example*. London: Allen and Unwin.

Kolde, G. 1981. *Sprachkontakte in gemischtsprachigen Städten. Vergleichende Untersuchungen über Voraussetzungen und Formen sprachlicher Interaktion verschiedensprachiger Jugendlicher in den Schweizer Städten Biel/Bienne und Fribourg/Freiburg i.Ue.* Wiesbaden: Steiner (ZDL-Beihefte.37).

———. 1983. "Rapporto tra apprendimento della lingua e sviluppo dell'identità: aspetti di psicologia sociale nella politica scolastica delle lingue in regioni mistilingui." In *Atti del convegno internazionale: L'apprendimento precoce della seconda lingua*. Bolzano, May 13–15, 1982. Bolzano (Educazione bilingue 8), pp. 163–85.

Koller, W. 1980. "Zum Sprachverhalten von in Norwegen lebenden Schweden und von in der Deutschschweiz lebenden Deutschen." In *Sprachkontakt und Sprachkonflikt*, ed. H. P. Nelde. Wiesbaden: Steiner, pp. 487–92 (ZKL-Beiheft. 32).

Kühn, P. 1980. "Deutsche Sprache in der Schweiz." In *Lexikon der Germanistischen Linguistik*, ed. H. P. Althaus et al. 2d ed. Tubingen: Niemeyer, pp. 531–36.

Lötscher, A. 1983. *Schweizerdeutsch. Geschichte, Dialekte, Gebrauch*. Frauenfeld, Stuttgart: Huber.

Lüdi, G. 1981. "Migration interne et intégration linguistique en Suisse." In *Etre migrant*, ed. A. Gretler et al. Berne, Frankfort: M. Lang, pp. 125–37.

Lüdi, G., and B. Py. 1984. *Zweisprachig durch Migration. Einführung in die Erforschung der Mehrsprachigkeit am Beispiel zweier Zuwanderergruppen in Neuenburg/Schweiz*. Tübingen: Niemeyer.

Lugon, C. 1983. *Quand la Suisse Française s'eveillera*. Genève: Editions Perret-Gentil.

Lurati, O. 1976. *Dialetto et italiano regionale nella Svizzera italiana*. Lugano.

Lutz, F., and J. C. Arquint. 1982. "Die rätoromanische Schweiz." In *Die viersprachige Schweiz*, ed. R. Schläpfer, pp. 253–300.

Matthews, R. J. H. 1979. "Bilingualism in a Swiss Canton. Language Choice in Ticino." In *Sociolinguistic Studies in Language Contact: Methods and Cases*, ed W. F. Mackey and J. Ornstein. The Hague, pp. 425–31.

McRae, K. D. 1964. *Switzerland: Example of Cultural Coexistence*. Toronto: Canadian Institute of International Affairs.

Merkelbach, Chr. 1979. "Communautés linguistiques en Suisse: quel dialogue?" *Zomar* 12:32–38.

Merkt, G. 1981. "Pour une intégration des dialectes alémaniques dans l'enseignement de l'allemand en Suisse romande." *Bulletin Cila* 33:73–86.

Meyer, K. 1939. *Die mehrsprachige Schweiz. Geschichtliche Voraussetzungen des eidgenössischen Sprachenfriedens*. Zürich.

Mörikofer, J. C. 1836. *Die schweizerische Mundart im Verhältnis zur hochdeutschen Schriftsprache, aus dem Gesichtspunkte der Landesbeschaftenheit, der Sprache, des Unterrichts, der Nationalität und der Literatur*. Frauenfeld: Chr. Beyel. (Anonymous.)

Müller, H. P. 1977. *Die schweizerische Sprachenfrage vor 1914. Eine historische Untersuchung über das Verhältnis zwischen Deutsch und Welsch bis zum 1. Weltkrieg*. Wiesbaden: Steiner.

Müller, M., and L. Wertenschlag. 1984. *Los emol. Schweizerdeutsch verstehen.* Berlin: Langenscheidt.

Panizzolo, P. 1982. *Die schweizerische Variante des Hochdeutschen.* Marburg: Deutsche Dialektgeographie 108.

Pichard, A. 1978. *La Romandie n'existe pas. Six portraits politiques: Fribourg, Genève, Jura, Neuchâtel, Valais, Vaud.* Lausanne.

Planta, J. M. von. 1957. *Unsere Sprache und wir. Von der vielsprachigen Schweiz zum Sprachziel des Abendlandes.* Frauenfeld: Huber.

Ris, R. 1978. "Sozialpsychologie der Dialekte und ihrer Sprecher." In *Grundlagen einer dialektorientierten Sprachdidaktik*, ed U. Ammon et al. Weinheim: Basel, pp. 93–115.

———. 1979. "Dialekte und Einheitssprache in der deutschen Schweiz." *International Journal of the Sociology of Language* 21:41–61.

Rubattel, Chr. 1976. "Recherches sur les langues en contact." *Etudes en linguistique appliquée*, N.S., 21:20–32.

Schäppi, P. 1971. "Der Schutz sprachlicher und konfessioneller Minderheiten im Recht von Bund und Kantonen. Das Problem des Minderheitenschutzes." Ph.D. diss., Zürich.

Schilling, R. 1970. *Romanische Elemente im Schweizerhochdeutschen.* Mannheim: Bibliographisches Institut (Duden-Beiträge.38).

Schläpfer, R., ed. 1982. *Die viersprachige Schweiz.* Zürich, Koln: Benziger.

Schliessl, A. 1965. "Le Français en Suisse romande. Calques de l'allemand et romandismes à pourfendre." *Vie et Langage* 158:263–66.

Schmid, C. 1982. "Diversity, National Identity and Political Socialization in Switzerland." *International Journal of Political Education* 5:57–74.

Schwarzenbach, R. 1969. *Die Stellung der Mundart in der deutschsprachigen Schweiz. Studien zum Sprachbrauch der Gegenwart.* Frauenfeld: Huber. (Beiträge zur schweizerdeutschen Mundartforsch.17.)

Schwarzenbach, R., and H. Sitta. 1983. "Mundart und Hochsprache in der deutschen Schweiz." *Bulletin Cila* 38:62–71.

Schweizerisches Idiotikon. *Wörterbuch der schweizerdeutschen Sprache.* (1881 foll.) Frauenfeld.

Scope. 1973. *Die Fremdsprachenkenntnisse der Schweizer. Repräsentativerhebung.* Luzern.

Simon, W. B. 1969. "Multilingualism, A Comparative Study." In *Studies in Multilingualism*, ed. N. Anderson. Leyden, pp. 11–25.

Sonderegger, S. 1963. "Volks- und Sprachgrenzen in der Schweiz im Frühmittelalter. Mit besonderer Berücksichtigung der Burgundisch-alemannischen Grenze. Der sprachgeschichtliche Aspekt." *Schweizerische Zeitschrift für Geschichte* 13:493–534.

———. 1977. "Sprachgrenzen und Sprachgrenzlandschaften in der Schweiz." Berichte des 12 Internat. Kongresses für Namenforschung, Bern, 1975. Louvain: Peeters, Vol. 1, 277–92.

———. 1982. "Zur geschichtlichen Entwicklung eines schweizerischen Sprachbewusstseins in der frühen Neuzeit. Innsbrucker Beiträge zur Kulturwissenschaft." *Germanist.Reihe*, Vol. 13. *Zur Situation des Deutschen in Südtirol*, ed. H. Moser, pp. 51–61.

Sprachatlas der deutschen Schweiz. (1962 foll.). Ed. R. Hotzenköcherle, Vols. 1–4. Bern.

Stalder, F. J. 1819. *Die Landessprachen der Schweiz oder Schweizerische Dialektologie, mit kritischen Anmerkungen beleuchtet. Nebst der Gleichnissrede von dem verlorenen Sohne in allen Schweizermundarten.* Aarau: Sauerländer.

Steinberg, J. 1976. *Why Switzerland?* Cambridge: Cambridge University Press.

Stricker, H. 1980. "Zum Problem der etappenweisen Verdeutschung Unterrätiens (aus rätoromanischer Sicht)." In *Historische Übergänge im alemannischen Sprachraum.* München, pp. 67–77.

Strübin, E. 1976. "Zur Schweizerdeutschen Umgangssprache." *Schweizerisches Archiv für Volkskunde* 72:97–145.

Tappolet, E. 1901. Über den Stand der Mundarten in der deutschen und französischen Schweiz." *Mitteilungen der Gesellschaft für deutsche Sprache in Zürich.* Vol. 6.

———. 1913. "Die alemannischen Lehnwörter in den Mundarten der französischen Schweiz." *Kulturhistorisch-linguistische Untersuchung. Programm zur Rektoratsfeier der Universität Basel.* Basel.

Thilo, E. 1941. *Note sur l'égalite et sur l'usage des langues nationales en Suisse.* Lausanne: Roth.

Thomke, H. 1978. "Mundart und Schriftsprache in der Schule." *Schweizer Monatshefte* 58:875–84.

Trümpy, H. 1955. *Schweizerdeutsche Sprache und Literatur im 17. und 18. Jahrhundert.* Basel: Krebs.

Viletta, R. 1978. *Abhandlung zum Sprachenrecht mit besonderer Berücksichtigung des Rechts der Gemeinden und des Kantons Graubünden.* Vol. 1: *Grundlagen des Sprachenrechts.* Zürich. (Zürcher Studien zum öffentlichen Recht. 4.)

Vocabulario dei dialetti della Svizzera Italiana. (1953 foll.) Lugano.

Vouga, J. P. 1978. *Romands, Alémaniques, Tessinois.* Neuchâtel: La Baconnière.

Wartburg, W. von. 1940. "Entstehung und Wesen der mehrsprachigen Schweiz." *Schweizer Monatshefte* 20:8–17.

Weilenmann, H. 1925. *Die vielsprachige Schweiz. Eine Lösung des Nationalitätenproblems.* Basel, Leipzig: Rhein-Verlag.

Weinreich, U. 1952. "Research Problems in Bilingualism. With Special Reference to Switzerland." Ph.D. diss., Columbia University.

———. 1953. *Languages in Contact: Findings and Problems.* New York.

Werlen, I. Forthcoming. "Zur Einschätzung von schweizerdeutschen Dialekten." In *Probleme der schweizerischen Dialektologie.* Fribourg: Editions universitaires.

Zimmer, R. 1977. "Dialekt—Nationaldialekt—Standardsprache. Vergleichende Betrachtungen zum deutsch-französischen Kontaktbereich in der Schweiz, im Elsass und in Luxemburg." *Zeitschrift für Dialektologie und Linguistik* 44:145–57.

Zimmerli, J. 1891, 1899. *Die deutsch-französische Sprachgrenze in der Schweiz.* Geneva and Basel: H. Georg.

Zinsli, P. 1964. *Vom Werden und Wesen der mehrsprachigen Schweiz. Rückblick und Ausblick.* Bern. (Schriften des Deutschschweizerischen Sprachvereins1.)

Zwicky, M. 1978. *Modärns Schwyzertütsch. Passe partout. Méthode audiovisuelle.* Fribourg.

BILINGUALISM AND BILINGUAL EDUCATION IN THE UNITED STATES

Studies of language behavior in the United States generally begin with a description of the linguistic pluralism that characterizes the society, and has characterized it from its earliest days. Heinz Kloss (1977), for example, writes of an "American bilingual tradition," by which he means not only that many different language communities have contributed to the social makeup of the nation, but also that there has been a degree of tolerance for the use of several languages for official purposes (especially for schooling, administration, and the courts). Similarly, Christina Bratt Paulston (1981), Shirley Brice Heath and Charles Ferguson (1981), Joshua A. Fishman (1966), and others present the picture of a linguistically diverse nation, with new language groups being absorbed into the society even up to the present moment.

Such characterizations serve to combat the curious but pervasive myth of a linguistically monolithic United States, with everyone speaking or in the process of learning to speak English. While we might agree that the misperception rests on historical distortion, we should also understand that it represents a widespread language orientation: however much the United States may be characterized as a linguistically plural nation, such pluralism is both undervalued and transitory. To say that it is a bilingual or multilingual society is to make a descriptive statement, not a normative one, as Nancy Faires Conklin and Margaret A. Lourie suggest: "Americans may be a polyglot people, speaking many languages and many varieties of English. But for the most part we have conducted our public life as if we were all monolingual English speakers" (1983:xiii). That the United States has never declared English to be the official language should not lead us to doubt its primacy over all other languages. Indeed, this shows only its overwhelming strength: such attempts at officialization are generally regarded as superfluous and therefore rejected. Any discussion of language behavior in the

United States must begin with the acknowledgment of one fundamental social
fact: the perception that English is the most important and powerful language in
the world makes development of bilingual proficiency in the general population
appear to be a luxury, and intensifies the pressure for persons of non-English-
speaking background to discard their language in favor of English.

In this chapter, we will try to understand how linguistic diversity and normative
English monolingualism coexist in the United States, and explain how this situation developed. First, we will present a brief sociolinguistic profile, which
will include a picture of where the major language "islands" are located, an
examination of the nature and numerical strength of different language communities, and an appraisal of the prestige levels of different languages in relation
to English. Next, we will give a historical account of ethnic group relations in
the United States with a view to understanding why some groups tend to retain
their language longer than others. This will include, as well, a short history of
bilingual education programs and policy developments. We will then turn our
attention to an assessment of the present situation: What are the research trends
in the areas of group and individual bilingualism, second-language acquisition,
and language teaching? What are the recent policy developments that would
affect language behavior and education? What are the alternatives in bilingual
education programming? What movement is there toward the development of a
comprehensive language policy? What are the prospects for language maintenance and language shift and for the development of a general bilingual proficiency in the U.S. population? Finally, we will offer a short list of important
sources of information on language communities, language politics, bilingual
education, and language teaching in the United States.

SOCIOLINGUISTIC CONTEXT

It is important at the outset of this discussion to understand something of the
language dynamics of U.S. society. This entails, first, a word about the de-
mographics of language communities and the extent to which they have been
able to maintain their languages. Then we will examine some of the social and
political forces that act on language communities and that influence them toward
language maintenance or language shift.

Language Demographics

An analysis of the 1980 census published by the U.S. Bureau of the Census
(1980; cf. Waggoner, 1984) shows the minority language population (MLP) of
the country to number about 34.6 million persons, or a little more than 15 percent
of the total U.S. population of 226,361,000. The MLP can be defined as those
persons who speak a language other than English at home or who live in households in which at least one person speaks a non-English language. Of course,
not all such persons can be considered "bilingual" in the common sense of the

term (where ''bilingual'' is taken to mean a person who understands *and produces* the language to a certain degree of proficiency). Still, the census reports show that about 23 million people speak a non-English language at home, and about 18.6 million persons speak English and another language—that is, they are ''bilinguals'' (Garcia, 1985:149).

About 45 percent of the MLP is in the Spanish-language group (15.5 million); this group is followed in size by the French and German (3 million each), Italian (2.6 million), and Polish (1.3 million) communities. Of the general population, about 28 percent is eighteen years old or younger. But for the MLP, 33 percent is under eighteen. Most notable in this group are the Spanish (40 percent children) and the Vietnamese (46 percent children). This is significant, of course, for a number of public policy concerns, especially education. MLP children constitute 17 percent of the school-age population. Approximately 8 million children live in minority language families, and more than half of these speak the minority language at home. Reports on the 1980 census and the English Language Proficiency Survey (ELPS) show that the number of minority language-speaking children rose 27 percent from 3.8 million in 1976 to 4.5 million in 1982, and that the number of limited-English-proficient (LEP) children rose from 2 million to 2.4 million in the same period (Bell, 1984). The most recent studies of the census predict that the MLP, most notably the Hispanic and Asian groups, will continue to increase at a steady rate at least until the year 2000 (Brown et al., 1981; Oxford et al., 1981; U.S. Bureau of the Census, 1983; Wong, 1985).

As important as the number of minority language speakers is the geographical distribution of the different language communities. One of the most important factors in language maintenance is the physical position of these communities in relation to speakers of the dominant language (Conklin and Lourie, 1983; Paulston, 1985). Of particular significance has been the relative insulation and isolation these groups have been able to achieve. Kloss (1966) calls this the existence of ''language islands.'' In spite of a considerable amount of cultural and linguistic diffusion—an understandable result of the value placed in the society on all kinds of mobility—the major language communities of the United States can be associated with more or less definite geographical areas. We will try to point these out now.

It is fitting that the greatest part of the MLP are Spanish-speakers, since up until the last century more than half the areas of the United States was controlled by either Spain or Mexico. The areas of greatest Hispanic influence historically are also those where the largest Spanish-speaking communities are found today. *Chicanos*, or Mexican-Americans, are closely identified with the five Southwestern states of California, Texas, Arizona, New Mexico, and Colorado. Within these states, Chicanos are found mainly in urban *barrios* in large cities such as Los Angeles, San Antonio, El Paso, and San Francisco. Diffusion out of the Southwest, which has resulted in significant concentrations of Chicanos, is due in large part to economic factors; Chicano communities in the Plains and the Midwest, for example, have grown where migrant farm laborers and agricultural factory workers decided to settle. Chicanos constitute about 60 percent of the U.S. Hispanic community (Brown et al., 1981). *Puerto Ricans* have migrated to the mainland in large numbers starting in the 1960s, mainly as a result of poor economic conditions on the island. There are slightly more than 3 million insular Puerto Ricans, and about 2 million on the mainland, of whom almost 60 percent live in New York City. Most of the rest live in large cities of the Northeast, although growing communities can be found elsewhere, especially the Midwest and the West Coast. Perhaps as many as 85 percent of these Puerto Ricans have Spanish as their mother tongue (Brown et al., 1981; Zentella, 1981; Conklin and Lourie, 1983). Cubans came to the United States in large numbers for the first time following the 1959 revolution. This first wave of about eight hundred thousand persons consisted mainly of educated, landowning members of the middle and upper classes. About half of these immigrants settled in Dade County, Florida. A later influx of 125,000 Cubans, participants in the 1980 Mariel Boat Lift, added somewhat to the large Cuban community around Miami; but, perhaps because they were poorer and less well educated than the older immigrants, Florida communities were less tolerant of this group. As a result, they were scattered in a variety of locations around the country; many of them have since returned to Cuba. *Central and South Americans* and *other Spanish-speakers* may total up to 2.5 million persons. These immigrants, many of whom have entered the country as refugees, tend to be scattered throughout the country, though they appear to prefer settling in some of the established Hispanic communities (the *barrios* of San Francisco, New York, and Miami, for example, while primarily Chicano, Puerto Rican, and Cuban, respectively, serve as refuges for large numbers of other Spanish-speakers as well). This tendency for Spanish-speaking immigrants to seek out and settle in Hispanic enclaves is an important factor in the persistence of Spanish-language islands into the indefinite future.

The European language groups—the Germans, French, Italians, Poles, Scandinavians, and others—have been less successful in maintaining identifiable language islands. There are perhaps as many as 50 million people of *German* heritage in the United States today, the second largest ethnic heritage group in the country, after the Anglo-Irish (Gilbert, 1981). Yet, about 90 percent of that group is monolingual in English (Veltman, 1983:43). The large German communities that developed along the Eastern seaboard and in the Midwest starting in the middle of the nineteenth century have retained much of their ethnic distinctiveness, but not their language. Those groups best able to achieve a high degree of language maintenance, like the so-called Pennsylvania Dutch or the Amish, can do so because their language is also a religious language; but the link of German with the religion of the mainstream communities, so strong in the early Catholic and Lutheran churches, has virtually disappeared (Ruiz, 1985). There are still a few German-English bilingual communities, most notably in the Midwest (Conklin and Lourie, 1983:32). Generally, however, the relatively large concentrations of persons of German heritage which still exist are not so much language islands as ethnic-cultural ones. *French-speakers* are concentrated in areas where France and French Canada have had historical influence. While the greatest number of these persons is to be found in Louisiana (where the 1976 census found more than half a million French-English bilinguals), evidence of French influence persists in the Midwest along the Mississippi River and in the Northeast. It is interesting to note that Louisiana and New England share common sources of French speakers: each has been influenced by Europeans, Canadians, and West Indians. Calvin Veltman (1983) calculates that 65.6 percent of those of French heritage in the United States are English monolinguals. The other European groups can also be identified with certain regions. *Italians* formed urban communities in the large cities of the Northeast and the Great Lakes; very old Italian sections persist in Boston, New York City, Philadelphia, and Chicago (Correa-Zoli, 1981). *Poles and other Slavic groups* are also found in large numbers in these areas, as well as in Texas and California (Henzl, 1981). The vast majority of Scandinavian-Americans are either *Swedish* or *Norwegian*; these have clustered in the upper Midwestern states, though there are still identifiably Scandinavian communities in New York and the Pacific Northwest (Conklin and Lourie, 1983:35–37). In 1976, there were about 3.1 million persons of Scandinavian background in the United States, with an English monolingualism rate of over 86 percent (Veltman, 1983:43).

We need to mention two other groups of non-English-language background which tend to develop language islands. The *Asian* population of the United States grew by 142 percent between 1970 and 1980 (Wong, 1985). The largest increases occurred in the Filipino, Chinese, and Korean groups; there was also an influx of new immigrant groups during this time—most notably the Vietnamese and the Hmong. Of the 3.7 million Asians, 59 percent are foreign-born and two-thirds speak the language at home. Asians currently constitute 1.5 percent of the U.S. population; trends in immigration and birth rate suggest that this figure will be over 4 percent by the year 2000. In 1980, 64 percent of Asians lived in three states—California, Hawaii, and New York; 40 percent were concentrated in the four metropolitan areas of Los Angeles—Long Beach, San Francisco-Oakland, New York City, and Honolulu. These groups are expected to remain so concentrated until at least the year 2000 (Oxford et al., 1981). About half of the almost eight hundred thousand *Native Americans* in the United States live on reservations. Perhaps as many as one-third of the population speaks one of the two hundred or so Native American languages that still exist. The largest of these communities, the Navajo, number about ninety thousand persons. Because of their isolation and their use of native language in traditional religious practice, Native Americans tend to retain their language more successfully than most groups. On the other hand, the small number of speakers within most of these language communities and the movement of the young people away from reservations could mean a more rapid tendency to language shift in the future. Tragically, because the great majority of these languages have no writing system, language shift for Native Americans has in the past often meant language death (Nichols, 1985; Leap, 1981; Conklin and Lourie, 1983).

Language Status

Status has not been conferred in any official sense on English or any other language in the United States, except perhaps in a few isolated cases at the state or local level. Instead, there has evolved a language ideology that regards language as a form of social power: the status of a language in the United States is determined by its perceived utility. Fishman takes this position:

English for our masses is a lingua franca rather than a thing of beauty, elegance, precision, purity, or greatness. "It works"; it is an instrumentality; but as such, it is not an object of love, affection, devotion, emotion. For good or for evil, we have developed a civilization that is not sentimental about language, languages, or even about its own language (1981:516; cf. Fishman, 1966:30; Marckwardt, 1958:133).

One might speak of a sort of unconscious linguistic stratification that has developed in the United States, with English at the top and all other languages arranged in some order below it. But the situation is more complicated than that. Only certain varieties or forms of English—so-called Standard American English, for example, or British-influenced forms—have prestige. These are seen to be important for technology and business, for literature, and for worldwide communications. That the power of English is recognized throughout the world, a fact attested to by its widespread use as an additional language (Fishman, Cooper, and Conrad, 1977), only serves to add to the prestige of its international, standardized forms, and to subordinate other varieties, in the United States. The most obvious case of a subordinated variety is Black English, considered by some not to be a language at all. The fact that any well-developed linguistic arguments have been offered for its status as a full-fledged language (see, for example, Labov, 1972) has not diminished the resistance by the general population to its public use. Such resistance was also faced by other English varieties—Chicano English, Appalachian speech, and others—though perhaps to a lesser degree. This is because intolerance for these varieties has little to do with their status *as languages* or even with acknowledgments of their communicative richness; it has to do primarily with their lack of status *as purveyors of social power*. What subordinated varieties of English have in common is that they are perceived to have little or no potential for advancing their users toward some social good. Discarding these languages in favor of Standard English is considered a prudent, practical decision, essential for any economic and social mobility.

What can be said of this status with respect to non-English languages in the United States? Here, we must make some crucial distinctions. Ferguson and Heath distinguish between *ethnic* languages and *foreign* languages (1981:xxxiv). By this they mean, on the one hand, the languages used as mother tongues by non-English speakers and, on the other, languages learned in school as formal subjects. At least since the late nineteenth century, there has been a consistent intolerance for the public use of ethnic languages, with a concomitant rise in foreign language interest and study. How is this explained?

One should note, first, that this distinction operates on many levels. It is, for example, an academic distinction: with the formalization of foreign language curricula beginning in the 1880s, an emphasis on reading and writing of the highly standardized modern languages became the central feature of foreign language teaching. Mother tongues, which were often regional varieties of the World Standard languages found in textbooks and valued primarily as means of oral communication, came to be devalued by the educational establishment. The present antagonism between foreign language and bilingual education teachers is traceable in part to this academic bias (Ruiz, 1985). But if the distinction between ethnic and foreign languages is an academic one, it is probably more of a social-political-ideological one. Ethnic languages are potential threats socially, economically, and perhaps even militarily, precisely because they are attached to a language community. Efforts to maintain a non-English mother tongue have often been viewed as an act of separatism, of disloyalty; significantly, they are also seen as detracting from, and perhaps incompatible with, efforts to learn English. That is why bilingual education, which is designed to use the mother tongue as one of the media of instruction, has become such a controversial subject: some regard it as an effort to maintain a non-English language (largely, they are mistaken) and, therefore, as a program that retards English-language achievement. The ability to speak English, or at least the earnest desire to learn it, is regarded by some as the essence of citizenship in the United States.

On the other hand, the suspicion of disloyalty is removed from the study of foreign languages (except in the most hysterically xenophobic of times, such as the late 1910s and 1920s). Indeed, the U.S. military may well be the most prolific and efficient trainer of foreign language specialists. Furthermore, the Modern Language Association has recently reported an increase in interest in studying foreign languages in colleges and universities; the largest increases occurred in the study of the languages of the United States' three greatest ideological and commercial competitors—Japanese, Russian, and Chinese (Maeroff, 1984). There is a strange irony at work in a society in which the effort to retain one's first language is construed as disloyal, while the study of a second language is regarded as patriotic. But, we should not forget, it is also pragmatic: it is acknowledgment of the status differences between ethnic and foreign languages. Foreign languages are "standards"; ethnic languages are "vernaculars." Studying the one is an "elite" activity; maintaining the other is a "folk" act. The extent to which we emphasize foreign language study over ethnic language maintenance is evidence of the perception that the former is an act of acquiring power, and the latter an act of powerless sentimentality.

Finally, let us consider one other distinction. S. O. Garcia says the following:

What is accepted in the United States is *bilingualism*, that is, the use of two languages by individuals, but not *diglossia*, that is, the enduring societal arrangement for the existence of two languages, each having its secure, legitimate, and widely implemented functions (1985:147).

This is an interesting point, and it is related to what we have said above. Ethnic languages are attached to communities, the existence of which is an important contributor to diglossia. Foreign languages are not attached to communities, at least not intimately. The distinction between bilingualism and diglossia could perhaps be more generally stated in its application to the United States as a distinction between *diversity* and *pluralism*. The first of these is developed by individual initiative, and is considered an essential ingredient of American democracy; the second constitutes group activity and is regarded with great suspicion. The bias toward individualism in the United States may have its advantages in some areas of social life, but it is problematic in the development of language capacity. Diglossia is essential to long-term, stable bilingualism, as countless sociolinguists have told us; yet, it is not to be encouraged in the United States. This no doubt explains why the U.S. language student, even after long periods of training in our best universities, is deficient in conversational skills (Benderson, 1983). But, then, it is apparently not conversational skills that are valued; it is foreign language literacy to which prestige is attached.

We may summarize by restating our original thesis: status is attached to those languages, those language varieties, those dimensions of language capacity, and those activities related to language which are perceived to be of high utility. Standard English is preferred to regional or functional varieties. Foreign languages are preferred to ethnic languages. Literacy skills are preferred to conversational skills. These are all associated with the acquisition of power, which is the primary orientation of language ideology in the United States.

HISTORICAL CONTEXT

The sociolinguistic dynamics which we have just described need a historical framework in which to be understood. Language prestige and language attitudes, concerns with language maintenance and language shift, the development of a language ideology, as well as explanations of current events and projections for the future, all require historical perspective. We will try to give this first by presenting a brief account of ethnic group relations, and then by offering an abbreviated history of bilingual education in the United States.

Ethnic Group Relations

The nature of the contact among ethnic groups is a key to understanding differences in language attitude and behavior. Ferguson and Heath draw attention to the differences that tend to characterize groups in different categories—immigrant and indigenous groups, for example. Navajos tend to resist linguistic assimilation more than Italian-Americans, and they are on the whole more successful in their efforts (Veltman, 1983). This is at least in part because the immigrant is urged to adopt an attitude, motivated let us say by a sense of obligation or gratitude toward one's host, of yielding to the majority; the conditions of conquest and annexation being obviously different from those of immigration, the response of the indigenous person is predictably different. But, having said that much, the analysis becomes much more complicated. The conditions of contact among ethnic groups and between majority and minority groups affect everyone, majority groups as well. It is a whole complex of conditions which creates the status differences we have discussed above, which are in turn major factors in language attitudes and behavior. Let us consider only two examples.

Germans came to the United States in large numbers starting in the 1830s. From the Eastern Seaboard, they migrated into the major metropolitan areas of the Midwest—Chicago, St. Louis, Cincinnati, Indianapolis, Milwaukee, and others. Their communities flourished. They established schools, churches, and community organizations, and were generally well-respected citizens. By the 1850s, they were being elected to important civic offices and were being courted by interests in the public domain. This was important in cities such as St. Louis, where Germans constituted "a considerable portion of [the] active business and manufacturing community, holding a great amount of the wealth of [the] city, and contributing largely to its revenues" (St. Louis Public Schools, 1876:114). The German language became a popular course in the public schools, both because it was the language of a large portion of the community and because it was an important language for literature and science. Though complaints were heard occasionally about the strength of German influence by other ethnic groups (Pierce, 1936:385) and by some nationalist "protective" organizations (Kloss, 1977:70), the strength of the German communities and the German language in the public schools increased steadily until the beginning of World War I.

We get a completely different picture as we move to consider the Chicanos of the Southwest in precisely the same period. Thousands of Mexican citizens became Mexican-Americans with the end of the Mexican War and the signing of the Treaty of Guadalupe-Hidalgo on February 2, 1848. The United States' victory was expensive in lives; thirteen thousand U.S. soldiers died in the war. While the Treaty guaranteed certain rights to the Mexican tenants, many of them eventually lost their land and their status. Their language and their culture came to be depreciated by the controlling Anglo community. Mexican children were discouraged from going to school and were often segregated in their own schools when they did go. Public schools suppressed the Spanish language; many of them imposed "no-Spanish" rules, by which anyone overheard speaking Spanish on the school grounds was detained, fined, reported, or in other ways punished for this violation. These practices have continued up to very recently (U.S. Commission on Civil Rights, 1972).

What accounts for the differences in these two communities and the response of the majority group toward them? Four factors appear to be significant: (1) the nature of the initial contact, (2) economic strength, (3) racial traits, and (4) religious tradition. The early German immigrants were political refugees, inclined to feel favorably about the freedoms afforded by their new country. Furthermore, the small German communities that existed in the eighteenth century before the great influx of immigrants had demonstrated their loyalty by registering in significant numbers in the Revolutionary and Continental Armies (Leibowitz, 1971:6). The Mexicans, on the other hand, had been a problem to the United States and the inhabitants of the Southwestern territories before their conquest. Not only were they, along with the Indians, a major force in preventing westward expansion (and therefore in the realization of the promise of "manifest destiny"), but they were also suspected of undermining the efforts of Southern slave-owners by harboring fugitives (McWilliams, 1949). When they officially became part of the United States, the attitude on both sides was one of hostility engendered by a bitter and bloody war. Mexicans were the enemy, regardless of their legal status; today's "Remember the Alamo" bumper stickers are testimony to the fact that the hostility abides even now among some. This shows the strength of war in its effect on ethnic group interrelations and language status. It has affected the Mexican group from the beginning; it would have a similar effect on Germans in World War I: the immediate dismantling of German-language programs at the beginning of the war would have an impact such that the language would not recover even up to now.

The economic and political strength of the German communities of the Midwest helped to create an attitude of tolerance, even accommodation, for them. It appears, however, that economic power preceded, perhaps made possible, their political influence. The St. Louis reports show that the study of German language in public schools was encouraged by the authorities because it was important to draw the considerable resources of the German communities out of the private schools. There were similar patterns of accommodation in other cities of the Midwest. Whatever economic power the Mexicans of the Southwest had was soon eroded through legal and political maneuvering. The intolerance for Spanish was influenced by the fact that it was the language of a poor, disenfranchised group.

Physically, Germans were indistinguishable from the dominant white majority, which after all was a blend of the older Northern and Western European ethnic groups. Mexicans, on the other hand, were highly visible because of their darker features and their Indian background. This association with the Native American was a significant dimension of the discrimination against the Mexican-American. The Indian was the ultimate enemy to the white majority of the Southwest. Furthermore, Indians had a separate legal status; in some states, for example, it was legal to exclude Indians from the public schools (Weinberg, 1979); categorizing Mexican-Americans as Indians had the effect of justifying segregation of them as well. It was not until 1954 (in the case of *Pete Hernandez, Petitioner vs. Texas*) that Mexican-Americans were legally established as "Caucasians." That is not a categorization which many Chicanos are willing to accept for themselves, however; nor does it prevent discrimination based on a perception of racial difference on the part of the dominant group. It appears that differential evaluations based on race were also behind the acceptance of the language of the Germans and the suppression of the language of the Mexicans.

The Protestant tradition in the United States has been dominant from its earliest days. The exclusion of Catholic influences from the society has been a concern of individuals, private organizations, and public agencies (Kloss, 1977:27). This anti-Catholic orientation placed Mexicans at an immediate disadvantage. Germans were more balanced as to religion. This was important for the German Catholics, since at times they could form a coalition of interest with Lutherans when they felt threatened. Perhaps the most celebrated case of Lutheran-Catholic cooperation in the German community was the campaign against the Bennett Law of Wisconsin in the late 1880s. This was perceived to be an anti-parochial school measure. Since the two churches operated extensive private school systems by that time, they were able to work together and gather support from other sectors of the German community to get the law repealed. Still, this would not be the last battle fought against anti-Catholic bias.

These two examples show some of the complexity in providing a history of intergroup relations. A complicated array of conditions dictate in any particular era which of these, or other, factors will be the strongest in determining social status. These conditions are different for each group. Early Asian groups, which did well economically, were discriminated against nonetheless, perhaps primarily because of racial and religious bias; Eastern and Southern European immigrants of the turn of the century were generally sympathetic to American democratic government, yet they were viewed with suspicion; and the Germans themselves became social outcasts, in spite of all their favorable traits, when their country of origin became the enemy of the United States. Perhaps the case of the Germans should serve as an example of how there is no sure road to the attainment of social status in the United States, though some roads—particularly those that lead to an agglutination of power—are surer than others.

Bilingual Education

An important element in the history of ethnic group relations is an examination of how they, and their languages, have been treated in the schools. Bilingual schooling, by which we mean the use of two languages as media of instruction in the curriculum, is a relatively old phenomenon in the United States. It has its roots, no doubt, in the need for religious instruction in the communities themselves, coupled with the urge to accommodate the language of the dominant society. As a more generalized educational approach, it is probably as old as the public school itself. One of the earliest recorded programs was developed by Germans in Cincinnati in 1840 (Kloss, 1977:157–58). This program, which experimented with different patterns of German-English instruction, served as model and resource for other programs throughout the Midwest. For example, it furnished five specially trained bilingual teachers for the St. Louis public schools in 1864–65, the first year of their German-English program. The St. Louis program grew rapidly, so that in its tenth year 73 percent of its students were studying German in forty-five schools (St. Louis Public Schools, 1876:113). Other programs in the Midwest developed and grew just as rapidly. Chicago, Milwaukee, Indianapolis, Louisville, and other cities had significant programs, often supported by bureaucratic structures designed to administer them. Other language groups benefited from the German successes. In Milwaukee, Polish, Italian, and Norwegian, along with German, were studied; Czech, French, Spanish, Dutch, and other languages were used in public schools throughout the country, from Baltimore to San Francisco. These programs persisted until the outbreak of World War I.

The war brought an end to German study in the public schools. But it had more general effects as well. The period between the world wars can rightly be described as the most xenophobic in the history of the United States. Between 1918 and 1935, almost half of the states would pass laws hostile to foreign language study in schools. The most well known of these was Nebraska's Siman Law of 1919; it was ruled unconstitutional in the celebrated 1923 decision *Meyer vs. Nebraska* on the grounds that it inappropriately allowed the state to impose curricular decisions on private as well as public schools. Still, the hostility toward foreign languages, coupled with a strong push toward Americanization attitudes, had a negative effect on foreign language study until the 1950s (Ruiz, 1985). Bilingual education, where one of the languages is a mother tongue to the students, would not reemerge with any strength until the 1960s.

The most important programs of the modern era were those developed by the Cuban community of Dade County, Florida, in the early 1960s. These programs were motivated by two considerations: the need to be successful in an English-speaking country for as long as the refugees might be here; and the need for the children to retain a sense of Cuban identity and Spanish-language proficiency, since they fully expected to return within a short time. The Cuban programs served to foster an attitude of acceptability for such programs benefiting other groups. Chicanos and Puerto Ricans lobbied steadily for a general bilingual education measure. Finally, two bills that had been introduced by legislators from Texas and New York were combined and passed into law in 1968 as Title VII of the Elementary and Secondary Education Act of 1965. Commonly known as the Bilingual Education Act (BEA), it provided $7.5 million in 1969, its first year of operation. This resulted in seventy-six demonstration projects, all but one of which was geared toward Spanish-speakers. The 1968 BEA was vague in its description of what the programs should entail; consequently, a great variety of programs were developed. Its two main provisions were that the children benefiting from the program should be limited in their ability to speak English and that they should be from households earning $3,000 a year or less. Beyond that, it was not very specific.

The BEA has been revised and reauthorized three times since 1968—in 1974, 1978, and 1984. The 1974 version defined bilingual education as a program to help children acquire English proficiency; funds were to be used "to demonstrate effective ways of providing for children of limited English-speaking ability, instruction designed to enable them, while using their native language, to achieve competence in the English language." This has come to be the standard definition of a "transitional" bilingual program, where the child's language is used only until such time as he or she is able to perform ordinary classwork in English. This narrow view of bilingual education may have been influenced by the *Lau vs. Nichols* Supreme Court decision earlier in 1974. There, the Court found that the San Francisco school system had violated the civil rights of approximately eighteen hundred Chinese children by teaching them exclusively in a language they did not understand—English. While the Court mandated no particular remedy, the implementing rules formulated by the Department of Health, Education, and Welfare urged transitional bilingual education as an acceptable remedy. Therefore, the notion of bilingual education as a program to teach English to non-English speakers was now codified in administrative rules and crystallized in the public mind.

The revisions of 1978 did nothing to alter this view of bilingual education. Their most significant achievement was to change the target population from "limited-English-speaking" (LES) to "limited-English-proficient" (LEP). This had the practical effect of expanding the eligible population to those who had reading and writing deficiencies as well.

The 1984 BEA was heavily influenced by the ideas of staff members of the Reagan Administration who had doubts about the effectiveness of bilingual programs. Their view was that there was not enough evidence to support the exclusive use of transitional bilingual education to remedy the English deficiencies of these children (Baker and deKanter, 1983). The draft proposal submitted for the Administration by the Secretary of Education for consideration by Congress included four major changes in the law: it was to provide basic grants for building the capacity of local education agencies to treat LEP children; it encouraged the involvement of state authorities in the development and evaluation of projects; it would give priority to those children whose "usual language" was a non-English language; and it would provide funding for "special alternatives" which would serve as experiments in programming. All four of these changes made it into the final version, reported out of committee on October 2, 1984 (House of Representatives, 1984). Perhaps the most controversial change is the one providing for "special alternatives," since by that the proposers meant especially programs that would not use the child's mother tongue as a medium of instruction. The impact of this change, however, was diminished by the provision that not more than 10 percent of the total funds expended in any year could be used for alternative programming. Still, it has provided for the possibility that bilingual education in the United States can be a program where only one language is used for the purpose of developing proficiency in one language— English. One might well ask what justifies calling this kind of education "bilingual."

One should not assume from this discussion that developments in bilingual education policy have been only at the federal level. Nothing could be more untrue. By 1984, perhaps as many as twenty-two states had passed bilingual education legislation (reported figures vary: see, for example, Bell, 1984, who says twenty-two states had passed such laws, and Ambert and Melendez, 1985, who report twenty states with bilingual acts). This is significant, since in the United States the primary responsibility for education falls on state and local jurisdictions. One should also note, however, that the vast majority of state statutes provide for narrow, transitional programs almost exclusively.

The initial enthusiasm for bilingual education seems to have waned significantly in the mid–1980s. The $7.5 million appropriation of 1969 which reached its highwater mark at $171.7 million in 1980 was reduced by more than $30 million in the first three Reagan years (Toch, 1984; cf. Arias and Navarro, 1981, whose figures vary slightly from Toch's). Most informed observers anticipate much deeper cuts in the second Reagan term, the $4 million increase in 1985 appropriations being viewed almost universally as an election year aberration.

The condition of bilingual education in the United States is confusing. Advocates of a broader conception of bilingual education—Joshua Fishman, Rudolph Troike, and others—argue going beyond transitional bilingual education to maintenance and even enrichment bilingual education where the object is for everyone, minority and majority child alike, to have an opportunity to learn a second language while maintaining the mother tongue. Yet, these advocates are rarely represented in official policy; instead, the laws are influenced by middle-level staff members of the federal bureaucracy, many of whom have little formal background in bilingual education research or policy development. This may be the reason why the United States is moving toward bilingual education programming that does not seek to develop either a bilingual individual or a bilingual society, that is not "bilingual" in any common sense of the word. Instead, the trend is toward a policy of Anglification for all. Perhaps this trend is explained by our traditional hostility toward linguistic pluralism, and our depreciation of ethnic languages; perhaps it is merely a manifestation of our pragmatism: insuring English proficiency in these children empowers them in ways not afforded them by their own language.

THE PRESENT CONTEXT

We should now turn to a consideration of the current situation in respect to bilingualism and bilingual education in the United States. First, we will discuss the major research trends in bilingualism and second-language acquisition and teaching; next, we will examine some of the alternatives in bilingual education programming; then we will consider to what extent a consensus exists for a comprehensive national language policy; finally, we will speculate on the prospects for bilingualism in the United States.

Research Trends

Second-Language Acquisition. Program development in the United States has been influenced strongly by the work of researchers such as Stephen Krashen, Jim Cummins, and Tracy Terrell, who advance communicative approaches to second-language acquisition and teaching. The common principle that underlies this work can be stated as follows: a language is more readily acquired when it is used as a medium for the communication of meaningful messages than when it is used as a target for learning. This means that emphasis is placed on the function of language rather than on its form. This is in contrast to earlier behaviorist theories which emphasize conscious learning of correct forms of language in order that the learner acquire good habits. Communicative theorists consider the memorization and repetition drills employed in these approaches to be anxiety-producing and therefore a hindrance to real acquisition. The communicative approach would develop as close to a natural language environment as possible for the second-language classroom in order to reduce anxiety and encourage the production of large amounts of meaningful messages. For the bilingual classroom, this suggests a justification for the use of both languages as media of instruction rather than primarily as subjects.

Bilingualism. Wallace E. Lambert's (1981) distinction between additive and subtractive bilingualism is useful in considering the results of different kinds of school programs. Additive bilingualism characterizes the student who has been able to maintain the mother tongue while adding technical proficiency as well as communicative competence and an appreciation of the value system inherent in a second language. Subtractive bilingualism characterizes a student who, as a result of a school program, has lost proficiency in the mother tongue and has replaced it with a second language. This distinction is more descriptive of the results of bilingual programs than the more common maintenance-transition distinction. More generally, work by sociolinguists demonstrates that individual bilingualism must be supported by the operation of diglossic norms within the speech community or the larger society (Kjolseth, 1972). At the very least, this means that each of the languages of the bilingual must have a definite, substantive function in order for both to be maintained. For the classroom, this implies the necessity of functional differential of language use. A common technique in bilingual programs, translation from one language to another of the same material, is a violation of this principle, as is the assigning of purely directive or disciplinary functions to one language in the classroom.

Use of First Language as Medium. The traditional assumption in bilingual education is that both the mother tongue and the second language should be used as media of instruction. This is based on another assumption: that children can learn best through a language they understand. Recently, this assumption has been called into question (Baker and deKanter, 1983). It has been the object of research in a series of studies commissioned by the National Institute of Education referred to as the Significant Bilingual Instructional Features (SBIF) project.

Researchers found the use of the child's first language an essential part of effective programs: "in the most powerful educational environments for producing bilingualism, both languages are used as the medium of instruction" (Cazden, 1984:15–16). Furthermore, "when instruction is delivered in a language a child only minimally can understand, the result frequently is frustration, boredom, hostility, or withdrawal. Thus, access to learning is impeded at the very least, resulting in failure or falling behind in school work" (Tikunoff and Vazquez-Faria, 1982).

Importance of the Ethnic Culture in Instruction. SBIF researchers also found that use of the student's home culture as a mediator of instruction was a component of effective programs for the bilingual student (Tikunoff and Vazquez-Faria, 1982). This suggests reverting to an earlier emphasis on bicultural education and using cultural elements, such as affect and values, which go beyond merely material culture.

Effectiveness of Bilingual Approaches. The effectiveness of bilingual education has increasingly been called into question in recent days. Some have called for a national experiment to provide more definitive guidelines for future direction (Rotberg, 1984). Others have seen enough; they recommend diverting bilingual education funds to other approaches (Twentieth Century Fund, 1983; Baker and deKanter, 1983). Yet, advocates of bilingual education still present convincing arguments on its benefits (Troike, 1981). One problem in resolving this issue is that the question of effectiveness is determined by what one takes the goals of the program to be. It is clear that Fishman, Troike, Tikunoff and Vazquez-Faria, and others take a broad view of the goals of bilingual education: to increase equal educational opportunity; to enhance the child's self-esteem; to create better articulation between the home and the school experience; to develop and enhance skills in two languages. Baker and deKanter and members of the Twentieth Century Task Force, among others, take a much narrower view: proficiency in English. Resolution of this problem will be difficult, since it is not to be adjudicated strictly by marshalling empirical evidence.

Programmatic Alternatives

Courtney Cazden (1984) demonstrates the great variety of programs called "bilingual." There is wide variation in the ratio of first- to second-language use; the functions allocated to the two languages; the number of adults in the classroom and program; the nature and quantity of curriculum materials; daily schedules; the composition of the classrooms; the statement of objectives; the management styles of the directors; the role of parent advisory committees; and other factors. It is no wonder that researchers have a difficult time comparing results across programs and that the general public is confused. This section discusses only the most common program alternatives.

Transitional Bilingual Education. We have already discussed this topic briefly. It is designed to prepare the student as quickly as possible for entrance into the regular all-English curriculum. An important component of this alternative, as it is for most of the other varieties of bilingual education, is formal English-as-a-second-language (ESL) instruction. The first language is generally used extensively in the early part of the program and is phased out more or less gradually as English becomes the dominant curricular medium.

Maintenance Bilingual Education. This program is designed to maintain the student's proficiency in the mother tongue while adding proficiency in English. The ratio of first to second language use varies. English is generally taught as a subject from early on. There are very few true maintenance programs in the United States.

Enrichment Bilingual Education. This alternative has been proposed by Fishman and others. It transcends maintenance programs in that it is designed to add to the linguistic repertoires of both English-speakers and non- or limited-English-speakers. This program holds promise for making bilingual education a generally accepted curricular alternative, since it has benefits for both majority and minority groups. Up to now, federal bilingual education funds could not be used to teach foreign languages to English speakers. It remains to be seen whether any enrichment programs will be funded under the "special alternatives" provision of the new BEA.

Immersion Programs. It is far more likely that immersion programs will be funded under this provision. Researchers in the Department of Education have expressed an interest in conducting experiments in "structured immersion," by which they mean the use of English for instructional purposes only, though use of the mother tongue by the student would be allowed. Calls for immersion experiments have been motivated by a recognition of the success of such programs in Canada. However, there are important differences in the goals of these programs and in the sociolinguistic dynamics of the two countries (Hernandez-Chavez, 1984). Some of those most familiar with the Canadian programs have alerted us to the dangers of a hasty application to the United States, particularly for the purpose of teaching English to minority language speakers. Wallace Lambert, for example, considers that it would have been "inappropriate" for immersion programs to have been offered to French students in Canada. That would have led, ultimately, to a displacement of French by English, which is generally "viewed as the more useful, prestigious, or otherwise more valuable language" in North America (1984:8–9). If they are to be tried at all, they should be designed for the purpose of teaching majority English speakers a minority language. Up to this point, that is what the few immersion classrooms in the United States have been designed for. A recent report reveals that immersion programs have been developed in twenty-seven schools in eleven cities involving 5,421 students and 245 teachers; only three languages have been used: Spanish, French, and German (California State Department of Education, 1984:140–43).

Language Policy Development

The development of a comprehensive national language policy has never been attempted in the United States. One of the reasons has been our concern for freedom of speech, a fundamental constitutional guarantee. Another reason is that, in a federal system, the authority of the central government to make policies of that sort that would be binding on the states is questionable. Furthermore, we should understand that the development of such policies involves very complicated processes; many nations that have acted in this way have spent decades sorting out the details of implementation.

Still, there is evidence that a national consensus toward the development of a comprehensive language policy is building. A major immigration bill narrowly rejected by the 1984 Congress contained a section that would have declared English the official language of the country. In addition, several states have recently passed laws officializing English. Furthermore, much of the groundwork has already been laid. Work by the President's Commission on Foreign Language and International Studies (1979) and by the task forces of the Modern Language Association and the American Council of Learned Societies (Brod, 1980) and position statements by the Academy for Educational Development and the Edward W. Hazen Foundation (1982) might easily form the bulk of supporting documents for such a policy. But to the extent that a *de facto* policy already exists, its general orientation can be described by saying that the United States regards English to be the language of use for all official purposes, other languages being permissible to protect constitutional guarantees; non-English languages are valued for commercial, scholarly, and military-diplomatic purposes; capacity in these languages is to be developed in nonnative speakers; maintenance of a non-English language is not acceptable. Debate of a national language policy could begin with a consideration of the advantages and disadvantages of such an orientation.

Prospects for Bilingualism

A discussion of the prospects of bilingualism in the United States must come to grips with two facts. First, there is compelling evidence of rapid and massive language shift among non-English language communities: "The data everywhere suggest that children in all minority language groups (except, of course, the Navajo) are moving inexorably toward English monolingualism. The rate is very rapid" (Veltman, 1983:140; cf. Correa-Zoli, 1981; Gilbert, 1981). This is so in spite of the existence of 581 bilingual education programs in 106 different languages (U.S. Department of Education, 1984), media in a variety of languages (Keller, 1983), more than sixty-five hundred mother-tongue schools providing instruction in fifty-three different languages (Fishman, 1984), and a host of other institutions designed, at least in part, to maintain ethnic languages. Second, U.S. schools are notoriously bad at developing language capacity, particularly oral capacity, in students (Benderson, 1983). The recent increases in foreign language enrollment mean nothing if we cannot teach students once they are in the classrooms. If what Glenn G. Gilbert says about French and German is true of other languages, that their future "lies almost entirely in their function as foreign languages, not as first or second languages'' (1981:271), there apparently is no future.

The future is bleak indeed. Hope lies only in a complete change of orientation toward the nature and role of languages in the United States. Broadly stated, the new orientation would bring us to regard language communities and their languages not as problems to be resolved but as resources to be managed, preserved, and developed. To the extent that we devalue languages and their speakers, we make ourselves less able to appreciate the value of any language, even our own. The development of a "language-competent society," a phrase that recurs in recent commission reports and position statements, can no longer be regarded as a matter of technology or pedagogical expertise; it is difficult to imagine this society having any more of those commodities. It is a matter, now, of a change in basic orientation.

NOTE ON INFORMATION SOURCES

There are several very good sources of information on bilingualism and bilingual education in the United States. The National Clearinghouse for Bilingual Education can provide information by telephone. It also has two valuable publications: *Forum*, a newsletter, which is available free and is printed on a bimonthly basis; and *Focus*, a paper series, the titles of which can also be obtained through the Center. The Center for Applied Linguistics publishes books and papers of interest and importance to the scholarly community; it also oversees the ERIC Clearinghouse for Linguistics which publishes papers and monographs in hard copy and microfiche. The National Center for Bilingual Research, funded through the National Institute of Education, also publishes and makes available at nominal cost the results of its projects. The major language professional organizations such as the Modern Language Association, the National Association for Bilingual Education, and the Teachers of English to Speakers of Other Languages all have regular journals and newsletters that present current research and news items. Finally, the Georgetown University Round Table on Languages and Linguistics publishes its proceeding every year; its offerings have much of interest to those seeking information on bilingualism and bilingual education in the United States.

ACKNOWLEDGMENTS

I wish to acknowledge Joan Strouse, Julia Richards, Dianne Bowcock, Maria Dalupan, and Nancy Hornberger for their help in the preparation of this chapter. I also want to thank Gerald Ward for his technical assistance.

BIBLIOGRAPHY

Academy for Educational Development and the Edward W. Hazen Foundation. 1982. "A New Direction for Bilingual Education in the 1980s." *Focus*, No. 10 (National Clearinghouse for Bilingual Education).

Ambert, Alba N., and Sarah E. Melendez. 1985. *Bilingual Education: A Sourcebook*. New York: Garland Publishing, Inc.

Arias, M. Beatriz, and Richard Navarro. 1981. "Title VII, Bilingual Education: Developing Issues of Diversity and Equity." *IFG Policy Perspectives* (Stanford Institute for Research on Educational Finance and Governance). Autumn.

Baker, Keith, and Adriana A. deKanter. 1983. *Bilingual Education: A Reappraisal of Federal Policy*. Lexington, Mass.: D. C. Heath.

Bell, Terrell H. 1984. *The Condition of Bilingual Education in the Nation*. Washington, D.C.: U.S. Department of Education.

Benderson, Albert. 1983. "Foreign Languages in the Schools." *Focus*, No. 12 (Educational Testing Service).

Brod, R. I. 1980. *Language Study for the 1980s: Reports of the MLS-ACLS Language Task Forces*. New York: Modern Language Association of America.

Brown, George H., Nan L. Rosen, Susan T. Hill, and Michael A. Olivas. 1981. *The Condition of Education for Hispanic Americans*. Washington, D.C.: National Center for Education Statistics.

California State Department of Education. 1984. *Studies on Immersion Education: A Collection for United States Educators*. Sacramento: California State Department of Education.

Cazden, Courtney. 1984. *Effective Instructional Practices in Bilingual Education*. Washington, D.C.: National Institute of Education.

Conklin, Nancy Faires, and Margaret A. Lourie. 1983. *A Host of Tongues: Language Communities in the United States*. New York: Free Press.

Correa-Zoli, Yole. 1981. "The Language of Italian Americans." In *Languages in the USA*, ed. C. A. Ferguson and S. B. Heath. New York: Cambridge University Press, pp. 239–56.

Fallows, James. 1983. "Immigration—How It's Affecting Us." *The Atlantic Monthly*, November, pp. 45–106.

Ferguson, Charles A., and Shirley Brice Heath, eds. 1981. *Language in the USA*. New York: Cambridge University Press.

Fishman, Joshua A. 1966. "The Historical and Social Contexts of an Inquiry into Language Maintenance Efforts." In *Language Loyalty in the United States*, ed. J. A. Fishman et al. The Hague: Mouton.

———. 1981. "Language Policy: Past, Present, and Future." In *Language in the USA*, ed. C. A. Ferguson and S. B. Heath. New York: Cambridge University Press.

———. 1984. "Sociolinguistic Perspectives on Second Language Acquisition." Paper presented at the 13th annual Linguistics Symposium, "Current Approaches to Second Language Acquisition." Milwaukee, March 29–31.

Fishman, Joshua A., R. L. Cooper, and A. W. Conrad. 1977. *The Spread of English: The Sociology of English as an Additional Language*. Rowley, Mass.: Newbury House.

Garcia, S. O. 1983. "Sociolinguistics and Language Planning in Bilingual Education for Hispanics in the United States." *International Journal of the Sociology of Language* 44:43–54.

———. 1985. "Bilingualism in the United States: Present Attitudes in Light of Past Policies." In *The English Language Today*, ed. Sidney Greenbaum. Oxford: Pergamon Press, pp. 147–58.

Gilbert, Glenn G. 1981. "French and German: A Comparative Study." In *Language in the USA*, ed. C. A. Ferguson and S. B. Heath. New York: Cambridge University Press, pp. 257–72.

Henzl, Vera M. 1981. "Slavic Languages in the New Environment." In *Language in the USA*, ed. C. A. Ferguson and S. B. Heath. New York: Cambridge University Press, pp. 291–321.

Hernandez-Chavez, Eduardo. 1984. "The Inadequacy of English Immersion Education as an Educational Approach for Language Minority Students in the United States." In *Studies on Immersion Education: A Collection for United States Educators.* Sacramento: California State Department of Education, pp. 144–83.

House of Representatives, 98th Congress. 1984. *Education Amendments of 1984.* October 2.

Keller, Gary D., ed. 1983. "Chicano Cinema: Research, Reviews, and Resources." Special issue of *Bilingual Review/Revista bilingüe* 10:2 and 3 (May-December).

Kjolseth, Rolf. 1972. "Bilingual Education Programs in the United States: For Assimilation or Pluralism?" In *The Language Education of Minority Children*, ed. B. Spolsky. Rowley, Mass.: Newbury House.

Kloss, Heinz. 1966. "German-American Language Maintenance Efforts." In *Language Loyalty in the United States*, ed. J. A. Fishman et al. The Hague: Mouton.

———. 1977. *The American Bilingual Tradition*. Rowley, Mass.: Newbury House.

Labov, William. 1972. *Language in the Inner City: Studies in the Black English Vernacular*. Philadelphia: University of Pennsylvania Press.

Lambert, Wallace E. 1981. *Faces and Facets of Bilingualism*. Washington, D.C.: Center for Applied Linguistics.

———. 1984. "An Overview of Issues in Immersion Education." In *Studies on Immersion Education: A Collection for United States Educators*. Sacramento: California State Department of Education, pp. 8–30.

Leap, William L. 1981. "American Indian Languages." In *Language in the USA*, ed. C. A. Ferguson and S. B. Heath. New York: Cambridge University Press.

Leibowitz, Arnold H. 1971. *Educational Policy and Political Acceptance: The Imposition of English as the Language of Instruction in American Schools*. Washington, D.C.: Center for Applied Linguistics, ERIC Clearinghouse for Linguistics.

Maeroff, Gene I. 1984. "Interest in Foreign Languages Rises." *New York Times*, October 24.

Marckwardt, Albert H. 1958. *American English*. New York: Oxford University Press.

McWilliams, Carey. 1949. *North from Mexico*. Philadelphia: J. J. Lippincott.

Nichols, John. 1985. "Codification of Native American Languages." Paper presented at the Colloquium on Ethnicity and Public Policy, Green Bay, Wisconsin, May 9–10.

Oxford, R., L. Pol, D. Lopez, P. Stupp, M. Gendell, and S. Peng. 1981. "Projections of Non-English Language Background and Limited English Proficient Persons in the United States to the Year 2000: Educational Planning in the Demographic Context." *NABE Journal* 5, 3:1–29.

Paulston, Christina B. 1981. "Bilingualism and Education." In *Language in the USA*, ed. C. A. Ferguson and S. B. Heath. New York: Cambridge University Press, pp. 464–85.

———. 1985. "Linguistic Consequences of Ethnicity and Nationalism in Multilingual Settings." Paper presented at the Conference on the Educational Policies and the

Minority Social Groups Experts' Meeting organized by CERI/OECD, Paris, January 16–18.

Pierce, Bessie. 1936. *History of Chicago*. New York: A. A. Knopf.

President's Commission on Foreign Language and International Studies. 1979. *Strength Through Wisdom: A Critique of U.S. Capability*. Washington, D.C.: U.S. Government Printing Office.

Rotberg, Iris C. 1984. "Bilingual Education Policy in the United States." *Prospects* 14, 1:133–47.

Ruiz, Richard. 1985. *Language Teaching in American Education*. Washington, D.C.: National Institute of Education.

St. Louis Public Schools. 1876. *Annual Report of the Board of Directors of the St. Louis Public Schools for the Year Ending August 1, 1875*. St. Louis: St. Louis Public Schools.

Tikunoff, W., and J. Vazquez-Faria. 1982. "Successful Instruction for Bilingual Schooling." *Peabody Journal of Education* 59, 4:234–71.

Toch, Thomas. 1984. "The Emerging Politics of Language." *Education Week* 3, 20, February 8.

Troike, Rudolph. 1981. "A Synthesis of Research on Bilingual Education." *Educational Leadership* 14:498–504.

Twentieth Century Fund. 1983. *Report of the Twentieth Century Task Force on Federal Elementary and Secondary Education Policy*. New York: Twentieth Century Fund.

U.S. Bureau of the Census. 1983. *Condition of Hispanics in America Today*. Washington, D.C.: U.S. Bureau of the Census, September.

U.S. Commission on Civil Rights. 1972. *The Excluded Student: Educational Practices Affecting Mexican Americans in the Southwest* (Report III). Washington, D.C.: U.S. Government Printing Office.

U.S. Department of Education. 1984. *Department of Education Grant Report*. Washington, D.C.: Department of Education, November 29.

Veltman, Calvin. 1983. *Language Shift in the United States*. Berlin: Mouton.

Waggoner, Dorothy. 1984. "Minority Language Populations from the 1980 Census." *Forum* (National Clearinghouse for Bilingual Education), 7, 5:5–7, October/November.

Weinberg, Meyer. 1979. *A Chance to Learn*. New York: Cambridge University Press.

Wong, Sau-ling. 1985. "The Language Needs of Asian Immigrants and Refugees in the United States." Paper presented at the Colloquium on Ethnicity and Public Policy, Green Bay, Wisconsin, May 9–10.

Zentella, Ana Celia. 1981. "Language Variety Among Puerto Ricans." In *Language in the USA*, ed. C. A. Ferguson and S. B. Heath. New York: Cambridge University Press.

Lufuluabo Mukeba

SOME ASPECTS OF BILINGUALISM AND BILINGUAL EDUCATION IN ZAIRE[1]

Before colonization, Central Africa was inhabited mainly by the Bantu people but also by non-Bantu people. Some groups lived in the forest, and others lived in the savanna. Some of them shared political organizations, without having similar sociocultural values. Others shared similar sociocultural values as well as a similar political organization. Through geographical proximity, migration, or resettlement, they merged or split.

The colonial period brought about a fundamental change, with the incorporation of all the groups into one single political and economic organization. It has been reported that 250 cultural groups in Zaire speak 250 languages. How have these unrelated groups communicated in this "Tower of Babel?" How has society, historically, attempted to organize their linguistic behavior through the educational institution?

As anthropologists and political scientists did in the past, sociolinguists are focusing on the existence of subsystems within the larger context and the use of key concepts like tribe, ethnicity, and cultural pluralism in their attempt to explain the language situation of plural societies.

This chapter draws on articles, books, and dissertations on Zaire. Its purpose is (1) to describe the linguistic situation of Zaire's cultural groups in their historical contact, and (2) to show the relationship—if any—between the social organization and the school system as they deal with language problems.

DESCRIPTION OF ETHNIC GROUPS

1. *The Northern Uplands and Forest Fringe Non-Bantu Peoples*. Twenty percent of the population that speak non-Bantu languages stretch across the Northern Uplands (Ngbandi, Ngbaka) to the far northeast (Zande, Mangbetu).

2. *The Bantu of the Cuvette.* Living north and south of the Zaire River from Kinshasa to Kisangani are a large number of diverse Bantu-speaking groups: the Ngombe and the Mongo.

3. *Bantu Speakers of the Eastern Forest and Plain* (the Lega) and *the Eastern Highland* (the Shi) stretch along the territory's eastern frontier in the areas just west of the great lakes of Central Africa.

4. *The Bantu Peoples of the Savanna.* In southeastern Zaire, stretching between Kinsangami and Upper Katanga are the Bemba and the Kaonde communities; and in the southwestern communities, the Lunda.

5. *The Bantu Peoples of the Southern Uplands.* Stretching across much of the north and west of the copper belt are the southern savanna Luba communities subcategorized as Luba-Katanga (Luba-Katanga proper, Kaniok), Luba-Kasai (Luba-Lulua, Kete, Luntu), and Songye.

6. *The Bantu Peoples of the Kwango Kasai.* The Tio, Sakata, the Yans-Mbum, and the Lele communities stretch south and north of the lower Kasai River and the Kwa River. Living between the Kwango River and the Kasai River are the Yaka, the Mbala, the Pende, and the Chokwe communities.

7. *The Kongo People* occupy all of Lower Congo and are also a Bantu-speaking community.

This sketchy presentation of the various ethnic communities gives a selective outline of most of the commonly known groups, and in many instances related groups have been included in the major ones.

As suggested by Bruce Fetter (1983:125–26), the people of Zaire were organized in a wide variety of political units in precolonial times: empires, kingdoms, and states. Relatively large states developed in the savannas, whereas the political entities of the forest tended to be smaller. In some areas, the larger political unit was the village. Despite political fragmentation and geographical segmentation, the various groups shared a common culture.

ETHNIC GROUPS AND THEIR RELATIONSHIP

The varied origins of the Congolese created differences of detail in their patterns of subsistence and mode of sociopolitical organization. Nevertheless, their migration and resettlement were conducive to interpenetration of communities with new traditions and the transfer of aspects of culture from one community to another. Shifting cultivation due to limited fertility of the soil in the equatorial forest and other parts of Zaire and the comparatively simple agricultural technology resulted in a continuous relocation of villages.

According to Jan Vansina (1963:375), trade was conducted over greater distances either between culturally different peoples within a single state or between neighboring peoples. Another type of trade, the long-distance trade involving the exchange of European goods, was introduced in Central Africa in the fifteenth century. By the end of the nineteenth century, the whole of Central Africa was covered by a web of regional trade systems that furnished ivory and slaves in the Congo. Along these trade routes and the connected regional circuits, the practice of cultivating imported American plants spread. Maize and manioc were introduced in Central Africa around the end of the sixteenth century and by 1900 had covered almost the entire Congo area.

Fetter shows how business arrangements made in the savanna kingdoms between foreign traders and local traders connected to the Indian Ocean slave market resulted in the coalescence of some of the well-known Zairian "tribes." These included Lumpungu's Bena Lulua Kingdom.

Despite the political diversity, much of the territory was part of a single natural transportation network, the basin of the Congo River. By the nineteenth century when Europeans learned of the extent of these trading networks, they began to see the Congo as a single unit of trade and, ultimately, of colonization (Fetter, 1983: 126).

The porterage system that was introduced in Central Africa, with the European penetration for the transportation of goods overland to the coast, was one of the determinants that played a part in bringing ethnic groups into contact. In 1893, some eighty thousand loads (of 65 pounds each) were carried by porters. The lower Congo population could not supply enough workers, so men had to be brought in from other regions (Fehderau, 1966:31).

The creation of a network of colonial infrastructure also contributed to the mixing of populations. The Belgian colonizers created administrative centers (capital of colony, capital of province, headquarters of district, headquarters of territory). Most of these administrative centers ultimately became cities. The missionaries' central and boarding schools, along with their health care facilities, constituted another locus of opportunity for the Congolese of different backgrounds. Trading centers along the rivers and towns acquired a population of people from many "tribal" areas. As work opportunities increased, many Africans were encouraged—sometimes forced—to leave their homes to take positions that could not be filled by local people. Many orphaned children and "homeless" adults were brought from Upper Congo regions to be educated and to work in Lower Congo government centers. The organization of the Congolese Army (*Force Publique*) was also instrumental in bringing together people from many different regions (Fehderau, 1966:33–34). Africans who had received their training in rural areas soon became discontented with village life. Many school leavers succumbed to the attractions of higher salaries in colonial centers where they worked for the government or for private companies (Fetter, 1982:11).

In the absence of adequate statistics on the ethnic identification of speakers of specific languages, only the roughest estimates can be made. About 80 percent of the population speaks Bantu languages. The remaining 20 percent of the population in the northernmost portion and in the east along the Uele River speaks Adamawa-Eastern and Sudanic languages.

Linguistically, Zaire is a very complex area in Africa. A recent investigation (Mutombo, 1984:27–47) has distinguished almost 250 languages. One should agree with Donald G. Morrison et al. (1972:15) that language distribution is difficult to assess in Africa because scholars disagree on whether a particular designation refers to a dialect, a single language, or a group of closely related languages. The number of independent languages spoken corresponds only approximately to the number of ethnic groups (Kaplan, 1979: 122). This number may be reduced if mutually intelligible languages are treated together. By the same token, while creating the "myth of a Congolese Tower of Babel" as Fabian (1983:179) calls it, this number dramatizes the importance of bilingualism and bilingual education.

With the emergence of Swahili, Ciluba, Lingala, and Kikongo as lingua francas, the nineteenth century was crucial in the current language configuration in Zaire. Swahili was introduced into the country especially by the Zanzibari Swahilis during the slaving operations of the nineteenth century and is spoken extensively in the northeast, east, and south, more specifically in the Shaba region, in Kivu, and in Haut Zaire. Lingala developed along the Congo River in the 1880s in response to the need for a common language, and it is now used extensively in the north and northwest, more specifically in Kinshasa, the capital city; in Northern Bandundu; in the Equator Region; and in part of Upper Zaire. Lingala is also the language of the Zairian National Army and of Zairian modern music. Its use as the dominant lingua franca is growing particularly with the encouragement of President Mobutu. Kikongo is used primarily in the narrow neck of territory between Kinshasa and the Atlantic Ocean. A modified form, Kituba, is spoken in the region immediately east of Kinshasa, Bandundu region. Ciluba, sometimes spelled Tshiluba, emerged primarily as an ethnic language and spread in the 1890's in the Kasai under the missionaries' activities before the colonial administration had the time to look into the matter. It is used in Western Kasai and Eastern Kasai, located in southcentral Zaire, where it has enjoyed considerable diffusion among all the neighboring groups. Ciluba is sometimes confused in some literature with Kiluba, a closely related language spoken in Shaba. These four languages have been recognized since colonial times as national languages for certain government functions such as elementary education, proceedings of the lower courts of justice, radio and TV broadcasting, and local government administration at the township and village levels (Bokamba, 1976:116) in their respective areas where local languages, despite their limited scope, have a high survival rate and are not in imminent danger of extinction. Despite some attempts (Bruhn, 1984:3), there are no accurate statistics on the four major Zairian languages apart from some impressionistic estimates (Bokamba, 1977:120). No really precise statistics exist concerning the number and distribution of speakers of two or more languages in the nations of the world. This can be accounted for partly by the fact that there is no widely accepted definition of the concept of bilingualism (Grosjean, 1982:2).

The Belgians were able to introduce French as the official language and even to attempt some use of Flemish (Ellington, 1973:20) but without much success. Indeed, Zaire was the only African colony under the administration of a bilingual colonial power, thus making an already complex linguistic situation even more difficult. Spoken countrywide by about 4 percent of the population in 1975 (Faik et al., 1977:3), French enjoys all the prestige of being the language spoken by a minority; it is believed to be the unifying language. David Dalby (1980:42) is correct in observing that, although a European language may be retained as the official and main language in Africa south of the Sahara, it is evident that African languages will play an increasingly important role. Although French is used widely as a second language by the educated elite of Zaire, it has nowhere supplanted any indigenous African language.

BILINGUALISM

Two types of bilingualism should be distinguished. The first type describes bilingualism in Zairian languages and is termed mass bilingualism, that is, the use by an entire population or a section of the population of two or more linguistic systems (Marcellesi, 1981:5). This type of bilingualism is discussed under several headings: Bantu and non-Bantu (Bokamba, 1981:5), generalized bilingualism, and African bilingualism (Cam and Le Boul, 1976a:5; Houis, 1962:111).

The second type of bilingualism in Zaire is institutional (Houis, 1962:112) or state bilingualism (Cam and Le Boul, 1976a:5). It spreads throughout the country and coincides with the distribution of state apparatuses and agents, the private modern sector, and missionary work and schooling. This type deals with speakers of Zairian language(s) and French.

According to B. Kimputu (1978:44), Zairians belong to several speech communities at the same time: (1) the ethnic speech community, where the communication involves speakers from the same ethnic group and the local language is used; (2) the larger speech community, where the interaction involves speakers from different ethnic backgrounds who can communicate in a regional language or a lingua franca; and (3) the Francophone speech community, where the interaction involves speakers who have reached the eighth grade (Faik et al., 1977:5).

Every trip, change of location, transfer, or relationship outside the speech community involving some duration of time results in some acquisition of an additional language (Kimputu, 1978:48). Useful to the understanding of bilingualism in Zaire are some concepts discussed by Kimputu in his survey of some Kinshasa students (1978:54). The L1 (first language) is the first language acquired during the speaker's childhood. This may be the parents' tongue, the lingua franca, or even French. The PT (parents' tongue) is the ethnic language of the speaker's mother or father. The EL (ethnic language) may be the speaker's first language if that person's early childhood was spent in his or her ethnic community. The ML (major language) is the dominant language, the most used in the speaker's everyday life. This ML is not necessarily his or her L1 or EL. It may well be a lingua franca or French. The L1 was at the same time the PT of 50.4 percent of the students (Kimputu, 1978:60); 4.7 percent had two L1's simultaneously. This is often the case in urban areas where the EL is spoken at home while the lingua franca is used outside the home. The L1 only was spoken by 0.9 percent, and 49 percent had an L1 different from their EL.

Zairian languages are learned informally at home, or through contacts with members of a speech community (Cam and Le Boul, 1976a:17). Their formal acquisition through the school system is limited to a few years of elementary school and concerns only a few Zairian languages, mainly the four lingua francas. A total of 14.6 percent of the students were able to learn Zairian languages through the school system. Excluding French, the rate of bilingualism in Kimputu's respondents was 2.5 languages, and by including French it was 3.5. Both Lingala and Swahili were almost never reported as ethnic languages, although Lingala is sometimes considered a regional language (Kimputu, 1978:71–72). Ciluba and Kikongo are ethnic languages, L1, regional languages and lingua francas (Kimputu, 1978:76–77).

In 1975, it was estimated that 4 percent of Zairians could speak French. The speakers include party officials, administrators, government and corporation officials, intellectuals, teachers, lawyers, doctors, civil servants, technicians, journalists, grade school and college students, and a few businessmen. For every French speaker from a rural area, there were thirteen from an urban area in 1955–57. The study estimated that French speakers were between fifteen and forty-four years old in 1975. For one female French speaker, there were forty males in 1955–57. French is mostly used between educated Zairians who do not have any common Zairian language and by a very few Zairian college graduate couples, particularly those who studied in Europe and who are in interethnic marriages.

BILINGUAL EDUCATION

Colonial Education[2]

During the Congo Free State period, the international nature of the European personnel established a multilingual reality despite the government's unilingual policy. French instruction lagged or was nonexistent. However, French was declared the official language of the Congo Free State. Government instruction to administrators, army officials, and school officials constantly enjoined the use of French with Congolese. French was a required subject in the government *colonies scolaires* established by the 1890 Education Act and in almost all secular vocational schools (*écoles professionnelles*). Only in the schools for clerks was French to be the language of instruction. Instruction in French was not required by the 1892 Education Act. The 1906 *Concordat*, an agreement between the colonial government and the Vatican which covered among other things Catholic mission schools, stipulated that subsidized Catholic schools could establish, in agreement with the colonial government, their own school curriculum as long as the national languages (French and Flemish) were included.

Leopold's policy of attempting to diffuse French throughout the Congolese population failed because many officials did not enforce the official language policy even in the *colonies scolaires*. The Belgian directors of Catholic schools often differed with the administration on the use of a European language, and some of them did not speak French. The Governor-General found their efforts inadequate. At Kisantu, instruction was carried out in Kikongo. The White Fathers moved directly from Swahili to Latin. Many Catholic missionaries spoke Flemish—and like the Protestants—used French only poorly as a second language. Others were reluctant to propagate French because of the conflict in Belgium between the Flemings and the Walloons.

Interconfessional rivalry was the major impetus for what little French was offered in Catholic parochial schools. Catholic missionaries were forced to offer one modern European language to compete with Protestants for converts. Beginning in 1905, four of the nine Catholic mission orders (Redemptorists, Jesuits, Sacred Heart Fathers, and the Belgian Holy Ghost Fathers) finally introduced French in urban schools, or on mission stations for advanced pupils out of fear that Protestant-trained people would get the best jobs. European languages were to be dropped when there was no Protestant competition.

The Colonial Charter of 1908 transferred sovereignty from Leopold II to the Belgian Parliament. Inasmuch as the 1890 and 1892 Education Acts and the 1906 Concordat remained in effect after annexation, most Catholic schools were not subsidized until World War II, and therefore were not covered by this legislation. Catholic missionaries ignored the provisions of the 1890 Education Act and the 1906 Concordat. French was an unnecessary intermediary, particularly as it made available nonreligious ideas and the skills for employment outside the mission orbit.

Some Protestant missionaries in the 1880's and 1890's, wishing to teach a world language, introduced their maternal English which they found easier than French. Political consideration, however, led Leopold to forbid the diffusion of English. The government threatened to supervise the curriculum, and consequently, by the early 1890's the Protestant missionaries had discontinued formal English instruction in their schools. While he did not legally prohibit their teaching English, he did not require that they use the French language. With the curtailment of English instruction, a number of Protestants—principally the Baptists and the Disciples of Christ—shifted to French, and despite the fact that few of them spoke this language, some of their schools, beginning in the early 1890's, became the leading centers of French instruction. However, the government did not and could not give them favored treatment in order to encourage other schools to offer French as well. Although a minority of Protestant missionaries propagated a European language, it did not mean that French became a required subject or the medium of instruction. The majority of Protestant missionaries, like their Catholic counterparts, were not in favor of teaching a modern European language. French-language instruction remained a topic for discussion in Protestant circles. At the fifth General Conference of Protestant Missionaries in 1909, some maintained that French instruction was a necessity to keep boys from going to the Jesuit Station to study French so as to get jobs with the state and the railways. But the majority view disagreed and recommended concentration on the Bible in the vernacular.

Thus, the learning of French was regarded by both Protestants and Catholics as a means for African mobility, as well as a threat to missionary goals and white supremacy.

The 1925 Education Plan recommended that preference be given to the commercial language if it were related to the mother tongue and if it were not a mere lingua franca. With the 1929 Education Code, the government officially dropped the obligatory national languages (i.e., French and Flemish) from most subsidized schools. French was to be a required subject in upper primary schools and post-primary normal and vocational schools located in urban areas. Only post-primary schools for clerks were to use French as the language of instruction (Yates, 1980:271–73).

With the revised curricula of 1929 and 1938, French was to be introduced as a subject in the primary school from the third grade and as a medium of instruction at the secondary school level, the formerly used indigenous language becoming a subject (Polomé, 1968:302). The 1948 reorganization of education continued to make French a required subject beginning with the third grade only in urban schools and the medium of instruction only in the schools for clerks, now called *écoles moyenness*, and in the newly created six-year academic secondary schools for the Congolese. Flemish became a required subject as well, beginning with the tenth grade. The use of regional languages as the media of instruction was stressed by the 1948 Education Code (Yates, 1980, 273–76).

The creation of the metropolitan-type schools in 1954 inaugurated the use of French as the medium of instruction at the primary level from the first year on, and the lingua franca was taught only as subject. In interracial schools, all teaching was done in French, and Dutch (Flemish) was taught as a second language. Until 1954, most missionaries persisted in using the vernacular as the medium of instruction (Ndoma, 1977: 101–205). The use of French at all levels of formal education was not enforced until 1958–59 (Bokamba, 1976:112).

Postcolonial Education

At the time of independence in 1960, the percentage of the school-age population enrolled was 98.26 percent in primary schools; 1.7 percent in secondary schools; and 0.04 percent in post-secondary schools (Coleman and Ngonkwey, 1983: 57). More than 70 percent of the primary schools provided only the first two grades (George, 1966:48). Instruction was in the vernacular, not only for broader diffusion of Christianity but to avoid what was considered useless elitist pretensions and aspirations. As then envisaged, the avowed aim of education was "to produce better Africans, and not copies of Europeans who could never be more than humans of a third category'' (Hanley in Coleman and Ngonkwey, 1983:58).

During the first five years or so of independence, there was neither time nor inclination to reconsider language policy. It was sufficient to hold tenaciously to French as the language of national unity when unifying factors were scarce (Ellington, 1973: 20). But in 1961–62, under the strong influence of UNESCO, French became the language of instruction in all primary schools (Coleman and Ngonkwey, 1983:58).

The primary education reform of 1961–62 was adopted in 1963 and introduced at the beginning of the 1963–64 school year. The reform called for teaching in French as soon as possible, with the vernacular languages used only during a very brief period after children entered school. In many places, the primary program was given in the local language until the third, fourth, or (in some instances) the fifth year (George, 1966:83–84). The program provided one period per week for the teaching of Congolese languages and culture from third grade to sixth grade. This teaching of Congolese languages and culture was optional, however, (Cam and Le Boul, 1976b:53). A number of schools did not teach them. In a study evaluating the 1963 reform, Cam and Le Boul (1976b:35–62) reveal that:

- 89.36 percent of elementary school teachers were using a Congolese language at recess with fellow teachers, despite the regulation.
- 62.66 percent of teachers let students do the same.
- 60 percent of teachers were equipped with teaching materials for the teaching of Congolese languages mostly published between 1935 and 1960.
- 6.89 percent of the teachers did not have any materials at all.
- Where the program was interpreted as being optional, 83.55 percent of teachers did teach Congolese languages, 72.4 percent did it to explain French words, and 70.21 percent did it to explain ideas.
- The teaching of Congolese languages was limited to the major language of the classroom or to the lingua franca of the area.
- Few textbooks in Congolese languages were available for students; juvenile literature was nonexistent.

In 1974, the government initiated a new program aimed at reintroducing and reinforcing instruction in Congolese languages, more specifically the four lingua francas from first grade with French beginning only in third grade as a subject.

In the early 1970's, Zaire was characterized by the policy of authenticity which, in matters of education, was translated into "going local" linguistically, as Ellington (1973:20) puts it. Within a relatively brief period, the "return to authenticity" changed the names of the Congo River, the country, streets, and cities as well as the personal names of Zaire's nearly 21 million citizens.

The proposal came after the first conference of Zairian linguists in May 1974.

The Centre de Linguistique Théorique et Appliquée (CELTA) was charged, among other things, with working on manuals and textbooks. According to Alain Tashdjan (1981:51–54), the actual instruction (in the form of lingua francas) did not meet the needs of the political decision. No teacher training was planned, no budget was allocated to implement the program, and no information campaign was initiated in the community to make people aware of the sociocultural and socioeconomic importance of the reform. Furthermore, already established prejudices and attitudes against Zairian languages and in favor of French were not dealt with. As of 1976, a reversal was seen in the 1974 reform with the reintroduction of French beginning in the first grade, even if this was oral French.

An aspect of the problem of the 1974 reform seldom discussed is the fact that the task of curriculum development was assigned to CELTA, which was already a French Project created for other purposes. CELTA is part of a cooperative project for the expansion of standard French and is one of the Centers/Institutes for Applied Linguistics founded during the 1960s at the Francophone African universities with French technical assistance. The aim of these Centers was to improve and increase the teaching of French in Francophone countries through a series of contrastive, statistical, and sociolinguistic studies of the major local African languages in order to gauge their relative impact on French and studies on lexical varieties of French in Africa (Brann, 1982:353–59). Apparently, these were two different projects involving competing vested interests.

LANGUAGE AND RELIGION

About one-half of the Zairian population are Christians. Of these, about three-quarters are Roman Catholic and one-quarter Protestant. Most of the non-Christians adhere to either traditional religions or syncretic sects (Background Notes, U.S. Department of State, 1981:3).

Religion has never been a key issue in the lives of Zairians, and less in regard to language problems. Nevertheless, during the colonial period, both Protestant and Catholic missionaries took different approaches to the studies of Congolese languages (Bokamba, 1977:197). It was not uncommon to hear about "Protestant" as well as "Catholic" Lingala, Ciluba, Kikongo. Generally, Catholic and Protestant missionaries used the same language, although very often in different dialects (Ndoma, 1984:194).

According to Barbara A. Yates, most Catholic missionaries in their proselytizing methods used a single native language in religious services, schools, communication, and the preparation of written materials. Thus, the Redemptorists and the Jesuits in the Lower Congo adopted Kikongo, the Sacred Heart Fathers and the White Fathers in Eastern Congo used Swahili, while the Scheutists spoke Ciluba in Kasai and Lingala on the Upper River.

Protestants preferred the vernacular spoken by the largest number of people near the mission station. They worked with individuals and wanted each of them to have direct access to the Scriptures in the vernacular. Therefore, Protestant missionaries rejected the use of regional languages.

At the beginning of the twentieth century, Catholics gave more attention to local languages in an effort to compete with neighboring Protestant stations. Some Protestant missionaries had second thoughts about the efficiency of their policy. They realized that the use of maternal languages increased costs and strained human resources. Protestant societies agreed that each society should be established in a different language area.

DOUBLE OVERLAPPING DIGLOSSIA

French enjoys the prestige of being the official language and the medium of instruction. As Yates (1980:278) argues, in the Congo proficiency in French has been an easily discernible public badge of social esteem. As in the colonial past, the possession of skills in an international language like French will continue to provide an entree to economic opportunities and social mobility in contemporary Zaire. French-language skills will continue to be an economic asset and a status symbol differentiating the elite from the masses.

Less prestige and low status are still attached to fluency in African languages in general. Ethnic and local languages in particular fall into the category of subordinate languages. They are native to the area where they are spoken and are associated with rural life, poverty, illiteracy, and ignorance. They have been reduced to low status by the rise of the four lingua francas introduced to the area at a later period.

The position of the four lingua francas (Ciluba, Kikongo, Lingala, and Swahili) is ambiguous. They are superordinate in relation to the ethnic languages. But in relation to French, they are subordinate. Only rudimentary literacy is possible in them. The lingua francas of Zaire are now involved in what Ralph Fasold (1984:45) calls two diglossic systems: as the High languages with the various Zairian ethnic languages as Lows, and as Low languages with French as the High. This intersection between two developing diglossia situations described by Abdulaziz Mkilifi (1978:134) is named double overlapping diglossia by Fasold (1984:45).

Their prestige has been increasingly growing. This is particularly the case with Lingala, which is becoming, to some extent, a language of social mobility, economic opportunity, and political promotion. The status of Lingala is a peculiar one and deserves special attention.

LANGUAGE ATTITUDES

The discussion of language attitudes in Zaire here will be limited to the four lingua francas.

Swahili is probably the language with the most positive attitudes from many people in Zaire. It is said to be the language of deference and politeness, a language spoken in a soft manner (Kimputu, 1978:277). Part of the positive attitudes toward Swahili can be accounted for by the fact that it is neither the language of a particular ethnic group nor a language identified with a specific area of the country, being used in three regions of the country out of eight. The only negative attitude toward Swahili came from missionaries during the colonial period. They associated it with Islamic influence.

Lingala, in general, is associated with mixed attitudes. Although it is for the most part not an ethnic language, it is sometimes associated with people coming from the Region of Equateur. Politically, people would like to know it to be able to understand the political rhetoric mostly delivered in that language. At the same time, if they do not agree with the politics delivered in Lingala, they express their discontent with both the form and content of the discourse.

Lingala has been the language of the military for about half a century. As pointed out by Irving Kaplan (1979:250–53), a negative aspect about the Zairian Army has been its lack of affinity to local populations. The military forces, highly visible in all areas of the country, is not an institution to which ordinary citizens felt any great attachment or one in which they had any great pride. Very often the exact opposite has been true—citizens often felt alienated from or abused by the military. The present-day military forces, a descendant of the colonial *Force Publique*, retained an aura of separateness and, like the colonial forces, has often been thought of as an instrument of repression. Because it was the army that was called on to deal with the many ethnic disturbances, secessions, and student riots, the people involved in those events thought of the army as the enemy. Public opinion of the military sometimes creates a negative attitude toward Lingala. Recent literature on language in Zaire (Mutombo, 1984:37) has associated Lingala with swindling, fraud, and oppression.

A number of Zairians object to Lingala on the basis that it lacks forms of politeness and respect, and consider Lingala a "poor" language (Ellington, 1973:20–21). Yet, every Zairian likes the popular music of Zaire whose lyrics are mostly in Lingala; they like to see Kinshasa, the big capital city, and then their attitude is positive.

Ciluba is said to be a difficult language, not softly spoken, a language of the most tribalist and arrogant of Zairians, and lacking forms of politeness (Kimputu, 1978:243, 277). Both Ciluba and Kikongo have been more narrowly identified with particular ethnic groups, and are consequently less appealing despite their vitality and large number of speakers (Ellington, 1973:20). Kikongo is perceived as carrying a bad accent (Kimputu, 1978:244).

LANGUAGE MAINTENANCE AND LANGUAGE SPREAD

Languages in Africa appear to have a high survival rate, and very few are in imminent danger of extinction. This is confirmed by the fact that maintenance is often characteristic of bilingual communities. The survey by Kimputu (p. 65) revealed that 93 percent of the students had a very good knowledge of their first languages. Two languages had a particularly high rate: Lingala (97.5 percent) and Ciluba (97 percent). The maintenance of Ciluba has often been overstated. Kimputu (p. 66) accounts for its "excellent" maintenance by the profound dedication of its native speakers. He adds that the Luba speakers consider it a moral obligation to pass it on from parents to their offspring. More than maintenance, this seems to be a case of language loyalty. The situation of Lingala is one of language spread rather than language maintenance.

Language shift is known particularly among ethnic groups represented by very few speakers in urban areas. These speakers do not always have the opportunity to use their language (Kimputu, 1978:68). Language shift also occurs with interethnic marriages or exogamy. In his study, Kimputu found that almost half of the students born from such marriages spoke the father's language, and another half spoke the mother's language. Only 26.8 percent of children from such marriages spoke both languages. Urbanization is another factor causing language shift. Many young people born in urban areas have only a passive knowledge of their ethnic language.

RESEARCH ON BILINGUALISM AND BILINGUAL EDUCATION

Research on bilingualism and bilingual education was not an important part of the Belgian tradition. Maurice Van Overbeke's 1972 bibliography is indicative of that trend. In his preface to Albert Verdoodt's bibliography of Belgium's linguistic problems (1973), Pierre De Bie reports how rare the academic approach is and how difficult an objective examination of linguistic problems is in Belgium.

There was much discussion over language questions in the Belgian Congo. Nevertheless, as was the case in Belgium, the term "bilingualism" was rarely mentioned. Besides a terminological or definitional problem, it was also an epistemological one. One of the few titles is F. Seaus' *Het problem van het bilinguisme in Belgische Kongo* (cf. Verbeke, 1966:107).

At the former Lovanium University in Kinshasa, unrelated research efforts in bilingualism and bilingual education were undertaken. First, research was begun at the Faculty Institute of Psychology and Pedagogy where, under R. Verbeke, psychometric studies were conducted to examine the impact of bilingualism on students' intelligence and achievement since the 1960s. Second, Professor W. Bal at the Faculty of Philosophy and Letters was the pioneer in studies and research on language interferences, contrastive studies, and studies on varieties of French. After his retirement, these efforts continued, particularly with the launching of a sociolinguistics course and the creation of the Centre de Linguistique Théorique et Appliquée (CELTA). Today CELTA is the major institution in research on bilingualism and bilingual education in Zaire. Unfortunately, these efforts have remained scattered without coordination between the two schools. The main problem remaining is that the Department of African Linguistics at the Faculty of Letters has not yet played its full role of leading efforts in bilingualism and bilingual education. The focus in this department is still on "descriptivism," not on applied linguistics, particularly African-language teaching.

INFORMATION SOURCES

Because of the political economy of publishing and the sophistication of the information system, resource centers for materials and reference publications on languages and education in Africa in general and in Zaire in particular are available through computer data bases in Europe or the United States. Although CELTA has published some bibliographies, these are so limited that they will not be considered here. Only Belgium and France, where substantial sources on Zaire are located, will be considered.

Because of the long colonial history, until some time ago Belgium was the headquarters of any information on Zaire. Recent years, however, have witnessed a decrease both in interest and budget devoted to Zaire owing to competition with other countries (France, the United States), as well as a need to balance Belgium's cooperation with other African countries. The major information source center was the Royal Museum of Central Africa (MURAC) at Tervuren which published the *Bibliographie Ethnographique* with linguistic, sociolinguistic, education, and teaching sections, along with the *Annales*, publishing articles or monographs from the Department of Linguistics of the Museum. The Museum publication budgets are being cut dramatically.

The Centre d'Etude et de Documentation d'Afrique (CEDAF) in Brussels, of recent creation, is probably one of the leading resource information centers on Africa and mainly on Zaire. Indexes, bibliographies, and resources in many areas such as education are found. Most of their materials cover the period since 1959.

In France, with all the importance given to cultural investments, the Centre National de la Recherche Scientifique (CNRS) and the Centre de Documentation en Sciences Humaines (CDSH) appear to be the two major resource information centers with special sections and issues devoted to Africa. They are sponsored by the Association des Universités Partiellement/Entièrement de Langue Française (AUPELF), the agency of the Francophone dealing with interuniversity affairs, and the Agence de Coopération Culturelle et Technique (ACCT), an intergovernmental Francophone body. On behalf of these bodies, the Association d'Etudes Linguistiques Interculturelles Africaines (AELIA) and the Centre International de Recherche et d'Etude en Linguistique Fondamentale et Appliquée (CIRELFA) publish reference and resource information of vital importance, and directories of microfiches, microfilms, indexes, abstracts, and bibliographies. Among other sections, one on *sciences de l'éducation* and another on *sciences du langage* are available. The Conseil International de la Langue Française (CILF) is another institution publishing inventories of African-language studies.

Both in Belgium and France, dissertation indexes and abstracts are nonexistent.

NOTES

1. The country now called Zaire will be referred to in this chapter as (a) Central Africa for the precolonial period, (b) Congo Free State for King Leopold II's era (1885–1908), (c) Belgian Congo for the period of the Belgian colonization (1908–1960), and (d) Congo or Zaire for the period from 1960 to the present.

2. This section draws heavily from Barbara A. Yates (1980).

BIBLIOGRAPHY

Abdulaziz Mkilifi, M. H. 1978. "Triglossia and Swahili-English Bilingualism in Tanzania." In *Advances in the Study of Societal Multilingualism*, ed. J. F. Fishman. The Hague: Mouton, pp. 129–52.

Africa South of the Sahara: 1980–1981. 1980. London: Europa Publications.

Bokamba Eyamba, G. 1976. "Authenticity and the Choice of a National Language: The Case of Zaïre." *Présence Africaine*, Nos. 99/100, pp. 104–43.

———. 1977. "The Impact of Multilingualism on Language Structures: The Case of Central Africa." *Anthropological Linguistics* 19, 5:181–203.

Brann, Conrad M. B. 1982. "French Lexicography in Africa: A Three-Dimensional Project." *Journal of Modern African Studies* 20, 2:353–59.

Bruhn, Thea C. 1984. *Zaire: Country Status Report.* Language/Area Reference Center, Center for Applied Linguistics, Washington, D.C.

Cam, Tran Hong, and Le Boul, Monique. 1976a. *Une Enquête sur le Plurilinguisme au Zaïre.* Centre de Linguistique Théorique et Appliquée. Lubumbashi (Zaïre).

———. 1976b. *Le Bilinguisme Scolaire au Zaïre.* Centre de Linguistique Théorique et Appliquée. Lumbashi (Zaire).

Coleman, James S., and Ndolamb Ngonkwey. 1983. "Zaire: The State and the University." In *Politics and Education: Cases from Eleven Nations*, ed. R. Murray Thomas. Oxford: Pergamon Press, pp. 155–78.

Dalby, David. 1980. "African Languages." In *Africa South of the Sahara, 1980–81.* London: Europa Publications.

Ellington, John. 1973. "What Is Authentic?" *Africa Report* (July-August): 20–22.

Fabian, J. 1986. *Language and Colonial Power.* Cambridge: Cambridge University Press.

Faîk, Sully. 1979. "Le Français au Zaïre." In *Le Français hors de France*, ed. Albert Valdman. Paris: Honoré Champion, pp. 441–72.

Faîk, Sully, et al. 1977. *Le Zaïre: Deuxième Pays Francophone du Monde?* Quebec: International Center for Research on Bilingualism.

Fasold, Ralph. 1984. *The Sociolinguistics of Society.* New York: Basil Blackwell, Inc.

Fehderau, Harold W. 1966. "The Origin and Development of Kituba (Lingua Franca Kikongo)." Ph.D. diss., Cornell University.

Feltz, Gaetan. 1980. "Un Echec de l'Implantation Scolaire en Milieu Rural." *Canadian Journal of African Studies* 13, 3:441–59.

Fetter, Bruce. 1983. *Colonial Rule and Regional Imbalance in Central Africa.* Boulder, Colo.: Westview Press, 1983.

George, Betty. 1966. *Educational Development in the Congo (Leopoldville).* Washington, D.C.: U.S. Government Printing Office.

Grosjean, François. 1982. *Life with Two Languages: An Introduction to Bilingualism*. Cambridge, Mass.: Harvard University Press.

Haugen, Einer, J. Derrick McClure, and Derrick Thomson, eds. 1981. *Minority Languages Today*. Edinburgh: Edinburgh University Press, 1981.

Houis, Maurice. 1962. "Aperçu Sociologique sur le Bilinguisme en Afrique Noire." *Notes Africaines* (Dakar, Senegal), no. 96, pp. 107–13.

Kachru, Braj B. 1982. "Bilingualism." In *Annual Review of Applied Linguistics, 1980*, ed. Robert B. Kaplan. Rowley, Mass.: Newbury House.

Kaplan, Irving. 1979. *Zaire: A Country Study*. Washington, D.C.: U.S. Government Printing Office.

Kazadi, Ntole. 1981. "La Linguistique Africaine Face à sa Nouvelle Situation." *Bulletin de l'AELIA* (Paris), No. 4 (March), pp. 59–63.

Kimputu, B. 1978. "La Situation Sociolinguistique à Kinshasa." Doctoral thesis, University of Provence (Aix-Marseille I), France.

Marcellesi, Jean-Baptiste. 1981. "Bilinguisme, Diglossie, Hégémonie: Problèmes et Tâches." *Languages* 15, 6 (March): 5–11.

Morrison, Donald George, et al., eds. 1972. *Black Africa: A Comparative Handbook*. New York: Free Press.

Mutombo Huta, M. 1984. "Pour ou Contre l'Unicité Linguistique au Zaire." *Analyses Sociales* 1, 4 (July-August): 27–47.

Ndoma, Ungina. 1977. "Some Aspects of Planning Language Policy in Education in the Belgian Congo, 1906–1960." Ph.D. diss., Northwestern University.

———. 1984. "National Language Policy in Education in Zaire." *Language Problems and Language Planning* 8, 2 (Summer): 172–84.

Nyembwe Ntita, T. 1980. "Le Français et les Langues Nationales au Zaïre, Problématique d'une Approche Sociolinguistique." Thèse, Université Catholique de Louvain, Louvain-la-Neuve (Belgium).

Polomé, Edgar. 1968. "The Choice of Official Language in the Democratic Republic of the Congo." In *Language Problems of Developing Nations*, ed. J. A. Fishman. New York: Wiley.

Population Reference Bureau, Inc. 1984. *1984 World Population Data Sheet*. Washington, D.C.

Show, Bryant P. 1984. "Force Publique, Force Unique: The Military in the Belgian Congo, 1914–1939." Ph.D. diss., University of Wisconsin, Madison.

Tashdjan, Alain. 1981. "Les Langues Nationales et l'Enseignement Primaire au Zaïre: Une Réforme et ses Difficultés. Ed. Jean-Pierre Caprile. *Bulletin de l'AELIA* (Paris), No. 4 (March): 51–57.

U.S. Department of State, Bureau of Public Affairs. 1981. *Background Notes: Zaire*. Washington, D.C.

Van Overbeke, Maurice. 1972. *Introduction au Problème du Bilinguisme*. Bruxelles: Editions Labor.

Vansina, Jan. 1963. "Long-Distance Trade-Routes in Central Africa." *Journal of African History* 3, 3:375–90.

Verdoodt, Albert. 1973. *Problèmes Linguistiques Belges: Introduction à la Bibliographie et Guide pour la Recherche*. Louvain, Belgium: Centre de Recherche Sociologique, Institut de Linguistique.

Verebeke, Ronald. 1966. "Langues Véhiculaires de l'Enseignement en Afrique Noire:

Problématique du Choix et Implications Pédagogiques.'' *Présence Africaine*, No. 60: 101–16.

Yates, Barbara A. 1980. ''The Origins of Language Policy in Zaire.'' *Journal of Modern African Studies* 18, 2: 257–79.

GLOSSARY

Arabization: the spread of Arab culture, language and religion.

bidialectalism: the ability to speak two distinct dialects, such as Black English and standard English.

bilingualism: the ability to speak two different languages.

cholofication: the process by which South Americans of Indian background assimilate into the dominant Hispanic culture.

code: a general term which refers to language, dialect or stylistic varieties.

codification: standardizing the orthography and system of writing.

code-mixing: a form of speech in which the speaker will mix two codes within the same utterance.

code-switching: a process of changing or switching from one variety of language or dialect to another.

contact language: a language used for everyday contacts between people of different language backgrounds; a lingua franca.

continuum: the term refers to the linguistic characteristic that there is no sharp or distinct break between the standard (high form, acrolect) and the non-standard (low form, basilect) varieties of a creole. Rather, there is a gradual or continuous progression (mesolect) from basilect to acrolect.

creole: a pidgin that has acquired native speakers.

diglossia: the co-existence of two dialects in functional distribution; one a literary prestige version, like classical Arabic and a spoken version, like colloquial Arabic.

exogamy: marrying outside one's own ethnic group, clan or other social unit.

heteroglossist: someone who studies other languages.

ikastolas: Basque schools.

interlanguage: the version of a language spoken by a second language learner before he has mastered it. Interlanguage is hence marked by errors.

koine-dialect: a lingua franca which develops out of a mixture of several languages.

language death: the disappearance of a language.

language shift: the abandonment, by a group, of one language and the adoption of another; e.g., immigrants to the United States.

lexicon: all the words in a language.

lingua franca: "language of the franks"; originally, a mixed language used for trade and crusades in the Mediterranean. It is now used generally to mean contact language.

link language: lingua franca.

mesolect: see continuum.

metalanguage: language used to describe or discuss a language.

microlect: a subset of a dialect.

morpheme: the smallest meaningful unit of speech; it may be a word or a part of a word (un-friend-ly).

morphology: the study of the smallest meaningful units of language and of their formation into words.

mother tongue: native language.

multilingualism: the ability to speak several different languages; the existence of several languages within a nation.

patois: a regional dialect, but usually used in the sense of an illiterate or nonstandard variety.

phoneme: the smallest significant unit of sound in a particular language.

phonology: the study of the sound system of a language.

pidgin: a contact language which develops out of a mixture of several languages. A pidgin has no native speakers.

reduplication: a morphological process in which there is a repetition of part of the word.

semilingualism: a controversial term for the claim that bilingual speakers may not be fully proficient in either language. This claim is undocumented.

speech revival: the revival of a dead language, such as Hebrew.

standardization: a process of language planning by which one or more dialects of a language are turned into a standard language with generally accepted word choice, spelling and grammar.

standard language: that dialect of a language which has literary and cultural prestige, appears in grammars and dictionaries, and is accepted by its speakers to be the proper variety.

suffix: a formative added to the end of a word to modify its meaning or to form a new derivative (dog-s, work-ing).

taalstryd: Afrikaans for language battle, i.e. the fight for Afrikaans as a standard official language.

vernacular: daily speech as distinguished from literary standard.

Christina Bratt Paulston

BIBLIOGRAPHICAL ESSAY

Bilingual education goes back almost as far as historical records. Before 2000 B.C. there is evidence of important bilingual schools in which the native Akkadian and the traditional Sumerian were taught. The prophet Daniel, selected for a scribal education by Nebuchadnessar, was taught to communicate in languages other than his native Hebrew. Roman children studied under Greek tutors, and influences of Latin and Greek remain to our own day. Glyn Lewis pursues these issues in "Bilingualism and Bilingual Education—The Ancient World to the Renaissance" (1977), and a very interesting account it is. The article contains numerous references to historical studies. Heinz Kloss explores the history of bilingualism and bilingual education specifically in the United States in *The American Tradition* (1977). As the author comments in the Preface, the content will seem strange even to the American reader. Historical fact does not always correspond to the myth of the melting pot.

More recent developments on the international scene are explored in a number of sources. A good place to start is with B. Spolsky and R. L. Cooper's fifteen *Case Studies in Bilingual Education* (1978) from around the world. From the same year we also have a special issue of the *International Review of Education* on "Language of Instruction in a Multi-Cultural setting" (24:3). There are a number of Proceedings from conferences on international bilingual education: R. Troike and N. Modiano, eds., *Proceedings of the First Inter-American Conference on Bilingual Education* (1975); J. E. Alatis, ed., *International Dimensions of Bilingual Education* (1978); and T. Husén and S. Opper, eds., *Multicultural and Multilingual Education in Immigrant Countries* (1983), which all span a wide range of cases and issues. Two recent works are B. Spolsky ed., *Language and Education in Multilingual Settings* (1986), which deals mostly with theoretical issues, and S. Churchill, *The Education of Linguistic and Cul-*

tural Minorities in the OECD Countries (1986) which considers the European situation.

One work which considers the vernacular, that is, a nonstandard language in bilingual education, is B. Hartford, A. Valdman, and C. R. Foster, eds. (1982) in *Issues in International Bilingual Education: The Role of the Vernacular*. Issues like those raised in the chapter on Jamaica surface, but there are also psychological perspectives, concerns with linguistic description, but particularly neo-Marxist views on curriculum and teacher training, and other conflictual viewpoints. The neo-Marxist perspective, while long common in Europe, is a fairly recent notion in the study of bilingual education in the United States. Marxism saw conflict of interest only in terms of socioeconomic class, while neo-Marxism adds the concept of ethnic groups and provides a viable alternative analysis and interpretation of the phenomenon of bilingual education.

For the reader who is interested in bilingualism and bilingual education in the United States, there are a number of sources. The best is probably C. Ferguson and S. Heath's *Language in the USA* (1981) which *inter alia* discusses American English, languages before and after English, that is, Amerindian and immigrant languages and language in education. Also useful is the Center for Applied Linguistics' five-volume series on *Bilingual Education: Current Perspectives* (1977): Volume 1, Social Science; Volume 2, Linguistics; Volume 3, Law; Volume 4, Education; and Volume 5, Synthesis.

One aspect of bilingualism that is not covered in the present volume is the spread of English as a language of wider communication in the world. Today there are more nonnative speakers of English than there are native, and J. A. Fishman, R. Cooper, and A. Conrad, eds. documents this phenomenon in *The Spread of English* (1977).

Finally, the phenomenon of bilingualism can be studied from several perspectives. M. Albert and L. Obler consider it from a viewpoint of neurolinguistics in their *The Bilingual Brain* (1978). F. Grosjean takes a more social approach in considering what it is like to grow up with two languages in his *Life with Two Languages: An Introduction to Bilingualism* (1982). W. E. Lambert considers bilingualism from the perspective of psychology in *Language, Psychology, and Culture* (1972), a collection of his classic work. Also well known is James Cummins' "The Influence of Bilingualism on Cognitive Growth" (1976).

There is also the work in anthropology, the well-known Sapir-Whorf hypothesis which holds that the structure of the language one speaks influences the way one perceives the world. Although this is an attractive idea to nonlinguists, most linguists remain skeptical, but let the readers themselves explore Whorf's *Language, Thought, and Reality* (1956).

BIBLIOGRAPHY

Alatis, J. E., ed. 1978. *International Dimensions of Bilingual Education*. Washington,
   D.C.: Georgetown University Press.
Albert, M., and L. Obler. 1978. *The Bilingual Brain*. New York: Academic Press.
Center for Applied Linguistics. 1977. *Bilingual Education: Current Perspectives*. Vol.
   1, Social Science. Arlington, Va.
———. 1977. *Bilingual Education: Current Perspectives*. Vol. 2, Linguistics. Arlington,
   Va.
———. 1977. *Bilingual Education: Current Perspectives*. Vol. 3, Law. Arlington, Va.
———. 1977. *Bilingual Education: Current Perspectives*. Vol. 4, Education. Arlington,
   Va.
———. 1977. *Bilingual Education: Current Perspectives*. Vol. 5, Synthesis. Arlington,
   Va.
Churchill, S. 1986. *The Education of Linguistic and Cultural Minorities in the OECD
   Countries*. San Diego: College-Hill Press.
Cooper, R. L., ed. 1982. "A Framework for the Study of Language Spread." *Language
   Spread: Studies in Diffusion and Social Change*. Arlington, Va.: Center for Ap-
   plied Linguistics, and Bloomington, Ind.: Indiana University Press.
Cummins, J. 1976. "The Influence of Bilingualism on Cognitive Growth: A Synthesis
   of Research Findings and Explanatory Hypothesis." *Working Papers on Bilin-
   gualism*, No. 9: 1–43. Olse: University of Toronto.
Ferguson, C., and S. Heath, eds. 1981. *Language in the USA*. Cambridge: Cambridge
   University Press.
Fishman, J. A., R. Cooper, and A. Conrad, eds. 1977. *The Spread of English*. Rowley,
   Mass.: Newbury House.
Grosjean, F. 1982. *Life with Two Languages: An Introduction to Bilingualism*. Cam-
   bridge, Mass.: Harvard University Press.
Hartford, B., A. Valdman, and C. R. Foster, eds. 1982. *Issues in International Bilingual
   Education: The Role of the Vernacular*. New York: Plenum Press.

Husén, T., and S. Opper, eds. 1983. *Multicultural and Multilingual Education in Immigrant Countries*. Oxford: Pergamon Press.

Kloss, H. 1977. *The American Tradition*. Rowley, Mass.: Newbury House.

Lambert, W. E. 1972. *Language, Psychology, and Culture*. Stanford, Calif.: Stanford University Press.

Lewis, Glyn. 1977. "Bilingualism and Bilingual Education." In *Frontiers in Bilingual Education*, eds. B. Spolsky and R. Cooper. Rowley, Mass.: Newbury House.

Spolsky, B., ed. 1986. *Language and Education in Multilingual Settings*. Clevedon: Multilingual Matters Ltd.

Spolsky, B., and R. Cooper, eds. 1978. *Case Studies in Bilingual Education*. Rowley, Mass.: Newbury House.

Troike, R., and N. Modiano. 1975. *Proceedings of the First Inter-American Conference on Bilingual Education*. Washington D.C.: Center for Applied Linguistics.

Whorf, B. L. 1956. *Language, Thought, and Reality*. Cambridge, Mass.: MIT Press.

AUTHOR INDEX

LANGUAGE INDEX

SUBJECT INDEX

ABOUT THE CONTRIBUTORS

AFOLAYAN, ADEBISI. Professor, Department of English Language, University of Ife, Ile-Ife, Nigeria.

ALBÓ, XAVIER. Professor, Centro de Investigacion y Promocion del Campesinado, La Paz, Bolivia.

ARNBERG, LENORE. Research Associate, University of Stockholm, Institute of Linguistics, Department of Research on Bilingualism, Stockholm, Sweden.

BENTAHILA, ABDELÂLI. Professor, Department of English, Faculty of Arts, University Sidi Mohamed Ben Abdellah, Fez, Morocco.

BURNABY, BARBARA. Burnaby Language Consulting, Toronto, Ontario, Canada.

CORVALÁN, GRAZIELLA. Directora Adjunta, Centro Paraguayo de Estudios Sociologicos, Asunción, Paraguay.

CRAIG, DENNIS R. Professor of Language, University of the West Indies, Faculty of Education, Mona, Kingston, Jamaica.

DORIAN, NANCY C. Professor of Linguistics, Department of Anthropology, Bryn Mawr College, Bryn Mawr, Pa., USA.

ELGIBALI, ALAA. Instructor, Language Center, Kuwait University, Kuwait.

ESCOBAR, ALBERTO. Professor, Instituto de Estudios Peruanos, Lima, Peru.

GENESEE, FRED. Associate Professor, Department of English as a Second Language, University of Hawaii, Honolulu, Hawaii, USA.

GOPINATHAN, S. Professor, Department of Comparative Studies, Institute of Education, Republic of Singapore.

HYLTENSTAM, KENNETH. Professor, University of Stockholm, Institute of Linguistics, Department of Research on Bilingualism, Stockholm, Sweden.

KOLDE, GOTTFRIED. Professor, Departement des langues et litterature allemandes, Université de Genève, Geneva, Switzerland.

LINGUISTIC MINORITIES PROJECT: Xavier Couilland, Marily Martin-Jones, Verity Saifullah Khan, Anna Morawska, Euan Reid, Greg Smith. University of London, Institute of Education, London, UK.

MODIANO, NANCY. Professor, Escuela Desarrollo Regional La Cabana, Chiapas, Mexico.

MUKEBA, LUFULUABO. Instructor, Teacher Training College, Kinshasa, Zaire.

NAHIR, MOSHE. Professor, Department of Near Eastern and Judaic Studies, and the Department of Linguistics, University of Manitoba, Winnipeg, Manitoba, Canada.

PAULSTON, CHRISTINA BRATT. Professor of Linguistics, Department of General Linguistics, University of Pittsburgh, Pittsburgh, Pa., USA.

RUIZ, RICHARD. Assistant Professor, Educational Foundation and Administration, University of Arizona, Tucson, Ariz., USA.

SCOTTON, CAROL MYERS. Professor, Linguistics Program, University of South Carolina, Columbia, S.C.

SHORISH, M. MOBIN. Associate Professor of Comparative Education and Economics of Education, Department of Educational Policy Studies, University of Illinois of Urbana-Champaign, Champaign, Ill., USA.

SIGUAN, MIGUEL. Professor, Instituto de Ciencias de la Educación, Universidad de Barcelona, Barcelona, Spain.

SRIVASTAVA, R. N. Professor and Head, Department of Linguistics, University of Dehli, Delhi, India.

SWING, ELIZABETH SHERMAN. Associate Professor of Education, St. Joseph's University, Philadelphia, Pa., USA.

TAI, JAMES H.-Y. Associate Professor of Chinese and of Linguistics, Southern Illinois University, Carbondale, Ill., USA.

THOMASON, SARAH GREY. Professor of Linguistics, Department of General Linguistics, University of Pittsburgh, Pittsburgh, Pa., USA.

YOUNG, DOUGLAS. Professor, Department of Education, University of Cape Town, Cape Town, Republic of South Africa.